Further praise for *The Crusades*

'Asbridge takes care, in this scholarly survey of medieval crusading activity from the 11th to the 13th centuries, to give the Muslim perspective as much weight as the Christian. He can't help but tell a ripping yarn, often breezily dramatic, whipping the narrative along' Iain Finlayson, *The Times*

'Stuffed with the kind of splendidly colourful anecdotes that only the medieval era can supply. Asbridge departs radically – and successfully – from tradition [and] brilliantly exposes Muslim strategies and motivations' James McConnachie, *Sunday Times*

'A compelling narrative that resonates inescapably with contemporary events . . . Masterful' Malise Ruthven, *Observer*

'A truly comprehensive history of holy war in the Holy Land. Emphasizing the dramatic Third Crusade and its heroic antagonists, Richard the Lionheart and Saladin, the narrative reads like an adventure story, albeit one that is both factual and instructive' *Publishers Weekly*

'Today the crusades are all too topical, though mostly, Asbridge observes, for the wrong reasons: interesting as they are, he says, their place is in the past. That doesn't stop them being exciting, stirring, moving, horrific and a whole lot of other things as well though: this book gives us narrative history at its best' *Scotsman*

'Thomas Asbridge brings all the colour and drama of this violent era resolutely alive in *The Crusades*, presenting this clash of civilisations from both the Christian and Islamic viewpoints' *Oxford Times*

'There is more here than a historical account . . . *The Crusades* tells a new, no less interesting, story as well: how the memory of the Crusades was formed in modern times' *Wall Street Journal*

'Asbridge widens his vista to the entire 1195–1291 duration of the crusading era. With perceptive commentary about spiritual motivations behind crusading and perspectives from contemporary Islamic sources, Asbridge constructs a comprehensive, sophisticated and arresting analytic st, whether recreati

Also by Thomas Asbridge

THE FIRST CRUSADE
THE GREATEST KNIGHT

THE
CRUSADES

The War for the
Holy Land

THOMAS ASBRIDGE

**SIMON &
SCHUSTER**

London · New York · Sydney · Toronto · New Delhi

First published in Great Britain by Simon & Schuster UK Ltd, 2010
First published in paperback in Great Britain by Simon & Schuster UK Ltd, 2012

This edition published in Great Britain by Simon & Schuster UK Ltd, 2020

1 3 5 7 9 10 8 6 4 2

Simon & Schuster UK Ltd
1st Floor
222 Gray's Inn Road
London WC1X 8HB

www.simonandschuster.co.uk
www.simonandschuster.com.au
www.simonandschuster.co.in

Simon & Schuster Australia, Sydney
Simon & Schuster India, New Delhi

A CIP catalogue record for this book
is available from the British Library.

Paperback ISBN: 978-1-4711-9643-0
eBook ISBN: 978-1-84983-770-5

Typeset in Electra by M Rules
Printed and bound by CPI Group UK, Croydon, CR0 4YY

MIX
Paper from
responsible sources
FSC® C020471
www.fsc.org

For my father
Gerald Asbridge

CONTENTS

LIST OF MAPS

ATLANTIC

OCEAN

Boulogne
FLANDERS
Amiens
Caen Rouen Rheims
NORMANDY
Paris
Chartres
Troyes
Tours Blois
Poitiers Dijon
Cluny
FRANCE Lyons
Clermont

Bordeaux

LEON AND CASTILE

PORTUGAL

Toledo

ARAGON
Toulouse LANGUEDOC
Montpellier

Barcelona

Cologne
GERMAN
Bouillon
Mainz Prague
Trier
LORRAINE Worms Regensb
Toul ALSACE EMPIRE
Basel ALPS

Milan
LOMBARDY Venice
Valence Piacenza
PROVENCE Genoa Bologna
Pisa

CORSICA
Rome
Ostia
Salerr
SARDINIA

Me d i t e r r

Tunis SICIL

MALTA

Western Europe and
the Mediterranean
(Land over 1000 metres/3281 feet is shaded)

0   100   200   300 miles
0   100 200 300 400 500 km

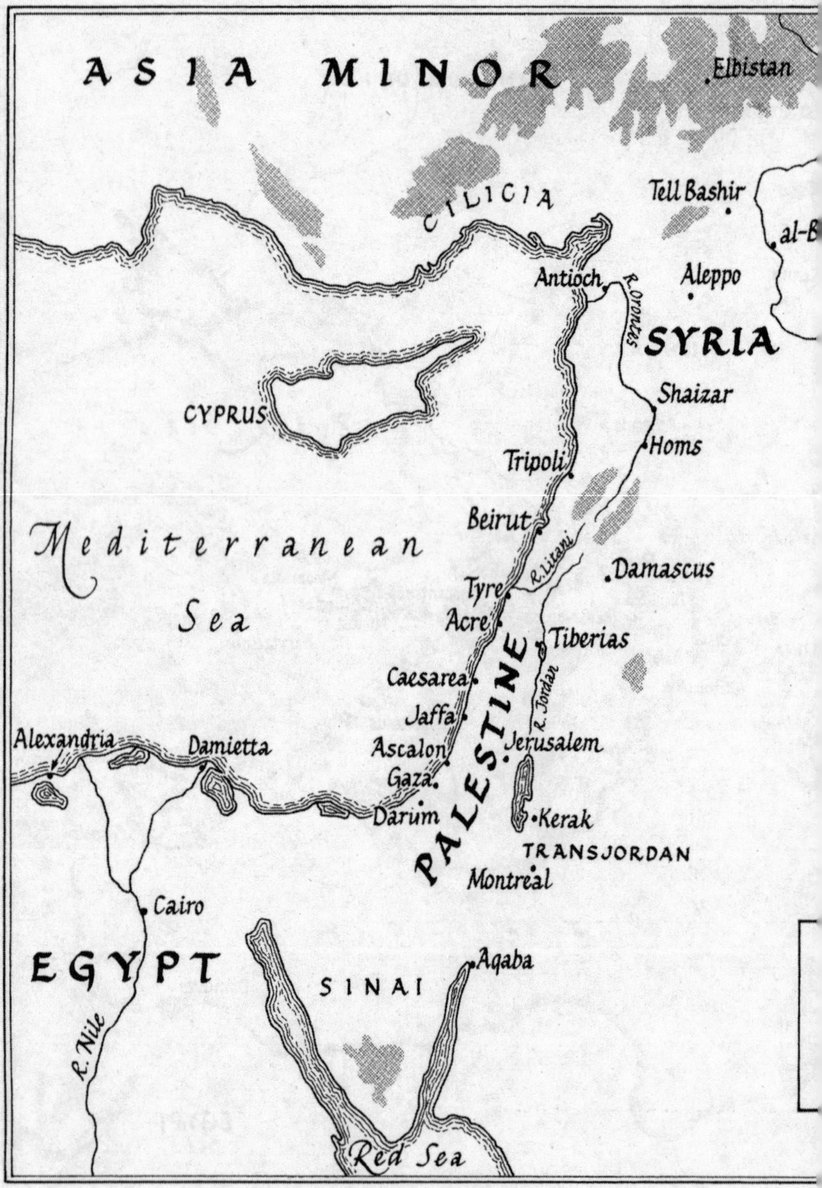

ASIA MINOR

Elbistan

CILICIA

Tell Bashir

al-B

Antioch

R. Orontes

Aleppo

SYRIA

Shaizar

CYPRUS

Homs

Tripoli

Beirut

Mediterranean

Sea

R. Litani

Damascus

Tyre

Acre

Tiberias

Caesarea

R. Jordan

PALESTINE

Jaffa

Alexandria

Damietta

Ascalon

Jerusalem

Gaza

Darum

Kerak

TRANSJORDAN

Montreal

Cairo

EGYPT

R. Nile

Aqaba

SINAI

Red Sea

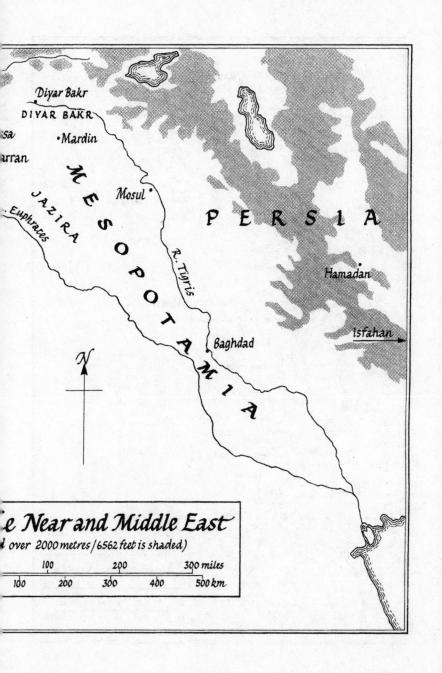

Diyar Bakr

DIYAR BAKR

sa

·Mardin

arran

·Euphrates

JAZIRA

MESOPOTAMIA

Mosul·

R. Tigris

Baghdad

N

PERSIA

Hamadan

Isfahan →

e Near and Middle East

d over 2000 metres / 6562 feet is shaded)

| 100 | 200 | 300 miles |
| 100 | 200 | 300 | 400 | 500 km |

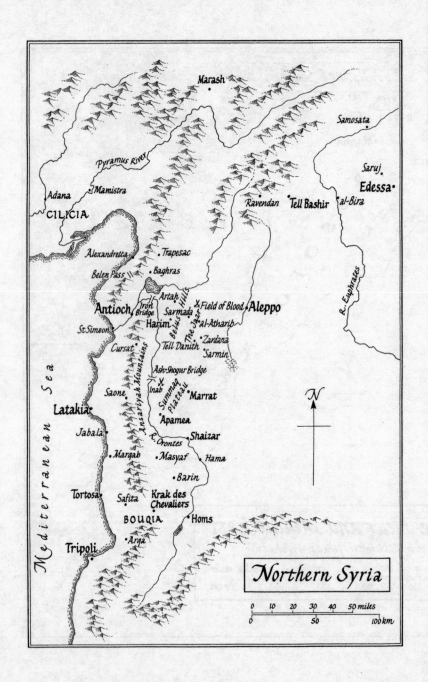

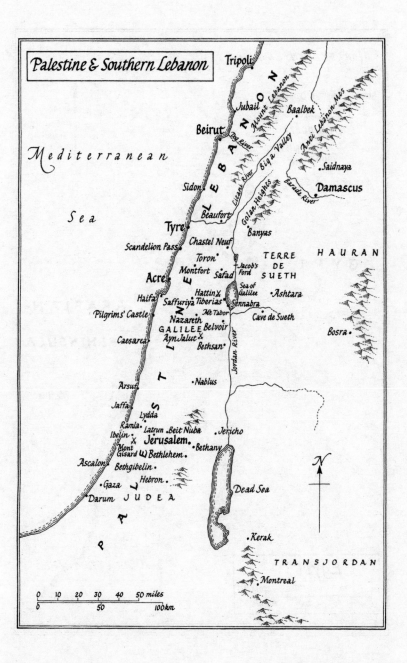

Palestine & Southern Lebanon

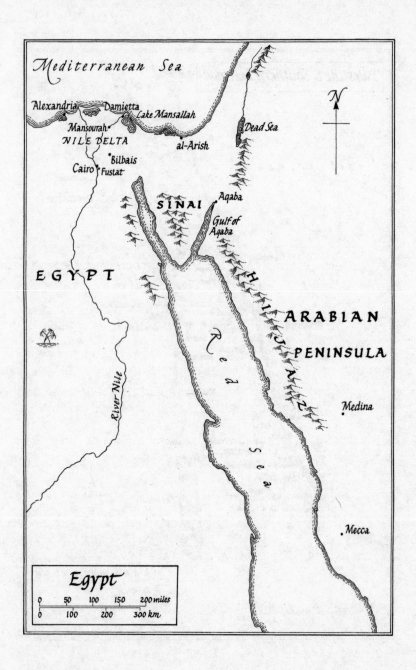

Mediterranean Sea

Alexandria · Damietta · Lake Mansallah
Mansourah · al-Arish
NILE DELTA
Cairo · Bilbais
· Fustat

Dead Sea

SINAI
Aqaba
Gulf of
Aqaba

EGYPT

H I J A Z

ARABIAN

PENINSULA

Medina

River Nile

Red Sea

Mecca

N

Egypt

0   50   100   150   200 miles
0   100   200   300 km

FOREWORD

In recent months, I have had the good fortune to travel across the Near and Middle East, and Europe, filming a documentary series for the BBC based on this book. Although a few of the locations I visited were new to me, most were familiar from previous trips connected to my decades-long research into crusading history. Yet in every place, I had a powerful sense that I was engaged in something that, for me, was novel, challenging and profoundly illuminating. I was seeking to convey my abiding passion for the crusades – to tell the story of these holy wars – in the very places in which the drama (and sometimes horror) of these events played out.

Over the years, I have sought in countless lectures and classes to communicate the febrile amalgam of faith and violence that powered the First Crusade, but it is something else entirely to stand in Jerusalem's Holy Sepulchre itself and describe the pious joy experienced by blood-splattered crusaders as they finally entered this most sacred Christian shrine in 1099. And I felt the same electrifying sense of connection within the Aqsa Mosque, speaking of how the great Sultan Saladin wept as he led Friday prayer in that very building on 3 July 1192, grief-stricken that he would have to abandon Jerusalem.

I would not claim that these experiences have somehow afforded me unique or groundbreaking insights into the crusading era, or that suddenly I am now better placed to achieve an empathetic understanding of the protagonists involved. In the end, a location alone (often altered from its medieval state) can only take you so far, and one has to turn back to the historical sources, be they textual or material. But my imagination has been sparked, and my enthusiasm for crusading history – already an obsession for considerably more than half my life – re-energised. In particular, I have been moved to ponder the ways in which we remember, and sometimes forget, events.

A few weeks ago, I walked into Sainte-Chapelle – the towering shrine built by King Louis IX of France in the heart of Paris – an hour before dawn. This structure was a technological miracle in its day; built to house Louis' prized collection of Passion relics (among them Christ's Crown of Thorns), its delicate stone columns and lofty vaults support seemingly impossible expanses of vibrant stained glass. Normally thronging with visitors, all transfixed by its beauty and high-Gothic splendour, the chapel now stood dark and deserted. As the sun rose and light slowly began to pour in through the dazzling windows, I was struck by the rare certainty that King Louis – a man who dedicated his life to the war for the Holy Land more than 700 years ago – had walked through this self-same space. Sainte-Chapelle survives as a talisman of Louis' memory, evoking his unswerving religious dedication; it is a celebrated icon of French history and national identity. But there are other places, just as intimately associated with this crusader monarch's life, which have been all but forgotten.

Mansourah, on the Nile Delta, where King Louis waged an epic struggle for control of Egypt in the thirteenth century, is now a sprawling, industrialised city. Rather improbably, the site of Louis' crusader camp beside the Nile remains as an isolated and forlorn pocket of agricultural land, overlooked by three chimneys pumping out clouds of noxious yellow smoke. No one comes here to see – let alone film – this place, where the Christian army was crushed by the emerging might of the Mamluks, and where the king himself was eventually unmanned by such an extreme case of dysentery that he had to cut a hole in his breeches. It was a peculiarly jarring, yet affecting, experience to stand in this spot and describe on camera how, at dusk on 4 April 1250, wounded and abandoned crusaders desperately tried to crawl to the few vessels still moored on the river-bank once the Muslims broke into their camp, only to be hunted down and slaughtered without mercy.

I experienced a similar feeling – one of briefly resurrecting a forgotten moment from the distant past – when recounting the story of another massacre, this time enacted by crusaders, upon the sandy plains beyond the northern Israeli city of Acre. Having spent a number of years carrying out an especially close study of all the firsthand accounts for this particular event, I am perhaps just a little too familiar with the appalling and grisly details of how, in the midst of the Third Crusade, Richard the Lionheart marched some 2,700 Muslim captives out of the city and then had them butchered in cold blood. For me, at least, it proved impossible not to ponder the terrible sense of fear and confusion that must have been rife amongst these prisoners in the moments before their deaths; before the crusaders set upon them 'with stabbings and blows of swords', as one witness put it.

Of course, one of the primary aims of my work has been to stress that the crusades were not simply a catalogue of ceaseless battles and campaigns. It is only too easy, through selected presentation of the evidence, to conceive of this as an age of 'total war' between Islam and the West; an era of embittered conflict, fuelled by ingrained hatred and cycles of reciprocal violence. This certainly is the vision of the crusades used to promote the notion of an inevitable clash of civilisations between Europe and the Muslim world. But in the course of the war for the Holy Land, pragmatic reality and political, military and commercial expediency meant that 'crusader' settlers were actually brought into frequent contact with the native peoples of the Levant, including Muslims. As such, the crusades created one of the frontier environments in which Europeans were able to interact with and absorb 'eastern' culture. This was not a cosy environment of harmonious concord, but given the prevailing realities of the wider world, this should be no surprise. The medieval West itself was wracked by inter-Christian rivalry and interminable martial strife; endemic social and religious intolerance were also on the rise. By these standards, the uneasy mixture of contact and simmering conflict visible in the 'crusader' Levant was not that remarkable.

One of the greatest benefits of working on this television series is that it has brought privileged access to the physical remnants – or material culture – of the medieval crusading age, many of which speak to this notion of inter-cultural contact. As a scholar used to seeing the past chiefly through textual evidence, it is enormously exciting to actually handle objects that survive from this era, especially those drawn from everyday life. In Israel, I found myself examining an array of 'crusader' coins minted by western Christian settlers in the Near East, ranging from fairly crude coppers – one of which might have bought a few loaves of bread – to precious gold issues. The most fascinating of these were a series that, at first glance, look like Islamic coins, replete with Arabic inscriptions and purporting to be issued by the Egyptian Caliph al-Amir who ruled between 1101 and 1130. In reality, they are 'fakes', produced by Christian rulers as imitation Muslim gold coins (of slightly debased weight) in or order to allow settlers to more readily and rapidly incorporate themselves into the commercial fabric of the Levant. The fact that – in the midst of the crusading age – western settlers were minting coins marked with Islamic text (and some that even bore the name of the Prophet Muhammad) speaks volumes about the importance of trans-cultural trade and the capacity for necessity to trump ideology.

I also have been granted access by the British Library to one of their greatest treasures: the Melisende Psalter. This small, finely wrought prayer book was probably crafted in the 1130s as a gift for Queen Melisende of Jerusalem from her husband, King Fulk. Indeed, it may well have been a peace offering, designed to help calm the waters after the couple had become embroiled in a matrimonial spat that almost ended in full civil war. This exceptionally beautiful artefact stands testament to the capacity for cultural fusion in the crusader states. Produced by at least seven different artisans, it exhibits elements of English, French, Byzantine, eastern Christian and even Islamic influence. Perhaps most spectacular of all are its ivory covers, which are now kept separately from the rest of the prayer book. Carved in minute detail and inset with semi-precious stones, they depict scenes of kingship and Christian piety: on the one cover moments from the life of King David himself, including the battle against Goliath; on the other, a monarch (likely Fulk himself) decked out in Byzantine imperial garb so as to appear more magisterial, carrying out diverse acts of devotion and charity, from clothing the poor to tending the sick. An excellent reproduction of this latter cover appears in the plate section within this book. What makes this object so captivating is that it connects us to the personal story of Melisende's and Fulk's joint reign, but it also reveals something about the wider world in which they lived.

One of the aims of the BBC series has been to answer that most fundamental of questions: how do we know that? To do so, I have gone back to a range of medieval manuscripts – often to the earliest surviving copy anywhere in the world – to reveal the historical sources we use to reconstruct the crusading era. Perhaps the greatest coup was gaining entry to the Aqsa Mosque Archive in Jerusalem to view an early thirteenth-century copy of Baha al-Din's biography of Saladin. This is a fantastically informative document, throwing unique light onto Saladin's personality and the course of his confrontation with Richard the Lionheart during the Third Crusade, written by a man who knew the sultan well and witnessed much of what he described. And what makes the Aqsa manuscript so special is that it was almost certainly no later copy, like most medieval texts, but an original, actually penned by Baha al-Din himself. To hold it and realise that I had in my hands the work of one of Saladin's closest intimates was simply extraordinary.

The final strand of evidence incorporated into the series has been that drawn from archaeology. Just four days ago, beneath a scorching desert sun, I visited the ruins of al-Wu'ayra castle (known in the West as the Valley of Moses) – a small, twelfth-century 'crusader' fortification just outside ancient Petra (Jordan). During the early stages of western settlement, European Christians tried to colonise this isolated and inhospitable region, but adapting to such an unfamiliar environment proved to be no simple matter. Excavations have uncovered sixteen rock-cut graves within the fortress from this period, and analysis of the human skeletal remains they contained suggest that the settlers were unable to gather enough fresh fruit and vegetables to balance their diets, and that their relatively pale skins also led them to suffer from a deficit of folic acid. At al-Wu'ayra I examined fragile fragments of skull from a small baby who, all those centuries ago, had died between the ages of six to nine months. The bones bore stark evidence of the lesions (almost sponge-like deformations) associated with extreme Vitamin C deficiency, or scurvy.

The work of adapting this book to become a documentary series has been enormously enjoyable and I feel hugely privileged to have been involved in such a remarkable project. The experience has certainly enriched my own understanding of the crusades and deepened my love of this era of our history. My hope is that, by revealing what now survives of the world inhabited by the crusaders and Muslims who waged the medieval war for the Holy Land – drawing upon the sense of place and evidence from texts, material culture and archaeology – a television series will emerge that does justice to this enthralling and thought provoking subject.

Thomas Asbridge
6 November 2011
West Sussex

INTRODUCTION

THE WORLD OF THE CRUSADES

Nine hundred years ago the Christians of Europe waged a series of holy wars, or crusades, against the Muslim world, battling for dominion of a region sacred to both faiths – the Holy Land. This bloody struggle raged for two centuries, reshaping the history of Islam and the West. In the course of these monumental expeditions, hundreds of thousands of crusaders travelled across the face of the known world to conquer and then defend an isolated swathe of territory centred on the hallowed city of Jerusalem. They were led by the likes of Richard the Lionheart, warrior-king of England, and the saintly monarch of France, Louis IX, to fight in gruelling sieges and fearsome battles; passing through verdant forests and arid deserts, enduring starvation and disease, encountering the fabled emperors of Byzantium and marching beside forbidding Templar knights. Those who died were thought of as martyrs, while survivors believed that their souls had been scourged of sin by the tempest of combat and trials of pilgrimage.

The advent of these crusades stirred Islam to action, reawakening dedication to the cause of *jihad* (holy war). Muslims from Syria, Egypt and Iraq fought to drive their Christian foes out of the Holy Land – championed by the merciless warlord Zangi and the mighty

Saladin; empowered by the rise of Sultan Baybars and his elite *mamluk* slave soldiers; sometimes aided by the intrigues of the implacable Assassins. Years of conflict inevitably bred greater familiarity, even at times grudging respect and peaceful contact through truce and commerce. But as the decades passed, the fires of conflict burned on and the tide slowly turned in Islam's favour. Though the dream of Christian victory lived on, the Muslim world prevailed, securing lasting possession of Jerusalem and the Near East.

This dramatic story has always fired the imagination and fuelled debate. And, over the centuries, the crusades have been subject to startlingly varied interpretations: held up as proof of the folly of religious faith and the base savagery of human nature, or promoted as glorious expressions of Christian chivalry and civilising colonialism. They have been presented as a dark episode in Europe's history – when ravening hordes of greedy western barbarians launched unprovoked, acquisitive attacks upon the cultured innocents of Islam – or defended as just wars sparked by Muslim aggression and prosecuted to recover Christian territory. The crusaders themselves have been depicted as both land-hungry brutes and pilgrim soldiers inspired by fervent piety; and their Muslim rivals portrayed as vicious and tyrannical oppressors, ardent fanatics or devout paragons of honour and clemency.

The medieval crusades have also been used as a mirror to the modern world, both through the forging of tenuous links between recent events and the distant past, and via the dubious practice of historical parallelism. Thus, during the nineteenth century the French and English appropriated the memory of the crusades to affirm their imperial heritage; while the twentieth and twenty-first centuries have witnessed a deepening tendency within some sections of the Muslim world to equate modern political and religious struggles with holy wars witnessed nine centuries earlier.

This book explores the history of the crusades from both the Christian and Muslim perspectives – focusing, in particular, upon the contest for control of the Holy Land – and examines how medieval contemporaries experienced and remembered the crusades.* It draws upon the wonderfully rich mine of available written evidence (or primary sources) from the Middle Ages: the likes of chronicles, letters and legal documents, poems and songs; recorded in languages as diverse as Latin, Old French, Arabic, Hebrew, Armenian, Syriac and Greek. Beyond these texts, the study of material remains – from imposing castles to delicate manuscript art and minuscule coins – has thrown new light on the crusading era. Throughout, original research has been informed by the great outpouring of modern scholarship in the field witnessed over the past fifty years.[1]

Containing the history of the crusades to the Holy Land between 1095 and 1291 in a single, accessible volume is a massive challenge. But it does offer enormous opportunities. The chance to trace the grand sweep of events, uncovering the visceral reality of human experience – through agony and exultation, horror and triumph; to chart the shifting fortunes and perceptions of Islam and Christendom. It also makes it possible to ask a series of crucial, interlocking and overarching questions about these epochal holy wars.

Issues linked to the origins and causes of the war for the Holy Land are of fundamental importance. How did two of the world's great religions come to advocate violence in the name of God, convincing their followers that fighting for their faith would open the gates to Heaven or Paradise? And why did endless thousands of Christians and Muslims answer the call to crusade and *jihad*, knowing full well that

---

* Even in the modern era many histories of the crusades written by 'western' scholars have been coloured (consciously or unconsciously) by a degree of bias, because most present this era from a Christian standpoint. This innate partiality might manifest itself relatively subtly – in the decision to describe the outcome of a battle as a victory or defeat, a triumph or disaster. In this account, which is divided into five parts, I have made a deliberate attempt to counteract this tendency by switching the point of view from western European Christian to Near Eastern Muslim in each major section. The book's core, covering the Third Crusade, alternates between its two major protagonists – Saladin and Richard the Lionheart.

they might face intense suffering and even death? It is also imperative
to consider whether the First Crusade, launched at the end of the
eleventh century, was an act of Christian aggression, and what
perpetuated the cycle of religious violence in the Near East for the
two hundred years that followed.

The outcomes and impact of these holy wars are equally
significant. Was the crusading era a period of unqualified discord –
the product of an inevitable 'clash of civilisations' – or one that
revealed a capacity for coexistence and constructive cross-cultural
contact between Christendom and Islam? We must ask who, in the
end, won the war for the Holy Land and why, but more pressing still
is the question of how this age of conflict affected history, and why
these ancient struggles still seem to cast a shadow over the world to
this day.

MEDIEVAL EUROPE

In the year 1000, the county of Anjou (in west-central France) was
ruled by Fulk Nerra (987–1040), a brutal and rapacious warlord. Fulk
spent most of his fifty-three years in power locked in near-constant
struggle: fighting on every front to retain control of his unruly county;
scheming to preserve his independence from the feeble French
monarchy; and preying upon his neighbours in search of land and
plunder. He was a man accustomed to violence, both on and off the
battlefield – capable of burning his wife at the stake for adultery and
of orchestrating the ruthless murder of a royal courtier.

But for all the blood on his hands, Fulk was also a committed
Christian – one who recognised that his brutish ways were, by the
tenets of his faith, inherently sinful, and thus might lead to his eternal
damnation. The count himself admitted in a letter that he had
'caused a great deal of bloodshed in various battles' and was therefore
'terrified by the fear of Hell'. In the hope of purifying his soul, he
made three pilgrimages to Jerusalem, more than 2,000 miles away.

On the last of these journeys, now an old man, Fulk was said to have been led naked to the Holy Sepulchre – the site of Jesus' death and resurrection – with a leash around his neck, being beaten by his servant while he begged Christ for forgiveness.[2]

What drove Fulk Nerra to make such drastic gestures of repentance, and why was his story filled with such feral turmoil? Even people in the eleventh century were shocked by the count's unbridled sadism and outlandish acts of devotion, so his career evidently was an extreme example of medieval life. But his experiences and mindset were reflective of the forces that shaped the Middle Ages and gave birth to the crusades. And it would be people like Fulk – including many of his own descendants – who stood in the front line of these holy wars.

Western Europe in the eleventh century

Many of those who lived in the same early eleventh-century world as Fulk Nerra feared that they were witnessing the last dark and desperate days of humanity. Apocalyptic dread reached its height in the early 1030s, when it was thought the millennial anniversary of Jesus' death would presage the Last Judgement. One chronicler wrote of this time: 'Those rules which governed the world were replaced by chaos. They knew then that the [End of Days] had arrived.' This palpable anxiety alone helps to explain Fulk's penitent mentality. But as far as the count and his contemporaries were concerned, it had not always been so. They harboured a collective memory of a more peaceful and prosperous past; a golden age when Christian emperors ruled in God's name, bringing order to the world in accordance with His divine will. This rather hazily imagined ideal was by no means a perfect recollection of Europe's history, but it did encapsulate some shards of truth.

Roman imperial rule had provided stability and affluence in the West until the late fourth century CE (Common Era). In the East the Roman Empire lived on until 1453, ruled from the great city of Constantinople, founded in 324 by Constantine the Great – the first emperor to convert to Christianity. Today, historians refer to this enduring realm as Byzantium. In the West between the fifth and the seventh centuries power devolved on to a bewildering array of 'barbarian' tribes, but around the year 500 one of these groups, the Franks, established control over north-eastern Gaul, giving rise to a kingdom known as Francia (from which the modern nation of France took its name).* By 800, a descendant of these Franks, Charlemagne (768–814), had united such a huge swathe of territory – encompassing much of modern France, Germany, Italy and the Low Countries – that he could lay claim to the long-dormant title of emperor of the West. Charlemagne and his successors, the Carolingians, presided over a short-lived period of renewed security, but their empire crumbled under the weight of succession disputes and repeated invasions by Scandinavian Vikings and eastern European Magyars. From the 850s onwards, Europe was again ripped apart by political fragmentation, warfare and unrest. The embattled kings of Germany still sought to claim the imperial title and a royal house in France survived in a desperately emasculated state. By the eleventh century Constantine and Charlemagne had passed into legend, the embodiments of a distant era. In the course of medieval European history, many a Christian king sought to emulate and imitate their supposed achievements – among them some who would fight in the crusades.

By the time of Fulk Nerra, the West was gradually emerging from this post-Carolingian age of decline (despite the predictions of Armageddon), but in terms of political and military power, and social

---

* France proved to be a major centre of crusade enthusiasm and recruitment when the wars for the Holy Land began in 1095. Even so, not all crusaders were French, but contemporaries who wrote about this era – especially those, like Muslims, who were looking in from outside western Europe – tended to brand all Christian participants in these holy wars as 'Franks' (in Arabic, *Ifranj*). It therefore has become common practice to describe the crusaders and those western Europeans who settled in the Near East as the Franks.

and economic organisation, most regions were still highly fragmented. Europe was not partitioned into nation states in the modern sense of the word. Instead, the likes of Germany, Spain, Italy and France were divided into many smaller polities, ruled over by warrior-lords, most of whom were bound by only loose ties of association and loyalty to a crown monarch. Like Fulk, these men bore titles such as *dux* and *comes* (duke and count) that harkened back to Roman and Carolingian times, and were drawn from the ranks of a nascent military aristocracy – the increasingly dominant class of well-equipped, semi-professional fighting men who came to be known as knights.

Eleventh-century Europe was not in a state of fully fledged anarchy, but the ravening violence of feud and vendetta was commonplace, and lawlessness endemic. Society was highly localised. Nature's grip over the West had yet to be loosened, with vast swathes of land still blanketed in forest or left open and uncultivated, and most major road systems dated back to imperial Rome. It was common, in such a world, to go through life without travelling more than fifty miles from one's birthplace – a fact that made Fulk Nerra's repeated journeys to Jerusalem, and the later popularity of crusading in the distant Holy Land, all the more extraordinary. Mass communication also did not exist as it would be understood today, because most people were illiterate and printing had not yet been invented.

Nevertheless, in the course of the central Middle Ages (between 1000 and 1300), western civilisation began to show sure signs of development and expansion. Urbanisation slowly gathered pace, and growth in the population of towns and cities helped to stimulate economic recovery and the revival of a monetary-based economy. Among those communities who spearheaded a resurgence in long-distance trade were the seaborne merchants of Italy, based in cities like Amalfi, Pisa, Genoa and Venice. Other groups demonstrated a marked propensity for military conquest. The Normans of northern France (descendants of Viking settlers) were especially energetic in the mid-eleventh century: colonising Anglo-Saxon England; and seizing southern Italy and Sicily from the Byzantines and North African Arabs. Meanwhile, in Iberia, a number of Christian realms began to push their borders south, reconquering territory from the Muslims of Spain.

As western Europeans began to look beyond their early medieval horizons, the forces of commerce and conquest brought them into closer contact with the wider world, and with the great civilisations of the Mediterranean: the ancient 'eastern Roman' Byzantine Empire and the sprawling Arab-Islamic world. These long-established 'superpowers' were historic centres of wealth, culture and military might. As such, they tended to regard the West as little more than a barbarian backwater – the dismal homeland of savage tribesmen who might be fierce fighters, but were essentially just an uncontrollable rabble, and thus posed no real threat. The coming of the crusades would help to overturn this dynamic, even as it confirmed many of these prejudices.[3]

Latin Christendom

Ancient Roman rule undoubtedly had a profound effect upon all aspects of western history, but the empire's most important and enduring legacy was the Christianisation of Europe. Constantine the Great's decision to embrace Christianity – then a minor eastern sect – after experiencing a 'vision' in 312 CE, catapulted this faith on to the world stage. Within less than a century Christianity had displaced paganism as the empire's official religion, and through the agency of Roman influence 'Christ's message' spread across Europe. Even as the political state that had given it impetus faltered, the Christian faith gained in strength. Europe's new 'barbarian' chieftains converted and soon began to claim that they had a divinely ordained right to rule over their tribes as kings. The mighty unifier Charlemagne styled himself as a 'sacral', or sacred, ruler – one who held the right and responsibility to defend and uphold the faith. By the eleventh century, Latin Christianity (so-called because of the language of its scripture and ritual) had penetrated to almost every corner of the West.*

A central figure in this process was the pope in Rome. Christian tradition maintained that there were five great fathers – or patriarchs – of the Church spread across the Mediterranean world at Rome, Constantinople, Antioch, Jerusalem and Alexandria. But the bishop of Rome – who came to call himself 'papa' (father) or pope – sought to claim pre-eminence among all these. Throughout the Middle Ages, the papacy struggled not only to assert its ecumenical (worldwide) 'rights', but also to wield meaningful authority over the ecclesiastical hierarchy of the Latin West. The decline of the Roman and Carolingian Empires disrupted frameworks of power within the Church, just as it had done within the secular sphere. Across Europe, bishops enjoyed centuries of independence and autonomy from papal control, with most prelates owing their first allegiance to local political rulers and the 'sacral' kings of the West. By the early eleventh century, popes were straining simply to make their will felt in central Italy, and in the decades that followed they would sometimes even find themselves exiled from Rome itself.

Nonetheless, it would be a Roman pope who launched the crusades, prompting tens of thousands of Latins to take up arms and fight in the name of Christianity. This remarkable feat, in and of itself, served to extend and strengthen papal power, but the preaching of these holy wars should not be regarded as a purely cynical, self-serving act. The papacy's role as the progenitor of crusading did help to consolidate Roman ecclesiastical authority in regions like France and, to begin with at least, crusader forces looked as though they might follow the pope's commands, functioning almost as papal armies. Even so, more altruistic impulses probably also were at work. Many

---

* The adherents of this Latin branch of Christianity – which today is more commonly known as Roman Catholicism – are more accurately described in a medieval setting as 'Latins'.

medieval popes seem earnestly to have believed that they had a wider duty to protect Christendom. They also expected, upon death, to answer to God for the fate of every soul once in their care. By constructing an ideal of Christian holy war – in which acts of sanctified violence would actually help to cleanse a warrior's soul of sin – the papacy was opening up a new path to salvation for its Latin 'flock'.

In fact, the crusades were just one expression of a much wider drive to rejuvenate western Christendom, championed by Rome from the mid-eleventh century onwards in the so-called 'Reform movement'. As far as the papacy was concerned, any failings within the Church were just the symptoms of a deeper malaise: the corrupting influence of the secular world, long enshrined by the links between clergymen and lay rulers. And the only way to break the stranglehold enjoyed by emperors and kings over the Church was for the Pope finally to realise his God-given right to supreme authority. The most vocal and extreme proponent of these views was Pope Gregory VII (1073–85). Gregory ardently believed that he had been set on Earth to transform Christendom by seizing absolute control of Latin ecclesiastical affairs. In pursuit of this ambition, he was willing to embrace almost any available means – even the potential use of violence, enacted by papal servants whom he called 'soldiers of Christ'. Although Gregory went too far, too fast and ended his pontificate in ignominious exile in southern Italy, his bold strides did much to advance the twinned causes of reform and papal empowerment, establishing a platform from which one of his successors (and former adviser), Pope Urban II (1088–99), could instigate the First Crusade.[4]

Urban's call for a holy war found a willing audience across Europe, in large part because of the prevailing religious atmosphere in the Latin world. Across the West, Christianity was an almost universally accepted faith and, in contrast to modern secularised European society, the eleventh century was a profoundly spiritual era. This was a setting in which Christian doctrine impinged upon virtually every facet of human life – from birth and death, to sleeping and eating, marriage and health – and the signs of God's omnipotence were clear for all to see, made manifest through acts of 'miraculous' healing, divine revelation and earthly and celestial portents. Concepts such as love, charity, obligation and tradition all helped to shape medieval attitudes to devotion, but perhaps the most powerful conditioning influence was fear; the same fear that made Fulk Nerra believe that his soul was in peril. The Latin Church of the eleventh century taught that every human would face a moment of judgement – the so-called 'weighing of souls'. Purity would bring the everlasting reward of heavenly salvation, but sin would result in damnation and an eternity of hellish torment. For the faithful of the day, the visceral reality of the dangers involved was driven home by graphic images in religious art and sculpture of the punishments to be suffered by those deemed impure: wretched sinners strangled by demons; the damned herded into the fires of the underworld by hideous devils.

Under these circumstances, it was hardly surprising that most medieval Latin Christians were obsessed with sinfulness, contamination and the impending afterlife. One extreme expression of the pressing desire to pursue an unsullied and perfected Christian life was monasticism – in which monks or nuns made vows of poverty, chastity and obedience, and lived in ordered communities, dedicating themselves to God. By the eleventh century, one of the most popular forms of monastic life was that advocated by the Burgundian monastery of Cluny, in eastern France. The Cluniac movement grew to have some 2,000 dependent houses from England to Italy and enjoyed far-reaching influence, not least in helping to develop and advance the ideals of the Reform movement. Its power was reaching an apex in the 1090s, when Urban II, himself a former Cluniac monk, held the papal office.

Of course, the demands of monasticism were beyond the means of most medieval Christians. And for ordinary laymen and women, the path to God was strewn with the dangers of transgression, because many seemingly unavoidable aspects of human existence – like pride, hunger, lust and violence – were deemed sinful. But a number of interconnected salvific 'remedies' were available (even though their theoretical and theological foundations had yet fully to be refined). Latins were encouraged to confess their offences to a priest, who would then allot them a suitable penance, the performance of which supposedly cancelled out the taint of sin. The most common of all penitential acts was prayer, but the giving of alms to the poor or donations to religious houses and the performance of a purgative devotional journey (or pilgrimage) were also popular. These meritorious deeds might also be undertaken outside the formal framework of penance, either as a sort of spiritual down payment, or in order to entreat God, or one of his saints, for aid.

Fulk Nerra was operating within this established belief structure when he sought salvation in the early eleventh century. One remedy he pursued was the foundation of a new monastery within his county of Anjou, at Beaulieu. According to Fulk's own testimony, he did this 'so that monks would be joined together there and pray day and night for the redemption of [my] soul'. This idea of tapping into the spiritual energy produced in monasteries through lay patronage was still at work in 1091, when the southern French noble Gaston IV of Béarn decided to donate some property to the Cluniac house of St Foi, Morlaàs, in Gascony. Gaston was an avowed supporter of the Reform papacy, had campaigned against the Moors of Iberia in 1087 and would go on to become a crusader. The legal document recording his gift to St Foi stated that he acted for the benefit of his own soul, that of his wife and children, and in the hope that 'God may help us in this world in all our needs, and in the future grant us eternal life'. In fact, by Gaston's day most of western Christendom's lay nobility enjoyed similar well-established connections with monasteries, and this had a marked effect upon the speed at which crusade enthusiasm spread across Europe after 1095. Partly, this was because the vow undertaken by knights committing to the holy war mirrored that taken by monks – a similarity that seemed to confirm the efficacy of fighting for God. More important still was the fact that the papacy, with its links to religious houses like Cluny, relied upon the monasteries of the Latin West to help spread and support the call to crusade.

The second path to salvation embraced by Fulk Nerra was pilgrimage, and, given his multiple journeys to Jerusalem, he evidently found this particular form of penitential devotion especially compelling – later writing that the cleansing force of his experiences left him in 'high spirits [and] exultant'. Latin pilgrims often travelled to less distant locations – including major centres like Rome and Santiago de Compostela (in north-east Spain), and even local shrines and churches – but the Holy City was fast emerging as the most revered destination. Jerusalem's unrivalled sanctity was also reflected in the common medieval practice of placing the city at the centre of maps depicting the world. All of this had a direct bearing upon the exultant reaction to crusade preaching because the holy war was presented as a form of armed pilgrimage, one that had Jerusalem as its ultimate objective.[5]

Warfare and violence in Latin Europe

In launching the crusades the papacy sought to recruit members of one social grouping above all others: the knights of Latin Europe. This military class was still at an early stage of development in the eleventh century. The fundamental characteristic of medieval knighthood was the ability to fight as a mounted warrior.* Knights were almost always accompanied by at least four or five followers who

---

* By modern standards, eleventh-century warhorses were relatively small – indeed, at an average twelve hands in height, today most would be classified as little more than ponies. Even so, they were cripplingly expensive to purchase and just as costly to maintain (requiring feed, horseshoes and the care of a dedicated squire). Most knights also needed at least one additional lighter mount upon which to travel. But small as they were, these warhorses still gave warriors huge advantages during hand-to-hand combat in terms of height, reach, speed and mobility. As equipment, fighting techniques and training improved, knights mounted on a stirruped (and therefore more stable) saddle also developed the ability to carry a heavy spear or lance couched underarm and learned to cooperate in a massed charge. The sheer brute force of this type of attack could utterly overwhelm an unprepared enemy.

could act as servants – tending to their master's mount, weaponry and welfare – but who also were capable of fighting as foot soldiers. When the crusades began, these men were not members of full-time standing armies. Most knights were warriors, but also lords or vassals, landholders and farmers – who would expect to give over no more than a few months in any one year to warfare, and even then did not usually fight in established, well-drilled groups.

The standard forms of warfare in eleventh-century Europe, familiar to almost all knights, involved a mixture of short-distance raiding, skirmishing – which was usually a ragged affair, characterised by chaotic close-quarter combat – and sieges of the many wood- or stone-based castles littered throughout the West. Few Latin soldiers had experience of large-scale pitched battles, because this form of conflict was incredibly unpredictable and therefore generally avoided. Virtually none would have fought in a protracted, long-range campaign of the sort involved in crusading. As such, the holy wars in the East would require the warriors of Latin Christendom to adapt and improve some of their martial skills.[6]

Before the preaching of the First Crusade, most Latin knights still regarded acts of bloodshed as inherently sinful, but they already were accustomed to the idea that, in the eyes of God, certain forms of warfare were more justifiable than others. There also was some sense that the papacy even might be capable of sanctioning violence.

At first sight, Christianity does appear to be a pacifistic faith. The New Testament Gospels record many occasions when Jesus seemed to reject or prohibit violence: from his warning that he who lived by violence would die by violence, to the Sermon on the Mount's exhortation to turn the other cheek in response to a blow. The Old Testament also appears to offer clear guidance on the question of violence, with the Mosaic Commandment: 'Thou shall not kill.' In the course of the first millennium CE, however, Christian theologians pondering the union between their faith and the military empire of Rome began to question whether scripture really did offer such a decisive condemnation of warfare. The Old Testament certainly seemed equivocal, because as a history of the Hebrews' desperate struggle for survival, it described a series of holy wars sanctioned by God. This suggested that, under the right circumstances, even vengeful or aggressive warfare might be permissible; and in the New Testament, Jesus had said that he came to bring not peace but a sword, and had used a whip of cords to beat moneylenders out of the Temple.

The most influential early Christian thinker to wrestle with these issues was the North African bishop St Augustine of Hippo (354–430 CE). His work laid the foundation upon which the papacy eventually built the notion of crusading. St Augustine argued that a war could be both lawful and justifiable if fought under strict conditions. His complex theories were later simplified to produce just three prerequisites of a Just War: proclamation by a 'legitimate authority', such as a king or bishop; a 'just cause', like defence against enemy attack or the recovery of lost territory; and prosecution with 'right intention', that is, with the least possible violence. These three Augustinian principles underpinned the crusading ideal, but they fell far short of advocating the sanctification of war.

In the course of the early Middle Ages, Augustine's work was judged to demonstrate that certain, unavoidable, forms of military conflict might be 'justified' and thus acceptable in the eyes of God. But fighting under these terms was still sinful. By contrast, a Christian holy war, such as a crusade, was believed to be one that God actively supported, capable of bringing spiritual benefit to its participants. The chasm separating these two forms of violence was only bridged after centuries of sporadic and incremental theological experimentation. This process was accelerated by the martial enthusiasm of the post-Roman 'barbarian' rulers of Europe. Their Christianisation injected a new 'Germanic' acceptance of warfare and warrior life into the Latin faith. Under the Carolingians, for example, bishops began sponsoring and even directing brutal campaigns of conquest and conversion against the pagans of eastern Europe. And by the turn of the millennium it had become relatively common for Christian clergy to bless weapons and armour, and the lives of various 'warrior saints' were being celebrated.

During the second half of the eleventh century, Latin Christianity began to edge ever closer towards the acceptance of holy war. In the early stages of the Reform movement, the papacy began to perceive the need for a military arm with which to reinforce its agenda and manifest its will. This prompted a succession of popes to experiment with the sponsoring of warfare, calling upon Christian supporters to defend the Church in return for vaguely expressed forms of spiritual reward. It was under the forceful guidance of Pope Gregory VII that the doctrine and application of sacred violence jumped ahead. Intent upon recruiting a papal army that owed its allegiance to Rome, he set about reinterpreting Christian tradition. For centuries theologians had characterised the internal, spiritual battle that devoted Christians waged against sin as the 'warfare of Christ', and monks were sometimes described as the 'soldiers of Christ'. Gregory twisted this idea to suit his purpose, proclaiming that all lay society had one overriding obligation: to defend the Latin Church as 'soldiers of Christ' through actual physical warfare.

Early in his pontificate, Gregory laid plans for a grand military enterprise that can be regarded as the first real prototype for a crusade. In 1074 he tried to launch a holy war in the eastern Mediterranean in aid of the Greek Orthodox Christians of Byzantium, who were, he claimed, 'daily being butchered like cattle' by the Muslims of Asia Minor. Latins fighting in this campaign were promised a 'heavenly reward'. His grandiose project fell flat, eliciting very limited recruitment, perhaps because Gregory had boldly pronounced his intention to lead the campaign in person. The pope's 1074 formulation of the link between military service to God and the resultant spiritual recompense still lacked specificity. But in the early 1080s, with the conflict with the German emperor in full flow, Gregory took a critical step towards clarification. He wrote that his supporters should fight the emperor and face 'the danger of the coming battle for the remission of all their sins'. This seemed to indicate that participation in this holy struggle had the same power to purify the soul as other forms of penance because it promised, just like a pilgrimage, to be both difficult and perilous. As yet, this more logical explanation for the redemptive quality of sanctified violence did not take hold, but it set an important precedent for later popes. In fact, the very novelty of Gregory's radical approach to the militarisation of Latin Christendom caused condemnation among some contemporaries, and he was accused in ecclesiastical circles of dabbling in practices 'new and unheard of throughout the centuries'. His vision was so extreme that, when his successor Pope Urban II offered a more measured and carefully constructed ideal, he appeared almost conservative in comparison and thus prompted less criticism.[7]

Gregory VII had taken Latin theology to the brink of holy war, arguing that the Pope had the clear right to summon armies to fight for God and the Latin Church. He also went some considerable way to grounding the concept of sanctified violence within a penitential framework – an idea that would be part of the essence of crusading. Nonetheless, Gregory cannot be regarded as the prime architect of the crusades because he manifestly failed to construct a compelling and convincing notion of holy war that resonated with the Christians of Europe. That would be the work of Pope Urban II.

THE MUSLIM WORLD

From the end of the eleventh century onwards, the crusades pitted western European Franks against the Muslims of the eastern Mediterranean. This was not because these holy wars were launched, first and foremost, to eradicate Islam, or even to convert Muslims to the Christian faith. Rather, it was a consequence of Islam's dominion over the Holy Land and the sacred city of Jerusalem.

The early history of Islam

According to Muslim tradition, Islam was born in c. 610 CE when Muhammad – an illiterate, forty-year-old Arab native of Mecca (in modern Saudi Arabia) – began to experience a series of 'revelations' from Allah (God), relayed by the Archangel Gabriel. These 'revelations', regarded as the sacred and immutable words of God, were later set down in written form to become the Koran. During his lifetime, Muhammad set out to convert the pagan polytheist Arabs of Mecca and the surrounding Hijaz region (on the Arabian Peninsula's western coast) to the monotheistic faith of Islam. This proved to be no easy task. In 622 the Prophet was forced to flee to the nearby city of Medina, a journey which served as the starting date for the Muslim calendar, and he then waged a bloody and prolonged war of religion against Mecca, finally conquering the city shortly before his death in 632.

The religion founded by Muhammad – Islam, meaning submission to the will of God – had common roots with Judaism and Christianity. During his life, the Prophet came into contact with adherents of these two faiths in Arabia and the eastern Roman Empire and his 'revelations' were presented as the perfecting refinement of these earlier religions. For this reason, Muhammad acknowledged the likes of Moses, Abraham and even Jesus as prophets, and a whole *sura* (or chapter) of the Koran was dedicated to the Virgin Mary.

During Muhammad's own life, and in the few years immediately following his death, the warring tribes of the Arabian Peninsula were united under the banner of Islam. Over the next few decades, under the guidance of a series of able and ambitious caliphs (the Prophet's successors) these Muslim Arabs proved to be an almost unstoppable force. Their incredible martial dynamism was married to a seemingly insatiable appetite for conquest – a hunger sustained by the Koran's explicit demand for the Muslim faith and the rule of Islamic law to be spread unceasingly across the world. The Arab-Islamic approach to the subjugation of new territories also eased the path to exponential growth. Rather than requiring total submission and immediate conversion to Islam, the Muslims allowed 'Peoples of the Book', such as Jews and Christians, to continue in their faiths in return for the payment of a poll tax.

In the mid-630s ferocious armies of highly mobile, mounted Arab tribesmen began to pour out of the Arabian Peninsula. By 650 they had achieved startling success. With mercurial speed, Palestine, Syria, Iraq, Iran and Egypt were absorbed into the new Arab-Islamic state. Over the next century the pace of expansion slowed from this breakneck pace, but inexorable gains continued, such that in the mid-eighth century the Muslim world stretched from the Indus River and the borders of China in the east, across North Africa to Spain and southern France in the west.

In the context of crusading history, a critical stage in this whole process was the capture of Jerusalem in 638 from the Greek Christians of Byzantium. This ancient city came to be revered as Islam's third-holiest site, after Mecca and Medina. In part this was due to Islam's Abrahamic heritage, but it was also dependent upon the belief that Muhammad had ascended to Heaven from Jerusalem during his 'Night Journey', and the associated tradition identifying the Holy City as the focus for the impending End of Days.

It was once popular to suggest that the Islamic world might have swept across all Europe, had not the Muslims been twice thwarted in their attempts to capture Constantinople (in 673 and 718) and then defeated in 732 at Poitiers by Charlemagne's Frankish grandfather Charles the Hammer. In fact, important as these reversals were, a fundamental and profoundly limiting weakness within Islam had already shown its face: intractable and embittered religious and political division. At their core, these issues related to disputes over the legitimacy of Muhammad's caliphal successors and the interpretation of his 'revelations'.

Problems were apparent as early as 661, when the established line of 'Rightly Guided Caliphs' ended with the death of 'Ali (the Prophet's cousin and son-in-law) and the rise of a rival Arab clan – the Umayyad dynasty. The Umayyads moved the capital of the Muslim world beyond the confines of Arabia for the first time, settling in the great Syrian metropolis of Damascus, and they held sway over Islam until the mid-eighth century. However, this same period witnessed the emergence of the Shi'a (literally the 'party' or 'faction'), a Muslim sect who argued that only descendants of 'Ali and his wife Fatima (Muhammad's daughter) could lawfully hold the title of caliph. Shi'ite Muslims initially set out to contest the political authority of the mainstream Sunni form of Islam, but over time the schism between these two branches of the faith took on a doctrinal dimension, as Shi'ites developed distinct approaches to theology, religious ritual and law.[8]

The fragmentation of the Muslim world

Over the next four centuries, the divisions within the Muslim world deepened and proliferated. In 750 a bloody coup brought Umayyad rule to an end, propelling another Arab dynasty – the Abbasids – to power. They shifted the centre of Sunni Islam even further from the Arabian homelands, founding a spectacular new capital in Iraq: the purpose-built city of Baghdad. This visionary measure had profound and far-reaching consequences. It heralded a comprehensive political, cultural and economic reorientation on the part of the Sunni ruling elite, away from the Levantine Near East to Mesopotamia – the cradle of ancient civilisation between the mighty Euphrates and Tigris Rivers, sometimes known as the Fertile Crescent – and further east into Persian Iran and beyond. Abbasid patronage also transformed Baghdad into one of the world's great centres of scientific and philosophical learning. For the next five hundred years the heart of Sunni Islam lay, not in Syria or the Holy Land, but in Iraq and Iran.

However, Abbasid ascendancy coincided with the gradual dismemberment and fragmentation of the monolithic Islamic state. The Muslim rulers of Iberia (sometimes known as the Moors) broke away to establish an independent realm in the eighth century; and, over the decades, the rift between the Sunni and Shi'a strands of Islam gradually intensified. Communities of Shi'ite Muslims continued to live, largely in peace, alongside and among Sunnis across the Near and Middle East. But in 969 a particularly assertive

Shi'ite faction seized control of North Africa. Championed by a dynasty known as the Fatimids (because they claimed descent from Fatima, Muhammad's daughter), they set up their own rival Shi'ite caliph, rejecting Sunni Baghdad's authority. The Fatimids soon proved themselves to be potent adversaries – conquering large swathes of the Near East from the Abbasids, including Jerusalem, Damascus and sections of the eastern Mediterranean coastline. By the late eleventh century, the Abbasids and Fatimids regarded each other as avowed foes. Thus, by the time of the crusades, Islam was riven by an elemental schism – one that prevented the Muslim rulers of Egypt and Iraq from offering any form of coordinated or concerted resistance to Christian invasion.

Even as the enmity between the Sunnis and Shi'ites hardened, the degree of influence exercised by both the Abbasid and Fatimid caliphs dwindled. They remained as nominal figureheads – in theory retaining absolute control over religious and political affairs – but in practice executive power came to be wielded by their secular lieutenants: in Baghdad, the sultan; in Cairo, the vizier.

A further, dramatic change transformed the world of Islam in the eleventh century – the coming of the Turks. From around 1040, these nomadic tribesmen from Central Asia – noted for their warlike character and agile skill as mounted archers – began to seep into the Middle East. One particular clan, the Seljuqs (from the steppes of Russia, beyond the Aral Sea), spearheaded the Turkish migration. Having adopted the religion of Sunni Islam, these fearsome Seljuqs declared their unswerving allegiance to the Abbasid caliph and readily supplanted the now sedentary Arab and Persian aristocracy of Iran and Iraq. By 1055, the Seljuq warlord Tughrul Beg had been appointed as sultan of Baghdad and could claim effective overlordship of Sunni Islam; a role which members of his dynasty would hold as a hereditary right for more than a century. The advent of the Seljuq Turks brought a new, vital lease of life and unity to the Abbasid world. Their restless energy and martial ferocity soon brought sweeping gains. To the south, the Fatimids were driven back and

Damascus and Jerusalem reconquered; notable victories were scored against the Byzantines in Asia Minor; and a Seljuq splinter group eventually founded their own independent sultanate in Anatolia.

By the early 1090s the Seljuqs had reshaped the Sunni Muslim world. Tughrul Beg's able and ambitious grandson Malik Shah held the office of sultan and, together with his brother Tutush, enjoyed relatively secure rule of Mesopotamia and most of the Levant. This new Turkish empire – sometimes referred to as the Great Seljuq Sultanate of Baghdad – was forged through ruthless despotism and the presentation of the Shi'ites as dangerous, heretical enemies against whom Sunnis must unite. But when Malik Shah died in 1092, his mighty realm quickly collapsed amid succession crises and chaotic civil war. His two young sons fought to be named sultan, contesting control of Iraq and Iran; while in Syria, Tutush sought to seize power for himself. When he died in 1095, his sons Ridwan and Duqaq likewise squabbled over their inheritance, snatching Aleppo and Damascus respectively. At this same time, conditions in Shi'ite Egypt were little better. Here, too, the precipitous deaths of the Fatimid caliph and his vizier in 1094 and 1095 brought sudden change, culminating in the rise of a new vizier of Armenian heritage, al-Afdal. Thus, in the very year that the crusades began, Sunni Islam was in a turbulent state of disarray and a new ruler of Fatimid Egypt was just finding his feet. There is no evidence to suggest that Christians in the West knew of these manifold difficulties, so they cannot be regarded as a definite trigger for the holy war to come. Even so, the timing of the First Crusade was remarkably propitious.[9]

The Near East at the end of the eleventh century

The endemic disunity afflicting Islam at the end of the eleventh century would exert a profound influence over the course of the crusades. So too did the Near East's distinctive cultural, ethnic and political make-up. In truth, this region – the battleground in the war for the Holy Land – cannot be spoken of as a Muslim world. The relatively tolerant approach to subjugation adopted during the early Arab-Islamic conquests meant that, even centuries later, the Levant still contained a very high proportion of indigenous Christians – from Greeks and Armenians to Syrians and Copts – as well as pockets of Jewish population. Nomadic communities of Bedouins also continued to range widely across the East – migrant Arabic-speaking Muslims, who had few fixed allegiances. This long-established pattern of settlement was overlaid by a numerically inferior Muslim ruling elite, itself made up of Arabs, some Persians and the newly arrived Turks. The Near East, therefore, was little more than a fractured patchwork of disparate social and devotional groupings, and not a purebred Islamic stronghold.

As far as the main powers within the Muslim world were concerned, the Levant was also something of a backwater – notwithstanding the political and spiritual significance attached to cities like Jerusalem and Damascus. For Sunni Seljuqs and Shi'ite Fatimids, the real centres of governmental authority, economic wealth and cultural identity were Mesopotamia and Egypt. The Near East was essentially the border zone between these two dominant spheres of influence, a world sometimes to be contested, but almost always to be treated as a secondary concern. Even during the reign of Malik Shah, no fully determined effort was made to subdue and integrate Syria into the sultanate, and much of the region was left in the hands of power-hungry, semi-independent warlords.

Thus, when Latin crusading armies arrived in the Near East to wage what essentially were frontier wars, they were not actually invading the heartlands of Islam. Instead, they were fighting for control of a land that, in some respects, was also a Muslim frontier, one peopled by an assortment of Christians, Jews and Muslims who, over the centuries, had become acculturated to the experience of conquest by an external force, be it at the hands of Byzantines and Persians, or Arabs and Turks.

Islamic warfare and jihad

In the late eleventh century, the style and practice of Muslim warfare were in a state of flux. The traditional mainstay of any Turkish fighting force was the lightly armoured mounted warrior, astride a fleet-footed pony, armed with a powerful composite bow that enabled him to loose streams of arrows from horseback. He might also be equipped with a light lance, single-edged sword, axe or dagger. These troops relied upon speed of movement and rapid manoeuvrability to overcome opponents.

The Turks classically employed two main tactics: encirclement – whereby an enemy was surrounded from all sides by a fast-moving, swirling mass of mounted warriors, and bombarded with ceaseless volleys of arrows; and feigned retreat – the technique of turning tail in battle in the hope of prompting an opponent to give fevered chase, the indiscipline of which would break their formation and leave them vulnerable to sudden counter-attack. This style of combat was still favoured by the Seljuqs of Asia Minor, but the Turks of Syria and Palestine had begun to adopt a wider array of Persian and Arab military practices, adjusting to the use of more heavily armoured mounted lancers and larger infantry forces, and to the needs of siege warfare. By far and away the most common forms of warfare in the Near East were raiding, skirmishing and petty internecine struggles over power, land and wealth.[10] In theory, however, Muslim troops could be called upon to fight for a supposedly higher cause – that of holy war.

Islam had, from its earliest days, embraced warfare. Muhammad himself prosecuted a series of military campaigns while subjugating Mecca, and the explosive expansion of the Muslim world during the seventh and eighth centuries was fuelled by an avowed devotional obligation to spread Islamic rule. The union of faith and violence within the Muslim religion, therefore, was more rapid and natural than that which gradually developed in Latin Christianity.

In an attempt to define the role of warfare within Islam, Muslim scholars turned to the Koran and the *hadith*, the 'traditions' or sayings associated with Muhammad. These texts provided numerous examples of the Prophet advocating 'struggle in the path of God'. In the early Islamic period there was discussion about what this 'struggle' or *jihad* (literally 'striving') actually involved – and the debate continues to this day. Some, like the Muslim mystics, or *Sufis*, argued that the most important or 'Greater *jihad*' was the internal struggle waged against sin and error. But by the late eighth century, Sunni Muslim jurists had begun to develop a formal theory advocating what is sometimes termed the 'Lesser *jihad*': 'rising up in arms' to wage physical warfare against the infidel. To justify this they cited canonical evidence, such as verses from the ninth *sura* of the Koran, including: 'Fight the polytheists totally as they fight you totally', and *hadith*, such as Muhammad's declaration that: 'A morning or an evening expedition in God's path is better than the world and what it contains, and for one of you to remain in the line of battle is better than his prayers for sixty years.'

Legal treatises from this early period declared that *jihad* was an obligation incumbent upon all able-bodied Muslims, although the duty was primarily seen as being communal, rather than individual, and the responsibility for leadership ultimately rested with the caliph. Making reference to the likes of the *hadith* 'The gates of Paradise are under the shadow of the swords', these treatises also affirmed that those fighting in the *jihad* would be granted entry to the heavenly Paradise. Jurists posited a formal division of the world into two spheres – the *Dar al-Islam*, or 'House of Peace' (the area within which Muslim rule and law prevailed); and the *Dar al-harb*, or 'House of War' (the rest of the world). The express purpose of the *jihad* was to wage a relentless holy war in the *Dar al-harb*, until such time as all mankind had accepted Islam, or submitted to Muslim rule. No permanent peace treaties with non-Muslim enemies were permissible, and any temporary truces could last no more than ten years.

As the centuries passed, the driving impulse towards expansion encoded in this classical theory of *jihad* was gradually eroded. Arab tribesmen began to settle into more sedentary lifestyles and to trade with non-Muslims, such as the Byzantines. Holy wars against the likes of Christians continued, but they became far more sporadic and often were promoted and prosecuted by Muslim emirs, without caliphal endorsement. By the eleventh century, the rulers of Sunni Baghdad were far more interested in using *jihad* to promote Islamic orthodoxy by battling 'heretic' Shi'ites than they were in launching holy wars against Christendom. The suggestion that Islam should engage in an unending struggle to enlarge its borders and subjugate non-Muslims held little currency; so too did the idea of unifying in defence of the Islamic faith and its territories. When the Christian crusades began, the ideological impulse of devotional warfare thus lay dormant within the body of Islam, but the essential framework remained in place.[11]

Islam and Christian Europe on the eve of the crusades

A charged and vexatious question remains: did the Muslim world provoke the crusades, or were these Latin holy wars acts of aggression? This fundamental enquiry requires an assessment of the overall degree of threat posed to the Christian West by Islam in the eleventh century. In one sense, Muslims were pressing on the borders of Europe. To the east, Asia Minor had served for generations as a battleground between Islam and the Byzantine Empire; and Muslim armies had made repeated attempts to conquer Christendom's greatest metropolis – Constantinople. To the south-west, Muslims continued to rule vast tracts of the Iberian Peninsula and might one day push north again, beyond the Pyrenees. In reality, however, Europe was by no means engaged in an urgent struggle for survival on the eve of the crusades. No coherent, pan-Mediterranean onslaught threatened, because, although the Moors in Iberia and the Turks in Asia Minor shared a common religious heritage, they were never united in one purpose.

In fact, after the first forceful surge of Islamic expansion, the interaction between neighbouring Christian and Muslim polities had been relatively unremarkable; characterised, like that between any potential rivals, by periods of conflict and others of coexistence. There is little or no evidence to suggest that these two world religions were somehow locked in an inevitable and perpetual 'clash of civilisations'. From the tenth century onwards, for example, Islam and Byzantium developed a tense, sometimes quarrelsome respect for one another, but their relationship was no more fraught with conflict than that between the Greeks and their Slavic or Latin neighbours to the west.

This is not to suggest that the world was filled with utopian peace and harmony. The Byzantines were only too happy to exploit any signs of Muslim weakness. Thus, in 969, while the Abbasid world fragmented, Greek troops pushed eastwards, recapturing much of Asia Minor and recovering the strategically significant city of Antioch. And with the advent of the Seljuq Turks, Byzantium faced renewed military pressure. In 1071, the Seljuqs crushed an imperial army at the Battle of Manzikert (in eastern Asia Minor), and though historians no longer consider this to have been an utterly cataclysmic reversal for the Greeks, it still was a stinging setback that presaged notable Turkish gains in Anatolia. Fifteen years later, the Seljuqs also recovered Antioch.

Meanwhile, in Spain and Portugal, Christians had begun to reconquer territory from the Moors, and in 1085 the Iberian Latins achieved a deeply symbolic victory, seizing control of Toledo, the ancient Christian capital of Spain. Nevertheless, at this stage, the Latins' gradual southward expansion seems to have been driven by political and economic stimuli and not religious ideology. The conflict in Iberia did become more heated after 1086, when a fanatical Islamic sect known as the Almoravids invaded Spain from North Africa, supplanting surviving indigenous Moorish power in the peninsula. This new regime reinvigorated Muslim resistance, scoring a number of notable military victories against the Christians of the north. But Almoravid aggression cannot really be said to have sparked the crusades, because the Latin holy wars launched at the end of the eleventh century were directed towards the Levant, not Iberia.

So what did ignite the war between Christians and Muslims in the Holy Land? In one sense the crusades were a reaction to an act of Islamic aggression – the Muslim conquest of sacred Jerusalem – but this had taken place in 638, and thus was hardly a fresh offence. At the start of the eleventh century, the Church of the Holy Sepulchre, thought to enclose the site of Christ's crucifixion and resurrection, had been partially demolished by the volatile Fatimid ruler known to history as the Mad Caliph Hakim. His subsequent persecution of the local Christian population lasted for more than a decade, ending only when he declared himself a living God and turned on his own Muslim subjects. Tensions also seem to have been running high in 1027, when Muslims reportedly threw stones into the compound of the Holy Sepulchre. More recently, Latin Christians attempting to make devotional pilgrimages to the Levant, of whom there continued to be many, reported some difficulties in visiting the Holy Places, and spread stories of eastern Christian repression in Muslim Palestine.

Two Arabic accounts offer important but divergent insights into these issues. Ibn al-'Arabi, a Spanish Muslim pilgrim who set out for the Holy Land in 1092, described Jerusalem as a thriving centre of religious devotion for Muslims, Christians and Jews alike. He noted that Christians were permitted to keep their churches in a good state of repair, and gave no hint that pilgrims – be they Greek or Latin – were suffering abuse or interference. By contrast, the mid-twelfth-century Aleppan chronicler al-'Azimi wrote that: 'The people of the Syrian ports prevented Frankish and Byzantine pilgrims from crossing to Jerusalem. Those of them who survived spread the news about that to their country. So they prepared themselves for military invasion.' Clearly, al-'Azimi at least believed that Muslim attacks triggered the crusades.[12]

In fact, on the basis of all the surviving evidence, the case could be argued in either direction. By 1095 Muslims and Christians had been waging war against one another for centuries; no matter how far it was in the past, Islam undoubtedly had seized Christian territory, including Jerusalem; and Christians living in and visiting the Holy Land may have been subjected to persecution. On the other hand, the immediate context in which the crusades were launched gave no obvious clue that a titanic transnational war of religion was either imminent or inevitable. Islam was not about to initiate a grand offensive against the West. Nor were the Muslim rulers of the Near East engaging in acts akin to ethnic cleansing, or subjecting religious minority groups to widespread and sustained oppression. There may at times have been little love lost between Christian and Muslim neighbours, and perhaps there were outbreaks of intolerance in the Levant, but there was, in truth, little to distinguish all this from the endemic political, military and social struggles of the age.

I

THE COMING
OF THE
CRUSADES

I

HOLY WAR, HOLY LAND

On a late November morning in the year 1095, Pope Urban II delivered a sermon that would transform the history of Europe. His rousing words transfixed the crowd that had gathered in a small field outside the southern French town of Clermont, and in the months that followed his message reverberated across the West, igniting an embittered holy war that would endure for centuries to come.

Urban declared that Christianity was in dire peril, threatened by invasion and appalling oppression. The Holy City of Jerusalem was now in the hands of Muslims – 'a people . . . alien to God', bent upon ritual torture and unspeakable desecration. He called upon Latin Europe to rise up against this supposedly savage foe as 'soldiers of Christ', reclaiming the Holy Land and releasing eastern Christians from 'servitude'. Enticed by the promise that this righteous struggle would purge their souls of sin, tens of thousands of men, women and children marched out of the West to wage war against the Muslim world in the First Crusade.[1]

POPE URBAN AND THE IDEA OF CRUSADING

Urban II was perhaps sixty years old when he launched the First Crusade in 1095. The son of northern French nobility, and a former cleric and Cluniac monk, he became pope in 1088, at a time when the papacy, reeling from a rancorous and protracted power struggle with the emperor of Germany, stood on the brink of overthrow. So parlous was Urban's position that it took him six years to reassert control over Rome's Lateran Palace, the traditional seat of papal authority. Yet, through cautious diplomacy and the adoption of measured, rather than confrontational, policies of reform, the new pope oversaw a gradual renaissance in the prestige and influence of his office. By 1095 this slow rejuvenation had begun, but the papacy's notional right to act as head of the Latin Church and spiritual overlord to every Christian in western Europe was still far from realised.

It was against this background of partial recovery that the idea of the First Crusade was born. In March 1095 Urban was presiding over an ecclesiastical council in the northern Italian city of Piacenza when ambassadors from Byzantium arrived. They bore an appeal from the Greek Christian Emperor Alexius I Comnenus, a ruler whose astute and assertive governance had arrested decades of internal decline within the great eastern empire. Exorbitant programmes of taxation had refilled the imperial treasury in Constantinople, restoring Byzantium's aura of authority and munificence, but Alexius still faced an array of foreign enemies, including the Muslim Turks of Asia Minor. He thus dispatched a petition for military aid to the council in Piacenza, urging Urban to send a detachment of Latin troops to help repel the threat posed by Islam. Alexius probably hoped for little more than a token force of Frankish mercenaries, a small army that could be readily shaped and directed. In fact, over the next two years, his empire would be practically overrun by a tide of humankind.

The Greek emperor's request appears to have chimed with notions already fermenting in Urban II's mind, and through the spring and summer that followed the pope refined and developed these ideas, envisaging an endeavour that might fulfil a broader array of ambitions: a form of armed pilgrimage to the East, what is now called a 'crusade'. Historians have sometimes characterised Urban as the unwitting instigator of this momentous venture, suggesting that he expected only a few hundred knights to answer his call to arms. But in reality he seems to have had a fairly shrewd sense of the potential scale and scope of this enterprise and to have laid the foundations of widespread recruitment with some assiduity.

Urban recognised that developing the idea of an expedition to aid Byzantium offered a chance not only to defend eastern Christendom and improve relations with the Greek Church, but also to reaffirm and expand Rome's authority and to harness and redirect the destructive bellicosity of Christians living in the Latin West. This grand scheme would be launched as part of a broader campaign to extend the reach of papal influence beyond the confines of central Italy, into Urban's birthplace and homeland, France. From July 1095 onwards he began a lengthy preaching tour north of the Alps – the first such visit by a pope for close to half a century – and announced that a major Church council would be held in November at Clermont, in the Auvergne region of central France. Through the summer and early autumn Urban visited a succession of prominent monasteries, including his own former house of Cluny, cultivating support for Rome and preparing the ground for the unveiling of his 'crusading' idea. He also primed two men who would play central roles in the coming expedition: Adhémar, bishop of Le Puy, a leading Provençal churchman and an ardent supporter of the papacy; and Count Raymond of Toulouse, southern France's richest and most powerful secular lord.

By November the pope was ready to reveal his plans. Twelve archbishops, eighty bishops and ninety abbots congregated in Clermont for the largest clerical assembly of Urban's pontificate. Then, after nine days of general ecclesiastical debate, the pope announced his intention to deliver a special sermon. On 27 November, hundreds of spectators crowded into a field outside the city to hear him speak.[2]

The sermon at Clermont

At Clermont Urban called upon the Latin West to take up arms in pursuit of two linked goals. First, he proclaimed the need to protect

Christendom's eastern borders in Byzantium, emphasising the bond of Christian fraternity shared with the Greeks and the supposedly imminent threat of Muslim invasion. According to one account, he urged his audience 'to run as quickly as you can to the aid of your brothers living on the eastern shore' because 'the Turks . . . have overrun them right up to the Mediterranean Sea'. But the epic endeavour of which Urban spoke did not end with the provision of military aid to Constantinople. Instead, in a visionary masterstroke, he broadened his appeal to include an additional target, one guaranteed to stir Frankish hearts. Fusing the ideals of warfare and pilgrimage, he unveiled an expedition that would forge a path to the Holy Land itself, there to win back possession of Jerusalem, the most hallowed site in the Christian cosmos. Urban evoked the unparalleled sanctity of this city, this 'navel of the world', stating that it was 'the [fountain] of all Christian teaching', the place 'in which Christ lived and suffered'.[3]

In spite of the undoubted resonance of these twinned objectives, like any ruler recruiting for war the pope still needed to lend his cause an aura of legitimate justification and burning urgency, and here he faced a problem. Recent history offered no obvious event that might serve to focus and inspire a vengeful tide of enthusiasm. Yes, Jerusalem was ruled by Muslims, but this had been the case since the seventh century. And, while Byzantium may have been facing a deepening threat of Turkish aggression, western Christendom was not on the brink of invasion or annihilation at the hands of Near Eastern Islam. With no appalling atrocity or immediate threat to draw upon, Urban chose to cultivate a sense of immediacy and incite a wrathful hunger for retribution by demonising the enemy of his proposed 'crusade'.

Muslims therefore were portrayed as subhuman savages, bent upon the barbaric abuse of Christendom. Urban described how Turks 'were slaughtering and capturing many [Greeks], destroying churches and laying waste to the kingdom of God'. He also asserted that Christian pilgrims to the Holy Land were being abused and exploited by

Muslims, with the rich being stripped of their wealth by illegal taxes, and the poor subjected to torture:

The cruelty of these impious men goes even to the length that, thinking the wretches have eaten gold or silver, they either put scammony in their drink and force them to vomit or void their vitals, or – and this is unspeakable – they stretch asunder the coverings of all the intestines after ripping open their stomachs with a blade and reveal with horrible mutilation whatever nature keeps secret.

Christians living under Muslim rule in the Levant were said to have been reduced to a state of 'slavery' by 'sword, rapine and flame'. Prey to constant persecution, these unfortunates might suffer forced circumcision, protracted disembowelment or ritualised immolation. 'Of the appalling violation of women', the pope reportedly reflected, it would be 'more evil to speak than to keep silent'. Urban appears to have made extensive use of this form of graphic and incendiary imagery, akin to that which, in a modern-day setting, might be associated with war crimes or genocide. His accusations bore little or no relation to the reality of Muslim rule in the Near East, but it is impossible to gauge whether the pope believed his own propaganda or entered into a conscious campaign of manipulation and distortion. Either way, his explicit dehumanisation of the Muslim world served as a vital catalyst to the 'crusading' cause, and further enabled him to argue that fighting against an 'alien' other was preferable to war between Christians and within Europe.[4]

Pope Urban's decision to condemn Islam would have dark and enduring consequences in the years to come. But it is important to recognise that, in reality, the notion of conflict with the Muslim world was not written into the DNA of crusading. Urban's vision was of a devotional expedition sanctioned by Rome, focused first and foremost upon the defence or reconquest of sacred territory. In some ways his choice of Islam as an enemy was almost incidental, and there is little to suggest that the Latins or their Greek allies truly saw the Muslim world as an avowed enemy before 1095.*

The pulse-quickening notion of avenging the 'execrable abuses' enacted by demonised Muslims may have captivated Urban's audience at Clermont, but his 'crusading' message contained a further, even more powerful, lure; one that addressed the very nature of medieval Christian existence. Bred upon a vision of religious faith that emphasised the overbearing threat of sin and damnation, the Latins of the West were enmeshed in a desperate, lifelong spiritual struggle to purge the taint of corruption from their souls. Primed to seek redemption, they were thus enthralled when the pope declared that this expedition to the East would be a sacred venture, participation in which would lead to 'the remission of all their sins'. In the past, even 'just war' (that is, violence that God accepted as necessary) had still been regarded as innately sinful. But now Urban spoke of a conflict that transcended these traditional boundaries. His cause was to possess a sanctified quality – to be a holy war, not simply condoned by 'the Lord', but actively promoted and endorsed. According to one eyewitness, the pope even averred that 'Christ commands' the faithful to enlist.

Urban's genius was to construct the idea of 'crusading' within the framework of existing religious practice, thus ensuring that, in eleventh-century terms at least, the connection he established between warfare and salvation made clear, rational sense. In 1095, Latin Christians were accustomed to the idea that punishment owed through sinfulness might be cancelled out by confession and the performance of penitential activities, like prayer, fasting or pilgrimage. At Clermont, Urban fused the familiar notion of a salvific expedition with the more audacious concept of fighting for God, urging 'everyone of no matter what class . . . knight or foot-soldier,

---

* It is a popular misconception that crusading was a form of forceful evangelism. In fact, to begin with at least, religious conversion was not an essential element of crusading ideology.

rich or poor' to join what was to be, in essence, an armed pilgrimage. This monumental endeavour, laden with danger and the threat of intense suffering, would take its participants to the very gates of Jerusalem, Christendom's premier pilgrimage destination. As such, it promised to be an experience imbued with overwhelming redemptive potency; functioning as a 'super' penance, capable of scouring the spirit of any transgression.

From the rape of the Holy City by an alien enemy to the promise of a new path to redemption, the pope conjured a persuasive and emotive blend of images and ideas in support of his call to arms. The effect on his audience appears to have been electric, leaving 'the eyes of some bathed with tears, [while others] trembled'. In what must have been a pre-planned move, Adhémar, bishop of Le Puy, was the first to step forward to commit to the cause. On the following day the bishop was proclaimed papal legate (Urban's official representative) for the coming expedition. As its spiritual leader, he was expected to promote the pope's agenda, not least the policy of détente with the Greek Church of Byzantium. At the same time, messengers arrived from Raymond of Toulouse proclaiming the count's own support for the cause. Urban's sermon had been a resounding success, and over the next seven months he followed it up with an extended preaching tour, which saw his message crisscross France.[5]

And yet, in spite of the fact that Clermont must be regarded as the First Crusade's moment of genesis, it would be wrong to regard Urban II as the sole architect of the 'crusading ideal'. Previous historians have rightly emphasised his debt to the past, not least in relation to Pope Gregory VII's pioneering exploration of holy war theory. But it is equally important to recognise that the idea of the First Crusade – its nature, intentions and rewards – underwent ongoing, largely organic development throughout the expedition. Indeed, this process even continued after the event, as the world sought to interpret and understand such an epochal episode. It is all too easy to imagine the First Crusade as a single, well-ordered host, driven on to Jerusalem by Urban's impassioned preaching. In reality, the months and years that followed November 1095 saw disjointed waves of departure. Even what we commonly term the 'main armies' of the crusade began the first phase of their journey not as a single force, but rather as a rough conglomeration of smaller contingents, gradually feeling their way towards shared goals and systems of governance.

Within a month of the pope's first sermon, popular (and often unsanctioned) preachers had begun to proclaim the call to crusade across Europe. In their demagogic hands some of the subtleties surrounding the spiritual rewards associated with the expedition – what would come to be known as the crusading 'indulgence' – seem to have been eroded. Urban had likely intended that the remission offered would only apply to the temporal punishment for confessed sins; a rather complex formula, but one that adhered to the niceties of Church law. Later events suggest that many crusaders thought they had been given assured guarantees of heavenly salvation and thus believed that those who died during the campaign became sacred martyrs. Such notions continued to inform thinking about the crusading experience for centuries to come, establishing a gnawing rift between official and popular conceptions of these holy wars.

Notably, Pope Urban II did not invent the term 'crusade'. The expedition he launched at Clermont was so novel, and in some ways still so embryonic in its conception, that there was no word with which it could be described. Contemporaries generally termed this 'crusade' simply an *iter* (journey) or *peregrinatio* (pilgrimage). It was not until the close of the twelfth century that more specific terminology developed, in the form of the word *crucesignatus* (one signed with the cross) for a 'crusader', and the eventual adoption of the French term *croisade*, which roughly translates as 'the way of the cross'. For the sake of convention and clarity, historians have adopted the term 'crusade' for the Christian holy wars launched from 1095 onwards, but we should be aware that this lends a somewhat misleading aura of coherence and conformity to the early 'crusades'.[6]

The call of the cross

In the months that followed the Council of Clermont, the crusading message spread throughout western Europe, evoking an unprecedented reaction. While Pope Urban broadcast his message throughout France, bishops from across the Latin world who had attended his original sermon took the call back to their own dioceses.

The cause was also taken up by popular, rabble-rousing preachers, largely unsanctioned and unregulated by the Church. Most famous and remarkable of these was Peter the Hermit. Probably originating from a poor background in Amiens (north-eastern France), he became renowned for his austere, itinerant lifestyle, repellent appearance and unusual eating habits – one contemporary noted that 'he lived on wine and fish; he hardly ever, or never, ate bread'. By modern standards he might be deemed a vagabond, but among the poorer classes of eleventh-century France he was revered as a prophet. Such was his sanctity that his followers even collected the hairs of his mule as relics. A Greek contemporary noted: 'As if he had sounded a divine voice in the hearts of all, Peter the Hermit inspired the Franks from everywhere to gather together with their weapons, horses and other military equipment.' He must have been a truly inspirational orator – within six months of Clermont he had gathered an army, largely made up of poor rabble, numbering in excess of 15,000. In history this force, alongside a number of other contingents from Germany, has become known as the 'People's Crusade'. Spurred on by crusading fervour, its various elements set off for the Holy Land in spring 1096, months before any other army, making ill-disciplined progress towards Constantinople. Along the way, some of these 'crusaders' concluded that they might as well combat the 'enemies of Christ' closer to home, and thus carried out terrible massacres of Rhineland Jews. Almost as soon as the People's Crusade crossed into Muslim territory they were annihilated, although Peter the Hermit survived.[7]

This first wave of the crusade may have ended in failure, but, back in the West, larger armies were gathering. Public rallies, in which massed audiences were bombarded with emotive rhetoric, prompted fevered recruitment, and crusading enthusiasm also seems to have been propagated more informally through kinship groups, networks of papal supporters and the links between monastic communities and the nobility. Historians continue to dispute the numbers involved, primarily because of the unreliability of wildly inflated contemporary estimates (some of which exceed half a million people). Our best guess is that somewhere between 60,000 and 100,000 Latin Christians set off on the First Crusade, of which 7,000 to 10,000 were knights, perhaps 35,000 to 50,000 infantry troops and the remaining tens of thousands non-combatants, women and children. What is certain is that the call to crusade elicited an extraordinary response, the scale of which stunned the medieval world. Not since the distant glories of Rome had military forces of this size been assembled.[8]

At the heart of these armies were aristocratic knights, the emerging martial elite of the Middle Ages.* Pope Urban knew only too well the anxiety of these Christian warriors, trapped in a worldly profession imbued with violence, but taught by the Church that sinful warfare would lead to damnation. One contemporary observed:

> God has instituted in our time holy wars, so that the order of knights and the crowd running in their wake . . . might find a new way of gaining salvation. And so they are not forced to abandon

---

* Typically, the first crusader knights wore what, by the standards of the day, was heavy armour: a conical steel helmet over a mail hood or coif, and a thigh-length mail shirt over a padded jerkin – all of which could hope to stop a glancing blow, but not a solid cut or thrust. For this reason, a large metal-bound wooden shield was also commonly deployed. The standard mêlée weapons were the lance – used couched or thrown over arm – and a one-handed, double-edged long sword, perhaps two feet in length. These heavy, finely balanced blades were more useful as bludgeoning tools than as sharp-edged cutting weapons. Knights and infantrymen also commonly made use of longbows – about six feet in length and capable of delivering arrows to a distance of 300 yards – while some also adopted rudimentary forms of crossbow.

secular affairs completely by choosing the monastic life or any religious profession, as used to be the custom, but can attain some measure of God's grace while pursuing their own careers, with liberty and in the dress to which they are accustomed.

The pope had constructed the idea of an armed pilgrimage at least in part to address the spiritual dilemma threatening the knightly aristocracy, and he also knew that, with the nobility on board, retinues of knights and infantry would follow, for even though the crusade required a voluntary commitment, the intricate web of familial ties and feudal obligation bound social groups in a common cause. In effect, the pope set off a chain reaction, whereby every noble who took the cross stood at the epicentre of an expanding wave of recruitment.

Although no kings joined the expedition – most being too embroiled in their own political machinations – the crème of western Christendom's nobility was drawn to the venture. Members of the high aristocracy of France, western Germany, the Low Countries and Italy, from the class directly below that of royalty, these men often bore the titles of count or duke and could challenge or, in some cases, even eclipse the power of kings. Certainly they wielded a significant degree of independent authority and thus, as a group, can most readily be termed 'princes'. Each of these leading figures commanded their own military contingents, but also attracted much looser, more fluid bands of followers, based on the bonds of lordship and family and perpetuated by common ethnic or linguistic roots.

Count Raymond of Toulouse, the most powerful secular lord in south-eastern France, was the first prince to commit to the crusade. An avowed supporter of the Reform papacy and ally of Adhémar of Le Puy, the count almost certainly had been primed by Urban II even before the sermon at Clermont. In his mid-fifties, Raymond was the expedition's elder statesman; proud and obdurate, boasting wealth and far-reaching power and influence, he assumed command of the Provençal-southern French armies. Later legend suggested that he had already campaigned against the Moors of Iberia, even that he had made a pilgrimage to Jerusalem, during which one of his eyes had been pulled out of his head as punishment for refusing to pay an exorbitant Muslim tax on Latin pilgrims. Indeed, the count was said to have returned to the West carrying his eyeball in his pocket as a talisman of his hatred for Islam. Fanciful as these tales may have been, Raymond nonetheless had the experience and, more importantly, the resources to vie for overall secular command of the crusade.[9]

The count's most obvious rival for that position was a forty-year-old southern Italian Norman, Bohemond of Taranto. As the son of Robert 'Guiscard' (Robert 'the Wily'), one of the Norman adventurers who conquered southern Italy during the eleventh century, Bohemond gained an invaluable military education. Fighting alongside his father during the 1080s in a four-year Balkan campaign against the Greeks, Bohemond learned the realities of battlefield command and siege warfare. By the time of the First Crusade he had an unequalled martial pedigree, prompting one near-contemporary to describe him as 'second to none in prowess and in knowledge of the art of war'. Even his Byzantine enemies conceded that he had an arresting physical presence:

> Bohemond's appearance was, to put it briefly, unlike that of any other man seen in those days in the Roman world, whether Greek or barbarian. The sight of him inspired admiration, the mention of his name terror . . . His stature was such that he towered almost a full cubit over the tallest men. He was slender of waist and flanks, with broad shoulders and chest, strong in the arms . . . The skin all over his body was very white, except for his face which was both white and red. His hair was lightish-brown and not as long as that of other barbarians (that is it did not hang on his shoulders) . . . His eyes were light-blue and gave some hint of the man's spirit and dignity . . . There was a certain charm about him [but also] a hard, savage quality in his whole aspect, due, I suppose, to his great height and his eyes; even his laugh sounded like a threat to others.

But for all his lion-like stature, Bohemond lacked wealth, having been disinherited by his acquisitive half-brother in 1085. Driven by rapacious ambition, he thus took the cross in the summer of 1096 with at least one eye upon personal advancement, nursing dreams of a new Levantine lordship to call his own. Bohemond was accompanied on crusade by his nephew, Tancred of Hauteville. Barely twenty, with little real experience of war, this young princeling nonetheless had an unquenchable dynamism (and could apparently speak Arabic), and he quickly assumed the position of second in command of the relatively small but redoubtable army of southern Italian Normans that followed Bohemond into the East. In time Tancred would become one of the foremost champions of the crusading cause.[10]

The leading southern French and Italian Norman crusaders were all allies of the Reform papacy, but after 1095 even some of the pope's most embittered enemies joined the expedition to Jerusalem. One such was Godfrey of Bouillon, from the region of Lorraine. Born around 1060, the second son to the count of Boulogne, he could trace his lineage back to Charlemagne (later legend even had it that he was born of a swan) and was said to have been 'taller than the average man . . . strong beyond compare, with solidly built limbs and stalwart chest, [with] pleasing features [and] beard and hair of medium blond'. Godfrey held the title of duke of Lower Lorraine, but proved unable to assert real authority over this notoriously volatile region and probably took the cross with some thought of starting a new life in the Holy Land. Despite his reputation for despoiling Church property and his limited military background, in the years to come Godfrey would demonstrate an unswerving dedication to the crusading ideal and a gift for clear-headed command.

Godfrey stood at the forefront of a loose conglomerate of troops from Lorraine, Lotharingia and Germany and was joined by his brother, Baldwin of Boulogne. Reportedly darker-haired but paler-skinned than Godfrey, Baldwin was said to have a piercing gaze. Like Tancred, he would emerge from relative obscurity during the course of the crusade, demonstrating a bullish tenacity in battle and an almost insatiable appetite for advancement.

These five princes – Raymond of Toulouse, Bohemond of Taranto, Godfrey of Bouillon, Tancred of Hauteville and Baldwin of Boulogne – played pivotal roles in the expedition to reclaim Jerusalem, leading three of the main Frankish armies and shaping the early history of the crusades. A fourth and final contingent, made up of the northern French, also joined the campaign. This army was dominated by a tight-knit kinship group of three leading nobles: the well-connected Robert, duke of Normandy, eldest son of William the Conqueror and brother to William Rufus, king of England; Robert's brother-in-law Stephen, count of Blois; and his namesake and cousin, Robert II, count of Flanders.

For these potentates, their followers and perhaps even the poorer classes, the process of joining the crusade involved a dramatic and often emotional ceremony. Each individual made a crusading vow to journey to Jerusalem, similar to that for a pilgrimage, and then marked their status by sewing a representation of the cross on to their clothing. When Bohemond of Taranto heard the call to arms, his reaction was apparently immediate: 'Inspired by the Holy Ghost, [he] ordered the most valuable cloak which he had to be cut up forthwith and made into crosses, and most of the knights who were [there] began to join him at once, for they were full of enthusiasm.' Elsewhere, some took this ritual to extremes, branding their flesh with the sign of the cross, or inscribing their bodies or clothing with blood.

The process of identification through a visible symbol must have served to separate and define the crusaders as a group, and the pilgrim vow involved certainly brought crusaders an array of legal protections for their property and persons. The contemporary descriptions of these moments of dedication tend to stress spiritual motivation. We might doubt this evidence, given that it is almost always provided by churchmen, except for the fact that it is supported by a wealth of legal documents, produced either by, or at the behest of, men placing their affairs in order before departing for Jerusalem. This material seems to confirm that many crusaders did indeed see their actions in a devotional context. One crusader, Bertrand of Moncontour, was so inspired that he decided to give up lands which he was withholding illegally from a monastery in Vendôme because 'he believed that the Way of God [the crusade] could in no way benefit him while he held these proceeds of theft'.

The documentary evidence also reflects an atmosphere of fear and self-sacrifice. Prospective crusaders seem to have been deeply apprehensive about the long and dangerous journey they were undertaking, but were at the same time willing to sell virtually all their possessions to fund their participation. Even Robert of Normandy was forced to mortgage his duchy to his brother. The once fashionable myth that crusaders were self-serving, disinherited, land-hungry younger sons must be discarded. Crusading was instead an activity that could bring spiritual and material rewards, but was in the first instance both an intimidating and extremely costly activity. Devotion inspired Europe to crusade, and in the long years to come the First Crusaders proved time and again that their most powerful weapon was a shared sense of purpose and indestructible spiritual resolution.[11]

BYZANTIUM

From November 1096 onwards the main armies of the First Crusade began to arrive at the great city of Constantinople (Istanbul), ancient gateway to the Orient and capital of the Byzantine Empire. For the next six months the various contingents of the expedition passed through Byzantium on their way to Asia Minor and the frontier with Islam. Constantinople was a natural location for the diverse forces of the crusade to gather, given that it stood on the traditional pilgrim route to the Holy Land and that the Franks had travelled east with the express intention of aiding their Greek brethren.

The ambitions of Alexius

The Byzantine Emperor Alexius I Comnenus had already witnessed the disordered collapse of the People's Crusade, and it usually is argued that he viewed the advent of the main crusade with equal disdain and suspicion. His daughter and biographer Anna Comnena wrote that Alexius had 'dreaded [the arrival of the Franks], knowing as he did their uncontrollable passion, their erratic character and their irresolution, not to mention their greed'. Elsewhere she described the crusaders as 'all the barbarians of the West' and was particularly scathing in her descriptions of Bohemond as 'a habitual rogue' who was 'by nature a liar'. Drawing upon her vituperative rhetoric, historians have often depicted the early Greco-Latin encounters of 1096–7 as being stained by deep-seated mistrust and ingrained hostility. In fact, Anna Comnena's account, written decades after the event, was heavily coloured by hindsight. To be sure, currents of wary circumspection, even of antipathy, pulsed beneath the surface of crusader–Byzantine relations. There were even occasional outbreaks of ill-tempered infighting. But to begin with, at least, these were eclipsed by instances of constructive cooperation.[12]

To truly understand the First Crusaders' journey through Byzantium and beyond, the preconceptions and prejudices of both the Franks and the Greeks must be reconstructed. Many imagine that in terms of wealth, power and culture European history has always been dominated by the West. But in the eleventh century the focal point of civilisation lay to the east, in Byzantium, inheritor of Greco-Roman might and glory; continuator of the known world's most enduring empire. Alexius could trace his imperial heritage back to the likes of Augustus Caesar and Constantine the Great, and for the Franks this imbued the emperor and his realm with a near-mystical aura of majesty.

The crusaders' arrival at Constantinople served only to reinforce this impression. Standing before its colossal outer walls – four miles long, up to fifteen feet thick and sixty feet tall – there could be no doubt that they beheld the heart of Christian Europe's great superpower. For those fortunate enough to be granted entry to the capital itself, the wonders only multiplied. Home to perhaps half a million citizens, this metropolis dwarfed the largest city in Latin Europe tenfold. Visitors could marvel at the domed Basilica of St Sophia, Christendom's most spectacular church, and gaze at the giant triumphal statues of Alexius' legendary forebears. Constantinople also was home to an unrivalled collection of sacred relics, including Christ's crown of thorns, locks of the Virgin Mary's hair, at least two heads of John the Baptist and the bones of virtually all the Apostles.

It is little wonder that most crusaders expected, quite naturally, that their expedition would begin in the service of the emperor. For his part, Alexius offered the Frankish armies a cautious welcome, shepherding them from the borders of his empire to his capital, ever under a watchful eye. He viewed the crusade as a military tool to be used in the defence of his realm. Having requested aid from Pope Urban in 1095, he was now confronted by a swarm of Latin crusaders. But for all their supposed unruly savagery, he recognised that the Franks' brutish vitality might be harnessed in the interests of the empire. Wielded with care and control, the crusade might prove to be the decisive weapon in his struggle to reconquer Asia Minor from the Seljuq Turks. Both Greeks and Latins were thus primed for collaboration, but the seeds of discord were present nonetheless. Most Franks expected the emperor to assume personal command of their armies, leading them as part of a grand coalition to the gates of Jerusalem itself. Alexius had no such plans. For him the needs of Byzantium, not those of the crusade, would always be paramount. He would furnish the Latins with aid and happily capitalise on any successes they enjoyed, not least if they enabled him to repulse the threat from Islam and perhaps even reclaim the strategically vital Syrian city of Antioch. But he would never expose his dynasty to overthrow, or his empire to invasion, by conducting a protracted campaign in the distant Holy Land. This disjuncture of aims and expectations would, in time, prove to have tragic consequences.

In service of the emperor

Determined to stamp his authority on the Franks, Alexius took full advantage of the crusader host's fragmented nature, dealing with each prince individually as they arrived at Constantinople. He also played upon his great capital's imposing magnificence to intimidate the Latins. On 20 January 1097 one of the first princes to arrive, Godfrey of Bouillon, was invited in the company of his leading nobles to an audience with Alexius at the opulent imperial Palace of the Blachernae. Godfrey apparently found the emperor 'seated, as was his custom, looking powerful on the throne of his sovereignty, not getting up to offer kisses [of greeting] to the duke nor to anyone'. Maintaining this air of regal majesty, Alexius required Godfrey solemnly to promise that 'whatever cities, countries or forts he might in future subdue, which had in the first place belonged to the Roman Empire, he would hand over to the officer appointed by the emperor'. This meant that any territory captured in Asia Minor and even beyond would be handed over to the Byzantines. The duke then offered the emperor an oath of vassalage, creating a reciprocal bond of allegiance which confirmed Alexius' right to direct the crusade, but also entitled Godfrey to expect imperial aid and counsel. In a characteristic show of Byzantine munificence, the emperor sweetened this act of capitulation by showering the Frankish prince with gifts of gold and silver, along with precious purple fabrics and valuable horses. With the deal done, Alexius promptly whisked Godfrey and his army across the Bosphorus Strait – the narrow finger of water connecting the Mediterranean with the Black Sea and separating the European and Asian continents – in order to avoid the potentially destabilising build-up of Latin troops outside Constantinople itself.

In the succeeding months virtually all the leading crusaders followed Duke Godfrey's example. In April 1097 Bohemond of Taranto appeared to make peace with his former Greek enemy, willingly acceding to the

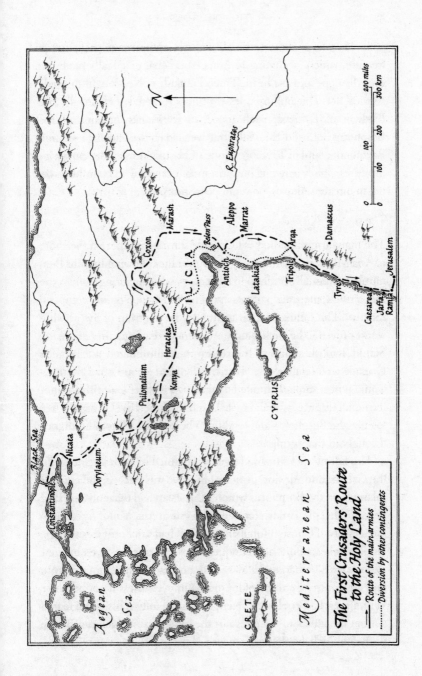

The First Crusaders' Route
to the Holy Land
— Route of the main armies
······ Diversion by other contingents

Black Sea

Constantinople
Nicaea
Dorylaeum
Philomelium
Konya
Heraclea
CILICIA
Coxon
Marash
Belen Pass
Antioch
Aleppo
Marrat
Latakia
Arqa
Tripoli
Damascus
Tyre
Caesarea
Jaffa
Ramla
Jerusalem

R. Euphrates

CYPRUS

Aegean Sea

CRETE

Mediterranean Sea

0   100   200   220 miles
0   100   200   300 km

oath. He was lavishly rewarded with an entire room packed with treasure, which, according to Anna Comnena, practically made his eyeballs pop from his head. Three Frankish nobles sought to evade Alexius' net. The ambitious lesser princes, Tancred of Hauteville and Baldwin of Bologne, each made an immediate crossing of the Bosphorus to avoid the oath, but were later persuaded to submit. Raymond, count of Toulouse, alone stubbornly resisted the emperor's overtures, finally agreeing only to a modified pact which saw him vow not to threaten Alexius' power or possessions.[13]

The siege of Nicaea

The main armies of the First Crusade started to gather on the shore of Asia Minor in February 1097, and over the following months their numbers gradually built up to perhaps 75,000, including some 7,500 fully armed, mounted knights and a further 35,000 lightly equipped infantry. The timing of their arrival on the doorstep of the Muslim world proved to be most propitious. Months earlier Kilij Arslan, the Seljuq Turkish sultan of the region, had annihilated the People's Crusade with relative ease. Thinking that this second wave of Franks would pose a similarly limited danger, he set off to deal with a minor territorial dispute far to the east. This blunder left the Christians free to cross the Bosphorus and establish a beachhead without hindrance throughout that spring.

The Latins' first Muslim target was defined by their alliance with the Greeks, and Alexius' primary objective was Nicaea, the city just inland from the Bosphorus which Kilij Arslan had brazenly declared his capital. This Turkish foothold in western Asia Minor threatened the security of Constantinople itself, but it had stubbornly resisted the emperor's best efforts at reconquest. Now Alexius deployed his new weapon: the 'barbarian' Franks. They arrived at Nicaea on 6 May to find an imposing stronghold. One Latin eyewitness described how 'skilful men had enclosed the city with such lofty walls that it feared neither the attack of enemies nor the force of any machine'. These thirty-foot-high battlements, nearly three miles in circumference, incorporated more than one hundred towers. More troubling still was the fact that the western edge of the city was built against the shores of the massive Askanian Lake, thus allowing the Turkish garrison, which probably numbered no more than a few thousand, to receive supplies and reinforcements even if they were encircled on land.

The Christians came close to suffering a damaging reversal in the first stage of their siege. Having now recognised the threat to his capital, Kilij Arslan returned from eastern Asia Minor in late spring. On 16 May he tried to launch a surprise attack upon the armies ranged before Nicaea, pouring out from the steep, wooded hills to the south of the city. Luckily for the Franks, a Turkish spy caught in their camp betrayed the Seljuqs' plans when threatened with torture and death. When the Muslim assault began the Latins were ready and, through sheer weight of numbers, soon forced Kilij Arslan to retreat. He escaped with most of his army intact, but his military prestige and the morale of Nicaea's garrison suffered grave damage. Hoping to accentuate enemy desperation, the crusaders decapitated hundreds of Turkish dead, parading the heads upon spikes before the city and even throwing some over the walls 'in order to cause more terror'. This sort of barbarous psychological warfare was common in medieval sieges and certainly not the preserve of the Christians. In the coming weeks the Nicaean Turks retaliated with macabre tenacity, using iron hooks attached to ropes to haul up any Frankish corpses left near the walls after skirmishes and then hanging these cadavers from the walls to rot, so as 'to offend the Christians'.[14]

Having repulsed Kilij Arslan's attack, the crusaders adopted a combined siege strategy to overcome Nicaea's defences, employing two styles of siege warfare simultaneously. On one hand, they established a close blockade of the city's landward walls to the north, east and south, hoping to cut off Nicaea from the outside world, gradually grinding its garrison into submission through physical and psychological isolation. As yet, however, the Franks had no means of severing westward lines of communication via the lake, so they also actively pursued the more aggressive strategy of an assault siege. Early attempts to storm the city with scaling ladders failed, so efforts centred upon creating a physical breach in the walls. The crusaders built some stone-throwing machines, or mangonels, but these were of limited power, incapable of propelling missiles of sufficient size to inflict significant damage to robust battlements. Instead, the Latins used light bombardment to harass the Turks and, under cover of this fire, attempted to undermine Nicaea's walls by hand.

This was potentially lethal work. To reach the foot of the ramparts troops had to negotiate a deadly rain of Muslim arrows and stone missiles, and, once there, they were exposed to attack from above by burning pitch and oil. The Franks experimented with a range of portable bombardment screens to counter these dangers, with varying degrees of success. One such contraption, proudly christened 'the fox' and fashioned from oak beams, promptly collapsed, killing twenty crusaders. The southern French had more luck, constructing a sturdier, sloping-roofed screen which allowed them to reach the walls and begin a siege mine. Sappers dug a tunnel beneath the southern battlements, carefully buttressing the excavation with timber supports as they went, before packing the void with branches and kindling. At dusk around 1 June 1097 they set this wood alight, leaving the whole structure to collapse, bringing down a small section of the defences above. Unfortunately for the Franks, the Turkish garrison managed to repair the damage overnight and no further progress was made.

By mid-June, with the crusaders enjoying no noteworthy progress, it fell to the Byzantines to tip the balance. Stationed a day's journey to the north, Alexius had maintained a discreet but watchful distance from the siege, while dispatching troops and military advisers to assist the Latins. Most notable among these was Taticius, a cool-headed veteran of the imperial household born of half-Arab, half-Greek parentage, known for his loyalty to the emperor.* It was not until

---

* Both a eunuch and an able general, Taticius was said to have had his nose sliced off earlier in his military career and now wore a golden replica in its place.

mid-June that Alexius made the defining contribution to Nicaea's investment. In response to requests from the crusader princes, he portaged a small fleet of Greek ships twenty miles overland to the Askanian Lake. At dawn on 18 June this flotilla sailed towards Nicaea's western walls, trumpets and drums blaring, as the Franks launched a coordinated land-based assault. Utterly horrified, with the noose closing around them, the Seljuq troops within were said to have been 'afraid almost to death, and began to wail and lament'. Within hours they sued for peace and Taticius and the Byzantines took possession of the city.

The capture of Nicaea marked the high point of Greco-Frankish cooperation during the First Crusade. There were some initial grumbles among the Latin rank-and-file about the lack of plunder, but these were soon silenced by Alexius' decision to reward his allies with lavish quantities of hard cash. Later western chronicles played up the degree of tension present after Nicaea's fall, but a letter written home by the leading crusader Stephen of Blois later that same summer made it clear that an atmosphere of friendship and cooperation endured. The emperor now held an audience with the Frankish princes to discuss the next stage of the campaign. The crusaders' route across Asia Minor was likely agreed and the city of Antioch identified as an objective. Alexius' plan was to follow in the expedition's wake, mopping up any territory it conquered and, in the hope of maintaining control over events, he directed Taticius to accompany the Latins as his official representative, along with a small force of Byzantine troops.

Throughout that spring and summer Alexius furnished the Latins with invaluable advice and intelligence. Anna Comnena noted that Alexius 'warned [them] about the things likely to happen on their journey [and] gave them profitable advice. They were instructed in the methods normally used by the Turks in battle; told how they should draw up a battle-line, how to lay ambushes; advised not to pursue far when the enemy ran away in flight.' He also counselled the crusade leadership to temper blunt aggression towards Islam with an element of pragmatic diplomacy. They followed his advice, seeking to exploit Muslim political and religious disunity by dispatching envoys by ship to the Fatimid caliphate in Egypt to discuss a potential treaty.[15]

As the crusaders left Nicaea in the last week of June 1097, Alexius could look back over the preceding months with some satisfaction. The Frankish horde had been channelled through his empire without major incident and a grave blow struck against the Seljuq Kilij Arslan. In spite of occasional moments of friction, with the magisterial presence of the emperor close at hand, the Latins had proved themselves to be both cooperative and subservient. The question was how long the spell would hold now that the crusade was marching on to the Holy Land and away from the heart of Byzantine authority.

ACROSS ASIA MINOR

Without Alexius' leadership the Franks had to wrestle with the issues of command and organisation. Essentially their army was a composite force, one mass made up of many smaller parts, united by a common faith – Latin Catholicism – but drawn from across western Europe. Many had been enemies before the expedition began. They even faced a profound communication barrier: the northern French crusader Fulcher of Chartres remarked, 'Who ever heard such a mixture of languages in one army?'

This disparate mass needed to be guided by a resolute hand. Indeed, the dictates of military logic suggested that without a clear, individual commander the crusade surely would be doomed to disintegration and collapse. But from the summer of 1097 onwards, the expedition had no single leader. The papal legate, Adhémar of Le Puy, could claim spiritual primacy, and the Greek Taticius certainly offered guidance, but in practice neither wielded total power. In fact, the crusaders had to feel their way towards an organisational structure through a process of experimentation and innovation, relying heavily upon the unifying influence of their shared devotional goal. Against all expectations, they achieved significant success. Their most valuable decision-making tool proved to be group discussion, normally anathema to military enterprise. From now on a council, made up of the leading Frankish princes – men such as Raymond of Toulouse and Bohemond of Taranto – met to discuss and agree policy. Early on they created a common fund through which all plunder could be channelled and redistributed. They also had to decide how best to negotiate the crossing of Asia Minor.

Because of its vast size, the crusade could not realistically move forward as a single army. Stretched out along the Roman roads and pilgrim routes that lay ahead, a single column of 70,000 people might take days to pass a given point. Foraging for food and supplies as they went, they would also scourge the surrounding countryside like a plague of locusts. But the Christians could ill afford to break into smaller contingents, travelling separately as they had en route to Constantinople, because Kilij Arslan and the Seljuq Turks still posed a very real threat. The princes eventually chose to divide their forces in two, while maintaining relatively close contact during the march.[16]

The Battle of Dorylaeum

On 29 June 1097, Bohemond's southern Italian Normans and Robert of Normandy's army set off, trailed at some distance by Godfrey of Bouillon, Robert of Flanders and the southern French. The plan was to rendezvous some four days' march to the south-east, at Dorylaeum, an abandoned Byzantine military camp. Kilij Arslan, however, had other ideas. After his humiliation at Nicaea he had amassed a full-strength army and was now hoping to ambush the crusaders as they crossed his lands. Their division into two armies gave him an opportunity to strike. On the morning of 1 July he attacked Bohemond's and Robert's leading force in an area of open ground at the junction of two valleys near Dorylaeum. One member of Bohemond's army recalled the horror of the moment as the Turks suddenly came into sight and 'began all at once to howl and gabble and shout, saying with loud voices in their own language some devilish word which I do not understand . . . screaming like demons'. Kilij Arslan had come with a throng of lightly armed but agile Seljuq horsemen, hoping to wreak havoc among the slower-moving crusader ranks, encircling like a whirlwind and shattering their formation with an unceasing hail of missiles. The Latins were certainly shocked by their opponents' tactics. One eyewitness in the thick of the fighting wrote: 'The Turks were howling like wolves and furiously shooting a cloud of arrows. We were stunned by this. Since we faced death and since many of us were wounded, we soon took flight; nor is this remarkable, because to all of us such warfare was unknown.'

Some may have fled, but, astonishingly, Bohemond and Robert were able to rally their troops and set up a makeshift camp beside a marsh. Instead of chaotic retreat, they chose to hold their ground, establish a defensive formation and wait for reinforcement. For half a day they relied upon weight of numbers and superior armour to resist the continuing Turkish assault. To strengthen their resolve in the face of this swarm, the crusaders passed a morale-boasting phrase down the line: 'Stand fast together, trusting in Christ and the victory of the Holy Cross. Today may we all gain much booty.' Occasionally, however, enemy troops did break through:

> The Turks burst into the camp in strength, striking with arrows from their horn bows, killing pilgrim foot-soldiers, girls, women, infants and old people, sparing no one on grounds of age. Stunned and terrified by the cruelty of this most hideous killing, girls who were delicate and very nobly born were hastening to get themselves dressed up, offering themselves to the Turks, so that at least, roused and appeased by love of their beauty, the Turks might learn to pity their prisoners.

Even so, the crusader line held firm. In the medieval age effective generalship was heavily dependent upon force of personality, the power to inspire obedience, and it is much to Bohemond's and Robert's credit that they were able to control their troops in the face of such aggression. After five appalling hours, the main crusading force arrived and Kilij Arslan was forced to retreat. Casualties were high, with perhaps as many as 4,000 Christians and 3,000 Muslims killed, but the attempt to terrify the crusaders into routing had failed. From this point on Kilij Arslan avoided them. The nomadic Seljuqs of Asia Minor had not been defeated, but their resistance was broken, opening the route across Anatolia.[17]

Contacts and conquests

After Dorylaeum the crusaders faced a different kind of enemy during their three-month march to Antioch. Thirst, starvation and disease plagued them throughout the summer of 1097 as they passed a series of settlements abandoned by the Turks. According to one chronicler, at one point the lack of water became so acute that:

Overwhelmed by the anguish of thirst as many as 500 people died. In addition horses, donkeys, camels, mules, oxen and many animals suffered the same death from very painful thirst. Many men, growing weak from the exertion and the heat, gaping with open mouths and throats, were trying to catch the thinnest mist to cure their thirst. Now, while everyone was thus suffering with this plague, [a] river they had longed and searched for was discovered. As they hurried towards it each was keen because of excessive longing to arrive first amongst the great throng. They set no limit to their drinking, until very many who had been weakened, as many men as beasts of burden, died from drinking too much.

It may seem remarkable that the deaths of animals were described in almost equal detail to those of men, but all the contemporary sources share this obsession with horses and pack animals. The army relied upon the latter to transport equipment and supplies, while knights depended upon their mounts in battle. In the past historians emphasised the military advantage enjoyed by crusader knights because of their larger, stronger, European horses, but, in truth, most of these died even before Syria was reached. A Frankish eyewitness later noted that because of this 'many of our knights had to go as foot-soldiers, and for lack of horses we had to use oxen as mounts'.[18]

Crusaders occasionally fell foul of more unusual dangers. Godfrey of Bouillon, for one, was attacked and severely wounded by a savage bear while hunting. He was lucky to survive. These perils and hardships seem to have prompted more careful planning of the journey's next leg. Upon reaching the fertile south-eastern corner of Asia Minor the crusaders began forging alliances with the local Armenian Christian population, who until then had been living under Turkish rule. At Heraclea, Tancred and Baldwin of Boulogne were sent south into Cilicia, while the main army took the northern route via Coxon and Marash. Both groups made contact with indigenous Armenian Christians, but Tancred and Baldwin went further, establishing an allied resource centre that helped to supply the entire crusade in the months to come, and securing a more direct route into Syria for the armies of reinforcements that the Franks were expecting to join them at Antioch.

In the aftermath of this Cilician expedition Baldwin decided to break off from the main crusade to seek his fortune in the eastern borderlands between Syria and Mesopotamia. He saw an opportunity to establish his own independent Levantine lordship and, leaving with a small company of just one hundred knights, began a campaign of brutal conquest and unceasing self-advancement that revealed his skills both as a military commander and as a wily political operator. Styling himself as the 'liberator' of Armenian Christians from the yoke of oppressive Turkish rule, Baldwin swiftly established control over a swathe of territory running east to the River Euphrates. His burgeoning reputation then earned him an invitation to ally with Thoros, the ageing Armenian ruler of Edessa, a city in the Fertile Crescent, beyond the Euphrates. The two were actually joined as adoptive father and son by a curious public ritual: both men stripped to the waist, and then, as Thoros embraced Baldwin, 'binding him to his naked chest', a long shirt was placed over them to seal their union. Unfortunately for Thoros, this ceremony did little to temper Baldwin's ruthless ambition. Within a few months his Armenian 'father' had been murdered, probably with Baldwin's tacit approval. The Frank then seized control of the city and surrounding region to create the first crusader state in the Near East – the county of Edessa.[19]

Meanwhile, the armies of the First Crusade regrouped on the borders of northern Syria in early October 1097; they had survived the crossing of Asia Minor, albeit with major losses. The events of the following century would prove that this in itself was an extraordinary achievement, as successive crusades foundered in this region. But a gargantuan task that would eclipse even these trials now stood before them: the siege of Antioch.

2

SYRIAN ORDEALS

In early autumn 1097 the First Crusaders crossed into northern Syria, arriving at one of the great cities of the Orient, the fortified metropolis of Antioch. They had at last reached the borders of the Holy Land, and now, to the south, perhaps just three weeks' march away, Jerusalem itself beckoned. But the most direct route to the Holy City, the ancient pilgrim road, ran through Antioch before tracing the coastline of the Mediterranean into Lebanon and Palestine, past a succession of potentially hostile Muslim-held cities and fortresses.

Historians have always maintained that the Franks had no choice but to capture Antioch before continuing their journey south – that the city stood as an immutable barrier to the progress of their expedition. This is not entirely true. Later events suggest that the crusaders could in theory have bypassed the city. Had they been solely focused upon reaching Jerusalem with maximum speed, they might have negotiated a temporary truce to neutralise the threat posed by Antioch's Muslim garrison, leaving them free to advance with minimum disruption. The fact that the Latins chose instead to besiege Antioch says much about their planning, strategy and motivation.[20]

The city of Antioch

First and foremost, Antioch appears to have been the core target of the crusader-Byzantine alliance. Founded in the year 300 BCE by Antiochus, one of Alexander the Great's generals, the city was ideally placed to tap into trans-Mediterranean trade. Famed as a vibrant crossroads between East and West, Antioch became the third city of the Roman world, a centre of commerce and culture. But during the first explosion of Islamic expansion in the seventh century CE, this bastion of the eastern empire was lost to the Arabs. A resurgent Byzantium secured Antioch's reconquest in 969, but the advent of the rampaging Seljuq Turks saw the city once again slip out of Christian control in 1085. Only too aware of this complex history, Alexius I Comnenus coveted Antioch, dreaming of the day when this city would be the cornerstone of a new era of Greek dominion over Asia Minor. It was for this reason that he continued to support the Franks through the summer of 1097 and beyond, hoping to harness the unprecedented influx of crusading manpower and reclaim the prize of Antioch.

The decision to target the city was thus an expression of ongoing Greco-Latin cooperation; however, the crusaders were not simply doing the bidding of their allies. Antioch, like Jerusalem, had a deeply rooted devotional significance. Tradition held that it was the site of the first Christian church founded by St Peter, chief of the Apostles, and the city still contained a magnificent basilica dedicated to the saint. It was also home to one of the five patriarchs, the leading powers of Christendom. Its liberation therefore chimed with the expedition's spiritual goals. In time, however, it would also become clear that crusade leaders like Bohemond and Raymond of Toulouse harboured their own more secular, self-serving ambitions for Antioch, aspirations that might clash with Byzantine expectations.

Beyond the issues of Latin–Greek relations and territorial conquest, the attempt to seize Antioch reveals a profound truth about the crusaders. They were not, as some medieval and modern commentators have imagined, a wild horde of uncontrolled barbarians, swarming without forethought to Jerusalem. The events of 1097 prove that their actions were, at the very least, informed by a vein of strategic planning. They prepared for Antioch's investment with some care, seizing a number of satellite settlements to act as centres of logistical supply and cultivating maritime contacts to ensure naval aid, some of which appear to have been organised months in advance. The Franks were also fully expecting to be reinforced at Antioch by Greek troops under Alexius as well as successive waves of western crusaders, and thus secured the safest, most direct route from Asia Minor to Syria across the Belen Pass. Everything about their behaviour in the autumn of 1097 indicates that the Franks were determined to conquer Antioch, though they recognised that this would be no simple task.

Even so, when the crusaders marched up to the city's walls in late October they were daunted by the sheer scale of its defences. One Frank wrote in a letter to Europe that at first sight the city seemed 'fortified with incredible strength and almost impregnable'. Antioch lay nestled between the Orontes River and the foot of two mountains – Staurin and Silpius. In the sixth century the Romans enhanced these natural features with a circle of some sixty towers joined by a massive enclosing wall – three miles long and up to sixty feet in height – running along the banks of the Orontes, and then up and across Staurin and up Silpius' precipitous slopes. Hundreds of feet above the city proper, near the peak of Mount Silpius, a formidable citadel crowned Antioch's fortifications. By the late eleventh century this defensive system had been weathered by time and ravaged by earthquakes, but it still presented an awesome obstacle to any attacking force. Indeed, a Frankish eyewitness was prompted to write that the city would 'dread neither the attack of machine nor the assault of man even if all mankind gathered to besiege it'.[21]

The crusaders nonetheless had one advantage: Muslim Syria was in a parlous state of disarray. Riven by power struggles since the collapse of Seljuq unity in the early 1090s, the region's Turkish

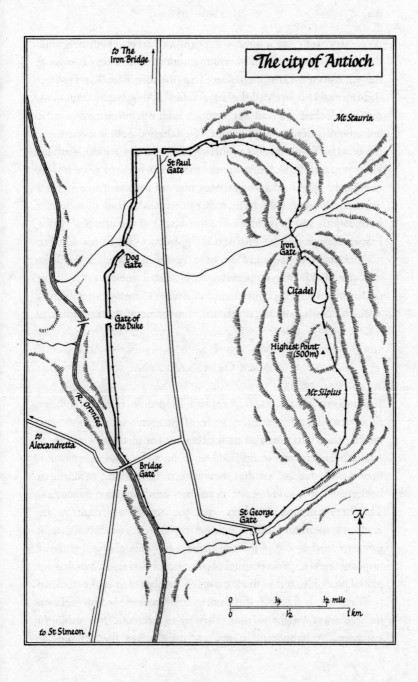

The city of Antioch

to The
Iron Bridge

Mt Staurin

St Paul
Gate

Dog
Gate

Iron Gate

Citadel

Gate of
the Duke

Highest Point
(500m)

Mt Silpius

R. Orontes

to
Alexandretta

Bridge
Gate

St George
Gate

N

0   ¼   ½ mile
0   ½   1 km

to St Simeon

potentates were more interested in pursuing their own petty infighting than in offering any form of rapid or concerted Islamic response to this unexpected Latin incursion. The two young feuding brothers Ridwan and Duqaq ruled the major cities of Aleppo and Damascus, but were locked in a civil war. Antioch itself was governed as a semi-autonomous frontier settlement of the faltering Seljuq sultanate of Baghdad by Yaghi Siyan, a conniving, white-haired Turkish warlord. He commanded a well-provisioned garrison of perhaps 5,000 troops, enough to man the city's defences but not sufficient to repel the crusaders in open battle. His only option was to trust in Antioch's fortifications and hope to survive the advent of the crusade. As the Franks approached he dispatched appeals for aid to his Muslim neighbours in Aleppo and Damascus, as well as to Baghdad itself, in the hope of attracting reinforcement. He also trained a watchful eye on the many Greek, Armenian and Syrian Christian members of Antioch's cosmopolitan population, wary of betrayal from within.

A WAR OF ATTRITION

Upon their arrival, the Latins had to decide upon a strategy. Discouraged by the massive scale of Antioch's fortifications and lacking the craftsmen and materials required to build weapons of assault siege warfare – scaling ladders, mangonels or movable towers – they quickly recognised that they were in no position to storm its battlements. But, as at Nicaea, an attrition siege presented difficulties. The sheer length of Antioch's walls, the rugged topography of the enclosing mountains and the presence of no fewer than six main gateways leading out of the city made a full encirclement virtually impossible. As it was, a council of princes decided upon a strategy of partial blockade, and in the last days of October their armies took up positions before the city's three north-western gates. As time went on the crusaders sought to police access to Antioch's two southern entrances. A temporary bridge was built across the Orontes to facilitate access to the south, and a series of makeshift siege forts developed to tighten the noose. But one entrance remained, the Iron Gate – perched in a rocky gorge between Staurin and Silpius, out of the crusaders' reach. Unguarded, it offered Yaghi Siyan and his men a crucial lifeline to the outside world throughout the long months that followed.

From the autumn of 1097 onwards the Franks committed themselves to the grinding reality of a medieval encirclement siege. The day-to-day business of this form of warfare might involve frequent small-scale skirmishing, but in essence depended not upon a battle of arms, but rather upon a test of physical and psychological endurance. For both the Latins and their Muslim foes morale was critical, and each side readily employed an array of gruesome tactics to erode their opponent's mental resilience. After winning a major battle in early 1098 the crusaders decapitated more than one hundred Muslim dead, stuck their heads upon spears and gleefully paraded them before the walls of Antioch 'to increase the Turks' grief'. Following another skirmish the Muslims stole out of the city at dawn to bury their dead, but, according to one Latin eyewitness, when the Christians discovered this:

> They ordered the bodies to be dug up and the tombs destroyed, and the dead men dragged out of their graves. They threw all the corpses into a pit, and cut off their heads and brought them to our tents. When the Turks saw this they were very sad and grieved almost to death, they lamented every day and did nothing but weep and howl.

For his part, Yaghi Siyan ordered the public victimisation of Antioch's indigenous Christian population. The Greek patriarch, who had long resided peacefully within the city, was now dangled by his ankles from the battlements and beaten with iron rods. One Latin recalled that 'many Greeks, Syrians and Armenians, who lived in the city, were slaughtered by the maddened Turks. With the Franks looking on, they threw outside the walls the heads of those killed with their catapults and slings. This especially grieved our people.' Crusaders taken prisoner often suffered similar maltreatment. The archdeacon of Metz was caught 'playing a game of dice' with a young woman in an orchard near the city. He was beheaded on the spot, while she was taken back to Antioch, raped and killed. The following morning, both of their heads were catapulted into the Latin camp.

Alongside these malicious exchanges, the siege revolved around a struggle for resources. This grim waiting game, in which each side sought to outlast the other, depended upon supplies of manpower, materials and, most fundamentally of all, food. With logistical considerations paramount, the crusaders were in the weaker position. The incomplete blockade meant that the Muslim garrison could still access external resources and aid. The larger crusading army, however, rapidly denuded their immediate resources and had to range ever further afield into hostile territory in pursuit of provisions. As the campaign continued, harsh winter weather compounded the situation. In a letter to his wife, the Frankish prince Stephen of Blois complained: 'Before the city of Antioch, throughout the whole winter we suffered for our Lord Christ from excessive cold and enormous torrents of rain. What some say about the impossibility of bearing the heat of the sun throughout Syria is untrue, for the winter there is very similar to our winter in the West.' One contemporary Armenian Christian later recalled that, in the depths of that terrible winter, 'because of the scarcity of food, mortality and affliction fell upon the Frankish army to such an extent that one out of five perished and all the rest felt themselves abandoned and far from their homeland'.[22]

The suffering in the Frankish camp reached its height in January 1098. Hundreds, perhaps even thousands, perished, weakened by malnourishment and illness. It was said that the poor were reduced to eating 'dogs and rats . . . the skins of beasts and seeds of grain found in manure'. Bewildered by this desperate predicament, many began to question why God had abandoned the crusade, His sacred venture.

Amidst an increasingly malevolent atmosphere of suspicion and recrimination, the Latin clergy proffered an answer: the expedition had become tainted by sin. To combat this pollution, the papal legate Adhémar of Le Puy prescribed a succession of purgative rituals – fasting, prayer, almsgiving and procession. Women, the supposed repositories of impurity, were simultaneously expelled from the camp. In spite of these measures, many Christians fled northern Syria, preferring an uncertain journey back to Europe over the appalling conditions at the siege. Even the demagogue Peter the Hermit, once the impassioned mouthpiece of crusading fervour, tried to desert. Caught attempting to escape under cover of night, he was unceremoniously dragged back by Tancred. Around the same time, the crusaders' Greek guide Taticius left the expedition, apparently in search of reinforcements and provisions in Asia Minor. He never returned, but the Byzantines on Cyprus did send some supplies to the Franks outside Antioch.

A hardened core of crusaders survived the manifold privations of that bitter winter and, with the arrival of spring, the balance of the siege began to shift slowly in their favour. The system of foraging centres established by the Franks played a part in easing the situation at Antioch: resources arrived from as far afield as Cilicia and, later, from Baldwin of Boulogne at Edessa. More significant still was aid transported across the Mediterranean and siphoned through the northern Syrian ports of Latakia and St Simeon, which the Latins had now occupied. On 4 March a small fleet of English ships arrived at the harbour of St Simeon, carrying food, building materials and craftsmen. A few days later, Bohemond and Raymond of Toulouse successfully escorted this valuable cargo back from the coast in the face of heavy opposition from Antiochene Muslim troops. The resultant influx of materials allowed the Franks to close a key loophole in their investment.

Up to this point Yaghi Siyan's men had been able to use the city's Bridge Gate with relative impunity, and thus had control of the roads leading to St Simeon and Alexandretta. The Christians now fortified a derelict mosque on the plain in front of this entrance, creating a basic siege fort which they christened La Mahomerie (The Blessed Mary), from which they could police the surrounding area. Count Raymond offered to shoulder the burden of garrisoning this outpost at exorbitant cost to his treasury, but his motives may not have been entirely altruistic. At the start of the siege, southern Italian Norman troops had occupied ground in front of the St Paul Gate and were thus primed to make a swift incursion into the city, if and when it fell. This gave Bohemond a good chance of staking a claim to the city because, earlier in the expedition, the princes had agreed to abide by the rules of 'right by conquest' – whereby captured property belonged to the first claimant or occupier. By positioning his own men in front of Antioch's other main entrance, the Bridge Gate, Raymond was now ideally placed to challenge his rival.

Within a month the Franks had improvised another siege fort, fortifying a monastery near Antioch's last accessible portal, the Gate of St George. Tancred agreed to man this post, but only in return for a hefty payment of 400 silver marks. Having begun the crusade in the second rank of nobles, shadowed by his uncle Bohemond's renown, Tancred was now beginning to emerge as a significant figure in his own right. Following his adventures in Cilicia, the honour of this command and the wealth it brought served both to enhance his status and lend him a degree of autonomy.[23]

BETRAYAL

By April 1098 the crusaders had tightened the cordon around Antioch. Yaghi Siyan was still able to bring in some supplies through the Iron Gate, but his ability to harry the Franks had been severely curtailed. It was now the turn of the Muslim garrison to face isolation, dwindling resources and the spectre of defeat. Throughout the siege, however, the crusaders were haunted by a gnawing fear: the prospect of a unified Muslim relief army marching to Antioch's aid, trapping them between two enemies.

The Latins had already benefited from the crippling factionalism that afflicted Muslim Syria. Unwilling to put aside their differences – and perhaps mistaking the crusaders for Byzantine mercenaries – Duqaq of Damascus and Ridwan of Aleppo had responded to Yaghi Siyan's entreaties by sending separate, uncoordinated forces to combat the Franks in December 1097 and February 1098. Had these two great cities united their resources that winter they probably would have trounced the First Crusade before the walls of Antioch. As it was, the Latins successfully repelled both of their armies, although not without significant loss.

The crusaders also knew full well that Near Eastern Islam was sundered by an even more elemental schism – that between Sunnis and Shi'ites – and on the advice of Alexius Comnenus had sought to exploit this division by establishing contact with the Shi'ite Fatimids of North Africa back in the summer of 1097. This approach elicited a response in early February 1098, when an embassy from al-Afdal, vizier of Egypt, arrived in the Christian camp outside Antioch to discuss the possibility of some form of negotiated settlement with the First Crusaders. The visit of these Muslim envoys was neither fleeting, nor secretive. They remained in the crusaders' camp for at least a month, and their presence was reported widely by Latin eyewitness sources. And yet the welcoming of this embassy seems to have occasioned little, if any, criticism. Stephen of Blois for one showed no embarrassment when writing to his wife that the Fatimids had 'established peace and concord with us'. The crusaders and Egyptians reached no definitive agreement at Antioch, but the latter did offer promises of 'friendship and favourable treatment', and in the interests of pursuing just such an entente, Latin envoys were sent back to North Africa, charged with 'entering into a friendly pact'.

Until the early summer of 1098 the First Crusaders had successfully employed diplomacy and pre-emptive military intervention to stave off a direct Muslim counter-attack. In late May, however, a dread-laden rumour began to circulate: a new enemy was abroad. It seemed that the sultan of Baghdad had finally responded to Antioch's desperate appeals for aid by raising a huge relief force. On 28 May scouts returned to the Frankish camp to confirm that they had seen a '[Muslim] army swarming everywhere from the mountains and different roads like the sands of the sea'. This was the fearsome Iraqi general Kerbogha of Mosul, marching at the head of some 40,000 Syrian and Mesopotamian troops. He was less than one week from Antioch.[24]

The news that Sunni Islam had at last united against the crusaders horrified the Latin princes. Seeking to conceal these grim tidings from the masses for fear of inciting panic and desertion, they convened an emergency council to discuss a course of action. Although the encirclement of the city had tightened and Yaghi Siyan's resistance was weakening, no swift end to the siege was yet in sight. The Franks were in no position to confront Kerbogha in a full-scale battle – they were outnumbered by as many as two to one and faced a severe shortage of horses with which to mount a cavalry offensive. After all the bitter struggles and sacrifices of the preceding months, it now appeared that the Christian army would be crushed against Antioch's walls by the oncoming wave of Muslim attack.

At this moment of crisis, with the crusade facing devastation, Bohemond stepped forward. He argued that, in light of their predicament, whoever could engineer Antioch's fall should have legal right to the city, and after much debate this was generally agreed with the proviso that it should be returned to the Emperor Alexius if he came to claim it. With the bargain in place, the wily Bohemond revealed his hand. He had, it transpired, made contact with a renegade inside Antioch, an Armenian tower commander named Firuz, who was prepared to betray the city.

A few days later, on the night of 2–3 June, a small group of Bohemond's men used an ox-hide ladder to climb an isolated section of the city's south-eastern wall, where Firuz was waiting. Even with the traitor's help, this sortie was so risky that Bohemond himself chose to wait below, for had an alarm been raised the isolated advance party would surely have been butchered. As it was, the guards of the three nearest towers were rapidly and silently dispatched and a small postern gate opened below. Up to this point stealth had been essential, but with the first breach made Bohemond sounded bugles to initiate a second, coordinated attack on Antioch's citadel. The calm night air was suddenly shattered as the Franks screamed out their battle cry: 'God wills it! God wills it!' As the growing tumult punctured the darkness, the city's garrison was thrown into a state of utter confusion and some of the eastern Christians still living in Antioch turned on their Muslim overlords and rushed to open the city's remaining gates.

With resistance crumbling, the crusaders poured into Antioch, straining to release eight months of pent-up anger and aggression. Amid the gloom of the approaching dawn, the chaotic slaughter began. One Latin contemporary noted that 'they were sparing no Muslim on the grounds of age or sex, the ground was covered with blood and corpses and some of these were Christian Greeks, Syrians and Armenians. No wonder since (in the darkness) they were entirely unaware of whom they should spare and whom they should strike.' Afterwards, one crusader described how 'all the streets of the city on every side were full of corpses, so that no one could endure to be there because of the stench, nor could anyone walk along the narrow paths of the city except over the corpses of the dead'. Amongst all this uncontrolled bloodshed, and the looting that followed it, Bohemond ensured that his blood-red banner was raised above the city, the customary method of staking claim to captured property. Raymond of Toulouse, meanwhile, raced through the Bridge Gate to occupy all the buildings in the area, including the palace of Antioch, establishing a significant Provençal foothold within the city. Only the citadel, perched high above on the crest of Mount Silpius, remained in Muslim hands, under the command of Yaghi Siyan's son. The governor himself fled in terror, only to be caught and decapitated by a local peasant.[25]

Bohemond's devious plan had succeeded, ending the first siege of Antioch, but there was little chance to celebrate. On 4 June, just one day after the city's fall, the vanguard of Kerbogha's army arrived. With Muslim troops flooding in, Antioch was soon surrounded, leaving the First Crusaders trapped within.

THE BESIEGED

The second siege of Antioch, in June 1098, was the crusade's greatest crisis. The Latins had avoided a battle on two fronts, but they now found themselves besieged within Antioch's walls. Denuded of resources during the first investment, the city could offer them little in the way of food or military supplies. And, with its citadel in enemy hands, its mighty defences were fatally undermined. The entire expedition was on the brink of destruction.

The crusaders' one fragile spark of hope was that the long-awaited Byzantine army might arrive under the command of Alexius Comnenus to save them. Unbeknownst to the Franks, however, events had conspired to snuff out even this faint prospect of deliverance. On 2 June, just before Antioch fell to the Latins, the crusader prince Stephen of Blois adjudged that the Christians had no chance of survival and decided to flee. Feigning illness, he escaped north and set off to recross Asia Minor. His departure must have been enormously damaging to morale, but Stephen caused even more harm to the expedition's prospects, and to the crusading movement as a whole.

In central Anatolia he came across Emperor Alexius and his army encamped at the town of Philomelium. Throughout the siege of Antioch the crusaders had been expecting Greek reinforcements, but Alexius had been preoccupied recapturing the coastline of Asia Minor. When Stephen reported that the Franks by now had most likely been defeated, the emperor elected to retreat to Constantinople. At this crucial moment Byzantium failed the crusade, and the Greeks were never fully forgiven. Stephen returned to France only to be branded a coward by his wife.

The First Crusaders were thus abandoned to face Kerbogha's horde alone. The Mosuli general proved to be a formidable adversary. The Franks saw him as the officially appointed 'commander-in-chief of the sultan of Baghdad's army', but it would be wrong to imagine that Kerbogha was merely the servant of the Abbasid caliphate. Nursing his own expansive ambitions, he recognised that a war against the Franks at Antioch offered the perfect opportunity to seize control of Syria for himself. Kerbogha had spent six months carefully laying the military and diplomatic foundations for his campaign, piecing together an immensely intimidating Muslim coalition. Armies from across Syria and Mesopotamia committed to the cause, including a force from Damascus, but most were driven not by overriding hatred for the Christians, nor by spiritual devotion, but by fear of Kerbogha, a man who now seemed destined to rule the Seljuq world.

In early June 1098 Kerbogha approached the second siege of Antioch with diligent care and purposeful resolution. Establishing his main camp a few miles north of the city, he made contact with the Muslims holding the citadel and began amassing forces in and around the fortress on the eastern, less precipitous slopes of Mount Silpius. Soldiers were also deployed to blockade the Gate of St Paul in the north of the city. Kerbogha's initial strategy was based on an aggressive frontal assault, channelled through Antioch's citadel and its environs. By 10 June he was ready to launch a blistering attack. Over the next four days he poured in wave after wave of troops as Bohemond led the Franks in a desperate hand-to-hand struggle to retain control of the city's eastern walls. This was the most intense and unrelenting combat the crusaders had ever experienced. Literally lasting from dawn till dusk without pause, in the words of one eyewitness, 'a man with food had no time to eat, and a man with water no time to drink'. Nearing exhaustion, utterly petrified, some Latins reached breaking point. A crusader later recalled that 'many gave up hope and hurriedly lowered themselves with ropes from the wall tops; and in the city soldiers returning from the [fighting] circulated widely a rumour that mass decapitation of the defenders was in store'. By day and night the rate of desertion increased, and soon even well-known knights like Bohemond's brother-in-law were joining the ranks of the so-called 'rope-danglers'. At one point word spread that the princes themselves were preparing to flee, and Bohemond and Adhémar of Le Puy were forced to bar the city's gates to prevent a general rout.

Through sheer bloody-minded determination, those who remained managed to cling on to their positions. Then, on the night of 13–14 June, a shooting star appeared to fall out of the sky into the Muslim camp. The crusaders interpreted this as a favourable omen, because the very next day Kerbogha's men were seen retreating from the slopes of Mount Silpius. But the Muslim redeployment was probably driven by hard strategy. Having failed to break Frankish resistance through frontal assault, Kerbogha switched to a less direct approach. Skirmishing still occurred on a daily basis, but from 14 June the Muslim besiegers focused their energy on encircling Antioch. The bulk of the Abbasid army remained in the main camp to the north, but large detachments of troops were now posted to blockade the Bridge Gate and the St George Gate. By tightening this cordon, severing Latin contact with the outside world, Kerbogha hoped to starve the crusaders into submission.

Food had been scarce ever since the Franks entered Antioch. Now, however, shortages intensified and the Latins were soon racked by unprecedented levels of suffering. One Christian contemporary described these days of horror:

> With the city thus blockaded on all sides, and [the Muslims] barring their way out all round, famine grew so great amongst the Christians that in the absence of bread they . . . even chewed pieces of leather found in homes which had hardened or putrefied for three or six years. The ordinary people were forced to devour their

leather shoes because of the pressure of hunger. Some, indeed, filled their wretched bellies with roots of stinging nettles and other sorts of woodland plants, cooked and softened on the fire, so they became ill and every day their numbers were lessened by death.

Immobilised by fear and starvation, with morale crumbling, the First Crusaders seemingly had no avenue of escape and little prospect of survival. In these bleakest of days, most believed that defeat was imminent.[26]

Historians have long argued that at this point the course of Antioch's second siege, indeed the fortunes of the entire crusade, were transformed by a single dramatic event. On 14 June a small group of Franks, led by a peasant visionary named Peter Bartholomew, began digging in the Basilica of St Peter. Bartholomew claimed that an apparition of the apostle St Andrew had revealed to him the resting place of an extraordinarily powerful spiritual weapon: the spear that pierced the side of Christ on the cross. One of the men who joined the search for this 'Holy Lance', Raymond of Aguilers, described how:

We had been digging until evening when some gave up hope of unearthing the Lance ... But the youthful Peter Bartholomew, seeing the exhaustion of our workers, stripped his outer garments and, clad only in a shirt and barefooted, dropped into the hole. He then begged us to pray to God to return His Lance to [the crusaders] so as to bring strength and victory to His people. Finally, in His mercy, the Lord showed us His Lance and I, Raymond, the author of this book, kissed the point of the Lance as it barely protruded from the ground. What great joy and exultation then filled the city.

The discovery of this small metal shard, an apparent relic of Christ's Passion, was long believed to have had an electrifying effect upon the crusaders' state of mind. Interpreted as an irrefutable indication of

God's renewed support, an assurance of victory, it supposedly spurred the Latins to take up arms and confront Kerbogha in open battle. Another Frankish eyewitness described the impact of this Holy Lance: 'And so [Peter] found the lance, as he had foretold, and they all took it up with great joy and dread, and throughout all the city there was immense rejoicing. From that hour we decided on a plan of attack, and all our leaders forthwith held a council.'[27]

In fact, the impression fostered by this account – that the Christians, their spirits suddenly rejuvenated by an ecstatic outpouring of faith, made an urgent and immediate move to engage their enemy – is profoundly misleading. Two whole weeks separated the discovery of the Lance from the battle eventually fought against Kerbogha.

Peter Bartholomew's 'discovery' certainly had some effect on crusader morale. To modern sensibilities the story of his visions might seem fantastical, his claim to have uncovered a genuine remnant of Christ's own life fraudulent, even ludicrous. But to eleventh-century Franks, familiar with the concepts of saints, relics and miraculous intervention, Peter's experiences rang true. Conditioned by a well-ordered system of belief, in which the saintly dead acted as God's intercessors on Earth, channelling His power through sacred relics, most were willing to accept the authenticity of the Holy Lance. Among the leaders of the crusade only Adhémar of Le Puy seems to have harboured any doubts, and these probably stemmed from Peter's lowly social status. But buoyed though their spirits may have been by the advent of this relic, the Latins remained paralysed by fear and uncertainty through the second half of June. The unearthing of the Lance was not the overwhelming catalyst to action, much less a focal turning point in the fortunes of the First Crusade.[28]

By 24 June the crusaders were on the brink of collapse and so dispatched two envoys to seek parley with Kerbogha. Historians have tended to follow uncritically the Latins' own explanation for this embassy, characterising it as an exercise in bravado. In reality, it was more probably a forlorn attempt to negotiate terms of surrender. A non-partisan eastern Christian source described how 'the Franks became threatened with a famine [and thus] resolved to obtain from Kerbogha a promise of amnesty on condition that they deliver the city into his hands and return to their own country'. A later Arabic chronicle appears to substantiate this version of events, asserting that the crusader princes 'wrote to Kerbogha to ask for safe conduct through his territory, but he refused, saying: "You will have to fight your way out."'

With this, any chance of escaping Antioch evaporated. Recognising that their only hope now lay in open battle, no matter how bleak the odds, the Latin princes initiated preparations for a final, suicidal confrontation. In the words of one Latin contemporary, they had decided that 'it was better to die in battle than to perish from so cruel a famine, growing weaker from day to day until overcome by death'.[29]

In those final days the Christians carried out last-ditch preparations. Ritual processions, confessions and communion were undertaken by way of spiritual purgation. Meanwhile, Bohemond, now elected commander-in-chief of the army, set about concocting a battle plan. On paper, the Franks were hopelessly outclassed, numbering perhaps 20,000 including non-combatants. Their elite force, the heavily armoured mounted knights, had also been crippled by a dearth of horses, and most were now forced to fight astride pack animals or on foot. Even the German Count Hartmann of Dillingen, once a proud and wealthy crusader, was reduced to riding a donkey so diminutive that it left his boots dragging in the dirt. Bohemond thus had to develop an infantry-based strategy designed to confront the enemy with maximum speed and ferocity.

For all its size, Kerbogha's army did have two potential weaknesses. With the bulk of his force still cautiously encamped some distance to the north, the troops encircling Antioch were relatively thinly spread. At the same time, Kerbogha's men lacked the Latins' sense of a desperate common cause, being bound by only the thinnest veneer of unity. Should the Muslims start to lose confidence in their general, cracks might appear.

By 28 June 1098 the crusaders were ready for battle. At dawn that day they began marching out of the city while clergy lining the walls offered prayers to God. Most believed that they were marching to their deaths. Bohemond had chosen to sally out of the Bridge Gate, crossing the Orontes to confront the Muslim troops guarding the plains beyond. If they were to avoid being stopped in their tracks and cut down to a man, rapidity and cohesion of deployment would be essential. As the gates opened an advance guard of Latin archers let fly raking volleys of arrows to beat back the enemy, clearing the way across the bridge. Then, with Bohemond holding the rear, the Franks marched forward in four closely ordered battle groups, fanning out into a rough semi-circle and closing to engage the Muslims.

As soon as the Bridge Gate was opened, Kerbogha, encamped to the north, was alerted by the raising of a black flag above the Muslim-held citadel. At this moment he could have committed his main force, hoping to catch the crusaders as they exited the city and shatter their formation. As it was, he hesitated. This was not, as legend later had it, because he was frivolously engaged in a game of chess. Rather, Kerbogha hoped to strike a killer blow, allowing the Franks to deploy outside the city so that he could crush them en masse, bringing the siege of Antioch to a swift and triumphant conclusion. This strategy had some merit, but it required a cool head. Just when the general should have held his position, letting the crusaders advance to fight a battle on ground of his choosing, he lost his nerve. Sensing that the Latins were gaining a slim advantage in the fracas beside the city, he ordered his entire army to make a panicked and disordered advance.

His timing was appalling. The Franks had survived a succession of searing counter-attacks from the Muslim forces that had been blockading Antioch, including a potentially lethal assault from the rear by troops left to guard the southern gateway of St George. Christian casualties were mounting, but Bohemond nonetheless pressed forward to seize the initiative, and Muslim resistance began to collapse. Kerbogha's main force arrived just as the tide of battle was turning. Unnerved by their failure to overrun the supposedly bedraggled Latin army, the Muslims fighting near the Bridge Gate took flight. They ran straight into the serried ranks of their advancing comrades, causing havoc. At this, the defining moment of the battle, Kerbogha failed to rally his men. With their formation in tatters, one by one the various Abbasid contingents cut their losses and fled the field. The brutal shock of the crusaders' indomitable resolve had exposed the fractures embedded within the Muslim army. An outraged Muslim chronicler later wrote that: 'The Franks, though they were in the extremity of weakness, advanced in battle order against the armies of Islam, which were at the height of their strength and numbers, and they broke the ranks of the Muslims and scattered their multitudes.'[30]

Barely a fraction of his mighty host had been slain, yet Kerbogha was forced into a shameful retreat. Abandoning the riches of his camp, he fled in disgrace towards Mesopotamia. In the wake of the battle the Muslim garrison of Antioch's citadel surrendered. The huge city was, at last, truly in Latin hands. The Battle of Antioch was a stunning victory. Never before had the crusade come so close to destruction, and yet, against all expectation, Christendom had triumphed. Not surprisingly, many saw the hand of God at work, and an array of spectacular miracles was reported. An army of ghostly Christian martyrs, clad all in white and led by soldier saints, appeared out of the mountains to aid the Franks. Elsewhere, Raymond of Aguilers himself carried the Holy Lance in among the southern French contingent led by Bishop Adhémar. It was later said that the sight of the relic paralysed Kerbogha. With or without such divine intervention, piety played a central role in these events. The crusaders unquestionably fought amid an atmosphere of fervent spiritual conviction, urged on by priests marching among them, chanting and reciting prayers. Above all, it was their shared sense of devotional mission, fused with an almost primal sense of desperation, which bound the Latins together during this terrible confrontation and enabled them to withstand and even repel their fearsome enemy.

DELAY AND DISSIPATION

In the immediate aftermath of this remarkable success, hopes grew of a swift and triumphant conclusion to the crusade. As it was, the expedition lost direction and momentum as its leaders squabbled over the spoils of Syria. The heat of midsummer ignited an epidemic of disease, and many in the army who had survived the terrible privations of the preceding months now died from illness. Even the nobility were not immune and, on 1 August, Adhémar of Le Puy, who in his role as papal legate had been a voice for reason and conciliation, succumbed.

Throughout this period, the expedition was gripped by an embittered dispute over Antioch's future that stalled any further progress towards Palestine. Bohemond wanted the city for himself and was now strongly placed to press his claim. It was he who had engineered Antioch's fall in the crusade's hour of need; his banner that flew above the city walls at dawn on 3 June. Within hours of Kerbogha's defeat he had cemented his position by seizing personal control of the citadel, despite Raymond of Toulouse's best efforts to beat him to the prize. Bohemond now sought unequivocal recognition from his fellow princes of his legal right of possession, in spite of the promises they had made to the Byzantine emperor. Mindful of the fact that Alexius had forsaken them at Philomelium, most acquiesced, but once again it was Raymond who offered opposition, trumpeting the expedition's outstanding obligations to the Greeks. An embassy was dispatched to Constantinople entreating the emperor to lay claim to Antioch in person, but when he failed to appear an impasse was reached.

Bohemond has often been cast as the villain of this episode – his greed and ambition contrasted with Raymond's selfless dedication to justice and the crusading cause. Although Bohemond undoubtedly had an eye to personal advancement, the situation was not quite so clear-cut. In the absence of Greek reinforcement, one of the Frankish princes would need to stay behind in Syria to govern and garrison Antioch, lest the Frankish blood spilled in the name of its conquest be squandered. From one perspective it could be argued that the crusaders were lucky that Bohemond was willing to shoulder this burden, forgoing the immediate completion of his pilgrimage to Jerusalem. At the same time, Raymond of Toulouse's altruistic reputation does not bear close scrutiny. He may have been willing to deliver Antioch to Byzantium, but he was also driven by dreams of power. For the remainder of the crusade the count's behaviour was governed by two entwined, sometimes conflicting aspirations: the desire to carve out a new lordship of his own in the Levant, and a concomitant wish to be recognised as the crusade's leader.

It was with the latter goal in mind that Raymond cultivated a close association with the visionary Peter Bartholomew and the cult of the Holy Lance. Inspired by what appears to have been authentic devotion to this relic, the Provençal count took Peter under his wing and became the Lance's chief supporter. In the coming months, as the crusaders looked back over the dramatic events of Antioch's second siege and their seemingly miraculous victory over Kerbogha, Raymond and his supporters helped to promote the idea that the Lance had played a critical role in securing their survival. At the same time, Peter continued to report an ongoing succession of visions and was soon acting as the self-styled mouthpiece of God. According to the peasant prophet, St Andrew had revealed to him that 'the Lord gave the Lance to the count' in order to single out Raymond as the leader of the First Crusade.[31]

In August, the evolution of the Lance's cult and attendant promotion of Raymond's political career took rather macabre turns. In life, Adhémar of Le Puy had expressed doubts about the Lance's authenticity. But just two days after the papal legate's death, Peter

Bartholomew proclaimed that he had experienced his first visitation from Adhémar's spirit and the process of appropriating his memory began. The bishop was buried in the Basilica of St Peter, within the very hole in which the Holy Lance had been discovered. The physical fusion of the two cults – a masterstroke of manipulation – was reinforced once Peter began relaying Adhémar's 'words' from beyond the grave, revealing that he now recognised the Lance as genuine and that his soul had been severely punished for the sin of having doubted the relic, suffering whipping and burning. Alongside this apparent volte-face on the Holy Lance, the bishop's spirit began to back Count Raymond's political ambitions. Indeed, Adhémar soon 'declared' that his former vassals should transfer their allegiance to the count and that Raymond should be authorised to hand-pick the expedition's new spiritual leader.

As the First Crusade idled away that long Syrian summer, the cult of the Holy Lance took hold and the popularity and influence of Raymond of Toulouse and Peter Bartholomew rose in tandem. Even so, by early autumn the count still had not managed to oust Bohemond from Antioch, nor was he in a position to declare himself outright leader of the crusade. What Raymond needed was greater leverage. From late September onwards he led a series of campaigns into the fertile Summaq plateau region to the south-east. These operations have often been misrepresented as foraging expeditions, even as attempts to initiate an advance on Palestine, but in reality Raymond's goal was the establishment of his own independent enclave to counter and threaten Bohemond's control of Antioch.

Part of this process involved the conquest of Marrat, the region's major town. It surrendered after a hard-fought winter siege and Raymond swiftly initiated a programme of Christianisation and settlement, converting mosques and installing a garrison. But shortly afterwards the Latin lines of supply faltered, and some of the count's poorest followers began to starve. This moment saw one of the crusade's most appalling atrocities. According to one Frank:

Our men suffered from excessive hunger. I shudder to say that many, terribly tormented by the madness of starvation, cut pieces of flesh from the buttocks of Saracens lying there dead. These pieces they cooked and ate, savagely devouring the flesh while it was insufficiently roasted.

A Latin eyewitness noted that 'this spectacle disgusted as many crusaders as it did strangers'. Uncomfortable as it may be to acknowledge, these chilling acts of barbarism – which even Frankish chroniclers saw fit to condemn – did bring the Latins some short-term benefit. Among Syrian Muslims the crusaders' reputation for savagery now gained currency, and in the succeeding months many local emirs sought to negotiate with their fearsome new enemies rather than risk annihilation.[32]

Meanwhile, as the months of dispute and inaction ground on and a succession of councils of the Latin princes proved unable to resolve the argument over Antioch, popular sentiment among ordinary crusaders began to harden. Pressure was growing for the princes to put aside their differences and focus instead upon the interests of the expedition as a whole. Events came to a head at Marrat in early January 1099 with an extraordinary outbreak of civil disobedience. Dismayed by the fact that even Raymond of Toulouse, champion of the Holy Lance, preferred to contest control of Syria rather than march on to Jerusalem, a mob of poor Franks began to demolish Marrat's fortifications with their bare hands, ripping down its walls stone by stone. Facing this protest, Raymond finally recognised that he could not hope to lead the crusade and rule Antioch at the same time. On 13 January he made the symbolic gesture of marching south from Marrat barefoot, clad simply as a penitent pilgrim, leaving the town and his hopes of conquest in ruins behind him. Bohemond, meanwhile, remained at Antioch. The dream of achieving independent rule of the city had at last been realised, but his ambition had contributed to months of destructive delay for the crusade, and more importantly, caused severe and enduring damage to Latin relations with the Byzantine Empire.

Appearing to have prioritised the holy war, Raymond enjoyed a groundswell of support and, for a time, he seemed to become the crusade's acknowledged leader. He took the rather calculated step of using hard cash to ensure that his new drive towards Palestine received the endorsement of fellow princes. Not all could be bribed – Godfrey of Bouillon, for one, stood aloof – but Robert of Normandy and even Tancred now shifted their allegiance to the Provençal camp for 10,000 and 5,000 *solidi* (gold coins) apiece. They, and many other Christians, joined the advance south towards Lebanon.

Raymond of Toulouse's pre-eminence now seemed assured, and it might have remained so had he continued to focus solely upon the task of reaching Jerusalem. In truth, however, beneath the appearance of simple dedication the count still yearned to create a new Provençal lordship in the East. In mid-February 1099 he committed the crusade to an unnecessary and ultimately futile siege of the small Lebanese fortress of Arqa and sought to browbeat the neighbouring Muslim city of Tripoli into submission. Officially Raymond's excuse was that the expedition needed to pause to allow those remaining crusaders still stationed in and around Antioch, including Godfrey of Bouillon, to catch up. But even when this was achieved the count still refused to press on southwards. After two wasteful months of siege at Arqa, the masses were already restless when Raymond's prestige was dealt a disastrous blow.

The count's close association with Peter Bartholomew and the Holy Lance had been instrumental in securing his recognition as commander of the crusade. But as the months passed, Peter proved to be an increasingly volatile ally, given to extreme and unpredictable visionary experiences. By spring 1099 his ravings had become ever more fantastical and when, in early April, he reported that Christ had instructed him to oversee the immediate execution of thousands of 'sinful' crusaders, the spell broke. Not surprisingly, doubts were now openly expressed about the self-styled prophet and the relic he purportedly discovered, with the criticism spearheaded by a Norman cleric, Arnulf of Chocques, keen to reaffirm northern French influence.

Apparently convinced of the reality of his experiences, Peter volunteered to undergo a potentially lethal trial by fire to prove his own honesty and the Lance's authenticity. He spent four days fasting to purify his soul before the test. Then, on Good Friday, before a crowd of crusaders, dressed in a simple tunic and bearing the relic of the Holy Lance, Peter willingly walked into an inferno – blazing 'olive branches stacked in two piles, four feet in height, about one foot apart and thirteen feet in length'.

There are differing accounts of what happened next. Peter's supporters maintained that he emerged from the conflagration unscathed, only to be fatally crushed by a fevered mob of onlookers. Other more sceptical observers described how:

> The finder of the Lance quickly ran through the midst of the burning pile to prove his honesty, as he had requested. When the man passed through the flames and emerged, they saw that he was guilty, for his skin was burned and they knew that within he was mortally hurt. This was demonstrated by the outcome, for on the twelfth day he died, seared by the guilt of his conscience.

However they were inflicted, Peter Bartholomew perished from the injuries received on the day of his ordeal. His demise shattered belief in his prophecies and left the efficacy of the Holy Lance in grave doubt. It also inflicted grievous damage to Count Raymond's reputation. Raymond tried to hold on to power, but by early May, with even his own southern French supporters clamouring for the march south into Palestine to continue, he was forced to back down, abandoning Arqa and his Lebanese project. As the Franks set out from Tripoli on 16 May 1099, the phase of Provençal domination of the crusade came to end; from now on

Raymond would, at best, have to share power with his fellow princes. At last, after more than ten months of delay and disillusionment, the First Crusade began its final advance on the Holy City of Jerusalem.[33]

3

THE SACRED CITY

As the last phase of the march to Jerusalem began, the First Crusaders were possessed by a new sense of urgency. Any thoughts of conquering other towns and ports on the journey through Lebanon and Palestine were abandoned, and the Franks, now driven by the determined desire to complete their pilgrimage to the Holy City, advanced with resolute speed. It was not devotion alone that drove the Frankish pace; strategic necessity also played its part. Back in the spring, during the siege of Arqa, the issue of diplomatic relations with Egypt had re-emerged when Latin emissaries sent to the Vizier al-Afdal a year earlier rejoined the expedition in the company of Fatimid representatives. Much had changed in the intervening period. Capitalising upon the tremors of fear that shook the Sunni Seljuq world after Kerbogha's defeat at Antioch, al-Afdal had seized Jerusalem from the Turks in August 1098. This radical transformation in the balance of Near Eastern power prompted the crusader princes to seek a negotiated settlement with the Fatimids, offering a partition of conquered territory in return for rights to the Holy City. But talks collapsed when the Egyptians bluntly refused to relinquish Jerusalem. This left the Franks facing a new enemy in Palestine and a race against time. The crusaders now had to cover the remaining

200 miles of their pilgrimage with maximum rapidity, before al-Afdal could muster an army to intercept them or properly organise Jerusalem's defences.

As they traced the Mediterranean coastline south, the crusaders' passage was eased by the willingness of local semi-independent Muslim rulers to negotiate short-term truces, even on occasion to offer markets in which to purchase food and supplies. Cowed by the Latins' reputation for brutish invincibility earned at Antioch and Marrat, these emirs were happy to avoid confrontation. Passing by the major settlements of Tyre, Acre and Caesarea, the Franks encountered only limited resistance and were deeply relieved to find a succession of narrow coastal passes unguarded. In late May the expedition turned inland at Arsuf, taking a direct route across the plains and up into the Judean hills. They paused only briefly when approaching Ramla, the last real bastion on the road to the Holy City, but found it abandoned by the Fatimids. At last, on 7 June 1099, Jerusalem came into view. One Latin contemporary described how 'all the people burst into floods of happy tears, because they were so close to the holy place of that longed-for city, for which they had suffered so many hardships, so many dangers, so many kinds of death and famine'. Al-Afdal's inaction had allowed the expedition to advance south from Lebanon in less than a month.[34]

IN HEAVEN AND ON EARTH

After nearly three years, and a journey of some 2,000 miles, the crusaders had reached Jerusalem. This ancient city, Christendom's sacred heart, pulsated with religion. For the Franks it was the holiest place on Earth, where Christ had suffered his Passion. Within its lofty walls stood the Holy Sepulchre, the church erected in the fourth century CE under the Roman Emperor Constantine to enclose the supposed sites of Golgotha and of Jesus' Tomb. This one shrine encapsulated the very essence of Christianity: the Crucifixion,

Redemption and Resurrection. The crusaders had marched east from Europe in their thousands to reclaim this church – many believing that if the earthly city of Jerusalem could be recaptured it would become one with the heavenly Jerusalem, a Christian paradise. Feverish prophecies abounded of the imminent onset of the Last Days of Judgement centred on the Holy City, imbuing the Latin expedition with an apocalyptic aura.

But across more than 3,000 years of history, Jerusalem had become immutably entwined with two other world religions: Judaism and Islam. These faiths also treasured the city, reserving particular reverence for the area known either as the Temple Mount, or *Haram as-Sharif*, a raised enclosure in its eastern reaches, containing the Dome of the Rock and the Aqsa mosque, and abutted by the Wailing Wall. To Muslims this was the city from which Muhammad made his ascent to heaven, the third-holiest site in the Islamic world. But it was also the seat of the Israelites, where Abraham offered to sacrifice his son and the two Temples were built.

Just as it is today, Jerusalem became a focus of conflict in the Middle Ages precisely because of its unrivalled sanctity. The fact that it held critical devotional significance for the adherents of three different religions, each of whom believed that they had inalienable and historic rights to the city, meant that it was almost predestined to be the scene of war.

The task ahead

The First Crusade now faced a seemingly insurmountable task – the conquest of one of the known world's most fearsomely fortified cities. Even today, amid the urban sprawl of modern expansion, Jerusalem is able to convey the grandeur of its past, for at its centre lies the 'Old City', ringed by Ottoman walls closely resembling those that stood in the eleventh century. If one looks from the Mount of Olives in the east, stripping away the clutter and bustle of the twenty-first century, the great metropolis that confronted the Franks in 1099 comes into focus.

The city stood isolated, amid the Judean Hills, on a section of raised ground, with deep valleys falling away to the east, south-east and west, enclosed within an awesome two-and-a-half-mile circuit of battlements, sixty feet high and ten feet thick. Realistically, the city could only be attacked from the flatter ground to the north and south-west, but here the walls were reinforced by a secondary curtain wall and a series of dry moats. Five major gates, each guarded by a pair of towers, pierced this roughly rectangular system of defences. Jerusalem also possessed two major strongholds. In the north-western corner stood the formidable 'Quadrangular Tower', while midway along the western wall rose the Tower of David. One Latin chronicler described how this dread citadel was 'constructed of large square stones sealed with molten lead', noting that if 'well supplied with rations for soldiers, fifteen or twenty men could defend it from every attack'.[35]

As soon as the crusaders arrived at Jerusalem a worrying rift within their ranks became apparent, as their armies divided in two. Since the siege of Arqa, Raymond of Toulouse's popularity had been in decline and, now, abandoned by Robert of Normandy, the count was left struggling even to retain the allegiance of the southern French. Raymond positioned his remaining forces on Mount Zion, south-west of the city, to threaten the southern Zion Gate. The campaign's emerging leader, Godfrey of Bouillon, meanwhile moved to besiege the city from the north, between the Quadrangular Tower and Damascus Gate. Enjoying the support of Arnulf of Chocques, the priest who had helped to discredit the Holy Lance, Godfrey was joined by the two Roberts and Tancred. In strategic terms, the division of troops had some merit, exposing Jerusalem to attack on two fronts, but it was also the product of gnawing discord.

This was all the more troubling because the Franks could not pursue a long-drawn-out encirclement siege at Jerusalem, as they had at Antioch. The vast length of the city's perimeter wall meant that, with limited manpower at their disposal, enforcing an effective blockade would be impossible. More pressing still was the issue of time. The crusaders had taken an enormous, if arguably necessary,

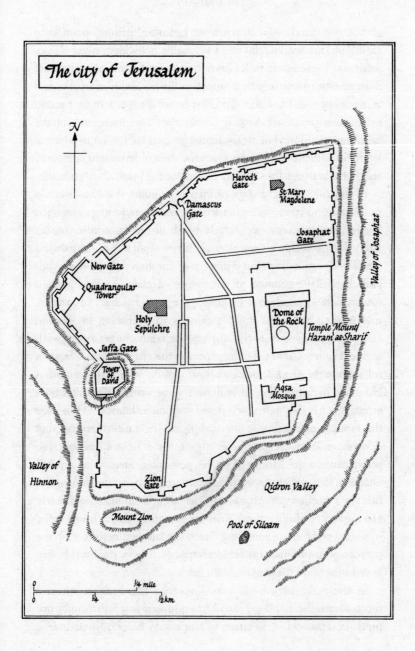

The city of Jerusalem

N

Herod's Gate

St Mary Magdelene

Damascus Gate

Josaphat Gate

New Gate

Quadrangular Tower

Holy Sepulchre

Dome of the Rock

Temple Mount Haram as-Sharif

Jaffa Gate

Tower of David

Aqsa Mosque

Valley of Hinnon

Zion Gate

Qidron Valley

Mount Zion

Pool of Siloam

Valley of Josaphat

0   ¼ mile
0   ¼   ½ km

gamble by marching at speed from Lebanon, without pausing to secure their rear or to establish any reliable network of supply. They were now hundreds of miles from their nearest allies, all but cut off from reinforcement, logistical support or the possibility of escape. And all the while they knew that al-Afdal was racing to prepare his Fatimid forces, bent upon relieving the Holy City and stamping out the Christian invasion. The near-suicidal audacity of the Latin advance left them with but one option: crack the shell of Jerusalem's defences and fight their way into the city before the Egyptian army arrived.

In this final, fraught stage of their expedition, the Franks could muster around 15,000 battle-hardened warriors, including some 1,300 knights, but this army was largely bereft of the material resources needed to prosecute an assault siege. The overall size of the garrison they faced is unknown, but it must have numbered in the thousands and certainly contained an elite core of at least 400 Egyptian cavalrymen. Jerusalem's Fatimid governor, Iftikhar ad-Daulah, meanwhile, had been quite assiduous in preparing to face an offensive, laying waste to the surrounding region by poisoning wells and felling trees, and expelling many of the city's eastern Christian inhabitants to prevent betrayal from within. When the crusaders launched their first direct assault on 13 June, just six days after their arrival, the Muslim defenders offered staunch resistance. At this stage the Franks possessed only one scaling ladder, a pitiful arsenal, but desperation and the prophetic urgings of a hermit encountered wandering on the Mount of Olives persuaded them to chance an attack. In fact, Tancred spearheaded a fierce strike on the ramparts in the city's north-western quadrant that almost achieved a breach. Having successfully raised their sole ladder, Latin troops sped upwards, seeking to mount the walls, but the first man to grab the parapet promptly had his hand chopped off by a mighty Muslim sword stroke and the onslaught foundered.

In the wake of this dispiriting reversal the Frankish princes reconsidered their strategy, electing to postpone any further offensive until the appropriate weapons of war could be constructed. As a frantic search for materials began, the crusaders started to feel the effects of the baking Palestinian summer. For the time being at least, food was not the main cause of concern, as grain had been brought from Ramla. Instead, it was water shortages that began to weaken Latin resolve. With all the nearby watering holes polluted, the Christians were forced to scour the surrounding region in search of drinkable liquid. One Frank recalled rather forlornly: 'The situation was so bad that when anyone brought foul water to camp in vessels, he was able to get any price that he cared to ask, and if anyone cared to get clear water, for five or six pennies he could not obtain enough to satisfy his thirst for a single day. Wine, moreover, was never, or very rarely, even mentioned.' At one point some of the poor died after gulping down filthy marsh water contaminated with leeches.[36]

Luckily for the crusaders, just as these shortages were beginning to take hold help arrived from a seemingly unheralded quarter. In mid-June a six-ship-strong Genoese fleet made anchor at Jaffa, a small natural harbour on the Mediterranean coast that was Jerusalem's nearest port. Their crew, which included a number of skilled craftsmen, made their way to join the siege of the Holy City, laden with an array of equipment, including 'ropes, hammers, nails, axes, mattocks and hatchets'. At the same time, the Frankish princes used intelligence garnered from local Christians to locate a number of nearby forests and soon began ferrying in timber by the camel-load. These two developments transformed Latin prospects, putting them in a position to build siege machinery. For the next three weeks they threw themselves into a furious programme of construction, fashioning siege towers, catapults, battering rams and ladders, almost without pause, but always with one eye upon the impending arrival of al-Afdal's relief army. Meanwhile, inside Jerusalem, Iftikhar ad-Daulah looked to the arrival of his master, even as he oversaw the assembly of scores of his own stone-throwing devices and the further strengthening of the city's walls and towers.

Amid all these determined preparations both besiegers and besieged paused only to exchange morale-sapping acts of barbarism. Wooden crosses were regularly dragged up on to the city walls to be desecrated through spitting and even urination in full sight of the enraged crusaders. For their part, the Franks made a point of executing any captured Muslims, usually through decapitation, in front of Jerusalem's garrison. During one particularly gruesome episode the crusaders took this tactic to a new extreme. Having caught a Muslim spy in their midst, the Christians once again sought to intimidate their enemy by throwing him back into the city, just as they had done with other victims in earlier sieges. But according to one Latin contemporary, on this occasion the unfortunate captive was still alive: 'He was put into the catapult, but it was too heavily weighed down by his body and did not throw the wretch far. He soon fell onto sharp stones near the walls, broke his neck, his nerves and bones, and is reported to have died instantly.'[37]

In early July, with the construction of their siege weapons nearing completion, the Franks received word that a Fatimid relief force was gathering, and the need to achieve a swift victory became even more pressing. In this moment of desperation, spiritual revelation served once again to bolster morale and empower the expedition with a sense of divine sanction. A Provençal priest-visionary, Peter Desiderius, now prophesied that the Holy City would succumb to an assault if the crusaders first underwent three days of ritual purification. Just as at Antioch, there followed a series of sermons, public confessions and masses. The army even made a solemn, barefoot procession around the city's walls bearing palm fronds, although the Fatimid garrison showed little respect for this ritual, peppering the crusader ranks with arrows when they came into range. By the end of the second week of July, with their siege machines completed and their spirits strengthened by pious fervour, the crusaders were ready to launch their attack.

THE ASSAULT ON JERUSALEM

The crusaders' assault on Jerusalem began at first light on 14 July 1099. To the south-west, Raymond of Toulouse and his remaining

Provençal supporters were positioned on Mount Zion, while Duke Godfrey, Tancred and the other Latins held the plateau to the north of the city. As horn blasts called the Franks to war on both fronts, Muslim troops peering into the half-light over the northern parapet suddenly realised that they had been duped. Godfrey and his men had spent the preceding three weeks constructing a massive siege tower directly in front of the city's Quadrangular Tower. Watching this three-storey behemoth rise day by day to a height of some sixty feet, the Fatimid garrison had naturally set about reinforcing their defences in the north-western corner of the city. This was just what Godfrey had hoped for. His siege tower had actually been built with a secret technological refinement: it was capable of being broken down into a series of portable sections and then rapidly re-erected. During the night of 13–14 July the duke used the cover of darkness to move this edifice more than half a mile to the east, beyond the Damascus Gate, to threaten an entirely new section of wall. According to one crusader:

> The Saracens were thunderstruck next morning at the sight of the changed position of our machines and tents ... Two factors motivated the change of position. The flat surface offered a better approach to the walls for our instruments of war, and the very remoteness and weakness of this northern place had caused the Saracens to leave it unfortified.

Having thus deceived his enemy, Godfrey's first priority was to break through the low outer wall that protected Jerusalem's main northern battlements, for without achieving such a breach his great siege tower could not be deployed up against the city itself. The Franks had constructed a monstrous, iron-clad battering ram to smash a path through the outer defences and now, under cover of Latin mangonel fire, scores of crusaders struggled to haul this weapon forward, all the while facing the Muslim garrison's own strafing missile attacks. Even mounted as it was upon a wheeled platform, the ram was desperately unwieldy, but after hours of exertion it was finally manoeuvred into position. With one last mighty charge the Franks sent it crashing into the outer wall, creating a massive fissure; indeed, the ram's momentum propelled it so far forward that the Fatimid troops atop the ramparts feared that it might even threaten the main walls, and thus rained 'fire kindled from sulphur, pitch and wax' down upon the dreadful weapon, setting it alight. At first the crusaders rushed in to extinguish the flames, but Godfrey soon recognised that the charred remains of the ram would block the advance of his great siege tower. So, in an almost comically bizarre reversal of tactics, the Latins returned to burn their own weapon, while the Muslims vainly sought to preserve its obstructive mass, pouring water from the ramparts. Eventually, the Christians prevailed and by the end of the day the northern Franks had succeeded in penetrating the first line of defence, opening the way for a frontal assault on the main walls.

To the south-west of the city, on Mount Zion, the Provençals enjoyed less success. This sector of Jerusalem's walls was reinforced by a dry moat rather than a curtain wall, so over the preceding weeks Raymond of Toulouse had instituted a fixed payment of a penny for every three stones thrown into this ditch as infill, ensuring the rapid neutralisation of this obstacle. At the same time, he oversaw the construction of his own wheeled siege tower and on 14 July, in concert with Godfrey's offensive, this colossal engine of war was deployed. Inching its bulk towards the walls, the southern French troops came into range of enemy volleys and met an oppressive torrent of Fatimid missiles. Believing that the main Frankish assault would come from Mount Zion, Iftikhar ad-Daulah had concentrated his defensive firepower in this quadrant and his men now unleashed an incessant barrage. A Latin eyewitness described how 'stones hurled from [catapults] flew through the air and arrows pelted like hail', while the advancing siege tower was targeted by viciously effective firebombs 'wrapped with ignited pitch, wax and sulphur, tow, and rags [and] fastened with nails so that they stuck wherever they hit'. Having failed to reach the walls, with the onset of dusk Raymond ordered a humiliating retreat.[38]

After a restless night of fearful anticipation for defenders and attackers alike, battle recommenced. The southern French once again set about driving forward their tower, but after some hours the intensity of the continued Muslim bombardment took its toll and the Provençal engine began to collapse and burn. With their offensive stymied, Raymond's men fell back to Mount Zion in a state of 'fatigue and hopelessness'. But the simple fact that Jerusalem's garrison had faced an assault on two fronts stretched Fatimid resources, leaving the northern walls vulnerable. There, on the second day of fighting, Godfrey and his men began to make significant progress. Having breached the outer wall, they now heaved their wheeled siege tower towards this gap and the main battlements beyond. With the sky darkened by the furious exchange of missiles, the lofty edifice, packed with Franks, advanced inexorably. Casualties were appalling. One Latin chronicler recalled that 'death was present and sudden for many on both sides'. Perched on the tower's top storey to direct operations, Godfrey himself was desperately exposed. At one point, a flying mangonel stone practically decapitated a crusader standing at his side.

Catapulted firebombs careened into the Frankish tower, but, shielded by slick hide-swathed wattle screens, these failed to catch and the siege engine held solid, inching ever forwards. At last, near noon, it passed through the rift in the outer defences to reach the main walls. With the crusaders now just yards from the ramparts and both sides exchanging frenzied volleys of smaller-scale missile weapons, the Fatimids made a final attempt to stem the assault, employing their own 'secret' weapon. They had prepared a huge wooden spar, soaked in a combustible material, akin to Greek fire (a naphtha-based incendiary compound), which could not be extinguished by water. This beam was set alight and then hefted over the walls to land in front of Godfrey's engine as a flaming barrier. Luckily for the Latins, they had been tipped off by local Christians about the one weakness of this terrible, impervious fire: it could be quenched by vinegar. Godfrey had thus stocked the tower with a supply of vinegar-filled wineskins, and these were now used to douse the flaming conflagration. As Franks on the ground dashed in to pull away the smouldering timber, the path ahead to the battlements was at last opened.

The success of the Latin offensive now depended on gaining an actual foothold on the city's ramparts. The immense height of the siege tower gave the Franks a significant advantage – at this point the main walls rose to about fifty feet – allowing Godfrey and his men in the top storey to rain down a stream of suppressing fire upon the defenders. Suddenly, in the midst of fierce fighting, the crusaders realised that a nearby defensive tower and a portion of the battlements were burning. Whether through the use of flaming catapult missiles or fire arrows, the Franks had succeeded in igniting the main wall's wooden substructure. This blaze 'produced so much smoke and flame that not one of the citizens on guard could remain near it' – in panic and confusion the defenders facing the crusaders' siege tower broke into retreat. Realising that this opening might last only moments, Godfrey hurriedly cut loose one of the wattle screens protecting the tower, fashioning a makeshift bridge across to the ramparts. As the first group of crusaders poured on to the walls, scores of Franks raced forward below with scaling ladders and began climbing up to reinforce their position.

Once Godfrey and his men achieved this first dramatic breach, the Muslim defence of Jerusalem collapsed with shocking rapidity. Terrified by the crusaders' brutal reputation, those stationed at the northern wall turned and fled in horror at the sight of the Franks cresting the battlements. Soon the entire garrison was in a state of chaotic disorder. Raymond of Toulouse was still struggling on Mount Zion, his troops seemingly on the brink of defeat, when the incredible news of the breakthrough arrived. Suddenly Muslim defenders on the southern front, who only moments before had been fighting with venom, began to desert their posts. Some were even seen jumping, terrified, from the walls. The Provençals wasted no time in rushing into the city to join their fellow crusaders, and the sack began.[39]

The horror of 'liberation'

Soon after midday on 15 July 1099 the First Crusaders achieved their long-cherished dream – Jerusalem's conquest. Surging through the streets in blood-hungry, ravening packs, they overran the Holy City. What little Muslim resistance remained melted away before them, but most Franks were in no mood to take prisoners. Instead, three years of strife, privation and yearning coalesced to fuel a rampaging torrent of barbaric and indiscriminate slaughter. One crusader joyfully reported:

> With the fall of Jerusalem and its towers one could see marvellous works. Some of the pagans were mercifully beheaded, others pierced by arrows plunged from towers, and yet others, tortured for a long time, were burned to death in searing flames. Piles of heads, hands and feet lay in the houses and streets, and men and knights were running to and fro over corpses.

Many Muslims fled towards the *Haram as-Sharif*, where some rallied, putting up futile resistance. A Latin eyewitness described how 'all the defenders retreated along the walls and through the city, and our men went after them, killing them and cutting them down as far as the [Aqsa mosque], where there was such a massacre that our men were wading up to their ankles in enemy blood'. Tancred gave his banner to a group huddled on the roof of the Aqsa, designating them as his captives, but even they were later slain in cold blood by other Franks. So gruesome was the carnage that, according to one Latin, 'even the soldiers who were carrying out the killing could hardly bear the vapours rising from the warm blood'. Other crusaders ranged through the city at will, slaughtering men, women and children, both Muslims and Jews, all the while engaging in rapacious looting.[40]

Neither Latin nor Arabic sources shy away from recording the dreadful horror of this sack, the one side glorying in victory, the other appalled by its raw savagery. In the decades that followed Near Eastern Islam came to regard the Latin atrocities at Jerusalem as an act of crusader barbarity and defilement, demanding of urgent vengeance. By the thirteenth century, the Iraqi Muslim Ibn al-Athir estimated the number of Muslim dead at 70,000. Modern historians long regarded this figure to be an exaggeration, but generally accepted that Latin estimates in excess of 10,000 might be accurate. However, recent research has uncovered close contemporary Hebrew testimony which indicates that casualties may not have exceeded 3,000, and that large numbers of prisoners were taken when Jerusalem fell. This suggests that, even in the Middle Ages, the image of the crusaders' brutality in 1099 was subject to hyperbole and manipulation on both sides of the divide.

Even so, we must still acknowledge the terrible inhumanity of the crusaders' sadistic butchery. Certainly, some of Jerusalem's inhabitants were spared; Iftikhar ad-Daulah for one took sanctuary in the Tower of David and later negotiated terms of release from Raymond of Toulouse. But the Frankish massacre was not simply a feral outburst of bottled rage; it was a prolonged, callous campaign of killing that lasted at least two days and it left the city awash with blood and littered with corpses. In the midsummer heat the stench soon became intolerable, and the dead were dragged out beyond the city walls, 'piled up in mounds as big as houses' and burned. Even six months later a Latin visiting Palestine for the first time commented that the Holy City still reeked of death and decay.

The other unassailable truth of Jerusalem's conquest is that the crusaders were not simply driven by a desire for blood or plunder; they were also empowered by heartfelt piety and the authentic belief that they were doing God's work. Thus that first, ghastly day of sack and slaughter concluded with an act of worship. In a moment which perfectly encapsulated the crusade's extraordinary fusion of violence and faith, dusk on 15 July 1099 saw the Latins gather to give tearful thanks to their God. A Latin contemporary rejoiced in recounting that, 'going to the Sepulchre of the Lord and his glorious Temple, the clerics and also the laity, singing a new song unto the Lord in a high-sounding voice of exultation, and making offerings and most humble supplications, joyously visited the Holy Place as they had so long desired to do'. After years of desperate suffering and struggle, the First Crusaders' terrible work was done: Jerusalem was in Christian hands.[41]

AFTERMATH

The crusaders' thoughts soon turned to the fate of their new conquest. Having travelled 2,000 miles to claim Jerusalem for Latin Christendom, it was clear to all that the city would now have to be governed and defended. The clergy contended that a site of such rarefied sanctity should not be subjected to the rule of a secular monarch, arguing instead for the creation of a Church-run ecclesiastical realm, with the Holy City as its capital. But because Jerusalem's Greek patriarch had died recently in exile in Cyprus, there was no obvious candidate to champion this cause. Raymond of Toulouse eyed the position of Latin king, but his popularity had been waning since Arqa and, on 22 July 1099, Godfrey of Bouillon, chief architect of the crusaders' victory, took up the reins of power. In a gesture of conciliation to the clergy he accepted the title of 'Advocate of the Holy Sepulchre', implying that he would merely act as Jerusalem's protector.[42]

His ambitions foiled once again, a furious Count Raymond made an abortive attempt to retain personal control of the Tower of David, before abandoning the Holy City in a fit of pique. In his absence, the Norman French crusader Arnulf of Chocques, critic of the Holy Lance, was selected as Jerusalem's new patriarch designate. The idea of installing a Latin in this sacred post ran roughshod over the rights of the Greek Church, signalling a clear break with the policy of cooperation with Byzantium. As yet, Arnulf's election remained unconfirmed, being subject to approval from Rome, but this did not stop him from engendering a rather shameful atmosphere of religious intolerance. Within months, the same eastern Christian 'brethren' that the Franks had been charged to protect during their holy war were subjected to persecution, as Armenians, Copts, Jacobites and Nestorians were expelled from the Church of the Holy Sepulchre.

The new order cemented its position by cultivating its own relic cult, destined to banish the sullied memory of the Holy Lance. Around 5 August a piece of the True Cross was unveiled. This relic, probably a rather battered silver and gold crucifix, was believed to contain a chunk of wood from the actual cross upon which Christ had died. It had apparently been hidden through generations of Muslim rule by Jerusalem's indigenous Christian population. Seized upon by Arnulf and his supporters, this supposed remnant of Jesus' life soon became the totem of the new Latin realm of Jerusalem, a symbol of Frankish victory and of the efficacy of the crusading ideal.

The last battle

Neither the patriarch nor Godfrey of Bouillon had much opportunity to relish their new-found status. In early August news arrived that al-Afdal had landed at the southern Palestinian port of Ascalon, having assembled an army of some 20,000 ferocious North Africans. The vizier was just days away from marching forth to reclaim Jerusalem for Islam. After all their trials and suffering, the Franks, beset by factionalism and woefully outnumbered, now faced the very real prospect of annihilation and the unravelling of their remarkable achievements.

Rather than wait to be besieged, Godfrey decided to risk everything on a pre-emptive strike against the Fatimids. On 9 August he left the Holy City, his troops marching barefoot as penitent soldiers of Christ, accompanied by Patriarch Arnulf and the relic of the True Cross. Over the next few days Godfrey managed to cobble together a grudging, last-ditch Latin alliance, which saw Raymond of Toulouse rejoin the fray. The massed ranks of the once great Frankish host had now been whittled down to an elite, hardened core of crusade survivors, numbering perhaps 1,200 knights and 9,000 infantrymen in total. This army marched south towards Ascalon on 11 August, but towards the end of the day they captured a group of Egyptian spies who revealed al-Afdal's battle plan as well as the size and the disposition of his forces. Recognising that they would be outnumbered two to one, the crusaders chose to rely upon an element of surprise to even the odds. At dawn the next day they launched a sudden attack on the still-sleeping Fatimid troops, quartered before Ascalon. Overconfident, al-Afdal had failed to post sufficient watchmen, leaving the Franks free to scythe through rank upon rank of stunned Muslim troops. As Latin knights drove into the heart of their camp, seizing al-Afdal's personal standard and most of his possessions, the battle quickly turned into a rout:

> In their great fright [the Fatimids] climbed and hid in trees, only to plunge from boughs like falling birds when our men pierced them with arrows and killed them with lances. Later the Christians uselessly decapitated them with swords. Other infidels threw themselves to the ground grovelling in terror at the Christians' feet. Then our men cut them to pieces as one slaughters cattle for the meat market.[43]

In a state of horrified shock, al-Afdal escaped into Ascalon and immediately set sail for Egypt, leaving the crusaders to crush any lingering resistance and mop up a lavish horde of booty, including the vizier's own precious sword. The First Crusade had survived its final test, but the petty rivalry that had divided its leaders for so long now exacted a costly price. Terrified and abandoned, Ascalon's garrison was more than ready to surrender that August, but they demanded to negotiate with Raymond of Toulouse, the one Frank known to have upheld his promises during the sack of Jerusalem. Fearful that the Provençal count might thereby establish his own independent coastal lordship, Godfrey interfered and negotiations collapsed. This squandered opportunity left Ascalon in the hands of Islam. In the decades to come a resurgent Fatimid navy proved able to defend this Palestinian foothold, leaving the nascent kingdom of Jerusalem dangerously exposed to Egyptian attack.

The return to Europe

After the victory at Ascalon, most crusaders considered their work to be done. Against all odds and expectations they had survived the gruelling pilgrimage to the Holy Land, secured the 'miraculous' reconquest of Jerusalem and repelled the might of Fatimid Egypt. Of the tens of thousands who had taken the cross years earlier, only a fraction remained, and now the vast majority of these looked to return home to the West. By summer's end they had joined Robert of Normandy and Robert of Flanders in taking ship from Syria, leaving Godfrey with just 300 knights and some 2,000 infantrymen to defend Palestine. Tancred was the only major crusader prince to remain, his eyes open to the opportunity of establishing his own independent lordship in the East.

Few, if any, crusaders returned to Europe laden with riches. The plunder amassed at Jerusalem and Ascalon seems to have been swiftly consumed by travel costs, and many reached their homelands in a state of near-penniless destitution, afflicted by sickness and exhaustion. Many carried with them a different form of sacred 'treasure' – relics of the saints, pieces of the Holy Lance and the True Cross, or simple palm fronds from Jerusalem, the badge of their completed pilgrimage. Peter the Hermit, for one, reached France with relics of John the Baptist and the Holy Sepulchre itself, and duly founded an Augustinian priory near Liège in their honour. Almost all were assured a degree of renown for their exploits, and it became common for these crusaders to be celebrated with the nickname 'Hierosolymitani', or 'travellers to Jerusalem'.

Of course, there were hundreds, even thousands, of Franks who did not return to a 'hero's welcome'; those who, like Stephen of Blois, had abandoned the expedition before its completion and thus failed to fulfil their pilgrim vows. These 'deserters' were greeted by a withering tide of public opprobrium. Stephen was openly chastised by his wife Adela. He, and many like him, sought to overcome the stain of this ignominy by enlisting in a new venture – the 1101 crusade. Since 1096, Pope Urban II had been encouraging waves of Latin reinforcements to set out for the Levant. Urban died in the summer of 1099, just before news of Jerusalem's capture reached Rome, but his successor, Paschal II, soon took up the call, promoting a large-scale expedition to bring military aid to the nascent Frankish settlements in the East. Buoyed by tales of the First Crusade's victories, this campaign enjoyed extraordinary levels of recruitment, drawing upon the ranks of the disgraced and thousands of new enthusiasts. Armies that at least matched the size of those amassed in 1096–7 marched to Constantinople, where they were joined by the veteran prince Raymond of Toulouse, recently arrived in Byzantium to renew his alliance with Emperor Alexius.

Despite its apparent martial strength, the 1101 crusade proved to be a shocking debacle. Forsaking the advice of both Stephen of Blois and Raymond of Toulouse, this expedition ignored the need for unified action. Instead, no fewer than three separate armies set out to cross Asia Minor, and each met its doom at the hands of a potent coalition of local Seljuq Turkish rulers, now only too aware of the threat posed by a crusader invasion. Having vastly underestimated the scale of enemy resistance, the 1101 crusaders were wiped out in a succession of devastating military encounters. Of those few who survived, only a handful, including Stephen and Raymond, limped on to Syria and Palestine, and even then they achieved nothing of substance.[44]

Perhaps surprisingly, these reversals did little to dampen enthusiasm back in Latin Europe for the notion of 'crusading'. Indeed, many contemporaries actually argued that the failure of the 1101 campaign, supposedly born out of sinful pride, simply served to reinforce the miraculous nature of the First Crusade's achievements. And yet, despite papal attempts to experiment with this new form of sanctified warfare and to associate the memory of the First Crusade

with different theatres of conflict, the start of the twelfth century was
not marked by an explosion of crusading enthusiasm. In fact, it would
be decades before the Frankish West roused itself to launch
expeditions in defence of the Holy Land on the scale of those
witnessed between 1095 and 1101. This left the Latins who had
remained in the Levant after Jerusalem's conquest dangerously
isolated.

IN MEMORY AND IMAGINATION

The success of the First Crusade stunned Latin Christendom. For
many, only the hand of God could explain the crusaders' survival at
Antioch and their ultimate triumph at Jerusalem. Had the expedition
been thwarted in the Near East, the very notion of crusading would
probably have fallen into abeyance. As it was, the victory fired
enthusiasm for this new form of devotional warfare for centuries to
come, and the First Crusade became perhaps the most widely
recorded event of the Middle Ages.

Configuring the memory of the crusade in Latin Europe

The work of memorialising the crusade began almost immediately,
as a number of participants sought, in the first years of the twelfth
century, to document and celebrate the campaign. The most
influential of these, the *Gesta Francorum* (the *Deeds of the Franks*),
was written in Jerusalem around 1100, most likely by a noble-born
southern Italian Norman crusader of some education. While this
account does appear to have been informed by the personal
experiences of its anonymous author, it cannot be regarded as pure
eyewitness evidence, akin to the likes of a diary. Instead, the author
of the *Gesta Francorum* adopted a new approach to the recording of
the past, one that was just starting to emerge in medieval Europe as
an alternative to the traditional year-on-year chronicle. Distilling the
experiences of thousands of participants into a single, overarching

narrative, he constructed the first *Historia* (narrative history) of the crusade, recounting a tale of epic scope and heroic dimensions. Other crusade veterans, including Raymond of Aguilers, Fulcher of Chartres and Peter Tudebode, drew upon the *Gesta Francorum* as a kind of base text around which to construct their own narrative accounts – a form of plagiarism commonplace in this era. Modern scholars have turned to this corpus of evidence, and to the letters written by crusaders during the campaign, to recreate a Latin perspective of the expedition. And by cross-referencing this close testimony with non-Frankish sources (by Muslims, Greeks, Levantine Christians and Jews), they have sought to build up the most accurate possible picture of what really happened on the First Crusade – what might be termed an empirical reconstruction.[45]

In the first decade of the twelfth century, however, a number of Latins living in Europe set out to write – or more accurately to rewrite – the history of the crusade. Three of these – Robert of Rheims, Guibert of Nogent and Baldric of Bourgueil – were particularly important because of the widespread popularity and significance of the accounts they authored. All three were highly educated Benedictine monks living in northern France, with no first-hand experience of the holy war outside Europe. Working almost simultaneously, but apparently without any knowledge of the other two, each of these three monks composed new accounts of the First Crusade, using the *Gesta Francorum* as the basis for their work. According to their own words, they took on this labour because they believed the *Gesta* was written in a 'rough manner' that used 'inelegant and artless language'. Yet, Robert, Guibert and Baldric went far beyond simply polishing the *Gesta*'s medieval Latin. They added new details to the story, sometimes gleaning this information from other 'eyewitness' texts, like that of Fulcher of Chartres, elsewhere drawing from the oral testimony of participants or perhaps from their own imaginings. Crucially, at a fundamental level, all three also reinterpreted the First Crusade.

Robert of Rheims, for example, utilised a far richer and more learned palette of scriptural allusion than that employed in the *Gesta Francorum*. He used these quotations from, or parallels with, the Old and New Testaments to position the crusade within a better-defined Christian context. Robert also emphasised the expedition's miraculous nature, arguing that its success was not achieved because of the efforts of man, but through the divine agency of God's will. In addition, Robert recast the whole story of the crusade. The *Gesta* preserved only an oblique reference to Urban II's preaching of the campaign and was structured so as to present the siege and conquest of Antioch as the pinnacle of endeavour, covering events at Jerusalem almost as an afterthought. By contrast, Robert began his history with an extended account of the pope's sermon at Clermont (which Robert claimed to have witnessed in person) and placed far greater stress upon the Holy City's capture. In this way, he portrayed the expedition as a venture instigated, directed and legitimated by the papacy, and affirmed that the crusade's ultimate goal was Christendom's repatriation of Jerusalem.

Of course, Robert's history did not alter the events of the First Crusade in any material sense; neither did the accounts penned by Guibert and Baldric. But their work is of fundamental importance to the understanding of the crusades as a whole, because, in comparison to texts like the *Gesta Francorum*, it was read far more widely by medieval contemporaries. As such, these Benedictine reworkings served to shape the way people recalled and thought about the crusade in the twelfth and thirteenth centuries. Robert of Rheims' history was especially admired – the equivalent of a medieval bestseller among the learned elite. It was also used as a source for the most famous *chanson de geste* (epic poem) about the expedition, the *Chanson d'Antioche*, whose 10,000 lines of Old French immortalised the crusaders as legendary Christian heroes. Written in the popular *chanson* form – which fast became the most widely disseminated means in western Europe of recounting 'historical' events – the *Chanson d'Antioche* was designed to be recited publicly in a vernacular language familiar to a lay audience. As such, it too did much to mould the prevailing memory of the First Crusade in Latin Christendom.

From the first wave of 'eyewitness' accounts, through to the likes of Robert of Rheims' *Historia* and the *Chanson d'Antioche*, the process of memorialising the crusade had a gradual but far-reaching effect upon the imagined reality of events: promoting Godfrey of Bouillon as the expedition's sole leader; imbedding the memory of the Holy Lance's 'miraculous' impact; and consolidating the idea that 'martyred' crusaders were guaranteed a heavenly reward. Perhaps the most historically charged reconfiguration and manipulation involved the events at Jerusalem on and after 15 July 1099. The Latins' sack of the Holy City could be readily interpreted by Christian contemporaries as the decisive moment of divinely sanctioned triumph, or by Muslims as an act of unqualified savagery that revealed the Franks' innate barbarism. It certainly is striking that Christian accounts made no attempt to limit the number of 'infidels' killed when Jerusalem fell – if anything, they gloried in the event. They also revelled in the scene of carnage at the Aqsa mosque. The *Gesta Francorum* noted that the crusaders were left wading up to their ankles in blood by the work of butchery. However, another 'eyewitness', Raymond of Aguilers, expanded on this image. Lifting a scriptural quote from the New Testament Book of Revelation, he declared that the Franks 'rode in [enemy] blood to the knees and bridles of their horses'. This more extreme image gained wide acceptance and was repeated by numerous western European histories and chronicles in the course of the twelfth century.[46]

The First Crusade and Islam

For all its violent conquests, the First Crusade elicited a surprisingly muted response within the Muslim world. The campaign generated no outpouring of Arabic testimony to match the veritable flood of comment in Latin Christian texts. Indeed, the first surviving Arabic chronicles to describe the crusade in any detail were written only around the 1150s. Even in these works, composed by the

Aleppan al-Azimi and the Damascene Ibn al-Qalanisi, the coverage was relatively brief – little more than a skeleton narrative overview, covering the crossing of Asia Minor and events in Antioch, Marrat and Jerusalem, peppered with occasional condemnations of Frankish atrocities. These included a comment on the incalculable number of Antiochenes 'killed, taken prisoner and enslaved' when the city fell in early June 1098, and the observation that 'a great host [of Jerusalem's populace] were killed' during the crusaders' sack of the Holy City.

By the 1220s, the Iraqi historian Ibn al-Athir was more fulsome in his censure, recording that 'in the Aqsa mosque the Franks killed more than 70,000, a large number of them being *imams*, religious scholars, righteous men and ascetics, Muslims who had left their native lands and come to live a holy life in this august place'. He then described how the crusaders looted the Dome of the Rock. Ibn al-Athir added that a deputation of Syrian Muslims came to the Abbasid caliph in Baghdad in late summer 1099 to beg for aid against the Franks. They were said to have recounted stories of suffering at Latin hands 'which brought tears to the eye and pained the heart', and to have made a public protest during Friday prayer, but, despite all their entreaties, little was done, and the chronicler concluded that 'the rulers were all at variance ... and so the Franks conquered the lands'.[47]

How should this apparent lack of historical interest in the First Crusade within Islam be interpreted? In western Europe the expedition was widely celebrated as an earth-shatteringly significant triumph, but in the Muslim world of the early twelfth century it seems barely to have registered as a tremor. To an extent, this may be attributed to the desire of Islamic chroniclers to limit references to Muslim defeats, or to a general disinterest in military events on the part of Islamic religious scholars. But it is surprising, nonetheless, that the most contemporaneous Arabic accounts do not show clearer traces of anti-Latin invective or contain more vocal demands for vengeful retribution.

A few isolated Muslim voices did call for a collective response to the First Crusade in the years immediately following Jerusalem's capture, among them a number of poets whose Arabic verses were repeated in later collections. Al-Abiwardi, who lived in Baghdad and died in 1113, described the crusade as 'a time of disasters' and proclaimed that 'this is war, and the infidel's sword is naked in his hand, ready to be sheathed again in men's necks and skulls'. Around the same time, the Damascene poet Ibn al-Khayyat, who had earlier lived in Tripoli, described how the Frankish armies had 'swelled in a torrent of terrifying extent'. His verses expressed regret at the willingness of Muslims to be pacified by Christian bribes and weakened by internecine rivalry. He also exhorted his audience to violent action: 'The heads of the polytheists have already ripened, so do not neglect them as a vintage and a harvest!' The most interesting reaction was that of 'Ali ibn Tahir al-Sulami, a Muslim jurist who taught in the Grand Umayyad Mosque in Damascus. Around 1105 he appears to have delivered a number of public lectures on the merits of *jihad* and the urgent need for a resolute and collective Islamic response to the First Crusade. His thoughts were recorded in a treatise, the *Book of Holy War* (*Kitab al-Jihad*), sections of which survive to this day. But despite al-Sulami's prescient assessment of the threat posed by the Franks, his calls for action, like those of the poets, went unheeded.[48]

The stark absence of a concerted Islamic reaction to the coming of the crusades can be explained in a number of ways. In general, Near and Middle Eastern Muslims seem to have had only a limited understanding of who the First Crusaders were and why they came to the Holy Land. Most imagined that the Latins were actually Byzantine mercenaries, engaged in a short-term military incursion, not driven warriors devoted to the conquest and settlement of the Levant. These misconceptions helped to blunt Islam's response to the events of 1097 to 1099. Had the Muslims recognised the true scale and nature of the crusade, they might have been inspired to put aside at least some of their own quarrels to repel a common enemy. As it was, the fundamental divisions remained. A deep-seated fracture still separated the Sunnis of Syria and Iraq and the Shi'ite Fatimids of Egypt. Rivalry between the Turkish rulers of Damascus and Aleppo continued unabated. And in Baghdad, the Seljuq sultan and Abbasid caliph were preoccupied with their own Mesopotamian power struggles.

Over the next century some of these problems were resolved and enthusiasm for a *jihad* against the invading Franks spread across the Muslim world of the eastern Mediterranean. To begin with, however, the Latins who invaded the Levant faced no determined pan-Islamic counter-attack. This gave western Christendom a crucial opportunity to consolidate its hold on the Holy Land.

4

CREATING THE CRUSADER STATES

The First Crusade brought Latin Christendom control of Jerusalem and of two great Syrian cities, Antioch and Edessa. In the wake of these astounding achievements, a new outpost of the western European world was born in the Near East, as the Franks expanded and consolidated their hold over the Levant. In the Middle Ages, this region was sometimes referred to as 'Outremer', the land beyond the sea, while today the four major settlements that emerged in the first decades of the twelfth century – the kingdom of Jerusalem, the principality of Antioch and the counties of Edessa and Tripoli – are frequently described as the 'crusader states'.[49]

At its core, the crusading movement, for centuries to come, would be dominated by the need to defend these isolated territories, this island of western Christendom in the East. With the benefit of hindsight, it is all too easy to forget that the basic survival of the crusader states hung in the balance in the years that followed the First Crusade. That expedition had achieved the impossible – the recapture of the Holy City – but amid the exultant drive towards that singular goal the crusaders had largely ignored the need for systematic conquest. The first generation of Frankish settlers in Outremer thus inherited a disjointed patchwork of poorly resourced towns and cities, and their fragile 'new world' teetered on the brink of extinction. In 1100 the future of the crusader states seemed desperately uncertain, and all the bloody triumphs of the crusade stood to be erased.[50]

PROTECTOR OF THE HOLY CITY

This problem was immediately apparent to Godfrey of Bouillon, the first Frankish ruler of Jerusalem. Possessing only meagre resources in terms of military manpower, with most of Palestine as yet unconquered and the forces of both Abbasid and Fatimid Islam cowed but far from broken, his initial prospects were bleak. Godfrey's first priorities were to expand the Latin foothold in the Holy Land and to secure maritime communications with the West. To fulfil both needs he targeted Arsuf, the small Muslim-held fortified port town just north of Jaffa, but, despite a hard-fought siege in autumn 1099, he failed to secure its capture.

Godfrey returned to the Holy City in early December only to be confronted by a new danger – civil war. Given the contested nature of his elevation and his apparent decision to forgo a regal title, Godfrey's authority over the Frankish territories in Palestine was open to challenge. Tancred's continued presence already posed something of a problem, but the real possibility of internal overthrow solidified on 21 December 1099 with the advent of a powerful delegation of Latin 'pilgrims'. Bohemond of Taranto and Baldwin of Boulogne had travelled south from Antioch and Edessa to fulfil their crusading vows by venerating the Holy Places. They were accompanied by the new papal legate to the Levant, Archbishop Daimbert of Pisa, a man driven by personal ambition and an unflinching belief in the power of the Church. Each of these potentates harboured hopes of ruling Jerusalem, as either a secular or an ecclesiastical realm, and their appearance presented an obvious, if unspoken, threat. And yet, through political pragmatism, Godfrey managed to turn their arrival to his advantage. After celebrating the Feast of the Nativity at

Bethlehem, he elected to turn on Arnulf of Chocques and side with Daimbert. By backing the archbishop's candidacy for the patriarchal seat, Godfrey stemmed the immediate threat from Bohemond and Baldwin and secured the much-needed naval support from the Pisan fleet of 120 ships that had accompanied Daimbert to the Near East. This new pact was not without its price – the donation of a section of the Holy City to the patriarch and the promise of a Pisan quarter in the port of Jaffa.

Baldwin and Bohemond returned to their northern lordships in January 1100, and over the next six months the latter bolstered Frankish authority over Syria at the expense of Byzantium by expelling the Greek patriarch of Antioch and installing a Latin in his place. However, in the course of a rather rash campaign beyond his principality's northern frontier in July 1100, Bohemond was set upon by a force of Anatolian Turks and taken prisoner. The great crusader general would spend the next three years in captivity, dividing his time, rumour later had it, between courting a glamorous Muslim princess named Melaz and praying for the intervention of St Leonard, the Christian patron saint of prisoners.

In Palestine, Godfrey enjoyed a modicum of success deploying the Pisan fleet to intimidate Muslim-held Arsuf, Acre, Caesarea and Ascalon in early 1100, with each coastal settlement agreeing to make tribute payments to the Franks. Tancred, meanwhile, was busy carving out his own semi-independent lordship in Galilee, capturing Tiberias from the Muslims with relative ease. Upon the departure of the Pisan fleet in spring and the arrival of a new Venetian naval force in the Holy Land in mid-June, Godfrey's reliance upon Patriarch Daimbert lessened. But before he could capitalise upon this new opportunity to exercise sovereign authority, the duke was taken ill, apparently after feasting upon oranges while being entertained by the Muslim emir of Caesarea. There was some suspicion of poisoning, but in all likelihood Godfrey contracted a disease akin to typhoid during what was, even by Levantine standards, a scorching hot summer. On 18 July he undertook the rituals of confession and communion for one last time and then, in the words of one Latin contemporary, 'secured and protected by a spiritual shield' the crusading conqueror of Jerusalem, still little more than forty years of age, 'was taken from this light'. Five days later, in reverence of his status and achievements, Godfrey's body was buried within the entrance to the Holy Sepulchre.[51]

GOD'S KINGDOM

Godfrey of Bouillon's death in July 1100 left the newborn Frankish realm of Jerusalem in a state of turmoil. Godfrey's wish seems to have been that lordship of the Holy City pass to his younger brother, Baldwin of Boulogne, the first Latin count of Edessa. But Patriarch Daimbert continued to harbour his own vision for Jerusalem; one in which the city would become the physical embodiment of God's kingdom on Earth, capital of an ecclesiastical state with the patriarch at its head. Had he been present at the moment of Godfrey's demise this dream might have found some purchase in reality. But Daimbert just then was engaged, alongside Tancred, besieging the port of Haifa. Supporters of Godfrey's bloodline, including Arnulf of Chocques and Geldemar Carpinel, seized this chance to act, occupying the Tower of David (the strategic key to dominion over Jerusalem) and dispatching messengers north to summon Baldwin.

The news reached Edessa around mid-September. The count, now in his mid-thirties, was said to be 'very tall [and] quite fair of complexion, with dark brown hair and beard, [and an] aquiline nose', his regal bearing only faintly marred by a prominent upper lip and slightly receding chin. Given Baldwin's quality and nature – his voracious appetite for power and advancement, his genius for hard-hearted enterprise – the invitation from Palestine represented a stunning opportunity. Even his chaplain, the First Crusade veteran Fulcher of Chartres, was forced to admit that Baldwin 'grieved somewhat at the death of his brother, but rejoiced more over his inheritance'. In the weeks that followed, Baldwin quickly settled the county's affairs. To ensure that this, his first Levantine lordship, would remain in Frankish hands and subject to his own authority, Baldwin installed his cousin and namesake, Baldwin of Bourcq (a little-known First Crusader), as the new count of Edessa. He seems to have recognised Baldwin of Boulogne as his overlord at this point.[52]

Setting out from the northern reaches of Syria with just 200 knights and 700 infantrymen in early October, Baldwin travelled via Antioch and then repelled a sizeable intercepting Muslim force led by Duqaq of Damascus near the Dog River in Lebanon. Once in Palestine, Baldwin moved quickly to outmanoeuvre Tancred and Daimbert, sending ahead one of his most trusted knights, Hugh of Falchenberg, to make contact with Godfrey's supporters in the Tower of David and to orchestrate a fitting welcome to the Holy City. When Baldwin at last reached Jerusalem on 9 November, he was greeted by jubilant and, most likely, stage-managed celebrations, replete with cheering crowds of Latin, Greek and Syrian Christians. In the face of this apparent outpouring of popular support, Daimbert could do little to intercede. Skulking in the small Mount Zion monastery just outside the city walls, the patriarch absented himself on 11 November when Baldwin was formally declared Jerusalem's new ruler.

As yet, however, Baldwin was unable to claim the title of king; first he would have to undergo a coronation. This centuries-old rite usually involved a crown wearing, but this was not, as might be imagined, the centrepiece of the ceremony. That honour fell to the ritual of anointment, the moment when holy chrism (oil) was poured upon a ruler's head by one of God's representatives on Earth, such as an archbishop, patriarch or pope. It was this act that set a king apart from other men; that imbued him with the numinous power of divine sanction. To achieve this elevation, Baldwin needed to reach some form of accommodation with the Church.

His rule began with a show of forceful intent: a month-long raiding campaign along the realm's southern and eastern frontiers, securing pilgrim routes and harassing the Egyptian garrison at Ascalon. To his subjects and neighbours alike it was obvious that Baldwin brought a new sense of purpose and power to the Latin kingdom. Daimbert duly recognised that he was better off holding on to office under this new regime than risking deposition from the patriarchal throne. On 25 December 1100, in the Church of the Nativity at Bethlehem – a date and place steeped in symbolism – the patriarch crowned and anointed Baldwin of Boulogne as the first Frankish king of Jerusalem. By this act Daimbert effectively ended any notion that the crusader realm might live on as a theocracy. His submission also averted a potentially catastrophic civil war.

But the patriarch was not long saved by this concession. In the months and years that followed, Baldwin I moved with calculated efficiency to stamp out any residual challenge to his authority and to realign the Latin Church in his favour. Fortunately for the king, his most significant secular rival, Tancred, left Palestine in the spring of 1101 to take up the regency of Antioch during Bohemond's imprisonment. Later that year, Daimbert was deposed when it was discovered that he had embezzled money sent from Apulia to fund the defence of the Holy Land. After a brief return to power in 1102, Daimbert's fortunes waned and the patriarchal seat passed to a succession of papally sanctioned candidates, culminating in 1112 with the reinstatement of Baldwin's long-term ally, Arnulf of Chocques. These patriarchs were never wholly subservient to the crown, but were willing to engage in active and mutual cooperation with the king as he sought to consolidate Frankish control over Palestine.

One key feature of this collaboration was the management and cultivation of the cult associated with the Jerusalemite relic of the True Cross discovered by the First Crusaders in 1099. In the first years of the twelfth century the Cross became a totem of Latin power in the Levant. Borne by either the patriarch or one of his leading clergymen into a succession of battles against Islam, it quickly acquired a reputation for miraculous intervention; soon it was said that, in the presence of the Lord's Cross, the Franks were invincible. [53]

Creating a kingdom

Having secured his accession, Baldwin I was confronted by one overwhelming difficulty. In reality, the kingdom over which he now ruled was little more than a loose network of dispersed outposts. The Franks held Jerusalem alongside the likes of Bethlehem, Ramla and Tiberias, but in 1100 these were still just isolated pockets of Latin settlement. Even here, the ruling Franks were vastly outnumbered by the indigenous Muslim population and by eastern Christian and Jewish communities. The bulk of Palestine remained unconquered and in the hands of semi-autonomous Islamic potentates. Worse still, the Latins had barely begun to assert control over the Levantine coastline, controlling only Jaffa and Haifa, neither of which offered an ideal natural harbour. Only by subjugating Palestine's ports could Baldwin hope to secure lines of communication with western Europe, open his kingdom to Christian pilgrims and settlers, and tap into a potentially bounteous conduit of trade between East and West. Internal security and the need for territorial consolidation, therefore, were paramount.

A Latin eyewitness, Fulcher of Chartres, reflected upon this situation:

> In the beginning of his reign Baldwin as yet possessed few cities and people ... Up to that time the land route [to Palestine] was completely blocked to our pilgrims [and those Franks who could] came very timidly in single ships, or in squadrons of three or four, through the midst of hostile pirates and past the ports of the Saracens ... Some remained in the Holy Land, and others went back to their native countries. For this reason the land of Jerusalem remained depopulated [and] we did not have more than 300 knights and as many footmen to defend [the kingdom].

The perils associated with these problems were reflected in the testimony of early Christian pilgrims who did reach the Near East.

Saewulf, a pilgrim (most likely from Britain) who documented his journey to Jerusalem at the very start of the twelfth century, described the prevailing lawlessness of the Judean hills in disturbing detail. The road between Jaffa and the Holy City, he noted, 'was very dangerous . . . because the Saracens are continually plotting an ambush . . . day and night always keeping a lookout for someone to attack'. En route he saw 'countless corpses' left to rot or to be 'torn up by wild beasts' because no one would risk stopping to organise proper burials. Things had improved somewhat by around 1107, when another pilgrim, a Russian known as Daniel the Abbot, visited the Holy Land, but he still complained bitterly that it was impossible to travel through Galilee without the protection of soldiers.

Perhaps the most striking demonstration that the Holy Land had yet to be truly conquered came in the summer of 1103 when, during a routine hunting trip near Caesarea, Baldwin I was attacked by a small Fatimid raiding party that had seemingly marched into Latin territory at will. Caught in the thick of the fighting, the king was struck by an enemy lance, and, although the precise nature of his injuries is unclear – one account had him stabbed 'in the back near the heart', another 'pierced through the thigh and kidneys' – they were certainly grave. A Latin contemporary described how 'at once streams of blood gushed ominously from this wound . . . his face began to grow pale [and] at length he fell from his horse to the ground as if dead'. Thanks to the careful ministrations of his physician, after a protracted convalescence Baldwin recovered, but he continued to be troubled by this injury for the remainder of his life.[54]

Ultimately, Baldwin I was forced to dedicate much of the first decade of the twelfth century to the consolidation of his hold over Palestine, employing a mixture of pragmatic flexibility and icy resolve in his dealings with the Muslim inhabitants of the Holy Land. He received an early boost when a Genoese fleet arrived in Jaffa, possibly alongside ships from Pisa, just before Easter 1101. These sailors had come east probably with a mind to aid in the consolidation and defence of the Levant and to explore new avenues for commerce.

They brought a much-needed naval element to Baldwin's campaign of conquest and, in return, he offered them generous terms: a third share of any booty taken and a semi-independent trading enclave, to be held 'by perpetual and hereditary right', within any settlement taken with Italian aid. With the deal struck, Baldwin was ready to go on the offensive.

His first target, Arsuf, had staunchly resisted a land-based assault from Godfrey of Bouillon in December 1099. Now Baldwin was able to enforce a siege from the sea and, after just three days, its Muslim populace sued for peace on 29 April 1101. The king was magnanimous, granting them safe conduct, bearing any goods they could carry, as far as Ascalon. Success had been achieved without loss of Christian life.

Baldwin then turned his attention to Caesarea, twenty-odd miles to the north. This once bustling Greco-Roman settlement had faded over centuries of Muslim rule; its aged walls still stood, but the city's celebrated port had long since been destroyed and all that remained was a small, shallow harbour. Baldwin sent a legation to the emir of Caesarea, urging him to capitulate or face a merciless siege; but, holding out hope of Fatimid reinforcement, the town's Muslim inhabitants stoutly rejected any notion of a negotiated surrender. At Arsuf, the Latin king had shown clemency to a submissive foe; here, in the face of such brazen obstinacy, he sought to make a brutal demonstration. Moving in around 2 May 1101, he began bombarding Caesarea with mangonels. Its garrison put up stern resistance for fifteen days, but Frankish troops eventually managed to storm the city's buckling defences with the aid of scaling ladders. Baldwin now allowed the full wanton fury of his troops to be unleashed on Caesarea's terrified populace. Christian troops scoured the city, street by street, house by house, giving no quarter, butchering most of the male population, enslaving the women and children and plundering every shred of loot they could find. One Latin observer wrote:

How much property of various kinds was found there it is impossible to say, but many of our men who had been poor became rich. I saw a great many of the Saracens who were killed there put in a pile and burned. The fetid odour of their bodies bothered us greatly. These wretches were burned for the sake of finding the gold coins which some had swallowed.

Not since the sack of the Holy City itself in 1099 had the Levant witnessed such avaricious barbarity. The wealth seized was substantial – the Genoese alone, upon receiving their allotted third, were able to distribute forty-eight *solidi* of Poitou and two pounds of valuable spices to each of 8,000 men – and the spoils must also have done much to restock the royal treasury. In addition, the Italians were given an emerald-green bowl, the *Sacro Catino*, once believed to be the Holy Grail, which remains in Genoa's Cathedral of San Lorenzo to this day. Baldwin I, meanwhile, made a point of sparing the emir and *qadi* (judge) of Caesarea in order to secure a hefty ransom. A cleric also named Baldwin, notorious for having branded a cross on his forehead at the start of the First Crusade, was then appointed as the new Latin archbishop of Caesarea.[55]

This conquest sent a stark message to the remaining Muslim settlements in Palestine: resistance would bring annihilation. Before long this notion smoothed the way to the most significant conquest of Baldwin's early reign. In April 1104 he laid siege to the port of Acre, some twelve miles north of Haifa, home to Palestine's largest and most sheltered harbour. Fighting alongside a seventy-ship-strong Genoese fleet, the king began an assault siege, and the Muslim garrison, isolated from any possible Fatimid reinforcement, soon capitulated, requesting the same terms of surrender given at Arsuf. Baldwin readily acquiesced; indeed, he even allowed Muslim citizens to remain in Acre in return for payment of a form of poll tax. With limited loss of life, he had acquired a valuable prize – a port offering relatively secure anchorage, whatever the season, that could act as a vital channel for maritime communication and commerce with western Europe.[56] Before long, Acre became the Latin kingdom's trading capital.

In the years that followed, Baldwin continued gradually to extend and consolidate his control over the Mediterranean seaboard. Beirut was captured in May 1110, this time with the aid of Genoese and Pisan ships. Later that year Baldwin targeted Sidon, which for some time had been bribing the Frankish king with lavish tributes of gold to secure immunity. With the able support of a large contingent of recently arrived Norwegian crusader-pilgrims, under their young king Sigurd, Baldwin laid siege to Sidon in October and forced its surrender by early December, once again on terms of safe conduct and a provision to allow some members of the Muslim population to remain in peace, working the land under Latin rule.

In the course of this first decade, Baldwin I brought a real measure of territorial security to his nascent kingdom and forged a crucial lifeline back to the Christian west. Nonetheless, two cities remained beyond his grasp. To the north, the strongly fortified port of Tyre stood as a stubborn Muslim outpost, separating Acre from Sidon and Beirut; it survived a concerted Frankish siege in 1111 largely because its emir switched allegiance from Egypt to Damascus, securing valuable reinforcement. Unable to achieve its capture, Baldwin isolated Tyre by building fortresses inland at Toron and south along the coast at a narrow cliff pass known as Scandelion.

To the south, Ascalon likewise slipped through Baldwin's fingers. In the spring of 1111 he threatened to besiege the city, frightening its latest emir, Shams al-Khilafa, into adopting a remarkable policy of political realignment. The emir first bought peace with the promise of a tribute of 7,000 dinars. With al-Afdal, the Fatimid vizier of Egypt, rumbling his objections back in Cairo, al-Khilafa decided that his best hope of political survival lay in a dramatic switch of allegiance. Breaking with the Fatimid caliphate, he travelled to Jerusalem to broker a new deal with Baldwin I and, having pledged his loyalty to the Latin kingdom, was left in power as a semi-independent client ruler. Soon afterwards a Christian garrison of 300 troops was installed in Ascalon, and for some months it seemed that Baldwin's pragmatism had finally closed the doorway between Egypt and Palestine. The unfortunate Shams al-Khilafa did not live long beyond that summer. A group of Ascalonite Berbers, still loyal to the Fatimids, attacked him while he was out riding. Badly wounded, he fled to his house, but was hunted down and butchered. Before King Baldwin could come to its aid, the Christian garrison was similarly dispatched. Having been sent al-Khilafa's head, al-Afdal swiftly reimposed Fatimid control over Ascalon.[57]

Servants to the crown

Baldwin I demonstrated a gift for forceful governance in his role as king of an expanding realm. Throughout the first phase of his reign he took great care to ensure that the balance of power in Latin Palestine lay with the crown and not with the nobility. In this he had a particular advantage over fellow monarchs back in the West in that he was, in relative terms at least, beginning with a clean slate. Not having to deal with an imbedded aristocracy, enmeshed within centuries-old systems of lordship and landholding, Baldwin could shape the new kingdom of Jerusalem to his advantage.

A central feature of his approach was the maintenance of a powerful royal domain – the territory owned and directly administered by the crown. Kings in Europe might inherit realms in which many of the richest and most powerful territories had long since been parcelled out to nobles, to be governed as fiefs in the name of the crown but ruled in semi-autonomous fashion. Baldwin I kept many of Palestine's most important settlements within his domain, including Jerusalem, Jaffa and Acre, creating very few new lordships. Frequently whittled away by the high mortality rate of the warfare-strewn Levant, the aristocracy also had little opportunity to assert hereditary claims to the fiefs that were available. The king also made frequent use of money fiefs, rewarding service with cash rather than land.

The early history of two lordships – Haifa and Tiberias – is particularly illustrative of Baldwin's management of, and attitude to, his leading vassals. Once Tancred left for Antioch in 1101, Baldwin divided the overpowerful principality of Galilee in two. Geldemar Carpinel, a southern French crusader who had been in Godfrey of Bouillon's service, was given Haifa in March 1101, perhaps in return for his support of Baldwin's claim to the throne. Geldemar was killed in battle just six months later and, over the next fifteen years, the lordship of Haifa passed through the hands of three further men, none of whom were related. In this way, authority over the port consistently reverted to the crown, and on each occasion Baldwin was able to redistribute the reward of this fief as he chose.

Tiberias, meanwhile, was given to one of the king's closest followers, Hugh of Falchenberg, the knight from Flanders who had probably joined Baldwin during the First Crusade. Hugh served the kingdom well, but soon fell foul of the region's military insecurity and was killed by an arrow during an ambush in 1106. Tiberias then passed to a northern Frenchman, Gervase of Bazoches, who became one of Baldwin's favourites and was appointed as royal seneschal (in charge of financial administration and the judiciary). Within two years, however, Gervase was captured by Damascene troops during a Muslim raid on Galilee.

Of course, not all of Baldwin I's vassals met with precipitous or gruesome deaths. Along the northern coast of Palestine, on the border with Lebanon and far from the immediate reach of Jerusalem, the king created some new lordships. One of these, Sidon, he gave to the great rising star of his reign, Eustace Garnier. A knight, probably of Norman origin, Eustace had likely served Baldwin while still in Edessa, and certainly fought for him against the Egyptians in 1105. From relative obscurity, Eustace quickly amassed a potent clutch of lordships, including Caesarea and, through marriage to Emma (the well-connected daughter of Patriarch Arnulf of Chocques), the town of Jericho. Eustace was, however, an exception. On the whole, Baldwin seems to have created a loyal and effective noble class that was, as yet, largely subservient to the crown.[58]

FACING ISLAM

Of course, in the early years of his reign Baldwin I could ill afford to focus simply upon the consolidation of his hold over Palestine; one watchful eye remained trained upon his Muslim neighbours, most notably the Shi'ite Fatimids of Egypt. Their vizier al-Afdal had been humbled by the First Crusaders, but with the port of Ascalon – the stepping stone between Palestine and Egypt – still in Fatimid hands, the door stood open for a counter-attack on the kingdom of Jerusalem.

The Battles of Ramla

In May 1101, soon after Baldwin's violent subjugation of Caesarea, news arrived of an Egyptian invasion. Al-Afdal had dispatched a large force that was now advancing on the Holy City under the command of one of his leading generals, the former governor of Beirut, Sa'ad al-Daulah. Baldwin rushed south, but rather than seek open battle he elected to hold his ground amid the relative security of Ramla and wait for the Fatimids' next move. For the next three months a tense stalemate held, with Sa'ad waiting at Ascalon for the right moment to pounce and Baldwin nervously patrolling the region between Jaffa and Jerusalem. Finally, in the first week of September, with the fighting season drawing to a close, the Egyptians began a definitive advance.

Eschewing a reactive policy of defence, Baldwin decided to confront the enemy head-on, ordering an immediate mobilisation at Jaffa. This was a brave decision given the worrying paucity of warriors at his disposal. Even after summoning troops from across the kingdom and ordering that every eligible squire be knighted, he was left with just 260 knights and 900 footmen. Latin estimates of Muslim manpower at this point vary widely – from 31,000 to 200,000 – and seem grossly inflated. No reliable Arabic testimony survives, but it is likely that the Franks were heavily outnumbered that autumn.

Marching out of Jaffa on 6 September to intercept the Fatimids on the plains south of Ramla, the Christians seem to have been possessed by a sense of desperate determination. Among them was the king's chaplain, Fulcher of Chartres, who later wrote that 'we earnestly prepared to die for the love of [Christ]', taking solace from the presence of the relic of the True Cross carried in their midst.

The atmosphere at dawn the following day was laden with echoes of the First Crusade. With Sa'ad al-Daulah's forces spotted 'from a distance . . . shimmering in the plain', the king apparently fell to his knees before the True Cross, confessed his sins and received mass. Fulcher recalled the rousing battle speech his monarch then delivered:

> Come then, soldiers of Christ, be of good cheer and fear nothing, [but] fight, I beseech you, for the salvation of your souls . . . If you should be slain here, you will surely be among the blessed. Already the gate of the kingdom of Heaven is open to you. If you survive as victors you will shine in glory among the Christians. If, however, you wish to flee, remember that France is indeed a long distance away.

With that the Franks began advancing at speed, taking the fight to the Egyptians, arrayed in five or six divisions. Baldwin, astride his fleet-footed mount fittingly named Gazelle, led a reserve force, ready to attack once the shape of the fracas became clear. Riding close to his king throughout, Fulcher of Chartres later evoked the chaotic horror of the battle that followed, writing that 'the number of the foe was so great and they swarmed over us so quickly that hardly anyone could see or recognise anyone else'. The Latin vanguard was soon decimated, with Geldemar Carpinel among the slain, and the whole army was quickly encircled.

With the Christians on the brink of defeat, Baldwin committed his reserve, riding alongside the True Cross. At the force of his attack rank upon rank of Fatimid troops buckled. Fulcher watched as the king himself skewered a leading Egyptian emir in the belly with his lance, and a large portion of the Muslim force turned in flight. It was probably in this shock assault that Sa'ad al-Daulah was killed. One Latin contemporary believed that victory was assured by a miracle associated with the True Cross in which a Muslim commander was choked to death just as he was about to attack the bishop carrying the relic. This story seems to have circulated through the army, and certainly contributed to the burgeoning cult surrounding the Cross, but in reality the whole encounter was close run and inconclusive. Fulcher testified that the field was cloaked with weapons, armour and the bodies of both Muslim and Christian dead, estimating the enemy's losses at 5,000, but conceding that eighty Frankish knights and a larger number of infantry were killed. And while Baldwin was able to retain control of the plain and of the run-down sections of the Fatimid force that had routed in the direction of Ascalon, terrified survivors of the Latin vanguard were, at the same time, streaming back towards Jaffa, hotly pursued by Muslim troops who believed they had carried the day.

So great was the confusion that two Frankish escapees from the battle actually declared a defeat upon reaching Jaffa, 'saying that the king and all his men were dead'. With about 500 Fatimid troops riding on the port, Baldwin's traumatised queen (then residing in Jaffa) quickly dispatched a messenger north to Antioch by ship, begging Tancred to bring aid. Luckily for the Franks, the people of Jaffa rejected any notion of an immediate surrender, and the very next day King Baldwin, having camped at the battlefield as a statement of victory, arrived on the coast. At first sight, the remaining Fatimid soldiers outside Jaffa thought the approaching army was their own and happily rode out in greeting; realising their mistake and the grave reversal of fortune that must have occurred, they fled. A second messenger was immediately sent north to declare the king alive and victorious.[59]

Through a mixture of strategic resolution and good fortune, Baldwin had prevailed against the odds, but any sense of triumph or security was to be short-lived. Egypt's abundant wealth meant that al-Afdal had the resources to mount a second invasion of Palestine almost immediately. With the coming of spring in 1102 and the start of the new fighting season, another Fatimid army gathered at Ascalon, this time under the command of al-Afdal's son, Sharaf al-Ma'ali. In May the Egyptians marched once again on Ramla, skirmishing with the fifteen knights guarding its small fortified tower and raiding the nearby Church of St George at Lydda.

Baldwin I was, at this point, at Jaffa, seeing off the last members of the ill-fated 1101 crusade who had recently celebrated Easter in Jerusalem. William of Aquitaine managed to take ship to the West, but Stephen of Blois, Count Stephen of Burgundy and many others were less fortunate: having set sail, they encountered unfavourable winds and were forced to turn back. They were beside the king, therefore, when rumours of this latest Egyptian offensive arrived around 17 May. Baldwin now made the most calamitous decision of his life. Believing that the news from Ramla heralded the presence of a small Fatimid expeditionary force rather than a full-scale field army, he rashly elected to prosecute a speedy retaliatory attack. In the company of his own household and a clutch of crusaders – including the two Stephens, Hugh of Lusignan and Conrad, constable of Germany – he rode from Jaffa, seemingly brimful with confidence. His force contained a mere 200 knights and no infantry.

Once on the plains of Ramla the full might of the Egyptian army came into view and Baldwin realised the terrible reality of his miscalculation. Facing thousands of Muslim troops (one estimate put them at 20,000), the Franks now had no hope of victory and precious little chance of survival. Sharaf al-Ma'ali rushed to engage the king's tiny force the moment it was spotted. Baldwin attempted to mount a valiant charge, but the odds were hopeless; quickly surrounded, the carnage began. Within minutes the bulk of his force had been slain. Among the dead were the First Crusader Stabelo, once Godfrey of Bouillon's chamberlain, and the 1101 crusader Gerbod of Windeke. Amid the confusion, another veteran of the First Crusade, Roger of

Rozoy, managed to break through with a small group of men and race back towards Jaffa. Meanwhile, with the enemy closing in for the kill, Baldwin beat a fighting retreat to Ramla with a handful of survivors, taking meagre sanctuary in its fortified tower.

That evening, Baldwin found himself in a desperate predicament. Knowing full well that dawn would bring a crushing Fatimid assault and certain death or capture, he made what must have been a tortured decision: to abandon his army and seek escape under cover of night. In the company of five of his most faithful and fearsome retainers he stole out of the encircled fort, probably in some form of disguise and via a small postern gate, but he was soon challenged by Muslim troops. In the darkness a bloody, chaotic mêlée began. According to one contemporary, a Frankish knight named Robert 'went to the front with drawn sword, mowing down the [enemy] to right and left' but he momentarily lost hold of his weapon and was quickly overwhelmed. As another two of his companions fell, Baldwin fled, borne away astride his swift horse, Gazelle. He now had with him a single surviving follower, Hugh of Brulis (of whom there is no further record).

The Egyptians quickly launched a frantic hunt for the fugitive monarch. Sensing that he was only moments away from capture, the king sought sanctuary and concealment in an overgrown thicket of canes, but his pursuers set light to the undergrowth. Baldwin barely managed to escape, suffering minor burns in the process. He spent the next two days on the run, in fear of his life. Bewildered, short of food and water, he first tried to find a way through the wild Judean foothills to Jerusalem, but retreated at the sight of numerous Fatimid patrols combing the area. On 19 May 1102 he turned north-west to the coast and eventually found his way to Arsuf and a modicum of safety. Throughout this period Baldwin must have been plagued by feelings of humiliation and doubt; he had no way of knowing what fate had befallen his abandoned comrades at Ramla, nor whether Jaffa or even the Holy City might have capitulated in his absence. It is testament to the physical and psychological trauma of the preceding days that, once at Arsuf, his first concern was to eat, drink and sleep. As one Latin contemporary observed, 'this was required by the human side of his nature'.

The next day brought better fortune. Hugh of Falchenberg, lord of Tiberias, arrived at Arsuf with eighty knights, having heard of the Egyptian assault. Commandeering an English pirate ship anchored nearby, the king sailed south towards Jaffa, while Hugh marched south along the coastline. Baldwin found Jaffa in a parlous state, besieged on land by Sharaf al-Ma'ali's forces and at sea by an Egyptian fleet of thirty vessels, come north from Ascalon. Boldly flying his royal banner from his own ship to bring heart to Jaffa's garrison, the king narrowly evaded the Fatimid flotilla to reach the harbour. Once on land, the news he encountered was grim indeed.

Jaffa had come close to capitulation. Unsure of the king's whereabouts and the fate of his army at Ramla, and surrounded on all sides, the port's populace were already in desperate straits. But then Sharaf al-Ma'ali employed a devious tactic. In life, Gerbod of Windeke had apparently borne a passing resemblance to the king. The Muslims now mutilated his corpse, cutting off his head and legs and, having dressed these grisly remains in the purple of royalty, paraded them before Jaffa's walls, declaiming Baldwin's death and demanding immediate surrender. Many, including the queen, who once again found herself ensconced in Jaffa, were taken in by this ruse, and began planning to flee the port by ship. It was at this very moment that Baldwin's ship appeared from the north. The king's timely arrival buoyed morale and seems to have shaken Sharaf's resolve. The bulk of the Fatimid army now retreated some distance towards Ascalon, apparently to prepare siege machinery for a full-scale assault, but this gave the Franks an invaluable breathing space within which to regroup.

Baldwin had arrived in time to save Jaffa, but he was too late to intervene in the events at Ramla. On the morning after his escape, Muslim troops stormed Ramla's town walls and moved in to surround the fortified tower which now held the remnants of Baldwin's force.

The Fatimids began an intense assault siege of this rudimentary structure, undermining its walls and setting fires to smoke out its occupants. By 19 May the trapped Franks were in a hopeless predicament; abandoned by the king, confronting defeat, they chose, in the words of one Latin contemporary, 'to be destroyed while defending honourably [rather] than to choke and die a wretched death'. Charging from the tower, they mounted a suicidal last stand and were promptly butchered almost to a man. One of the few to survive was Conrad of Germany, who fought with such ferocity, cutting down any who came within sword length, that in the end he was left standing, ringed by the dead and dying. Awestruck, the Fatimid troops offered him the chance to surrender on the promise that he would be spared and taken as a captive to Egypt. Conrad left behind him many who were less fortunate, among them Stephen of Blois, whose death at Ramla finally put to rest the shame of his cowardice at Antioch four years earlier.

The disaster at Ramla proved to be the low point in Frankish fortunes that year. At the start of June 1102 Baldwin rallied troops from across the kingdom, including a contingent from Jerusalem bearing the True Cross. His forces were also boosted by the arrival of a sizeable pilgrim fleet. Now in command of a full field army, Baldwin launched an immediate counter-attack on the ill-prepared Egyptians. Sharaf's indecisive generalship had already sewn the seeds of discontent among the Fatimids; in the face of this sudden Frankish assault, they were soon routed. The number of Muslim fatalities was limited and the pickings after the battle were rather paltry – some camels and asses – but the 'crusader' kingdom had, nonetheless, been saved.[60]

Between Egypt and Damascus

In these fragile, formative years the Latins of Jerusalem were extremely fortunate that no alliance existed between Shi'ite Egypt and the great Sunni Syrian power of Damascus. Had Baldwin faced such a combined threat in 1101 or 1102, the meagre resources of his kingdom might have been overwhelmed. As it was, Duqaq of Damascus pursued a subdued policy of détente with Frankish Palestine for the remainder of his life. Stung by the memory of defeat at the Dog River, content to allow the Christians to block Fatimid ambitions in the Holy Land, Duqaq maintained a stance of neutrality. But with his premature death in 1104 at the age of just twenty-one, Damascus was to adopt a new policy.

After a brief but ugly contest, Duqaq's leading lieutenant, the *Atabeg** Tughtegin, took control of the city. As husband to Duqaq's scheming widowed mother, Safwat, he had long waited in the wings; indeed, it was even rumoured that Duqaq's untimely demise had been the result of poisoning organised by Tughtegin himself. Now, the *atabeg*'s gift for devious political intrigue and his casual, at times chillingly capricious, attitude to brutality propelled him into power. In 1105 the *atabeg* accepted a renewed overture for military cooperation from Egypt. Fortunately for the Franks, however, this unprecedented Sunni– Shi'ite coalition had its limits. Perhaps still harbouring doubts about his new allies, Tughtegin stopped short of organising a full-scale Damascene invasion of Palestine. Instead, he contributed a force of 1,500 archers when al-Afdal sent a third army, under another of his sons, north to Ascalon in the summer of 1105.

With an Egyptian fleet also harrying Jaffa, Baldwin I recognised that the port would soon be besieged and his realm once again destabilised. Stealing the initiative, he summoned the patriarch of Jerusalem and the True Cross and moved to engage the Fatimid army head-on near Ramla. On this occasion he commanded around 500 knights and 2,000 infantry, but even so they must have been significantly outnumbered. For the third time in four years, however, Egyptian martial indiscipline allowed Baldwin to rout his enemy and

---

* *Atabegs* were usually appointed as the guardians of princes, but often served as regional governors or commanders-in-chief.

secure a narrow victory. The casualties on both sides were roughly equal, but the encounter nonetheless had a ruinous effect on Fatimid morale. The Muslim ruler of Ascalon was slain in the battle; Baldwin ordered the emir's decapitation and then had his severed head taken to Jaffa and brandished before the Egyptian fleet to encourage their hasty departure.

Egypt continued to threaten Frankish Palestine, but al-Afdal launched no further large-scale offensives and certainly never achieved significant success. For the moment Damascus had been partially neutralised. Tughtegin adopted a more nuanced, predominantly non-aggressive approach to his dealings with Jerusalem. He was certainly not averse to defending Damascene interests with force when he considered them to be under threat, and he also prosecuted frequent punitive raids into Christian territory. But at the same time he agreed a succession of limited-term pacts with Baldwin, primarily directed at easing the path of mutually beneficial trade between Syria and Palestine.

The most enduring consequence of these dealings was the formulation of a partial armistice (confirmed by written treaty) around 1109. This remarkable accord related to the region east of the Sea of Galilee – known by the Franks as the Terre de Sueth (or Black Lands) because of its dark basalt soil – centred on the fertile arable lands of the Hauran, and extending north into the Golan Heights and south of the Yarmuk River. Baldwin and Tughtegin agreed to establish what in essence was a partially demilitarised zone in this area, allowing Muslim and Christian farmers to cooperate in the exploitation of the land. The produce of the Terre de Sueth was then split into three parts, with one portion retained by the resident peasants and the remainder divided between Jerusalem and Damascus. This arrangement remained in place for much of the twelfth century.[61]

In the first five years of his reign, however, King Baldwin's own survival, and arguably that of his entire realm, had been in doubt. Only through flashes of gifted leadership and the good fortune of

Muslim disunity and Fatimid martial ineptitude had the Latins prevailed.

LATIN SYRIA IN CRISIS (1101–8)

In the first chill months of 1105, Tancred, the celebrated veteran of the First Crusade, had every reason to despair. He found himself in command of the Latin principality of Antioch at a time when that newborn realm seemed in its death throes. Six months earlier, the Franks' reputation for invincibility had been shattered when Antioch's army suffered a frightening and humiliating defeat at the hands of Islam. In response, Tancred's famed uncle, and Antioch's supposed prince, Bohemond, had fled the Levant, stripping the city of its resources even as he rushed to set sail for the West. With the principality crumbling before him, beset by rebellion and invasion on every front, Tancred faced the spectre of ruination. Seven years earlier, he had witnessed first hand the horror of Antioch's siege and the terrible cost of its seizure by the crusade. Now, it seemed, the faltering Frankish enclave created by that conquest was doomed to collapse.

Little, if any, of the blame for this crisis could be laid at Tancred's feet. In the spring of 1101 he had travelled north from Palestine to act as Antioch's regent after Bohemond's imprisonment. In the two years that followed Tancred quickly restored a sense of stability and security to the principality, demonstrating both vigour and competence. Shortly before his capture, Bohemond had allowed the fertile plains of Cilicia, north-west of Antioch, to slip out of his grasp. Hoping for greater autonomy, the region's Armenian Christian population had switched allegiance to the Byzantine Empire, but Tancred beat them back into submission with a brief but vicious campaign. Not content simply to recoup his uncle's losses, Tancred then sought to expand the principality. Like the kingdom of Jerusalem, Antioch needed to control the ports of the eastern Mediterranean seaboard, but Latakia, home to Syria's best natural harbour, remained in Greek hands despite Bohemond's intermittent efforts. After a protracted siege, however, the town fell to Tancred in 1103.

Tancred seems to have relished the new-found opportunities and authority his position offered; certainly he made no effort to orchestrate the speedy release of his uncle. This task was instead taken up by Bohemond's recent ecclesiastical appointee, Patriarch Bernard, and by Baldwin of Bourcq, now count of Edessa. Together they set about amassing the vast ransom demanded by Bohemond's captor, the Danishmendid emir – 100,000 gold pieces. The Armenian Kogh Vasil, lord of two cities in the Upper Euphrates, gave one-tenth of this sum in return for promises of alliance, but in the words of one rather scandalised eastern Christian contemporary, 'Tancred gave nothing.' Eventually, in May 1103, Bohemond was freed. The consequences for Tancred were galling; not only did he have to hand over the reins of power in Antioch, he was also compelled to relinquish his own conquests in Cilicia and Latakia.[62]

The Battle of Harran (1104)

With his own liberty and authority restored, Bohemond sought to build upon his friendship with Count Baldwin II of Edessa. Over the next twelve months the two united in a series of campaigns designed to subdue the territory between Antioch and Edessa and to isolate and harass Aleppo. It was probably with the latter goal in mind that they launched an expedition east of the Euphrates in spring 1104. Dominion over this region would have secured the county of Edessa's southern frontier while hampering Aleppan communication with Mesopotamia. As it was, they encountered fierce opposition from a sizeable Muslim army, led by the Seljuq Turkish rulers of Mosul and Mardin.

Battle was joined on the plains south of Harran around 7 May. Bohemond and Tancred held the right flank, while Baldwin II commanded Edessa's forces on the left, alongside his cousin Joscelin of Courtenay (a well-connected northern French aristocrat who arrived in the Levant after 1101 and had received a lordship centred on the major fortress town of Tell Bashir). In the fighting that followed, the Edessene troops became detached from the rest of the army – overcommitting to a charge, they fell foul of a ferocious counter-attack and were routed. Baldwin and Joscelin were taken captive as thousands of their compatriots were killed or imprisoned. Bohemond and Tancred led a chastened retreat towards Edessa, where the latter was left in charge of defending the city.

Harran was a shocking reversal for the Franks. Battlefield losses through casualties and captivity were significant, but the greatest damage was psychological. This defeat shifted the balance of power and confidence in the northern reaches of the Levant; it now dawned on the indigenous peoples of Syria that the Latins were not, after all, indomitable. A near-contemporary Muslim writing in Damascus reflected that '[Harran] was a great and unparalleled victory . . . it discouraged the Franks, diminished their numbers and broke their power of offence, while the hearts of the Muslims were strengthened.' In fact, Muslims, Greeks and Armenians all seized the opportunity to turn the tide in their favour, and it was Antioch, not Edessa, that suffered most. The Byzantines reoccupied Cilicia and Latakia, although the latter's citadel may have remained in Frankish hands. To the south-east the towns of the Summaq region expelled their Latin garrisons, turning to Aleppo for leadership. In a final indignity, the strategically critical town of Artah followed suit soon after. Guardian of the main Roman road inland, lying barely one day's march north-east of Antioch, Artah was regarded by contemporaries as the city's 'shield'. By the late summer of 1104, the principality had been decimated; all that remained of this once burgeoning realm was a small nucleus of territory around Antioch itself.[63]

Early that autumn, Bohemond made an unexpected decision. Recalling Tancred from Edessa, he convened a council in the basilica of St Peter and announced his intention to leave the Levant. The real motives behind this move are hard to unravel. Publicly Bohemond avowed that, in order to save Latin Syria, he would

recruit a new Frankish army in western Europe. He may also have
expressed his determination to fulfil his vows to St Leonard (to whom
he had appealed while in prison) by making a pilgrimage to the
shrine of his relics at Noblat, in France. Privately, however, he seems
to have had little intention of making a swift return to Outremer,
planning, instead, to raise a force with which to attack the Byzantine
Empire head-on in the Balkans. This might have the effect of
distracting Alexius Comnenus, perhaps forestalling a direct Greek
assault on Antioch, but Bohemond's strategy probably owed more to
his desire to conquer new territory in the Adriatic and the Aegean,
and to his dream of sitting upon the throne of mighty
Constantinople itself.

Bohemond's disenchantment with the fragility of Antioch's
position is further evidenced by his calculated appropriation of the
city's remaining wealth and manpower before departing. Even the
contemporary Latin writer Ralph of Caen, normally a promoter of
Bohemond's cause, observed that 'he carried off the gold, silver, gems
and clothing [leaving the city] to Tancred without protection, wages
and mercenaries'. Bohemond set sail from the shores of Syria around
September 1104. During the First Crusade, he had trained the full
force of his military genius and avaricious guile upon Antioch's
conquest. Now, as he turned his back upon the Levant, he must have
known that he was abandoning his old prize to a desperately bleak
and uncertain future.[64]

On the brink of collapse

So it was that Tancred began the year 1105 in a state of beleaguered
penury, prince-regent of a realm bound for destruction. In the fire of
this crisis, the defining challenge of his career, he proved his mettle.
Blending charm and coercion, he won the support of Antioch's
indigenous population for an emergency tax, restocking the treasury
and financing the fresh recruitment of mercenaries. He also sought
to replenish further his resources by exploiting fully the one positive
consequence of the debacle at Harran, Antioch's nominal lordship

over the county of Edessa. Calling 'all the Christian men' of northern Syria to arms, stripping Edessa, Marash and Tell Bashir of all but token garrisons, he had by early spring assembled an army of some 1,000 knights and 9,000 foot soldiers. Tancred's unshakable resolution and incisive strategic acuity now came to the fore.

Facing such a plethora of enemies, he recognised that he could neither fight on every front nor fall back upon a policy of inert defence. Instead he employed targeted, proactive aggression, selecting his quarry with great care. In mid-April he marched on Artah, engineering a decisive confrontation with Ridwan of Aleppo. This was an audacious gamble. Overcoming this foe in pitched battle might allow Tancred to regain the initiative and rekindle the Franks' martial authority, but he must have known that the Aleppans would outnumber his own forces, perhaps three to one, and that any defeat would mark the end of Latin dominion over Syria.

Before leaving Antioch the Christians undertook rites of spiritual purification, including a three-day fast, purging their souls of sin in a preparation for death that echoed crusading practice. Tancred then crossed the Orontes at the Iron Bridge and moved in to besiege Artah. Once Ridwan took the bait, advancing with a reported 30,000 troops, Tancred backed off. The centrepiece of his strategy was to capitalise upon his close knowledge of the local terrain and to exploit his growing appreciation of Muslim tactics. The route between Artah and the Iron Bridge passed through an area of flat but rocky ground, over which horses could not easily gallop, before reaching an open plain. It was to this second zone that Tancred retreated and, on 20 April 1105, Ridwan pursued. One Latin contemporary described the battle that followed:

The Christians held their positions as if torpid . . . then, when the Turks had passed the rough ground, Tancred charged into their midst as if having been roused from sleep. The Turks quickly retreated, hoping, as was their custom, to turn about while fleeing and shoot. However, their hopes and their tricks were foiled . . . the

[Franks'] spears struck them in the back and the path arrested their flight. Their horses were useless.

In the ensuing battle, the Latins ploughed into the packed ranks of terrified Muslim troops, dispatching the enemy almost at will as Aleppan resistance crumbled. Horrified, Ridwan scurried away to safety as best he could, losing his banner in the process, and Tancred was left the victor on the field, enriched with spoils and glory.

The Battle of Artah marked a watershed in the history of the northern crusader states. Over the next few years Tancred readily recouped the losses suffered after Harran. Artah was immediately reoccupied and the Summaq plateau soon followed suit. Ridwan sued for peace, trying to position himself as a subservient ally, and, with the frontier zone between Antioch and Aleppo secured, Tancred was able to direct his attention elsewhere. By 1110 he had effected long-term Antiochene dominion over Cilicia and Latakia at the expense of the Greeks. At the same time, he shored up the principality's southern defences against another potentially aggressive Muslim neighbour, the town of Shaizar, by seizing the neighbouring ancient Roman settlement of Apamea. In personal terms, the success of 1105 also served to legitimise Tancred's position; before long he was ruling less as Bohemond's regent and more as a prince in his own right. In this, however, he was also aided by a concurrent decline in the fortunes of his famed uncle.[65]

Bohemond's crusade

Bohemond of Taranto sailed for Europe in autumn 1104. It was later rumoured among the Greeks that he employed a bizarre form of trickery to avoid capture by Byzantine agents during his voyage across the Mediterranean. Feigning his own death, Bohemond was said to have travelled west in a coffin punctured with concealed air holes. To complete the ruse, he was entombed alongside the rotting carcass of a strangled cockerel to ensure that his own 'corpse' emitted a suitably revolting putrefactive odour. Indeed, Emperor Alexius' daughter,

Anna Comnena, even allowed herself a note of admiration for Bohemond's indomitable 'barbarian' spirit when she wrote, 'I wonder how on earth he endured such a siege on his nose and still continued to live.'

Whatever his mode of transport, Bohemond's arrival in Italy in early 1105 was greeted with a clamorous outpouring of adulation. The self-styled hero of the First Crusade had returned. He soon won the support of Pope Urban's successor, Paschal II, for a new crusading expedition, one which Bohemond proceeded to promote in Italy and France for the next two years. Along the way he fulfilled his vow to visit the shrine of St Leonard at Noblat, depositing a gift of silver shackles as a sign of gratitude for his release from imprisonment in 1103. He also appears to have sponsored the copying and dispersal of a rousing narrative account of the First Crusade, akin to the *Gesta Francorum*, which promoted his own achievements and helped to blacken the name of the Greeks. With his fame in the ascendant and his recruiting rallies attracting large enthusiastic crowds, Bohemond secured a marriage alliance which propelled him into the highest echelons of the Frankish aristocracy. In the spring of 1106 he was wed to Princess Constance, daughter of the king of France; around the same time one of the king's illegitimate daughters, Cecilia, was betrothed to Tancred. Bohemond used the occasion of his own nuptials at Chartres to promote his new crusade, launching a stinging attack on his proclaimed enemy, Alexius Comnenus – supposed betrayer of the crusaders in 1098 and 1101, and invader of Antioch.

By the end of 1106 Bohemond had returned to southern Italy to supervise the ongoing construction of a crusading fleet, having recruited many thousands of men to his cause. But despite the size of the force that gathered in Apulia one year later – some 30,000 men to be carried by a fleet of more than 200 ships – historians have long disputed the nature of this expedition. The current consensus maintains that this campaign, which targeted the Greek Christian empire of Byzantium, cannot be regarded as a fully fledged crusade, or at the very least should be branded as a distortion of the crusading ideal. The expedition obviously bore some striking similarities to the First Crusade, with participants taking a vow, bearing the symbol of a cross and expecting to receive a remission of sins. The nub of the debate, however, depends on papal involvement. Surely, so it is argued, the pope would never knowingly have awarded the privileged status of a crusade to an expedition against fellow Christians; rather, it was Bohemond, twisted by ambition and hatred, who deceived Paschal II, pretending that his armies would fight in the Levant.

This view of events is riddled with significant problems. The bulk of contemporary evidence suggests that the pope was aware of Bohemond's intentions and nonetheless supported him, even dispatching a papal legate to accompany and endorse the preaching campaigns in France and Italy. Even in the unlikely case that the pope was misled, there can be no doubt that a huge number of lay recruits accepted the idea of joining a crusade against the Greeks. In fact, the tendency to sideline Bohemond's expedition as a perversion of crusading is symptomatic of a more fundamental misconception: a belief that the ideas and practices of crusading had already coalesced to create a uniform ideal. For most people living in western Europe in the early twelfth century, this new type of devotional warfare had no finite identity and was still subject to continual, organic development. As far as they were concerned, crusades did not need to be directed against Muslims, and many readily accepted the idea of waging a holy war against Alexius Comnenus once he had been deemed the enemy of Latin Christendom.

However the background to the 1107–8 'crusade' against Byzantium is viewed, the expedition itself proved to be a shambolic disaster. Crossing the Adriatic in October 1107, the Latins laid siege to the city of Durazzo (in modern Albania), regarded by contemporaries as 'the western gate of the [Greek] empire'. But, in spite of his military pedigree, Bohemond was outwitted by Alexius, who deployed his forces to cut the invaders' supply lines while carefully avoiding direct confrontation. Weakened by hunger, unable to break Durazzo's defences, the Latins capitulated in September 1108. Bohemond was forced to accede to a humiliating peace accord, the Treaty of Devol. By the terms of this agreement, he was to hold Antioch for the remainder of his life as the emperor's subject, but the Greek patriarch was to be restored to power in the city and the principality itself to be all but emasculated by the cession of Cilicia and Latakia to Byzantium.

As it was, this agreement was not implemented and thus had little bearing upon future events, because Bohemond never returned to the Levant. After sailing back to southern Italy in the autumn of 1108, he appears only fleetingly in historical records, his reputation broken, his grand dreams and ambitions shattered. Constance bore him a son, also named Bohemond, around 1109, but by 1111 the once great commander of the First Crusade was ailing, and on 7 March he died in Apulia. At Antioch, Tancred remained in power, perhaps still nominally as regent, but with his authority uncontested among the Franks. From the perspective of Outremer, one positive did emerge from Bohemond's later career: his Balkan campaign diverted Greek resources from the Levant, allowing Tancred to assert lasting control over Latakia and Cilicia.[66]

TO RULE IN THE HOLY REALM

Tancred's drive to expand the principality of Antioch and to augment its wealth and international influence accelerated after 1108, and he showed a ruthless willingness to use any and all means in pursuit of these ambitions, even if that meant fighting fellow Latins while engaging Muslim allies. For the next five years he worked tirelessly, drawing upon a seemingly inexhaustible pool of martial energy to engage in near-constant campaigning. Beleaguering his neighbours and opponents through a mixture of territorial conquest, political coercion and economic exploitation, Tancred came close to forging an Antiochene empire in the Levant.

The counties of Edessa and Tripoli

Between 1104 and 1108 Antioch was the effective overlord of the county of Edessa. Once Tancred assumed control of the principality in autumn 1104, he installed his brother-in-law and fellow southern Italian Norman First Crusader Richard of Salerno as regent of Edessa. Even though Richard proved unpopular, Antiochene influence went unchecked while Count Baldwin II remained in captivity.

Antioch certainly made no effort to orchestrate the count's release. In the summer of 1104, when Baldwin's captors first sought to organise the terms of his ransom, even Bohemond demurred. Rather than repay the energy Baldwin had expended to secure Bohemond's own freedom in 1103, the prince preferred to retain control of Edessa's considerable agrarian and commercial resources, estimated to value in excess of 40,000 gold bezants per annum. Once at the helm of Frankish Syria, Tancred continued to enjoy these revenues and to ignore Baldwin's plight.

By 1107 the count's companion, Joscelin of Courtenay, lord of Tell Bashir, had been ransomed by the populace of that town, and in the following year Joscelin successfully negotiated Baldwin's release from Mosul. It was the Turkish warlord Chavli, the latest ruler of Mosul, who finally agreed terms; but with an eye to the fragility of his own position and the ongoing internecine struggles within Near Eastern Islam, Chavli demanded not only a cash ransom and hostages, but also a promise of military alliance.

When Baldwin sought to reclaim Edessa in the summer of 1108, a tense standoff ensued. Having enjoyed access to the wealth and resources of the county for four years, Tancred had no intention of simply handing over a territory which he had saved from conquest, and he now sought to pressure Baldwin into taking an oath of subservience; after all, he argued, historically Edessa had been the vassal of the Byzantine duchy of Antioch. The count refused, not least because he had already sworn allegiance to Baldwin of Boulogne in

1100. With neither side willing to give ground, conflict seemed inevitable.

In early September both men raised armies. Less than ten years after Jerusalem's conquest, Baldwin and Tancred – fellow Latins and veteran crusaders – were now ready and willing to crush one another in open war. More shocking still was the fact that Baldwin marched forth to this struggle alongside his new ally, Chavli of Mosul, and some 7,000 Muslim troops. When battle was joined, probably near Tell Bashir, Tancred, although outnumbered, managed to hold the field. But with some 2,000 Christian dead on both sides, Patriarch Bernard, the ecclesiastical overlord of both Antioch and Edessa, stepped in to calm frayed tempers and adjudicate. When witnesses publicly attested that Tancred had actually promised Bohemond in 1104 that he would relinquish control of Edessa upon Baldwin's release, the Antiochene ruler was forced grudgingly to back down. The city of Edessa itself may have been repatriated, but the embedded hatred and rivalry remained. Tancred stubbornly refused to hand over territory in the northern reaches of the county and was soon pressing Baldwin to make tribute payments in return for peace with Antioch.[67]

With this dispute still simmering, Tancred's acquisitive gaze settled upon the nascent county of Tripoli. In the immediate aftermath of the First Crusade his old rival Raymond of Toulouse had sought to carve out his own Levantine lordship centred on the northern reaches of modern-day Lebanon. The challenge confronting Raymond was considerable, for unlike the founders of other Latin settlements he had no crusader conquests to build upon, and the region's dominant city, Tripoli, remained in Muslim hands.

Nonetheless, Raymond made some progress, capturing the port of Tortosa in 1102, with the aid of a Genoese fleet and survivors from the 1101 crusade. Two years later he conquered a second port to the south, Jubail, resplendent with Roman ruins. Meanwhile, on a hill outside Tripoli, Raymond constructed a doughty fortress, christened Mount Pilgrim, thereby securing effective control of the surrounding region. Yet, despite his tenacious efforts, when the count died in his mid-sixties on 28 February 1105, Tripoli itself remained unconquered.

In the years that followed, two men sought to press claims to Raymond's legacy. His nephew, William Jordan, the first to arrive in Outremer, continued to pressure Tripoli while also overcoming the neighbouring town of Arqa. In March 1109, however, Raymond's son Bertrand of Toulouse reached the Holy Land, determined to assert his rights as heir. When he brought a sizeable fleet to reinforce the siege of Tripoli, the two claimants squabbled over rights to the city, even though it had yet to be captured, and William Jordan quit Mount Pilgrim for the north. The emergent county of Tripoli looked as if it might founder amid bitter dynastic squabbling.

In the end, however, the contest for control of Tripoli involved far more than the simple issue of inheritance; it became the centrepiece of a wider struggle for dominion over the crusader states. Realising that he would need an ally if he was to have any hope of claiming Tripoli, William Jordan turned to Tancred, offering to become his vassal. Not surprisingly, Tancred seized this sudden opportunity to expand Antiochene influence southwards; should Tripoli fall under his sway and his designs upon Edessa come to fruition, then the principality might rightly claim to be Outremer's leading power. Modern historical analysis has persistently underestimated the significance of this episode, the assumption being that the kingdom of Jerusalem was automatically and immediately recognised as the overlord of the Frankish East at the start of the twelfth century. True, the Holy City had been the focus of the First Crusade, and Baldwin of Boulogne was the only Latin ruler in the Levant to assume the title of king, but his realm encompassed Palestine, not the entire Near East. Each of the four crusader states was founded as an independent polity and Jerusalem's pre-eminent status among them had never been formally ratified. A current of rivalry had coloured relations between Baldwin and Tancred ever since they contested control of Cilicia in 1097; now, in 1109, Tancred's brash assertiveness offered a challenge to Baldwin's authority that would determine the balance of power in the Latin Levant.

Over the next twelve months, Jerusalem's monarch resolved this political crisis with stunning finesse, roundly outplaying his old opponent. To his credit, Baldwin made no attempt to counter Antiochene ambition with direct force of arms, preferring instead to promote and harness the notion of Frankish solidarity in the face of Muslim adversaries. Employing diplomatic guile, he affirmed Jerusalemite supremacy even as he advanced Outremer's defensive security.

In the summer of 1109 Baldwin called the rulers of the Latin East to assist Bertrand of Toulouse at the siege of Tripoli. On the face of it, this was to be a grand Frankish alliance, dedicated to the subjugation of an intransigent Muslim outpost. The king himself marched north with some 500 knights; Tancred, together with 700 knights, arrived in the company of his new ally, William Jordan; and Baldwin II of Edessa and Joscelin likewise brought a sizeable force. Alongside Bertrand's Provençal navy and a Genoese fleet, this represented a formidable assembly. And yet, entrenched animosity and fractious suspicion rippled beneath the surface of this coalition.

Of course, the subtext to the whole affair – as all the key players must well have known – was the issue of power among the Franks. Would Baldwin I allow Antioch's burgeoning influence to go unchecked, and if not, what manner of riposte would the king employ? With the gathering complete, the king enacted his canny scheme. Having already taken Bertrand of Toulouse under his wing, extracting an oath of fealty in exchange for Jerusalem's support, he now convened a general council to resolve the dispute over Tripoli's future. Baldwin I's masterstroke was to comport himself not as a wrathful, overbearing overlord, nor as Tancred's conniving rival, but rather as an impartial arbiter of justice. In the words of one Latin contemporary, the king listened to 'all the injuries of both sides' along with a jury of 'his loyal men' and then enacted reconciliation. Raymond of Toulouse's heirs were 'made friends', with Bertrand given rights to the bulk of the county, including Tripoli, Mount Pilgrim and Jubail, and William placated with Tortosa and Arqa. What is more, Baldwin II and Tancred were said to have been 'reconciled' on the understanding that Antioch would relinquish control of all remaining Edessene territory. By way of compensation, Tancred was reinstated as the lord of Haifa and Galilee.

The king appeared to have achieved an equitable settlement, restoring harmony to Outremer. The coalition forces were certainly able to prosecute Tripoli's investment with renewed vigour, bludgeoning the city's Muslim garrison into submission by 12 July 1109. In reality, however, Tancred had been stymied and humbled. He made no effort to claim his lordship in the kingdom of Jerusalem, not least because this involved an oath of subservience to Baldwin I. The king, meanwhile, despite maintaining a façade of impartiality, had served his own interests, protecting his relationship with Edessa and positioning his own favourite as the new ruler of a Tripolitan county. He cannot have been overly dejected when, soon after Tripoli's capitulation, William Jordan was 'pierced through the heart in a secret attack and died', leaving Bertrand in a position of uncontested authority.

In May 1110 Baldwin I seized an opportunity to consolidate further his status as overlord of the Latin Levant. That spring, Muhammad, the Seljuq sultan of Baghdad, finally reacted to the Frankish subjugation of the Near East. He dispatched a Mesopotamian army to begin the work of reclaiming Syria under the command of Maudud, a capable Turkish general who recently had come to power in Mosul. The first target was the county of Edessa. In the face of this threat, the Latins united, and the swift arrival of a large coalition army from Jerusalem, Tripoli and Antioch forced Maudud to break off his short-lived siege of Edessa. King Baldwin I used the opportunity presented by this gathering of the ruling Frankish elite to call a second council of arbitration, this time with the sole focus of addressing the ongoing dispute between Tancred and Baldwin of Bourcq. According to one Christian contemporary, resolution was to be achieved, 'either by a fair trial or by agreement of a council of magnates'. Knowing that he was unlikely to receive anything approaching 'fair' treatment, Tancred had to be persuaded to attend by his closest advisers and, once the council began, his fears were soon confirmed. With King Baldwin presiding in judgement, Tancred was accused of inciting Maudud of Mosul to attack Edessa and of allying with Muslims. These charges were almost certainly manufactured and, notably, no mention was made of either Baldwin of Bourcq's own alliance with Mosul in 1108 or Baldwin I's dealings with Damascus. Facing the united opprobrium of the council and threatened with ostracism from the Frankish community, Tancred was once again forced to back down. From this point on, he seems to have stopped demanding tribute from Edessa.

Antioch's submission had not been formalised and, in the years to come, the principality would make renewed attempts to assert its independence. Throughout the early decades of the twelfth century this secular power struggle was also mirrored by a protracted and embittered squabble over ecclesiastical jurisdiction between the Latin patriarchs of Antioch and Jerusalem. Nonetheless, in 1110 King Baldwin had, for the time being at least, affirmed his own personal authority and established Jerusalem's position as the pre-eminent secular power in Outremer.[68]

Tancred's legacy

In spite of the political setbacks of 1109 and 1110, the closing years of Tancred's life proved to be a triumph. With unabated vigour he pushed the principality's frontiers to the limit and subdued his Muslim neighbours, fighting for months on end almost without pause. In this period, Tancred confronted a significant strategic quandary that has been largely ignored by modern historians. For Tancred, as for all medieval military commanders, topography was a key consideration. By 1110 the principality had expanded its borders to two natural boundaries. To the east, on the frontier between Antioch and Aleppo, Frankish power now extended to the foot of the

Belus Hills, a craggy spine of arid, low-altitude fells. To the south, towards Muslim Shaizar, the principality stretched to the edge of the Summaq plateau and to the Orontes River valley. As it stood, the physical barriers running along these two border zones offered both Latin Antioch and its Muslim neighbours a relatively equal balance of power and security.[69]

Tancred could have settled for this situation, allowing the status quo to be maintained, engendering the possibility of long-term coexistence. Instead, he chose the risks and potential rewards of continued expansion. In October 1110 he crossed the Belus Hills, prosecuting a taxing winter expedition that led to the capture of a string of settlements in the Jazr region (east of the Belus Hills), including al-Atharib and Zardana. This left barely twenty miles of open, undefended plains between the principality and Aleppo. Then, in the spring of 1111, he moved to apply a similar degree of pressure to the south, initiating construction of a new fortress on a hill close to Shaizar. To begin with, at least, Ridwan of Aleppo and the Muslim rulers of Shaizar, the Munqidh clan, responded to this aggression with conciliatory submission, offering tribute payments totalling 30,000 gold dinars in return for peace.

There was a well-established precedent for this form of financial exploitation. In eleventh-century Iberia, the Christian powers of the north had gradually come to dominate the fractured Muslim city-states of the south, establishing complex networks of annual tribute payments. This system famously culminated in the peaceful occupation of the peninsula's long-lost capital, Toledo (central Spain), in 1085.

Tancred may well have harboured similar plans to reduce Aleppo and Shaizar to the point of collapse, but his policies had a dangerous edge. Apply too much pressure, demand overly exorbitant protection payments, and the quarry might be driven to risk retaliation. In the case of Aleppo, the mixture of intimidation and exploitation proved effective and culminated in a sustained period of submission. But in 1111, Tancred pressed Shaizar too far and the Munqidh clan readily allied with Maudud of Mosul when he led a second Abbasid army into Syria that September. Threatened with an invasion of the Summaq region, Tancred mustered every possible ounce of Antiochene manpower. He also called for aid from his fellow Latins and, despite the tensions which had recently divided their ranks, the armies of Jerusalem, Edessa and Tripoli assembled once more. This composite force took up a defensive position at Apamea, and by patiently holding its ground, blunted Maudud's attempts to provoke a decisive battle and eventually forced his retreat.

Tancred once again had repulsed a threat to the principality's survival, but any hopes of securing the conquest of either Aleppo or Shaizar came to nothing when, after years of tireless campaigning, his health failed him at the age of thirty-six. The early twelfth-century Armenian Christian historian Matthew of Edessa lavished elegiac praise upon Tancred when recording his death in December 1112, writing that 'he was a saintly and pious man and had a kind and compassionate nature, manifesting concern for all the Christian faithful; moreover he exhibited a tremendous amount of humility in his dealings with people'. This panegyric conceals Tancred's darker traits: his unquenchable hunger for advancement; his gift for political intrigue; and his willingness to betray or battle all around him in pursuit of power. It was these qualities, allied to his boundless dynamism, that lent Tancred his remarkable potency and enabled him to forge an enduring Frankish realm in northern Syria. If justice be done, history should regard Tancred, not his infamous uncle Bohemond, as the founder of the principality of Antioch.[70]

OVERLORD OF OUTREMER (1113–18)

Tancred's death came at a time of more general change in the shape and balance of power in the Near East, brought on by a mixture of dynastic succession and political intrigue. At Antioch itself, power passed to Tancred's nephew, Roger of Salerno, son of the First

Crusader Richard of Salerno. Roger was soon woven into the fabric of Frankish society as a series of high-level marriage alliances bound together the ruling elite of Outremer. This complex web of familial connections ushered in a new phase of heightened interdependence among the crusader states. Roger himself married the sister of Baldwin of Bourcq, count of Edessa, while Joscelin of Courtenay, lord of Tell Bashir, was wed to Roger's sister. Bertrand of Toulouse's death early in 1112 led to the accession of his youthful son, Pons, as count of Tripoli. He soon distanced himself from the traditional Toulousean policy of subservience to Byzantium and antipathy to Antioch and, at some point between 1113 and 1115, married Tancred's widow, Cecilia of France. Pons remained a dependant of Jerusalem, but Cecilia's dowry brought him a significant Antiochene lordship in the Ruj valley, one of only two southern approach routes to Antioch itself. The wider significance of these shifts in personnel and allegiance was twofold: on the one hand, they promised to engender a new era of Frankish cooperation in the face of external threats; on the other, they reopened old questions about the balance of power in Outremer and, most notably, the relationship between Antioch and Edessa.

Strength in unity

The bonds of Latin unity were soon tested by the ongoing threat of Iraqi invasion. In May 1113 Maudud of Mosul, now Baghdad's foremost military commander, led a third Abbasid army into the Near East, and on this occasion he turned away from Syria to invade Palestine. The frequency and ferocity of Frankish raiding upon Damascene lands to the north and east of Galilee appear to have convinced Tughtegin that he must now turn his back on any form of enduring rapprochement with Jerusalem. In the last week of May he led a sizeable army to join Maudud, and together they marched into Galilee.

When news of this threat reached Baldwin I at Acre, he dispatched an urgent call for reinforcement to his new neighbours, Roger and

Pons. The king now had a difficult decision to make. Should he wait for the full strength of the Frankish alliance to assemble, leaving Maudud and Tughtegin free to ravage the north-eastern reaches of the realm, or risk an immediate move to counter their incursion with only limited military resources? In mid- to late June he settled upon the second course of action. Baldwin's precipitous behaviour was widely criticised by contemporaries – indeed, even his chaplain noted that the king was denounced by his allies for 'rush[ing] against the enemy in a rash and disorderly manner without waiting for their advice and aid' – and Baldwin has been similarly condemned in modern historiography. In the king's defence, he does not seem to have acted with the same damaging impetuosity shown in 1102. Details of events in the summer of 1113 are sketchy, but it would appear that Baldwin advanced from Acre to establish an advanced base from which to patrol Galilee and not with the express intention of confronting the enemy in pitched battle.

Unfortunately for the king, on 28 June his army was battered by a surprise attack. Normally so assiduous in his use of scouts and the garnering of intelligence, Baldwin appears to have camped near the al-Sennabra bridge, a crossing over the River Jordan just south of the Sea of Galilee, without realising that his foes were stationed nearby, across the eastern shore. When Muslim foragers discovered his position, Maudud and Tughtegin launched a lightning assault. Pouring across the bridge, they quickly overran the shocked Franks, killing 1,000 to 2,000 men, including some thirty knights. Baldwin himself fled in disgrace, losing his royal banner and his tent, key symbols of his regal authority.

Chastened, Baldwin retreated to the slopes of Mount Tabor, above Tiberias, where he was soon joined by the armies of Antioch and Tripoli. He now adopted a far more cautious strategy, holding his forces in this defensible position, policing the region but avoiding direct confrontation. For nearly four weeks the two sides remained in the area, testing one another's resolve, but in the face of such a large Latin force Maudud and Tughtegin could not afford to march south en masse to Jerusalem and were only able to launch a series of wide-ranging raids. In August, the Muslim allies crossed back over the Jordan, leaving, in the words of one Damascene chronicler, 'the enemy humbled, broken, defeated and dispirited'. As evidence of their triumph they sent a gift of plunder, Frankish prisoners and the heads of the Christian dead to the sultan in Baghdad. Baldwin had survived, albeit with considerable damage to his reputation.[71]

Maudud fatefully elected to spend early autumn in Damascus. Having attended Friday prayers with Tughtegin at the Grand Mosque on 2 October 1113, the Mosuli commander was walking through a courtyard when he was ambushed and mortally wounded by a lone attacker. The assailant was summarily decapitated and his corpse later burned, but neither his identity nor his motive was ever precisely ascertained. The suspicion was that he had been an adherent of a secretive Nizari sect. This splinter faction of the Isma'ili branch of Shi'a Islam, originally from north-eastern Persia, had begun to play a notable role in Near Eastern politics at the start of the twelfth century. With limited resources, they gained power and influence by murdering their enemies and, because it was rumoured that their adherents were addicted to hashish, a new word emerged to describe them – Assassins. During Ridwan ibn Tutush's life they gained a significant foothold in Aleppo, but after his death in 1113 they were driven out of the city. The Assassins then found a new ally in Tughtegin, and for this reason the *atabeg* was suspected of having been complicit in Maudud's assassination. The true extent of Tughtegin's involvement is unclear, but the rumour alone was enough to isolate him from Baghdad and to promote a new rapprochement between Damascus and Jerusalem.[72]

For the Franks, the crisis of 1113 proved beyond doubt the necessity for unified resistance to Muslim aggression; it also reaffirmed the wisdom of a cautious defensive strategy. Taken together, the events of 1111 and 1113 established a pattern of Latin military practice that was to persist for much of the twelfth century: in the face of a strong invading force, the Franks would unite; mustering at a defensible location, they would seek to police the threatened region and to disrupt the enemy's freedom of movement, all while staunchly avoiding the unpredictability of open battle.

It was precisely this approach that Roger, prince of Antioch, adopted initially in 1115 when facing the first real threat of his reign. The only difference was that, on this occasion, he enjoyed the support not only of his Latin compatriots, but also of the Muslim potentates of Syria. With Aleppo now in a state of some disarray, the sultan of Baghdad saw an opportunity to take control of the city and thereby reassert his authority over the Near East. To this end, he sponsored a new expedition across the Euphrates, this time led by a Persian commander, Bursuq of Hamadan.

The prospect of such direct intervention prompted an unprecedented reaction from the feuding Muslim rulers of Syria. Tughtegin allied with his son-in-law, Il-ghazi of Mardin, the leading member of a Turcoman dynasty known as the Artuqids, who held sway over the Diyar Bakr region of the Upper Tigris River. Together, Tughtegin and Il-ghazi took temporary control of Aleppo and dispatched an embassy to Antioch to request peace talks. At first, Roger greeted this approach with some suspicion, but he was soon won over, perhaps by the entreaties of one of his leading vassals, Robert fitz-Fulk the Leper, who held a major lordship on the principality's eastern frontier and had developed a close friendship with Tughtegin. A treaty of military cooperation was duly sealed early that summer and preparations for Bursuq's invasion began.

Upon reaching Syria and discovering that Aleppo was now closed to him, Bursuq followed the example of Maudud of Mosul in 1111 and sought support from Shaizar for an attack on Antioch's southern frontier. Roger, meanwhile, responded in kind by marching 2,000 troops to a holding position at Apamea, probably in the company of Baldwin II of Edessa. There the extraordinary pan-Levantine alliance assembled. Tughtegin, true to his word, joined Roger with some 10,000 men, while Baldwin I and Pons of Tripoli arrived later in August. These arrayed forces, so often themselves combatants, held their ground throughout the summer, successfully intermingling Latin and Muslim troops without apparent difficulty.

Facing such a sizeable and entrenched opposing force, Bursuq did his best to provoke open battle, sending skirmishers to harass the allied camp and leading raids into the Summaq plateau. It is testament to the difficulty of maintaining discipline in the face of such provocation that Roger threatened to blind anyone breaking ranks. The Latins, alongside their Damascene fellows, duly held to their position. Thwarted, Bursuq retreated from Shaizar and, with the danger to Syria now apparently passed, the grand coalition broke up.

Roger returned to Antioch, but in the first days of September Bursuq's withdrawal was revealed as a ruse. Having fallen back towards Hama to await the dissolution of the defending army, he now circled around, cutting a swathe through the northern reaches of the Summaq. With the principality in real danger of being overrun, Roger found himself in an unsettling predicament, isolated from his allies. Only Baldwin of Edessa remained, having held troops in the principality throughout the summer as something akin to a client ruler of Antioch. Should Roger dutifully await the reassembly of the Latin–Muslim coalition, leaving Bursuq to roam the Syrian countryside with impunity, or risk swift, independent action? In essence, his dilemma replicated that faced by Baldwin I two years earlier and, in spite of the evident lessons of that encounter, on 12 September 1115 the prince of Antioch gathered his army at Rugia and marched to intercept the enemy. This was a rather foolhardy act of bravado. Leading some 500 to 700 knights and perhaps 2,000 to 3,000 infantry, he stood to be outnumbered by at least two to one. The Latins seem to have put their faith in an Antiochene relic of the True Cross carried in their midst by the bishop of Jabala and to have undertaken a series of purifying spiritual rites, but even so Roger must have recognised that he was gambling the future of Frankish Syria.

On this occasion it was the Christians who enjoyed the benefit of fortune and the sharper edge of military intelligence. Moving through the Ruj valley, Roger camped at Hab, all the while searching for signs of Bursuq's army. On the morning of 14 September scouts brought news: the enemy was camped nearby in the valley of Sarmin, unaware of their approach. Roger launched a surprise attack, panicking the Muslims into a chaotic retreat on to the flanks of a nearby hill known as Tell Danith, where they were soon overrun. With Bursuq in full flight, Roger savoured a famous victory. So plentiful was the loot plundered from the captured Muslim camp that the triumphant prince needed three days to distribute it among his men. Roger had broken the rules of engagement and won; but in doing so he had set a worrying precedent for hot-headed impetuosity.[73]

Baldwin of Boulogne's last years

King Baldwin I reaffirmed his own propensity for audacious, even visionary, exploits later that same autumn. East, beyond the banks of the River Jordan and between the Dead Sea and the Red Sea, lay an arid, inhospitable and largely unpopulated region. Today it roughly conforms to the modern borders of Jordan; in the twelfth century it became known as Transjordan. Desolate as it might have been, it acted as an essential channel for trade and communication between Syria and the cities of Egypt and Arabia. Baldwin had already ventured into the area in 1107 and again in 1113 on limited, exploratory campaigns. Now, towards the end of 1115, he made a bold attempt to initiate Frankish colonisation of the area as a first step towards controlling trans-Levantine traffic. Marching with just 200 knights and 400 infantry to a tell-like outcrop known locally as Shobak, he constructed a makeshift castle christened Montreal, or the Royal Mountain. He then returned to the region the following year to establish the small outpost on the Red Sea coast at Aqaba. By these steps Baldwin began a process of territorial expansion that would benefit the kingdom in years to come.

After a severe bout of infirmity in winter 1116–17, Baldwin spent months convalescing, but by the start of 1118 he was ready to contemplate new military endeavours. That March he mounted an ambitious raiding campaign into Egypt, reaching the eastern branches of the Nile. In the midst of success, he suddenly fell desperately ill; the old wound received in 1103, from which he had never fully recovered, had now reopened. Deep in enemy territory, the great king found himself in such terrible pain that he was unable to ride a horse, and so, borne upon an improvised litter, he began a tortured journey back towards Palestine. A few days later, on 2 April 1118, he reached the tiny frontier settlement of al-Arish, but could go no further and there, having confessed his sins, he died.

The king had been determined that his body not be left in Egypt and so, after his death, his careful, if rather gruesome, instructions to his cook Addo were precisely followed in order to prevent his corpse rotting in the heat.

> Just as he had resolutely asked, his belly was cut [open], his internal organs were taken out and buried, his body was salted inside and out, in the eyes, mouth, nostrils and ears [and] also embalmed with spices and balsam, then it was sewn into a hide and wrapped in carpets, placed on horseback and firmly tied on.

The funeral party bearing his remains reached Jerusalem that Palm Sunday and, in accordance with his last wishes, King Baldwin I was buried in the Church of the Holy Sepulchre, beside his brother Godfrey of Bouillon.[74]

Although the First Crusaders prosecuted the initial invasion of the Levant, the real task of conquering the Near East and creating the crusader states was carried out by the first generation of settlers in Outremer. Of these, the greatest individual contributions were undoubtedly made by King Baldwin I and his rival Tancred of Antioch. Together these two rulers steered the Latin East through a period of extreme fragility, during which the myth of Frankish invincibility in battle cracked and the first intermittent signs of a Muslim counter-offensive surfaced. Between 1100 and 1118, perhaps even more than during the First Crusade, the real significance of

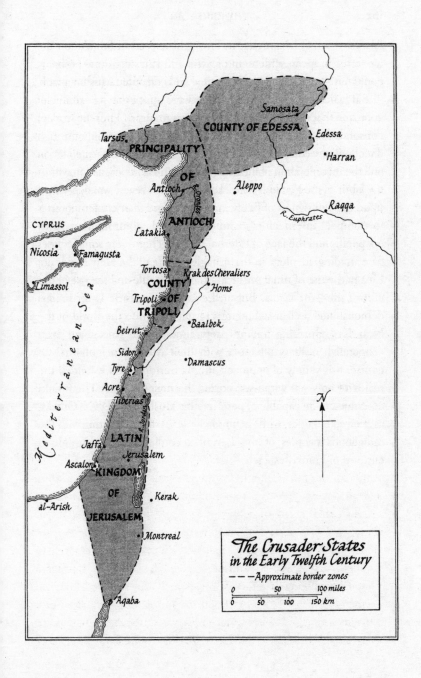

The Crusader States
in the Early Twelfth Century

--- Approximate border zones

Islamic disunity became clear, for in these years of foundation the western European settlement of Syria and Palestine quite probably could have been halted by committed and concerted Muslim attack.

Baldwin's and Tancred's successes were built upon a flexibility of approach that mixed ruthlessness with pragmatism. Thus the work of consolidation and subjugation was carried out not simply through direct military conquest, but also via diplomacy, financial exploitation and the incorporation of the indigenous non-Latin population within the fabric of the Frankish states. Latin survival likewise was dependent upon the willingness of Baldwin, Tancred and their contemporaries to temper internecine competition and confrontation with cooperation in the face of external threats. There were some echoes of 'crusading' ideology in the struggle to defend the Holy Land, not least in the use of ritual purification before battle and the rise of the cult of the True Cross. But at the same time, early Latin settlers demonstrated a clear willingness to integrate into the world of the Near East, pursuing trading pacts, limited-term truces and even cooperative military alliances with their Muslim neighbours. Of course, this variety of approach simply mirrored and extended the reality of holy war witnessed during the First Crusade. The Franks continued to be capable of personifying Muslims, and even Greeks, as avowed enemies, while at a broader level still interacting with the indigenous peoples of the Levant according to the normalised customs of Frankish society.

5

OUTREMER

Just before first light on 28 June 1119 Prince Roger of Antioch gathered his army in readiness for battle. His men huddled together to listen to a sermon, partake of mass and venerate the Antiochene relic of the True Cross – girding their souls for the fight ahead. In the days leading up to this moment, Roger had reacted with decisive resolution to news of an impending Muslim invasion. After years of passively enduring Antiochene expansionism and repeated demands for exorbitant tribute, Aleppo had suddenly moved on to the offensive. Mustering a force – perhaps in excess of 10,000 men – the city's new emir, the Artuqid Turk Il-ghazi, marched on the border zone with Frankish Antioch. Facing this threat, Roger could have waited for reinforcements from his Latin neighbours, including Baldwin of Bourcq (who had assumed the Jerusalemite crown in 1118). Instead, the prince assembled around 700 knights, 3,000 infantry and a corps of Turcopoles (Christianised mercenaries of Turkish birth) and crossed to the eastern flanks of the Belus Hills. Roger camped in a valley near the small settlement of Sarmada – which he believed was well defended by enclosing rocky hills – and that morning was about to initiate a swift advance, hoping to catch his enemy unawares and replay his success of 1115. Unbeknownst to the prince, however, on the preceding evening scouts had revealed the Christians' position to Il-ghazi. Drawing upon local knowledge of the surrounding terrain, the Artuqid commander dispatched troops to approach Roger's camp from three different directions and, as one Arabic chronicler attested, 'as dawn broke [the Franks] saw the Muslim standards advancing to surround them completely'.[75]

THE FIELD OF BLOOD

With bugles sounding an urgent call to arms through the ranks, Roger rushed to organise his forces for combat, a cleric bearing the True Cross beside him. As Il-ghazi's men closed in, there was just time to assemble the Latin host beyond the confines of the camp. In the vain hope of regaining the initiative, Roger ordered the Frankish knights on his right flank to deliver a crushing heavy charge and, at first, they appeared to have stemmed the Aleppan advance. But as battle was joined along the line, a contingent of Turcopoles stationed on the left wing buckled, and their rout splintered the Latin formation. Outnumbered and encircled, the Antiochenes were gradually overrun.

Caught at the heart of the maelstrom, Prince Roger was left horribly exposed, but 'though his men lay cut down and dead on all sides . . . he never retreated, nor looked back'. One Latin eyewitness described how, 'fighting energetically . . . [the prince] was struck by a [Muslim] sword through the middle of his nose right into his brain, and settling his debt to death [beneath] the Holy Cross he gave up his body to the earth and his soul to heaven'. The unfortunate priest carrying the True Cross was likewise cut down, although it was later said that the relic exacted its own miraculous revenge for this killing, causing all the Muslims nearby to suddenly become 'possessed by greed' for its 'gold and precious stones' and thus to begin butchering one another.

As resistance collapsed, a few Franks escaped westwards into the Belus Hills, but most were slaughtered. A Muslim living in Damascus described it as 'one of [Islam's] finest victories', noting that, strewn across the battleground, the enemy's slain horses resembled hedgehogs 'because of the quantity of arrows sticking into them'. So terrible was this defeat, so great the number of Christian dead, that the Antiochenes thereafter dubbed the site '*Ager Sanguinis*', the Field of Blood.

The Latin principality, stripped of its ruler and army, stood open to further assault. Il-ghazi, nonetheless, made no real attempt to conquer Antioch itself. Traditionally, he has been criticised broadly for not seizing an ideal opportunity to capture the Frankish capital. Yet, in truth, Antioch was weakened, but far from helpless. Its extraordinarily formidable fortifications meant that, even with limited manpower to hand, the city could resist conquest by an external enemy. Il-ghazi possessed neither the time to prosecute a grinding siege, nor the men to garrison the city should it fall. Aware that Frankish reinforcements from the south would likely arrive within weeks, and with Aleppan strategic interests foremost in his mind, Il-ghazi chose instead to focus upon the Jazr border zone east of the Belus range, retaking al-Atharib and Zardana. By early August he had reoccupied this buffer zone, safeguarding Aleppo's survival as a Muslim power.

In the meantime, Latin armies from Jerusalem and Tripoli reached Antioch, and King Baldwin II prepared for a counter-strike. Rallying the remnants of the principality's fighting manpower, he confronted Il-ghazi on 14 August 1119 in an inconclusive battle near Zardana. The Muslim army, recently bolstered by Damascene troops, was driven from the field, and, with momentum faltering, Il-ghazi drew his campaign to a close. Christian losses were high and among those captured was Robert fitz-Fulk the Leper, lord of Zardana. Brought to Damascus, he might have hoped for clemency from his friend and former ally Tughtegin, but when Robert refused to renounce his religion, the *atabeg* flew into a rage and beheaded him 'by a stroke of his sword'. Rumour had it that Tughtegin had Robert's skull fashioned into a gaudy, gold-plated, jewel-encrusted goblet.[76]

King Baldwin II's arrival in northern Syria secured the Frankish principality's immediate survival, but Outremer as a whole now had to confront the Field of Blood's terrible aftermath. The territorial losses were grave – beyond Il-ghazi's conquests, Muslim Shaizar exploited Christian weakness to overrun all of the Summaq plateau, barring the outpost at Apamea – but Antioch had recovered from an even bleaker position after the defeat at Harran in 1104. The true significance of 1119 lay in the prince's death. Never before had an incumbent Latin ruler fallen in battle and, worse still, Roger died childless, leaving Antioch prone to a crippling succession crisis. With few options available, Baldwin stepped into the breach. The claim of Bohemond of Taranto's nine-year-old son and namesake, Bohemond II, then living in Italy, was resurrected, with the king agreeing to act as regent until the young prince-designate reached his majority at the age of fifteen.

In a wider sense, the Field of Blood was a deeply unsettling shock for Latin Christendom. This was not the first Frankish reversal. In the afterglow of the 'miraculous' First Crusade, earlier setbacks had already cast their shadow: the collapse of the 1101 Crusade; Baldwin I's defeat in the second Battle of Ramla; the mauling at Harran. But in the wake of 1119 – the 'sorrow of sorrows', which 'took away joy and went beyond the bounds and measure of all misery' – a troubling question that cut to the heart of the belief system that underpinned crusading and the settlement of Outremer was unavoidable. If holy war truly was the work of God, sanctioned and empowered by His divine will, then how could defeat be explained? The answer was sin – success for Islam in the war for dominion of the Levant was a punishment, mandated in Heaven, for Christian transgression. The sinner, or scapegoat, at the Field of Blood was deemed to be Prince Roger, now branded as an adulterer and a usurper. In the future, the notion of sin as a cause of defeat would gain ever wider currency, and other individuals and groups would be targeted to explain the vagaries of war.[77]

COUNTERING MISFORTUNE

In one sense, the alarm caused by the Field of Blood proved to be unfounded. The threat posed by Aleppo soon abated and Il-ghazi died in 1122 without scoring another telling victory against the Franks. Over the next two decades Near Eastern Islam remained disunited, mired in internal power struggles – and thus little concerted thought was given to waging *jihad* against Outremer. Indeed, the Latins made a number of significant conquests in this period. Baldwin II recouped Antioch's losses in the Summaq and east of the Belus Hills. A foothold in another strategically sensitive border zone – this time between Jerusalem and Damascus – was secured when the Franks occupied the fortified town of Banyas, situated to the east of the River Jordan's headwaters, standing guard over the Terre de Sueth. In 1142 the Jerusalemite crown also supported the construction of a major new castle in Transjordan. This fortress, Kerak, perched upon a narrow ridge amid the Jordanian desert, grew to become one of the great 'crusader' strongholds of the Levant and was designated as the region's administrative centre.

Nonetheless, the crusader states were plagued by instability in the years that followed the Field of Blood. This was born largely of misfortune rather than entrenched Muslim aggression, as captivity and untimely death robbed the Latins of a series of leaders, igniting succession crises and engendering civil strife. Taken prisoner during a chance Muslim attack in April 1123, King Baldwin II spent sixteen months in captivity before being ransomed, during which time a coup in Palestine was narrowly avoided. Bohemond II arrived in 1126 to assume control of Antioch and was married to Baldwin II's daughter Alice, but the young prince was slain during a raid into Cilicia just four years later, leaving behind an infant girl, Constance, as heir. Alice spent the early 1130s intriguing to seize power in the principality. Baldwin II's own death from illness in 1131, closely followed by the demise of his ally and successor as count of Edessa, Joscelin of Courtenay, also eradicated the last vestiges of Outremer's old guard. Against this background of incipient weakness, the need for an injection of strength and support became ever more pressing.[78]

The Military Orders

The emergence of two religious orders combining the ideals of knighthood and monasticism played a vital role in buttressing the Frankish Levant. In about 1119, a small band of knights, led by a French nobleman named Hugh of Payns, dedicated themselves to the charitable task of protecting Christian pilgrims to the Holy Land. In practical terms, at first this meant patrolling the road from Jaffa to Jerusalem, but Hugh's group quickly gained wider recognition and patronage. The Latin patriarch soon acknowledged their status as a spiritual order, while the king himself gave them quarters in Jerusalem's Aqsa mosque, known to the Franks as the Temple of Solomon, and from this site they gained their name: the Order of the Temple of Solomon, or the Templars. Like monks, they made vows of poverty, chastity and obedience, but, rather than dedicate themselves to lives of sheltered devotion in isolated communities, they took up sword, shield and armour to fight for Christendom and the defence of the Holy Land.

As the Templars' leader (or master), Hugh of Payns travelled to Europe in 1127 in search of validation and endorsement for his new order. Formal recognition by the Latin Church came in January 1129, at a major ecclesiastical council held at Troyes (Champagne, France). In the years to come, this official seal of approval was further garlanded by papal support and extensive privileges and immunities. The Templars also earned the endorsement of one of the Latin world's great religious luminaries, Bernard of Clairvaux. As abbot of a Cistercian monastery, Bernard was renowned for his wisdom and trusted as an adviser in all the courts of the West. The combination of political and ecclesiastical power that he wielded was unprecedented, but in physical terms Bernard was a wreck, forced to have an open latrine trench dug next to his pew in church so that he could relieve the symptoms of an appalling chronic intestinal affliction.

Around 1130 Bernard composed a treatise – titled *In Praise of the New Knighthood* – extolling the virtues of the Templars' way of life. The abbot declared the order to be 'most worthy of total admiration', lauding its brethren as 'true knights of Christ fight[ing] the battles of their Lord', assured of glorious martyrdom should they die. This lyrical exhortation played a central role in popularising the Templar movement across Latin Europe, garnering acceptance for a revolutionary offshoot of crusade ideology that in many ways was the ultimate distillation and expression of Christian holy war.

The example set by the Templars encouraged another charitable religious movement founded by Latins in the Near East to embrace militarisation. Since the late eleventh century, Jerusalem's Christian quarter had contained a hospital, funded by Italian merchants and devoted to the care of pilgrims and the sick. With the Holy City's conquest by the First Crusaders and the associated influx of pilgrim traffic, this institution, dedicated to John the Baptist and so known as the Hospital of St John, grew in power and importance. Recognised as an order by the pope in 1113, the Hospitallers, as they came to be known, began to attract widespread international patronage. Under the guidance of its master, Raymond of Le Puy (1120–60), the movement appended a martial element to its ongoing medical functions, emerging by the mid-twelfth century as the second Military Order.

Over the course of the twelfth and thirteenth centuries, the Templars and Hospitallers stood at the heart of crusading history, playing leading roles in the war for the Holy Land. In the central Middle Ages, Latin lay nobles commonly sought to affirm their devotion to God by giving alms to religious movements, often in the form of title to land or rights to its revenue. The mercurial popularity of the Military Orders therefore brought them rich donations in Outremer and across Europe. Despite their relatively humble origins – immortalised in the Templars' case by their seal, depicting two impoverished knights riding a single horse – both were soon endowed with enormous wealth. They also attracted a steady stream of recruits, many of whom became highly trained, well-equipped warrior-monks (as knights or lower-ranking sergeants). Most medieval European war bands were startlingly amateurish, accustomed only to fighting in short seasonal campaigns and predominantly composed of poorly drilled, lightly armed irregulars. The Templars and Hospitallers, by contrast, could levy expert full-time standing forces: in effect, Latin Christendom's first professional armies.

The Military Orders became supranational movements. Primarily focused on the protection of the crusader states, they nonetheless developed an array of other European military, ecclesiastical and financial interests, including a prominent role in the Iberian frontier wars against Islam. In the Levant their unprecedented military and economic might brought them a concomitant degree of political influence. Both orders enjoyed papal patronage, gaining independence from local secular and ecclesiastical jurisdictions, and so had the potential to destabilise the Latin East's sovereign polities. As rogue powers, they might question or even countermand crown authority, or ignore patriarchal edicts and episcopal instruction. For now, though, this danger was more than balanced by the transformative benefits of their involvement in Outremer's defence.

Together, the Templars and Hospitallers brought a desperately needed influx of manpower and martial expertise to crusader states starved of military resources. Crucially, they also possessed the wealth to maintain, and in time extend, Outremer's network of forts and castles. From the 1130s onwards, the lay lords of the Latin East began ceding control of fortified sites to the orders, often allowing them to develop semi-independent enclaves in border zones. Command of the castle of Baghras gave the Templars a dominant position in the northern reaches of the Antiochene principality. Rights to Safad in

Galilee and to Gaza in southern Palestine brought the order similar rights and responsibilities. The Hospitallers, meanwhile, gained centres at Krak des Chevaliers, perched above the Bouqia valley between Antioch and Tripoli, and at Bethgibelin, one of three strongholds built in southern Palestine to defend Jerusalem and exert military pressure upon Muslim-held Ascalon.[79]

Turning to Christendom

After 1119 the Levantine Franks also began to look beyond their own borders for aid. In theory at least, eastern Christians should have been one obvious source of assistance.* Encircled by Islam and distant as it was from western Europe, Outremer needed a neighbouring ally if it was to achieve long-term survival. Yet, although the crusader states shared a common Christian faith with the Byzantine Empire – the Mediterranean superpower feared and respected by the Muslim world – since Jerusalem's conquest the Greeks had contributed precious little to the war for the Holy Land. The embittered dispute over Antioch lay at the heart of this failure to secure imperial support and, if unaddressed, this problem looked set to cripple the Frankish Levant for decades to come. In 1137, after long years of distraction elsewhere in Byzantium, Alexius I's son and heir, Emperor John II Comnenus, marched into Syria to reassert Greek influence over what he considered the eastern fringes of his realm. John managed to impose theoretical suzerainty over Antioch, and from this point forward the principality's relations with the rest of Outremer were always balanced by its ties to Constantinople. But in military terms the empire's contribution was disappointing, with expeditions against Aleppo and Shaizar ending in failure. John returned to the East in

---

* Around this time the rising Armenian Christian Roupenid dynasty began expanding out of their power base in the Taurus Mountains. They would eventually become one of the Levant's major powers, but despite the maintenance of generally cordial relations with Edessa, the Roupenids' desire to establish a kingdom in Cilicia brought them into conflict with Antioch.

late summer 1142, probably planning to create a new Byzantine polity at Antioch ruled directly by his youngest son Manuel. As it was, John died in a hunting accident in Cilicia in April 1143 – a sudden catastrophe that brought the Greek expedition to an immediate halt.[80]

In fact, Outremer turned most frequently to western Christendom for assistance after the Field of Blood. In January 1120, at a general assembly of the kingdom of Jerusalem's secular and ecclesiastical leaders in Nablus (north of the Holy City), the crisis facing the crusader states was discussed. This resulted in the first direct appeal to Pope Calixtus II for a new crusade to the Holy Land and a further entreaty to Venice. The Italian mercantile republic responded by sending a fleet of at least seventy ships east in autumn 1122 under the crusading banner. With Venetian help the Jerusalemite Franks captured the heavily fortified city of Tyre in 1124 – one of Palestine's last remaining Muslim-held ports and a major centre of Mediterranean shipping and commerce.* King Baldwin II sought to rally another crusade for a projected attack on Damascus in 1129, but despite recruiting a sizeable party of western knights, the campaign itself proved to be a fiasco.

Intent upon forging closer links with the Latin West and keen to solve their own succession crises, the Levantine Franks also looked to secure eligible European husbands for a number of Outremer's heiresses. In the crusader states, as in much of medieval Christendom, there was a perceived need for male rule; secular lords,

---

* The Venetians received a startling variety of concessions from the kingdom of Jerusalem in return for their assistance. These included: a third of the city and lordship of Tyre, plus an annual payment of 300 gold bezants from the royal revenues of Acre; exemption from all taxation, barring that owed for carrying pilgrims to the Holy Land; the right to use Venetian measures in trade; and a parcel of property in every town of the realm (made up of a street and a square, plus a church, bakery and bathhouse) to be held in perpetuity. Baldwin II later managed to engineer some adjustments to the agreement – most notably, that land in the lordship of Tyre would be held by the Venetians as fiefs, with military service owing to the crown – but the deal, nonetheless, transformed Venice into the commercial powerhouse of the Frankish Levant.

from kings to counts, were expected to lead, or at least direct, their armies in times of war, and military command generally was deemed to be the preserve of men. Ideally, marriage candidates would be high-born aristocrats – men willing to commit to the defence of the Holy Land and possessed of the social standing to bring new wealth and manpower to the East. One such figure was Raymond of Poitiers – the duke of Aquitaine's second son and a relation of France's Capetian king – who was married to Constance of Antioch in 1136, bringing a long period of political turbulence in northern Syria to an end. An even more influential union was orchestrated in the late 1120s. King Baldwin II had four daughters with his Armenian wife Morphia, but no sons, and therefore he sought a match for his eldest child Melisende to secure the royal succession. After protracted negotiations, in 1129 the princess duly wed Count Fulk V of Anjou, one of France's most eminent potentates with ties to the monarchs of England and France.

Upon Baldwin II's death, Fulk and Melisende were consecrated and crowned on 14 September 1131. Perhaps twenty-two years of age, the new queen was the first ruler of Jerusalem to be born of mixed (Latin-Armenian) parentage. As such, she was the living embodiment of a new oriental Frankish society. Around 1134, however, Latin Palestine was brought to the brink of civil war by a dispute over crown rights. Resentful of the new king's decision to appoint his own handpicked supporters to positions of wealth and influence, and his growing estrangement from Melisende, Jerusalem's established Frankish aristocracy set out to curb Fulk's authority by forcing him to rule jointly with the queen. After a decidedly frosty period, during which the king apparently 'found that no place was entirely safe among the kindred and partisans of the queen', the royal couple were reconciled. From this point forward, Melisende started to play a central role in governing the realm, and her position was further consolidated after Fulk's death in 1143, when she was appointed as joint ruler with her young son Baldwin III.

In the longer term, these events helped to reshape the nature and extent of royal authority in Palestine. Baldwin I and Baldwin II had often ruled almost as autocrats, but as the twelfth century progressed it became clear that the Latin nobility could limit the absolute might of the monarchy. Over time, the crown rulers of Frankish Jerusalem engaged in a greater degree of consultation with their leading nobles, and the council of the realm's most important landholders and ecclesiastics, known as the Haute Cour (High Court), became Palestine's most important forum for legal, political and military decision making.[81]

A CRUSADER SOCIETY?

One of the rarest and most beautiful treasures to survive from the crusading era is a small prayer book, thought to have been made in the kingdom of Jerusalem during the 1130s and now residing in London's British Library. Bound between two ornate ivory covers decorated with carvings of unsurpassed delicacy, its pages contain a series of magnificent and deeply emotive illuminations illustrating the life of Jesus. The work of many master craftsmen, a piece of the highest attainable quality, the book was designed as a personal guide to Christian life and religious observance – detailing saints' days, listing prayers – that technically would be called a psalter. Taken simply on its own terms, it is a masterpiece of medieval art.

Yet what sets this remarkable remnant of a distant age apart is its provenance. For this psalter is thought to have been commissioned by King Fulk of Jerusalem as a gift for his wife, Melisende; perhaps even as a peace offering to salve the wounds opened in 1134. As such, it offers us an extraordinary, tangible connection to Outremer and the world of Melisende. The notion of seeing, perhaps even of touching, an item that belonged to the queen, particularly one so intimately related to her daily life, is stirring enough.

But Melisende's Psalter has far more to tell us; indeed, its mere existence opens up a furious debate that cuts to the heart of crusading history. For the book's construction and decoration seem to speak of an artistic culture in which Latin, Greek, eastern Christian and even Islamic styles have intermingled, fusing to create a new and unique form; what might be termed 'crusader art'. At least seven artisans, labouring in the workshop of the Church of the Holy Sepulchre, collaborated in the Psalter's production (including a Byzantine-trained artist bearing the distinctly Greek-sounding name Basilius, who signed one of the internal images). The images wrought upon its ivory covers are broadly Byzantine in form, but are enclosed within densely packed geometric borders suggestive of Islamic influence. Other elements of the manuscript exhibit different influences: the text has been attributed to a French hand; the numerous decorated capital letters that introduce pages are western European in conception; and the detailed calendar contained within is English.[82]

Does this psalter reflect wider truths about the nature of life in the Frankish Levant? Was the society inhabited by Melisende and her contemporaries itself distinct in character and quality; and was this 'crusader' world one of perpetual war – a closed community of religious and ethnic intolerance – or a melting-pot of cross-cultural interchange? This debate has the potential to offer profoundly instructive insights into the reality of medieval life. It is also among the most heated in all crusade history. Over the last two hundred years historians have presented wildly divergent visions of the relationship between Frankish Christians and the indigenous peoples of the Near East, with some emphasising the forces of integration, adaptation and acculturation and others depicting the crusader states as oppressive, intolerant colonial regimes.

Given the relative paucity of a surviving body of medieval evidence that sheds light on Outremer's social, cultural and economic context, it is not surprising that the image put forward of the crusader states has often revealed more about the hopes and prejudices of our own world than the mentality and mores of the medieval past. For those who believe in the inevitability of a 'clash of civilisations' and a global conflagration between Islam and the West, the crusades and the societies they begat can serve as grim proof of mankind's innate propensity to savagery, bigotry and tyrannical repression of an enemy 'other'. Alternatively, the evidence of transcultural fusion and peaceful coexistence in Outremer can be harnessed to underpin the ideal of *convivencia* (literally 'living together'), to suggest that peoples of differing ethnic and religious backgrounds can live together in relative harmony.[83]

Despite all of these manifest complexities, the world of Outremer demands close and careful examination, because it has such integral bearing upon the fundamental issues of crusade history, opening up a pair of pressing questions: was the Frankish conquest and colonisation of the Near East unusual because it occurred in the context of holy war, or actually quite unremarkable? And did the creation of the crusader states change the history of western Europe – accelerating cross-cultural contact and the diffusion of knowledge; serving as a breeding ground for greater familiarity and understanding between Latin Christians and Muslims?

Life in Outremer

A number of elementary facts conditioned the nature of life in the crusader states. Outremer's foundation did not bring about a widespread displacement of the Levant's indigenous population. Instead, Frankish settlers governed polities whose populations reflected that region's historic diversity – a mixture of Muslims, Jews and eastern Christians. This latter group included a bewildering number of Christian rites, among them Armenians, Greeks, Jacobites, Nestorians and Copts; as well as 'Syrian' (or Melkite) Christians, who were Greek Orthodox but spoke Arabic. The distribution and relative representation of these different peoples varied considerably across the crusader states because of established settlement patterns: with a preponderance of Armenians in the county of Edessa and Greeks in the principality of Antioch; and probably a higher proportion of Muslims in the kingdom of Jerusalem.

The Latins ruled over these native subjects as an elite, heavily outnumbered minority. Linguistic difference seems to have remained as a defining and dividing factor. The common spoken tongue adopted by the Latins was Old French (with Latin used in formal documentation) and, while some settlers did learn Arabic and other eastern languages like Greek, Armenian, Syriac and Hebrew, most did not. Many Franks resided in urban and/or coastal communities – and thus in relative isolation from the agrarian indigenous population. In rural inland settings, western lords generally lived in separate manor houses, largely cut off from their subjects, but the pragmatic necessity of sharing scarce resources like water sometimes prompted increased contact. In general, small rural settlements tended to have a coherent devotional identity, so that one village might be made up of Muslims, another of Greeks (the same is true in parts of the Near East today). But large towns and cities were more multicultural.

So the Franks evidently ruled over, and in some cases lived among, a diverse range of 'eastern' peoples. Did the Latins stand aloof, or integrate themselves into this richly variegated setting? According to King Baldwin I's chaplain Fulcher of Chartres, writing in the 1120s, they seem quickly to have undergone a high degree of acculturation:

> Consider, I pray, and reflect how in our time God has transformed the Occident [West] into the Orient. For we who were Occidentals have become Orientals. He who was a Roman or a Frank has in this land been made into a Galilean or a Palestinian. He who was of Rheims or Chartres has now become a citizen of Tyre or Antioch. We have already forgotten the places of our birth.

Admittedly, Fulcher was writing the equivalent of a recruitment manifesto; seeking to new lure new Latin settlers to the East. But even with this proviso in mind, his testimony seems to indicate openness to the idea of assimilation. Fulcher went on to describe another mode of cross-cultural contact – intermarriage. Unions between Franks and eastern Christian Greeks and Armenians were relatively commonplace, and sometimes served to cement political alliances. Queen Melisende of Jerusalem herself was a product of just such a marriage. Frankish men might also wed Muslim women who converted to Christianity. But marriages between Latins and Muslims seem to have been extremely rare. At a council held in Nablus in 1120, soon after the crisis caused by the Field of Blood, the Frankish hierarchy instituted a series of laws explicitly forbidding fraternisation. The punishments for sex between Christians and Muslims were severe: a man would be castrated; a consenting woman would have her nose cut off. These were the first such examples of encoded prohibition in the Latin world. The same batch of legislation also banned Muslims from wearing clothing 'in the Frankish custom'. The import of these rulings is debatable, in part because any law can be read in a positive or negative light. Do the Nablus decrees reflect a world of intense segregation, where such acts would be unimaginable; or were these laws created to restrict what had become a common practice? Certainly, there is no evidence to indicate that these edicts were put into action, nor were they carried over into Outremer's thirteenth-century law codes.

When they first captured cities like Antioch and Jerusalem and decided to settle in the Near East, the Latins had to develop the means to rule their new lordships by establishing administrative frameworks. In general, their approach was to import many practices from the West, while adopting and adapting some Levantine models. This process was probably driven by the pragmatic need rapidly to set up a functioning system, rather than any particular desire to embrace new forms of government. Regional considerations also influenced decisions. In the principality of Antioch, with its history of Greek rule, the main city official was a *dux* (duke), an institution drawn from a Byzantine template; in the kingdom of Jerusalem, a similar role was performed by a Frankish-style viscount.

Eastern Christians certainly played some role in local and even regional government; so, too, on occasion, did Muslims. Most Muslim villages seem to have been represented by a *ra'is* – the equivalent of a headman – just as they had been under Turkish or Fatimid rule. Through a single reference, it is known that in 1181 the Muslim citizens of Tyre also had their own *ra'is* named Sadi. A similarly isolated piece of evidence indicates that in 1188 the Latin-held Syrian port of Jabala had a Muslim *qadi* (judge). It is impossible to gauge the true extent of this type of representation.[84]

Perhaps the most fascinating source of evidence for the nature of life in Outremer is Usama ibn Munqidh's *Book of Contemplation*, a collection of tales and anecdotes by a northern Syrian Arab nobleman who watched the war for the Holy Land unfold through the twelfth century. Usama's text is crammed with direct comments on (and incidental details about) contact with the Franks and life in the crusader states. His interest was almost always in the bizarre and unusual, so the material he recorded has to be used with some caution; nonetheless, his work is an invaluable mine of information. On the question of orientalised Latins, he wrote: 'There are some Franks who have become acclimatized and frequent the company of Muslims. These are better than those who have just arrived from their homelands, but they are the exception, and cannot be taken as typical.' In the course of his life, Usama encountered Franks who had taken to eating Levantine food and others who frequented *hammam* (bathhouses) that were open to Latins and Muslims alike.

One of the most surprising revelations to emerge from Usama's writings is the normalised, almost day-to-day nature of his encounters with Franks. While some of these took place in the context of combat, many meetings were of an amicable and courteous form. This may well have been a function of Usama's high social class, but it is clear that Latins did establish friendships with Muslims. In one case, Usama described how 'a respected knight [in King Fulk's army] grew to like my company and he became my constant companion, calling me "my brother". Between us there are ties of amity and sociability.' Nonetheless, there was an undertone to this tale, one that reverberated through many of the stories related in the *Book of Contemplation*: an inbred sense of Muslim cultural and

intellectual superiority. In the case of his knightly friend, this came
to the fore when the Frank offered to take Usama's fourteen-year-old
son with him back to Europe so that the boy could receive a proper
education and 'acquire reason'. Usama thought this preposterous
proposition revealed 'the Franks' lack of intelligence'.

Another seemingly unlikely association enjoyed by Usama ibn
Munqidh was his amicable relationship with the Templars. According
to Usama:

> When I went to visit the holy sites in Jerusalem, I would go in and
> make my way up to the Aqsa mosque, beside which stood a small
> mosque that the Franks had converted into a church. When I went
> into the Aqsa mosque – where the Templars, who are my friends,
> were – they would clear out that little mosque so that I could pray
> in it.

Usama evidently had no difficulty either in making a pilgrimage to
the Holy City or in finding a mosque in Frankish territory within
which to perform his canonically mandated daily prayers. Did this
right to worship extend to Muslims living under Latin rule; indeed,
was Outremer's non-Frankish population as a whole treated equitably,
or subjected to oppression and abuse? One fact is clear: in the Latin
East, the primary division was not between Christians and Muslims,
but between Franks (that is to say, Latin Christians) and non-Franks
(be they eastern Christian, Jewish or Muslim). This second group of
subjected indigenous peoples was made up mostly of peasants and
some merchants.[85]

In legal terms, non-Franks were generally treated as a separate
class: for serious breaches of law they were subject to the 'Burgess'
court (just like non-noble Latins), and here Muslims were allowed to
take oaths on the Koran; but civil cases came before the *Cour de la
Fonde* (or Market Court), specifically instituted for non-Franks. The
constitution of this body favoured eastern Christians because it was
manned by a jury of two Franks and four Syrians, with no Muslim

representation. Outremer's Latin law codes also seem to have assigned harsher punishments to Muslim offenders.

Much of the historical debate about the treatment of subjected Muslims has centred on the day-to-day issues of rights to worship and financial exploitation. In this regard, the evidence provided by the Iberian Muslim traveller and pilgrim Ibn Jubayr is enlightening. During a grand journey in the early 1180s that took in North Africa, Arabia, Iraq and Syria, Ibn Jubayr passed through the kingdom of Jerusalem, visiting Acre and Tyre before taking ship to Sicily. Of his journey through western Galilee he wrote:

> Our way lay through continuous farms and ordered settlements, whose inhabitants were all Muslims, living comfortably with the Franks. God protect us from such temptation. They surrender half their crops to the Franks at harvest time, and pay as well a poll-tax of one dinar and five qirat for each person. Other than that, they are not interfered with, save for a light tax on the fruits of trees. Their houses and all their effects are left to their full possession.

This account seems to indicate that a large, sedentary Muslim population lived in relative peace within Latin Palestine, paying a per-capita levy (like the poll-tax imposed by Islamic rulers on their non-Muslim subjects) and a produce tax. Surviving evidence for the level of taxation imposed within Islamic polities around this same time suggests that Muslim peasants and farmers were no worse off living under Frankish Christian rule. In fact, Ibn Jubayr even suggested that Muslims were more likely to be treated with 'justice' by a 'Frankish landlord' and to suffer 'injustice' at the hands of 'a landlord of [their] own faith'. This did not mean that he approved of peaceful coexistence or abject submission to Latin rule. At one point he noted that 'there can be no excuse in the eyes of God for a Muslim to stay in any infidel county, save when passing through it'. But principled objections such as this actually lend further credence to the positive observations he chose to record.[86]

Ibn Jubayr also reported that subjected Muslims had access to mosques and rights to prayer in Acre and Tyre. On the basis of this sliver of evidence, it is impossible to state categorically that all Muslims living in Outremer enjoyed similar devotional liberty. Broadly speaking, the most that can be suggested is that outnumbered Frankish settlers had a vested interest in keeping their native subjects content and in situ, and the conditions of life for indigenous eastern Christians and Muslims did not prompt widespread civil unrest or migration. By the contemporary standards of western Europe or the Muslim East, non-Franks living in the crusader states were probably not particularly oppressed, exploited or abused.[87]

One mode of contact that undoubtedly brought together Levantine Franks and Muslims was trade. There were sure signs of vibrant commercial enterprise during the first hundred years of Latin settlement. Italian merchants from Venice, Pisa and Genoa played leading roles in this process, establishing enclaves in Outremer's great ports and coastal cities and creating a complex network of trans-Mediterranean trade routes. These pulsing arteries of commerce, linking the Near East with the West, enabled Levantine products (such as sugar cane and olive oil) and precious goods from the Middle East and Asia to reach the markets of Europe. As yet, the bulk of trade flowing out of the Orient still passed through Egypt, but, even so, Outremer's economic development proved extraordinarily lucrative: it paved the way for cities like Venice to become the leading mercantile powers of the Middle Ages; and through customs and levies, it also helped to stock the treasuries of Antioch, Tripoli and Jerusalem. This does not mean that the Latin settlements in the East should be regarded as exploitative European colonies. Their establishment and survival may have depended, in part, upon the likes of Genoa; but they were not set up, in the first instance, as economic ventures. Nor did they serve the interests of 'western homelands' as such, because the financial benefits accrued by the 'state' tended to stay in the East.

The passage of goods from the Muslim world to the Mediterranean ports of the Frankish Levant was crucial not only to the Latins. It also became one of the linchpins of the wider Near Eastern economy: vital for the livelihoods of Muslim merchants plying the caravan routes to the East; critical to the incomes of Islam's great cities, Aleppo and Damascus. These shared interests produced interdependency and promoted carefully regulated (and thus essentially 'peaceful') contact, even at times of heightened political and military conflict. In the end – even in the midst of holy war – trade was too important to be disrupted.

Historians often present 1120 as a year of crisis and tension in the Levant. After all, the Field of Blood was fresh in the memory, and it was in this year that the council of Nablus prescribed harsh punishments for intercultural fraternisation. But in 1120 Baldwin II also instituted scything commercial tax cuts in Jerusalem. According to Fulcher of Chartres (who was then living in the Holy City), the king declared that 'Christians as well as Saracens were to have freedom to come in or go out to sell whensoever and to whomsoever they wished.' According to Muslim testimony, around the same time, Il-ghazi – the victor at the Field of Blood – abolished tolls in Aleppo and agreed terms of truce with the Franks. The degree of coordination between these two supposed enemies is impossible to determine, but both were obviously making strident attempts to stimulate trade. In fact, the tenor and scope of Latin–Muslim commercial contacts appear largely to have been unaffected by the rising tide of *jihadi* enthusiasm within Islam. Even Saladin, the 'champion' of the holy war, forged close links with the seaborne merchants of Italy when he became ruler of Muslim Egypt. Keen to promote profitable trade and to secure ready supplies of shipbuilding timber (which was difficult to source in North Africa), he endowed the Pisans with a protected commercial enclave in Alexandria in 1173.[88]

Knowledge and culture

Another form of exchange was also taking place in Outremer during the twelfth century: the transmission of Muslim and eastern

Christian knowledge and culture among members of the Latin intellectual elite. The evidence for this form of 'dialogue' in Jerusalem is limited, but in Antioch, with its long-embedded traditions of scholasticism, the situation was quite different.[89] The city and its environs were home to numerous eastern Christian monastic houses, predating the crusades and famed as centres of intellectual life. Here, some of the great minds of the Christian world gathered to study and translate texts on theology, philosophy, medicine and science that were written in languages such as Greek, Arabic, Syriac and Armenian. With the creation of the crusader states, Latin scholars naturally began to congregate in and around the city. In about 1114 the famous philosopher and translator Adelard of Bath visited, perhaps staying for two years. A decade later, Stephen of Pisa – the Latin treasurer of the Church of St Paul – was carrying out groundbreaking studies. In the course of the 1120s he produced some of the most important Latin translations ever to originate in the Levant. Stephen was most famous for his translation of al-Majusi's *Royal Book* – an extraordinary compendium of medical lore – that later helped to advance knowledge in western Europe.[90]

The extent to which this medical knowledge influenced actual practice in the Latin Levant is debatable. Usama ibn Munquidh wrote with relish about the peculiar and sometimes distinctly alarming techniques used by Frankish doctors. In one case a sick woman was diagnosed as having 'a demon inside her head'. Usama apparently watched as the attending Latin physician first shaved her head and then 'took a razor and made a cut in her head in the shape of a cross. He then peeled back the skin so that the skull was exposed and rubbed it with salt. The woman died instantaneously.' Usama concluded dryly: 'I left, having learned about their medicine things I had never known before.' Latin settlers in the crusader states seem to have recognised that Muslims and eastern Christians possessed advanced medical knowledge; and some, like the Frankish royal family in Jerusalem during the second half of the twelfth century, retained the services of non-Latin doctors. But there were some centres of excellence operated by western Christians, including the massive hospital in Jerusalem dedicated to St John and run by the Hospitaller Military Order.

The artistic fusion of Melisende's Psalter was echoed in buildings erected in the crusader states around this time, most famously in the massive reconstruction programme undertaken at the Holy Sepulchre in Jerusalem, during the reigns of Fulk and Melisende. When the Franks first conquered Palestine this church was in a state of some decay. Through the 1130s and 1140s the Latins rejuvenated this most sacred site, designing a suitably majestic structure that, for the first time, would enclose all the various shrines associated with Christ's Passion: including the Calvary chapel (on the supposed site of his crucifixion) and his burial tomb or Sepulchre. By this time, the church was also closely associated with the Frankish crown rulers of Jerusalem, being the venue for coronations and the burial site of kings.

In overall configuration, the new plan for the Holy Sepulchre adhered to the western European 'Romanesque' style of the early Middle Ages, and bore some similarity to other major Latin pilgrim churches in the West, including that found in Santiago de Compostela (north-western Spain). The 'crusader' church did have some distinctive features – including a large domed rotunda – but many of these peculiarities resulted from the building's unique setting, and from its architects' ambition to incorporate so many 'holy places' under one roof. The Church of the Holy Sepulchre standing today is still, broadly speaking, that of the twelfth century, but almost all of the interior 'crusader' decoration has been lost (as have the royal tombs). Of the extensive Latin mosaics only one remains – almost hidden on the ceiling, within the dim confines of the Calvary chapel – depicting Christ in Byzantine style. The main entryway to the building, through grand twinned portals on the south transept, was crowned by a pair of lavishly sculpted stone lintels: one, on the left, showing scenes from Jesus' final days, including the Last Supper; the other, a complex geometric web of interwoven vine-scrolling, dotted with human and mythological figures. These lintels remained in situ until the 1920s, when they were removed to a nearby museum for preservation. Throughout, the sculpture on the south façade appears to incorporate Frankish, Greek, Syrian and Muslim influences.

The new 'crusader' church was consecrated on 15 July 1149, exactly fifty years to the day after Jerusalem's reconquest. This building set out to proclaim, honour and venerate the unique sanctity of the Holy Sepulchre – Christendom's spiritual epicentre. It also stood as a bold declaration of Latin confidence, affirming the permanency of Frankish rule and the might of its royal dynasty; and as a monument that celebrated the achievements of the First Crusade, even as it bore splendid testimony to Outremer's cultural diversity.[91]

God's land of faith and devotion

The 'crusader' Church of the Holy Sepulchre was just one expression of the intense devotional reverence attached to Jerusalem, and to the Holy Land as a whole. For the Franks, this Levantine world – through which Christ himself had walked – was itself a sacred relic, where the air and earth were imbued with the numinous aura of God. It was inevitable that the religious monuments built in this hallowed land, and the expressions of faith carried out among its many holy places, would be coloured by an especially febrile piety. Latin religious life was also affected by the fact that many of the indigenous peoples of the Near East (including eastern Christians, Muslims and Jews) shared this sense of zealous adoration.

Through the twelfth century, the most common western European visitors to Outremer were not crusaders; they were pilgrims. Thousands came from Latin Christendom, making landfall at ports like Acre – the human equivalent of the precious cargo shipped from east to west; others came from the likes of Russia and Greece. Some stayed as lay settlers or became monks, nuns or hermits. Only a few religious houses were erected on entirely undeveloped sites, but many disused locations were revitalised (such as the Benedictine convent of St Anne in Jerusalem), and Latin monasteries that pre-dated the crusades, like Notre-Dame de Josaphat (just outside the Holy City), enjoyed a massive boost in popularity and patronage.

Acts of devotion also brought Franks into contact with the native inhabitants of the Levant. Some Latins sought to get closer to God by living ascetic lives of isolation in areas of wilderness like Mount Carmel (beside Haifa) and the Black Mountain (near Antioch); there they mingled in loose communities with Greek Orthodox hermits. One of the most remarkable examples of religious convergence occurred at the Convent of Our Lady at Saidnaya (about fifteen miles north of Damascus). This Greek Orthodox religious house, deep in Muslim territory, possessed a 'miraculous' icon of the Virgin Mary which had been transmuted from paint into flesh. Oil supposedly flowed from the icon's breasts and this liquid was treasured for its incredible healing properties. Saidnaya was a well-established pilgrimage destination, popular with eastern Christians and Muslims (who revered Mary as the mother of the prophet Jesus). From the second half of the twelfth century onwards, it also was visited by a number of Latin pilgrims – some of whom took phials of the Virgin's 'miraculous' oil back to Europe – and the shrine proved to be particularly popular among the Templars.

Just as some Franks were permitted to pass through Islamic lands to reach Saidnaya, so were Muslim pilgrims occasionally able to access sacred sites in Outremer. In the early 1140s, Unur of Damascus and Usama ibn Munqidh were allowed to visit the Dome of the Rock in Jerusalem. Around this same time, Usama also travelled to the Frankish town of Sebaste (near Nablus) to see the crypt of John the Baptist (and, as previously noted, he claimed to have made frequent trips to the Aqsa mosque). In the early 1180s, the Muslim scholar 'Ali al-Harawi was able to make a thorough tour of

Islamic religious sites in the kingdom of Jerusalem, and later wrote an Arabic guide to the area. On the basis of these few potentially isolated incidences, however, it is impossible accurately to gauge the real extent of Muslim pilgrim traffic.

In spite of these various forms of devotional interaction, the underlying religious atmosphere was still characterised by a marked degree of intolerance. Frankish and Muslim writers continued to denigrate one another's faiths, commonly through accusations of paganism, polytheism and idolatry. Relations between Latin and Levantine Christians also continued to be shaded by tension and distrust. The crusaders' conquest of the Near East put an effective (if not permanent) end to the region's established Greek Orthodox ecclesiastical hierarchy. New Latin patriarchs were appointed in Antioch and Jerusalem, and Latin archbishops and bishops were installed all across Outremer. The leaders of this Latin church made strident efforts to defend their ecclesiastical jurisdiction and to curtail what they regarded as the dangers of cross-contamination between western and eastern Christian rites, particularly with regard to monasticism.[92]

The Frankish East – Iron Curtain or open door?

The crusader states were not closed societies, wholly isolated from the Near Eastern world around them, nor uniformly oppressive, exploitative European colonies. But by the same token, Outremer cannot accurately be portrayed as a multicultural utopia – a haven of tolerance in which Christians, Muslims and Jews learned to live together in peace. In most regions of the Latin East, at most times in the twelfth century, the reality of life lay somewhere between these two polar opposites.

The ruling western European minority showed some pragmatic willingness to accommodate and incorporate non-Franks into the legal, social, cultural and devotional fabric of Outremer. Economic imperatives – from maintaining a subjected native workforce to facilitating the passage of trade – also promoted a degree of equitable interaction. Theoretically, two conflicting paradigms might be expected to have shaped 'crusader' society: on the one hand, the softening of initial antipathies over time, through gradually increasing familiarity; and, on the other, the potentially counteractive force of mounting *jihadi* enthusiasm within Islam. In reality, neither trend was so clear cut. From the start, Franks and Muslims engaged in diplomatic dialogue, negotiated pacts and forged trade links; and they continued to do so as the twelfth century progressed. And even as the decades passed, writers of all creeds persistently fell back on traditional stereotypes to express seemingly immutable suspicion and loathing of the 'other'.[93]

Franks, eastern Christians and Muslims living in the Near East may have come to know each other a little better in the course of the twelfth century, but this did not lead to real understanding or enduring harmony. Given the prevailing realities of the wider world, this should be no surprise. The medieval West itself was racked by inter-Latin rivalry and interminable martial strife; endemic social and religious intolerance was also on the rise. By these standards, the uneasy mixture of pragmatic contact and simmering conflict visible in the Levant was not that remarkable. And while the ethos of holy war may have influenced the nature of Frankish society, Outremer does not seem to have been defined by the crusading ideal.

For all this, the Latin settlement of the Near East did give rise to a remarkable, albeit not entirely unique, society – one that was subject to a distinctive range of forces and influences. The patterns of life in Outremer show some signs of acculturation and the surviving evidence of artistic and intellectual endeavour bears the hallmarks of cultural fusion. But this is likely to have been the result of undirected and organic development, not a deliberate drive towards assimilation.

ZANGI – TYRANT OF THE EAST

It was once popular to suggest that Muslim attitudes towards Outremer underwent a critical shift with the rise of the Turkish despot Zangi in 1128. That year certainly was one of change in Near Eastern politics. It began with the death of the Damascene ruler Tughtegin, who, in time, was succeeded by a string of ineffectual emirs of the Burid dynasty, placing Damascus on the path to internal decay and debility. That June, Zangi, the *atabeg* of Mosul, exploited the endemic factionalism afflicting northern Syria to seize control of Aleppo, ushering in a new era of secure, energetic rule.

Said to be 'handsome, brown-skinned, with beautiful eyes', Zangi was a truly remarkable individual. Even in a brutal, conflict-ridden age, his capacity for untempered violence was legendary, his insatiable hunger for power unequalled. One Muslim chronicler offered this forbidding, awestruck description of the *atabeg*: 'He was like a leopard in character, like a lion in fury, not renouncing any severity; not knowing any kindness . . . he was feared for his sudden attacking; shunned for his roughness; aggressive, insolent, death to his enemies and citizens.' Born around 1084 to a prominent Turkish warlord, Zangi grew up amid the inferno of civil war, surviving in an environment of near-constant warfare, awash with betrayal and murder, by learning to be resourceful, cunning and exceptionally ruthless. He came to prominence in the 1120s, earning the support of the Seljuq sultan of Baghdad, and by 1127 had been appointed as governor of Mosul and military adviser and commander to the sultan's two sons.

Zangi had a well-earned, and no doubt carefully cultivated, reputation for cruelty and callous, even arbitrary, brutality. He believed wholeheartedly in the power of abject fear, both to inspire loyalty in his subjects and to drive his enemies into submission. One Arabic chronicler conceded that the *atabeg* used terror to control his troops, noting that he 'was tyrannical [and] would strike with indiscriminate recklessness', observing that 'when he was unhappy with an emir he would kill him or banish him and leave that individual's children alive but castrate them'.[94]

Given his fearsome qualities, we might expect Zangi to have transformed Islam's fortunes in the war for the Holy Land. In the past, he has certainly been presented as a figure of central importance to the history of the crusades – as the first Muslim leader to strike a decisive blow against the Franks, the progenitor of an Islamic 'counter-crusade' who rekindled the fires of *jihad*, a towering *mujahid* (holy warrior) and champion of this new era. Yet for all this, through virtually his entire career Zangi's real impact upon, and interest in, the world of the crusades were negligible. In part, this might be explained by simple geopolitics. The *atabeg* bestrode the Near and Middle East like a colossus, with one foot resting in Mosul and the other planted west of the Euphrates, in Aleppo. Out of necessity, he was forced to divide his time, energy and resources between these two spheres of influence – Mesopotamia and Syria – and was thus never able truly to focus upon fighting the Franks. But even this rationale, often trumpeted to defend Zangi's *jihadi* credentials, is somewhat misleading, because it is predicated upon two faulty assumptions.

For Turkish warlords like Zangi, the Near East (including Syria and Palestine) and the Middle East (particularly Iraq and Iran) were not of equal political value and significance. The *atabeg*'s career demonstrates that, in the first half of the twelfth century, the heartland of Sunni Islam remained in Mesopotamia. It was there, in cities such as Baghdad and Mosul, that the greatest wealth and power were to be won. For Zangi, and many of his contemporaries, the battle against the Franks in the west was almost akin to a frontier war and, as such, of only intermittent and tangential interest.

What is more, when the *atabeg* did concern himself with Levantine affairs, his primary objective proved not to be the eradication of the crusader states, but the conquest of Damascus. Through the 1130s, in between long periods of absence in

Mesopotamia, Zangi made repeated attempts to push the sphere of Aleppan influence south towards this goal, seeking to absorb Muslim-held settlements like Hama, Homs and Baalbek that had become Damascene dependencies. Throughout Zangi showed a ready willingness to break vows, turn on allies and terrorise enemies in pursuit of his goals. In 1139 the ancient Roman city of Baalbek (in Lebanon's fertile Biqa valley) was pummelled into submission after a scouring assault and finally surrendered on the promise that its troops would be spared. Intent upon sending a chillingly clear message to any Syrian Muslims resisting his authority, Zangi reneged on these terms and crucified Baalbek's garrison to a man. Then, to ensure the city's continued loyalty, he appointed another up-and-coming member of his entourage as its governor, the Kurdish warrior Ayyub ibn Shadi, a man whose family would come to increasing prominence in the course of the twelfth century.

During this same period, Zangi employed a mixture of diplomatic intrigue and overt military pressure in his dealings with Damascus itself, hoping to engineer the capital's submission and eventual capture. His cause was only abetted by the chaotic, blood-drenched feuding that gripped the city for much of the 1130s. Despite the continued survival of the Burid dynasty in the form of a succession of feeble figureheads, real power in Damascus gradually devolved upon Unur – a Turcoman military commander who had served Tughtegin as a *mamluk* (slave soldier). It was he who now had to face the spectre of Zangid aggression. In the wake of Baalbek's savage conquest, Zangi laid siege to Damascus in December 1139, maintaining a loose cordon and launching intermittent attacks over the next six months. Even the *atabeg* was reluctant to launch a full-strength assault against a city of such profound historical significance for Islam, hoping instead to slowly squeeze Damascus into submission.

Yet, as the noose tightened in 1140, Unur rejected calls for surrender. Rather than submit to Zangid domination, he turned to a non-Muslim power for aid, dispatching an ambassador to

Jerusalem to seal a new alliance against Aleppo. In an audience with King Fulk, Zangi was portrayed as 'a cruel enemy, equally dangerous to both [Latin Palestine and Damascus]', and a munificent monthly tribute of 20,000 gold pieces was promised in return for Frankish assistance in combating this menace. In addition, Banyas (which had been retaken by the Muslims in 1132) would be ceded to Jerusalem.

Convinced both of the value of these extremely generous terms and of the benefits of forestalling Zangi's conquest of Syria, Fulk led an army north to relieve Damascus. With his operations against the city stalled, this threat was enough to prompt the *atabeg*'s retreat. He returned to Mosul, once more turning his attention to Mesopotamian affairs.[95]

Zangi against the Franks

Throughout the 1130s Zangi showed little or no interest in the prosecution of an anti-Frankish *jihad* and any attacks launched against the Latins in this period were either almost incidental or related to his advance into southern Syria. The *atabeg*'s only notable offensive against Outremer came in July 1137, when he targeted the fortress of Barin (to the west of Hama and the Orontes). But even this campaign should not be misconstrued, because Zangi's primary intention was to use Barin as a ready staging post for his aggression against Muslim Homs. The *atabeg*'s first concern was to further his southward expansion towards Damascus, not to deliver a mortal blow to the crusader states.

During the early 1140s Zangi focused almost exclusively on events east of the Euphrates, seeking to expand his power base in Iraq and to consolidate relations with the Seljuq sultan of Baghdad. From 1143 the *atabeg* was particularly concerned with subjugation of the Artuqid princes and minor Kurdish warlords to the north, in Diyar Bakr. Facing this aggression, one Artuqid, Qara Arslan of Hisn Kaifa, forged a pact with Joscelin II of Edessa (who succeeded his father in 1131), offering to relinquish territory to the Franks in return for aid. In autumn 1144, believing his county to be safe from attack, Joscelin duly led a large Edessene army to Qara Arslan's assistance. This move, born of an imperfect appreciation of Zangi's ambitions and capabilities, would have a profound impact upon Outremer's history.

Soon after the count's departure, the few troops that remained in Edessa alongside its Latin archbishop were stunned by Zangi's arrival outside their walls. The *atabeg* had long valued precise, up-to-date intelligence, happily expending a small fortune to maintain an extensive network of spies and scouts across the Near and Middle East. He therefore learned almost immediately of Joscelin's absence and the weakening of Edessa's garrison. Sensing a rare, and probably unexpected, opportunity, Zangi switched targets from Diyar Bakr to the Frankish capital. His war band, already equipped with siege weaponry, reached the city by forced march in late November and immediately initiated a devastating investment. For the next four weeks the Christians within strove to endure incessant bombardment and repeated assaults by armoured towers and teams of sappers, but the defenders' position was all but hopeless.

Learning of the attack, Joscelin II tried to assemble a relief force at Tell Bashir. Melisende responded immediately to his pleas for assistance, sending troops north, but, for reasons that remain unclear, Raymond of Antioch prevaricated. With the count still desperately trying to prepare a counter-strike, the dreadful news of Edessa's fall arrived. On 24 December 1144, Zangi's miners collapsed a huge section of the city's towering fortifications. With Muslim troops flooding through the breach, the Christians fled in terror towards the citadel. Amid the resultant panic hundreds were crushed to death, the Latin archbishop among them, even as the *atabeg*'s soldiers set about their grisly work. One Armenian native of the city wrote that the Muslims 'ruthlessly shed an enormous amount of blood, neither respecting the age of elderly people, nor taking pity on the innocent, lamb-like children'. Those few who reached the inner fortress held out for a further two days, but by 26 December the entire city was in the hands of Islam.

Zangi's conquest of Edessa may have been largely opportunistic, but it was still an unmitigated catastrophe for the Franks. The strategic consequences alone were profoundly alarming. With its principal city lost, the surrounding Latin county stood on the brink of total ruination. Should this most northern of crusader states fall, contact and communication between the Muslim powers in Mesopotamia and Syria would become far more fluid and secure. In this context, the principality of Antioch's future looked bleak indeed: its northern neighbour and ally transformed into an enemy; its rival, Aleppo, resurgent. The danger of a domino effect, in which weakness and vulnerability seeped southwards, bringing the successive collapse of each remaining Latin polity, was only too obvious. The Frankish chronicler William of Tyre reflected upon the 'ominous disaster' of 1144, observing that there was now a real prospect of the Muslim world 'overrunning the entire East unchecked'.*

The psychological impact of this event was perhaps even more significant. Never before had one of Outremer's four great capitals fallen to Islam. Edessa, the first eastern city to be seized by the crusaders, had stood inviolate for almost half a century. Its sudden unheralded loss sent a tremor of fear and apprehension pulsing through the Latin Levant, severely undermining confidence and morale. Any lingering sense of Christian invincibility evaporated; the dream of Outremer – of a permanent, divinely wrought resettlement of the Holy Land – lay shattered. And, to make matters worse, Zangi, so long a looming threat, could be expected to capitalise upon his victory, galvanising Islam to ever greater efforts in the war for dominion of the Near East.

As this dire news filtered back to the West, the renowned Abbot

---

* William of Tyre was born in the Levant in c. 1130 and went on to become chancellor of the Latin kingdom of Jerusalem and archbishop of Tyre. Between around 1174 and 1184 William wrote an invaluable overarching narrative account of Outremer's history from the time of the First Crusade.

Bernard of Clairvaux echoed these dreadful concerns, affirming in a letter that: 'The earth is shaken because the Lord of heaven is losing his land . . . the enemy of the Cross has begun to lift his sacrilegious head there and to devastate with the sword that blessed land, that land of promise.' Bernard warned that sacred Jerusalem, 'the very city of the living God', might itself be overrun. The only answer for the Latin East, indeed for western Christendom as a whole, was to launch a new crusade.[96]

6

CRUSADING REBORN

Edessa's downfall shocked the Levant. In 1145 Frankish and Armenian envoys travelled to Europe to broadcast the calamitous news, and to spell out the threat of annihilation now hanging over all the Christians of the Near East. In response, the Latin world launched a huge military expedition that has been dubbed the Second Crusade.[97] For the first time western kings took up the fight and, in a great upsurge of recruitment, some 60,000 troops marched east to save Outremer. At the same time, the wars of the cross were borne into new theatres of conflict in Iberia and the Baltic. This was a massive and unprecedented explosion of crusade enthusiasm – outstripping even that witnessed after 1095. Could this fervour guarantee success? And how would the rebirth of Christian holy war affect the future history of the crusades?

EARLY TWELFTH-CENTURY CRUSADING

Latin Europe's fervent reaction to the preaching of the Second Crusade can only be understood properly against a backdrop of earlier twelfth-century developments in crusading. The First

Crusaders' 'miraculous' conquest of the Holy Land in 1099 established a fragile Latin outpost in the Levant and seemed to provide conclusive proof that God endorsed this novel fusion of pilgrimage and warfare. Under the circumstances, one might expect the opening decades of the twelfth century to have been marked by a flood of 'crusading' activity, as western Europe rushed to embrace this extension of Christian holy war and to defend Outremer. This was not the case. The memory of the First Crusade certainly burned brightly, but the years leading to 1144 witnessed only a sporadic clutch of small-scale crusades. In part this was because many regarded the First Crusade as a singularly astonishing event that was essentially unrepeatable. Drawing upon centuries of hindsight, later historians identified the mass armed pilgrimage stimulated by Pope Urban II's preaching in 1095 as the first of an ongoing succession of crusades and, thus, as the start of a crusading movement. But this 'future' was by no means apparent in the early twelfth century and the idea of crusading had yet to coalesce.

To some extent, this relative lack of enthusiasm and limited ideological refinement can be explained by mitigating factors. The papacy's ability to harness and develop crusading was curtailed by a succession of crippling upheavals: the onset of a papal schism between 1124 and 1138 that saw the appointment of a number of alternative anti-popes; and the mounting pressure upon Rome from the rival powers of imperial Germany to the north and the emerging Norman kingdom of Sicily to the south. Some of these problems lingered at the time of the Second Crusade, and the pope was not even able to enter Rome in 1145. Similar convulsions afflicted the secular laity. Germany was racked by internal rivalry, with two dynasties, the Hohenstaufen and the Welfs, challenging for power. England, meanwhile, was unhinged by civil war during the tumultuous reign of King Stephen (1135–54), the son of the First Crusader Stephen of Blois. Under the Capetian dynasty, the French monarchy enjoyed greater stability, but only now was beginning to manifest its authority beyond the heartlands of royal territory centred on Paris.

One feature of crusade ideology may also have served to constrain recruitment. Preachers of the First Crusade may have played upon a sense of spiritual or social obligation to repatriate the Holy Land, but at an essential level the 1095 expedition resonated with Latin Christians because it was presented as an intensely personal devotional enterprise. Thousands took the cross seeking redemption of sin through the pursuit of holy war. Crusading was driven by religious devotion, but a self-serving form of devotion. Given the particularly arduous, dangerous, frightening and expensive nature of armed pilgrimages to the East, participation in a crusade represented an extreme path to salvation. For many, more obvious and immediate penitential activities – prayer, alms-giving, localised pilgrimage – were often preferable. The decades and centuries to come would prove that, in general, only seismic catastrophes married to forceful preaching and active involvement of the upper aristocracy could produce large-scale crusades.

This should not lead us to imagine that there were no crusades between 1101 and 1145. Some members of the Church, and of the laity, undoubtedly made sporadic attempts to replicate or imitate the First Crusade in this period, preaching or participating in ventures that included some, or all, of the features that would eventually become more stable elements in the make-up of a crusade: papal promulgation; the taking of a defined vow and the symbol of the cross; the promise of a spiritual reward (or indulgence) in return for military service. But, at the same time, the fundamental nature of crusading remained relatively fluid and ill defined. Basic questions such as who was empowered to invoke a crusade, what rewards could be offered to participants and against whom this form of sanctified warfare might be waged were left largely unresolved.

Two significant crusades to the Holy Land were launched in the 1120s, but while the Venetian crusade (1122–4) was certainly enacted by Pope Calixtus II, the Damascus expedition of 1129 appears to have been preached in Europe by Hugh of Payns with little or no papal involvement. In this same period, crusades were initiated in geographical regions outside the Levant and against enemies other than Near Eastern Muslims. Long established as a theatre of Muslim–Christian conflict, Iberia soon witnessed campaigns akin to crusades. The leader of a joint Catalan and Pisan offensive against the Balearic Islands (1113–15) bore the sign of the cross on his shoulder, while the pope offered a full remission of sins to all those who died in the 1118 Aragonese attack on Zaragoza. Calixtus II, who had been papal legate to Spain and was thus familiar with Iberian affairs, took a major step towards formalising the role of crusading on the peninsula. He issued a papal letter in April 1123 encouraging recruits to take a vow to fight in Catalonia with 'the sign of the cross on their clothes' in return for 'the same remission of sins that we conceded to the defenders of the eastern Church'.

Non-Muslims were likewise targeted. Bohemond of Taranto's crusade (1106–8) was waged against Christian Byzantium. In 1135 Pope Innocent II even sought to extend crusade privileges to those fighting against his political enemies, affirming that his allies would be granted 'the same remission . . . which Pope Urban decreed at the council of Clermont for all who set out for Jerusalem to free the Christians'.

For all these references to the 'remission of sins' awarded to the First Crusaders, the actual formulation of the spiritual rewards being offered remained vague and equivocal. Questions that might trouble theologians and even warriors – Would participation remit all sins or only those confessed? Was martyrdom guaranteed to all those who died on crusade? – had yet to be answered definitively. It was Bernard, abbot of Clairvaux and supporter of the Templars, who dealt with one of the thorniest theological consequences of crusading. With the preaching of the First Crusade, the papacy had, in a sense, unwittingly opened Pandora's Box. The call for a crusading army to manifest God's divine will on earth might suggest that God actually needed man, and therefore could not be truly omnipotent – a train of thought that obviously had explosive potential. Bernard countered this problem with typical intellectual agility. He argued that God only pretended to be in need as an act of charity, deliberately engineering the threat to the Holy Land so that Christians could have another

chance to tap into this new mode of spiritual purification. In one step
the abbot defended the idea of crusading and promoted its devotional
efficacy. Bernard would play a central role in the promulgation of the
Second Crusade, but in the first instance the work of launching the
expedition was undertaken by others.[98]

LAUNCHING THE SECOND CRUSADE

In 1145 the Levantine Christian petitions for European aid targeted
both ecclesiastical and secular leaders. One recipient of the appeals
was Pope Eugenius III, a former Cistercian monk and protégé of
Bernard of Clairvaux, who had just ascended to the papal office that
February. Eugenius' situation was not ideal. From the start of his
pontificate, the new pope was mired in a long-running dispute with
the people of Rome over the secular governance of the city, and he
was forced to live in exile. Even as Eugenius laid plans to launch a
grand new crusade, he was forced to spend most of 1145 in Viterbo,
some fifty miles north of the Lateran Palace.

Emissaries from Outremer also visited Louis VII, the Capetian
monarch of France – one of the heartlands of crusade enthusiasm.
Now in his mid-twenties, Louis had been crowned in 1137, bringing
a lease of youthful vitality to the throne. He has often been described,
rather blandly, as pious. In fact, Louis' early reign had been marked
by heated disputes with Rome over French ecclesiastical
appointments and a caustic squabble with the count of Champagne.
Pope Eugenius' predecessor actually placed Capetian lands under
papal interdict (temporarily excommunicating the entire realm). In
1143, at the height of the conflict with Champagne, Louis' troops took
the brutal step of burning to the ground a church in Vitry containing
more than 1,000 people, an atrocity for which the king seems to have
shown remorse. By 1145 the young king had been reconciled with the
papacy, and his brand of fevered religious devotion possessed a
penitential streak. Moved by the news of Edessa's fate, he embraced

enthusiastically the idea of leading an army to relieve the crusader states.

Eugenius III and Louis VII seem to have laid coordinated plans to initiate a crusade, but to begin with these fell flat. The papal curia (administrative court) drafted an encyclical (general letter of proclamation) announcing a new call to arms on 1 December 1145, but this did not reach Louis in time for his Christmas court at Bourges (in central France). When the monarch declared his intention to take the cross and wage war in the Holy Land, the response was muted. Eugenius III reissued his encyclical, in almost identical form, three months later, and its message was broadcast to much greater effect at a second Capetian assembly in Vézelay at Easter 1146. From that moment the spark of crusading passion was reignited and for the next year or more it burned its way across Europe. The pope's official letter – conventionally known as *Quantum praedecessores* (the Latin words with which it began) – was essential to this process. Widely circulated throughout the Latin West between 1146 and 1147, recited at numerous public assemblies and mass rallies, it became the template for the preaching of the Second Crusade across Europe. The encyclical set out to fulfil two interlocking objectives: to define official papal thinking on the expedition, in particular specifying who, it was hoped, would participate and what privileges and rewards they would receive; and to stimulate recruitment by establishing the crusade's causes and appeal.

Half a century earlier, Pope Urban II had initiated the First Crusade with his sermon at Clermont, but because no exact record of this speech survives, attempts to reconstruct his ideas and intentions involve a degree of speculation. In contrast, while the genesis of the Second Crusade cannot be traced to a single grand address, extant copies of *Quantum praedecessores* do allow us to explore the thinking behind the expedition and the manner in which it was promoted with far greater precision.

One striking fact is immediately apparent from Eugenius' encyclical – the memory of the First Crusade was central to his vision of this new campaign. Seeking both to legitimate and to empower his own call to arms, the Pope made repeated references to the 1095 expedition. Eugenius stated that he was inspired to summon the Second Crusade by the example of 'our predecessor of happy memory, Pope Urban' and made it clear that the spiritual rewards now on offer were exactly the same as 'those instituted by our aforesaid predecessor'. Some of the ideas employed by Urban at Clermont were likewise echoed. Eugenius took care to emphasise repeatedly that he had a divine mandate, 'the authority given us by God', to initiate this holy war. He also depicted the crusade as a just response to Muslim aggression: affirming that Edessa had been 'taken by the enemies of the cross of Christ'; describing how clerics had been killed and saintly relics 'trampled under the infidels' feet'. These events were said to pose a 'great danger [to] all Christianity'.

At the same time, the themes of recollection and past precedent were redeployed in *Quantum praedecessores* in a manner that was both innovative and extraordinarily effective. The Pope declared that Christians should be moved to take the cross by the memory of their forebears who had sacrificed 'their own blood' to liberate Jerusalem 'from the filth of the pagans'. 'Those things acquired by the efforts of your fathers [should be] vigorously defended by you', he exhorted, for, if not, 'the bravery of the fathers will have proved to be diminished in the sons.' This potent imagery harnessed the collective memory of the First Crusade and sought to tap into notions of honour and familial obligation.

While explicitly projecting this new campaign as a recreation of the First Crusade, Eugenius' encyclical actually adjusted or developed many of Urban II's ideas. Enlisting the right type of crusaders (namely, those capable of fighting) in sufficient numbers had been an obvious problem from the start. The 1095 expedition was presented as a form of pilgrimage, but because this penitential practice was traditionally voluntary and open to all, the papacy found it difficult to restrict the number of non-combatant recruits – from women and children to monks and paupers. Crusades in the early twelfth century, meanwhile, had struggled to attract mass recruitment. By the 1140s there was an evident tension between the popular, ecstatic element of crusading and the increasing push towards prescribed definition and papal control. The Church would wrestle with this conundrum for decades to come, seeking to contain and direct enthusiasm without extinguishing fervour. *Quantum praedecessores* made a rather half-hearted attempt to address this issue, counselling that 'those who are on God's side and especially the more powerful and the nobles' should join the crusade, but the difficulty of balancing selectivity and mass appeal remained largely unresolved.

Eugenius also made significant refinements to the array of protections and privileges offered to those taking the cross. His encyclical proclaimed that, in a crusader's absence, the Church would protect 'their wives and children, goods and possessions', while legal suits regarding a crusader's property were banned 'until there is absolute certain knowledge of their return or death'. Likewise, interest on debts owed by a crusader was cancelled.

The area of greatest advance came with regard to the crusade indulgence. Where Urban II's 1095 formulation had lacked clarity, *Quantum praedecessores* provided specificity, affirming that the pope would 'grant remission of and absolution from sins' to participants, explaining that 'whosoever devoutly begins and completes so holy a journey or dies on it will obtain absolution from all his sins of which he has made confession with a contrite and humble heart'. Eugenius was not proposing a blanket guarantee of salvation, but he was delivering an assurance that the spiritual benefit of crusading could still be enjoyed even without death.

Through its precise formulation and broad dissemination, *Quantum praedecessores* shaped the Second Crusade, helping to ensure a greater degree of uniformity in preaching and going some considerable way to cement the notion that a legitimate crusade must be promulgated by the pope. The document is perhaps of even more elemental importance to crusade history because of its afterlife. The medieval papal curia was, by its nature, an institution that treasured retrospection. When wishing to formulate a decision or frame a pronouncement, Roman officials always looked to precedent. In this context, *Quantum praedecessores* became the benchmark for crusading, presenting an official memory of what Pope Urban II had supposedly preached in 1095 and enshrining certain ideas about the nature of the First Crusade itself. Into the second half of the twelfth century and beyond, the encyclical served to define the scope, identity and practice of crusading because future popes used the document as an exemplar. Many drew upon its style, format and substance; some simply reissued it unaltered.

For all this, Eugenius' encyclical was surprisingly unclear on one key issue: the precise goal of the Second Crusade. Edessa's fate was highlighted, but no explicit demand was made that the city be recaptured, and Zangi was not named as an enemy. Instead, the crusaders were exhorted 'to defend . . . the eastern Church' and free 'the many thousands of our captive brothers' currently in Muslim hands. This lack of specificity was probably the result of uncertainty about a strategically realistic goal in 1145 and 1146, but it exposed the expedition to future disputes over direction and focus.[99]

This shortcoming in *Quantum praedecessores'* formulation also was reflective of a more profound problem in the relationship between crusading and the crusader states. The two were, in fact, tragically ill matched. Crusades were essentially spiritually self-serving, devotional expeditions of finite duration, led by individuals with their own ambitions, agendas or aims (not least to complete a pilgrimage to the Holy Places). But to survive, the Frankish settlements in the East actually needed stable, obedient military reinforcements, willing to carry out the will of Outremer's rulers.

A SAINT SPEAKS – BERNARD OF CLAIRVAUX AND THE SECOND CRUSADE

Pope Eugenius III's encyclical *Quantum praedecessores* proclaimed the Second Crusade. The text of this letter, deliberately designed as a preaching tool that could be readily translated from Latin into the common vernacular tongues of the medieval West, stood at the core of the crusade message disseminated in 1146 and 1147. Yet, unable even to control central Italy, the pope was in no real position to launch an extended preaching campaign north of the Alps. He therefore turned to Bernard, abbot of Clairvaux.

Bernard was the most potent and influential preacher of the Second Crusade. Above all other churchmen, he must be credited for disseminating and popularising the message contained in *Quantum praedecessores*. Born in Burgundy around 1090, at the age of twenty-three he joined a community of Benedictine monks recently formed at Cîteaux and enjoyed a mercurial rise to prominence. After just two years he was instructed to establish a new Cistercian monastery (that is, one following the principles established at Cîteaux) at Clairvaux and his fame soon spread across the Latin West. Renowned as an orator and avid correspondent, exchanging frequent letters with many of the great political and ecclesiastical figures of his age, Bernard emerged as one of the most illustrious figures of the twelfth century.

The abbot's influence grew in tandem with that of the Cistercian order to which he belonged. Founded in 1098, this new monastic movement swept through Europe, advocating a fundamentalist interpretation of the Benedictine rule – the regulations governing monastic life – that ushered in a new atmosphere of austerity and simplicity. The Cistercians experienced exponential growth: from two houses in 1113 to 353 by 1151. By the mid-twelfth century, Cîteaux could challenge, even outshine, the influence of more established forms of monasticism, like that of Cluny. This shift was starkly apparent in the origins of individual popes, for while Urban II came from a Cluniac background, Eugenius III had been monk at Clairvaux before his election to the papal office.[100]

Bernard first preached the crusade during a grand Easter week assembly at Vézelay in 1146. The location of this gathering, jointly planned by the papacy and the French monarchy for the expedition's relaunch, was no accident. Nestled in the Burgundian heartlands of Cluniac and Cistercian monasticism, Vézelay was perfectly placed to host a recruitment rally. Already closely associated with the practice of pilgrimage as one of the starting points for the journey to Santiago de Compostela, it was also home to a magnificent abbey church, dedicated to Mary Magdalene.

The scale of the meeting held at Vézelay was unprecedented. While the 1095 council of Clermont had been a largely ecclesiastical affair, in 1146 the flower of north-western Europe's nobility came together. King Louis VII was joined by his beautiful, headstrong young wife, Eleanor, heiress to the immensely powerful duchy of Aquitaine. They had wed in 1137, when she was fifteen and Louis was about to ascend the throne (aged seventeen), but the initial warmth of their marriage waned somewhat as the king's piety deepened. Possessed of a marked lust for life, Eleanor was to accompany Louis on crusade, although the later legend that she rode at the head of an army of Amazons was apocryphal.

The king's brother, Robert, count of Dreux, likewise was present at Vézelay, as were a host of other Frankish potentates, many of whom had historic links to crusading. These included Count Thierry of Flanders, who probably had already made a pilgrimage to Jerusalem in the late 1130s, and Count Alphonse-Jordan of Toulouse, son to the crusade leader Raymond and kinsman of Tripoli's Latin rulers. The crowds of nobles were joined by so large a throng that the assembly had to be held outside the confines of the abbey church. From the vantage point of a hastily constructed wooden platform, Louis and Bernard delivered rousing, impassioned speeches on Easter Sunday. The French king's clothing was already emblazoned with a cross specially sent to him by the pope, and a witness recalled that, when the abbot finished his stirring oration: 'Everyone around began shouting for crosses. When [Bernard] had given out, we might even say had sown, the bundle of crosses which he had prepared, he was forced to tear up his clothes and sow them.' The clamour was apparently so great that the wooden dais collapsed, although luckily no one was injured (this in itself was interpreted as a sign of divine favour).

Vézelay was an enormous success, promoting an infectious sense of enthusiasm and excitement, but even so, for the crusade to reach its full potential the call to arms needed to be broadcast to an even wider audience. With this in mind, Bernard enacted a range of measures. Additional preachers were deputised to spread the word elsewhere in France, while scores of letters extolling the virtues of the crusade were dispatched to other regions, including England, northern Italy and Brittany. In these missives the abbot almost adopted the language of a salesman to promote the crusade. In one the expedition was characterised as a unique opportunity to overcome sin: 'This age is like no other that has gone before; a new abundance of divine mercy comes down from heaven; blessed are those who are alive in this year pleasing to the Lord, this year of remission . . . I tell you, the Lord has not done this for any generation before.' Another letter encouraged Christians 'not to let the chance pass you by' to fight for God and thereby earn as 'wages, the remission of their sins and everlasting glory'.[101]

Meanwhile, despite being in his mid-fifties and physically frail, Bernard himself embarked on an extended tour of north-eastern France, Flanders and Germany, sparking waves of recruitment wherever he went. In November 1146 the abbot met Conrad III, king of Germany, arguably the most powerful secular ruler in all Latin Christendom. Around fifty years old, he had not yet been crowned by the pope and was thus unable to claim the title of emperor enjoyed by his predecessors, but it seemed only a matter of time before this honour would be conferred. During the First Crusade, Rome and Germany had been embroiled in an acrimonious dispute that checked any hopes of direct imperial involvement in the expedition. But in the mid-twelfth century relations between the two powers were considerably improved. Conrad had shown himself to be a true and valued papal ally, not least against Norman Sicilian aggression in Italy; he had also demonstrated an affinity for the Holy Land, probably visiting the Levant in the 1120s. Nonetheless, Conrad was initially reluctant to take the cross, only too conscious that, in his absence, political rivals such as Welf, duke of Bavaria, might move to seize power. At their first meeting in Frankfurt, the king thus demurred when Bernard suggested that he enlist.

The abbot responded by throwing himself into a vigorous winter preaching campaign, delivering sermons at the likes of Freiburg, Zürich and Basel. His journey was said to have been accompanied by a multitude of miracles – more than two hundred cripples were apparently healed, demons cast out and one individual even raised from the dead. And, although Bernard could not speak German, and had to orate with the aid of an interpreter, his words were still capable of bringing 'floods of tears' to his audience. Through November and December, hundreds, if not thousands, committed to the cause. It surely was not coincidental that this journey took the abbot into southern German territory neighbouring Welf of Bavaria's domain, nor that it culminated in Duke Welf's own enrolment in the crusade.

Buoyed by this achievement, Bernard rejoined Conrad at Speyer on 24 December. In the course of that Christmas the abbot delivered a public sermon and then, on 27 December, was granted a private audience with the king. The following day, Conrad finally took the cross. Scholars continue to dispute the degree of influence exerted by Bernard at this critical moment, some arguing that he effectively goaded the king into joining against his will, others that Conrad's decision had long been premeditated. Certainly, contemporaries described how the abbot mixed his 'customary gentleness' with dire warnings of an imminent apocalypse to win over the king, but it was probably Welf of Bavaria's recruitment that proved decisive.

Notwithstanding this debate, Bernard of Clairvaux must still be regarded as the primary force behind the preaching of the Second Crusade. The abbot himself remarked that, through his efforts, the Latin armies had been 'multiplied beyond number', and that there was barely one man to every seven women left in the settlements through which he passed. There were, nonetheless, other individuals and influences at work in this period. The notions of memory and familial heritage emphasised in *Quantum praedecessores* evidently had a marked impact on recruitment. Louis VII had a bloodline connection to the First Crusade – his great-uncle, Hugh of Vermandois, had participated in the expedition. Analysis of others known to have joined the Second Crusade reveals that many had a similar crusading pedigree.[102]

Because of the nature of medieval textual evidence – which usually took the form of documents written by churchmen – the dominant surviving image of crusading tends to be innately coloured by an ecclesiastical perspective. By and large, scholars wishing to reconstruct the history of this age, of necessity rely upon material written by clerics and monks. And these sources are subject to obvious vagaries of bias and omission. But crusades involved the Church and the laity, so how can the secular outlook of knights and soldiers be gauged? One rewarding avenue is the study of popular songs sung in the vernacular rather than Latin. Such songs almost certainly played a role in bolstering recruitment and morale from the very start of the crusading era, but the first actual lyrics to survive date from the 1140s. One was the Old French song 'Knights, much is promised', recited by court singers, or troubadours, in the months following the Vézelay assembly. Its chorus and first verse ran:

> Who goes along with King Louis
> Will never be afraid of Hell,
> His soul will go to paradise,
> Where angels of the Lord do dwell.
>
> Edessa is taken, as you know,
> And Christians troubled sore and long.
> The churches there are empty now,
> And masses are no longer sung.
> O knights, you should consider this,

You who in arms are so renowned,
And then present your bodies to
One who for you with thorns was crowned.

This rare glimpse of the lay celebration and promotion of crusading chimes with some of the messages inherent in clerical preaching: the promise of spiritual rewards; the suffering of eastern Christendom; fighting in the service and imitation of Christ. But the language was more direct and the nuances differ. Louis VII was identified as the central leader, with no mention made of the pope. The complexities of the indulgence were replaced by a straightforward guarantee of a place in 'paradise'. And, in a later verse, Zangi was named as the endeavour's chief enemy. Even as the Church deployed *Quantum praedecessores* and Abbot Bernard broadcast the call to arms, the laity clearly had the capacity to shape their own vision of the Second Crusade.[103]

EXPANDING THE IDEAL

The loss of Edessa sparked the Second Crusade and, in 1147, the major armies under Louis VII of France and Conrad III of Germany set out to fight in the Levant. But the scope of crusading activity in the late 1140s was not limited to the Near East, for in this period Latin troops engaged in similar holy wars in Iberia and the Baltic. To some it seemed as if the entire West had taken up arms in a pan-European crusade. Pope Eugenius III himself wrote in April 1147 that 'so great a multitude of the faithful from diverse regions is preparing to fight the infidel ... that almost the whole of Christendom is being summoned for so great a task'. Two decades later, the Latin chronicler Helmold of Bosau (in the northern Baltic coast region of Germany) appeared to reinforce this view, writing that 'to the initiators of the expedition it seemed that one part of the army should be sent to the [Holy Land], another to Spain and a third against the Slavs who live next to us'. Some contemporaries thus presented the Second Crusade as a single grand enterprise, shaped and directed by its visionary 'initiators', Eugenius and the abbot of Clairvaux. In recent decades, modern historians have drawn upon this notion to suggest that the extraordinary range of crusading endeavour between 1147 and 1149 resulted from conscious, proactive planning on the part of the Roman Church. In this rendering of events the papacy had the power to shape and define crusading and it was the sheer elemental force of the Second Crusade's preaching – the tailored sophistication of *Quantum praedecessores'* message and Bernard's power to inspire – that prompted the unparalleled extension of crusading activity into new theatres after 1146.

The fighting in Iberia and the Baltic may not have had immediate bearing upon the war for the Holy Land, beyond some redirection of manpower and resources. But the consequences of this interpretation of the Second Crusade are far-reaching and fundamental, because they affect the future scale and nature of Christian holy war. Two questions are imperative. Did the Roman Church really take the vital initiative to expand crusading as part of a premeditated design, or was this development more accidental? And, by extension, was the pope actually in control of the crusading movement by the mid-twelfth century?

The notion that wars waged outside the Levant might be sanctified certainly was not unprecedented and, between 1147 and 1149, other conflict zones were undoubtedly drawn into the ambit of the Second Crusade. Through summer 1147, Saxon and Danish Christians fought as crusaders against their pagan neighbours, known as the Wends, in the Baltic region of north-eastern Europe. The impact of the Second Crusade was even more powerfully felt in Iberia. A fleet of some two hundred vessels, carrying crusaders from England, Flanders and the Rhineland, set sail for the Levant from Dartmouth in May 1147. These ships stopped en route in Portugal, and there assisted its Christian King Afonso Henriques in conquering Muslim-held Lisbon on 24 October. King Alfonso VII of León-Castile championed another Christian offensive, with Genoese aid, which enjoyed crusading status. This culminated in the capture of Almería, in far south-eastern Spain, in October 1147 and of Tortosa, in the north-east, in December 1148.

Christian troops were fighting under the crusading banner on multiple fronts in the late 1140s, but the idea that these disparate strands were woven into a single enterprise as part of an overarching, studied plan is faulty. When the events are scrutinised closely it becomes clear that chance and unstructured organic development were at work. The Baltic arm of the Second Crusade was actually the result of the Church superimposing the notion of crusading on top of a pre-existing conflict. At the Frankfurt assembly in March 1147, a Saxon delegation indicated to Bernard of Clairvaux that they were deeply reluctant to go to the Holy Land. Instead, these warriors were intent upon fighting closer to home against their pagan Wendish neighbours. The abbot realised that the Saxons could not be persuaded to participate in the main Near Eastern expedition, but Bernard was still keen to extend the papacy's power and influence over eastern European events. He therefore drew the Baltic campaign into the crusading sphere, promising its participants 'the same spiritual privileges as those who set out for Jerusalem', and in April 1147 Pope Eugenius issued an encyclical confirming this grant.

The Iberian elements of the Second Crusade also need to be re-evaluated. The crusading contribution of the capture of Lisbon was almost certainly the result of an unplanned decision to stop to fight in Portugal. The campaigns against Almería and Tortosa seem to have been appropriated to the crusading cause. Catalan, southern French and Genoese participants did apparently regard themselves as being engaged in a holy war with some parallels to the First Crusade. But no precise evidence exists of papal involvement in the planning or instigation of these wars and, in all probability, they were conceived and driven by Christian Iberia's secular rulers. The papal endorsement of these endeavours, which came in April 1148, was almost an afterthought, designed to bring Spain under the crusading umbrella.

Modern scholarship has too readily accepted the idea of the Second Crusade as an expression of the papacy's ability to expand and direct the crusading movement. In fact, the events of the late 1140s suggest that Eugenius, Bernard and the papal curia were still struggling to harness and control this form of sanctified warfare, even as they sought to assert the primacy of Rome within Latin Christendom.[104]

THE WORK OF KINGS

The inception of the Second Crusade was especially remarkable in one additional respect. Up to this point, crusading expeditions had been led in the field by prominent noblemen – counts, dukes and princes – drawn from the upper echelons of Latin society, but no western monarch had taken the cross.* The decision of King Louis VII of France and King Conrad III of Germany to answer *Quantum praedecessores'* call to arms thus set an important precedent, adding an enduring new dimension to crusading. The immediate consequences were marked. Recruitment was buoyed, partly through the power of royal endorsement and example and also because the hierarchical nature of medieval society prompted a chain reaction of enlistment. Crown involvement also enhanced the material resources deployed in the name of the cross, at least to some extent. A recent spate of failed western European harvests meant that even men of Louis' and Conrad's stature struggled to meet the full financial demands of so long and committed a campaign. Neither seems to have been able to impose general taxes within their

---

* Sigurd of Norway, who campaigned in the Levant in 1110, was a king, but he shared the Norwegian throne with two of his brothers.

respective realms, and turned instead to levying money from towns and churches, but this proved to be only partially successful and, within weeks of his departure, the French monarch was short of cash.

Royal participation came at a considerable price. In the past, most crusaders had sought to arrange their affairs before departure, but the manifold complexities involved in a king all but abandoning his realm for months, even years, had the potential to greatly extend the range and duration of these preparations. In 1147 regents were appointed to protect the throne and oversee day-to-day government, from law and order to the economy: in France, Abbot Suger of St Denis, a long-term Capetian ally and Louis' childhood tutor, was chosen; in Germany, Conrad's ten-year-old son, Henry, was designated as heir and the kingdom entrusted to a leading churchman, Abbot Wibald of Corvey and Stavelot.

The fractious nature of medieval European politics also meant that crown involvement in the crusade deepened and extended the potential for damaging antagonism between contingents. Northern–southern French tension alone had come close to stalling the First Crusade. While an ingrained sense of national identity had yet to take hold in either realm, in 1147 troops from France and Germany did travel to the Holy Land in separate hosts headed by their respective monarchs. Long-standing international rivalry and suspicion might easily have undermined the expedition. To begin with, at least, the two powers displayed reassuring signs of cooperation, coordination and communication. Louis met with Conrad's representatives to discuss preparations, in the presence of Bernard of Clairvaux, at a meeting at Châlons-sur-Marne on 2 February 1147. The French and Germans then held further separate planning assemblies at Étampes and Frankfurt.

The presence of these two kings on crusade likewise threatened to disrupt the delicate diplomatic equilibrium that held sway in mid-twelfth-century Latin Christendom. This issue was of greatest concern in relation to Roger II of Sicily, head of a formidable southern Italian Norman kingdom that was fast becoming one of the Mediterranean's great powers. In the 1140s the papacy and Byzantium were directly threatened by Roger's expansionist policies and therefore looked to their mutual ally, Germany, to counter Sicilian aggression. Conrad's decision to join the crusade threatened to disrupt this web of interdependence, exposing Rome and Constantinople to attack. Matters were complicated further by Louis VII's relatively amiable relations with King Roger, a fact which unsettled Eugenius III and made the Greeks wary of a Sicilian–French invasion plot. Manuel Comnenus – who had now assumed control of Byzantium – sent envoys to Louis VII and Conrad III in an attempt to pave the way for peaceful collaboration with the crusade, but doubts remained in the emperor's mind and the pope too was probably reluctant to see Conrad leave Europe.

Royal diplomacy also had a practical impact upon the route taken by the expedition. Given the state of western naval technology in the 1140s, transporting the entire crusade to the Levant by ship may have been impractical. Nonetheless, Roger II offered to carry French troops eastwards, but in the end this was refused because of the tension between Sicily and Byzantium. As with the First Crusade, the vast bulk of the 1147 expedition set out to follow the land route to the Near East, past Constantinople and across Asia Minor. This was to have grave consequences.

One further question remained: how would two of Latin Christendom's most powerful leaders interact with the rulers of the crusader states? Would Louis and Conrad allow themselves to be directed by a prince of Antioch, a count of Edessa, or even a king of Jerusalem? Or would the French and German monarchs pursue their own independent, and potentially conflicting, ambitions and agendas?

Notable as they were, the immediate to short-term effects of Louis' and Conrad's involvement in the 1146 to 1149 expedition paled in comparison to the wider historical significance of the union between crusading and medieval kingship. Both would be transformed by this intimate, often unsettling relationship over the decades and centuries to come. Outremer and western Christendom came to expect Europe's sovereigns to champion the crusading cause, but future expeditions involving Latin monarchs were subject to the same possibilities and problems – afforded wealth, resources and manpower; yet hamstrung by disunity and hampered by a lack of shared goals. Crusades involving kings proved to be ponderous, even unreactive to the needs of the Near East, and were always capable of destabilising European politics. At the same time, the ideal of holy war began to influence the practice of kingship across the Latin West. Commitment to the crusading cause became an essential duty for Christian rulers, a pious obligation that served to confirm their martial qualities, but one that also had to be managed alongside the business of government.[105]

ON THE ROAD TO THE HOLY LAND

Now enjoying a greater degree of security in Rome, Pope Eugenius III came to Paris at Easter 1147 to oversee the final preparations for the Second Crusade. That April a group of around one hundred Templar knights also joined the French crusading army. On 11 June 1147 the pope, alongside his mentor Abbot Bernard, presided over a heavily stage-managed public ceremony, held at the grand royal Church of St Denis, a few miles north of Paris, at which Louis made a dramatic, ritualised departure for the Holy Land. This gathering encapsulated the new royal dimension of crusading, but also provides an authentic insight into the young king's own burgeoning sense of personal piety. En route to the meeting at St Denis, Louis decided that he had to make an 'impromptu' two-hour tour of the local leper colony as a demonstration of his subservience to God, leaving both his glamorous wife, Eleanor of Aquitaine, and the pope literally waiting at the altar. The queen was said to have been 'almost fainting from emotion and the heat'.

When Louis finally arrived at St Denis, hushed crowds of nobles, packed into the aisles, watched in awe as 'he humbly prostrated himself on the ground and adored his patron saint, Denis'. The pope presented the king with his pilgrim staff and scrip (satchel), and Louis then raised the ancient *Oriflame*, believed to have been Charlemagne's battle-standard, the very symbol of French monarchy. In one moment, this impassioned performance sent out a succession of powerful interlocking messages: crusading was a genuine act of Christian devotion; Louis was a truly regal king; and the Roman Church stood at the centre of the crusading movement.[106]

The main armies of the Second Crusade began their journeys to the Levant in early summer 1147. Their intention was to recreate the glories of the First Crusade, travelling east overland through Byzantium and Asia Minor. After the ceremony at St Denis, Louis led the French from Metz; having assembled his German forces at Regensburg, Conrad III had set out in May. These staggered departures appear to have been purposefully coordinated, perhaps as a result of plans laid at Châlons-sur-Marne, the aim being to allow both contingents to follow the same route to Constantinople – through Germany and Hungary – without exhausting local resources. But despite this early promise of cooperation, and all the carefully nurtured dreams of reliving past exploits and achievements, the attempt to reach the Holy Land proved to be an almost unmitigated disaster.

In large part this was due to a failure to collaborate effectively with the Byzantine Empire. Half a century earlier, Alexius I Comnenus had helped to trigger the First Crusade and then succeeded in harnessing its strength to reconquer western Asia Minor. In 1147, the position and perspective of his grandson, Emperor Manuel, differed considerably. Manuel had had no interest in summoning this new Latin expedition and actually stood to lose power and influence now that it was in motion. In the West, Conrad III's absence freed Roger of Sicily to attack Greek territory, and the prospect of two vast Frankish armies marching through the empire, and past

Constantinople itself, filled Manuel with dread. To the east, meanwhile, the new crusade looked set to revitalise Outremer, stemming the recent resurgence of Byzantine authority in northern Syria; a concern that was only exacerbated by King Louis VII's familial connections to Prince Raymond of Antioch. For Manuel, the Second Crusade was a worrisome threat. As the Frankish armies approached the empire the emperor's concerns deepened to such an extent that he decided to secure his eastern frontier by agreeing a temporary truce with Ma'sud, the Seljuq sultan of Anatolia. To the Greeks this was a logical step that allowed Manuel to focus upon the thousands of Latin troops nearing his western borders. But, when they learned of the deal, many crusaders saw it as an act of treachery.

Problems began almost as soon as the Franks crossed the Danube and entered the empire. Conrad's large, unwieldy army conducted an ill-disciplined march south-east through Philippopolis and Adrianople, punctuated by outbreaks of looting and skirmishing with Greek troops. Desperate to safeguard his capital, Manuel hurriedly ushered the Germans across the Bosphorus. Initially, the smaller French contingent's advance progressed more peacefully, but, once camped outside Constantinople, the Franks became increasingly belligerent. News of Manuel's pact with Ma'sud was greeted with horror, derision and deep-seated mistrust. Godfrey, bishop of Langres, one of the crusade's leading churchmen, even sought to incite a direct attack on Constantinople, a scheme which King Louis rejected. The emperor did supply the crusaders with guides, but even they seem to have rendered only limited assistance.

Lacking the full support of Byzantium, the Latins needed, above all, to unite their own forces against Islam once in Asia Minor. Unfortunately, coordination between the French and German contingents broke down in autumn 1147. Conrad unwisely elected to forge ahead without Louis in late October, marching out from his staging post at Nicaea into an arid, inhospitable landscape that was controlled only loosely by the Greeks. The plan was, once again, to follow a similar route to that taken by the First Crusaders, but the

Seljuqs of Anatolia were better prepared than they had been in 1097. The German column, unaccustomed to Muslim battle tactics, soon fell foul of repeated harrying attacks from elusive, fast-moving bands of Turkish horsemen. Limping their way eastwards past Dorylaeum, with losses mounting and supplies dwindling, the crusaders finally decided to turn back. By the time they had retraced their steps to Nicaea in early November, thousands had perished and even King Conrad had been wounded. Morale was shattered. Many of the bedraggled survivors cut their losses and set out on the return journey to Germany.

Chastened, Conrad joined forces with the French, who by now had crossed the Bosphorus, to attempt a second advance. They successfully traced a different route south towards the ancient Roman metropolis of Ephesus, where the onset of illness forced the German king to remain behind. In late December, with rain and snow falling, Louis left the coast, leading his army along the Meander valley towards the Anatolian uplands. At first, military discipline held and early waves of Seljuq attacks were repulsed, but around 6 January 1148 the crusaders lost formation while trying to cross the imposing physical obstacle of Mount Cadmus and suffered a searing Turkish assault. Losses were heavy and Louis himself was surrounded, narrowly avoiding capture by taking refuge in a tree. Shaken by the experience, the king now asked the force of Templar knights that had joined his army back in France to lead the survivors in a tightly controlled march south-east to the Greek-held port of Adalia – a decision illustrative both of the crusaders' dire predicament and of the martial reputation already accrued by the Templar Order. Louis later sent a letter to the abbot of St Denis recalling these grim days: 'There were constant ambushes from bandits, grave difficulties of travel, daily battles with the Turks . . . We ourselves were frequently in peril of our life; but thanks to God's grace were freed from all these horrors and escaped.' Exhausted and hungry, the French reached the coast around 20 January. Some thought was given to marching onwards, but eventually Louis decided to sail to Syria with a portion of his army. Those left behind were promised Byzantine support, but most died from starvation or were killed during Turkish attacks. The French king reached Antioch in March 1148. Meanwhile, having recuperated in Constantinople, Conrad likewise decided to complete his journey east by sea and sailed to Acre.

The Second Crusaders who took the land route to the Near East, proudly hoping to emulate the 'heroism' of their forebears, had been crushed; thousands were lost to combat, starvation and desertion. The expedition had been broken even before it reached the Holy Land. Many blamed the Greeks for this terrible reversal, levelling accusations of treachery and betrayal. But, although Manuel had indeed offered Louis and Conrad only limited support, it was the Latins' own incaution in the face of heightened Turkish aggression that precipitated disaster. With both the Germans and French so roundly and ignominiously defeated, William of Tyre concluded that the crusaders' once 'glorious reputation [for] valour' now lay in tatters. 'Henceforward', he wrote, 'it was but a joke in the eyes of those unclean peoples to whom it had once been a terror.' Louis and Conrad had finally reached the Levant; the question now was whether their greatly weakened forces could hope to achieve anything of substance and rekindle the crusading flame.[107]

II

THE RESPONSE
OF ISLAM

7

MUSLIM REVIVAL

The half-century since the advent of the First Crusade had seen little sign of a united or determined Islamic response to the Christian conquest of the Holy Land. Jerusalem – the most sacred city in the Muslim world after Mecca and Medina – remained in Latin hands. And the elemental division between Sunni Iraq and Syria and Shi'ite Egypt endured. Barring occasional Muslim victories, most notably at the Field of Blood in 1119, the early twelfth century had been dominated by Frankish expansion and aggression. But in the 1140s it seemed as if the tide might be shifting, as Zangi, the *atabeg* of Mosul and Aleppo, and his family (the Zangid dynasty) took up the torch of *jihad*.

ZANGI – THE CHAMPION OF ISLAM

Zangi's capture of Edessa in 1144 was a triumph for Islam: what one Muslim chronicle described as 'the victory of victories'. When his troops stormed the city on 24 December, the *atabeg* initially allowed them to pillage and slaughter at will. But after this first wave of violence, he enforced an approach that was, at least by his standards, relatively temperate. The Franks suffered – every man was butchered and all women taken into slavery – but the surviving eastern Christians were spared and permitted to remain in their homes. Likewise, Latin churches were destroyed, but their Armenian and Syriac counterparts left untouched. Similar care was taken to limit the amount of damage inflicted upon Edessa's fortifications, and a rebuilding programme was undertaken immediately to repair weakened sections of the walls. Realising the strategic significance of his new acquisition, Zangi wished the city to remain habitable and defendable.

With Edessa in his possession, the *atabeg* could hope to unite a vast swathe of Syrian and Mesopotamian territory, stretching from Aleppo to Mosul. And for the Muslim world of the Near and Middle East, his startling achievement seemed to promise the dawn of a new era, one in which the Franks might be driven from the Levant. There can be no doubt that 1144 marked a turning point for Islam in the war for the Holy Land. Equally, it is clear that Zangi made energetic efforts to publicise his success as a blow struck by a zealous *mujahid* in the name of all Muslims.

Within Islamic culture, Arabic poetry had a long-established role in both influencing and reflecting public opinion. Muslim poets commonly composed works for public recitation, sometimes before massed crowds, mixing reportage and propaganda to comment upon current events. Poets who joined Zangi's court, some of them Syrian refugees from Latin rule, authored works celebrating the *atabeg*'s achievements, casting him as the champion of a wider *jihadi* movement. Ibn al-Qaysarani (from Caesarea) stressed the need for Zangi to reconquer the whole of the Syrian coastline (the *Sahil*), arguing that this should be the holy war's primary aim. 'Tell the infidel rulers to surrender . . . all their territories', he wrote, 'for it is [Zangi's] country.' At the same time, this notion of pan-Levantine conquest was twinned with a more precise objective, one that possessed an immediate devotional focus – Jerusalem. Edessa lay hundreds of miles north of Palestine, but its capture was nonetheless presented as the first step on the path to the Holy City's recovery. 'If the conquest of Edessa is the high sea', Ibn al-Qaysarani affirmed, 'Jerusalem and the *Sahil* are its shore.'

Many Muslim contemporaries appear to have accepted this projection of the *atabeg* as a *jihadi* warrior. The Abbasid caliph in Baghdad now conferred upon him the grand titles 'Auxiliary of the Commander of the Faithful, the Divinely Aided King'. Given that the Zangids were still, to an extent, outsiders – upstart Turkish warlords, with no innate right to rule over the established Arab and Persian hierarchies of the East – this caliphal endorsement helped to legitimate Zangi's position. The idea that the *atabeg*'s career had somehow been building to this single achievement also gained currency. Even a chronicler based in rival Damascus declared that 'Zangi had always coveted Edessa and watched for a chance to achieve his ambition. Edessa was never out of his thoughts or far from his mind.' On the basis of his 1144 victory, later Islamic chroniclers labelled him a *shahid*, or martyr, an honour reserved for those who died 'in the path of God' engaging in the *jihad*.

This is not to suggest that Zangi recognised the political value of espousing the principles of holy war only after his sudden success at Edessa. An inscription dated to 1138, from a Damascene *madrasa* (religious school) patronised by the *atabeg*, already described him as 'the fighter of *jihad*, the defender of the frontier, the tamer of the polytheists and the destroyer of heretics', and the same titles were again used four years later in an Aleppan inscription. The events of 1144 allowed Zangi to emphasise and expand upon this facet of his career, but even then *jihad* against the Franks remained as one issue among many. Within his own lifetime, the *atabeg* sought, first and foremost, to present himself as a ruler of all Islam; an aspiration highlighted by his decision to employ an array of honorific titles tailored to the differing needs (and distinct tongues) of Mesopotamia, Syria and Diyar Bakr. In Arabic he was often styled as *Imad al-Din Zangi* ('Zangi, the pillar of religion'), but in Persian he might present himself as 'the guardian of the world' or 'the great king of Iran', and in nomadic Turkish as 'the falcon prince'.[1]

There is precious little evidence to suggest that Zangi prioritised *jihad* above all other concerns before, or even after, 1144. He did take steps to consolidate his hold over the county of Edessa in early 1145, seizing the town of Saruj from the Franks and defeating a Latin relief force that had assembled at Antioch. But before long, he was to be found once again fighting fellow Muslims in Iraq. By early 1146 it was whispered that Zangi was preparing for a new Syrian offensive. Construction of siege weaponry began and, while officially these were for the *jihad*, an Aleppan chronicler admitted that 'some people thought that he was intending to attack Damascus'.

Zangi was now sixty-two and still in remarkably rude health. But on the night of 14 September 1146, during the siege of the Muslim fortress of Qalat Ja'bar (on the banks of the Euphrates), he suffered a sudden and unexpected assault. The details of the terrible attack are murky. Zangi was said to have retained numerous watchful sentries to guard against assassination, but somehow they were bypassed, and the *atabeg* was set upon in his own bed. The assailant was later cast variously as a trusted eunuch, slave or soldier and, not surprisingly, rumours also circulated that the bloody deed had been instigated by Damascus. The truth will probably never be known. An attendant who found Zangi grievously wounded recounted the scene:

> I went to him, while he was still alive. When he saw me, he thought that I was intending to kill him. He gestured to me with his index finger, appealing to me. I halted in awe of him and said, 'My lord, who has done this to you?' He was, however, unable to speak and died at that moment (God have mercy on him).[2]

For all his feral vitality and enduring ambition, the *atabeg*'s tumultuous career had been cut short. Zangi, lord of Mosul and Aleppo, conqueror of Edessa, lay dead.

The advent of Nur al-Din

Zangi's demise was a squalid, brutal and ignominious affair. Amid the shock of the moment, even his relatives gave little thought to honouring the deceased; the *atabeg*'s corpse was buried without ceremony and 'his stores of money and rich treasures were plundered'. Attention turned instead to the issues of power and succession.

Zangi's heirs moved swiftly: his eldest son, Saif al-Din, seized Mosul – affirmation that Mesopotamia was still seen as the true cradle of Sunni Islam; the *atabeg*'s younger son, Nur al-Din Mahmud, meanwhile, travelled west to assume control of his father's Syrian lands. This division of Zangid territory had notable consequences. Without direct interests in Iraq, Nur al-Din, the new emir of Aleppo, would be focused upon Levantine affairs, and thus perhaps better placed to pursue the *jihad*. At the same time, however, without access to the Fertile Crescent's wealth and resources, the strength of his Syrian realm might wane.

Nur al-Din came to power aged around twenty-eight. He was said to have been 'a tall, swarthy man with a beard but no moustache, a fine forehead and a pleasant appearance enhanced by beautiful, melting eyes'. In time he would attain power to eclipse even that held by his father, emerging as Latin Christendom's most feared and respected Muslim adversary in the Near East – a ruler who nurtured and re-energised the cause of Islamic holy war. Even William of Tyre was later moved to describe him as 'a wise and prudent man and, according to the superstitious traditions of his people, one who feared God'. But in 1146, the emir's position was precarious and the task set before him all but insurmountable.[3]

In the wake of Zangi's assassination, Syria was thrown into disarray. The brutal effectiveness of the *atabeg*'s despotism now became apparent as lawlessness broke out across large swathes of the Muslim Levant. Even a Damascene contemporary acknowledged that 'all the towns were in confusion, the roads became unsafe, after enjoying a grateful period of security'. With Nur al-Din's right and ability to rule as yet unproven, a number of Zangi's loyal lieutenants realigned their interests. Under pressure from Unur, the de facto ruler of Damascus, the Kurdish warlord Ayyub ibn Shadi surrendered Baalbek and moved to the southern Syrian capital. Nur al-Din retained the support of Aleppo's Zangid governor, Sawar, and the backing of Ayyub's brother, Shirkuh, but on balance the young emir's prospects for success, or even survival, were slim.

As emir of Aleppo, Nur al-Din found himself in control of one of the great cities of the Near East. Already in the twelfth century Aleppo had an almost unimaginably ancient history – the site of human settlement for at least seven thousand years. In physical terms, the metropolis governed by Nur al-Din from 1146 was dominated by an impressive walled citadel, rising out of the heart of the city, atop a steep-sided, 200-foot-high natural hill. One near-contemporary visitor noted that this 'fortress is renowned for its impregnability and, from far distance seen for its great height, is without like or match among castles' – even today it dominates the modern city. Aleppo's Great Mosque, a short distance to the west, was founded around 715 under the Umayyads, to which the Seljuqs had added a striking square minaret in the late eleventh century. The city was also a renowned commercial hub, home to a network of covered *souqs* (markets). Aleppo may not have been Syria's first city in the twelfth century, but it was a centre of political, military and economic power – as such it offered Nur al-Din a vital platform upon which to build his career.[4]

In 1146, amidst the chaotic vacuum of power that followed Zangi's murder, Nur al-Din needed to assert his authority. An opportunity to do just this soon presented itself, as urgent news of a sudden crisis arrived. The Frankish count of Edessa, Joscelin II, was making a desperate attempt to recover his capital. Leading a rapidly assembled force, he had marched on the city in October 1146 and, with the collusion of its native Christian population, breached Edessa's outer defences by night. The Muslim garrison fled to the heavily fortified citadel and were now closely besieged.

Nur al-Din reacted with urgent resolution, determined to prevent Edessa's loss to the Franks and to forestall any possibility of westward expansion by his brother Saif al-Din. Mustering thousands of Aleppan troops and Turcoman warriors, the emir prosecuted a lightning forced march through day and night, travelling at such an intense pace 'that [the Muslims'] horses dropped by the roadsides from fatigue'. This speed paid off. Lacking the manpower and siege engines to overcome the citadel, Joscelin's troops were still ranged within the lower city when Nur al-Din arrived. Trapped between two forces, the count immediately abandoned the city, escaping at the cost of heavy Latin losses. With Edessa back in his possession, the emir chose to make a blunt demonstration of his ruthless will. Two years earlier, Zangi had spared the city's eastern Christians; now, as punishment for their 'connivance' with the Franks, his son and heir scourged Edessa of their presence. All males were killed, women and children enslaved. One Muslim chronicler remarked that 'the sword blotted out the existence of all the Christians', while a shocked Syrian Christian described how, in the aftermath of this massacre, the city 'was deserted of life: an appalling vision, enveloped in a black cloud, drunk with blood, infected by the cadavers of its sons and daughters'. The once vibrant metropolis remained a desolate backwater for centuries to come.[5]

Grim as its impact was in Edessa, Nur al-Din's show of strength helped to cement his rule over Aleppo. On this occasion, the emir had followed his father's lead in relying upon brute force and fear to impose his authority. Over time, however, Nur al-Din proved capable of employing more subtle modes of governance – from consensual politics to the shaping of public opinion – alongside steely resolve. Like Zangi, he aspired to unite Aleppo and Damascus, but to begin with, at least, the emir cultivated an atmosphere of renewed cooperation with his southern Syrian neighbour. A marriage alliance was arranged between Nur al-Din and Unur of Damascus' daughter, Ismat. The Aleppan emir also made the magnanimous gesture of releasing a slave girl captured by Zangi at Baalbek in 1138, who had once been Unur's lover. In the opinion of one Muslim chronicler, 'this was the most important reason for the friendship between [Nur al-Din and the Damascene]'.

With the rebalancing of power that followed Zangi's death, Aleppo and Damascus were feeling their way towards a new relationship. No longer fearful of imminent Zangid invasion, Unur's authority was rejuvenated, and he began to sever his ties as a client ruler of the Franks. When one of his dependants, Altuntash of Bosra, sought to form a breakaway alliance with the kingdom of Jerusalem in spring 1147, Unur moved to intervene. Nur al-Din came south to lend support and together the two beat back a Latin attempt to occupy Bosra. This notable success earned Unur recognition from the rival caliphs of Baghdad and Cairo, with both sending robes of honour and diplomas of investiture. Against this backdrop, Damascus, rather than Aleppo, appeared in 1147 to be the dominant Syrian Muslim polity.

Nur al-Din spent that summer consolidating his position in the north and campaigning on the western border zone with Antioch. Chilling news then put the emir on the defensive. An 'innumerable' Latin army was reportedly 'making for the land of Islam'; it was said that so many Christians had joined the huge force that the West had been left empty and undefended. Alarmed by these tidings, Aleppo, and all its Muslim neighbours, sought to prepare for the Second Crusade, and the coming of a new war.[6]

COUNTERING THE CRUSADE

Over the next six months, reports of the German and French crusaders' experiences gradually filtered back to the Near East. One Damascene heard that 'a vast number of them perished' in Asia Minor, through 'killing, disease and hunger', and by early 1148 it was apparent that Ma'sud, the Seljuq sultan of Anatolia, had inflicted crippling losses upon the Franks. For Nur al-Din and Unur, anxiously waiting in Aleppo and Damascus, these tidings must have been a welcome, but surprising, relief. Their Turkish neighbours to the north-west – more often rivals than allies over recent decades – had blunted the Christian crusade even before it reached the Levant.

Even so, the danger was not past. That spring, Latin survivors (still numbering in their thousands) began to arrive in the ports of Syria and Palestine. The question now was, where would they strike? Nur al-Din readied Aleppo for an attack and his brother, Saif al-Din, brought reinforcements from Mosul later that summer. Yet against expectations the Frankish offensive, when it finally came in July 1148, was launched to the south against Damascus.

Reaching Antioch that March, King Louis VII of France had quarrelled with Raymond of Antioch. Edessa's recent devastation scuppered any lingering plans to attempt its immediate reconquest; instead Raymond advocated a campaign targeting Aleppo and Shaizar. The plan had considerable merit, offering an opportunity to strike against Zangid power while Nur al-Din was still consolidating his hold over northern Syria, but the French king rejected the scheme and promptly marched south to Palestine. The causes of Louis' decision have long been debated. He may have been short of funds, concerned about King Conrad of Germany's activities in the Latin kingdom, and keen to fulfil his own pilgrimage to Jerusalem. The heart of the matter, though, was probably a torrid scandal. Upon arriving in Antioch, Louis' young charismatic wife Eleanor of Aquitaine had spent a great deal of time in the company of her uncle, Prince Raymond. Rumour spread that they had begun a passionate, incestuous affair. Humiliated and appalled, the French monarch was forced to drag his wife out of the city against her will, an act that soured their relationship beyond repair and put an end to any hopes of cooperation between Antioch and the crusaders.

With Conrad having arrived in the Holy Land that April, the French and German contingents regrouped in northern Palestine in early summer. On 24 June a joint Latin council of the leading crusaders and Jerusalem's High Court was held near Acre to debate a future course of action, and Damascus was chosen as the new target. This decision was once viewed by scholars as an act of near-lunacy, given the Muslim city's recent alliance with Frankish Palestine and its resistance to Zangid ascendancy. But this view has been rightly challenged on the grounds that Zangi's death in 1146 reshaped the balance of power in Muslim Syria. Once Jerusalem's docile pawn against Aleppo, by 1148 Damascus had become a far more threatening and aggressive neighbour. As such, its neutralisation and conquest were a reasonable objective and the city's seizure might transform Outremer's prospects for long-term survival.[7]

In midsummer 1148, the Christian kings of Europe and Jerusalem advanced to Banyas and then marched on Damascus. Unur did his best to prepare the city, strengthening defences and organising troops and militia. Requests for aid were dispatched to his Muslim neighbours, including the Zangids. On 24 July the Franks approached through the dense, richly irrigated orchards south-west of Damascus. These tightly packed copses, enclosed by low mud walls, stretched some five miles from the city's suburbs. Traversable only via narrow lanes, they had long served as a first natural line of defence. The Muslims did their best to halt the Latin advance, launching skirmishing attacks and incessant arrow volleys from watchtowers and concealed vantage points amidst the trees, but the enemy pressed on.

By day's end the Franks had established a camp on the open ground in front of the city, from where they had access to the waters of the Barada River. In contrast to the likes of Antioch and Jerusalem, Damascus possessed no great encircling fortifications, but was protected at most by a low outer wall and the crowded jumble of its outlying suburbs. With the Christians now waiting on its very outskirts, the metropolis seemed horribly vulnerable. Unur ordered the streets to be barricaded with huge wooden beams and piles of rubble and, to raise morale, a mass gathering was held in the Grand Umayyad Mosque. One of Damascus' most sacred treasures, a revered copy of the Koran, once owned by the Caliph 'Uthman (an early successor to Muhammad), was displayed to the throng 'and the people sprinkled their heads with ashes and wept tears of supplication'.

For the next three days a desperate struggle was played out, as the Muslims battled to hold back the Franks, and both sides suffered heavy casualties in close, hard-fought combat. Reinforcements from the Biqa valley boosted Muslim resistance and, with the arrival of Nur al-Din and Saif al-Din anticipated, Unur played for time. He appears to have promised to renew tribute payments in return for an end to hostilities. Aware of the rivalries coursing beneath the surface of the Christian coalition, Unur also sought, rather deviously, to sow seeds of doubt and distrust. A message was apparently sent to the crusader kings warning of the Zangids' approach, while a separate envoy contacted the Levantine Franks, pointing out that their alliance with the westerners would only culminate in the creation of a new adversary in the East, for 'you know that, if they take Damascus, they will seize the coastal lands that you have in your hands'. The Christian ranks certainly seem to have been plagued by internal tensions, as Latin sources confirm that the Franks began arguing over who should have rights to the city if it fell.

Having made little progress and with doubts surfacing, the Franks held a council of war on the evening of 27 July. A somewhat panicked decision was made to move to the east of the city from where, it was believed, a direct attack might be more easily launched. In fact, this area of Damascus proved to be just as strongly defended, and the Christians now found themselves camped in an exposed, waterless position. Beneath the searing summer sun, their nerve broke. According to one Muslim eyewitness, 'reports reached the Franks from several quarters of the rapid advance of the Islamic armies to engage in the holy war against them, and they became convinced of their own destruction and the imminence of disaster'. Latin sources murmur of treachery within the army, of pay-offs by Unur and heated recriminations on all sides. On 28 July, the coalition of crusaders and Levantine Franks began an appallingly humiliating retreat, harried by Damascene skirmishers as they fled. King Conrad later wrote that the

Christians had 'retreated in grief with the siege a failure', while William of Tyre described the crusaders as being 'covered with confusion and fear'. The French and German kings spoke of plans to launch a second, better-equipped assault against Damascus, or of a possible campaign against Fatimid Ascalon, but no action was taken on either count. Conrad set sail for Europe in September and, after visiting the holy sites, Louis followed his lead in spring 1149. With relief, one Muslim chronicler declared that 'God saved the believers [in Damascus] from their evil.'[8]

As far as the Franks were concerned, the main Levantine thrust of the Second Crusade had ended in miserable defeat. After such grand, regal preparations, the Christians' plans had come to naught and the very concept of Latin holy war was now brought into question. The consequences of this grave setback for the popularity and practice of crusading would be felt long into the future. Despite the protracted debate over the wisdom of the Franks' decision to besiege Damascus, historians have tended to underplay the crusade's impact upon Near Eastern Islam. On the surface, the balance of power appeared unchanged – Unur remained in control of Damascus; the Christians had been repelled. But at the critical moment of danger, the Damascenes had been forced to appeal to Aleppo and Mosul. For a brief moment in the mid-1140s, Unur had seemed capable of checking Zangid ascendancy; now, in the aftermath of the Second Crusade, he had to accept an increasingly subservient relationship with Nur al-Din.

The Latin attack on Damascus in 1148 also contributed to a hardening of anti-Frankish sentiment among the wider Damascene populace. Before long, Unur and the Burid ruling elite reopened diplomatic channels with the kingdom of Jerusalem, but local support for the policy of alliance with Palestine was now in terminal decline.

The county of Edessa dismembered

Aleppo had escaped the Second Crusade unscathed and, if anything, the Latin expedition had bolstered Nur al-Din's position in northern

Syria. Certainly the crusade had done nothing to reverse the Zangid gains achieved in the county of Edessa. In the years that followed, the scattered remnants of what had been the first crusader state were gradually picked over by Islam. Facing pressure from three fronts – as Nur al-Din, Ma'sud of Konya and the Artuqids of Diyar Bakr all vied to seize Edessene territory – Count Joscelin II tried to buy a measure of security by agreeing a submissive truce with Aleppo. But when the count was captured in 1150, Nur al-Din paid scant notice of Joscelin's supposed status as a client-ally; the Frank was thrown into prison (and possibly blinded) and remained in confinement until his death nine years later.

Zangid supporters made the most of Joscelin's fall from power. Describing him as 'an intransigent devil, fierce against the Muslims and cruel', one Muslim chronicler noted that '[the count's] capture was a blow to all Christendom'. Expanding on this theme, the poet Ibn al-Qaysarani (now a member of Nur al-Din's court) affirmed that Jerusalem itself would soon be 'purified'.[9]

With Joscelin captive, his wife Beatrice sold off the remainder of the Latin county to the Byzantines, prompting a stream of Frankish and eastern Christian refugees to flee to Antioch. The countess settled in Palestine, where her children – Joscelin III and Agnes – later became prominent political figures. Even the Greeks proved unable to defend these isolated outposts and, with the fall of Tell Bashir to Nur al-Din's forces in 1151, the county of Edessa came to a final, irredeemable end. The Zangids had eradicated one of the four crusader states.

8

THE LIGHT OF FAITH

Nur al-Din emerged as the Near East's foremost Muslim leader in the aftermath of the Second Crusade. Over the course of his career, Nur al-Din would unite Syria, extend Zangid power into Egypt and score a series of victories against the Christian Franks. He became one of the greatest luminaries of medieval Islam, celebrated as a stalwart of Sunni orthodoxy and a champion of *jihad* against Latin Outremer. Indeed, the appellation by which he is known to history, 'Nur al-Din', literally means 'the Light of Faith'.

Muslim chroniclers of the age generally presented Nur al-Din as the very archetype of a perfect Islamic ruler – deeply pious, clement and just; humble and austere, yet cultured; valiant and skilful in battle, and committed to the war for the Holy Land. This view was most powerfully expressed by the great Iraqi historian Ibn al-Athir (d. 1233), writing in Mosul in the early thirteenth century, when that city was still governed by members of Nur al-Din's Zangid dynasty. Among his many works, Ibn al-Athir composed a voluminous account of human history, starting with the Creation, and even in this chronicle Nur al-Din was presented as the principal protagonist. 'The fame of his good rule and justice' was said to have 'encompassed the world', and 'his good qualities were numerous and his virtues abundant, more than this book can contain'.[10]

Modern historians have sought, with varying degrees of success, to reach beyond this panegyric to reconstruct an authentic vision of Nur al-Din, producing wildly divergent images. A central feature of this process has been the attempt to pinpoint a moment of transformation or spiritual epiphany in the emir's life, after which he assumed the mantle of the *mujahid*.[11] In the context of the crusades, two interlocking issues are imperative. Nur al-Din spent a fair portion of his life fighting against fellow Muslims – but was he acting for the greater good, unifying Islam in preparation for *jihad*, or was holy war simply a convenient veil behind which to construct a Zangid empire? And did Nur al-Din start out as an ambitious, self-serving Turkish warlord, only (at some point) to experience a deepening of his religious conviction and a quickening of his desire to prosecute the holy war? In part, these questions can be resolved by tracing the path of Nur al-Din's career – examining when and why he fought against the Latins; and assessing his dealings with the Sunni Muslims of Syria, the Shi'ite Fatimids of Egypt and the Greeks of Byzantium.

THE BATTLE OF INAB

In the summer of 1149 Nur al-Din launched an offensive against the Christian principality of Antioch, seeking to consolidate his burgeoning authority over northern Syria. Since late 1148 his troops had clashed with Antiochene forces in a number of small-scale encounters, but the results had been inconclusive. In June 1149, Nur al-Din capitalised upon the recent rapprochement with Unur of Damascus by calling for reinforcements, assembling a formidable invasion army, spearheaded by 6,000 mounted warriors. Historians have made little effort to understand the Aleppan ruler's motivations, assuming that he was simply seeking a confrontation with Prince Raymond of Antioch. But just like his predecessor Il-ghazi in 1119, Nur al-Din's actions probably had a more defined strategic purpose.

In 1149, Nur al-Din set out to conquer two Latin outposts – Harim and Apamea. The fortress town of Harim stood on the western fringe of the Belus Hills, in a commanding position overlooking the Antiochene plains. Just twelve miles from Antioch itself, Harim had been in Latin hands since the time of the First Crusade. The Belus range had long played a role in the struggle between Aleppo and the principality. Earlier in the twelfth century, when Antioch was in the ascendant, the Franks had occupied territory to the east of these craggy hills, offering a direct threat to Aleppan security. First Il-ghazi, and then Zangi, pushed them back, re-establishing a border that followed the natural barrier of the Belus. But Nur al-Din was not content with this state of equilibrium. He sought to capture Harim and gain a foothold beyond the barrier of the Belus range, thereby undermining the defensive integrity of Antioch's eastern frontier.

Nur al-Din also targeted Apamea, on the southern edge of the Summaq plateau. In the past, Antiochene dominion over the Summaq threatened the main routes of communication between Aleppo and Damascus, but Zangi had recaptured much of this area in the late 1130s. By 1149 the Franks retained only a meagre corridor of territory, hugging the Orontes valley south to the increasingly lonely outpost at Apamea. Nur al-Din's primary objective in 1149 seems have been the conquest of this fortified settlement, eradicating the lingering Latin presence in the Summaq region. Recent attempts to directly overrun Apamea, perched upon a lofty ancient earthen tell, had failed. Switching tack, Nur al-Din now sought to isolate the town – severing its main line of communication with Antioch by taking control of the ash-Shogur Bridge across the Orontes.

In June he advanced into this vicinity and began operations by laying siege to the small fort of Inab. When this news reached Antioch, Prince Raymond reacted swiftly, perhaps even impetuously. Later Latin tradition held that he set off immediately to relieve Inab, 'without waiting for the escort of his cavalry, [hurrying] rashly to that place', but this may have been something of an exaggeration because a Muslim contemporary based in Damascus reckoned that the Franks arrived with 4,000 knights and 1,000 infantry. Raymond's force also included a contingent of Assassins, led by his Kurdish Muslim ally, 'Ali ibn Wafa. Nur al-Din responded to the Antiochenes' approach on 28 June with caution, retreating from Inab to assess his enemy's strength, but his eyes were open for any chance to launch a counter-attack, and just such an opportunity soon presented itself.

Arriving in the environs of Inab, Raymond rather optimistically assumed that he had frightened off Nur al-Din's forces and successfully secured the region. He elected to camp that night on the open plain rather than withdraw to a place of safety – a fatal error. Having actually moved off only a short distance, Nur al-Din gathered intelligence of the Frankish numbers and their exposed position and immediately retraced his steps under the cover of night. As dawn broke on 29 June 1149 the Latins awoke to find themselves surrounded. Sensing that a famous victory was now within his grasp, the lord of Aleppo wasted no time in pressing the advantage, 'storm[ing] the camp as if he were besieging a city' in the words of one Christian. According to the Damascus Chronicle, Prince Raymond vainly sought to rally his men and mount a defence, 'but the Muslims split up into detachments which attacked them from various directions and swarmed over them'. Vicious hand-to-hand fighting ensued and, as the winds picked up, dust clouded the air, adding to the confusion. Outnumbered and encircled, the Franks soon buckled, but even as swathes of his troops fled the field, Raymond held his ground, fighting on to the end. One contemporary Arabic text described how 'the swords of Islam had the final word [and] when the haze dispersed [the Christians] lay upon the ground prostrate and dirt-befouled'.

The Muslims had prevailed and the full extent of their triumph became clear when Nur al-Din's men began combing the battlefield. There the Antiochene ruler Raymond 'was found stretched out amongst his guard and his knights; he was recognised and his head cut off and carried to Nur al-Din, who rewarded the bearer of it with a handsome gift'. It was rumoured that the prince had been cut down by a sword blow from the Kurdish warlord Shirkuh. Nur al-Din apparently had the Frank's head sealed within a silver trophy case and dispatched to Baghdad to celebrate the defeat of an enemy who, according to the Muslims, had 'acquired special repute by the dread which he inspired, his great severity and excessive ferocity'. Latin sources confirm that Raymond's corpse was decapitated, adding the grisly but practical observation that, when the Antiochenes finally returned to recover his mutilated body, it could only be identified by 'certain marks and scars'.[12]

The significance of the Battle of Inab in 1149 paralleled that of the Field of Blood thirty years earlier. The Frankish principality was again deprived of a potent ruler and, with no obvious adult male heir apparent, left leaderless and vulnerable. Nur al-Din was now in a dominant position, but his actions after Inab are revealing. Crucially, he made no determined attempt to subjugate Antioch itself, but instead sent a large portion of his army south to Apamea. Nur al-Din led the remainder of his troops on the principality's capital, but after a brief siege agreed to leave the city inviolate in return for a sizeable tribute payment of gold and treasure. Travelling to the coast, he took the symbolic step of bathing in the Mediterranean – a gesture affirming that Islamic power now stretched west to the sea.

The real work of conquest began around mid-July, with an assault on Harim. With its Latin garrison weakened after Inab, the town fell swiftly and steps immediately were taken to bolster its defences. Towards the end of that same month, Nur al-Din marched south to Apamea. Cut off from Antioch, with no hope of rescue, the Franks stationed there surrendered in return for a promise that their lives would be spared.

Like Il-ghazi in 1119, Nur al-Din had capitalised upon his defeat of the Antiochenes to achieve focused strategic goals – in this case, the neutralisation of Antioch and the assertion of Aleppan dominion over the lands east of the Orontes. He also forsook a potential opportunity to capture Antioch, perhaps in part because he lacked the manpower and material resources to overwhelm that city's immense fortifications and knew that Frankish reinforcements would arrive soon from Palestine. Certainly in 1119 and again in 1149 Antioch's conquest was not prioritised as an objective.

In spite of these evident similarities, the Battle of Inab was not a simple rerun of the Field of Blood. In 1119 King Baldwin II of Jerusalem had rushed to the principality's aid and, over the following years, recouped its territorial losses. His grandson, King Baldwin III, likewise travelled north to Syria in summer 1149, but proved unable to fully revive Antioch's fortunes. Apamea was never recovered and a brief attempt to retake Harim failed. With Nur al-Din's soldiers ensconced within striking distance of its capital, the principality's ability to threaten Aleppo was severely curtailed. Later that summer the Latins were pressed into a humiliating treaty with Nur al-Din that, by confirming Aleppan rights over the Summaq plateau and the territory east of the Belus Hills, tacitly acknowledged Antioch's emasculation.

Nur al-Din's underlying motivations and intentions in 1149 also differed fundamentally from those of Il-ghazi and this, in itself, exposes a deeper truth about the shifting balance of power in Syria. The Field of Blood had been an expression of Antiochene and Aleppan rivalry, a last-ditch attempt to stem the sweeping tide of Frankish territorial expansion eastwards. In stark contrast, and despite initial appearances, the campaign that culminated in the Battle of Inab was actually driven by inter-Muslim enmity. Nur al-Din set out to occupy Apamea not to stave off Frankish aggression, but rather to open a clear and unchallenged route south from Aleppo to his real target, the Burid-held city of Damascus. Driven back beyond the Orontes, the Antiochenes would be in no position to interfere in this greater game.

Generations of modern historians have misconstrued the causes and significance of Inab, some even maintaining that this victory

marked the vital moment of transformation for Nur al-Din into a
dedicated *jihadi* warrior. To be sure, the lord of Aleppo celebrated his
success against the Christians. One Muslim chronicler observed that
'the poets made much praise of Nur al-Din in congratulation for this
victory, as the killing of [Prince Raymond] had a great effect on both
sides', and went on to quote this verse by Ibn al-Qaysarani:

> Your swords have produced in the Franks a shaking
> Which makes the hearts of Rome beat fast.
> You have struck their chief a crushing blow with
>   them
> Which has destroyed his backbone and brought the
>   crosses low.
> You have cleansed the enemy's land of their blood
> In a cleansing that has made every sword polluted.

But to accept this propaganda at face value is to ignore the reality of
Nur al-Din's strategic focus in 1149: Damascus. Future events would
demonstrate that he was wholly content to leave Antioch in the
faltering grip of the Franks because, neutralised as a threat in the
theatre of Levantine conflict, the Latin principality served as a useful
buffer state between Aleppo and Greek Byzantium. In fact, in these
early years of his rule, Nur al-Din's overriding concern was the
conquest of Damascus.

Events in August 1149 initially seemed to offer Nur al-Din the
perfect opportunity to increase his influence within Muslim Syria.
After dining on a particularly hearty meal, his sometime ally and rival
Unur of Damascus was 'seized by a loosening of the bowels' which
developed into a debilitating bout of dysentery. By the end of the
month Unur was dead and Damascus plunged into a chaotic power
struggle. But any hopes of capitalising upon this misfortune
evaporated when news arrived of a second death, this time of Nur al-
Din's elder brother, Saif al-Din, on 6 September. Rushing to Iraq,
Nur al-Din briefly sought to stake a claim to Mosul, but was

eventually begrudgingly reconciled with his younger sibling, the heir designate Qutb al-Din Maudud. For now a chance to take control of Damascus had been missed. Faltering Burid rule endured in the city, but it would not be long before Nur al-Din's gaze once again turned south of Aleppo.[13]

THE ROAD TO DAMASCUS

In 1150 Latin Outremer was beset by adversity. Arguably there had never been a more propitious moment for the lords of Near Eastern Islam – and for Nur al-Din in particular – to strike at the heart of the crusader states, sweeping the Franks into the Mediterranean. The Christians had suffered, in swift succession, the Second Crusade's failure, defeat at Inab and the county of Edessa's dissolution. After 1149 their difficulties only deepened. Panicked calls to western Europe for a new crusade were made, but with recent humiliation fresh in the memory, they went unanswered. In Antioch, Prince Raymond's sudden death prompted yet another succession crisis because his son and heir, Bohemond III, was only five years old, and his widow Constance forcefully rejected her cousin King Baldwin III of Jerusalem's plans to marry her off to a suitor of his choosing. Like her mother Alice before her, Constance sought to control her own fate, but this left the principality without an incumbent male military commander for four years and saddled Baldwin III with oversight of Antioch. The young king's responsibilities were multiplied even further in 1152 by the murder of Raymond II of Tripoli by a band of Assassins. As the count's son and namesake, Raymond III, was just twelve years old, Baldwin was again forced to assume the mantle of guardian.

Still only in his early twenties, Baldwin III of Jerusalem was now charged with the rule of all three of the surviving crusader states. To make matters worse his relationship with his mother Melisende was crumbling. Together they had exercised joint rule of Jerusalem since

1145 (when the boy king reached his majority at the age of fifteen), and in the beginning the queen's wisdom and experience had been a welcome source of security and continuity. But as Baldwin grew into adulthood, his mother's presence at his side began to feel more stifling than reassuring. Melisende, for her part, had no intention of relinquishing power and still enjoyed widespread support within the realm. From 1149 onwards, relations between the two co-rulers soured, and by 1152 Latin Palestine was almost torn asunder by civil war. Ultimately, Baldwin was forced to drive Melisende from her lands in Nablus and then to actually besiege the queen in the Holy City itself to force her abdication and assert his own right to independent rule.

In spite of the endemic weakness of his supposed enemy, Nur al-Din did little to pursue directly the interests of the *jihad* against the Christians. Instead, he continued to direct the bulk of his energy and resources towards the seizure of Damascus. Those seeking to promote Nur al-Din as a hero of Islamic holy war – from medieval Muslim chroniclers to modern historians – have argued that this dogged focus upon the subjection of Syria was but a means to an end; that only by preventing Damascus from falling into Christian hands and uniting Islam could the lord of Aleppo eventually hope to achieve victory in the greater struggle against the Franks.[14] Zangi had long eyed the prize of Damascus, but was often drawn away by the affairs of Mesopotamia. For the next five years, Nur al-Din pursued this quarry with greater determination, bringing a nuanced array of tactics to bear. His father's primary weapons had always been intimidation and fear. He had butchered the populace of Baalbek after promising to spare their lives if they surrendered, in the vain hope of terrifying Damascus into submission. Nur al-Din had perhaps learned the lesson of this failure. He adopted a new approach, concerning himself with the battle for hearts and minds, as well as the force of arms.

Power in Damascus now lay in the hands of another member of the faltering Burid dynasty, Abaq, and his inner circle of advisers, but their grip over the city was far from secure. In April 1150 Nur al-Din responded to news of Latin incursions into the Hauran, the frontier zone between Jerusalem and Damascus, by calling upon Abaq to join him in repelling the Franks. Nur al-Din then marched his own army into southern Syria, advancing beyond Baalbek. Just as he had expected, Abaq prevaricated with 'specious arguments and dissimulation', while simultaneously dispatching envoys to forge a new pact with King Baldwin III.

Now camped north of Damascus, Nur al-Din took great care to ensure the continued discipline of his troops, preventing them 'from plundering and doing injury in the villages', even as he ratcheted up the diplomatic pressure on Abaq. Messages arrived in Damascus chiding the Burid ruler for turning to the Franks and for paying them tribute monies stolen from 'the poor and weak among [the Damascenes]'. Nur al-Din assured Abaq that he had no intention of attacking the city, but rather that he had been endowed by Allah with power and resources 'in order to bring help to the Muslims and to engage in the holy war against the polytheists' – to which Abaq replied bluntly that 'there is nothing between us except the sword'. Nur al-Din's firm but restrained approach seems, nonetheless, to have borne fruit, as public opinion inside Damascus began to turn in his favour. One Muslim resident even noted that 'prayers were continually being offered up for him by the people of Damascus'.

Nur al-Din backed away from this initial exchange, having made only relatively meagre gains. For all his brave posturing, Abaq eventually agreed to a renewed truce with Aleppo, officially acknowledging Nur al-Din as suzerain and ordering his name to be recited from the pulpit during Friday prayer and placed on Damascene coins. Symbolic as these gestures may have been, the piecemeal work of subduing Damascus with a minimum of bloodshed had begun. Over the next few years Nur al-Din maintained diplomatic and military pressure on the Burids while still seeking to avoid a direct assault on their city. His 'scrupulous aversion to the slaying of Muslims' continued to be noted by those living in

Damascus, and by 1151 many were rejecting Abaq's calls to muster against the Aleppans.

Around this time, Shirkuh ibn Shadi's brother, Ayyub, began to act as Nur al-Din's agent within the city. Ayyub had transferred allegiance to the Burid dynasty in 1146, but he now decided, with familiar political flexibility, to return to the Zangid fold, becoming a valuable voice of support within the Damascene court, while also winning over the local militias. By slow steps, Nur al-Din was transforming Damascus into a client-state. In October 1151 Abaq actually travelled north to Aleppo to declare his loyalty, tacitly acknowledging subjection in the hope of staving off full conquest. Nur al-Din merely used this as an excuse to employ even more devious and divisive propaganda – repeatedly writing, in the guise of a concerned overlord, to warn Abaq that various members of his own Damascene court were contacting Aleppo to plot Damascus' surrender.

In winter 1153–4, Nur al-Din finally intensified his campaign, moving to cut off northern grain shipments to Damascus. Food shortages soon took hold. In the spring, with internal discontent swelling, he sent an advance force south under Shirkuh and then in late April 1154 closed on the city in person. In the end, no real attack was necessary. A Jewish woman reportedly lowered a rope over the walls, allowing some Aleppan troops to mount the eastern battlements and to raise Nur al-Din's standard. As Abaq fled in horror to the citadel, the people of Damascus threw open the city's gates, offering their unconditional surrender.

Patience and restraint had brought Nur al-Din control of the historic seat of Muslim power – he now took care to maintain those principles. Abaq, in spite of fears, was treated with equanimity and rewarded with the fiefdom of Homs in return for relinquishing control of Damascus; he later moved to Iraq. An abundance of food started flowing into the city and Nur al-Din's generosity was affirmed by the 'abolition of duties on the melon market and the vegetable market'.

Nur al-Din's conquest of Damascus in 1154 was a striking achievement. With this act, he emerged from his father's shadow, succeeding where Zangi had repeatedly failed. Nur al-Din could now claim dominion over almost all Muslim Syria; for the first time since the crusades began, Aleppo and Damascus were united. And all this had been achieved without the gratuitous shedding of Muslim blood.

Damascus' subjugation has often been depicted as one of the crowning glories of Nur al-Din's career. Conscious himself of its significance, he began to make extensive use of the title *al-Malik al 'Adil* (The Just King). The notion also gained currency that his overthrow of another Islamic polity was a necessary precursor to the waging of holy war against the Franks. One Aleppan chronicler later wrote that 'from this point forward, Nur al-Din dedicated himself to *jihad*'.

This view of events does not bear close scrutiny. Nur al-Din probably did have a real aversion to killing fellow Muslims, but he also seems to have been keenly aware of his clemency's value in practical and propaganda terms. More importantly, despite having drawn upon anti-Latin sentiment to legitimise and empower his campaign against Burid Damascus, Nur al-Din launched no new *jihadi* offensive after 1154. The rhetoric had suggested that, with the kingdom of Jerusalem before him, the emir would unleash a wave of scalding aggression against the Franks. In fact, contemporary Arabic testimony reveals that Nur al-Din actually followed up his occupation of Damascus by agreeing new peace treaties with Latin Palestine. On 28 May 1155, 'terms of truce were agreed' with Jerusalem for one year. In November 1156 the pact was renewed for another year, this time with the stipulation 'that the tribute paid to [the Franks] from Damascus should be 8,000 dinars of Tyre'. Far from being focused upon holy war after 1154, Nur al-Din actually spent most of his time acquiring more Muslim-held territory – subjugating Baalbek and capitalising upon the death of Ma'sud, the Seljuq sultan of Anatolia, to absorb lands in the north. The treaties and tribute payments to the Christians, so disparaged in years gone by, now served to secure Nur al-Din's Damascene lands.[15]

Damascus – 'Paradise of the Orient'

Nur al-Din's seizure of Damascus may not have heralded an immediate *jihadi* revival, but it did mark a watershed in Zangid history. The dynasty now ruled Syria's greatest city – what one twelfth-century Muslim pilgrim described as the 'Paradise of the Orient . . . the seal of the lands of Islam'. Damascus is one of the oldest permanently inhabited settlements on Earth, with a history stretching back to c. 9000 BCE.

At Damascus' heart stood the Grand Umayyad Mosque – perhaps the most awe-inspiring Muslim structure of the age. Built on the site of a Roman Christian church dedicated to John the Baptist (which itself had replaced a massive Temple of Jupiter), the Grand Mosque was constructed on the orders of Caliph al-Walid in the early eighth century, at the extraordinary cost of full seven years' income from the Damascene treasury. Located within a huge rectangular walled compound – measuring some 525 feet by 320 feet – the lavishly decorated prayer hall was reached via an expansive courtyard whose walls displayed mosaic tableaux of unparalleled scale and magnificence: forty tonnes of glass were used in their creation. Although somewhat altered by centuries of damage and rebuilding (particularly after suffering significant fire damage in 1893), the Grand Mosque still can be visited today. The twelfth-century Iberian Muslim pilgrim Ibn Jubayr wrote lyrically, and at great length, about its 'perfection of construction, marvellous and sumptuous embellishment and decoration', describing its *mihrab* (prayer niche) as 'the most wonderful in Islam for its beauty and rare art'.

As the home of this wondrous mosque, Damascus was revered as a site of particular devotional significance within Islam. The city's sanctity was further enhanced by the presence nearby of a number of cave shrines – including one that was supposedly the birthplace of Abraham and another said to have been visited by Moses, Jesus, Lot and Job (all recognised as prophets in Islam). Members of Muhammad's family and inner circle had also been buried at Damascus, and, in addition, some believed that the Messiah himself would descend to Earth on the Day of Judgement by the city's 'white minaret', upon the East Gate.

Imbued as it was with historic and spiritual significance, the

Damascus conquered by Nur al-Din in 1154 needed rejuvenation. The emir set to work, fortifying the Seljuq citadel, west of the Grand Mosque (originally dating from the late eleventh century), and repaired and bolstered the city walls. With the advent of stable Zangid rule, the Damascene populace, which had declined in number to around 40,000, soon began to increase. Commerce was also stimulated and the Arab visitor al-Idrisi now remarked that:

> Damascus contains all manner of good things, and streets of various craftsmen, with [merchants selling] all sorts of silk and brocades of exquisite rarity and wonderful workmanship . . . That which they make here is carried into all cities and borne in ships to all quarters, and all the capitals both far and near . . . The city itself is the most lovely in all Syria and the most perfect for beauty.[16]

It is little wonder that, over time, Nur al-Din gradually shifted his seat of power from Aleppo to Damascus. Thus, while Shirkuh was appointed initially as the city's governor, after 1157 Damascus was confirmed as the new capital of Nur al-Din's expanding realm, and promoted as a focal point of Abbasid Sunni orthodoxy.

CHALLENGES

The 1150s saw little material advance for Islam in the *jihad* against the Franks. Even as Nur al-Din sought to subjugate Damascus, the Latins were enjoying their own renewal of fortune. Now confirmed as sole ruler, King Baldwin III swiftly scored a deeply significant victory for Jerusalem. For the last half-century the port of Ascalon had remained in Fatimid hands, offering the Muslim rulers of Egypt a strategic and economic foothold in southern Palestine. In 1150 Baldwin had overseen the construction of a fortress to the south of Ascalon, atop the ruins of the ancient settlement of Gaza, thus severing the Muslim port's landward communications with Cairo. In January 1153 the young king mustered the full force of his armies to descend on Ascalon itself, finally securing its surrender after a hard-fought, eight-month siege. What once had been the Fatimid gateway to the Holy Land now became a vital stepping stone for the further expansion of Latin ambitions southwards, towards Egypt itself. The consequences of this victory would be felt keenly in the years to come.

The principality of Antioch was also rejuvenated. After four years of sole rule, the young Princess Constance of Antioch at last settled upon a husband, although her chosen spouse brought neither wealth nor power to the match. In spring 1153 she wed Reynald of Châtillon, a handsome young French knight and crusader of aristocratic birth but limited material means. Having fought alongside Baldwin III in the early stages of Ascalon's siege, he gained the king's permission, as his overlord and Constance's guardian, for the union. Antioch's new prince soon revealed his mercurial nature. Having first furthered Byzantine interests by moving against the rising power of the Armenian Roupenid warlord Thoros (Leon I's son) in Cilicia, Reynald promptly allied with Thoros to lead a vicious raid on the Greek-held island of Cyprus. Often criticised by contemporaries and modern historians alike for his reckless ambition, lack of diplomacy and tempestuous brutality, Reynald nonetheless proved to be a formidable warrior who, in time, would offer staunch opposition to Islam.

The revitalisation of Jerusalem and Antioch meant that Nur al-Din faced pressure in two key frontier zones. In the north, events centred on Harim. Nur al-Din's control of this outpost – just a day's march from Antioch itself – since 1149 had all but neutralised the Frankish principality as a threat to Aleppo. In 1156 the Latins began conducting raids into its suburbs, but for now these were driven back successfully. Nur al-Din even had the grim pleasure of triumphantly parading the heads of Christians taken in these encounters through the streets of Damascus. Meanwhile, to the south, Baldwin III broke his truce with Nur al-Din in 1157, hoping to extend Jerusalemite authority over the Terre de Sueth. A series of largely inconclusive skirmishes followed, particularly in the region of Frankish-held

Banyas, although the Latin king narrowly avoided capture in June 1157 when caught in an ambush.

Around this time, however, events conspired to curtail Nur al-Din's capabilities. Syria had always been prone to earthquakes and now, in the late 1150s, the region was subjected to a succession of severe tremors, gravely damaging many Muslim-held settlements in the area between Aleppo and Homs. A contemporary chronicler in Damascus described how 'continuous earthquakes and shocks ... wrought destruction amongst the [Muslims'] castles, fortresses and dwellings in their districts and marches'. Throughout this dreadful period, Nur al-Din was forced to commit the bulk of his resources to rebuilding work, much of which was frustratingly undone by renewed seismic activity.

Then, in October 1157, Nur al-Din was struck down by a critical illness while lodging in the Summaq. The exact nature of this malady is unknown, but it was so extreme that the great emir soon began to fear for his life. Carried by litter to Aleppo, he quickly made arrangements for his will, designating one of his brothers, Nusrat al-Din, as heir and lord of Aleppo, while Shirkuh was to hold Damascus as his subject. Despite these provisions, civil unrest soon racked Muslim Syria, and Nur al-Din's condition deteriorated throughout the autumn. Although he survived this first onslaught, his health seems to have remained fragile and, in late 1158, he was again laid low for months by acute sickness, this time in Damascus. Unfortunately, we lack the close eyewitness testimony to gauge accurately the impact of these brushes with death upon Nur al-Din's state of mind. He is said to have experienced a spiritual awakening in these years, hereafter embracing a more ascetic lifestyle and adopting simpler garb. It is certainly true that, in spite of ongoing Levantine tensions, he took the time to perform the *Hajj*, the pilgrimage to Mecca, in late 1161.[17]

External threats

Spies soon brought the enemy word of Nur al-Din's debility – it was even rumoured that he was perhaps already dead – and the Franks quickly sought to exploit the confusion gripping the emir's lands.

Their strength was reinforced by the presence of Count Thierry of Flanders, a powerful western noble and veteran of the Second Crusade, who once again had taken the cross and come east. In the autumn of 1157 his troops joined an amalgamated Christian army – with elements from Antioch, Tripoli and Jerusalem and an Armenian force under Thoros – in marching on Shaizar. After a short siege the lower town fell, and the allies appeared to be on the brink of overrunning the citadel when a bitter argument erupted. Hoping to harness Thierry's wealth and resources for Outremer's defence, Baldwin III had promised the count hereditary lordship of Shaizar, but Reynald of Châtillon disputed the legality of this plan, claiming that the town belonged to Antioch. With neither side willing to back down, the Christian offensive ground to a halt and, amid mutual recriminations, the allies abandoned the siege, forsaking a rare opportunity to reassert Frankish authority over the southern Orontes. Despite this reversal, the Latins managed to regroup in early 1158. Gathering at Antioch they targeted Harim and, after an energetic siege, forced the surrender of its citadel. On this occasion there was no argument over rights and the town was returned to the principality, thereby restoring a measure of security to its eastern borders.

Byzantium also re-emerged as a force in the Near East in the period. Greek influence in the region had been in abeyance since the death of Emperor John Comnenus in 1143. Power had passed to his son, Manuel, who, after the debacle of the Second Crusade, had been preoccupied with affairs in Italy and the Balkans. In the late 1150s Manuel sought to restore relations with the Franks after the ill will and suspicion engendered in 1147–8 – reaffirming imperial authority in Antioch and Cilicia, and establishing closer ties with Frankish Palestine. Marriage alliances were the foundation of this process. In September 1158, King Baldwin III wed a highly placed member of the Comneni dynasty, Manuel's niece Theodora. She brought with her a lavish dowry in gold. The emperor then took the further step of marrying Bohemond III's sister, Maria of Antioch, in December 1161.

For Nur al-Din the implication of these unions was at once obvious and disquieting: the ancient eastern Christian opponent of Islam, Byzantium, would again be directing its legendary might towards the Levant. And, while the Latins stood as both a threat and annoyance to his ambitions, the lord of Aleppo and Damascus appears to have seen in the Greeks a more enduring and intractable menace. Awe, apprehension and resolution thus fused to condition Nur al-Din's response when Manuel Comnenus led a huge army into northern Syria in October 1158.

That autumn the emperor received Reynald of Châtillon's submission, accepting his penance for the recent assault on Cyprus, and brought the increasingly independent Roupenid Armenians to heel. In April 1159, with his recalcitrant subjects cowed, Manuel rode, in full majesty, through the gates of Antioch, surrounded by his resplendent Varangian Guard, attended by his servant, Prince Reynald. Even King Baldwin showed his humility by following some distance behind, mounted, but unadorned by any symbols of office. The message was obvious: as ruler of the eastern Mediterranean's Christian superpower, Manuel's eminence was unparalleled. Should he wish, he might carve a swathe through Syria.

Nur al-Din, only now in spring 1159 recovering from his second bout of infirmity, took this threat to heart, summoning troops from as far afield as Mosul to fight under the banner of *jihad* and strengthening Aleppo's fortifications. Even so, when the Christian armies assembled at Antioch in May under Manuel's leadership, readying themselves for a direct assault on Aleppo itself, the Muslims must have been significantly outnumbered. On the brink of such a dreadful confrontation a more bluntly bellicose Seljuq lord, of Zangi's ilk, might simply have embraced the coming struggle with proud defiance, and likely suffered decimation. In his dealings with Damascus, however, Nur al-Din had shown a gift for the subtleties of diplomacy. Now he set out to test Manuel's commitment to the prosecution of a costly campaign on Byzantium's far-eastern frontier. Dispatching envoys, Nur al-Din proposed a truce, offering to free some 6,000 Latin prisoners captured during the Second Crusade and to support the Greek Empire against the Seljuqs of Anatolia. To the dismay of his Frankish allies, the emperor quickly agreed these terms, ordering the immediate cessation of his campaign.

This startling turn of events is profoundly instructive. Manuel's behaviour could perhaps have been predicted – once again the interests of Byzantium had been prioritised above those of Outremer. But Nur al-Din's conduct revealed that he was no intransigent *jihadi* ideologue, bent upon conflict with Christendom. Instead, he had employed pragmatism to defuse a confrontation with one of Islam's true global rivals. Amid the dealings between Nur al-Din and Manuel, the crusader states almost seemed like an insignificant sideshow.

Throughout these years Nur al-Din's actions suggest that, in spite of his apparent spiritual awakening and emergent patronage of *jihad* propaganda, he continued to view Latin Outremer as simply one opponent among many within the complex and entangled matrix of Near and Middle Eastern power politics. At the start of the 1160s, he made no concerted attempt to exert direct military or diplomatic pressure on the Franks – indeed, the emir allowed two opportunities for action to pass by. In 1160 Reynald of Châtillon was captured by one of Nur al-Din's lieutenants and imprisoned in Aleppo (where he would remain for the next fifteen years), but rather than exploit a period of Antiochene weakness as the young Bohemond III came to power, Nur al-Din elected to agree a new two-year truce with Jerusalem. Then, in early 1163, when King Baldwin III died of illness aged just thirty-three, Nur al-Din again failed to react. One Latin chronicler put this down to the emir's innate sense of honour, writing that:

When it was suggested to [him] that while we were occupied with the funeral ceremonies he might invade and lay waste the land of his enemies, he is said to have responded, 'We should sympathise with their grief and in pity spare them, because they have lost a prince such as the rest of the world does not possess today.'

This quote from William of Tyre reflects the archbishop's deep-seated admiration for Baldwin III, but Arabic sources give no indication that Nur al-Din's decision making was influenced by compassion at this point. In part, his inaction can be explained by the fact that he had begun, as we shall see, to direct his attention south, towards Egypt. But it was also a function of his continuing preoccupations in Asia Minor and Mesopotamia, and of his failure to prioritise the *jihad* against the Franks.[18]

TRIAL AND TRIUMPH

From the spring of 1163 onwards, however, Nur al-Din's perception of his own role within the war for the Holy Land seems to have altered, prompting a deepening of his commitment to the cause. In May the emir led a raiding party into the county of Tripoli's northern reaches, making camp in the Bouqia valley – the broad plain between the Ansariyah Mountains to the north and Mount Lebanon to the south. News of his whereabouts spread, and the Franks of Antioch, recently reinforced by a group of pilgrims from Aquitaine and by Greek soldiers, decided to launch an attack under the command of the Templar Gilbert of Lacy.

Oblivious to this threat, an advance party of Zangid troops were shocked to see a large Christian army marching out of the foothills of the Ansariyah range. After a brief skirmish they were put to flight and raced back towards Nur al-Din's main encampment, hotly pursued by the enemy. A Muslim chronicler later described how the two forces 'arrived together', so that, overcome by surprise, 'the Muslims were unable to mount their horses and take up their weapons before the Franks were amongst them, killing and capturing many'. A Latin contemporary recorded that '[Nur al-Din's] army was almost annihilated [while] the prince himself, in despair of his very life, fled in utter confusion. All the baggage and even his sword were abandoned. Barefooted and mounted on a beast of burden, he barely

escaped capture.' Muslim sources confirm the scale of this defeat and
the ignominy of Nur al-Din's retreat, adding that, in his desperation,
he mounted a steed whose legs were still hobbled and was saved only
by the bravery of one of his Kurds, who rushed in to sever the tether
at the cost of his own life.

Stunned and humiliated, Nur al-Din scuttled back to Homs with
a handful of survivors. The horror of this unheralded disaster seems
to have left a scar on his psyche and the nature of his reaction over the
coming months is revealing. Filled with rage and impassioned
determination, he is said to have vowed: 'By God, I shall not shelter
under any roof until I avenge myself and Islam.' We might suspect this
to be pure invective, but it was followed by practical action. At
significant cost, Nur al-Din paid for the replacement of all weapons,
equipment and horses out of his own purse – a responsibility not
usually shouldered by Muslim warlords – so that 'the army was
restored as if it had not suffered any defeat'. He also ordered that the
lands of any slain soldiers be passed on to their families, rather than
reverting to his control. Most strikingly, when the Franks sought, later
that year, to agree a truce, the emir flatly refused.[19]

Nur al-Din now sought to build a coalition with the Muslims of
Iraq and the Jazira, gathering a mighty army to prosecute a retaliatory
attack on the Latins. Stories of his devout dedication to 'fasting and
praying' spread through the Near East, and he also began actively
recruiting the support of ascetics and holy men throughout Syria and
Mesopotamia, urging them to publicise the Latins' manifold crimes
against Islam. The impetus of *jihad* was gathering pace.

By the following summer, Nur al-Din was ready to strike, and his
strategic objectives were audacious. Numerical estimates of his forces
have not survived, but we know that he was followed by troops from
his own Syrian territories as well as those from the eastern cities of
Mosul, Diyar Bakr, Hisn Kifr and Mardin. He must have been
confident about the strength of his army, because he set out both to
make territorial conquests and to lure the Christians into a decisive
battle. Nur al-Din advanced on Harim, which had remained in

Antiochene hands since 1158, laying siege to its citadel and initiating a bombardment campaign with siege engines. As he must have expected, the Franks soon sought to make a counter-attack. In early August 1164 an army probably in excess of 10,000 men, including some 600 knights, marched from Antioch under the command of Prince Bohemond III, Count Raymond III of Tripoli and Joscelin III of Courtenay, alongside Thoros of Armenia and the Greek governor of Cilicia.

At news of their approach, Nur al-Din marched his army to the nearby Latin-held settlement of Artah, on the Antiochene plain, hoping to draw his enemy further away from the security of Antioch. Then, on 11 August, when the Christian allies made a nervous feint towards Harim, he closed to engage their forces on open ground. As the battle began, Nur al-Din's right flank made a feigned retreat, tempting the Latin knights into a hasty charge. Left isolated and vulnerable, the Christian infantry faced a ruinous assault and were swiftly overrun. With the tide of the battle moving in the Muslims' favour, the mounted Frankish elite reversed their headlong advance, only to find themselves enveloped as Nur al-Din's right wing halted its supposed flight to '[come] back on their heels', and his centre turned to engage them at close quarters. An Arabic chronicle described how '[the Christians'] spirits sank and they saw that they were lost, left in the middle, surrounded on all sides by the Muslims'. Aghast, a Latin contemporary conceded that: 'Overwhelmed and shattered by the swords of the enemy, [the Franks] were shamefully slain like victims before the altar . . . Regardless of honour all threw down their arms precipitately and ignominiously begged for life.' Thoros fled the field, but 'to save their lives even at the cost of shame and reproach', Bohemond, Raymond and Joscelin all surrendered; 'chained liked the lowest slaves, they were led ignominiously to Aleppo, where they were cast into prison and became the sport of the infidels'.

Nur al-Din's victory was absolute, the revenge for Bouqia sweet. He had thrashed the Syrian Franks, reaping an unprecedented harvest of high-level captives. Within days he returned to Harim which, now cut off from all hope of reinforcement, promptly surrendered. From this time onwards the town would remain in Muslim hands, leaving the principality of Antioch cowering behind an eastern frontier that had been definitively driven back to the River Orontes. Just as in 1149, after his triumph at Inab, Nur al-Din chose not to target the city of Antioch itself. The chronicler Ibn al-Athir later explained that the emir was deterred by the strength of its citadel and, more revealingly, by his reluctance to provoke a counter-attack from Antioch's overlord, Emperor Manuel, quoting Nur al-Din as saying, 'To have Bohemond as a neighbour I find preferable to being a neighbour of the ruler of Constantinople.' With this in mind, he soon agreed to release the young Antiochene prince in return for a hefty ransom; he refused, however, to give Raymond of Tripoli, Joscelin of Courtenay or his other princely prisoner, Reynald of Châtillon, their freedom.[20]

In October 1164 Nur al-Din turned his attention to the southern frontier with Jerusalem. There the pivotal town of Banyas was vulnerable, because its lord, the Constable Humphrey of Toron, was in Egypt with the king of Jerusalem. The emir moved in with heavy siege weaponry and began an investment, deploying a combination of incessant bombardment and sapping to weaken the fortress and break the will of its small garrison. Bribes may also have been used to buy off Banyas' commander. Within a few days, surrender on terms of safe conduct was secured and Nur al-Din installed his own well-supplied troops. Just as at Harim, the conquest of Banyas proved to be a permanent gain for Islam. The significance of this turning point in the regional balance of power was reflected in the punitive terms Nur al-Din now imposed on the Franks of Galilee – a share of the revenues of Tiberias and an annual tribute payment. Three years later, the emir followed up this success by destroying the Latin fortress at Chastel Neuf. This opened up a new corridor into Frankish Palestine, through the area of rolling hills known as Marj Ayun, between the Litani valley and the Upper Jordan. There could now be no question that Nur al-Din posed a real threat to Outremer.

THE DREAM OF JERUSALEM

Nur al-Din's actions in the 1160s suggest that he had adopted a more determined and aggressive stance in his dealings with the Franks, embracing and promoting an active *jihad* against them. Ever since his occupation of Damascus in 1154, Nur al-Din had sponsored a monumental building programme within the city, rejuvenating and reaffirming its status as one of the Near East's great centres of power and civilisation. This began almost immediately, with the construction of a new hospital, the *Bimaristan* – soon to become one of the world's leading centres of medical science and treatment – and a luxurious bathhouse, the *Hammam Nur al-Din*, which remains largely unaltered and can be visited to this day.

From the late 1150s onwards, however, these public works seem to have been increasingly imbued with a devotional dimension; one inspired by and/or designed to aver Nur al-Din's deepening sense of personal piety and his preoccupation with Sunni orthodoxy. In 1163 he financed the building of a new House of Justice, where he later sat for two days each week to hear the grievances of his subjects. This was followed by the construction of the *Dar al-hadith al-Nuriyya* – a new centre dedicated to the study of the life and traditions associated with Muhammad – headed by Nur al-Din's close friend, the renowned scholar Ibn 'Asakir, which the emir attended in person.

To promote Damascus as a hub of Sunni Islam, Nur al-Din built a new suburb, to the west of the city, to house pilgrims en route to Mecca, and in 1159 he founded the town of al-Salihiyya, just over one mile to the north, to shelter refugees from Palestine. Nur al-Din's Damascene court soon drew in experts in the fields of governance, law and warfare from across the Muslim world. Among them was the Persian intellectual Imad al-Din al-Isfahani, who would later write some of the most illuminating and lyrical Arabic histories of this era. Educated in Baghdad, he joined the emir as a *katib* (secretary/scholar) in 1167, later describing his new patron as 'the most chaste, pious, sagacious, pure and virtuous of kings'.

Throughout this period, Nur al-Din projected an image of himself as a devoted Muslim, the reviver of Sunni law and orthodoxy. Revealingly, the most potent and portable propaganda tool available to Nur al-Din – the coins he issued – bore the inscription 'The Just King'. From the early 1160s, however, he appears to have placed greater emphasis upon the role of *jihad* in his rule, proclaiming his virtues as a heroic *mujahid* in inscriptions adorning public monuments. The pre-eminent position of Jerusalem within the framework of *jihad* ideology also began to crystallise in this period. The emir's colleague Ibn 'Asakir helped to revitalise the tradition of writing texts extolling the Holy City's virtues and took to reciting these works to large public gatherings in Damascus. Poets in Nur al-Din's court composed widely disseminated works stressing the need not only to attack the Latins but also to reconquer Islam's third city. One wrote encouraging his patron to wage war on the Franks 'until you see Jesus fleeing from Jerusalem'. Ibn al-Qaysarani, who had also served Zangi, announced his wish that 'the city of Jerusalem be purified by the shedding of blood', proclaiming that 'Nur al-Din is as strong as ever and the iron of his lance is directed at the Aqsa.' The emir himself wrote to the caliph in Baghdad of his desire 'to banish the worshippers of the Cross from the Aqsa mosque'.

One further piece of evidence attests to Jerusalem's increasingly central role, both within the ideology propagated by Nur al-Din and, perhaps, within his own heartfelt ambitions. In 1168–9, he commissioned the master carpenter al-Akharini to carve a fabulously ornate *minbar* (wooden pulpit) that the emir hoped to place in the Aqsa mosque once the Holy City was retaken. Some years later, the Iberian Muslim traveller Ibn Jubayr remarked on the pulpit's extraordinary beauty when he passed through the Levant, asserting that its grandeur was unrivalled in the medieval world. This *minbar* was undoubtedly intended as a potent and public declaration of intent, emblazoned as it was with the description of the emir as 'the fighter of *jihad* in His path, the one who defends [the frontiers] against the enemies of His religion, the just king, Nur al-Din, the pillar of Islam and the Muslims, the dispenser of justice'. Yet, in some respects, it must in addition be viewed as an intensely personal, almost humble, offering to God, for it was also inscribed with the simple, emotive appeal: 'May He grant conquest to [Nur al-Din] and at his own hands.' Upon its completion, the emir installed the pulpit in Aleppo's Great Mosque, where, according to Imad al-Din, it lay 'sheathed like a sword in the scabbard', awaiting the day of victory, when Nur al-Din might achieve the dream of Jerusalem's recovery.[21]

How then should Nur al-Din be regarded? Do his attacks on the Franks after the humiliation at Bouqia and his dissemination of *jihad* ideology prove that he was possessed by an unequivocal commitment to holy war? Can the emir's own words, recorded in the Damascus Chronicle, be taken at face value? He was said to have declared:

> I seek nothing but the good of the Muslims and to make war against the Franks . . . [If] we aid one another in waging the holy war, and matters are arranged harmoniously and with a single eye to the good, my desire and purpose will be fully achieved.[22]

There was a marked difference between Nur al-Din's approach and focus in the 1140s and his activities in the 1160s. Comparison with the methods and achievements of his father Zangi is striking. But question marks and caveats remain. Given the context, and the complexities of human nature, any expectation of a singular solution – in which Nur al-Din was either wholly dedicated to *jihad* or purely self-serving – is surely flawed. Just as the Christian First Crusaders appear to have been moved by a mixture of piety and greed, Nur al-Din may well have recognised the political and military value of championing a religious cause, while still being impelled by authentic devotion. As upstart Turkish warlords in a Near and Middle Eastern world still underpinned by Arab and Persian elites, the Zangids' need for social, religious and political legitimation must have been pressing.

In the course of the twelfth century the notion of a rebirth of Islamic *jihad* took hold in the Levant, and this process accelerated almost exponentially during Nur al-Din's career. In 1105, when the Damascene preacher al-Sulami extolled the virtues of holy war, few responded. By the late 1160s the atmosphere in Damascus and Aleppo was transformed – Nur al-Din may well have cultivated and inspired this fervour; at the very least, he understood that a message emphasising the spiritual dimension of the struggles against Sunni Islam's enemies now would find a receptive audience.

9

THE WEALTH OF EGYPT

For much of the 1160s the conflict between Zangid Islam and the Levantine Franks centred on Egypt, as both powers tried to assert control over the Nile region. In strategic terms, dominion of Egypt might allow Nur al-Din effectively to encircle Outremer – with control of Aleppo and Damascus secured, the addition of Cairo could shift the balance of power in the Near East irrevocably in his favour. The division between Sunni Syria and Shi'ite Egypt had long undermined any hope of a concerted drive to defeat the Latins. If that rift was somehow overcome, Islam would stand united for the first time since the coming of the crusades.

The Nile's fabulous wealth was also alluring. The great river's annual August flood bestowed enormous fertility upon the arable land along its banks throughout the Nile Delta. In a good year, Egypt enjoyed an abundant agricultural surplus and, by association, bounteous tax revenues. The region likewise benefited from burgeoning trade between the Indian Ocean and the Mediterranean Sea, because the critical land route linking the two crossed Egypt. Popular with Italian and Byzantine merchants, the Nile region became one of the world's leading commercial hubs.

MEDIEVAL EGYPT

Egypt often is characterised as having been a Muslim territory in the age of the crusades, but this is a misleading simplification. The region was conquered in 641 CE during the first wave of Arab Islamic expansion, but the Arab ruling elite was largely concentrated in two centres: the port city of Alexandria, founded by Alexander the Great some 1,500 years earlier; and the new settlement of Fustat, established by the Arabs at the head of the Nile Delta. Elsewhere, Egypt's indigenous Coptic Christian population predominated. Over the centuries the Copts were Arabised in a cultural sense, for example taking on the Arabic language, but their adoption of the Islamic faith was far more gradual. Even in the twelfth century this Coptic Christian rural underclass remained.

From 969 Egypt was ruled by the Shi'ite Fatimid dynasty, who broke free from the Sunni Abbasid rulers of Baghdad. The Fatimids built a formidable navy, with which they came to dominate Mediterranean shipping. They also constructed a new capital city north of Fustat, which they named Cairo (meaning 'the Conqueror'), and established a rival Shi'ite caliph ('successor' to the Muslim Prophet Muhammad), challenging the universal authority of the Sunni caliph in Baghdad. By the twelfth century the walled city of Cairo was the political heart of Egypt. Here, two fabulously opulent, labyrinthine caliphal palaces stood as testament to the limitless wealth of the Fatimids – housing exotic menageries and hordes of court eunuchs. The city was also home to the tenth-century al-Azhar mosque, renowned as a centre of Islamic scholasticism and theological study, while at the end of a canal running to the Nile, on the small island of Roda, was the Nilometer, a carefully calibrated structure that allowed the great river's flood to be measured precisely and, therefore, the harvest predicted.

Cairo became the seat of Fatimid power, but ancient Alexandria retained its status as the focal point of Egypt's economy into the crusading era. Located on the Mediterranean coast to the west of the Nile Delta, possessed of the great wonder that was Pharos' Lighthouse, this port was perfectly positioned to exploit the trade in luxury goods such as spices and silks flowing from Asia, through the Red Sea and on to Europe. One Latin then living in Palestine observed that 'people from the East and the West flock to Alexandria, and it is a public market for both worlds'.

By the time of the crusades the ability of Fatimid caliphs to exercise real power over the Nile region had dwindled and, for the most part, Egypt was governed by the caliph's chief administrator, his vizier. After the death of the Vizier al-Afdal in 1121, however, this political system faltered and Cairo was soon gripped by intrigue. A noxious cycle of dissolute conspiracy, unbridled brutality and murder brought Fatimid Egypt to its knees. As one Muslim chronicler observed, 'in Egypt the vizierate was the prize of whoever was the strongest. The caliphs were kept behind the veil and viziers were the de facto rulers . . . It was rare for anyone to come to office except by fighting and killing and similar means.' Beset by political instability, the Nile region fell into decline, and the once great Fatimid fleet was left to decay. Against this backdrop of endemic weakness it was no wonder that the ruling powers of Syria and Palestine began to regard Egypt as a prime target.[23]

THE NEW BATTLEGROUND

In the early 1160s, Egypt was spiralling ever deeper into chaos. By 1163 nominal power lay in the hands of the eleven-year-old boy Caliph al-Adid (1160–71), while the vizierate was held by the former governor of Upper Egypt, Shawar. He came to power in early 1163, but within eight months had been overthrown by his Arab chamberlain, Dirgham. Shawar escaped with his life to Syria and, like so many of the usurpers before him, Dirgham 'put to death many of the Egyptian emirs to clear the lands of rivals'. After decades of infighting the country had now been all but stripped of its ruling elite. In this weakened state, Egypt was desperately vulnerable to the predations of its Christian and Muslim neighbours.

The kingdom of Jerusalem had for some years shown increasing interest in the region. Ascalon's conquest in 1153 opened the coastal road south from Palestine – known as the *Via Maris* – and, in 1160, King Baldwin III threatened an invasion, but halted his plans on the promise of a huge annual tribute of 160,000 gold dinars. Then, upon his untimely death in 1163, Baldwin (being childless) was succeeded by his younger brother, Amalric. The great Latin historian of Outremer, William of Tyre, who came to prominence under Amalric's patronage, recorded an intriguingly frank description of the new monarch. Aged twenty-seven, Amalric was said to be earnest and taciturn, 'a man of prudence and discretion', who lacked his predecessor's easy charm and eloquence, in part because he suffered from a mild stammer. Physically, Amalric 'was of goodly height', with 'sparkling eyes', a 'very full beard' and slightly receding blond hair. William praised his royal 'bearing', but acknowledged that, despite his extremely moderate consumption of food and wine, the king 'was excessively fat, with breasts like those of a woman hanging down to his waist'.[24]

One of Amalric's first goals as monarch was to reassert Jerusalem's dominance over Egypt, with an – albeit abortive – siege of the city of Bilbais, which lay upon the banks of one of the Nile's tributaries. Though the Latins were forced to retreat, over the coming years the Frankish king was to dedicate much of his energy and resources to the pursuit of power in Egypt.

Shirkuh ibn Shadi's Egyptian campaigns

Nur al-Din's attention was also being drawn south. Towards the end of 1163, the deposed vizier Shawar arrived in Damascus, hoping to secure political and military support for a counter-coup. Historians have sometimes lauded Nur al-Din's decision to support him as visionary, arguing that he readily embraced the opportunity to wage a new proxy war against the Latins on Egyptian soil, all the while dreaming of the moment when the rule of Aleppo, Damascus and Cairo might be united, encircling Frankish Palestine.

In fact, at first Nur al-Din was reticent. He was aware that protracted entanglement in North Africa would sap resources even as he sought to consolidate his hold over Syria, and he doubted Shawar's reliability as an ally (even though Shawar promised to reward Nur al-Din's aid with one-third of Egypt's grain revenues). But, after some months, the emir was persuaded to take action. Nur al-Din's choice was driven partly by strategic imperative, because, left unchecked, the Jerusalemite Franks might gain an unassailable foothold in the Nile region, with disastrous consequences for the overall balance of power in the Levant. He was, however, also responding to the ambitions of his long-standing Kurdish lieutenant, Shirkuh, who was something of a gnarled veteran, having joined Zangi in the 1130s and then remained loyal to Nur al-Din. Even a Latin contemporary conceded that, despite being blind in one eye because of a cataract, 'small of stature, very stout and fat [and] advanced in years', Shirkuh was feared and respected as 'an able and energetic warrior, hungry for glory and of wide experience in military affairs'. This wily old campaigner had already risen to a position of power within Nur al-Din's inner circle, but in Egypt he saw grander opportunities for advancement. Muslim chroniclers described him as being 'very eager' to lead forces into North Africa, and he played a pivotal role in galvanising and shaping 'Zangid' involvement in the region during the years to come.[25]

In April 1164, Nur al-Din entrusted Shirkuh with command of a sizeable, well-equipped force, instructing him to 'restore Shawar to his office'. At first the campaign proceeded well. The allies stormed into Egypt, seizing control of the town of Fustat, just south of Cairo. By late May Dirgham lay dead, slain by a stray arrow from one of his own men during a skirmish, and the caliph reinstated Shawar as vizier. But after this initial success, relations between the allies deteriorated. Shawar tried to buy off Shirkuh with the promise of 30,000 gold dinars in return for his departure from Egypt, but the Kurdish commander refused.

The newly installed vizier now demonstrated just the sort of elasticity of allegiance that Nur al-Din had feared, inviting Amalric of Jerusalem to come to Egypt's rescue on the promise of bounteous financial rewards. The Frankish king willingly obliged, marching to link up with Shawar in midsummer 1164 and lay siege to Shirkuh, who had taken refuge in Bilbais. The city was only weakly fortified, with a low wall and no fosse, but Shirkuh organised a disciplined defence and for three months a stalemate held. Then, in October, news of Nur al-Din's victories at Harim and Banyas reached Amalric, and he hurriedly negotiated a cessation of hostilities in Egypt, such that both Latins and Syrians were permitted to return to their own lands in peace, and Shawar was left in control of Cairo.

In the years that followed, Shirkuh was said to have 'continued to talk about the project of invading [Egypt]'. By 1167 the Kurdish warlord had amassed an invasion force to overthrow Shawar. Shirkuh was now acting with increasing independence, and, although Nur al-Din did dispatch several warlords to accompany him, the emir apparently 'disliked the plan' to attack Egypt. The campaign was also joined by a rising star of the Damascene court, Shirkuh's twenty-nine-year-old nephew, Yusuf ibn Ayyub. Renowned as one of Nur al-Din's favourite polo partners, Yusuf may have fought at the Battle of Harim in 1164 and was certainly appointed in the following year as Damascus' *shihna* (the equivalent of police chief), in which post he acquired a reputation for firm law enforcement and, perhaps less reliably, for extorting money from prostitutes.

In January 1167, Shirkuh led his force across the Sinai Peninsula. This threat prompted Shawar to make a renewed appeal for aid from Palestine, promising in his extreme desperation to pay the Franks the amazing sum of 400,000 gold dinars. Amalric duly marched into Egypt in February, and North Africa once again became the proxy battleground in a wider struggle between Muslim Syria and Outremer. The two sides clashed in an inconclusive battle that March at al-Babayn, in the desert far to the south of Cairo, and Yusuf later proved his competence as a military commander during a gruelling siege of Alexandria, but neither the Franks nor the Syrians were able to achieve a definitive victory.

Just as in 1164, Shirkuh limped back to Syria with little to show for his efforts. Shawar remained in power, and recent events had only served to augment Frankish influence in the region, as Amalric agreed a new pact with the vizier that guaranteed an annual tribute of 100,000 dinars and installed a Latin prefect and garrison within Cairo itself. Egypt was now a client-state of the kingdom of Jerusalem. But far from punishing Shirkuh for this failure, Nur al-Din rewarded him with the command of Homs and granted Yusuf ibn Ayyub lands around Aleppo. For now, at least, the lord of Damascus was evidently keen to redirect the energies of these two Kurdish commanders towards Syrian affairs, keeping them close at hand to check any tendencies to independence.

This situation might well have endured, to the ultimate frustration of Shirkuh's Egyptian ambitions, had Amalric not sought to overplay his hand. For a number of years the king had been trying to forge closer ties with Byzantium, in part to secure Greek participation in a joint invasion of North Africa, and the first fruits of this diplomacy came in late August 1167 when he married Emperor Manuel's niece, Maria Comnena. Detailed plans for a combined expedition were discussed, and William of Tyre was sent as royal envoy to Constantinople to finalise terms. By the time he returned in autumn 1168, however, Amalric had already taken action. The king had gambled that he could prevail without Greek aid and thus forestall any need to divide Egypt's riches with Manuel. Not content with Egypt's client status, Amalric sought to conquer the Nile. With the vocal encouragement of the Hospitallers, he launched a surprise invasion in late October, marching from Ascalon to attack Bilbais. The city fell after just a few days, on 4 November, and the Franks engaged in a bloody and rapacious sack, sparing few among its populace and looting at will.

In the wake of this opening victory, however, the Latin offensive unravelled. Amalric may have hoped that a sudden savage assault would shatter Egyptian resistance, but in fact his betrayal of the truce with Cairo and the shock caused by the Franks' unfettered ferocity at Bilbais hardened Muslim opposition throughout the Nile region. To make matters worse, the king now slowed the pace of his invasion, perhaps believing that the Vizier Shawar would readily surrender, and Amalric allowed himself to be stalled by offers of negotiation and promises of new tribute. In fact, the king's entire strategy in late 1168 had been predicated upon a dreadful miscalculation. Believing that the events of 1167 had driven a wedge between Cairo and Damascus, he thought that Shawar would be bereft of allies and thus vulnerable, but he had underestimated the vizier's diplomatic agility and Zangid ambition.

The return to the Nile

When the Franks attacked Egypt, Shawar dispatched a flurry of messages to Nur al-Din, begging for assistance and, notwithstanding his earlier misgivings about involvement in North African affairs, the emir now responded with sure and swift resolution. By early December 1168 a full-strength Syrian expeditionary force – including 7,000 mounted troops and thousands more infantrymen – had been assembled south of Damascus. Shirkuh was given overall command, a war chest of 200,000 dinars and full treasury funding to equip his army. But to curtail the Kurd's capacity for independent, self-serving action, Nur al-Din also took care to send a number of other trusted warlords, including the Turk Ayn al-Daulah. Despite their familial connection, Nur al-Din also seems to have placed considerable trust in Shirkuh's nephew, Yusuf ibn Ayyub, who apparently needed some persuading to return to the Nile, haunted as he was by dark memories of the Alexandrian siege.

When news reached Amalric that Shirkuh was marching across the Sinai at the head of 'an innumerable host', the Latin king was horrified. Rushing to muster his forces at Bilbais, Amalric marched east into the desert in late December, hoping to intercept the Syrians before they could join forces with Shawar. But he was too late. Scouts reported back that Shirkuh had already crossed the Nile and, judging that he would now be too heavily outnumbered, Amalric made the difficult and humiliating decision to retreat to Palestine empty-handed.[26]

Egypt, at last, lay open to Shirkuh, and he wasted little time in pressing his advantage. In the first days of January 1169 Shawar made desperate attempts to negotiate terms, but his base of political and military support was faltering. His policy of alliance with the Franks – which had included the deeply unpopular, even scandalous, provision of opening Cairo itself to Latin soldiers – lay in ruins. Shirkuh represented Sunni Syria, traditional enemy of the Shi'ite Fatimids, but for many in the Egyptian capital he was nonetheless preferable to the Christians of Jerusalem, and on 10 January the Caliph al-Adid appears privately to have indicated his own support for the Kurd. On a foggy morning eight days later, an unsuspecting Shawar rode out to continue talks in Shirkuh's camp, only to be attacked and unhorsed by Yusuf ibn Ayyub and another Syrian, Jurdik. Within a few hours the vizier had been executed and his head placed before the caliph. Even now, however, Syrian success was not assured. Riding into Cairo to be appointed as al-Adid's new chief minister, Shirkuh was confronted by an angry mob. Penned in among the Old City's narrow streets, he was said to have 'feared for his life', but in a moment of canny quick thinking he redirected the unruly throng to loot the late Shawar's mansion, and thereby managed to reached the caliphal palace in safety.

In theory, Shirkuh's elevation to the post of Fatimid vizier confirmed Zangid power in the Nile region, heralding a new era of Muslim unity in which Aleppo, Damascus and Cairo might join forces to prosecute the *jihad* against the Franks. Contemporary Muslim sources indicate that, in public at least, Nur al-Din celebrated Shirkuh's achievement, ordering his 'conquest of Egypt' to be proclaimed throughout Syria, even if the emir harboured concerns about the future loyalty of his lieutenant. In fact, Shirkuh's true intentions were never made manifest, for barely two months later he died of an acute, suppurating throat infection, having gorged himself on coarse meats.

Records detailing the emergence of Shirkuh's successor – both as commander of the Syrian expedition and as vizier – are confused and contradictory. He was survived by his Kurdish nephew, Yusuf ibn Ayyub, the veteran of al-Babayn and Alexandria, who might count on the support of most of his uncle's personal military entourage (or *askar*), made up of 500 *mamluks* (slave soldiers). But there were other, perhaps more obviously powerful claimants, including the pro-Zangid Turk, Ayn al-Daulah, and another of Shirkuh's lieutenants, the talented Kurdish warrior al-Mashtub. After days of debate and intrigue it was Yusuf who emerged victorious. Demonstrating a remarkable gift for the subtleties of court politics, Shirkuh's nephew played the other Syrian candidates against one another, using suggestion and innuendo, emerging as the compromise candidate. His spokesman and advocate throughout this process was Isa, a silver-tongued Kurdish jurist and *imam*. Only Ayn al-Daulah remained implacable, returning to Damascus with the promise that he would never serve such an upstart. At the same time, Yusuf showed the caliph and his inner circle of Egyptian advisers a different face – one that led them to believe that, as chief minister, he would prove pliable and ineffectual, an outsider who might later be readily overthrown to usher in a Fatimid resurgence. In late March 1169, his 'command of the [Syrian] troops and appointment as al-Adid's vizier' were duly confirmed.[27]

Whatever the Egyptian caliph's expectations, Yusuf ibn Ayyub soon revealed his true qualities, crushing an attempted palace coup and brutally suppressing a military revolt within months of taking office. Indeed, in the years that followed, it became clear that his ambitions far outstripped those of his uncle, Shirkuh. Capable, in turn, of extreme ruthlessness and principled magnanimity, gifted with political and military acuity, Yusuf's achievements would eclipse even those of his overlord Nur al-Din, in time earning him the grand appellation by which he is more commonly known to

history: *Salah al-Din*, 'the goodness of faith', or, in the western
tongue, Saladin.

SALADIN, LORD OF EGYPT (1169–74)

Despite the seismic impact he would have upon history and the war
for the Holy Land, no physical description of Saladin has survived. In
1169 few could have guessed that this thirty-one-year-old Kurdish
warrior would establish the Ayyubids (named for Saladin's father
Ayyub) as the new rising power within Islam. Some medieval
chroniclers, and many modern historians, have suggested that
Saladin's relationship with his Syrian overlord Nur al-Din soured
almost as soon as the former took up the office of Egyptian vizier; that
the shadows of imminent conflict between Cairo and Damascus were
immediately apparent. In reality, despite a limited degree of friction
during an initial period of adjustment, there is plentiful evidence to
suggest continued cooperation and little to indicate an early move, on
Saladin's part, to assert independence. The balance of power and
interplay of loyalty between these two potentates – champions of the
Zangid and Ayyubid dynasties – would, in time, become a pressing
issue, but in 1169 Saladin had more urgent concerns.[28]

Challenges

Upon succeeding his uncle as vizier to the Fatimid Caliph al-Adid,
Saladin's prospects for survival were bleak. During the preceding
fifteen years the vizierate had changed hands no fewer than eight
times; embittered factionalism, treachery, betrayal and murder were
all pervasive and ingrained features of Cairene politics. Saladin came
to this volatile, lethal environment as an isolated outsider – a Sunni
Kurd in a Shi'a world – backed by limited military and financial
resources. Few can have expected him to prevail.

In spring 1169, Saladin's first instinct was to gather swiftly around
him an inner core of loyal and able supporters. Throughout his career

he seems to have placed great faith in the fidelity of blood; all but alone in Egypt, he turned to his family, asking Nur al-Din to allow members of the Ayyubid line to quit Syria for the Nile. Within months Saladin was joined by his elder brother, Turan-Shah, and nephew, Taqi al-Din. They were later followed by others, including Saladin's father, Ayyub, and another, younger brother, destined to rise to prominence, al-Adil. As vizier, Saladin entrusted key positions of power within Egypt to his relations, but he also won over many of his late uncle Shirkuh's *askar*, who were known as the Asadiyya – a play on his full name, Asad al-Din Shirkuh ibn-Shadi.

These included the fellow Kurd al-Mashtub, who had himself challenged for the vizierate; the forceful and forthright *mamluk* Abu'l Haija the Fat, who in later life reached such an extreme of obesity that he had difficulty standing; and the astute, but rather brutish Caucasian eunuch Qaragush. In years to come these men would prove themselves to be among Saladin's most faithful lieutenants. He also began to assemble his own *askar*, the Salahiyya. Saladin even found some allies inside the fractious Fatimid court itself. The scribe, poet and administrator al-Fadil, a native of Ascalon, who had been employed by a number of viziers, now entered Saladin's service, becoming his secretary and close personal confidant. Al-Fadil was an avid correspondent, and copies of his letters today serve as a vital corpus of historical evidence.

Within months of assuming the vizierate, Saladin needed the support of these trusted allies as he faced a series of assaults on his position. He also revealed a capacity for nuanced political operation in dealing with these threats – one that would prove a signal characteristic of his career. When necessary, Saladin could act with pitiless determination, but he was also able to employ caution and diplomacy. In the early summer of 1169, Mutamin, the leading eunuch within the caliph's palace, sought to engineer a coup against Saladin, opening channels of negotiation with the kingdom of Jerusalem in the hope of prompting yet another Frankish invasion of Egypt to topple the Ayyubids. A secret envoy was dispatched from

Cairo, disguised as a beggar, but passing near Bilbais a Syrian Turk spotted that he was wearing new sandals whose fine quality jarred with his otherwise ragged appearance. With suspicions aroused, the agent was arrested and letters to the Franks discovered, sewn into the lining of his shoes, revealing the plot. Saladin curtailed the independence of the Fatimid court, executing the eunuch Mutamin in August and replacing him with Qaragush, who from this point forward presided over all palace affairs.[29]

Saladin's severe intervention elicited an outbreak of unrest among Cairo's military garrison. The city was packed with some 50,000 black Sudanese troops, whose loyalty to the caliph made them a dangerous counter to Ayyubid authority. For two days they rioted through the streets, marching on Saladin's position in the vizier's palace. Abu'l Haija the Fat was sent to stem their advance, but Saladin knew that he lacked the manpower to prevail in open combat and soon adopted less direct tactics. Most of the Sudanese lived with their families in the al-Mansura quarter of Cairo. Saladin ordered that the entire area be set alight, according to one Muslim contemporary leaving it 'to burn down around [the rebelling troops'] possessions, children and women'. With their morale shattered by this callous atrocity, the Sudanese agreed a truce, the terms of which were supposed to provide for safe passage up the Nile. But once out of the city and travelling south in smaller, disorganised groups, they fell victim to treacherous counter-attacks from Turan-Shah and were virtually annihilated.

Saladin continued to use cold-blooded retaliation when he thought the situation demanded it, but often he adopted more subtle, piecemeal methods to deal with his opponents. Once in office as Fatimid vizier, Saladin faced repeated pressure from the caliph in Baghdad, and from Nur al-Din in Damascus, to depose Egypt's Shi'ite caliph, a heretic in the eyes of Sunni orthodoxy. But Saladin resisted, making no incautious move to topple al-Adid, cultivating instead a mutually beneficial alliance with the young ruler – one that may even have been shaded by a degree of real friendship. Saladin's

position in the Nile region was far too precarious to risk direct
dynastic revolution. To endure as vizier he recognised that, to begin
with at least, he needed the measure of stability, and, even more
importantly, the bounteous financial benefaction attendant upon
caliphal support.

This policy proved its worth in late summer 1169. Still smarting
from the humiliation of his retreat from Egypt the preceding winter,
King Amalric of Jerusalem chose this moment to launch another
assault, this time targeting the port of Damietta, in the eastern reaches
of the Nile Delta, with the assistance of a massive Byzantine fleet.
This attack posed a grave threat to Saladin, yet he proved more than
capable of meeting the challenge. He raised and equipped a huge
army, funded by a truly colossal grant of 1,000,000 gold dinars from
al-Adid's treasury. Rather than command the relief of Damietta in
person, leaving Cairo prey to revolt, Saladin wisely deputised his
nephew, Taqi al-Din, while he remained in the capital. When this
force linked up with Syrian troops sent by Nur al-Din, Amalric found
himself outnumbered and, unable adequately to coordinate
Latin–Greek military operations, his offensive collapsed. This
Muslim victory effectively brought to an end the contest for control
of Egypt, waged against the Latins throughout the 1160s. The Franks
continued to dream of the Nile's conquest, but for now that region
remained in the grasp of Islam, and Saladin.[30]

Having withstood the early challenges of his first year as vizier,
Saladin – echoing Nur al-Din's approach to the exercise of power –
initiated programmes of civil and religious rejuvenation. Alexandria's
fortifications were strengthened, while in Cairo and its southern
suburb of Fustat new centres of Sunni Islamic law were erected.
Saladin later abolished non-Koranic taxation of trade in Egypt
(although he did hike up other forms of levy in order to make up for
the shortfall in state income). In November 1170 he also appeared to
take up the mantle of *mujahid*, leading his first invasion of Frankish
Palestine. At the head of a sizeable army, Saladin overran the small
Latin fortress of Darum, just south of Gaza, and skirmished with

King Amalric's hastily assembled relief force before marching to the shores of the Red Sea to occupy the port of Aqaba. While blows were evidently struck against the Christians during this campaign, Saladin's primary objective may have been to shore up the land route between the Nile region and Damascus, and it would probably be wrong to regard this venture as the first blossoming of his dedication to the holy war.

LIEUTENANT OR COMMANDER

As Saladin's control of Egypt solidified, his continued lack of independence came ever more sharply into focus. He was a Sunni warlord, possessed of growing power and resources, yet still only second in command to a Shi'ite caliph and bound by ties of subservience to Nur al-Din. Caution had served Saladin well to this point, but by late summer 1171, with his hold over Cairo secured, he was ready to oust the Fatimids. Even now, however, he moved with marked restraint, largely forsaking the traditional aberrations of Egyptian politics – bloody *coup d'état* and wholesale murder. This approach was, in part, made possible by the young Caliph al-Adid's failing health. Around the end of August he contracted a severe illness and, though barely twenty years old, was soon at death's door.[31]

On Friday 10 September 1171, Saladin took his first guarded step towards autonomy. For centuries, the name of the Shi'ite caliph had echoed through Egypt's mosques during Friday prayer, recited in honorific recognition of Fatimid authority. On this day, however, in Fustat, al-Adid's name was replaced with that of the Sunni Abbasid caliph of Baghdad. Saladin was testing the water, gauging whether open rebellion would follow, before showing his hand in Cairo itself, but no uprising ensued. The next day he presided over an imposing military parade in the capital, as virtually the entire might of his armies marched through the streets, prompting his secretary al-Fadil to record that 'no king of Islam had ever possessed an army to match this'. For his Egyptian subjects, and the Latin and Greek ambassadors who happened to be visiting Cairo at that point, the message was unambiguous. Saladin was now lord of Egypt. News of these events reached the dying al-Adid and he implored Saladin, still nominally his vizier, to come to his bedside, hoping to beg for the lives of his family. Fearing a plot, Saladin refused – although it was said that he later regretted this hard-hearted decision – and the caliph died on 13 September. Saladin made a great show of accompanying his body to its burial and took no steps to eliminate his offspring. Instead they were housed and cared for within the caliphal palace, but forbidden from having children so that their line would die out. Regardless of its piecemeal nature, the consequences of this revolution were dramatic. The days of the Fatimids were at an end; the religious and political schism that had divided Egypt from the rest of the Muslim Near East since the tenth century receded, leaving Saladin to pose as a champion of Sunni orthodoxy.

Given the caliph's near-legendary reputation for fabulous wealth, one of the immediate benefits of al-Adid's death for Saladin should have been a massive influx of hard cash. But upon occupying the Fatimid palace Saladin found a surprisingly small store of money, much of the reserves having been used to fund the late Vizier Shawar's exorbitant tributes to Jerusalem and Damascus, and Saladin's own defence of Damietta in 1169. What treasures he did find – a 'mountain' of rubies, a huge emerald and an assortment of giant pearls – were quickly auctioned off.

Saladin's abolition of the Fatimid caliphate and subjection of Egypt in 1171 were, at least in theory, not merely personal victories; they were also a triumph for his overlord, Nur al-Din, whose realm could now be said to stretch from Egypt to Syria and beyond. Certainly, both men were sent splendid ceremonial robes of victory by the caliph of Baghdad that autumn. But behind the façade of Sunni unity and ascendancy, signs of strain between the lord and his ever more powerful lieutenant were becoming apparent. With the unification of Aleppo, Damascus and Cairo and the resultant encirclement of the

Frankish kingdom of Jerusalem, Nur al-Din might have expected to draw upon the Nile's wealth and resources, and Saladin's military support, to launch an all-out offensive on Palestine. From autumn 1171, however, as the new lord of Egypt, Saladin began to act as a sovereign ruler in his own right. Since the days of Shirkuh's North African adventures, Ayyubid involvement in the region had always been gilded with a self-serving edge and, ultimately, Egypt's conquest had depended above all upon Saladin's own qualities: his acute political and military vision; his patience, guile and mercilessness. Now he might arguably claim to be Nur al-Din's equal and ally rather than his servant.

Open conflict was, in part, averted by Nur al-Din's preoccupations elsewhere in his realm. Syria and Palestine were struck yet again by a series of damaging earthquakes in the early 1170s, forcing the diversion of resources into extensive rebuilding programmes. In Iraq, the death of his brother, followed by the Abbasid caliph's demise, prompted Nur al-Din once more to involve himself in Mesopotamian affairs, while in the Jazira and Anatolia, new opportunities for territorial expansion similarly commanded his attention. Then, in 1172, a dispute with the Franks over trading rights along the Syrian coast triggered a number of punitive raids against Antioch and the county of Tripoli.

In spite of these distractions, Nur al-Din did seek Saladin's support in one crucial theatre of conflict, the Latin-held desert area east of the River Jordan known as Transjordan. This region was certainly a valuable prize: annexed in the early twelfth century by the construction of Frankish castles at Montreal and Kerak, it gave the Latins at least partial control over the main land route from Damascus to either Egypt or to Mecca and Medina, the sacred cities of the Arabian Peninsula. Saladin has been accused, both by some medieval chroniclers and a number of modern scholars, of failing to cooperate fully in two attempts to conquer this frontier zone in the early 1170s. This 'treachery' supposedly revealed that Saladin was driven by self-serving ambition rather than a desire to promote the wider interests of Islam. But did he really turn his back on Nur al-Din, wrecking an opportunity to triumph in the war for the Holy Land?

In late September 1171, soon after the Fatimid caliphate's abolition, Saladin marched into Transjordan with the apparent intention of launching a joint operation with Nur al-Din. As the latter came south from Damascus, Saladin laid siege to Montreal, but after a short period he suddenly decided to retreat to Egypt, and the two Muslim armies never combined. The Mosuli historian Ibn al-Athir, who supported Nur al-Din's Zangid dynasty, saw in these events a definitive moment of division between Saladin and his overlord, asserting that a 'deep difference' emerged between them. He maintained that, having reached Montreal, Saladin was warned by his advisers about the real strategic and political consequences of Transjordan's conquest. Counselled that the opening of a secure route from Damascus to Egypt would lead to Nur al-Din's seizure of the Nile region and cautioned that 'if Nur al-Din comes to you here, you will have to meet him and then he will exercise his authority over you as he wishes', Saladin fled.

The problem with Ibn al-Athir's account is that it relies upon the notion of Saladin as a naïve commander, devoid of foresight. Yet, on the evidence of his striking successes in Egypt, Saladin was no innocent, but a far-sighted and astute operator. He would surely have recognised in advance the wider ramifications of the Transjordan enterprise, long before actually arriving at Montreal itself. Frustratingly, the other surviving sources shed little additional light upon events: according to one account, Saladin excused himself by arguing that rebellion was brewing in Egypt, while another contemporary Arabic writer simply observed that 'something happened' to cause his precipitous return to Cairo.

Ibn al-Athir went on to accuse Saladin of abandoning a second joint venture before Nur al-Din could arrive, this time against Kerak in early summer 1173. While Saladin certainly did besiege that fortress at this point, he was probably acting independently of Damascus, as Nur al-Din was busy with the affairs of northern Syria and in no position to lead troops into Transjordan.[32]

The evidence against Saladin for the period between 1171 and 1173 is, on balance, inconclusive. He cannot be said categorically to have betrayed Nur al-Din, nor was he solely culpable for the failure to prevail in the *jihad*. Publicly at least Saladin affirmed his continued subservience to the Zangid dynasty after the end of Fatimid rule in 1171 – Nur al-Din was included in the Friday prayer and Egyptian coins were minted bearing his name alongside that of the Abbasid caliph.

In reality, any hostility brewing between Damascus and Cairo in the early 1170s was probably not primarily related to the issue of unified military action, but, rather, connected to the question of hard cash. Above all else, Nur al-Din wanted to tap into Egypt's riches and began demanding an annual tribute from the region. To this end he sent an official from Damascus to carry out a full audit of Egypt's revenue at the end of 1173. As the financial investigation proceeded apace in Egypt during the first months of 1174, tension mounted. Both Nur al-Din and Saladin mobilised troops, although it is not certain whether this was in preparation for a direct confrontation or a renewed attempt at collaboration. In all likelihood, both men were making a show of strength as a precursor to intense diplomatic wrangling, aware that this might in time escalate into open conflict. Discord was certainly in the air, as even Saladin himself later admitted to his biographer: 'We had heard that Nur al-Din would perhaps attack us in Egypt. Several of our comrades advised that he should be openly resisted and his authority rejected and that his army should be met in battle to repel it if his hostile move became a reality.' He apparently added, somewhat less convincingly, 'I alone disagreed with them, urging that it was not right to say anything of the sort.'[33]

Fate intervened to prevent what potentially would have been a hugely damaging Sunni civil war. While waiting for his auditor to report from Cairo, Nur al-Din fell ill in late spring 1174. Playing polo outside Damascus on 6 May, he was seized by some form of fit and, by the time he returned to the citadel, was clearly unwell. Suffering with what may have been angina, at first he stubbornly refused to call physicians. By the time his court doctor, al-Rahbi, arrived, Nur al-Din was huddled in a small prayer room, deep within the citadel, 'close to death . . . his voice barely audible'. When it was suggested that he be treated with bleeding, Nur al-Din bluntly refused, saying, 'you do not bleed a man of sixty', and in the face of this great ruler no one argued.

On 15 May 1174 Nur al-Din died, his body later being interred in one of the religious schools he had had built in Damascus. Even among his enemies the Franks, Nur al-Din was revered as 'a mighty persecutor of the Christian name and faith . . . a just and valiant prince'. He was the first Muslim leader since the advent of the crusades to unite Aleppo and Damascus. His vision and quickening sense of devotion had ushered in a new era of religious rejuvenation within the Sunni world, resuscitating the notion of *jihad* against Islam's enemies as an emblematic and imperative cause. And yet, at his death, the Franks remained unconquered, and the hallowed city of Jerusalem still lay in Christendom's grasp.[34]

10

HEIR OR USURPER

Nur al-Din's death in May 1174 appeared to furnish Saladin with a perfect opportunity to emerge from the shadow of Zangid Syrian overlordship, allowing the lieutenant to become leader, assert his right to fully independent rule and assume the mantle of champion in Islam's holy war against the Franks. It is only too easy to imagine the history of twelfth-century Near Eastern Islam as an era of linear progression; one in which a swelling tide of *jihadi* resurgence gathered pace under Zangi, Nur al-Din and, finally, Saladin – with the torch of leadership passing smoothly, and almost inevitably, from one Muslim 'hero' to another. This was certainly the impression fostered and energetically promoted by some Islamic contemporaries.

The central flaw in this admittedly alluring illusion is that Saladin was not proclaimed Nur al-Din's heir in 1174. Instead, Nur al-Din left behind an eleven-year-old son, al-Salih, who he hoped would take up the reins of power. The great Syrian lord was also survived by an assortment of other blood relations who might seek to protect and perpetuate Zangid ascendancy in the Near and Middle East. As such there was, in reality, no natural or immediate path to advancement open to Saladin in 1174. Instead he was presented with choices: to prioritise his hold over the Nile region, constructing a largely self-contained Egyptian realm; or to seek to emulate, or even eclipse, Nur al-Din's achievements, to become the premier Muslim leader in the Levant.

A HERO FOR ISLAM

Saladin embraced this latter objective with singular dedication and vigour. The fundamental question – similar to that asked of Nur al-Din – was why? Did Saladin seek power, forging a despotic, pan-Levantine Islamic Empire, to fulfil his own self-serving, personal ambition? Or was he driven by a higher cause, pursuing Muslim unification as a means to an end – the necessary precursor to success in the *jihad* against the Christian Franks? Some attempt to understand Saladin's motives and mentality has to be made, not least because of his profound importance as a historical figure, particularly in Islamic culture. In the modern world, Saladin has come to be regarded as the supreme Muslim champion of the crusading age; an extraordinarily powerful talisman of the Islamic past, viewed by many as a revered hero. The task of stripping away the layers of legend, propaganda and bias to explore the reality of his career is thus particularly sensitive and demands scrupulous and assiduous care.

In relative terms, the contemporary sources for Saladin's life are plentiful, but they are also problematic. A number of Muslim eyewitnesses wrote about his remarkable achievements, including two of his closest supporters – his secretary Imad al-Din al-Isfahani (from 1174) and his adviser Baha al-Din Ibn Shaddad (from 1188) – but both presented sanitised biographies of their master after the event. Their works are predicated upon the notion that Saladin was driven by heartfelt religious devotion to serve Islam and fight the Franks. According to Baha al-Din, Saladin's spiritual conviction deepened after he assumed power over Egypt in 1169, forgoing 'wine-drinking and turning his back on frivolity', and from this point forward he was supposedly driven pious by 'passion, constancy and zeal'. His commitment to the holy war was said to be absolute:

> Saladin was very diligent and zealous for the *jihad*. If anyone were to swear that, since his embarking upon the *jihad*, he had not expended a single dinar or dirham on anything but the *jihad* or support for it, he would be telling the truth and true in his oath. The *jihad*, his love and passion for it, had taken a mighty hold of his heart and all his being, so much so that he talked of nothing else [and] thought of nothing but the means to pursue it.

This highly favourable depiction is balanced, to some extent, by other evidence. The Iraqi chronicler Ibn al-Athir, a supporter of the rival Zangid dynasty, offered a more dispassionate view of Saladin. Manuscript copies also survive of the public and private correspondence written for Saladin by his scribe and confidant al-Fadil. This crucial (yet still relatively under-exploited) corpus of material offers valuable insights into Saladin's thinking and his own widespread use of propaganda and interest in image creation.[35]

It is also imperative to contextualise any judgements about Saladin's character and career. As a medieval ruler he operated within a violent and venomous political environment – to survive and advance it would have been virtually impossible for him always to act with pure-bred nobility, honour, justice and clemency. Indeed, few, if any, of history's great rulers could claim such qualities, whatever age they lived in.

It is, in fact, evident that Saladin was not simply a bloodthirsty tyrant. In seeking to usurp power from Nur al-Din's heirs, he could have followed the example set by Zangi, relying upon fear and brutality to amass and maintain power. Instead, Saladin chose to pursue policies that closely mimicked those of his former overlord, Nur al-Din – indeed, in this regard at least he could be said to have been Nur al-Din's true successor. Saladin's task in 1174 was essentially to recreate the achievements of the Zangids, but in reverse, subduing

Damascus, Aleppo and Mosul. To do so he employed a cautious fusion of military might and adept political manipulation. And throughout he set great store by notions of legitimacy and just cause. This need for validation was amplified by Saladin's social and ethnic background. What had been true for the Zangid Turks was doubly so for the Ayyubids as Kurdish mercenary warlords – all too easily they could be characterised as upstart outsiders in a Near and Middle Eastern world historically dominated by Arab and Persian Muslim ruling elites.

Throughout the 1170s and beyond, Saladin sought to legitimate his ascent to power and prominence by emphasising his roles as a defender of Islam and Sunni orthodoxy, and as the supposed servant of the Abbasid caliph of Baghdad. He also used the notion of *jihad* to justify the need for Islamic unity under one ruler. Just as Pope Urban II had harnessed the power of a feared and threatening Muslim enemy to unite western Europe in support of the First Crusade, so Saladin proved only too willing to present the Levantine Franks as menacing and inimitable foes.

At the same time, he evidently aspired to extend his own power and to create an enduring dynasty. In the 1170s he began styling himself as a 'sultan' (king or ruler), a title reflective of autonomous authority. He was also busy siring a new generation of potential heirs. Few details survive of the numerous wives and slave girls who begat his children, but already in 1174, at the age of thirty-six, he had five sons, the eldest of whom, al-Afdal, was born in 1170.

IN NUR AL-DIN'S WAKE

From summer 1174 it was not just Saladin who looked to exploit the power vacuum left in the Near East by Nur al-Din's demise. Members of the late emir's court and extended family – the Zangid dynasty – sought to assert either their own independence or their right to act, in effect, as his successor. Within months, the Zangid realm, so patiently constructed over twenty-eight years, fractured almost beyond recognition, ushering a bewildering array of protagonists on to the stage.

To the east in Mesopotamia, two of Nur al-Din's nephews held power – Saif al-Din in Mosul and Imad al-Din Zangi in nearby Sinjar. Both now began vying for control of territory west towards the Euphrates. In Syria, Nur al-Din's young son, al-Salih, became a political pawn as various factions claimed to be his 'protector'. The boy was eventually spirited away to Aleppo, where the eunuch Gumushtegin had emerged, through bloody intrigue, as the dominant force. Meanwhile, in Damascus a group of emirs, headed by the military commander Ibn al-Muqaddam, seized power. Not surprisingly, the Latins too saw a chance for action that summer. King Amalric's primary objective was the reconquest of Banyas, the frontier settlement lost to Damascus a decade earlier. He laid siege to the town for two weeks, but the onset of ill health prevented him from pressing any advantage, and he agreed a truce with Ibn al-Muqaddam in return for a cash payment and the release of some Christian captives.

This urgent flurry of activity gripped Syria, but in Egypt Saladin bided his time. In midsummer a Sicilian fleet attacked Alexandria, while in Upper Egypt surviving Fatimid emirs tried to incite rebellion. These threats were readily repulsed, but Saladin still approached the issue of the succession to Nur al-Din's realm with great caution. Overtly conscious of the need to counter accusations of despotic usurpation, Saladin forsook the blunt tools of invasion and violent suppression, instead employing guileful diplomacy against a backdrop of determined propaganda. One of his first acts was to write to al-Salih, declaring his own loyalty, affirming that the young ruler's name had duly replaced that of Nur al-Din during the Friday prayer in Egypt, and that Saladin stood ready and willing as a 'servant' to defend al-Salih against his rivals. In another letter, the sultan proclaimed that he would fight 'as a sword against [al-Salih's] enemies', warning that Syria was surrounded 'on all sides' by foes, such as the Franks, who had to be fought.

These two documents reveal that within weeks of Nur al-Din's death Saladin was publicising the official agenda under which he would operate through much of the 1170s. In the years to come he sought, with almost unfailing tenacity, to extend his own personal authority over the shattered remnants of Nur al-Din's realm. But always this grasping pursuit of power was veiled beneath the public avowal of twinned principles: that as al-Salih's appointed guardian Saladin laboured tirelessly, and without regard for his own reward, to preserve Zangid authority; and that this drive towards Islamic unity was of paramount importance precisely because the Muslim world was engaged in a historic struggle with an implacable Christian foe, who even now retained possession of the sacred city of Jerusalem.[36]

Of course, many of the sultan's contemporary opponents were only too aware that Saladin actually was trying to build his own empire, even if it was one constructed in the interests of *jihad*, and they were often willing to publicise their fears and accusations. Under these circumstances, Saladin relied upon the politics of fear to lend force to his programme of dissimulation. If matters proceeded peacefully in Syria, the sultan would have no excuse to intervene – somewhat ironically, in 1174 Saladin thus hoped that his rivals would act against al-Salih's interests and that the Franks would go on the offensive.

The occupation of Damascus

Given his base of operations in Egypt, Saladin's first objective in seeking to reconsolidate Nur al-Din's dominions under his own rule had to be Damascus. Seizing upon Ibn al-Muqaddam's decision to buy peace with the kingdom of Jerusalem at Banyas, the sultan now levelled allegations of weakness against the Damascene court, citing its failure to pursue the holy war as a probable cause to intervene in Syrian affairs. Nur al-Din's former secretary, the Persian scribe and scholar Imad al-Din al-Isfahani, recorded the exchange of correspondence that followed. Ibn al-Muqaddam chided Saladin, writing, 'let it not be said that you have designs upon the house of the one who established you [as] this does not befit your good character'. The sultan responded with a forceful assertion of his intentions:

> We choose for Islam and its people only what will unite them, and for the [Zangid] house only what will preserve its root and its branches . . . I am in one valley and those who think evil of me are in another . . . If we had inclined to any other path, we would not have chosen the way of consultation and writing.

This was the message that Saladin wished to broadcast throughout Syria, but, stirring as his words may have been, they were unlikely to sway policy on their own. In all probability it was fear of a potential alliance between Mosul and Aleppo that, by summer's end, prompted Ibn al-Muqaddam to side with Saladin, inviting him to come to the aid of Damascus. This was precisely the opportunity that the sultan had hoped for. Leaving his brother al-Adil to govern Egypt, Saladin marched into Syria in October 1174 equipped with two weapons: an army with which to overcome any pockets of resistance and, perhaps more importantly, tens of thousands of gold dinars to buy support. His entry into the ancient city on 28 October proved to be a peaceful affair.

One of Saladin's contemporary biographers described the day, taking care to emphasise the sultan's personal connection to Damascus, home of his youth, writing that 'he went straight to his house and people flocked to him rejoicing'. His lavish largesse likewise was highlighted: 'That same day he distributed huge sums of money to the people and showed himself pleased and delighted with the Damascenes, as they did with him. He went up into the citadel and his power was firmly established.' To emphasise the orthodox quality and magnanimity of his rule, Saladin went to pray in the Grand Umayyad Mosque, ordered the immediate revocation of non-Koranic taxation and forbade looting. He later justified his occupation of the city as a step on the road to retaking Jerusalem, arguing that 'to hold back from the holy war is a crime for which there can be no excuse'. But many remained unconvinced by Saladin's claims – Jurdik, his former ally in Egypt, for one, sided with Aleppo. Even the Franks living in Palestine were aware of the incipient power struggle and one Latin contemporary noted that Saladin's occupation of Damascus contravened 'the loyalty he owed to his lord and master [al-Salih]'.[37]

Nonetheless, in the closing months of 1174, a number of Syria's Muslim potentates decided to back Saladin – judging that this was their best chance of survival – and the sultan was able to extend his authority northwards in a series of largely bloodless campaigns, seizing control of Homs, Hama and Baalbek (where Ibn al-Muqaddam was duly rewarded for his support with a command). Once again, Saladin took great care to justify these conquests. After taking Homs he wrote in a public dispatch back to Egypt, 'our move was not made in order to snatch a kingdom for ourselves, but to set up the standard of the holy war'. His opponents in Syria had, he argued, 'become enemies, preventing the accomplishment of our purpose with regard to this war'. He also stressed that he had taken care not to damage the town of Homs itself, 'knowing how close it was to the unbelievers'. However, a more personal letter, written around the same time to his nephew Farrukh-Shah (an increasingly prominent lieutenant), seems to offer a less gilded view of events. Here Saladin bluntly criticised the 'feeble minds' of Homs' populace and acknowledged that cultivating his own reputation for justice and clemency was the 'key to the lands'. He even managed to joke about his future prospects. His primary objective was now Aleppo, the name of which in Arabic (*Halab*) also means 'milk'. Saladin forecast that city's imminent fall, writing that 'we have only to do the milking and Aleppo will be ours'.[38]

Stalking Aleppo

By the start of 1175, Saladin was certainly in a position to threaten Aleppo, but in spite of his rather bold prediction, that city proved to be an intractable obstacle, stalling the extension of his authority over all Syria for years to come. Aleppo's formidable citadel and strong garrison meant that any attempt at an assault siege would require patience and extensive military resources. But even if successful, such a direct approach likely would lead to a protracted and bloody conflict – not a conquest that would sit comfortably alongside Saladin's preferred image as a humble guardian of Islam. The sultan must have hoped that his opponents would give him grounds to attack the city, perhaps by abusing or even murdering al-Salih, but Gumushtegin was far too astute to make such an obvious blunder. The young Zangid heir, the seed of legitimacy, was more valuable alive as a puppet ruler within Aleppo. Indeed, Gumushtegin even persuaded the boy to deliver an emotive, tearful speech to the city's populace, begging for their protection against Saladin's tyranny.

To compound Saladin's problems, the rulers of Aleppo and Mosul put aside their differences in order to unite against the threatening tide of Ayyubid rule. Over the next year and a half Saladin remained in Syria, prosecuting a succession of limited and largely inconclusive sieges of Aleppo and its satellite settlements. In April 1175, and then again a year later in April 1176, he met Aleppan–Mosuli forces in pitched battle, winning convincing victories on both occasions. These two confrontations enhanced the sultan's burgeoning reputation as Islam's leading general, while proving the marked superiority of his increasingly experienced Egyptian and Damascene armies. But in practical terms they proved indecisive. Convinced that lasting dominion of Syria could not be achieved when stained with Muslim blood, Saladin sought to limit the degree of actual inter-Muslim combat that took place, relying upon troop discipline rather than martial ferocity to prevail and curtailing any harrying of his retreating foes once they had been driven from the field. His opponents were thus permitted to lick their wounds and regroup.

By the summer of 1176 the combination of tempered military aggression and incessant propaganda seemed to have run its course. Gumushtegin remained in control of Aleppo, alongside al-Salih, while Saif al-Din continued to govern Mosul, but these allies were forced, by steps, to agree to some concessions. Saladin's right to rule the Syrian territory he held to the south of Aleppo was acknowledged in May 1175, and this position was formalised subsequently by a caliphal diploma of investiture issued in Baghdad. When peace was settled in July 1176, Saladin recognised that he could no longer claim to be al-Salih's sole legal guardian (although the sultan did continue to present himself as the Zangid's servant), but by this point Aleppo had agreed, albeit in rather vague terms, to contribute troops to the holy war.

Throughout this period, Saladin had tried, with some success, to damage Gumushtegin's and Saif al-Din's reputations by repeatedly accusing them of negotiating with the Latins. Saladin often wrote to the caliph complaining that they had forged treacherous pacts with the Christians sealed by the exchange of prisoners. This echoed his condemnation of the submissive truce agreed with Jerusalem by Ibn al-Muqaddam in 1174. The sultan was trying to present his Syrian campaigns as a heartfelt, ideological struggle to unite Islam against a foreboding Frankish enemy. In fact, this was pure rhetorical invective, for Saladin himself agreed two truces with the Latins in this period.[39]

The Old Man of the Mountain

Saladin's attempts to subdue Syria in the mid-1170s were complicated by entanglements with the Assassins. By this time the Syrian wing of this secretive order was firmly ensconced in the Ansariyah Mountains and was flourishing under the leadership of a formidable Iraqi, Rashid al-Din Sinan, popularly known as the Old Man of the Mountain. Ruling the order for close to three decades in the later twelfth century, Sinan's reputation as a man of 'subtle and brilliant intelligence' gained wide currency among Muslims and Christians alike. William of Tyre believed that Sinan commanded the absolute loyalty and obedience of his followers, noting that 'they regard nothing as too harsh or difficult and eagerly undertake even the most dangerous tasks at his command'.[40]

The Assassins were an embedded, independent and largely

unpredictable force in Near Eastern affairs; and their chief weapon –
political assassination – continued to prove highly effective. Saladin's
drive to dominate Syria, and more specifically his campaigns against
Aleppo, brought him into the Assassins' orbit. In early 1175, Sinan
decided to target Saladin, probably at least in part on the prompting
of the Aleppan ruler Gumushtegin. With the sultan stationed outside
Aleppo, a group of thirteen knife-wielding Assassins managed to
penetrate the heart of his camp and launch an assault. Saladin's
bodyguards came to his aid, cutting down one assailant even as he
leapt to strike the sultan himself. Although the plot was foiled, there
were still fatalities among the Salahiyya. Soon afterwards, Saladin
wrote warning his nephew Farrukh-Shah to be watchful at all times,
and before long it became standard practice to place the sultan's own
tents within a fortified and heavily guarded enclosure, isolated from
the rest of the camp.

In spite of these precautions, the Assassins managed to strike again
in May 1176. While Saladin was visiting one of his emir's tents
four Assassins attacked, and this time came perilously close to
completing their murderous task. In the first sudden flurry of
movement, the sultan was struck and only his armour saved him from
a severe wound. Once again his men pounced on the killers,
butchering them to a man, but Saladin was left bloodied by a cut to
his cheek and badly shaken. From this point onwards, any members
of his entourage whom he did not personally recognise were
dismissed.

In August 1176 Saladin decided to deal with this troublesome
threat. He laid siege to the major Assassin castle of Masyaf, but after
less than a week he broke off the investment, retreating to Hama. The
motive for the sultan's departure and the details of any deal brokered
with Sinan remain mysterious. A number of Muslim accounts repeat
the story that, under the threat of an unwavering Assassin campaign
to murder members of his Ayyubid family, Saladin agreed to a pact of
mutual non-aggression with the Old Man. One Aleppan chronicler
offered an even more chilling explanation, describing how the sultan

was visited by Sinan's envoy. Once searched for weapons, this messenger was granted an audience with Saladin, but insisted upon conferring with him in private. The sultan eventually agreed to dismiss all but his two most skilful and trusted bodyguards – men he regarded as his 'own sons'.

> The envoy then turned to the pair of guards and said: 'If I ordered you in the name of my master to kill this sultan, would you do so?' They answered yes, and drew their swords saying: 'Command us as you wish.' Saladin was astounded, and the messenger left, taking them with him. And thereafter Saladin inclined to make peace with [Sinan].[41]

The reality of this tale may be doubted – if the Assassins had indeed had agents so close to Saladin they surely would have succeeded in killing him in 1175 or 1176 – but the story's implicit message was accurate. It was all but impossible to protect oneself permanently from the Assassins. By whatever means, Saladin and Sinan evidently achieved some form of accommodation in 1176, because the sultan never again attacked the order's mountain enclave and no further attempts were made on his life.

SALADIN'S AYYUBID REALM

In late summer 1176 Saladin brought almost two years of campaigning against Aleppo to an end. With a truce in place enshrining his possession of Damascus and the bulk of Syria, he willingly perpetuated the fiction of subservience to al-Salih. Across Saladin's dominions, the young ruler's name continued to appear on coinage and to be recited in Friday prayer. But the sultan did seek further to legitimise his own authority by marrying Nur al-Din's widow Ismat, daughter of Unur, the long-dead ruler of Burid Damascus. This was, first and foremost, a political union, for her hand allowed Saladin to connect himself to that city's two historic ruling dynasties, but real friendship, perhaps even love, seems to have blossomed between the couple.* By this time, the sultan had taken other steps to appropriate the machinery of Zangid government. Nur al-Din's secretary, Imad al-Din al-Isfahani, was taken into service and, alongside al-Fadil, soon became one of the sultan's closest confidants.

In September 1176 Saladin returned to Egypt. This move offered him something of a respite from the dangers and confrontations of recent months – he paused in Alexandria with his six-year-old son al-Afdal for three days in March 1177 to listen to tales of the Prophet Muhammad's life – but it was also reflective of a new reality in the sultan's life. Presiding over a realm that stretched from the Nile to the Syrian Orontes, he now faced all the practical difficulties attendant upon governing a geographically expansive kingdom in the medieval age. One overriding issue was communication. Facing the same problem, Nur al-Din had supplemented his network of horse-borne couriers and messengers with the extensive use of carrier pigeons, and Saladin now followed suit. He also maintained spies and scouts in Syria and Palestine to garner intelligence. Even so, no matter how they were transported, messages were always subject to possible enemy interception, and the sultan sometimes resorted to writing in code. A significant truth of living through this era, for Muslims and Christians alike, was that even within allied groups the transfer of information was hugely imprecise, while knowledge of enemy intentions and movements was often based upon pure guesswork. Ignorance, error and disinformation all served to shape decision making and, in the years to come, Saladin always struggled to maintain knowledge of events across the Muslim world, and to retain even a partial understanding of Frankish plans and actions. In this situation, al-Fadil's and Imad al-Din's roles as

---

* Ismat died in January 1186 when Saladin was himself suffering from severe illness. The sultan's closest advisers kept the news of his wife's demise from him for two months for fear of causing him shock and distress.

correspondents, communicators and propagandists were of paramount importance.

The union of Cairo and Damascus under Ayyubid rule also forced Saladin to embrace the use of lieutenants to govern in his absence. Throughout his career the sultan turned first to his blood relations to fill such posts, and sometimes this system of trusting his extended family worked well. In autumn 1176 he returned to find that his brother al-Adil and nephew Farrukh-Shah had governed Egypt with attentive prudence. In Syria, however, arrangements proved to be less satisfactory. Deputised as ruler of Damascus, Saladin's elder brother Turan-Shah proved to be an incompetent liability. Given to excessive financial liberality – infamously accruing personal debts of some 200,000 gold dinars at his death – he was also fond of life's more dissolute distractions. With Syria stricken by a protracted drought in the late 1170s, it gradually became clear that Turan-Shah would have to be replaced. By 1178 Saladin despairingly admitted that 'one can overlook small faults and keep silent about minor matters, but where the whole land is eaten up . . . this shakes the pillars of Islam'.

The sultan enjoyed greater success in his attempts to balance the use of physical and financial resources across the lands he now commanded. In 1177 he prioritised the Nile region, strengthening the defences of Alexandria and Damietta and initiating the construction of a massive fortified wall to enclose both Cairo and its southern suburb Fustat. He also took the costly but far-sighted decision to rebuild Egypt's once famous fleet. Some ship-building materials and sailors were brought in from Libya, but Saladin's quest for the best timber soon led him to forge commercial links with Pisa and Genoa. This was just one example of mounting international trade in military materials, technology and even weaponry between Ayyubid Islam and the West that continued even as the holy war intensified. The sultan's investment had striking strategic consequences, for within a few years he controlled a navy of sixty galleys and twenty transport vessels. Long bereft of any real power over mercantile and martial shipping in the

Mediterranean, Near Eastern Islam could once again vie for control of the sea.[42]

THE LEPER KING

Just as Saladin was consolidating his hold over Egypt and Damascus, a new Latin king of Jerusalem was finding his feet. In 1174 King Amalric had broken off from the siege of Banyas complaining of illness. In fact, he had contracted an extreme case of dysentery and, by July, the thirty-eight-year-old sovereign lay dead. He was succeeded by his son, Baldwin IV, a young monarch whose reign would be shadowed by tragedy and ever-deepening crisis. Baldwin's status at the moment of his precipitous elevation to the throne was peculiar. In 1163 Amalric had agreed, on the insistence of the High Court, to renounce his wife, Agnes of Courtenay (daughter of Count Joscelin II of Edessa), before assuming the crown of Jerusalem. The official grounds for the annulment of their marriage had been consanguinity – they were third cousins – but the underlying cause may have been suspicions that Agnes would seek to promote the interests of the now largely landless Courtenay clan in Palestine at the expense of the incumbent aristocracy. Amalric and Agnes had already produced two children, Baldwin and his elder sister Sibylla, and it was agreed that their legitimacy would be upheld, even though Amalric was soon remarried to the Byzantine princess Maria Comnena.

Baldwin IV's childhood and minority

Just two years old in 1163, Baldwin grew up in a dislocated familial environment. His mother Agnes also remarried almost immediately and, being largely absent from court, played little or no part in Baldwin's upbringing, while his stepmother Maria maintained a cool distance, more concerned to further the interests of her own offspring with Amalric. Even the infant Sibylla was effectively a stranger to the young prince, being brought up within the secluded walls of her aunt Yvetta's convent at Bethany.

In the end, one of Baldwin's closest childhood companions turned out to be the cleric and court historian William of Tyre. Appointed as tutor to the young prince around 1170, William was tasked to 'train [the heir designate] in the formation of character as well as to instruct him in the knowledge of letters' and a range of academic studies. William's history of the Latin East offers a poignant and intimate character sketch of Baldwin as a boy. Bearing a marked physical resemblance to his father, even to the extent of mirroring the king's gait in walking and his tone of voice, the prince was described as 'a good-looking child for his age', quick-witted, with an excellent memory, beloved of both learning and riding. Yet William also wrote with heart-rending honesty about a moment of dreadful revelation in Baldwin's life.

One day, when he was nine years old and living in William's household, the prince was playing with a group of noble-born boys. They were competing in a popular test of fortitude, 'pinching each other on the arms and hands with their nails, as children often do' to see who would cry out in pain. Despite their best efforts, no one was able to make Baldwin reveal the barest sign of discomfort. At first, it was assumed that this was simply a sign of his regal endurance, but William wrote:

> When this had happened several times and I was told about it . . .
> I began to ask him questions [and] came to realise that half of his
> right arm and hand was dead, so that he could not feel pinching or
> even biting. I began to feel uneasy in my mind . . . his father was
> told, and after the doctors had been consulted, careful attempts
> were made to help him with poultices, ointments and even charms,
> but all in vain. For with the passage of time we came to understand
> more clearly that this marked the beginning of a more serious and
> totally incurable disease. It is impossible to refrain from tears when
> speaking of this great misfortune.[43]

Baldwin was, in fact, suffering from the early stages of leprosy. It is unlikely that a definite diagnosis was made at this point. The finest physicians were employed to oversee the prince's care, including the Arab Christian Abu Sulaiman Dawud, and for the time being there seems to have been no further serious deterioration in his condition. So that Baldwin might still learn the quintessential knightly art of mounted warfare, Abu Sulaiman's brother was appointed as the boy's riding tutor. Trained to control a mount with his knees alone, leaving his working left arm free to wield a weapon, the prince became a remarkably skilful horseman.

Through the early 1170s Amalric sought a suitable husband for Princess Sibylla, hoping to secure the line of succession should an alternative to Baldwin prove necessary. But at the time of the king's own unexpected death in 1174, no match for Sibylla had yet been found, and the only surviving child from his marriage to Maria Comnena was another girl, the infant Isabella. In July 1174 Prince Baldwin was far from an ideal candidate for the throne. Born of a union that had later been dissolved, he was just thirteen (and thus two years short of adulthood by the laws of the kingdom) and was known to be suffering from some form of debilitating illness. Nonetheless, the High Court agreed to his elevation, and Baldwin was duly crowned and anointed by the patriarch of Jerusalem in the Holy Sepulchre on 15 July, the auspicious anniversary of that city's conquest by the First Crusaders.

Historians used to regard Baldwin IV's reign as an almost unmitigated disaster for the Latin East. Just as Saladin rose to power, emerging from Egypt to unite the Muslim world, so it was argued, Frankish Palestine was brought to its knees by a feeble and sickly monarch. Baldwin was criticised for selfishly retaining the crown long after the point when he should have abdicated, and blamed for ushering in an era of embittered and injurious factionalism, as Outremer's nobility schemed for power and influence.

The young king's reputation has been rejuvenated somewhat in recent years, with new emphasis being placed on the burden he shouldered due to deteriorating health, on the relative vitality of his early reign and on his determined efforts both to defend the realm and to find a viable successor. One truth, however, remains inviolate. The crusader states had been racked frequently by succession crises, often most deleteriously when a ruler died suddenly through battle, injury or ill health. Baldwin's case was different, and the damage wrought during his reign was deeper, precisely because he did not die. Lingering on the throne, often requiring executive authority to be wielded by a form of regent during bouts of extreme infirmity, the leper king's faltering rule eventually left Jerusalem in a precarious and vulnerable state of limbo.[44]

For the first two years of his reign Baldwin was a minor, and much of the work of government was directed by one of his cousins, Count Raymond III of Tripoli, acting as regent. Now in his early thirties, Raymond only recently had been released after nine years in Muslim captivity and was thus something of an unknown quantity. A slightly built, somewhat diminutive figure of swarthy complexion and piercing gaze, the count's stiff deportment was allied to a rather aloof demeanour. Cautious by nature, he nevertheless was driven by ambition, and his marriage to one of the kingdom's most eligible heiresses, Princess Eschiva of Galilee, marked him out as Jerusalem's greatest vassal. As regent, he adopted a conciliatory approach in dealing with the High Court and avoided direct confrontation with Saladin, agreeing terms of truce in 1175 during the sultan's drive towards Aleppo.

Raymond's overriding concern through these years was the succession, for soon after his coronation Baldwin IV's health went into terrible decline. Perhaps aggravated by the onset of puberty, his leprosy developed into the most grievous lepromatous form, and soon the telltale signs of the disease were unmistakeable, as his 'extremities and face were especially attacked, so that his faithful followers were moved with compassion when they looked at him'. In time, he would be left unable to walk, see, barely even to speak, but for now he was doomed to suffer a grim decline into physical disability, punctuated by bouts of severe, incapacitating illness. The social and religious stigma attached to leprosy was immense. Commonly perceived as a curse from God, indicative of divine disfavour, the disease was also believed to be extremely contagious, usually prompting the segregation of sufferers from society.[45] Baldwin's situation was deeply problematic – as a monarch he was vulnerable to criticism and unable to provide stable rule; and in dynastic terms he could not perpetuate the royal line, in part because contemporaries believed that sexual contact transmitted leprosy, but also because Baldwin's affliction rendered him infertile.

In many ways, hopes for the future thus rested with Baldwin's sister, Sibylla. Her youth and sheltered convent upbringing meant that she was not well positioned to follow in the footsteps of her grandmother Melisende by assuming regnal authority in her own right. Raymond of Tripoli thus busied himself with the ongoing search for a suitable husband for Sibylla. The candidate eventually chosen was William of Montferrat, a north Italian noble who was cousin to two of the most powerful monarchs in Europe, King Louis VII of France and the German Emperor Frederick Barbarossa (the nephew of the Second Crusader King Conrad III of Germany). Sibylla and William of Montferrat were married in late 1176, but in June 1177 he fell ill and died, leaving Sibylla a pregnant widow. She later gave birth to their son Baldwin (V) in either December 1177 or January 1178, and he became a potential heir to the Jerusalemite throne.

In the mid-1170s Raymond of Tripoli also supported William of Tyre's career, overseeing his appointment as royal chancellor and then as archbishop of Tyre, and in part this may explain the broadly positive account of Raymond's career in William's chronicle. It was from this privileged position, at the centre of the Latin kingdom's political and ecclesiastical hierarchies, that William observed and recorded Outremer's history.

Baldwin IV's early reign

In the summer of 1176 Baldwin IV reached his majority and Count Raymond's regency came to an end. The young monarch threw himself into the business of kingship despite the gradual downgrading of his leprosy, and immediately made his mark. Overturning Raymond's policy of diplomatic rapprochement, Baldwin refused to renew the truce with Damascus and in early August led a raiding party into Lebanon's Biqa valley, defeating Turan-Shah in a minor engagement. This shift in policy towards Islam was accompanied by a decline in influence for the count of Tripoli and, during the remainder of the decade, Baldwin tended to look elsewhere for guidance and support. Now returned to court, his mother Agnes of Courtenay seems to have established a close relationship with her once estranged son. She certainly became a significant influence in his life and before long her brother Joscelin III was appointed as royal seneschal, the highest governmental office in the realm, with purview of the treasury and regal property. After long years in Muslim captivity, Joscelin had just been released by Gumushtegin of Aleppo as part of a deal to secure support from Frankish Antioch.

This same pact brought liberty for another noble destined to shape Jerusalem's history, Reynald of Châtillon. He had been captured by Nur al-Din in 1161, when prince of Antioch, but much had changed during fifteen years of incarceration. The death of his wife Constance and the accession of his stepson Bohemond III in 1163 deprived Reynald of rule over the Syrian principality, but, at the same time, the wedding of his stepdaughter Maria of Antioch to the Byzantine emperor lent him an aura of prestige. He thus emerged from prison as a well-connected, battle-hardened veteran, albeit one who technically was landless. This anomaly was soon resolved by Reynald's marriage, blessed by King Baldwin, to Stephanie of Milly, the lady of Transjordan, which brought him lordship of Kerak and Montreal and a position on the front line in the struggle with Saladin.

As a Syrian prince, Reynald had a reputation for untamed violence, garnered from his attack on Greek-held Cyprus and his infamous attempts, around 1154, to extort money from the Latin patriarch of Antioch, Aimery of Limoges. The unfortunate prelate was beaten, dragged to the citadel and forced to sit through an entire day beneath the blazing summer sun, with his bare skin smeared in honey to attract swarms of worrisome insects. In the late 1170s, however, Reynald became one of Baldwin's most trusted allies, furnishing him with able support in the fields of war, diplomacy and politics.

With Egypt and Damascus united under Saladin and Baldwin IV's health faltering, the Palestinian Franks made repeated but ultimately fruitless attempts to secure foreign aid. During the winter of 1176 to 1177 Reynald of Châtillon was sent as a royal envoy to Constantinople to negotiate a renewed alliance with the Greek Emperor Manuel Comnenus. In September 1176 the Byzantines had been roundly defeated at the Battle of Myriokephalon (in western Asia Minor) by the Seljuq sultan of Anatolia, Kilij Arslan II (who had succeeded Ma'sud in 1156). In terms of manpower and territory, the losses inflicted upon the Greeks as a result of this reversal were relatively limited. But severe damage was done to Byzantine prestige in both Europe and the Levant, and Manuel spent much of the remainder of the decade retrenching his position. In the hope of reasserting Greek influence on the international stage, the emperor agreed to Reynald of Châtillon's overture, promising to provide naval support for a new allied offensive against Ayyubid Egypt. In return, the Latin kingdom was to accept subject status as a Byzantine protectorate and an Orthodox Christian patriarch restored to power in Jerusalem.

For a time, it seemed as if this venture might bear fruit. In late summer 1177 a Greek fleet duly arrived at Acre, and this coincided with the advent in the Levant of Count Philip of Flanders, son of the committed crusader Thierry of Flanders, at the head of a large military contingent. Philip had taken the cross in 1175 in response to the ever more frequent and vocal appeals from the Latins of Outremer for new western European crusades to the Holy Land. Yet despite his good intentions, Philip's expedition proved to be a fiasco. With final preparations afoot for an assault on Egypt, petty arguments broke out over who should have rights to the Nile region should it fall and, amid mutual recriminations, the projected campaign collapsed.

Disgruntled and alienated, the Byzantine navy set sail for Constantinople. In September 1177 Count Philip joined forces with Raymond III of Tripoli, and together they spent the winter trying and failing to capture first Hama and then Harim. A real chance to disrupt, perhaps even to overrun, Saladin's position in Egypt had been squandered. Having amassed a defensive force to counter the expected Christian invasion, the sultan suddenly found that he was no longer under threat.

CONFRONTATION

In late autumn 1177 Saladin initiated his first significant military campaign against the Latin kingdom of Jerusalem since Nur al-Din's death. Despite the importance of this expedition – the sultan's opening salvo in his self-appointed role as Islam's new *jihadi* champion – his precise motives and objectives are somewhat opaque. In all probability the 1177 offensive was not planned as a full-scale invasion of Palestine, targeting the reconquest of Jerusalem, but was instead an opportunistic raid. With his armies already assembled to defend against an expected attack, Saladin seized the chance to make a practical affirmation of his commitment to the holy war, seeking to assert his own martial dominance over the Franks, while providing a counterweight to their northern Syrian attack.

Saladin marched out of Egypt at the head of more than 20,000 horsemen, setting up a forward command post at the frontier settlement of al-Arish. Leaving behind his heavy baggage, he moved north into Palestine, reaching Ascalon around 22 November. There he found an alarmed Baldwin IV. With much of his realm's fighting manpower absent in the north alongside Philip of Flanders and Raymond III, the king had hurriedly mustered what troops he could at the coast. As one eastern Christian contemporary put it, 'everyone despaired of the life of the sick king, already half dead, but he drew upon his courage and rode to meet Saladin'. Baldwin was joined by

Reynald of Châtillon, his seneschal, Joscelin of Courtenay, a force of some 600 knights and a few thousand infantry, and the bishop of Bethlehem carrying the True Cross. This army made a brief show of confronting the Muslim advance, but, overwhelmingly outnumbered, the Franks soon withdrew behind the walls of Ascalon, leaving Saladin free to strike inland towards Judea.[46]

The Battle of Mont Gisard

The sultan now made a fateful miscalculation. Seemingly adjudging that the Franks would remain cowed and contained within Ascalon, he allowed his forces to fan out, raiding Latin settlements such as Ramla and Lydda, leaving behind no effective network of scouts to monitor Baldwin's movements. The young king, encouraged and aided by Reynald of Châtillon, was, however, in no mood to sit idly by as his realm was ravaged. Linking up with eighty Templar knights stationed at Gaza with their master, Odo of St Amand, Baldwin made the bold, perhaps even foolhardy decision to confront Saladin. As William of Tyre put it, '[the king] felt that it was wiser to try the dubious chances of battle with the enemy than to suffer his people to be exposed to rapine, fire and massacre'. This was a potentially deadly gamble.

On the afternoon of 25 November, the sultan was advancing to the east of Ibelin, with much of his army spread out across the surrounding coastal plain, when the Latin army made a sudden and unheralded appearance. Saladin's remaining troops were just then engaged in fording a small river near the hill known as Mont Gisard. When Reynald of Châtillon unleashed a near-immediate heavy cavalry charge on their broken ranks, the sultan proved unable to organise any effective defence and his numerically superior force was soon thrown into retreat. One Muslim contemporary admitted that 'the rout . . . was complete. One of the Franks charged Saladin and got close, almost reaching him, but the Frank was killed in front of him. The Franks crowded about him, so he departed in flight.'

While the sultan barely escaped the field, vicious fighting

continued. Fleeing for their lives, his soldiers abandoned their armour and weapons, even as the Latins hunted them down, giving dogged pursuit for more than ten miles until nightfall finally offered the Muslims some respite. There were heavy casualties on both sides, for even the triumphant Christians suffered 1,100 fatalities, while a further 750 injured were later brought to the Hospital of St John in Jerusalem. But, while the exact scale of Muslim losses remains unclear, the severe psychological damage inflicted was unquestionable. Saladin was deeply humiliated at Mont Gisard. His close friend and adviser Isa was taken prisoner by the Franks and spent a number of years in captivity before eventually being ransomed for the massive sum of 60,000 gold dinars. The sultan was forced to scurry from the scene, the misery of his own journey back to Egypt compounded by ten successive days of unusually intense, chilling rainfall and the discovery that the often fickle Bedouins had sacked his camp at al-Arish. Having suffered food and water shortages, Saladin finally limped out of the Sinai in early December 1177, shaken and bedraggled.

The inescapable truth was that his own incautious negligence had exposed the army to defeat and that, as a consequence, his reputation for assured military leadership had been tarnished. In public, Saladin did his best to limit the damage, arguing in correspondence that the Latins had actually lost more men in the battle and accounting for the slow speed of his return to Cairo by explaining that 'we carried the weak and the helpless and went slowly so that stragglers could [catch up]'. He also expended time and money rebuilding his army. Privately, however, Mont Gisard left its scars. Imad al-Din admitted that it had been 'a disastrous event, a terrible catastrophe', and, more than a decade later, the painful memory of this 'terrible reverse' endured, with the sultan acknowledging that it had been 'a major defeat'.[47]

The burden of blood

Any immediate prospect of avenging this injury was forced into the background by the need to address the festering issue of Turan-Shah's ineptitude. Saladin returned to Damascus in April 1178, relieving his brother of the governorship, but was then forced into an embarrassing and intractable predicament. By way of compensation for his demotion, Turan-Shah demanded lordship of Baalbek – the richly endowed ancient Roman city of Lebanon, located in the fertile Biqa valley. The problem was that the sultan had already awarded these lands to Ibn al-Muqaddam in token of gratitude for his aid in negotiating Damascus' surrender in 1174, and the emir was now understandably reluctant to relinquish his prize. The unravelling of this affair over the following months was revealing. On the one hand, it underscored a consistent problem that beset Saladin throughout his career. To build his 'empire', the sultan generally relied upon his family rather than selecting lieutenants on merit, but this trust sometimes proved to be ill-founded. Incompetent, unreliable and potentially even disloyal, figures like Turan-Shah were liabilities – capable of gravely damaging the grand dream of Ayyubid domination – yet time and again Saladin proved reluctant to turn against his blood relations. In seeking to resolve the Baalbek dilemma, the sultan also demonstrated that, to further his aims, he would willingly embrace devious and duplicitous politicking.

After a summer of failed diplomacy, Saladin moved on Baalbek in autumn 1178. According to Imad al-Din he began by 'flatter[ing] Ibn al-Muqaddam, for all his age, like a baby', but when this produced no result, the sultan blockaded the city throughout the coming winter. At the same time, Saladin initiated a programme of blatant propaganda to justify his intervention. Ibn al-Muqqadam was declared a dissident and variously accused in letters to Baghdad of employing an ineffective band of 'ignorant scum' to defend the frontier against the Franks, and later, of actually being in treacherous contact with these Christian enemies. By the following spring, the 'rebel' lord, his reputation blackened, had been ground into submission and a deal was brokered. Turan-Shah duly received his chosen reward of Baalbek, but even here his rule seems to have been incompetent and he was soon packed off to Egypt, where he died in

1180. Meanwhile, having bent to Saladin's will, Ibn al-Muqaddam was welcomed back into the fold. Richly endowed with lands to the south of Antioch and Aleppo, he remained loyal to the sultan for the rest of his career.[48]

The House of Sorrow

While still entangled in the Baalbek dispute, Saladin became aware of an alarming development in the border zone between Damascus and the kingdom of Jerusalem. Looking to capitalise upon the momentum gained by his victory at Mont Gisard, Baldwin IV had initiated a deeply threatening scheme, designed to bolster Palestine's defences and destabilise Ayyubid dominion of Syria.

To appreciate the significance of these events, some sense of how frontiers functioned in the twelfth century is necessary. In common with most of the medieval world, Muslim and Frankish territory in the Levant was rarely divided by the literal equivalent of a modern border, but instead, roughly delineated by frontier zones – areas of overlapping political, military and economic influence, where neither side exerted full sovereignty. The positioning of these areas of contested control, akin to no-man's-lands between realms, was often closely related to topographic/geographic features, be they mountains, rivers, dense forests or even deserts. And attempts by one polity to consolidate or extend influence in such a region could have profound bearing upon local stability and the overall balance of power between rivals.

In the early twelfth century, a case in point had been the Latin principality of Antioch's expansion of its sphere of authority eastwards, beyond the natural frontier zone with Aleppo, the low-lying, rocky Belus Hills. This intensified threat to Aleppo's survival ultimately prompted Muslim retaliation, culminating in the Battle of the Field of Blood in 1119. In the late 1170s a similar confrontation was looming between Baldwin IV and Saladin. During this period, the critical border zone between their respective realms lay to the north of the Sea of Galilee and broadly corresponded with the course of the

Upper River Jordan. Previously, the epicentre of the struggle for dominance here had lain in the north-east, at the fortress settlement of Banyas. But once it fell to Nur al-Din in 1164, Latin influence east of the Jordan diminished, and the resultant status quo favoured Muslim Damascus.

In October 1178, Baldwin IV made a bold new play for pre-eminence in the Upper Jordan border zone. His target was not the reconquest of Banyas, but rather the construction of an entirely new fortification on the west bank of the Jordan, beside an ancient crossing known to the Franks as Jacob's Ford and in Arabic as Bait al-Ahzan, the House of Sorrow (where, it was said, Jacob had mourned the supposed death of his son). With swamps upstream and rapids to the south, this ford was the only crossing of the Jordan for miles and, as such, acted as an important gateway between Latin Palestine and Muslim Syria, offering access to the fertile Terre de Sueth region. Crucially, Jacob's Ford was also just one day's march from Damascus.

Baldwin was hoping to tip the balance of regional power in favour of the Franks by building a major castle on this site. He was partnered by the Templars, who already held territory in northern Galilee, and together the crown and the order made a huge commitment to the project. Between October 1178 and April 1179 Baldwin actually moved his seat of government to the building site so as to be on hand as both supervisor and protector, setting up a mint to produce special coins with which to pay the massive workforce, and issuing royal charters on site.

This castle jeopardised Saladin's burgeoning Ayyubid Empire because it promised to serve the Franks as both a defensive tool and an offensive weapon. Medieval strongholds could rarely, if ever, hope to seal or blockade a frontier entirely – attacking armies might march around a fortress or, with sufficient manpower and resources, eventually force their way past its defences. But castles did provide a relatively secure environment in which to station armed forces, and these troops might be deployed to harass and hamper any attempt at invasion by an enemy. The presence of a Templar fortress at Jacob's

Ford would certainly have inhibited the sultan's ability to assault the Latin kingdom. Its garrison would also be in a position to raid Muslim territory, ransack trade caravans and threaten Damascus itself. And with his capital under threat, Saladin's ambitious plans to extend his authority over Aleppo and Mesopotamia would likely falter. The danger posed by the fortress being built beside the Jordan, therefore, was impossible to ignore. Unfortunately, with his troops entrenched at Baalbek, a direct military strike on Jacob's Ford was not really feasible, so initially the sultan sought to use bribery in place of brute force. He offered the Franks first 60,000 and then 100,000 dinars if they halted building work and abandoned the site. But, in spite of the fortune on offer, Baldwin and the Templars refused.

At first sight all the surviving written evidence seems to suggest that the castle at Jacob's Ford had been finished by April 1179, when the leper king handed command of the stronghold to the Templars. William of Tyre certainly described it as 'complete in all its parts' after having seen it with his own eyes that spring. Muslim eyewitnesses also confirmed this fact, with one Arabic source describing its walls as 'an impregnable rampart of stone and iron'. Until the 1990s, historians always assumed that this meant a fully fledged concentric castle – one with an inner and outer wall – had been built at Jacob's Ford, making it an incredibly formidable fortress. But, in 1993, the Israeli scholar Ronnie Ellenblum rediscovered the location of this long-lost Frankish fortress. His ongoing archaeological investigation of the site, at the head of an international team of experts, has reshaped our understanding of events and the interpretation of the written sources. Excavations have proved conclusively that in 1179 Jacob's Ford was not a concentric castle – in fact it had just one perimeter wall and a single tower, and was effectively still a building site. This suggests that to William of Tyre and his contemporaries a 'complete' fortress was one that was enclosed and defensible rather than fully formed, and that this particular stronghold was actually a work in progress.

Crucially for Saladin, this meant that Jacob's Ford was still relatively vulnerable and from spring 1179 onwards, with Baalbek

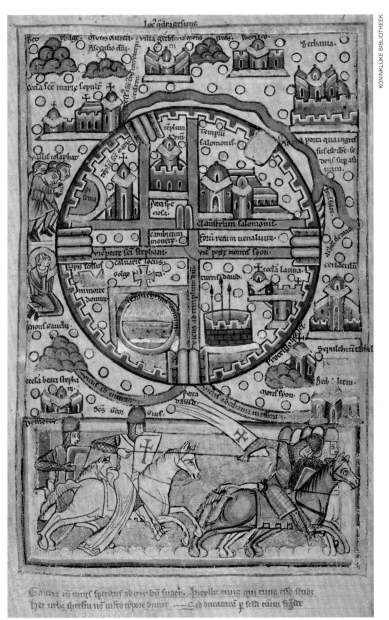

In the Middle Ages, just as it is today, Jerusalem was revered as a site of profound spiritual significance by Christians, Muslims and Jews, and the fate of this Holy City was bound inextricably to the history of the crusades. This late twelfth century map depicts the walled metropolis and its most sacred shrines – the Dome of the Rock, the Aqsa mosque and the Holy Sepulchre.

Pope Urban II
launched the First
Crusade in 1095.

Around 100,000 people joined the crusade, among them Duke Godfrey of
Bouillon and Adhémar of Le Puy, shown here setting out for the Holy
Land.

The great city of Antioch, built at the foot of Mount Silpius, was enclosed by a three-mile-long circuit of towering walls.

Once they broke into the city near dawn on 3 June 1098, the First Crusaders carried out an indiscriminate massacre, depicted here in a thirteenth-century manuscript illumination.

The city of Jerusalem

The Dome of the Rock, lying within the Haram as-Sharif or Temple Mount complex.

The Holy Sepulchre, which is thought to enclose the site of Jesus Christ's death and resurrection. It was here that the First Crusaders gave thanks after sacking Jerusalem on 15 July 1099.

Jerusalem's citadel, the Tower of David.

The Latin Christians of the kingdom of Jerusalem conquered the city of Tyre – home to one of the Levant's best harbours – in 1124 with the aid of Venetian sailors (seen here on the right). The naval support offered by the likes of Venice, Pisa and Genoa proved crucial to the foundation of the crusader states. This illumination comes from a manuscript of William of Tyre's *History of Outremer* that was produced in the second half of the thirteenth century.

Oez, estoit agrant merueille la cire de
furz t mout endenne. Vlpins qui mott
fut de clois isu tiez, si com len dit. li ou me in
en norerent mout quant ilorent la seiguio
rie du monde sol our for endenne os munic ha

The imposing citadel of Aleppo.

The Grand Umayyad Mosque of Damascus.

One of two ivory covers of the Melisende Psalter, the small but lavishly decorated prayer book thought to have been given by King Fulk of Jerusalem to his wife Queen Melisende around 1135. Here a king, clothed in Greek imperial raiment, enacts works of charity: clothing the poor; tending to the sick.

St Bernard of Clairvaux: one of the foremost spiritual figures of the twelfth century, supporter of the Templars and preacher of the Second Crusade.

The ornately carved pulpit commissioned by Nur al-Din and installed in Jerusalem's Aqsa mosque by Saladin in 1187. It was destroyed in a fire started by an Australian fanatic in 1969.

subdued, he returned to Damascus to address the problem of this fortress. The months that followed saw a series of inconclusive skirmishes, as both sides sought to size one another up. Saladin led an expeditionary force to test the strength of Jacob's Ford, but soon retreated when one of his commanders was killed by a Templar arrow. Nonetheless, during two other engagements the sultan's troops bested Baldwin's forces in minor battles. In one, the king's constable – his chief military adviser – was killed; in another, the Templar Master Odo of St Amand was taken captive along with 270 knights. These successes disrupted the Christians' military command structure and went some way to redressing the Muslim humiliation at Mont Gisard. With the scales tipping back in Saladin's favour, King Baldwin retreated to Jerusalem to regroup, while the sultan summoned reinforcements from northern Syria and Egypt.

By late August 1179 Saladin was ready to launch a full-scale attack on Jacob's Ford. On Saturday the 24th he began an assault-based siege, with the intention of breaking into the castle as rapidly as possible. There was no time for a lengthy encirclement, because the leper king was by now stationed nearby at Tiberias, on the shores of the Sea of Galilee, just half a day's march to the south-west. As soon as news of the attack reached him the king would begin assembling a relief army, so the siege was effectively a race, in which the Muslims struggled to crack the stronghold's defences before the Latins arrived. Taken together, contemporary written records and the archaeological evidence now being uncovered offer a vivid picture of what happened over the next five grim days. Saladin began by bombarding the fortress with arrows from east and west – hundreds of arrow heads have been recovered clustered on these fronts – looking to demoralise the Templar garrison. At the same time, specialist miners, probably from Syrian Aleppo, were sent to tunnel under the north-eastern corner of the walls, hoping to collapse the ramparts through the technique of sapping. A tunnel was quickly dug and packed full of wood, but once set alight it proved to be too small to cause a rupture in the walls above. In desperation, the sultan offered a gold dinar to each soldier carrying a goatskin of water from the river to extinguish the flames, and work then continued night and day to enlarge the mine. Meanwhile, Baldwin was preparing to march from Tiberias.

At dawn on 29 August the leper king set out with his host to relieve the fortress. Unbeknownst to him, at that same moment fires were being lit within Saladin's expanded siege mine. Its wooden pit props duly burned and the passageway caved in, bringing down the walls above. Saladin later wrote that, as the flames spread, the castle resembled 'a ship adrift in a sea of fire'. As his troops poured through the break in the walls desperate hand-to-hand combat ensued, while the garrison of elite Templar knights made a bloody, but ultimately futile last stand. In a last-ditch act of bravery the Templar garrison commander mounted his war horse and charged into the burning breach; one Muslim eyewitness later described how 'he threw himself into a hole full of fire without fear of the intense heat and, from this brazier, he was immediately thrown into another – that of Hell'.

With the castle's defences breached the Latin garrison was eventually overrun and a bloody sack followed. The human skeletal remains recently unearthed within the perimeter wall bear witness to the ferocity of the assault. One male skull showed evidence of three separate sword cuts, the last of which split the head, crushing the brain. Another had had his arm chopped off above the elbow before being dispatched. With much of the site now in flames, Saladin executed more than half of the garrison, amassing a mountain of plunder, including 1,000 coats of armour. By noon on that Thursday, racing northwards, Baldwin got his first despairing glimpse of smoke on the horizon – telltale evidence of the destruction at Jacob's Ford. He was just six hours too late.

In the two weeks that followed, Saladin dismantled the castle of Jacob's Ford, razing it to the ground stone by stone. Indeed, he later claimed to have ripped out the foundations with his own hands. Most of the Latin dead, along with their horses and mules, were thrown into the stronghold's capacious cistern. This was a rather ill-advised policy, as soon after a 'plague' broke out, ravaging the Muslim army and claiming the life of ten of Saladin's commanders. By mid-October, with his primary objective achieved, the sultan decided to abandon the seemingly cursed site, and Jacob's Ford became an abandoned, forgotten ruin.[49]

Saladin's successes in summer 1179 broke the tide of Frankish martial momentum that had been building since Mont Gisard. The Latins' attempt to seize the initiative in the Upper Jordan border zone and pressure Damascus was stymied. The sultan had protected his unification of Egypt and Syria. But the work of unifying Islam through the subjugation of Aleppo and Mosul remained incomplete.

11

THE SULTAN OF ISLAM

Although Saladin had achieved a series of victories against the Franks in 1179, in the early 1180s he returned to the business of empire building, devoting most of his energy and resources to consolidating his hold over Egypt and Damascus, and to extending his authority over the Muslims of Aleppo and Mosul. In spring 1180, with Syria suffering from the effects of continuing drought and famine, he agreed a two-year truce with the Latins – a pact which was evidently deemed to be advantageous to both sides, given that neither paid a monetary tribute to secure peace. This deal left Saladin free to tackle a range of issues within the Muslim world.

THE DRIVE TO DOMINATE

One of Saladin's first priorities was to counteract the growing power and influence of Kilij Arslan II, the Seljuq sultan of Anatolia. Kilij Arslan had been in an assertive mood since crushing the Byzantines at Myriokephalon in 1176, and could himself claim, with some justification, to be the true rising champion of Islamic *jihad*. Saladin broadcast propaganda designed to discredit the Seljuq leader, arguing that he was an opponent of Muslim unity – Saladin even explained his own truce with the Jerusalemite Franks in 1180 to Baghdad by claiming that he could not deal simultaneously with the grave threats posed by Kilij Arslan and the Latin Christians. In summer 1180, Saladin left his nephew Farrukh-Shah in control of Damascus, and led troops into the north, securing alliances with a number of cities in the Upper Euphrates region in order to contain Kilij Arslan's ambitions within Asia Minor. Saladin also used military pressure to force the latest Armenian ruler of Cilicia, Roupen III, to accept a non-aggression pact, effectively neutralising the Armenian Christians as opponents to Ayyubid expansion.

Around this time a series of deaths altered the political landscape. In 1180 the Byzantine Emperor Manuel Comnenus passed away, leaving behind him an eleven-year-old son and heir who, two years later, was supplanted by Manuel's cousin, Andronicus Comnenus. This period was marked by a gradual decline in relations between the Greeks and the crusader states that served Saladin's interests. In 1181 the Byzantines secured a peace treaty with the sultan, a first sign of their realignment towards neutrality in the Levant. Andronicus' seizure of power in 1182 was then accompanied by a massacre of Latins living and trading in Constantinople and the new emperor made little effort to re-establish cooperative ties with Outremer.

Similar shifts took place in the East. In 1180 the Abbasid caliph and his vizier also died. Aware that this might herald a dangerous decline in the support he enjoyed in Baghdad, Saladin carefully cultivated links with the new Caliph al-Nasir. The Zangids suffered their own losses. In summer 1180 Saif al-Din of Mosul died and was succeeded by his younger brother, Izz al-Din. More significantly still, late 1181 saw the death from illness of Nur al-Din's son and official heir, al-Salih, at the age of just nineteen. This event was of critical importance to Saladin's future ambitions. In recent years, al-Salih had begun to emerge as a potentially formidable opponent, following Gumushtegin's death as a result of court intrigue in Aleppo. As the figurehead of Zangid legitimacy, al-Salih represented the promise of dynastic continuity and enjoyed the abject loyalty of the Aleppan populace. Had he survived, al-Salih might have posed a serious challenge to Ayyubid ascendancy; at the very least, his continued presence would have weakened Saladin's claim to be the sole, rightful champion of Islam, and probably put paid to the sultan's hopes of absorbing northern Syria without open warfare. Although power in Aleppo soon passed to Saif al-Din's elder brother, Imad al-Din Zangi of Sinjar, al-Salih's demise nonetheless presented Saladin with a long-awaited opportunity to extend his power within the Muslim world.[50]

Saladin made careful preparations for a new campaign against the Zangids of Aleppo and Mosul. Having spent most of 1181 and early 1182 attending to the governance of Egypt, Saladin set out for Syria in spring 1182, leaving al-Adil and Qaragush in control of the Nile region. Alarmed by news that the sultan would be passing through Transjordan in May, and particularly fearful that the region's soon to be harvested corn crop might be destroyed, Reynald of Châtillon convinced Baldwin IV to assemble the kingdom's full military strength at Kerak. In the event, Saladin led his troops past the castle in close order, but without offering any attack, and no battle was joined.

The truce agreed with the Franks in 1180 had now lapsed and that summer the Ayyubids made a number of tentative attacks on the Latin kingdom of Jerusalem. As Saladin marched through Transjordan, from his base in Damascus Farrukh-Shah exploited the fact that Latin Galilee had been all but stripped of troops, capturing the Christians' small three-storey cave fortress, south-east of the Sea of Galilee, known as the Cave de Sueth, their last fortified outpost in the Terre de Sueth. Then, in July and August, the sultan led two expeditions against the Franks. The first, an invasion in force of Lower Galilee and a brief siege of the fortress at Bethsan, prompted King Baldwin to reassemble his army at Saffurya. This site, midway between Acre and Tiberias, replete with an abundant spring and fine pasturage, was a natural staging post for the Christian army. An inconclusive military engagement followed near Bethsan, fought beneath a roasting midsummer sun on 15 July. Baked alive, the Latin cleric carrying the True Cross died of heatstroke, while, even after they had recrossed the Jordan, Saladin's men found their first campsite unbearable; according to one eyewitness the brackish water and pestilential air meant that 'the market of the doctors did a roaring trade', and a further retreat towards Damascus was soon made.[51]

In August 1182 Saladin attacked again, this time targeting the coastal city of Beirut. The rebuilt Egyptian navy had already been put to use in 1179–80, harassing Latin shipping around Acre and Tripoli, but the sultan now deployed his fleet to launch a two-pronged offensive, besieging Beirut by land and sea. For three days his archers peppered the city while sappers sought to undermine its walls, but when Baldwin's relief force approached, Saladin broke off the assault, ravaging the surrounding countryside as he slipped back into Muslim territory.

Neither of these 1182 campaigns was truly determined, but they were, rather, opportunistic forays, designed to gauge Frankish strength and reactions, while inflicting damage and snatching any available territorial or material rewards at minimum risk and cost. As such, they set the tone for years to come. These demonstrations of apparent commitment to the *jihad* also allowed Saladin to justify his ongoing attempts to subdue Muslim Syria and Mesopotamia – fairly obviously his real priority. A series of letters from Saladin to the caliph in Baghdad reveal the vocal protestations and devious polemical arguments repeatedly put forward by the Ayyubids in this period. The sultan complained that he had shown his willingness to wage holy war against the Latins, but was constantly distracted from this cause by the threat of Zangid aggression – urgent necessity demanded Islamic unity and Saladin suggested that he should be empowered to subjugate any Muslims who refused to join him in the *jihad*. At the same time, the Zangid rulers of Aleppo and Mosul were characterised as rebellious enemies of the state. They were accused of seizing power on grounds of hereditary succession when, lawfully, command of these cities should have been in the gift of the caliph.

Izz al-Din of Mosul was said to have agreed a submissive eleven-year truce with Jerusalem (thus breaking the prescribed limit of ten years for pacts between Muslims and non-Muslims), promising to pay the Christians an annual tribute of 10,000 dinars. Similar accusations were later levelled at Imad al-Din Zangi in relation to his dealings with Antioch. Courting caliphal support and broader public opinion, with this onslaught of propaganda Saladin laid the groundwork for a major anti-Zangid offensive.

His cue for action came in late summer 1182, while still engaged in the brief siege of Beirut, when a message arrived from Keukburi of Harran, a Turkish warlord who had so far supported the Zangids and had fought against Saladin in 1176. Keukburi now invited the Ayyubids to cross the Euphrates, effectively proclaiming his willingness to switch sides.[52] In response, the sultan assembled an army and set out that autumn to prosecute a campaign in Iraq without renewing any truce with Jerusalem.

Saladin's campaigns against Aleppo and Mosul (1182–3)

In late September 1182 Saladin used Keukburi's invitation as a pretext to launch an expedition, marching eastwards to join the lord of Harran near the Euphrates, and then pushing on into the Jazira. In the months that followed, the sultan made quite strenuous efforts to limit the amount of open warfare with his Muslim rivals, preferring coercion, diplomacy and propaganda over the sword. Before long he was calling for additional funds from Damascus and Egypt with which to buy off his opponents. Even William of Tyre was aware that the sultan used profligate bribery to quickly subjugate 'almost the entire region ... formerly under the power of Mosul', including Edessa.[53]

In November Saladin marched on to threaten Mosul itself. Despite Keukburi's encouragement, the sultan was reluctant to commit to a difficult and bloody siege of the city, but his hopes of frightening Izz al-Din into submission went unrealised. With a stalemate holding as winter began, envoys from Caliph al-Nasir arrived, hoping to broker a peace. To Saladin's chagrin they adopted a neutral position, favouring neither the Ayyubid nor the Zangid position, and with little progress being made the sultan withdrew. In December he marched some seventy-five miles east to Sinjar, where he pressured the major fortified town into surrender and, after a brief pause through the worst winter weather, moved north-east into Diyar Bakr in early spring 1183, capturing the supposedly impregnable capital city in April, after which success the Artuqid ruler of Mardin agreed to a submissive alliance. In six months Saladin had isolated and all but emasculated Mosul, winning over much of the Jazira and Diyar Bakr through a mixture of force and persuasion. Throughout, the Zangids could do little to respond. Izz al-Din and Imad al-Din Zangi tried to organise a counter-attack in late February, but lacked both the resources and the nerve to see it through.

Saladin had made satisfying progress, but Mosul itself remained beyond his grasp. That spring he initiated an increasingly vociferous diplomatic onslaught, hoping to sway opinion in Baghdad in his favour. His letters to the caliph accused the Zangids of inciting the Franks to attack Ayyubid territory in Syria, even of funding the Christian war effort. The sultan also appealed to Caliph al-Nasir's own desire for political as well as spiritual power, declaring that the Ayyubids would force Mesopotamia to recognise caliphal authority. Saladin added, rather boldly, that if only Baghdad would endorse his claim to Mosul, he would be in a position to conquer Jerusalem, Constantinople, Georgia and Morocco. Around the same time, the sultan deviously tried to disrupt Zangid solidarity, contacting Imad al-Din Zangi to warn him that Izz al-Din of Mosul had supposedly offered to ally with the Ayyubids against Aleppo.

From late spring onwards Saladin shifted the focus of his campaign to Aleppo, recrossing the Euphrates to station troops around the city on 21 May 1183. Once again, the sultan hoped to avoid open warfare, but the Aleppans quickly demonstrated their willingness to defend their property, daily launching fierce attacks on his troops. Luckily for Saladin, Imad al-Din Zangi proved more malleable. Concluding that the Ayyubid hold over Syria was now unbreakable, and that his own isolated position was therefore untenable, the Zangid ruler secretly negotiated with the sultan. On 12 June he agreed terms, opening the gates of Aleppo's citadel to Saladin's troops, much to the shock of the local populace. By way of recompense, Imad al-Din Zangi received a parcel of territory in the Jazira, including his former lordship at Sinjar, while promising to furnish the sultan with troops whenever called upon. Jurdik – the Syrian warlord who had helped Saladin to arrest the Egyptian Vizier Shawar in 1169 – was also won over that summer. Since 1174 Jurdik had remained staunchly loyal to Aleppo, refusing to back the Ayyubids. Now, at last, he entered the sultan's service, becoming one of his most devoted and adept lieutenants.

Once in control of Aleppo, Saladin immediately sought to limit civil unrest and engender an atmosphere of unity. Non-Koranic taxes were abolished and, later that summer, a law was enacted ordering non-Muslims within the city to wear distinctive clothing, a measure seemingly designed to promote cohesion among Aleppo's Sunni and Shi'ite Muslims and to hasten their acceptance of Ayyubid rule.

Aleppo's occupation was a major achievement for Saladin. After almost a decade he had united Muslim Syria, and could now claim dominion over a swathe of territory between the Nile and the Euphrates. A number of surviving letters reveal the manner in which the sultan celebrated and publicised his success. As always, he also took care to justify his conquest, declaring that he would happily share leadership of Islam if he could, but noting that, in war, only one man could command. Aleppo's subjugation was described as a step on the road to the recapture of Jerusalem and he declared proudly that 'Islam is now awake to drive away the night phantom of unbelief'.[54]

Against the backdrop of this rhetoric, it was obvious by late summer 1183 that Saladin had, to some extent at least, to fulfil the promise implicit in his propaganda by attacking the Franks. To shore up the defences of northern Syria he agreed to a truce with Bohemond III of Antioch, securing extremely favourable terms for

Islam – including the release of Muslim prisoners and territorial concessions – before travelling south to Damascus to orchestrate a show of force against the kingdom of Jerusalem.

THE WAR AGAINST THE FRANKS

The balance of power in Frankish Palestine had shifted significantly in recent years. In the late 1170s, with King Baldwin IV's health worsening, a marriage alliance had been planned between his widowed sister Sibylla and the eminent French nobleman Duke Hugh III of Burgundy. King Louis VII of France's death in 1180, leaving his young son Philip Augustus as heir to the throne, upset this scheme, because the attendant power struggle in France meant Hugh was unwilling to abandon his dukedom. A new match for Sibylla, therefore, had to be found. At this point Raymond III of Tripoli and Bohemond III of Antioch seem to have decided that, in the interests of their own ambitions and Jerusalem's continued security, Baldwin IV needed to be edged from power. Around Easter 1180, the pair tried to orchestrate what was, in essence, a *coup d'état*, by forcing Sibylla to marry their chosen ally, Baldwin of Ibelin, a member of the increasingly powerful Ibelin dynasty. Had this match proceeded, the leper king might have been sidelined, but Baldwin IV was unwilling to forgo his influence over the succession. With the encouragement of his mother and uncle, Agnes and Joscelin of Courtenay, he seized the initiative. Before Raymond and Bohemond could intervene, the king wed Sibylla to his own preferred candidate, Guy of Lusignan, a noble-born Poitevin knight, recently arrived in the Levant.

In part Baldwin's choice was governed by necessity, as Guy was the only unmarried adult male of sufficiently high birth then present in Palestine. Guy's connection with Poitou – a region ruled by the Angevin King Henry II of England – may also have been a factor, for with Capetian France in disarray, England's importance as an ally was increased. Nonetheless, Guy's emergence as a leading political player was both sudden and unexpected. With his marriage to Sibylla, Guy of Lusignan became heir designate to the Jerusalemite throne. He would also be expected to fulfil the role of regent should Baldwin IV be incapacitated by his affliction. The question was whether Guy's precipitous elevation would alienate and embitter other leading members of the court, including Raymond of Tripoli and the Ibelins. Guy's qualities as a political and military leader also remained untested, as did his willingness to restrain his own ambitions for the crown while Baldwin IV lived on, clinging to power.[55]

The spur of Latin aggression

Saladin's decision to launch an offensive against Frankish Palestine in autumn 1183 was not simply triggered by a desire to affirm his *jihad* credentials. To an extent, his attacks were also a retaliatory response to recent Latin aggression. In late 1182, during the sultan's absence in Iraq, the Franks raided the regions surrounding Damascus and Bosra, retaking the Cave de Sueth.

To the south in Transjordan, Reynald of Châtillon initiated a more deliberately belligerent campaign; one for which he had been preparing, probably in concert with the king, for some two years. Saladin's intelligence network had warned that the lord of Kerak was planning an attack, but the sultan wrongly assumed that this would focus upon the route across the Sinai linking Egypt and Damascus, and so tasked al-Adil to strengthen the fortifications at the key muster point of al-Arish. In fact, Reynald's scheme was far bolder and more daring, even if it was, in strategic terms, less judicious. In late 1182 to early 1183, five galleys, constructed in sections at Kerak, were transported on camel-back to the Gulf of Aqaba, reassembled and launched on to the Red Sea. This was the first time in centuries that Christian ships had plied these waters. Reynald divided his fleet, with two vessels blockading the Muslim-held port of Aqaba, which he himself then attacked by land, and the remaining three galleys sent south, equipped with Arab navigators and manned by soldiers. Apparently, news of the extraordinary exploits of this small three-ship flotilla never reached the Franks. A sole Latin source recorded that, after their launch, 'nothing was heard of them and nobody knows what became of them', and, having inflicted some damage on Aqaba, Reynald returned home.

In the Muslim world, however, the shocking and unprecedented Red Sea expedition caused outrage. For weeks the three Christian galleys wreaked havoc upon the unsuspecting ports of Egypt and Arabia, harassing pilgrims and merchants, and threatening Islam's spiritual heartland, the sacred cities of Mecca and Medina. It was even rumoured that the Christians intended to steal Muhammad's body. Only when al-Adil portaged his own fleet from Cairo to the Red Sea were they hunted down. Forced to beach their vessels on the Arabian coast, the Christian crew fled into the desert, but, once cornered, 170 of them surrendered, probably in return for promises of safe conduct. In the event, however, their lives were not spared.

Informed of events while in Iraq, Saladin insisted that an example be made: officially, he argued that infidels who knew the paths to Islam's holiest sites could not be allowed to live; in private, of course, he must have been only too conscious of an uncomfortable truth. At this very moment of infamous crisis he, the self-proclaimed champion of the faith, was absent, fighting fellow Muslims. Thus, despite al-Adil's evident disquiet, the sultan demanded retribution for the 'unparalleled enormity' of the Latin prisoners' crimes and, according to Arabic testimony, insisted that 'the earth must be purged of their filth and the air of their breath'. Most of the captives were sent singly or in pairs to various cities and settlements across the Ayyubid realm and publicly executed, but two were held back for a still more ghastly fate. At the time of the next *Hajj* they were led to a site on the outskirts of Mecca, where traditionally livestock are offered for slaughter and their flesh given to feed the poor, and here the two unfortunate captives were butchered 'like animals for sacrifice' before a baying pilgrim throng. The defilement of Arabia had been punished and the sultan's image as Islam's resolute defender affirmed, but the bitter memory of the Franks' scandalous Red Sea campaign endured, and its architect, Reynald of Châtillon, now became a despised figure of hate.[56]

A rising tide of conflict?

When Saladin's attack on the kingdom of Jerusalem finally came in autumn 1183 it exposed profound weaknesses within Christian Palestine. That summer, Baldwin IV's health again deteriorated. By this stage leprosy had already left his body in ruins, as 'his sight failed and his extremities were covered in ulcerations so that he was unable to use either his hands or his feet'. No longer able to ride any distance, he had become accustomed to travelling upon a litter. Nonetheless, up to this point, William of Tyre attested that 'although physically weak and impotent, yet mentally he was vigorous, and, far beyond his strength, he strove to hide his illness and to support the cares of the kingdom'. Now in 1183, however, he was seized by some form of secondary infection, and 'attacked by [a] fever . . . he lost hope of life'. Unmanned by this infirmity, desperately fearful that Saladin would unleash a new attack yet wholly unsure where he would strike, the young king was in an appalling dilemma. Summoning his Jerusalemite forces, along with troops from Tripoli and Antioch, to assemble at Saffurya, he himself retired to Nazareth and temporarily passed executive power to his brother-in-law, the heir apparent, Guy of Lusignan.

As regent, Guy thus held the office of Frankish commander-in-chief when Saladin invaded Galilee in late September 1183. He stood at the head of one of the largest Frankish hosts ever assembled in Palestine – containing some 1,300 knights and 15,000 infantry – albeit one that was still dwarfed by the Muslim force. With little or no experience of directing such an army in the midst of full-blown warfare, Guy's abilities were sure to be taxed, but by the measure of military science he did an effective, if unspectacular job. When Saladin once again pillaged Bethsan, Guy made an ordered advance, using infantry to screen his mounted knights while on the move, and, barring minor skirmishes, avoided committing to a hasty pitched battle. Hoping to tempt the Latins into breaking formation, Saladin withdrew north a short distance, but no pursuit was forthcoming and the two sides took up defensive positions within a mile of one another, near the village of Ayn Jalut. A stalemate held for nearly two weeks, despite efforts on the sultan's part to provoke an attack, and in mid-October the Muslim army retreated across the Jordan. The Franks had survived the storm.

Throughout the campaign Guy followed the established principles of 'crusader' defensive strategy almost to the letter, maintaining troop discipline, seeking to limit enemy mobility by advancing to offer a threat, yet steering clear of risky confrontation. Yet, in spite of this cautious competence, he was roundly criticised by his rivals at court for allowing Saladin to raid the kingdom unchallenged, and chided for tentative timidity unbecoming of knightly culture. The reality was that, tactically sound as it might be, guarded inaction was rarely popular with Latin soldiers. Even established sovereigns and seasoned field commanders struggled to enforce orders that, on the face of it, appeared humiliating and cowardly – in 1115 Roger of Salerno had to threaten to blind his men to keep them in line, and, in the years to come, Richard the Lionheart would experience similar difficulties with troop control. Guy was an unproven general, newly risen to the regency, whose right to rule was open to question. What he needed most in autumn 1183 was a firm show of martial defiance, perhaps even a brazen military victory, to win over doubters and silence critics. At the very least, he had to demonstrate that he possessed the force of will to quell Jerusalem's independent-minded aristocracy. In effect, by doing what was right for the defence of the realm, Guy did himself a grave disservice. It is not surprising that his political opponents seized upon this opportunity to besmirch his reputation.[57]

After a brief pause, in late October 1183 Saladin moved south into Transjordan to besiege Kerak. This was a more determined attack, for he came equipped with heavy siege weaponry, including a number of siege engines with which to assail the castle, but it was also a convenient opportunity to rendezvous with his brother al-Adil, who had travelled from Egypt to assume lordship over newly conquered Ayyubid territory in northern Syria. The sultan's investment of Kerak also coincided, perhaps deliberately, with the celebration of a high-profile Frankish wedding between Humphrey IV of Toron and the king's half-sister, Isabella, presided over by Reynald of Châtillon, his wife Stephanie of Milly and Isabella's mother, Maria Comnena. Saladin may have had one eye on capturing such an eminent crop of Christian nobles, for their ransoms would prove a handsome boon.* A story later circulated that – even in the midst of the siege – Lady Stephanie courteously sent food from the nuptial banquet out to the sultan, and that in return he promised not to bombard that part of the fortress occupied by the newly-weds. If there is any truth to this tale, which is not mentioned in the Muslim sources, then Saladin's apparent gallantry may, in part, have been motivated by a desire to preserve the lives of such valuable hostages.

News of Kerak's siege reached the Latin court in Jerusalem at a moment when the Franks were already ensnared in dispute. Against expectations, the leper king's fever abated and a modicum of strength returned to Baldwin's enfeebled frame. In the aftermath of the events at Ayn Jalut, he and Guy of Lusignan squabbled over rights to the realm and, perhaps with his mind poisoned by the views of Raymond III and the Ibelin brothers, the young monarch turned on Guy, rescinding his regency. Even as Kerak lay under threat, Baldwin convened a council to discuss the selection of a new heir and, in the end, the choice fell to Sibylla's infant son by her first husband – the nephew and namesake of the king, Baldwin (V). On 20 November 1183, this five-year-old boy became heir designate, crowned and anointed as co-ruler in the Holy Sepulchre. Even William of Tyre

---

* Of course, given the entrenched enmity that already existed between Saladin and Reynald of Châtillon, and in light of the sultan's later treatment of him, it is likely that, in the lord of Kerak's case, Saladin would have had no intention of seeking a ransom for Reynald.

had to admit that 'the opinions of wise men over this great change were many and varied . . . for since both kings were hampered, one by disease and the other by youth, it was wholly useless'. The archbishop nonetheless made his own, thinly veiled, views apparent, concluding that this settlement had, at least, stifled any lingering hope harboured by the 'entirely incompetent' Guy of one day ascending to the throne.[58]

With this new arrangement sealed, Baldwin IV set out for Transjordan, hoping to relieve Kerak. In light of the king's continued frailty, he probably had to be carried upon a litter, and Raymond of Tripoli was appointed as field commander of the Frankish army. Despite the Latins' delayed reaction, Saladin had been unable to overcome Kerak's expansive dry moat and, with the Christian host approaching, the sultan abandoned his siege on 4 December 1183. Overall, his attack had proved half-hearted and he was certainly unwilling to confront the Franks in open battle. The leper king was thus able to enter the desert fortress in the guise of a victorious saviour.

That winter an open rift developed between Baldwin IV and Guy of Lusignan, and throughout the first half of 1184 the Latin kingdom remained in a weakened state of disunity. Saladin, however, focused upon the diplomatic struggle for Mosul and made no move to threaten the Franks until late summer. Around 22 August he initiated another siege of Kerak, but after the leper king mustered what remained of his waning strength to assemble a relief force the sultan retreated once again, establishing a well-defended camp some miles to the north. When the Latins made no effort to attack he moved on. After prosecuting a short-lived raiding campaign up the Jordan valley and a brief attack on Nablus, Saladin retired to Damascus.

Throughout his two expeditions against the kingdom of Jerusalem, in 1183 and again in 1184, Saladin pursued a strategy of cautious aggression, continuing to pressure and test the Franks, taking minimal risks and avoiding battle when the enemy refused to fight on his terms and at a site of his choosing. These encounters have often been presented as measured, gradually escalating steps on the path to all-out invasion, but they might equally be interpreted as tentative jabs in a struggle that was, as yet, of only secondary importance to the sultan. It is notable that, throughout the early 1180s, Saladin's *jihadi* offensives against the Latins were focused, almost exclusively, upon two specific regions which were of strategic, political and economic significance for the Ayyubid realm: Transjordan, the crucial land route linking Egypt and Damascus, which also served as a major thoroughfare for commercial caravans and pilgrim traffic to Arabia; and Galilee, the Latin-held region which posed the greatest threat to Damascus.

The truth is that, in this period, Saladin showed no determination to prosecute a decisive invasion of Palestine and made no dogged attempt to confront the Franks in open battle. In real terms, Latin dominion of Jerusalem remained unchallenged. The sultan did wage war against Outremer, but his efforts seem, at least in part, to have been driven by the need publicly to substantiate his declared dedication to *jihad* – on occasion his attacks appear almost as token gestures. Looking back with the benefit of hindsight, it is evident that, because of the Franks' extreme vulnerability, a committed Ayyubid offensive against the kingdom of Jerusalem might have brought Saladin outright victory, particularly in 1183–4. In the sultan's defence, however, it is far from certain that he actually knew the true, crippling depth of dissension and weakness to which the Christians had been brought.

It is also important to recognise that, while Arabic and Latin chronicles and biographies, concerned with political and military events, convey a sense of mounting tension between Christian Outremer and Ayyubid Islam in the 1180s, other contemporary sources offer a different perspective. The Iberian Muslim pilgrim and traveller Ibn Jubayr passed through the Holy Land in this precise period, joining a Muslim trade caravan from Damascus to Acre in autumn 1184 and witnessing a degree of cross-cultural contact and coexistence that he found extraordinary:

One of the astonishing things talked of is that though the fires of discord burn between these two parties, Muslim and Christian, two armies of them may meet and dispose themselves in battle array, and yet Muslim and Christian travellers will come and go between them without interference. In this connection we saw Saladin [depart] with all the Muslim troops to lay siege to the fortress of Kerak, one of the greatest Christian strongholds lying astride the road [to Mecca and Medina] and hindering the overland passage of the Muslims . . .

This sultan invested it, and put it to sore straits, and long the siege lasted, but still the caravans passed successively from Egypt to Damascus, going through the lands of the Franks without impediment from them. In the same way the Muslims continuously journeyed from Damascus to Acre [through Frankish territory], and likewise not one of the Christian merchants was stopped or hindered [in Muslim territory].

This fascinating and revealing evidence suggests that a pulsing current of commerce continued unabated throughout these years, connecting the two worlds of Christendom and Islam. Ibn Jubayr's testimony seems to belie any notion of these two rival powers being pitted against one another in a vehement and implacable conflict. If his vision of the Levantine world was representative – and it has to be remembered that Ibn Jubayr was an outsider who spent only a few months in the region – then Saladin's apparent failure urgently to prioritise *jihad* perhaps becomes more understandable.[59]

Whatever the true depth of enmity between Islam and the Franks, over the next year the crisis of leadership within the kingdom of Jerusalem deepened. In autumn 1184 Baldwin IV's condition once again deteriorated and it eventually became clear that he was dying. Despite his own continued misgivings about Raymond of Tripoli's loyalty, Baldwin appointed the count as regent – the only realistic alternative for the post being Reynald of Châtillon, who was closely engaged in the defence of Transjordan. Around mid-May 1185

Baldwin IV died at the age of just twenty-three, and was buried alongside his father Amalric in the Holy Sepulchre. For much of his troubled reign Baldwin struggled with a nightmarish predicament – aware that he was incapable of ruling effectively, yet unable to secure an acceptable replacement or to orchestrate a successful transfer of power, even as the threat of Muslim invasion increased. Throughout he showed great physical courage in enduring his disability. Even so, he failed to contain or control the ambitions of his most powerful subjects and suffered significant lapses of judgement, most notably in his decision to withdraw his support for Guy of Lusignan in late 1183. He must be remembered as a tragic figure – one who strove to defend the Holy Land, yet presided over a decade of perilous decline.

TRANSFORMATION

In 1185, Saladin once again turned his attention to the subjection of Muslim Mesopotamia. Renewed attempts to reach a negotiated settlement with Mosul in early 1184 had failed, even as the sultan continued to extend his influence in the region, winning the support of neighbouring Iraqi settlements through a mixture of intimidation, persuasion and outright bribery. By 1185, however, it was clear that a second expedition beyond the Euphrates would be necessary if Ayyubid authority was truly to be imposed, and Mosul bent to his will. With Syria and Egypt afforded a margin of protection by a one-year truce agreed with Raymond of Tripoli that spring, Saladin set out east from Aleppo with a large army in the company of Isa and al-Mashtub, and they were later joined by Keukburi.

Still concerned to uphold his image as a defender and unifier of Muslims, Saladin dispatched envoys to Baghdad to justify this campaign, drawing upon a now familiar array of allegations. At first, it seemed that Izz al-Din of Mosul would be willing to negotiate a settlement, but his attempts at diplomacy proved desultory and were probably designed simply to stymie Ayyubid military impetus. Before long, the sultan committed to a second siege of Mosul through the scorching summer. This proved to be a largely uneventful affair – indeed, progress was so slow that Saladin even considered a wildly ambitious plan to break Mosuli resistance by diverting the mighty River Tigris away from the city, cutting its water supply. In August he moved north to mop up easier conquests in the Diyar Bakr region of the Upper Tigris and by autumn most of Mesopotamia's Muslim potentates had either been won over to his cause or forced into submission. As yet, Izz al-Din remained unbowed, but his resistance appears to have been ebbing.

Facing mortality

It was at this point, on 3 December 1185, that the sultan fell ill with a fever and retired to Harran. As the weeks turned into months, his strength waned and the concerns of those around him deepened. Throughout this period, Imad al-Din, who had travelled east with Saladin, exchanged a stream of anxious letters with al-Fadil back in Damascus. Their words lay bare the deepening concern, fear and confusion that now gripped the Ayyubid world. Twice it seemed that the sultan's health was returning, and that the danger was past – at one point al-Fadil even happily reported that he had received a note written in Saladin's own hand – yet on both occasions the sultan relapsed. His court physicians, who had now arrived from Syria, were left to argue about possible treatments, even as Saladin's mind drifted in and out of lucidity and his body became emaciated. By his side throughout, Imad al-Din wrote that 'as [the sultan's] pain increased, so too did his hope in God's grace', and grimly observed that 'the spread of bad news . . . could not be concealed, especially when the doctors [came] out and said that there was no hope . . . then you could see people sending off their treasures'. In early 1186, al-Fadil wrote that in Damascus 'hearts [are] palpitating and tongues [are] full of rumours', begging that the sultan be brought back from the frontiers of his lands to the security of Syria.

In January, Saladin dictated his will and, by mid-February, al-Adil had arrived from Aleppo to lend his support, but also to be on hand to take up the reins of power should that prove necessary. Meanwhile, another Ayyubid slipped away from Harran to foment rebellion. Nasir al-Din, Shirkuh's son, seems to have harboured a cancerous jealousy of his cousin Saladin's rise to power in Egypt, a region which he himself might have claimed as Shirkuh's heir back in 1169. The gift of Homs had bought grudging loyalty in the 1170s, but with the sultan's demise seemingly imminent, Nasir al-Din now saw a chance for his own advancement. Quietly amassing troops in Syria, he laid furtive plans for the seizure of Damascus. His timing proved disastrous. In the final days of February, the sultan's condition turned a corner and he began to make a slow but lasting recovery. By 3 March Nasir al-Din was dead. Officially he had succumbed to a disease that worked 'faster than the blink of an eye', but rumour had it that he had been poisoned by one of Saladin's Damascene agents.

Saladin had been brought face to face with his own mortality in early 1186. It has often been suggested that he emerged a changed man, having paused to consider his life, his faith and his achievements in the many wars fought against the Franks and his fellow Muslims. Certainly some contemporaries represented this as a moment of profound transformation in the sultan's career, after which he dedicated himself to the cause of *jihad* and the pursuit of Jerusalem's recovery. At the height of his illness, he apparently vowed to commit all his energy to this end, regardless of the human and financial sacrifice exacted. Imad al-Din wrote that this affliction had been divinely appointed, 'to wake [Saladin] from the sleep of forgetfulness', and noted that the sultan subsequently consulted Islamic jurists and theologians about his spiritual obligations. Al-Fadil, who had lobbied against the Mosul campaign in the first place, now looked to convince Saladin to renounce aggression against Muslims. In practical terms, Saladin's infirmity forced him to accept a compromise with Mosul in March 1186. The Zangid ruler Izz al-Din remained in power, but recognised the sultan as overlord, including his name in the Friday prayer and promising to contribute troops to the holy war.[60]

Saladin's career to 1186

For modern scholars – most notably in the classic political biography of Saladin by Malcolm Lyons and David Jackson published in 1982 – Saladin's brush with death proved revelatory in another regard, for it raised the pointed question of how Saladin might be regarded by history had fate's course transected a different path, bringing his life to an end at Harran in early 1186. Lyons' and Jackson's swingeing conclusion that Saladin would be remembered as 'a moderately successful soldier [and] a dynast who used Islam for his own purposes' is instructive, if somewhat blunt. Up to this point, the sultan had made only a limited contribution to the *jihad*, spending some thirty-three months fighting against Muslims since 1174 and only eleven combating the Franks. He was a usurper with an obvious appetite for power and a marked facility for its accumulation – an aggressive autocrat who repeatedly seized Muslim territory to which he had no rightful claim and made fulsome use of propaganda to justify his actions and blacken the names of his opponents. Of course, not all historians have accepted this view of Saladin. Some still persist in suggesting that he was obsessed with the holy war against the Franks throughout his career – always building towards a full-scale attack on the kingdom of Jerusalem and ever seeking to bring his Christian enemies to battle – but, on balance, the contemporary evidence suggests that they are wrong.[61]

It is not surprising that Saladin's aims up to 1186 continue to be debated, because even contemporaries disputed this issue. Some praised the sultan. Writing shortly before his death (probably in 1185), William of Tyre believed that the Ayyubid ruler posed a grave and immediate threat to the continued survival of Outremer, but nonetheless commended him as 'a man wise in counsel, valiant in battle and generous beyond measure'.[62] Nevertheless, other opponents and supporters – from the pro-Zangid Iraqi chronicler Ibn al-Athir to the sultan's personal secretary al-Fadil – knew only too well that Saladin's lack of wholehearted dedication to the *jihad* left him dangerously exposed to accusations of self-serving empire building. Had the sultan died in early 1186 the question of his intentions would have remained unanswered. As it was, he lived on, with the call to holy war harkening in his ears.

12

HOLY WARRIOR

In the spring of 1186, with the worst of his illness behind him, Saladin – now some forty-eight years old – returned to Damascus. Much of the remainder of that year was given over to his protracted convalescence, and the calmer recreations of theological debate, hawking and hunting, as his physical vitality slowly rekindled. That summer, one marked distraction was provided by the prediction of an impending apocalypse. For decades, astrologers had foretold that, on 16 September 1186, a momentous planetary alignment would stir up a devastating wind storm, scouring the Earth of life. This bleak prophecy had circulated among Muslims and Christians alike, but the sultan nonetheless thought it ridiculous. He made a point of holding a candlelit, open-air party on the appointed night of disaster, even as 'feeble-mind[ed]' fools huddled in caves and underground shelters. Needless to say, the evening passed without event; indeed, one of his companions pointedly remarked that 'we never saw a night as calm as that'.

While his health gradually improved, Saladin looked to reorganise the balance and distribution of power within what could now be termed his Ayyubid Empire. One priority was the promotion of his eldest son al-Afdal as primary heir. The young princeling, now around sixteen, was brought north from Egypt to Syria. Entering Damascus to celebrations fit for a sultan, al-Afdal became nominal overlord of the city, although in the years to come Saladin often kept him by his side, tutoring him in the arts of leadership, politics and war. Two of Saladin's younger sons were similarly rewarded. Uthman, aged fourteen, was appointed ruler of Egypt, and the sultan's trusted brother al-Adil returned from Aleppo to the Nile region to act as the young boy's guardian and governor. Aleppo itself passed to the thirteen-year-old al-Zahir. The only problem spawned by this extensive reshuffle was Saladin's nephew Taqi al-Din. As governor of Egypt since 1183, he had shown worrying tendencies towards independent action. With the aid of Qaragush (whom Saladin had appointed to oversee the Cairene court in 1169), Taqi al-Din had laid plans for a campaign westwards along the North African coast that would have deprived the sultan of valuable troops. Rumours also abounded that, during the sultan's illness, Taqi al-Din had been preparing to declare his autonomy. In autumn 1186, Isa, ever the consummate diplomat, was tasked with the delicate mission of persuading him to relinquish his hold on Egypt and return to Syria. Arriving unexpectedly at Cairo, Isa was initially greeted with prevarication, but then apparently advised Taqi al-Din to 'Go wherever you want.' This seemingly neutral statement possessed an icily threatening undertone, and Saladin's nephew soon left for Damascus, where he was welcomed back into the fold and rewarded with his former lordship at Hama and further lands in the newly subdued region of Diyar Bakr.[63]

The question of Taqi al-Din's continued subservience reflected a wider issue. To sustain his burgeoning empire, Saladin relied upon the support of his wider family, but the sultan was also determined to protect the interests of his sons, the direct perpetuators of the Ayyubid bloodline. Saladin had to achieve a delicate balance – he needed to harness the drive and ambition of kinsmen like Taqi al-Din, because their energy was vital to the continued preservation and expansion of the realm; but at the same time, their independence had to be curbed. In Taqi al-Din's case, Saladin hoped to ensure loyalty by offering his nephew the prospect of continued advancement in Upper Mesopotamia.

ISLAM UNITED?

Saladin's attempts to shape the dynastic fortunes of the Ayyubid Empire in 1186 were, to some extent, a direct function of the increased power and territory he had now accumulated. Since emerging as a political and military force in 1169, he had masterminded the subjugation of Near Eastern Islam, extending his authority over Cairo, Damascus, Aleppo and large stretches of Mesopotamia. The Fatimid caliphate's abolition had brought the crippling division between Sunni Syria and Shi'ite Egypt to an end, ushering in a new era of pan-Levantine Muslim accord. These achievements, unparalleled in recent history, surpassed even those of Nur al-Din. On the face of it, Saladin had united Islam from the Nile to the Euphrates; his coinage, circulating throughout his realm and far beyond, now bore the inscription 'the sultan of Islam and the Muslims', stark proclamation of his all-encompassing, almost hegemonic authority. This image has often been accepted by modern historians – an attitude typified by one scholar's recent assertion that after 1183 'the rule of all Syria and Egypt was in [Saladin's] hands'.[64]

Yet the notion that Saladin now presided over a world of complete and enduring Muslim unity is profoundly misleading. His 'empire', constructed through a mixture of direct conquest and coercive diplomacy, was in truth merely a brittle amalgam of disparate and distant polities, many of which were administered by client-rulers whose allegiance might easily falter. Even in Cairo, Damascus and Aleppo – the linchpins of his realm – the sultan had to rely upon the continued fidelity and cooperation of his family, virtues that were never assured. Elsewhere, in the likes of Mosul, Asia Minor and the

Jazira, Ayyubid supremacy was largely ephemeral, dependent upon loose alliances and tainted by barely submerged antipathy.

In 1186 the spell held. But it did so only because Saladin had survived his illness and still possessed the wealth, might and influence to manifest his will. In the years that followed, the work of sustaining and governing such a geographically expansive and politically incongruent empire tested the sultan to breaking point. And the struggle to counteract the ingrained centrifugal forces that could so readily rip apart the Ayyubid Empire proved constant and consuming.

Even after some seventeen years of unrelenting struggle, Saladin's work was not done. Amidst the holy war to come, he could call upon a dedicated, loyalist core of battle-hardened troops, but for the most part the sultan stood at the head of a fragile, often restive, coalition, ever conscious that his realm might be disrupted by insurrection, rebellion or cessation. This fact was of paramount importance, for it shaped much of his thinking and strategy, often forcing him to follow the path of least resistance to seek swift, self-perpetuating victories. Contemporaries and modern historians alike have sometimes criticised Saladin's qualities as a military commander in this later phase of his career, arguing that he lacked the backbone to prosecute costly and prolonged sieges. In fact, he depended upon speed of action and ongoing success to maintain momentum, clear in the knowledge that if the Muslim war machine ground to a halt, it might well collapse.

At a fundamental level, Saladin's empire had also been forged against the backdrop of *jihad*; at every step he justified the extension of Ayyubid authority as a means to an end. Unity beneath his banner may have been bought at a heavy price, but he argued that it was directed at one sole purpose: the *jihad* to drive the Franks from Palestine and liberate the Holy City. This ideological impulse had proved to be an enormously potent instrument, fuelling and legitimising the motor of expansion, but it came at a near-unavoidable cost. Unless Saladin wished to be revealed as a fraudulent despot, all his promises of unbending devotion to the cause must now be fulfilled and the long-awaited war waged. Certainly, in the aftermath of his illness, and what may have been a period of deepening spirituality, the sultan's promulgation of the *jihad* became ever more active. Revered Islamic scholars like the brothers Ibn Qudama and Abd al-Ghani, both long-time proponents of Saladin's cause, were among those who contributed to a quickening of religious fanaticism. In Damascus, and across the realm, religious tracts and poems on the faith, the obligation of *jihad* and the overriding devotional significance of Jerusalem all were recited at massed public gatherings with increasing regularity. By the end of 1186, it appears that the sultan had not only recognised the political necessity for an all-out assault on the Latins, but had also embraced the struggle ahead at a personal level. This is borne out by the testimony of one of Saladin's few critics among contemporary Muslim commentators, the Mosuli historian Ibn al-Athir. Recording a war council from early 1187, the chronicler wrote:

One of [Saladin's] emirs said to him: 'The best plan in my opinion is to invade their territory [and] if any Frankish force stands against us, we should meet it. People in the east curse us and say, "He has given up fighting the infidels and has turned his attention to fighting Muslims." [We should] take a course of action that will vindicate us and stop people's tongues.'

Ibn al-Athir's intention was to censure Ayyubid expansionism, while evoking the tide of public pressure and expectation now attendant on the sultan. But he went on to suggest that Saladin experienced a brief, but significant, moment of self-realisation at this meeting. According to Ibn al-Athir, the sultan declared his determination to go to war and then mournfully observed that 'affairs do not proceed by man's decision [and] we do not know how much remains of our lives'. Perhaps it was the sultan's own sense of mortality that moved him to action; whatever the reason, a change does seem to have occurred. Real questions remain about the true extent of his determination to combat the Franks in the long years between 1169 and 1186, but regardless of what had gone before, in 1187 Saladin brought the full force of his empire to bear against the kingdom of Jerusalem. He was now doggedly resolved to bring the Christians to full and decisive battle.[65]

A KINGDOM UNDONE

This upsurge of Ayyubid aggression coincided with a deepening crisis in Latin Palestine. At some point between May and mid-September 1186 the young King Baldwin V of Jerusalem died, and a rancorous succession dispute erupted. Count Raymond of Tripoli, who had been acting as regent, schemed to seize the throne, but he was outmanoeuvred by Sibylla (Baldwin IV's sister) and her husband, Guy of Lusignan. Having won the support of Patriarch Heraclius, a large proportion of the nobility and the Military Orders, Sibylla and Guy managed to have themselves crowned and anointed as queen and king. Raymond tried to engineer an outright civil war, proclaiming Humphrey of Toron and his wife Isabella as the rightful monarchs of Jerusalem. But, perhaps mindful of the terrible damage that might be wrought should this claim be pursued, Humphrey declined to step forward.

As king, one of Guy's first steps was to buy time to restore some sense of order to the realm by renewing the treaty with Saladin until April 1187 in return for some 60,000 gold bezants. Guy was a divisive figure – Baldwin of Ibelin was so disgusted by his elevation that he gave up his lordship and moved to Antioch – and, as king, Guy's policy of putting family members from Poitou into positions of power caused further unease. To deal with his most powerful enemy, Raymond of Tripoli, Guy seems to have hatched a plan to seize the lordship of Galilee by force. But in response, Raymond took the quite drastic step of seeking protection from Saladin himself. Muslim sources indicate that many of the sultan's advisers were suspicious of this approach, but that Saladin rightly judged it to be an honest offer of alliance, the product of the desperate division that now afflicted the Franks. To the evident horror of many of his Latin contemporaries, Raymond welcomed Muslim troops into Tiberias, to bolster the town's garrison, and gave Ayyubid forces licence to travel unhindered through his Galilean lands. At this worst moment, the count perpetrated an act of treason, engendering even greater disunity among the Christians.

Then, in the winter months of 1186 and 1187, Reynald of Châtillon, lord of Kerak, contravened the truce with the Ayyubids by attacking a Muslim caravan travelling through Transjordan on its way from Cairo to Damascus. His motives remain open to debate, but basic greed probably combined with a realisation that Saladin was building towards a major offensive to spur Reynald into action. Certainly in the weeks that followed he made no effort to repair relations, bluntly refusing the sultan's demands for restitution of the stolen goods. Even without Reynald's raid, Saladin would almost certainly have refused that spring to renew the truce with Frankish Palestine, so the once popular contention that the lord of Kerak effectively ignited the war to come should probably be discarded. Nonetheless, Reynald's exploits did reinforce his status as the Muslim world's abhorred enemy. They also provided Saladin with a clear cause for war further to inflame the heart of Islam.

TO THE HORNS OF HATTIN

In the spring of 1187 Saladin began to amass his forces for an invasion of Palestine. Drawing troops from Egypt, Syria, the Jazira and Diyar Bakr, he assembled a massive army, with some 12,000 professional cavalrymen at its heart, supported by around 30,000 volunteers. One Muslim eyewitness likened them to a pack of 'old wolves [and] rending lions', while the sultan himself described how the dust cloud raised when this swarming horde marched 'dark[ened] the eye of the sun'. Marshalling such a huge force was a feat in itself – a muster point was appointed in the fertile Hauran region south of Damascus and, with soldiers coming from so far afield, the mobilisation took months to complete. The task was overseen by Saladin's eldest son, al-Afdal, in his first major command role.[66]

During the early stages of the 1187 campaign, Muslim strategy largely followed the pattern established by Ayyubid attacks in previous years. In April, the sultan marched into Transjordan to link up with forces advancing from North Africa, while prosecuting a series of punitive raids against Kerak and Montreal, including the widespread destruction of crops. But the Franks offered little or no reaction to this provocation. Meanwhile, on 1 May, al-Afdal participated in a combined reconnaissance and raiding mission across the Jordan, testing Tiberias' defences while Keukburi led a mounted assault force of around seven thousand to scout the Franks' own preferred muster point at Saffuriya. That night they were spotted by watchmen in Nazareth, and a small party of Templars and Hospitallers, then travelling through Galilee and led by the masters of both orders, decided to give battle. A bloody skirmish followed at the springs of Cresson. Vastly outnumbered, around 130 Latin knights and 300 infantry were killed or captured. The Templar Master Gerard of Ridefort was one of the few to escape, but his Hospitaller counterpart was among the dead. An early blow had been struck, buoying Muslim morale and denting Christian manpower. In the aftermath of this shocking defeat, with the overwhelming Ayyubid threat now impossible to ignore, King Guy and Raymond of Tripoli were begrudgingly reconciled, and the count broke off contact with Saladin.

In late May the sultan himself marched into the Hauran and, as the last troop contingents arrived, moved to the advance staging post of Ashtara, around a day's march from the Sea of Galilee. He now was joined by Taqi al-Din, returned from northern Syria, where a series of vicious raids had forced the Frankish Prince Bohemond III to agree terms of truce that safeguarded Aleppo from attack. Throughout June, Saladin made his final plans and preparations, carefully drilling his troops and organising battle formations, so that his immense army might function with maximum discipline and efficiency. Three main contingents were formed, with the right and left flanks under Taqi al-Din and Keukburi respectively, and a central force under Saladin's personal command. At last, on Friday 27 June 1187, the Muslims were ready for war. A crossing of the Jordan was made just south of the Sea of Galilee and the invasion of Palestine began.

In response to the terrible spectre of Islamic attack, King Guy had followed standard Frankish protocol, amassing the Christian army at Saffuriya. Given the unprecedented scale of Saladin's forces, the king had taken the drastic step of issuing a general call to arms, gathering together practically every last scrap of available fighting manpower in Palestine and using money sent by King Henry II of England to the Holy Land (in lieu of actually crusading) to pay for further mercenary reinforcements. A member of the sultan's entourage wrote that the Latins came 'in numbers defying account or reckoning, numerous as pebbles, 50,000 or even more', but, in reality, Guy probably pulled together around 1,200 knights and between 15,000 and 18,000 infantry and Turcopoles. This was one of the largest hosts ever assembled beneath the True Cross – the Franks' totemic symbol of martial valour and spiritual devotion – but it was, nonetheless, heavily outnumbered by the Muslim horde. In mustering this army, the Christian king had also taken a considerable gamble, leaving Palestine's fortresses garrisoned by the barest minimum of soldiers. Should this conflict end in a resounding Latin defeat, the kingdom of Jerusalem would stand all but undefended.[67]

Saladin's overriding objective was to achieve just such a decisive victory, drawing the Franks away from the safety of Saffuriya into a full-scale pitched battle on ground of his choosing. But all his experience of war with Jerusalem suggested that the enemy would not easily be goaded into a reckless advance. In the last days of June, the sultan climbed out of the Jordan valley into the Galilean uplands,

camping in force at the small village of Kafr Sabt (about six miles
south-west of Tiberias and ten miles east of Saffuriya), amidst an
expansive landscape of broad plains and undulating hills, peppered
with occasional rocky outcrops. He began by testing the enemy,
dispatching raiding sorties to ravage the surrounding countryside,
while personally reconnoitring Guy's encampment from a distance.
After a few days it became obvious that, as expected, a Latin reaction
would only be elicited by bolder provocation.

On 2 July 1187, Saladin laid his trap, leading a dawn assault on the
weakly defended town of Tiberias, where Christian resistance soon
buckled. Only the citadel held out, proffering precarious refuge to
Lady Eschiva, Raymond of Tripoli's wife. This news raced back to
Saffuriya (indeed, the sultan probably allowed Eschiva's messengers
to slip through) bearing entreaties for aid. Saladin's hope was that the
tidings of Tiberias' stricken condition would force Guy's hand. As
evening fell, the sultan waited to see whether this bait would bring
forth his quarry.

Lodged sixteen miles away, the Franks were locked in debate. At
a gathering of the realm's leading nobles, presided over by King Guy,
Count Raymond seems to have advised caution and patience. He
argued that the risk of direct confrontation with so formidable a
Muslim army must be avoided, even at the cost of Tiberias' fall and
his own spouse's capture. Given time, Saladin's host would break
apart, like so many Islamic forces before it, compelling the sultan to
retreat; then Galilee might be recovered, and Eschiva's ransom
arranged. Others, including Reynald of Châtillon and the Templar
Master Gerard of Ridefort, offered a different view. Counselling Guy
to ignore the traitorous, untrustworthy count, they warned of the
shame attendant upon cowardly inaction and urged an immediate
move to relieve Tiberias. According to one version of events, the king
initially elected to remain at Saffuriya, but, during the night, was
persuaded by Gerard to overturn this resolution. In fact, the most
decisive factor shaping Latin strategy was probably Guy's own
experience. Confronted with a near-identical choice four years

earlier, he had eschewed battle with Saladin and, in consequence, faced derision and demotion. Now, in 1187, he embraced bold pugnacity and, on the morning of 3 July, his army marched forth from Saffuriya.

Once news reached Saladin that the Franks were on the move, he immediately climbed back into the Galilean hills, leaving a small body of troops to maintain the foothold gained in Tiberias. The enemy were advancing eastwards in close order, almost certainly following the broad Roman road that ran from Acre to the Sea of Galilee, with Raymond of Tripoli in the vanguard, the Templars holding the rear and infantry screening the cavalry. A Muslim eyewitness described how 'wave upon wave' of them came into sight, remarking that 'the air stank, the light was dimmed [and] the desert was stunned' by their advance. Guy of Lusignan's precise objectives that first day are difficult to divine, but he may, rather

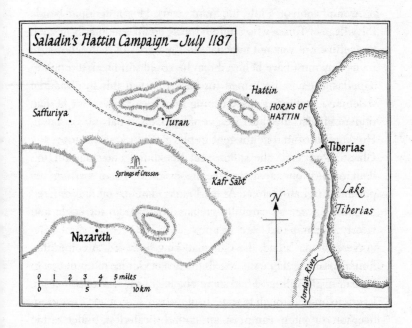

Saladin's Hattin Campaign – July 1187

optimistically, have hoped to reach Tiberias or at least the shores of the Galilean sea. The sultan was determined to prevent either eventuality. Sending skirmishers forward to harass the Christian column, he held the bulk of his troops on the open plateau north of Kafr Sabt, blocking their path.

Saladin rightly grasped that access to water would play a crucial role in this conflict. During high summer, soldiers and horses crossing such arid terrain might easily become dangerously dehydrated. With this in mind, he ordered any wells in the immediate region to be filled in, while ensuring that his own troops were well supplied from the spring at Kafr Sabt and with water ferried on camel-back from the Jordan valley below. Only the ample spring in the village of Hattin remained, on the northern fringe of the escarpment, and the approaches to this were now heavily guarded. The sultan had created what was, in effect, a waterless killing zone.[68]

Around noon on 3 July, the Franks paused for brief respite beside the village of Turan, whose minor spring could temporarily quench their thirst but was not adequate to the needs of many thousand men. Guy must have believed that he could still break through to Tiberias, for now he turned his back on even this insubstantial sanctuary, continuing the creeping march eastwards. But he had underestimated the sheer weight of numbers at Saladin's disposal. Holding his central contingent in place to block and hamper the Christian advance, the sultan sent Keukburi's and Taqi al-Din's flanking divisions racing to take possession of Turan, barring any possibility of Latin retreat. As the Franks marched on they entered the plateau area so carefully prepared by Saladin for battle and victory. The trap had been sprung.

Near the day's end, the Christian king hesitated. A committed frontal assault, either east towards the Sea of Galilee or north-east to Hattin, might still have had some chance of success, enabling the Latins to break through to water. But instead, Guy made the forlorn decision to pitch camp in an entirely waterless, indefensible position, a move that was tantamount to an admission of impending defeat. That night the atmosphere in the two armies could not have been more different. Hemmed in by Muslim soldiers 'so close that they could talk to one another' and so tightly that even 'a [fleeing] cat . . . could not have escaped', the Franks stood to in the heavy darkness, weakening each hour with terrible, unslaked thirst. The sultan's troops, meanwhile, filled the air with chants of '*Allah akhbar*', their courage quickening, 'having caught a whiff of triumph', as their leader made final assiduous preparations to deliver his *coup de grâce*.

Full battle was not joined with the coming of dawn on 4 July. Instead, Saladin allowed the Christians to make pitifully slow progress, probably eastwards along the main Roman road. He was waiting for the heat of the day to rise, maximising the withering effects of dehydration upon the enemy. Then, to further exacerbate their agony, Saladin's troops set scrub fires, sending clouds of stifling smoke billowing through the faltering Latin ranks. The sultan later chided that this conflagration was 'a reminder of what God has prepared for them in the next world'; it was certainly enough to prompt pockets of infantry and even some named knights to break ranks and surrender. One Muslim eyewitness remarked, 'the Franks hoped for respite and their army in desperation sought a way of escape. But at every way out they were barred, and tormented by the heat of war without being able to rest.'[69]

So far, Muslim skirmishers had continued to harass the enemy, but Saladin's deadliest weapon had not been unleashed. The preceding night he had distributed some 400 bundles of arrows among his archers and now, around noon, he ordered a full, scything bombardment to begin. As 'bows hummed and the bowstrings sang' arrows flew through the air 'like a swarm of locusts', killing men and horses, 'open[ing] great gaps in [the Frankish] ranks'. With the panicking infantry losing formation, Raymond of Tripoli launched a charge towards Taqi al-Din's contingent to the north-east, but the Muslim troops simply parted to defuse the force of their advance. Finding themselves beyond the fray, Raymond, Reynald of Sidon, Balian of Ibelin and a small group of accompanying knights thought better of returning to the battle and made good their escape. A Muslim contemporary wrote that:

When the count fled, [the Latins'] spirits collapsed and they were near to surrendering. Then they understood that they would only be saved from death by facing it boldly, so they carried out successive charges, which almost drove the Muslims from their positions despite their numbers, had it not been for God's grace. However, the Franks did not charge and retire without suffering losses and they were gravely weakened . . . The Muslims surrounded them as a circle encloses its central point.[70]

In desperation, Guy sought to make a last stand, beating a path north-east towards higher ground, where twinned rocky outcrops – the Horns of Hattin – stood guard over a saddle of land and a bowl-like crater beyond. Here, two thousand years earlier, Iron Age settlers had fashioned a rudimentary hill fort, and its ancient ruined walls still offered the Franks a degree of protection. Defiantly rallying his troops to the True Cross, the king pitched his royal red tent and prepared those knights who remained for a final, desperate attack. The Christians' only hope now lay in striking directly at the Ayyubid army's heart – at Saladin himself. For, should the sultan's yellow banner fall, the tide of battle might turn.

Years later, al-Afdal described how he watched alongside his father, in dread, as twice the Franks launched driving, heavy charges over the saddle of the Horns, spurring their horses directly towards them. On the first occasion they were barely held back, and the prince turned to see that his father 'was overcome by grief . . . his complexion pale'. Another eyewitness described the fearful damage inflicted upon the Latins when they were turned back to the Horns, as the pursuing Muslims' 'pliant lances danced [and] were fed on entrails' and their 'sword blades sucked away their lives and scattered them on the hillsides'. Even so, as al-Afdal recalled:

> The Franks regrouped and charged again as before, driving the Muslims back to my father [but we] forced them to retreat once more to the hill. I shouted, 'We have beaten them!' but my father rounded on me and said, 'Be quiet! We have not beaten them until that tent falls.' As he was speaking to me, the tent fell. The sultan dismounted, prostrated himself in thanks to God Almighty and wept for joy.

With the king's position overrun, the True Cross was captured and the last shreds of Christian resistance crumbled. Guy and all the Latin kingdom's nobles, bar those few who had escaped, were taken prisoner, along with thousands of Frankish survivors. Still thousands more had been slain.[71]

As the clamour of battle subsided, Saladin sat in the entryway to his palatial campaign tent – much of which was still being hurriedly erected – to receive and review his most important captives. Convention suggested that they be treated with honour and, in time, perhaps ransomed, but the sultan called forth two in particular for a personal audience: his adversary, the king of Jerusalem; and his avowed enemy, Reynald of Châtillon. With the pair seated beside him, Saladin turned to Guy, 'who was dying from thirst and shaking with fear like a drunkard', graciously proffering a golden chalice filled with iced julep. The king supped deeply upon this rejuvenating elixir, but when he passed the cup to Reynald, the sultan interjected, calmly affirming through an interpreter: 'You did not have my permission to give him drink, and so that gift does not imply his safety at my hand.' For, by Arab tradition, the act of offering a guest sustenance was tantamount to a promise of protection. According to a Muslim contemporary, Saladin now turned to Reynald, 'berat[ing] him for his sins and . . . treacherous deeds'. When the Frank staunchly refused an offer to convert to

Islam, the sultan 'rose to face him and struck off his head . . . After he was killed and dragged away, [Guy] trembled with fear, but Saladin calmed his terrors', assuring him that he would not suffer a similar fate, and the king of Jerusalem was led away into captivity.[72]

The sultan's personal secretary, Imad al-Din, summoned forth all his powers of evocation to depict the scene he witnessed as dusk fell over Galilee that evening. 'The sultan', he wrote, 'encamped on the plain of Tiberias like a lion in the desert or the moon in its full splendour', while 'the dead were scattered over the mountains and valleys, lying immobile on their sides. Hattin shrugged off their carcasses, and the perfume of victory was thick with the stench of them.' Picking his way across a battlefield that 'had become a sea of blood', its dust 'stained red', Imad al-Din witnessed the full horror of the carnage enacted that day.

> I passed by them and saw the limbs of the fallen cast naked on the field of combat, scattered in pieces over the site of the encounter, lacerated and disjointed, with heads cracked open, throats split, spines broken, necks shattered, feet in pieces, noses mutilated, extremities torn off, members dismembered, parts shredded.

Even two years later, when an Iraqi Muslim passed by the battle scene, the bones of the dead 'some of them heaped up and others scattered about' could be seen from afar.

On 4 July 1187, the field army of Frankish Palestine was crushed. The seizure of the True Cross dealt a crippling blow to Christian morale across the Near East. Imad al-Din proclaimed that 'the cross was a prize without equal, for it was the supreme object of their faith', and he believed that 'its capture was for them more important than the loss of the king and was the gravest blow they sustained in that battle'. The relic was fixed, upside down, to a lance and carried to Damascus.[73]

So many Latin captives were taken that the markets of Syria were flooded and the price of slaves dropped to three gold dinars. With the exception of Reynald of Châtillon, the only prisoners to be executed were the warriors of the Military Orders. These deadly Frankish 'firebrands' were deemed too dangerous to be left alive and were known to be largely worthless as hostages because they usually refused to seek ransom for their release. According to Imad al-Din, 'Saladin, his face joyful, was sitting on his dais' on 6 July, when some 100 to 200 Templars and Hospitallers were assembled before him. A handful accepted a final offer of conversion to Islam; the rest were set upon by a ragged band of 'scholars and Sufis . . . devout men and ascetics', unused to acts of violence. Imad al-Din looked on as the murder began.

> There were some who slashed and cut cleanly, and were thanked for it; some who refused and failed to act, and were excused; some who made fools of themselves, and others took their places . . . I saw how [they] killed unbelief to give life to Islam and destroyed polytheism to build monotheism.

Saladin's victory over the forces of Latin Christendom had been absolute. Just six days later he wrote a letter reliving his achievement, affirming that 'the gleam of God's sword has terrified the polytheists' and 'the domain of Islam has expanded'. 'It was', he asserted, 'a day of grace, on which the wolf and the vulture kept company, while death and captivity followed in turns'; a moment when 'dawn [broke] on the night of unbelief'. In time, he erected a triumphal Dome on the Horns of Hattin, the faint, ruined outline of which can still be seen to this day.[74]

THE FALL OF THE CROSS

In the aftermath of the triumph at Hattin, the door stood open to further Muslim success. The huge loss of Christian manpower on 4 July left the kingdom of Jerusalem in a state of extreme vulnerability, because its cities, towns and fortresses had been all but stripped of their garrisons. Nevertheless, the immense advantage for Islam might still have been squandered had Saladin not demonstrated such focused determination and been in a position to draw upon so deep a well of resources. As it was, through that summer, Frankish Palestine collapsed with barely a whimper.

Tiberias capitulated almost immediately and, within less than a week, Acre – Outremer's economic hub – had likewise surrendered. In the weeks and months that followed, Saladin directed most of his efforts to sweeping up Palestine's coastal settlements and ports, and from north to south the likes of Beirut, Sidon, Haifa, Caesarea and Arsuf fell in short order. Meanwhile, the sultan's brother, al-Adil, who had been alerted immediately after Hattin, swept north from Egypt to seize the vital port of Jaffa, even as other sorties won further successes inland. Ascalon offered stiffer resistance, but by September even that port had been forced into submission, and the fall of Darum, Gaza, Ramla and Lydda followed. Even the Templars eventually gave up their fortress at Latrun, in the Judean foothills en route to Jerusalem, in return for the release of their master, Gerard of Ridefort.

The mercurial speed and broad extent of these successes were due, in part, to the sheer weight of troop numbers and the array of reliable lieutenants, like al-Adil and Keukburi, at Saladin's disposal. This allowed a number of semi-autonomous Ayyubid war bands to range across the kingdom, significantly increasing the scale and pace of operations and prompting one Latin contemporary to observe that the Muslims spread 'like ants, covering the whole face of the country'. In truth, however, the shape of events through that summer was largely determined by Saladin's strategy. Conscious that Islamic unity could only be preserved by momentum in the field, he sought to diffuse Christian resistance by embracing a policy of clemency and conciliation. From the start, generous terms of surrender were offered to Frankish settlements – for instance, even Latin sources admitted that 'the people of Acre' were presented with an opportunity to remain in the town, living under Muslim rule, 'safe and sound, paying the tax which is customary between Christians and Saracens', while those who wished to leave 'were given forty days in which to take away their wives and children and their goods'.[75]

Similar terms seem to have been given to any town or fortress capitulating without resistance and, crucially, these deals were upheld. By keeping his word and not simply ransacking the Levant, Saladin quickly augmented his reputation for integrity and honour. This proved to be a powerful weapon, for when confronted with a choice of hopeless defiance or assured survival, most enemy garrisons surrendered. By this means, the kingdom of Jerusalem was conquered with startling rapidity and at minimal cost to resources. Nonetheless, this approach was not without its drawbacks. From July 1187 onwards, large swathes of the Latin population became refugees and, true to his promises, the sultan allowed them safe conduct to a port, from where, it was expected, they would take sail, perhaps to Syria or the West. In fact, hundreds and then thousands of Franks sought sanctuary in what became Palestine's sole remaining Frankish port – the heavily fortified city of Tyre.

Saladin was now confronted with a momentous choice. Much of the coastline and interior had been subjugated, but, as the summer waned, it was apparent that only one final push towards conquest might be possible before the onset of winter brought the fighting season to an end. A primary target needed to be identified. In strictly strategic terms, Tyre was the obvious priority: strengthening with each passing day, a bastion of Latin resistance, it offered a lifeline of naval communication with Outremer's surviving remnants to the north and with the wider Christian world beyond. As such, its continued defiance gifted the enemy a clawing foothold, from which an attempt to rebuild the shattered crusader kingdom might, in time, be launched. Nonetheless, the sultan elected to leave Tyre untouched, twice bypassing the port on his journeys north and south. The Iraqi chronicler Ibn al-Athir saw fit to criticise this decision, arguing that 'Tyre lay open and undefended from Muslims, and if Saladin had attacked it [earlier in the summer] he would have taken it easily', and some modern historians have followed this lead, suggesting a lack of foresight on the sultan's part. Such views depend, in large part, upon wisdom born of hindsight. In early September 1187, Saladin recognised that a protracted siege at Tyre might well bring his entire campaign to a grinding halt, causing the Ayyubid-led Islamic coalition to splinter. Rather than hazard this, the sultan prioritised his core ideological objective, turning inland to direct the full force of his army east, towards Jerusalem.[76]

To Jerusalem

Isolated amid the Judean hills, the Holy City's value as a military objective was limited. But decades of preaching and propaganda, engineered by Nur al-Din and Saladin, had reaffirmed Jerusalem's status as Islam's most sacred site outside Arabia. The city's compelling, almost mesmeric, spiritual significance now drew the Muslims on. For a war predicated upon the notion of *jihad* it was the inevitable and ultimate goal. Having sagely brought the Egyptian navy north to defend Jaffa against Christian counter-attack, and with the Latin outposts defending the eastern approaches to Judea readily subdued, Saladin's armies descended upon Jerusalem on 20 September 1187. The sultan had come with tens of thousands of troops and heavy siege weapons, ready for a prolonged confrontation, but despite being packed with refugees, the city was desperately short of fighting manpower. Within, Queen Sibylla and Patriarch Heraclius proffered some direction, but the real burden of leadership fell to Balian of Ibelin. After escaping from the disaster at Hattin, Balian had taken refuge in Tyre, but Saladin later granted him safe passage to the Holy City so that Balian might escort his wife Maria Comnena and her children to safety. The understanding was that Balian would remain in Jerusalem for just one night, but upon arrival he was quickly persuaded to renege on this agreement and stay on to organise resistance. With only the barest handful of knights at his disposal, Balian took the expedient step of knighting every noble-born male over the age of sixteen and a further thirty of Jerusalem's richer citizens. He also sought to strengthen the city's fortifications wherever possible. In spite of his best efforts, Muslim numerical superiority remained utterly overwhelming.

Saladin began his offensive with an attack on the western walls, but after five days of inconclusive fighting by the Tower of David, shifted focus to the more vulnerable northern sector, around the Damascus Gate – perhaps unwittingly following the precedent set by the First Crusaders. On 29 September, in the face of fierce but ultimately futile resistance, Muslim sappers achieved a major breach in Jerusalem's walls. The Holy City was now all but defenceless. Hoping for a miracle, Frankish mothers shaved their children's heads in atonement and the clergy led barefoot processions through the streets, but in practical terms nothing could be done; conquest was inevitable.

Saladin's intentions in September 1187

The sultan's reaction to this situation and the precise manner of Jerusalem's subjugation are immensely significant because they have been instrumental in shaping Saladin's reputation in history and in popular imagination. Some facts, attested in both Muslim and Christian sources, are irrefutable. Ayyubid troops did not sack the Holy City. Instead, probably on 30 September, terms of Latin surrender were agreed between the sultan and Balian of Ibelin, and, without further spilling of blood, Saladin entered Jerusalem on 2 October 1187. Over the centuries, great weight has been attached to this 'peaceful' occupation, and two interconnected notions have gained widespread currency. These events are seen to demonstrate a striking difference between Islam and Latin Christianity, because the First Crusade's conquest in 1099 involved a brutal massacre, whereas the Ayyubids' moment of triumph seems to reveal a capacity for temperance and human compassion. It has also been widely suggested that Saladin was only too conscious of the comparison with the First Crusade, being aware of what a negotiated surrender might mean for the image of Islam, for contemporary perceptions of his own career and for the mark he would leave upon history.[77]

The problem with these views is that they are not supported by the most important contemporary testimony. Two strands of evidence are vital – the account written by Imad al-Din, Saladin's secretary, who arrived in Jerusalem on 3 October 1187; and a letter from Saladin to the caliph in Baghdad, dating from shortly after Jerusalem's surrender. The point is not that this material should be trusted simply because it was authored by those closest to events, but rather that it offers an insight into how the sultan himself conceived of and wished to present what happened at the Holy City that autumn.

Both sources indicate that, by the end of September 1187, Saladin intended to sack Jerusalem. According to Imad al-Din, the sultan told Balian at their initial meeting: 'You will receive neither amnesty nor mercy! Our only desire is to inflict perpetual subjection upon you . . . We shall kill and capture you wholesale, spill men's blood and reduce the poor and the women to slavery.' This is confirmed in Saladin's letter, which noted that in response to the Franks' first requests for terms 'we refused point blank, wishing only to shed the blood of the men and to reduce the women and children to slavery'. At this point, however, Balian threatened that, unless equitable conditions of surrender were agreed, the Latins would fight to the very last man, destroying Jerusalem's Islamic Holy Places and executing the thousands of Muslim prisoners held inside the city. This was a desperate gambit, but it forced the sultan's hand, and begrudgingly he agreed a deal. The eyewitness sources reveal an underlying awareness that this accord might be perceived as a sign of Ayyubid weakness. In his letter, Saladin carefully justified his decision, stressing that his emirs had convinced him to accept a settlement so as to avoid any further unnecessary loss of Muslim life and to secure a victory that was already all but won. Imad al-Din reiterated this idea, describing at length a 'council meeting', during which the sultan sought the advice of his leading lieutenants.[78]

This evidence offers a glimpse of Saladin's own mindset in 1187. It suggests that his primary instinct was not to present himself as a just and magnanimous victor. Nor was he immediately concerned to parallel his own actions with those of the First Crusaders or, through some grand gesture, to reveal Islam as a force for peace. In fact, neither the sultan's letter nor Imad al-Din's account makes any explicit reference to the 1099 massacre. Instead, Saladin actually felt the need to explain and excuse his failure to butcher the Franks inside Jerusalem once a breach in the city's defences was made. This was because, above all else, he feared an attack upon his image as a warrior dedicated to the *jihad* – as a ruler who had forced Islam to accept Ayyubid domination on the promise of war against the Franks.

This insight might cause some re-evaluation of Saladin's character and intentions, but it should not prompt the pendulum to swing towards a total, polar opposite. The sultan's behaviour must be judged in its proper context, against contemporary standards. By this measure, Saladin's conduct in autumn 1187 was relatively lenient.[79] According to the customs of medieval warfare – which, broadly speaking, were shared and recognised by Levantine Muslims and Frankish Christians alike – the inhabitants of a besieged city who staunchly refused to capitulate right up until the moment that their fortifications were breached or overcome could expect harsh treatment. Typically, in such a situation, the defenders' opportunity to negotiate had passed and their men would be killed, their women and children enslaved. Even if the final settlement in Jerusalem was heavily influenced by Balian's threats, by the norms of the day the terms that Saladin did agree were generous – and, more important still, they were honoured.

The sultan also acted with a marked degree of courtesy and clemency in his dealings with his aristocratic 'equals' among the

Franks. Balian of Ibelin was forgiven for breaking his promise not to remain in Jerusalem, and an escort was even provided to take Maria Comnena to Tyre. Reynald of Châtillon's widow, Stephanie of Milly, was likewise released without any demand for ransom.

The conditions of surrender settled upon around 30 September contained a number of fundamental provisions. Jerusalem's Christian populace was given forty days to buy their freedom at a prescribed cost of ten dinars for a man, five for a woman and one for a child. In addition, they would be given safe conduct to the Latin outposts at Tyre or Tripoli and the right to carry away their personal possessions. Only horses and weaponry had to be left behind. After forty days those unable to pay the ransom would be taken captive. In the main, this agreement was followed and, in some instances, Saladin showed even greater generosity. Balian for instance was able, in return for one lump sum of 30,000 dinars, to secure the release of 7,000 Christians, and attempts appear to have been made to arrange a general amnesty for the poor.

Once enacted, the terms of capitulation resulted in a near-constant stream of refugees from Jerusalem, as bands of disarmed Franks were escorted to the coast. In practice, the system of ransoms proved to be an administrative nightmare for Saladin's officials. Imad al-Din admitted that corruption, including bribery, was rife, and he bemoaned the fact that only a fraction of the money owed was ever lodged in the sultan's treasury. Many Latins apparently slipped through the net: 'Some people were let down from the walls on ropes, some carried out hidden in luggage, some changed their clothes and went out dressed as [Muslim] soldiers.' The sultan's willingness to allow the Franks to depart with their possessions also limited the amount of plunder. Patriarch Heraclius apparently left the city weighed down with treasures, but 'Saladin made no difficulties, and when he was advised to sequestrate the whole lot for Islam, replied that he would not go back on his word. He took only the ten dinars from [Heraclius], and let him go to Tyre under heavy guard.' At the end of the allotted forty days, a total of 7,000 men and

8,000 women were said to have remained unransomed, and they were taken captive and enslaved.[80]

On balance, Saladin cannot be said to have acted with saintly clemency that autumn, but neither can he be accused of ruthless barbarism or duplicity. In the version of events he broadcast to the Muslim world, the sultan clearly presented himself as a *mujahid* willing, even eager, to put the Jerusalemite Franks to the sword, but it is impossible to determine whether this was his true intent. As it was, once confronted by Balian's threats, Saladin chose negotiation over confrontation and went on to show a considerable degree of restraint in his dealings with the Latins.

Jerusalem's triumphant reconquest marked the apogee of Saladin's career to date. Crucially, he could now draw upon this epochal achievement to legitimise his unification of Islam and to refute any charges of self-serving despotism. These two themes of astounding victory and 'innocence' affirmed permeated his letter to the caliph – they also formed the backbone of a further seventy letters written by Imad al-Din that autumn, publicising the Ayyubids' success.[81]

Jerusalem repossessed

The day of Jerusalem's formal surrender was selected with some care, so as to emphasise the sultan's image as a proven champion of the faith. Centuries earlier, Muhammad himself was said to have made his Night Journey to Jerusalem, ascending from there to Heaven on 2 October. Drawing clear parallels between his own life and that of the Prophet, Saladin chose that same date in 1187 to make his triumphal entrance. Once within the walls of the Holy City, the transformative work of Islamicisation began apace. Many Christian shrines and churches were stripped of their treasures and closed; some were converted into mosques, *madrasas* (teaching colleges) or religious convents. The fate of the Holy Sepulchre was debated intensely, with some advocating its total destruction. More moderate voices prevailed, arguing that Christian pilgrims would still continue to revere the site even if the building were razed to the ground, and Saladin was reminded that Umar, Jerusalem's first Muslim conqueror, had left the church untouched.

The spiritual dimension of Saladin's achievement was manifested most clearly in the assiduous care with which he and his men set about 'purifying' Jerusalem's holy places. Chief among these were two sites within the *Haram as-Sharif* (now also known as the Temple Mount) – the Dome of the Rock and the Aqsa mosque. In the eyes of Islam, the Franks had subjected both of these sacred buildings to the gravest desecration. Now this work was dutifully undone. Under Latin rule, the Dome – built by Muslims in the late seventh century and believed to house the rock upon which Abraham prepared to sacrifice his son and from which Muhammad ascended to heaven during his Night Journey – had been transformed into the *Templum Domini* (Church of Our Lord), its resplendent golden-hued dome adorned with a huge cross. This symbol was ripped down immediately, the Christian altar within and all pictures and statues removed, and rose water and incense used to cleanse the entire structure. After this, one Muslim eyewitness proudly proclaimed that 'the Rock has been cleansed of the filth of the infidels by the tears of the pious', emerging in a state of purity, like 'a young bride'. Later, an inscription was placed upon the Dome, commemorating the sultan's achievement: 'Saladin has purified this sacred house from the polytheists.'

Similar work was undertaken at the Aqsa mosque, which the Franks had first used as a royal palace and then reshaped as part of the Templars' headquarters. A wall covering the *mihrab* (a niche indicating the direction of prayer) was removed and the entire building rejuvenated, so that, in the words of Imad al-Din, 'truth triumphed and error was cancelled out'. Here the first Friday prayer was held on 9 October and the honour of delivering the sermon that day was hotly contested by orators and holy men. Saladin eventually chose Ibn al-Zaki, an *imam* from Damascus, to speak before the thronged, expectant crowd. Ibn al-Zaki's sermon appears to have stressed three interlocking themes. The notion of conquest as a form of purification was emphasised, with God praised for the cleansing 'of His Holy House from the filth of polytheism and its pollutions' and the audience entreated 'to purify the rest of the land from this filth which has angered God and His Apostle'. At the same time, the sultan was lavishly praised, acclaimed as 'the champion and protector of [God's] holy land', his achievements compared to those of Muhammad himself, and the efficacious nature of *jihad* exhorted with the words: 'Maintain the holy war; it is the best means which you have of serving God, the most noble occupation of your lives.'[82]

Saladin's achievement

The summer of 1187 brought Saladin two stunning victories. Seizing the moment after the Battle of Hattin, he reconquered Jerusalem, eclipsing the achievements of all his Muslim predecessors in the age of the crusades. Decades earlier, his patron Nur al-Din had ordered the construction of a staggeringly beautiful, ornate pulpit, imagining that he might one day oversee its installation within the sacred Aqsa. Now, in a final, telling act of appropriation, the sultan fulfilled his predecessor's dream and shouldered his legacy, bringing the pulpit from its resting place in Aleppo to Jerusalem's grand mosque, where it would remain for eight centuries.

Tellingly, even Saladin's contemporary Muslim critic Ibn al-Athir acknowledged the unrivalled glory of the sultan's accomplishments in 1187: 'This blessed deed, the conquering of Jerusalem, is something achieved by none but Saladin . . . since the time of Umar.' Al-Fadil, writing to the caliph in Baghdad, emphasised the transformative nature of the sultan's defeat of the Franks: 'From their places of prayer he cast down the cross and set up the call to prayer . . . the people of the Koran succeeded to the people of the cross.'[83] Eighty-eight years after the First Crusaders' stunning triumph, Saladin had repossessed the Holy City for Islam, striking a momentous blow against Outremer. He had reshaped the Near East and now seemed poised to achieve ultimate and enduring victory in the war for the Holy Land. But as news of these extraordinary events reverberated throughout the Muslim world and beyond, eliciting shock and awe, Latin Christendom was stirred to action. A vengeful lust for holy war awakened in the West and, once again, vast armies set out for the Levant. Soon Saladin would be forced to defend his hard-won conquests against a Third Crusade, battling a towering new champion of the Christian cause – Richard the Lionheart.

III

THE TRIAL OF
CHAMPIONS

13

CALLED TO CRUSADE

In late summer 1187, with Outremer still reeling from the cataclysm at Hattin and Saladin's dismemberment of Frankish Palestine proceeding apace, Archbishop Joscius of Tyre set sail for the West. He bore tidings of Christendom's calamitous defeat to the frail Pope Urban III, who promptly died of shock and grief. In the weeks and months that followed, the devastating news raced across Europe, eliciting alarm, anguish and outrage – triggering a new call to arms for the campaign known to history as the Third Crusade. The most powerful men in the Latin world took up the cross, from Frederick Barbarossa, mighty emperor of Germany, to Philip II Augustus, the astute young king of France. But it was Richard the Lionheart, king of England – one of the greatest warriors of the medieval age – who emerged as champion of the Christian cause, challenging Saladin's dominion of the Holy Land. Above all, the Third Crusade became a contest between these two titans, king and sultan, crusader and *mujahid*. After almost a century, the war for the Holy Land had brought these heroes to battle in an epic confrontation: one that tested both men to breaking point; in which legends were forged and dreams demolished.[1]

THE PREACHING OF THE THIRD CRUSADE

The injuries suffered by Christendom at Hattin and Jerusalem in 1187 moved the Latin West to action, rekindling fires of crusading fervour that had lain dormant for decades. After the failure of the Second Crusade in the late 1140s, Christian Europe's enthusiasm for holy war had waned dramatically. At the time, some began to question the purity of the papacy and the crusaders. One German chronicler described the Second Crusade in damning terms, writing: 'God allowed the Western Church, on account of its sins, to be cast down. There arose, indeed, certain pseudo-prophets, sons of Belial, and witnesses of the anti-Christ, who seduced the Christians with empty words.' Even Bernard of Clairvaux, arch-propagandist and passionate advocate of crusading, could offer scant consolation, merely observing that the setbacks experienced by the Franks were part of God's unknowable design for mankind. Christian sin was also advanced as an explanation for divine punishment – and, more often than not, the supposedly dissolute Franks living in the Levant were targeted as transgressors.[2]

Not surprisingly, attempts to launch major crusading expeditions after 1149 foundered. Muslim strength and unity in the Near East increased under Nur al-Din and Saladin, while Outremer faced a succession of crises: Prince Raymond of Antioch's death in the Battle of Inab; the defeat at Harim in 1164; the incapacitation of Baldwin the Leper King. Throughout, the Levantine Franks made ever more desperate and frequent appeals to the West for aid, and, while some few came to defend the Holy Land in minor campaigns, in the main the calls went unanswered.

Meanwhile, western monarchs, now crucial to any major crusading venture, had their own kingdoms to preserve and defend – tasks, so it was widely believed, that were themselves divinely appointed. Caught up in the concerns of politics, warfare, trade and economy, the prospect of spending months, even years, in the East crusading often proved less than inviting. Inertia rather than action predominated.

This problem was exacerbated by deepening rivalries between Latin Europe's leading powers. In 1152 power in Germany passed to the Hohenstaufen Frederick Barbarossa (or Red Beard), a veteran of the Second Crusade. Frederick assumed the title of emperor three years later, but spent decades trying to subdue warring factions within his own realm and seeking to secure control of northern Italy, all the while enmeshed in a rancorous conflict with the papacy and Norman Sicily. In France the Capetian dynasty retained the crown, but in terms of territorial dominion and political control the real authority wielded by King Louis VII and his son and successor Philip II Augustus (from 1180) was still severely constrained. The Capetians were challenged, above all, by the rise of the counts of Anjou.

In 1152, just a few short years after the disappointments of the Second Crusade, Louis VII's wife, Eleanor of Aquitaine, pushed for the annulment of their marriage – their union had produced two daughters, but no sons, and Eleanor derided Louis' desultory sexual appetite, likening him to a monk. Eight weeks later, she was wed to the more vigorous Count Henry of Anjou, a man twelve years her junior, who had already added the duchy of Normandy to his dominions. By 1154, he had ascended to the throne of England to become King Henry II, and together the pair created a new, sprawling Angevin 'Empire', uniting England, Normandy, Anjou and Aquitaine. Controlling most of modern-day France, their wealth and power far outstripped those of the French king, even though, nominally at least, they were still subjects of the Capetian monarch for their continental territories. Under the circumstances, it was all but inevitable that the Angevin and Capetian houses would become entrenched opponents. And throughout the mid- to late twelfth century, the festering antipathy and resentment between these two dynasties severely curtailed western participation in the war for the Holy Land. Locked into this struggle, Henry II of England proved unwilling or unable to honour repeated promises to go on crusade, usually providing financial support to Outremer by way of recompense.[3]

Only the truly epochal events of 1187 broke this deadlock, prompting real engagement. Old quarrels were not forgotten – indeed, Angevin–Capetian enmity had a profound effect upon the course of the Third Crusade. But the dreadful news from the Near East caused such uproar that the rulers of Latin Christendom not only heeded the call to arms; this time, they made good on their promises and actually went to war.

A *cause for weeping*

Upon his death on 20 October 1187, Pope Urban III was replaced by Gregory VIII, and by the end of the month a new papal encyclical – *Audita Tremendi* – had been issued, proclaiming the Third Crusade. As usual, care was taken to establish a justification for the holy war. The disaster at Hattin was described as 'a great cause for mourning [for] the whole Christian people'; Outremer, it was said, had suffered a 'severe and terrible judgement'; and the Muslim 'infidels' were depicted as 'savage barbarians thirsting after Christian blood and [profaning] the Holy Places'. The encyclical concluded that any sane man 'who does not weep at such a cause for weeping' must surely have lost his faith and his humanity.

Two new themes were sewn into this familiar, if particularly impassioned, exhortation. For the first time, evil was personified. Earlier calls to arms had projected Muslims as sadistic but faceless opponents. Now, Saladin was named specifically as the enemy and likened to the Devil. This move bespoke both greater familiarity with Islam and the mammoth scale of the blow struck by the sultan's 'crimes'. *Audita Tremendi* also set out to explain why God had allowed his people to 'be confounded by such great horror'. The answer was that the Latins had been 'smitten by the divine hand' as punishment for their sins. Franks living in the Levant were identified as the prime transgressors, having failed to show penitence after the fall of Edessa, but Christians living in Europe were also guilty. 'All of us [should] amend our sins . . . and turn to the Lord our God with penance and works of piety', the encyclical declared, '[and only] then turn our attention to the treachery and malice of the enemy.' In line with this theme of contrition, crusaders were encouraged to enlist not 'for money or worldly glory, but according to the will of God', travelling in simple clothing, with no 'dogs or birds', ready to do penance rather than 'to effect empty pomp'.

Audita Tremendi referred to the 'misfortunes . . . recently fallen upon Jerusalem and the Holy Land', but perhaps because news of Saladin's actual conquest of the Holy City had yet to reach the West, special emphasis was placed upon the physical loss at Hattin of the True Cross – the relic of Christ's cross. From this point forward, the recovery of the revered totem of the faith became one of the crusade's primary objectives.

In common with earlier crusading encyclicals, the closing sections of the 1187 proclamation detailed the spiritual and temporal rewards on offer to participants. They were assured full remission of all confessed sins, and those who died on campaign were promised 'eternal life'. For the duration of the expedition, they would enjoy immunity from legal prosecution and interest on debts, and their goods and families would be under the protection of the Church.[4]

Spreading the word

The unprecedented scale and significance of the disasters endured by the Franks in 1187 all but ensured a massive response in the West. Even in its barest form, the news carried to Europe by Joscius of Tyre had the power to terrify and inspire – indeed, before meeting the pope, the archbishop first made landfall in the Norman kingdom of Sicily and immediately convinced its ruler William II to send a fleet of ships to defend Outremer.

Nonetheless, *Audita Tremendi* set the tone for much of the preaching of the Third Crusade. In fact, the whole process of disseminating the crusading message was increasingly subject to centralised ecclesiastical and secular control, and the methods used to encourage recruitment ever more refined and sophisticated. The pope appointed two papal legates – Joscius of Tyre and Cardinal Henry of Albano, former abbot of Clairvaux – to orchestrate the call to the cross in France and Germany respectively. Large-scale recruitment rallies were also timed to coincide with major Christian festivals, with assemblies during Christmas 1187 at Strasbourg and Easter 1188 at Mainz and Paris, when crowds were already gathered and primed for a devotional message.

Preaching within the Angevin lands of England, Normandy, Anjou and Aquitaine was planned carefully at conferences at Le Mans in January 1188 and Geddington, in Northamptonshire, on 11 February. At the latter meeting Baldwin, archbishop of Canterbury, another former Cistercian abbot, took the cross himself and thereafter led the recruitment drive. He carried out an extensive tour of Wales, spreading the word, while also reinforcing Angevin authority over this semi-independent area, and ended up enlisting three thousand Welshmen 'skilled in the use of arrows and lances'.[5]

From this point forward, the act of crusading seems to have attained a more distinct identity, although it is not clear whether this was a response to centralised control or simply a by-product of gradual recognition and definition over time. Whereas previously crusaders had been variously dubbed pilgrims, travellers or soldiers of Christ, now, for the first time, documents began to describe them as *crucesignatus* (one signed by the cross) – the word that ultimately led to the terms 'crusader' and 'crusade'.

The Third Crusade was also publicised and popularised within secular society. In the course of the twelfth century, troubadours (court singers who often were themselves nobles) came to play increasingly important roles in aristocratic circles, and notions of courtly life and chivalry began to develop, particularly in regions such as south-western France. Forty years earlier, the first traces of courtly commentary about the Second Crusade had been apparent. Now, after 1187, troubadour songs about the coming holy war poured out, drawing upon, and in places extending, the message inherent in *Audita Tremendi*.

Conon de Béthune, a knight from Picardy who joined the Third Crusade, composed one such Old French verse between 1188 and 1189. Here, familiar themes were echoed – lamentation at the capture of the True Cross and the observation that 'every man ought to be downcast and sorrowful'. But elsewhere, new emphasis was placed upon the notions of shame and obligation. Conon wrote: 'Now we will see who will be truly brave . . . [and] if we permit our mortal enemies to stay [in the Holy Land] our lives will be shameful for evermore', adding that any who are 'healthy, young and rich cannot remain behind without suffering shame'. The Holy Land was also portrayed as God's imperilled patrimony (or lordship). This implied that, in the same way a vassal was obliged to protect his lord's land and property, Christians, as God's servants, should now rush to defend his sacred territory.[6]

The call to crusade prompted tens of thousands of Latin Christians to enlist. According to one crusader, 'such was the enthusiasm for the new pilgrimage that already [in 1188] it was not a question of who had received the cross, but who had not yet done so'. This was something of an exaggeration, as many more stayed in the West than set out for the Holy Land, but the expedition nonetheless caused a staggering upheaval in European society. Particularly in France, whole tranches of the local aristocracy led armed contingents to war. The involvement of kings proved critical, just as it had done in the 1140s, prompting a chain reaction of recruitment across the Latin West through ties of vassalage and obligation. Around 1189 the crusader Gauclem Faidit commented on this phenomenon, arguing in a song that: 'It behoves everyone to consider going there, and the princes all the more so since they are highly placed, for there is not one who can claim to be faithful and obedient to him if he does not aid [his lord] in this enterprise.'[7]

Yet even before the ominous news of Saladin's victories spread, before the fever of enthusiasm took hold, one leader made an immediate commitment to the cause. In November 1187 Richard Coeur de Lion (the Lionheart) took the cross at Tours – the first noble to do so north of Alps.

COEUR DE LION

Today Richard the Lionheart is one of the most widely remembered figures of the Middle Ages, recalled as England's great warrior-king. But who was Richard? This is a vexed question, because even in his own lifetime he became something of a legend. Richard certainly was aware of the extraordinary power of reputation and actively sought to promote a cult of personality, encouraging comparisons with the great figures of the mythic past such as Roland, scourge of the Iberian Moors, and King Arthur. Richard even set out on crusade with a sword named Excalibur, although admittedly he later sold it to pay for additional ships. By the mid-thirteenth century stories of his epic feats abounded. One author tried to account for Richard's famous appellation by explaining that he had once been forced to fight a lion with his bare hands. Having reached down the beast's throat and ripped out its still-beating heart, Richard supposedly ate the blood-dripping organ with gusto.

A contemporary eyewitness and ardent supporter offered this stirring portrait of his physical appearance:

> He was tall, of elegant build; the colour of his hair was between red and gold; his limbs were supple and straight. He had quite long arms, which were particularly convenient for drawing a sword and wielding it most effectively. His long legs matched the arrangement of his whole body.

The same source claimed that Richard had been endowed by God 'with virtues which seemed rather to belong to an earlier age. In this present age, when the world is growing old, these virtues hardly appear in anyone, as if everyone were like empty husks.' In comparison:

> Richard had the valour of Hector, the heroism of Achilles; he was not inferior to Alexander . . . Also, which is very unusual for one so renowned as a knight, Nestor's tongue and Ulysses' wisdom enabled him to excel others in every undertaking, both in speaking and acting.[8]

Perhaps not surprisingly, scholars have not always accepted this startling image of the Lionheart as an almost superhuman hero. As early as the eighteenth century, English historians were criticising Richard both as a monarch and as a man – accusing him of exploiting England for his own ends and of being possessed of a brutish and impulsive character. In recent decades the exceptional University of London scholar John Gillingham has reshaped the perception and understanding of the Lionheart's career. Gillingham acknowledged that Richard barely spent one year out of ten in England during his reign, but contextualised this fact, stressing that he had been not just a king of England, but the ruler of an Angevin Empire at a moment of crisis in Christendom. Likewise, the Lionheart's headstrong nature was recognised, but his image as a savage and tempestuous brute overturned. Richard is now generally regarded as having been a well-educated ruler, adept in politics and negotiation, and above all a man of action, beloved of warfare and imbued with a visionary flair for military command. Although much of this reassessment still holds true, in seeking to rejuvenate the Lionheart's reputation Gillingham may have overstated some of Richard's achievements on the Third Crusade, sparing him criticism when it was justified.[9]

Richard, count of Poitou, duke of Aquitaine

The Lionheart may have become king of England, but he was most assuredly not English by either birth or background. His native tongue was Old French, his heritage that of Anjou and Aquitaine. He was born in Oxford on 8 September 1157 to King Henry II of England and Eleanor of Aquitaine. With such parentage, the young prince was almost predestined to leave his mark on history, but Richard was not expected to inherit this vast Angevin realm; that glory fell to his elder brother, known to history as Henry the Younger. To begin with, at least, Richard was groomed to be a lieutenant, not a commander. In twelfth-century Europe, however, high rates of infant and adolescent mortality meant that a change in prospects was always possible.

As a boy, Richard was associated with Aquitaine. On the expectation that he would not inherit the throne of England, and perhaps through the influence of his mother, the young prince was designated as ruler of this vast region of south-western France. In 1169 Richard paid homage to the French King Louis VII for Aquitaine and then, in 1172 at the age of fifteen, he was installed formally as duke of Aquitaine (with the associated title of count of Poitou). Richard was further woven into the complex web of relations between the Angevin and Capetian dynasties through his betrothal, in 1169, to King Louis' daughter Alice – although the French princess spent her time from this point onwards in King Henry II's court rather than with Richard, and reputedly became Henry's mistress.

Aquitaine was among the wealthiest and most cultured regions of France – a flourishing centre of music, poetry and art – and these factors seem to have left their marks on Richard. He was a generous patron of troubadours and himself a keen singer, and a writer of songs and poetry. He likewise possessed an excellent knowledge of Latin and a good-natured, if acerbic, wit. His duchy was also notable for its associations with the legendary holy wars against Islam waged in Spain during the time of Charlemagne. Churches within the region claimed to house the body of Roland, the mighty hero of the campaign, and the very horn with which he had sought to summon aid against the Moors.

For all its veneer of civility, Aquitaine was a quarrelsome hotbed of lawlessness and civil discord – really it was just a loosely agglomerated collection of fiercely independent territories, peopled by powerful, recalcitrant families like the Lusignans. Given this, Richard looked set to rule a polity that was all but ungovernable, but he proved to be remarkably competent. Through the 1170s and 1180s he not only maintained order, quelling numerous rebellions, but even managed to expand his ducal territory at the expense of the county of Toulouse. These trials provided the Lionheart with valuable military experience, particularly in the field of siegecraft, and he revealed a marked aptitude for warfare.

Richard also had to contend with the fractious reality of contemporary politics. Throughout his early career, he was enmeshed in a complex, constantly shifting power struggle within the Angevin dynasty – with Henry II skilfully defending his own position against the rising power of his sons and the ambitions of his wife, while the Lionheart and his brothers squabbled over the Angevin inheritance as often as they united against their father. As early as 1173, Richard was involved in a full-scale rebellion against Henry II alongside his brothers. The Lionheart's status was transformed in 1183 when, in the midst of another rebellion, his brother Henry the Younger died, leaving Richard as Henry's eldest son and heir designate. Far from resolving the internecine feuding, this simply made Richard a clearer target for attacks and intrigue, as Henry sought to recover possession of Aquitaine and to rearrange the distribution of Angevin territory in favour of his youngest son John. Richard certainly did not prevail in all of these convoluted machinations, but by and large he held his own against Henry II, perhaps the most devious and adroit Latin politician of the twelfth century.

As an Angevin, Richard was also party to the continued rivalry with the Capetian monarchy and often found himself drawn into disputes with King Louis VII and then, after 1180, his heir Philip Augustus. The lingering matter of Richard's betrothal to Alice of France was also at issue, because Henry continued to use the proposed union as a diplomatic tool and no marriage had yet taken place. This pattern of confrontation looked set to continue in June 1187 when King Philip invaded Angevin territory in Berry, prompting Henry II and Richard to ally and move in for a counter-attack. A major pitched battle seemed imminent, but at the last minute a rapprochement was reached and a two-year truce brokered. But once this agreement was finalised, Richard suddenly switched sides, riding back to Paris with Philip in a deliberately public demonstration of friendship. This was an agile diplomatic manoeuvre that even the now-ageing Henry II had not foreseen, and the message it sent was clear. Should the Angevin monarch seek to deprive Richard of Aquitaine of his wider inheritance, the Lionheart was more than willing to break with his family and side with the Capetian enemy. Outplayed, Henry immediately sought to repair relations with Richard, confirming all his territorial rights. The old king won his son back into the Angevin fold and, for now, an uneasy standoff held, but the shadows of a more decisive confrontation involving Henry, Richard and Philip were looming.

Richard and the crusade

Barely a week later, Saladin defeated the Jerusalemite Franks at Hattin on 4 July 1187. By November that same year, Richard had taken the cross at Tours, evidently without consulting his father. Under the circumstances, the Lionheart's decision was extraordinary. In 1187 Richard was deeply immersed in the power politics of western Europe and had shown an absolute determination to retain the duchy of Aquitaine and assume control of the Angevin Empire after Henry II died. Richard then joined the crusade, seemingly without considering the consequences – a move that threatened his own prospects and those of his dynasty. King Henry was enraged by what he deemed to be an ill-considered and unsanctioned act of folly. Philip Augustus, too, was aghast at the prospect of such a potentially critical ally heading off to holy war. The Lionheart's enlistment in the Third Crusade promised to disrupt massively the delicately balanced web of power and influence in England and France. On the face of it, Richard had little to gain and everything to lose.

How then can this apparently anomalous deed be explained?

Aware, with the benefit of hindsight, that the West soon would be swept by crusade enthusiasm – indeed, that Henry II and Philip Augustus themselves would take the cross within a few months – scholars have all but passed over Richard's decision, presenting it as normative and inevitable. Yet, taken on its own terms and in context, his choice was quite the opposite.

Perhaps a multiplicity of factors was at work. Impulsiveness probably played its part. If the Lionheart had a weakness, it was his emerging streak of overconfident, reckless arrogance. Even one of Richard's supporters admitted that 'he could be accused of rash actions', but explained that 'he had an unconquerable spirit, could not bear insult or injury, and his innate noble spirit compelled him to seek his due rights'. In addition, Richard may well have been moved, like so many crusaders before him, by a heartfelt and authentic sense of religious devotion. Such feelings surely would have been intensified by his familial and seigneurial connections to Frankish Palestine, being the great-grandson of Fulk of Anjou, king of Jerusalem (1131–42), cousin to Queen Sibylla and former feudal overlord to the Poitevin, Guy of Lusignan. The Lionheart was also struggling to emerge from the shadow of his parents. Much of his life had been devoted to emulating and eclipsing the achievements of his father (and to a degree those of his mother). Before 1187 the fulfilment of that goal had lain in defending Aquitaine and succeeding to the Angevin realm. But Hattin and the launching of the Third Crusade opened up another path to greatness – a new chance to leave a lasting mark on history as a leader of men and a military commander, in a sacred war far beyond the confines of Europe. The crusade may also have appealed to Richard as an ardent warrior, born into a world in which ideas about knightly honour and chivalric conduct were beginning to coalesce. For the coming campaign would serve as the ultimate proving ground of prowess and valour.[10]

The true balance between these various stimuli is impossible to determine. In all likelihood, Richard himself would have been unable to define a singular motive or ambition that shaped his actions in late 1187. Certainly, in the years that followed, he showed flashes of anger and impetuosity. It also became clear that he was wrestling with a deep-seated crisis of identity and intention – striving to reconcile his roles as a crusader, a king, a general and a knight.

THE TAKING OF THE CROSS

The shock of Richard's enlistment in the Third Crusade prompted a political crisis, with Philip of France threatening to invade Angevin territory unless Henry II made territorial concessions and compelled the Lionheart to marry Philip's sister, Alice of France. On 21 January 1188 the Capetian and Angevin monarchs, Philip and Henry, met near the border castle of Gisors, in the company of their leading magnates, to discuss a settlement. But Archbishop Joscius of Tyre also attended the assembly. He proceeded to preach a rapturous sermon on the imperilled state of the Holy Land and the merits of the crusade, speaking 'in [such] a wonderful way [that he] turned their hearts to taking up the cross'. At this moment a cross-shaped image was supposedly seen in the sky – a 'miracle' which prompted many other leading northern-French lords to join the expedition, including the counts of Flanders, Blois, Champagne and Dreux.[11]

Amid an impassioned groundswell of crusading enthusiasm, Henry II and Philip Augustus made public declarations of their determination to fight in the Levantine holy war. It is not known whether one king pledged his willingness first, thus all but forcing the other to follow suit. What is certain is that, by the meeting's end, both were committed. The effectively simultaneous nature of this enrolment was telling, because it reflected a wider determination only to act in tandem. Angevin and Capetian alike had vowed to crusade in the East, but it was soon obvious that neither would leave Europe without the other. To do so would have been tantamount to political suicide – the abandonment of one's realm to the privations of a despised arch-enemy. The absolute necessity for coordinated action and synchronised departure had a profound effect on the Third Crusade, contributing to a series of interminable delays as the English and French monarchs eyed one another with suspicion and distrust.

Frederick Barbarossa and the German crusade

In 1187, Frederick Barbarossa, the Hohenstaufen emperor of Germany, was Europe's elder statesman. Through a mixture of tireless military campaigning and shrewd politicking, he had imposed an unprecedented degree of centralised authority over the notoriously independent-minded barons of Germany and reached advantageous accommodations with northern Italy and the papacy. Now in his mid-sixties, Frederick could claim dominion over a swathe of territory from the Baltic coast to the Adriatic and the Mediterranean. In terms of wealth, martial resources and international prestige, his power easily outstripped that of the Angevins and Capetians. Naturally, most contemporaries expected him to play a leading role in the Third Crusade.

The first call to arms in Germany was made at Barbarossa's 1187 winter court in Strasbourg. This secured a stream of eager recruits, but the emperor bided his time, gauging the scale of public support for the expedition, before taking the cross at a second great assembly at Mainz, on 27 March 1188, and announcing his firm intention to set out in just over one year. Frederick then made relatively swift but assiduous preparations for his departure: exiling his political enemy Henry the Lion; leaving his eldest son, Henry VI, in Germany as heir designate, while taking his second son, Frederick of Swabia, with him on crusade. Barbarossa marshalled his own economic resources, establishing a significant imperial war chest, but otherwise devolved financial responsibility for funding the expedition on to individual crusaders, requiring each participant to carry their own money east.

Some German crusaders sailed to the Levant – including those from Cologne, Frisia and, eventually, those under Duke Leopold V of Austria – but Frederick elected to lead the vast majority along the land route used by earlier expeditions. Hoping to ease the journey eastwards, he initiated diplomatic contacts with Hungary, Byzantium and even the Muslim ruler of Seljuq Anatolia Kilij Arslan II. On 11 May 1189, only marginally later than scheduled, he set out from Regensburg at the head of a massive army, including eleven bishops, around twenty-eight counts, some four thousand knights and tens of thousands of infantry.

The German crusaders made good progress on their march until they reached Byzantium in late June. There Emperor Isaac II Angelus had rejected Frederick's attempts to negotiate safe passage through Greek territory. Isaac had already formed a pact with Saladin agreeing to delay any crusader advance and was also nervous of Barbarossa's dealings with Kilij Arslan, suspecting that the pair might try to launch a combined offensive on Constantinople. Moving south-east, Frederick occupied the city of Philippopolis and then marched to Adrianople in November 1189, amidst open warfare with the Greeks. Barbarossa rested his army through the depths of winter, but left open the threat of a direct assault on the Byzantine capital. In February 1190, however, a compromise was reached with Isaac. Keeping their distance from Constantinople, the Germans travelled to Gallipoli, and from there crossed the Hellespont to Asia Minor in late March with the help of Pisan and Greek ships. Frederick's experience as a seasoned campaigner had proved its worth. Decisive and formidable as a leader, and a stern advocate of troop discipline, he had successfully guided the German crusade to the edge of the Muslim world.[12]

DELAYS IN ENGLAND AND FRANCE

Though they enlisted months before Frederick Barbarossa, the monarchs of England and France took far longer to set out on crusade. In fact, more than two and a half years passed before the main Angevin and Capetian armies even left their homelands. Preparations for the expedition were initiated in early 1188, but after a brief respite the two dynasties resumed their feuding. To make matters worse, Richard was distracted further by a rebellion in Aquitaine and warfare with the county of Toulouse.

From that spring onwards the Lionheart faced a series of probing attacks from Philip Augustus, while Henry waited on the sidelines doing little to intervene, happy to let his two younger rivals squabble among themselves. But by late autumn 1188 Richard had had enough of his father's double-dealing and deliberate prevarication over the succession. Convinced that the old king was about to declare John his heir – the prince having rather pointedly not taken the cross – the Lionheart switched sides, once again joining forces with Philip and making a dramatic public show of allegiance to the Capetian monarch in November. This time there was to be no reconciliation with Henry II.

Through that winter ill health immobilised the old king at the very moment when he needed to prove he could still dominate the field. With the balance of power shifting inexorably, scores of once loyal supporters among the Angevin aristocracy began to switch allegiance to Richard. When the Lionheart and Philip launched a blistering offensive against Normandy in June 1189, sweeping up a succession of castles as well as Le Mans and Tours, Henry had little option but to sue for peace. At a conference on 4 July 1189 he acceded to all terms, confirming Richard as his successor, agreeing to pay Philip a tribute of 20,000 marks and promising that together all three of them would set out on crusade the following Lent. By now Henry was physically shattered – barely able to sit astride his horse – but he was said still to have mustered the energy for one final, vituperative barb. Leaning forward to seal the accord by conferring the ritual kiss of peace upon his son, Henry apparently whispered, 'God grant that I may not die until I have had my revenge on you.' He was then borne away to Chinon on a litter, where he passed away two days later.[13]

Richard I, king of England

The events of early July 1189 transformed Richard the Lionheart from a scheming prince and wilful crusader into a royal monarch and ruler of the mighty Angevin dynasty. At Rouen, on 20 July 1189, he was installed as duke of Normandy and then, on 3 September 1189, crowned king of England in London's Westminster Abbey. Richard may have achieved his ambition through intrigue and betrayal, but once in power he assumed a more regal dignity, comporting himself with sober maturity. Visiting the abbey church at Fontevraud, where his father's body was laid in state, Richard was said to have shown no flicker of emotion. That summer he made a point of rewarding not only his own trusted supporters, men like Andrew of Chauvigny, but also those who had remained loyal to Henry II throughout, such as the famed knight William Marshal. Those who had turned away from the old king in his final months were shown less favour.

Richard's elevation also brought about a profound change in the tenor of his relationship with Philip Augustus. As allies the pair had defeated Henry II. Now, with Richard as head of the Angevin dynasty, they were pitted against one another as adversaries. The potential for rancour was heightened by the peculiarities of their respective standings. Richard was just shy of his thirty-second birthday when he became king, making him six years older than Philip. But the Lionheart was newly risen to the throne, while the young Capetian was experienced, having shouldered the burdens of monarchy for almost a decade. As crown rulers the two were equals, but in reality Richard possessed the more powerful realm, even though he was officially Philip's vassal for the Angevin lands in France such as Normandy, Anjou and Aquitaine. The two also were somewhat dissimilar in their natures and attributes. Richard was a man of war and action who was, nonetheless, politically astute. Philip was more single-minded in his dedication to the Capetian crown, subtle and cautious.

From the summer of 1189 onwards both rulers faced one overbearing question: when would they set out on crusade? The problem was that neither king was willing to leave without firm assurances of truce from the other and the arrangement of a carefully coordinated, simultaneous departure. In the end it was the best part of another year before they began their journey. During that time, a considerable number of French crusaders, including James of Avesnes and Henry of Champagne, went on ahead.

The years lost to delay through rivalry and dispute certainly had a marked impact upon the course of the Third Crusade, and it would be easy to censure the Angevin and Capetian rulers for not putting aside their differences in the wider interests of Christendom and the crusade. In truth, though, Richard and Philip still made significant sacrifices and took real risks to fight the holy war. As a recently crowned king, whose position was threatened by a grasping younger brother, John, the Lionheart might sensibly have stayed in the West to consolidate his authority. Instead, Richard tried to pull off a dangerous balancing act: departing for a long absence in the East, leaving trusted supporters, including his mother Eleanor of Aquitaine and William of Longchamp, to guard the Angevin realm. The English king also relied upon a near-constant stream of exchanged correspondence to keep abreast of events in Europe. Philip could have called off his crusade in mid-March 1190 when his wife died in childbirth, along with their twins. This left arrangements for the Capetian succession in a precarious state, with the king's three-year-old son Louis as the only extant heir, but, even so, Philip left France behind.

PREPARATIONS, FINANCES AND LOGISTICS

The Angevins and Capetians may have taken their time to start the crusade, but they at least made detailed and comprehensive campaign preparations. This meant that Richard I left Europe with the twelfth century's most organised and best-funded crusading army. Soon after taking the cross in January 1188, Henry II and Philip Augustus imposed a special crusading tax in both England and France, with the aim of amassing the fortune needed to finance their expeditions. Known as the Saladin Tithe, this levy of ten per cent on all movable goods was enforced by the threat of excommunication. Members of the Templar and Hospitaller orders were also drafted in to aid in gathering the duty.

Among those staying in the West, this unprecedented tax proved deeply unpopular, with voluble complaints raised within secular society and the ecclesiastical hierarchy alike. But in the Angevin Empire, at least, the tithe worked. Before his death, Henry II managed to amass around 100,000 marks. Richard then intensified and broadened money-raising efforts. According to one eyewitness, in England 'he put up for sale all he had, offices, lordships, earldoms, sheriffdoms, castles, towns, lands, everything'. The Lionheart was even supposed to have joked that he would have sold London if he could.[14]

The mountain of cash raised had a direct bearing upon the fortunes of the Third Crusade. In part this was because both Richard and Philip were expected to pay their soldiers' wages for the duration of the expedition, so a ready supply of money would be critical to the maintenance of morale and martial momentum. The Lionheart also made extensive but judicious use of his fiscal resources before leaving Europe to secure the logistical underpinnings of his campaign. Thanks to the unusually fastidious attitude towards record keeping in England, some details of these preparations can be recovered. In the financial year 1189-90 (then measured from Michaelmas on 29 September) Richard spent around £14,000 – the equivalent of more than half of the annual crown revenue from all England. He is also known to have ordered 60,000 horseshoes from the Forest of Dean and Hampshire, 14,000 cured pig carcasses, an abundant supply of cheeses from Essex and beans from Kent and Cambridgeshire, as well as thousands of arrows and crossbow bolts.

Philip Augustus had far less success implementing the Saladin Tithe. He lacked the absolute regnal authority enjoyed by English kings since the time of the Norman Conquest, nor could he rely upon the same developed governmental and administrative machinery at Henry's and Richard's disposal. Thus, although Philip's right to exact the levy was accepted at Paris in March 1188, within a year he had to withdraw the tax and actually apologised for ever having sought its imposition. The Capetian monarch therefore began the crusade with a considerably smaller war chest, even though the Lionheart does seem to have paid off the 20,000 marks his father promised Philip at the settlement of July 1189.

Careful economic planning and preparation were all the more imperative because the Angevins and Capetians decided to travel to the Levant by ship. This form of transport was potentially quicker and more efficient. Given the costs involved, it also drastically curtailed the ability of poor, ill-equipped non-combatants to follow the crusade. These factors suited Richard's and Philip's plans to lead more competent, professional armies to the East and to minimise the amount of time spent away from their respective realms. However, hiring or commissioning ships was an expensive business, involving massive upfront outlay even before the campaign was properly begun. And naval transport also carried with it considerable risks – such as difficulties of navigation and coordination, and the ever present threat of shipwreck.

Attention was needed if military discipline was to be maintained during a confined, uncomfortable and perilous sea journey. With this in mind, Richard enacted a detailed set of regulations in 1190, mandating harsh penalties for disorder: a soldier who committed murder would be tied to the corpse of his victim and thrown overboard (and if the offence took place on land, he would be tied to the body and buried alive); attacking someone with a knife would cost you your hand, while for hitting someone with a fist you would be plunged into the sea three times; thieves would be shaved of their hair, and then have boiling pitch and feathers poured over their heads 'so that [they] may be known'.[15]

In the course of the Third Crusade, Richard I and Philip Augustus managed, by and large, to negotiate all of the potential problems with naval transport. In doing so they established an important precedent and, from this point onwards, it became far more common for crusade armies to depend on sea travel to reach their objectives.

TO THE HOLY LAND

Richard I and Philip Augustus met to discuss final preparations for the crusade on 30 December 1189 and again on 16 March 1190. At last, on 24 June, the Lionheart took up his pilgrim scrip (satchel) and staff in a public ceremony at Tours, while the French king performed an identical ritual that same day at St Denis (following in the footsteps of his father Louis VII). On 2 July the two monarchs met at Vézelay and agreed to share any acquisitions made during the coming campaign. Then, on 4 July 1190, exactly three years after the Latin defeat at Hattin, the main Angevin and Capetian crusading armies set out together. To distinguish between the two hosts it had been decided that Philip's men would wear red crosses, while Richard's bore white. These two forces separated at Lyons on the understanding that they would regroup at Messina in Sicily before setting sail for the Levant.

Richard had been able to muster and equip a large host – drawing upon the resources of the expansive Angevin realm and the riches accumulated through the Saladin Tithe. He probably departed from Vézelay with a royal contingent of around 6,000 soldiers, although by the time he left Europe he may have accumulated a total force of 17,000 men. The Lionheart made his way south to Marseilles, whence he took ship down the Italian coast to arrive at Messina on 23 September, while a portion of his army sailed on directly to the Holy Land under the command of Archbishop Baldwin of Canterbury. Richard had also managed to prepare a fleet of some one hundred vessels from England, Normandy, Brittany and Aquitaine, which sailed round Iberia to rendezvous with the king in Sicily. Philip Augustus' personal contingent appears to have been far smaller. From Lyons he marched to Genoa and there negotiated terms of carriage to Sicily and the Near East, paying a hire price of 5,850 marks on ships for 650 knights and 1,300 squires. The Capetian king reached Messina in mid-September.

With winter fast approaching and the seas becoming more treacherous, it was decided that the onward journey to the Levant would have to wait until the following spring. In any case, Richard had political concerns to resolve. William II, king of Sicily, the Lionheart's brother-in-law through marriage to his sister Joanne, had died in November 1189, leaving Sicily in the grip of a succession dispute which, upon his arrival, Richard quickly resolved. Once peace had been restored, the crusaders spent the winter refitting their fleets and amassing further stores of weapons and equipment – Richard, for example, secured a supply of massive catapult stones. In this period the Lionheart also met with Joachim of Fiore, a Cistercian abbot who was gaining a notable reputation for prophecy. Joachim promptly announced a vision predicting Richard's capture of Jerusalem and the imminent onset of the Last Days of Judgement, apparently affirming that 'the Lord will give you victory over his enemies and will exalt your name above all the princes of the earth' – words that served merely to bolster the Lionheart's egotistical confidence.[16]

The ongoing problem of Richard's betrothal to Philip II's sister Alice of France was also resolved. The Lionheart had skirted around the issue since taking the English crown, despite the French king's repeated demands that the marriage take place. Now, with the journey to the Holy Land begun and Philip committed to the campaign, Richard revealed his hand. He had no desire or intention to wed Alice. Instead, a new marriage alliance had been arranged with Navarre – an Iberian Christian kingdom whose support would protect the southern Angevin Empire against the count of Toulouse during Richard's absence. In February 1191 the Navarrese heiress Princess Berengaria arrived in southern Italy, chaperoned by the Lionheart's indefatigable mother, Eleanor of Aquitaine, who was now in her seventies.

Philip Augustus was confronted with a *fait accompli*. When Richard threatened to produce witnesses who would testify to the fact that Alice had been Henry II's mistress and had borne the old king an illegitimate child, the Capetian monarch cut his losses. In return for 10,000 marks, he released the Lionheart from his betrothal. Open conflict had been averted, but Philip was humiliated and the whole sordid affair restoked his simmering hostility towards the Angevin king.

Finally, with the coming of spring, the sea lanes reopened and the crusading kings began the last stage of the journey to the Holy Land. Philip set sail on 20 March 1191 and on 10 April Richard's fleet followed suit, with Joanne and Berengaria among its passengers. Almost four years had passed since the Battle of Hattin. In that time much had changed in the Levant.

14

THE CONQUEROR CHALLENGED

Jerusalem's capture on 2 October 1187 was the crowning glory of Saladin's career – the fulfilment of a passionately held personal ambition and the realisation of a publicly avowed and doggedly pursued campaign of *jihad*. The Latin kingdom was on the brink of extinction, its ruler in captivity, its armies decimated. It is easy to imagine that, in the wake of such a titanic victory, the Muslim world would rally to the sultan's cause as never before, united in their admiration for his achievements, now almost abject in their acceptance of his right to lead Islam. Surely Saladin himself had earned a moment's pause, to look back on all that he had achieved, to celebrate as the first chill of autumn brushed the Holy City? In fact, the conquest of Jerusalem brought him little or no respite, but, rather, begat new burdens and new challenges.

IN THE AFTERMATH OF VICTORY

Jerusalem's repossession was a triumph, but it was not the end of the war against Latin Christendom. Saladin now had to balance the responsibilities of governing his expanded empire and completing the destruction of the Frankish settlements in the East, all while preparing to defend the Holy Land against the wrathful swarm of western crusaders who, he rightly guessed, would soon seek to avenge Hattin and retake Jerusalem. Even so, Saladin should have been in the ascendant in 1187. In reality, from this point on his strength gradually began to ebb. Amidst the bitter trials to come, he often seemed shockingly isolated – a once great general humbled, deserted by his armies, striving just to survive the storm of the Third Crusade.

Empires have always proved easier to build than to govern, but Saladin faced a profusion of difficulties after October 1187. Resources were of paramount importance. That autumn, Saladin's subjects and allies were exhausted, and the sultan's ill-managed financial resources were already drained by the costs of intense campaigning. In the following years, as the stream of wealth from new conquests turned from a torrent to a trickle, the Ayyubid treasury struggled to slake the greed of Saladin's followers, and it proved increasingly difficult to maintain huge armies in the field.

The seizure of the Holy City had other, less obvious, consequences. Saladin had assembled an Islamic coalition under the banner of *jihad*. But with the central goal of that struggle achieved, the jealousies, suspicions and hostilities that had lain dormant within the Muslim world began to resurface. In time, the sense of purpose that had briefly united Islam before Hattin dissolved. The historic success at Jerusalem also prompted some to wonder where Saladin would next train his all-conquering gaze – to fear that he would prove himself a tyrannical despot, bent upon overthrowing the established order, sweeping away the Abbasid caliphate to forge a new dynasty and empire.

As a Kurdish outsider who usurped authority from the Zangids, Saladin had never enjoyed the unequivocal support of Turkish, Arab and Persian Muslims. Nor could he claim any divine right to rule. Instead, the sultan had carefully constructed his public image as a defender of Sunni orthodoxy and a dedicated *mujahid*. Following the advice of counsellors like al-Fadil and Imad al-Din, Saladin had also taken pains to cultivate the support of the Abbasid Caliph al-Nasir in Baghdad, because his backing brought with it the seal of legitimacy. After 1187 the sultan persevered with this policy of showing deference to al-Nasir, but with Ayyubid might now seemingly unassailable, relations became increasingly strained.[17]

Driving the Franks into the sea

Saladin's overriding strategic concern in late 1187 was to sweep up the remaining Latin outposts in the Levant, sealing the Near East against any crusade launched from western Europe. But the work of eradicating the remaining vestiges of Frankish power promised to be neither swift nor easy. In the wake of the victory at Hattin, much of Palestine had been conquered, and the major ports of Acre, Jaffa and Ascalon were now in Muslim hands, but a number of Frankish strongholds in Galilee and Transjordan still held out. Elsewhere, the northern crusader states of Tripoli and Antioch were still intact, even though one of Saladin's potential opponents, Count Raymond III of Tripoli, had died from illness that September, having escaped the battlefield at Hattin and taken refuge in northern Lebanon.

The most pressing issue was Tyre. Through summer 1187 the port city had become a focal point of Latin resistance in Palestine, and Saladin had allowed thousands of Christian refugees to congregate within its walls. Tyre might well have fallen to the sultan's armies soon after Hattin had not command of its garrison and defences been seized by Conrad, the marquis of Montferrat. A northern Italian nobleman and brother of the late William of Montferrat (Sibylla of Jerusalem's first husband and father to Baldwin V), Conrad had been serving the latest Byzantine Emperor Isaac II Angelus in Constantinople. But after murdering one of Isaac's political enemies in early summer 1187, the marquis decided to cut his losses and make a pilgrimage to the Holy Land, arriving in Palestine in July 1187 – coincidentally just days after Hattin.

Conrad found Tyre in a beleaguered state. The marquis' arrival proved to be a major boon for the Franks and an unforeseen, troublesome intrusion for Saladin. Conrad was profoundly ambitious – guileful and unscrupulous as a political operator, competent and authoritative as a general – and he embraced the opportunity for advancement presented by Tyre's predicament, quickly assuming control. Galvanising the Latin populace to action, he immediately set about bolstering the city's already formidable fortifications. Saladin's decision to channel his energy into the siege of Jerusalem in September 1187 afforded the marquis a valuable breathing space; one which he put to good effect, drawing in the support of the Military Orders and Pisan and Genoese fleets to prepare Tyre for attack.

By early November, when Saladin finally marched on Tyre, he found the city to be all but invulnerable. Built upon an island and approachable by land only via a narrow man-made causeway, this compact fortress settlement was protected by double battlements. A Muslim pilgrim who visited a few years earlier commended its '[marvellous] strength and impregnability', noting that anyone 'who seeks to conquer it will meet with no surrender or humility'. Tyre was also renowned for its excellent deep-water anchorage, its northern inner harbour being protected by walls and a chain.[18]

For more than six weeks, into the depths of winter, Saladin laid siege to Tyre by land and sea, hoping to pummel Conrad into submission. Fourteen catapults were erected by the Muslims, 'and night and day [the sultan had them] constantly hurling stones into [the city]'. Saladin was also soon reinforced by leading members of his family: his brother and most valued ally, al-Adil; al-Afdal, the sultan's eldest son, heir apparent to the Ayyubid Empire; and al-Zahir, one of Saladin's younger sons, now designated as ruler of Aleppo, who received his first experience of battle at Tyre. The Ayyubid fleet, meanwhile, was summoned from Egypt to blockade the port. Yet, despite the sultan's best efforts, little progress was made. Around 30 December the Franks scored a notable victory, initiating a surprise naval attack and capturing eleven Muslim galleys. This setback seems to have dampened Ayyubid morale. A Templar later wrote in a dispatch to Europe that Saladin himself was so distressed that 'he cut the ears and tail off his horse and rode it through his whole army in the sight of all'. With the morale of his exhausted army faltering, the sultan decided to throw everything into one final offensive. On 1 January 1188, he unleashed a blistering frontal assault along the causeway, but even this was turned back. Beaten to a standstill, Saladin raised the siege, leaving Conrad in possession of Tyre.

Saladin has often been criticised for this failure. The Iraqi contemporary Ibn al-Athir offered a withering appraisal of the sultan's generalship, observing that: 'This was Saladin's custom. When a town held out against him, he would grow weary of it and the siege and leave . . . no one can be blamed in this matter except Saladin, for it was he who sent armies of the Franks to Tyre.' In part, the sultan's decision can be justified by the inherent weaknesses of his military regime. By the end of 1187, after months of campaigning, with Ayyubid resources stretched to breaking point and the loyalty of some of his allies wavering, Saladin was obviously struggling to keep soldiers in the field. Judging that his base of support depended on his continued ability to pay and reward his troops, reluctant to stick with the task and risk insurrection, he chose to move on to pursue less intractable quarry. In truth, though, the smarting humiliation at Tyre was telling. The sultan's earlier decision in September 1187 to prioritise the devotional and political objective of Jerusalem had possessed a certain logic. But by turning his back on an unconquered Tyre in January 1188, the sultan laid bare his limitations. For all the energy exerted in uniting Islam, all the preparations made for holy war, ultimately Saladin possessed neither the will nor the resources to complete the conquest of the Palestinian coastline. For the first time since Hattin it appeared that the all-conquering Ayyubids might fail to drive the Franks into the sea.[19]

Sweeping up pawns

Saladin spent the remainder of that winter resting in Acre. Anxious about the prospect of a Christian counter-offensive, he considered razing the city to the ground to prevent it falling into enemy hands, but eventually elected to leave this 'lock for the lands of the Coast' intact, summoning Qaragush from Egypt to oversee Acre's defence. From spring 1188 onwards, Saladin began to march through Syria and Palestine, seeking out vulnerable Latin settlements, outposts and fortresses, sweeping up relatively easy conquests. Passing through Damascus and the Biqa valley, that summer he launched attacks on the principality of Antioch and the northern reaches of the county of Tripoli. The major Syrian port of Latakia was captured, while down the coast the Muslim *qadi* (religious judge) of Latin-held Jabala engineered that port's surrender. The sultan also seized castles such as Baghras and Trapesac in the Amanus Mountains north of Antioch and Saone and Bourzey, in the southern Ansariyah range.

Saladin made significant gains in the northern crusader states, but showed a profound reluctance to commit to any prolonged investments. The imposing Hospitaller and Templar castles at Krak des Chevaliers, Marqab and Safita were all bypassed, and no real effort was made to threaten the Latin capitals of Tripoli and Antioch – with Saladin agreeing an eight-month truce with the latter (albeit on punitive terms) before returning to Damascus. The sultan then prosecuted a winter campaign in Galilee, securing the surrender of the region's last remaining Frankish strongholds: Templar-held Safad and Hospitaller Belvoir. Around the same time, Ayyubid troops captured Kerak in Transjordan, and six months later nearby Montreal capitulated. The key factor in these successes was Latin isolation. Surrounded, deep in what was now Muslim territory, the garrisons of all four of these mighty 'crusader' castles found themselves in hopeless situations. With no possible prospect of holding out indefinitely, they laid down their arms, allowing Saladin to consolidate his dominion over Palestine. Sweeping through the Levant, the sultan had maintained martial momentum throughout 1188, but at the cost of leaving Antioch inviolate and the county of Tripoli all but untouched.

In the course of that year's campaigning, Baha al-Din ibn Shaddad joined Saladin's inner circle of advisers. A highly educated Mosuli religious scholar trained in Baghdad, Baha al-Din had acted as a negotiator for the Zangids in 1186 when, in the wake of the sultan's severe illness, he agreed terms with Izz al-Din of Mosul. In 1188 Baha al-Din took advantage of the recent Muslim conquest of the Holy Land, making a pilgrimage to Mecca and then Jerusalem. It was at this point that Saladin invited Baha al-Din to join the Ayyubid court, evidently impressed by the Mosuli's piety, intellect and wisdom. When the two met, Baha al-Din presented a copy of his newly authored treatise on *The Virtues of Jihad* to the sultan and was then appointed as *qadi* of the army. He rapidly became one of Saladin's closest and most trusted counsellors, staying with him almost constantly throughout the years that followed. Baha al-Din later composed a detailed biography of his master, which now serves as a critically important historical source, particularly for the period after 1188.[20]

The loss of focus

Despite having laid plans to launch new, more determined offensives against Tripoli and Antioch with the onset of the new fighting season, Saladin failed to return to the north in 1189. Instead, seemingly worn down by the burden of rule and near-incessant campaigning, the sultan became uncharacteristically indecisive and ineffectual. With each passing month, the prospect of western retaliation loomed larger. Saladin certainly appears to have been aware that the Third Crusade was afoot – in a letter written later that year, his adviser Imad al-Din demonstrated an incredibly detailed and accurate understanding of the crusade's scope, organisation and objectives. Yet the sultan made no last-ditch attempt to overcome the likes of Tyre before the inevitable storm struck. Instead, inexplicably, he wasted the spring and early summer of 1189 in protracted negotiations over the fate of Beaufort, a relatively insignificant and isolated Latin fortress, perched in the mountains of southern Lebanon, high above the Litani River.

Another questionable decision proved still more costly. As victor on the field of battle at Hattin in July 1187, Saladin had taken Guy of Lusignan, the Latin king of Jerusalem, prisoner. In summer 1188, however, the sultan decided to release Guy from captivity (apparently after repeated appeals from Guy's wife Sibylla). The motive behind this seemingly injudicious act of magnanimity is difficult to divine. Perhaps Saladin judged Guy to be a spent force, incapable of rousing the Franks, or possibly hoped that he might cause dispute and dissension among the Christians, challenging Conrad of Montferrat's growing power in Tyre. Whatever his reasons, the sultan probably did not expect Guy to honour the promises he made in exchange for his release – to relinquish all claim to the Latin kingdom and immediately leave the Levant – pledges which Guy renounced almost as soon as he was at liberty.[21]

If Saladin did take Guy for a broken man, he was sorely mistaken. At first the Latin king struggled to make his will felt among the Franks, and Conrad twice refused him entry to Tyre. But by summer 1189, Guy was preparing to make an unexpectedly bold and courageous move.

THE GREAT SIEGE OF ACRE

The blistering heat of midsummer 1189 found Saladin still bent upon the conquest of the intractable stronghold of Beaufort. But in late August news reached him in the foothills of the Lebanese highlands that stirred feelings of dread and suspicion – the Franks had gone on the offensive. In 1187–8 Conrad of Montferrat had played a crucial role defending Tyre against Islam, yet he still baulked at the notion of initiating an aggressive war of reconquest. Secure within the battlements of Tyre, Conrad seemed content to await the advent of the Third Crusade and the great monarchs of Latin Europe – willing, by and large, to wait out the coming war, looking for any opportunity for his own advancement.

Now, the unlikeliest of figures decided to seize the initiative. The

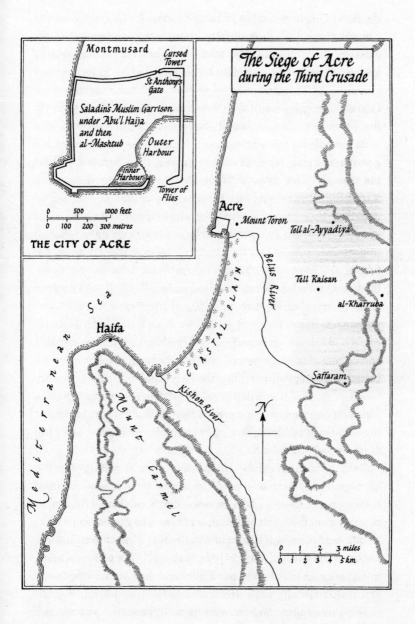

The Siege of Acre during the Third Crusade

THE CITY OF ACRE

Montmusard

Cursed Tower

St Anthony's Gate

Saladin's Muslim Garrison under Abu'l Haija and then al-Mashtub

Outer Harbour

Inner Harbour

Tower of Flies

0   500   1000 feet
0   100   200   300 metres

Acre

Mount Toron

Tell al-Ayyadiya

Belus River

Tell Kaisan

al-Kharruba

Mediterranean Sea

Haifa

Coastal Plain

Mount Carmel

Kishon River

Saffaram

N

0   1   2   3 miles
0   1   2   3   4   5 km

disgraced king of Jerusalem, Guy of Lusignan, whose ignominious defeat at Hattin had condemned his realm to virtual annihilation, was attempting the unthinkable. In the company of his redoubtable brother, Geoffrey of Lusignan, a recent arrival in the Levant, as well as a group of Templars and Hospitallers and a few thousand men, Guy was marching south from Tyre towards Muslim-held Acre. He seemed to be making a suicidal attempt to retake his kingdom.

At first Saladin greeted this move with scepticism. Believing that it was merely a feint designed to lure him away from Beaufort, he held his ground. This allowed King Guy to negotiate the narrow Scandelion Pass, where, one Frank wrote, 'all the gold in Russia' could not have saved them had the Muslims moved to block their advance. Realising his mistake, Saladin began a cautious advance south to Marj Ayun and the Sea of Galilee, waiting to assess the Christians' next move before turning west towards the coast. Benefiting from his enemy's circumspection, Guy followed the road south to arrive outside Acre on 28 August 1189.[22]

Acre was one of the great ports of the Near East. Under Frankish rule it had become an important royal residence – a vibrant, crowded and cosmopolitan commercial hub, and the main point of arrival for Latin Christian pilgrims visiting the Holy Land. In 1184 one Muslim traveller described it as 'a port of call for all ships', noting that 'its roads and streets are choked by the press of men, so that it is hard to put foot to ground' and admitting that '[the city] stinks and is filthy, being full of refuse and excrement'.

Built upon a triangular promontory of land jutting into the Mediterranean, Acre was stoutly defended by a square circuit of battlements. A crusader later observed that 'more than a third of its perimeter, on the south and west, is enclosed by the flowing waves'. To the north-east, the landward walls met at a major fortification, known as the Cursed Tower (where, it was said, 'the silver was made in exchange for which Judas the Traitor sold the Lord'). In the south-east corner the city walls stretched into the sea to create a small chained inner quay, and an outer harbour, protected by a massive wall running north–south that extended to a natural outcrop of rock – the site of a small fortification known as the Tower of Flies. The city stood at the northern end of a large bay arcing south to Haifa and Mount Carmel, surrounded by a relatively flat, open coastal plain, some twenty miles in length and between one and four miles in breadth. About one mile south of the port the shallow Belus River reached the coast.

The city stood at the gateway to Palestine – a bastion against any Christian invasion from the north, by either land or sea. Here Saladin's resilience, martial genius and *jihadi* dedication would be tested to the limit, as Islam and Christendom became caught up in one of the most extraordinary sieges of the crusades.[23]

Early encounters

When King Guy reached Acre his prospects were incredibly bleak. One Frankish contemporary remarked that he had placed his meagre force 'between the hammer and the anvil', another that he would need a miracle to prevail. Even the Muslim garrison apparently felt no fear and began jeering from Acre's battlements when they caught sight of the 'handful of Christians' accompanying the king. But Guy immediately demonstrated that he was developing a more acute sense of strategy; having surveyed the field that night, under the cover of darkness, he took up a position on top of a squat hill called Mount Toron. Some 120 feet high, lying three-quarters of a mile east of the city, this tell afforded the Franks a measure of natural protection and a commanding view over the plain of Acre. Within a few days a group of Pisan ships arrived. In spite of the punishing siege to come, many of the Italian crusaders on board had brought their families with them. These hardy men, women and children proceeded to land on the beach south of Acre and make camp.[24]

The measured pace of Saladin's advance to the coast almost had disastrous consequences. Outnumbered and exposed as he was outside Acre, Guy decided to risk an immediate frontal assault on the city even though, as yet, he had no catapults or other siege materials.

On 31 August the Latins attacked, mounting the walls with ladders, protected only by their shields, and might have overrun the battlements had not the appearance of the sultan's advance scouts on the surrounding plain prompted a panicked retreat. Over the next few days Saladin arrived with the remainder of his troops, and any hopes the Latins entertained of forcing a speedy capitulation of Acre evaporated; instead, they faced the dreadful prospect of a war on two fronts – and the near-certainty of destruction at the hands of the victor of Hattin.

Yet, at the very moment that Saladin needed to act with decisive assurance, he wavered. Allowing Guy to reach Acre had proved to be a mistake, but the sultan now made an even graver error of judgement. True, Saladin lacked overwhelming numerical superiority, but he outnumbered the Franks and, through a carefully coordinated attack in conjunction with Acre's garrison, he could have surrounded and overwhelmed their positions. As it happened, he adjudged a rapid, committed assault to be too risky and instead took up a cautious holding position on the hillside of al-Kharruba, about six miles to the south-east, overlooking the plain of Acre. Unbeknownst to the Latins, he managed to sneak a detachment of troops (presumably shielded by the darkness of night) into the city to bolster its defences and, while skirmishers were dispatched regularly to harass Guy's camp on Mount Toron, Saladin chose to hold back the bulk of his forces and wait patiently for reinforcement by his allies. On this occasion, such caution, so often the hallmark of the sultan's generalship, was inappropriate, the product of a significant misreading of the strategic landscape. One crucial factor meant that Saladin could ill afford to bide his time – the sea.

When Saladin reached Acre in early September 1189, the city was invested by Guy's army and the Pisans. But in the aftermath of Hattin and the fall of Jerusalem, it was almost inevitable that the Frankish siege of this coastal port would become the central focus of Latin Europe's retaliatory anger. During an inland siege, the king's forces could have been readily isolated from supply and reinforcement, and

Saladin's circumspection would have made sense. At Acre, the Mediterranean acted like a pulsing, unstemmable artery, linking Palestine with the West, and while the sultan waited for his armies to assemble, ships began to arrive teeming with Christian troops to bolster the besieging host. Imad al-Din, then in Saladin's camp, later described looking out over the coast to see a seemingly constant stream of Frankish ships arriving at Acre and a growing fleet moored by the shoreline 'like tangled thickets'. This spectacle unnerved the Muslims inside and outside the port, and to boost morale Saladin apparently circulated a story that the Latins were actually sailing their ships away every night and 'when it was light . . . [returning] as if they had just arrived'. In reality, the sultan's prevarication gave Guy a desperately needed period of grace in which to amass manpower.[25]

A significant group of reinforcements arrived around 10 September – a fleet of fifty ships, carrying some 12,000 Frisian and Danish crusaders as well as horses. The western sources describe its advent as a moment of salvation, a tipping point beyond which the Latin besiegers had at least some chance of survival. Among the new troops was James of Avesnes, a renowned warrior from Hainaut (a region on the modern border between France and Belgium). Likened by one contemporary to 'Alexander, Hector and Achilles', a skilled veteran in the art of war and the politics of power, James had been one of the first western knights to take the cross in November 1187.

In the course of September, crusaders continued to arrive, swelling the ranks of the Frankish army. Among their number were potentates drawn from the upper ranks of Europe's aristocracy. Philip of Dreux, the bishop of Beauvais, said to be 'a man more devoted to battles than books', and his brother Robert of Dreux came from northern France, as did Everard, count of Brienne, and his brother Andrew. They were joined by Ludwig III of Thuringia, one of Germany's most powerful nobles. By the end of the month even Conrad of Montferrat had decided, apparently at Ludwig's insistence, to come south from Tyre to join the siege, bringing with him some 1,000 knights and 20,000 infantry.[26]

Saladin too was receiving an influx of troops. By the second week of September the bulk of the forces summoned to Acre had arrived. Joined by al-Afdal, al-Zahir, Taqi al-Din and Keukburi, the sultan moved on to the plain of Acre, taking up position on an arcing line running from Tell al-Ayyadiya in the north, through Tell Kaisan (which later became known as the Toron of Saladin) to the Belus River in the south-west. Just as he settled into this new front, the Franks tried to throw a loose semi-circular cordon around Acre – running from the northern coast, through Mount Toron and across the Belus (which served as a water supply) to the sandy beach to the south. Saladin saw off this first Latin attempt at a blockade with relative ease. As yet, the crusaders lacked the resources to effectively seal off every approach to the city, and a combined assault by Acre's garrison and a detachment of troops under Taqi al-Din broke the weakest part of their lines to the north, enabling a camel train of supplies to enter the city via St Anthony's Gate on Saturday 16 September.

By mid-morning that day Saladin himself had entered Acre, climbing its walls to survey the enemy camp. Looking down from the battlements upon the thronged crusader host huddled on the plain below, now surrounded by a sea of Muslim warriors, he must have felt a sense of assurance. With the city saved, his patiently amassed army could turn to the task of annihilating the Franks who so arrogantly had thought to threaten Acre, and victory would be achieved. But the sultan had waited too long. For the next three days his troops repeatedly sought either to overrun the Latin positions or to draw the enemy into a decisive open battle, all to no avail. In the weeks since King Guy's arrival the swelling crusader ranks had dug into their positions, and they now repulsed all attacks. One Muslim witness described them standing 'like a wall behind their mantlets, shields and lances, with levelled crossbows', refusing to break formation. As the Christians clung with stubborn tenacity to their foothold outside Acre, the strain of the situation began to tell on Saladin. One of his physicians revealed that the sultan was so racked with worry that he barely ate for days. Frankish indomitability soon prompted indecision and dissension within Saladin's inner circle. With some advisers arguing that it would be better to await the arrival of the Egyptian fleet and others advocating that the approaching winter should be allowed to wreak its depredations upon the crusaders, the sultan wavered, and the attacks on the Christian lines ground to a halt. A letter to the caliph in Baghdad offered a positive summary of events – the Latins had arrived like a flood, but 'a path had been cut to the city through their throats' and they now were all but defeated – but in reality, Saladin must have begun to realise that the siege of Acre might prove difficult to lift.[27]

The first battle

The weeks that followed saw intermittent skirmishing, while Frankish ships continued to bring more and more crusaders to the siege. By Wednesday 4 October 1189 the Christians were numerous enough to contemplate going on the offensive, launching an attack on Saladin's camp in what was to be the first full-scale pitched battle of the Third Crusade. Leaving his brother Geoffrey to defend Mount Toron, King Guy amassed the bulk of the Frankish forces at the foot of the tell, carefully drawing up an extended battle line with the help of the Military Orders and potentates such as Everard of Brienne and Ludwig of Thuringia. With infantry and archers in the front ranks, screening the mounted knights, the Christians set out to cross the open plain towards the Muslims, marching in close order and at slow pace. This was to be no lightning attack, but, rather, a disciplined advance in which the crusaders tried to close with the enemy en masse, protected by their tightly controlled formation. Surveying the field from his vantage point atop Tell al-Ayyadiya, Saladin had ample time to arrange his own forces on the plain below, interspersing squadrons under trusted commanders like al-Mashtub and Taqi al-Din with relatively untested troops, such as those from Diyar Bakr on the Upper Tigris. Holding the centre with Isa, but looking to play a mobile command role, boosting morale and discipline where necessary, the sultan prepared to face the Franks.

The scene outside Acre at dawn that day was spectacular and unsettling. For more than two hours, thousands of crusaders in packed ranks, resplendent banners raised, advanced at walking pace, inching towards battle with Saladin's men. Soldiers on both sides must have struggled to hold their nerve. Then at last, around mid-morning, fighting began as the Christians' left flank reached the Muslim lines to the north, where Taqi al-Din was stationed. Hoping to lure the Franks into a formation-shattering charge, Taqi al-Din sent in skirmishers and then feigned a limited retreat. Unfortunately his manoeuvre was so convincing that Saladin believed his nephew was under real threat and dispatched troops from his centre to reinforce the north. This unbalancing of the line gave the crusaders an opportunity. Advancing with rigid discipline, they attacked the right of Saladin's central division 'as one man, horse and foot', quickly sending the inexperienced Diyar Bakris stationed there into full flight. Panic spread and the right half of the sultan's central division crumbled.

For a moment, Saladin looked to be on the verge of defeat. With the way suddenly open to the Muslim camp on Tell al-Ayyadiya, Franks began racing up the hill. A detachment of crusaders actually reached the sultan's personal tent, and one of Saladin's wardrobe staff was among those killed. But the very lure of victory and, of course, of booty, brought a reversal of fortune. In the thrill of the moment, the crusaders' formation, preserved until then with such care, broke apart: many turned to plundering, while the Templars doggedly pursued the retreating Muslims, only to discover that, unsupported, they had become separated from the main force. As they attempted a desperate withdrawal, Saladin rallied his troops. Accompanied by just five guards, he sped along the line, strengthening resolve and launching an attack on the retreating Templars. In the ensuing skirmish the brothers of that proud order were decimated. Their master, Gerard of Ridefort, the veteran of Hattin, was caught up in the midst of the fighting. With 'his troops being slaughtered on all sides', Gerard refused to flee to safety and was slain.

With the balance of the battle already shifting in Saladin's favour, two events sealed the Christians' fate. As combat raged on the plain between Mount Toron and Tell al-Ayyadiya, the Muslim garrison of Acre sallied out of the city, threatening both the crusaders' camp and their field army's rear. Sensing that they soon would be surrounded, struggling to maintain a semblance of formation, the Franks were close to panic. A small piece of misfortune pushed them over the edge. A group of Germans still engaged in pillaging Saladin's camp lost control of one of their horses and, as the animal bolted back towards Acre, they gave chase. The sight of another crusader detachment seemingly in full flight threw the Christian host into disarray; as fear coursed down the ranks, a fully fledged rout began. With thousands now racing for the relative safety of the Latin entrenchments, hotly pursued by Saladin's men, chaos reigned. 'On and on went the killing', wrote the eyewitness Baha al-Din, 'until the fugitives that survived reached the enemy camp.' Andrew of Brienne was cut to the ground while trying to halt the rout, and although he called out to his passing brother to save him, Count Everard was too terrified to stop. Elsewhere, James of Avesnes was unhorsed, but one of his knights gave up his own mount to enable James to escape and then turned to face his death. It even was said that King Guy rescued Conrad of Montferrat when the marquis became surrounded by Muslims.

Saladin proved unable to press home his advantage as the battle drew to a close. Latin troops stationed in the crusader camp fiercely resisted Muslim attempts to overrun their positions, and, perhaps more importantly, the sultan's camp was still in a state of confusion. When the crusaders fought their way on to the slopes of Tell al-Ayyadiya, scores of servants in the Muslim army had decided to cut their losses, loot whatever they could and flee. Just when Saladin needed to direct the full weight of his military might against the retreating Franks, large swathes of his army were engaged in chasing their own thieving domestics.

Nonetheless, on the face of it, this was a victory for Islam. The

Christians had come that morning seeking battle and had been defeated, leaving some 3,000 to 4,000 of their number dead or dying on the plains of Acre as darkness fell. The horror and humiliation of the day's events were brought home to the crusader host when a mutilated, half-naked figure crawled into camp in the middle of the night. This poor wretch, a knight named Ferrand, maimed in the course of the fighting, had hidden among his fallen comrades only to be stripped and left for dead by Muslim pillagers. When he eventually reached the safety of the Frankish lines 'he was so disfigured by his wounds that his people could not recognise him and he was barely able to persuade them to let him in'. The next morning Saladin chose to send his enemies a stark message: gathering the Christian dead, he pitched their remains into the Belus so that they floated downstream, into the Latin encampment. It was said that the stench from this mass of corpses lingered long after they were buried.[28]

Despite all this, the battle on 4 October did more lasting harm to Saladin's prospects. In terms of Muslim dead and injured losses had been minimal, but those members of the sultan's army that fled the field that day did not return – indeed, rumour had it that some of them did not stop running until they reached the Sea of Galilee – and they proved hard to replace. Worse still, the debacle in Saladin's camp crushed morale and sowed distrust. Baha al-Din noted that in the looting 'people lost vast sums' and that 'this was more disastrous than the rout itself'. Saladin made earnest attempts to recover as much lost property as possible, amassing a vast mound of plunder in his tent that could be reclaimed if people swore on oath that it was theirs, but the psychological damage had been done.

In the aftermath of the battle Saladin decided to review his strategy. After fifty days on the front line his troops were complaining of exhaustion, while he himself had begun to suffer from illness. Around 13 October his forces and baggage train began moving back from the contaminated battlefield to the more distant siege position of al-Kharruba to await the arrival of al-Adil. This was a tacit admission of failure; an acknowledgement that, in this first crucial phase of the siege, Saladin had been unable to dislodge the crusader force. By the logic of military science, the Franks had achieved the impossible – the successful establishment of an investment, deep in enemy territory, while facing an opposing field army. Historians have been consistently perplexed by this apparent anomaly. Yet the explanation is clear: the coastal nature of the siege certainly furnished the Franks with a vital lifeline, but, more significantly, the first exchanges of this conflict confirmed Saladin's deepening crisis of manpower while exposing his own inability to command with resolute determination. Falling back on his habitual avoidance of full-scale confrontation when lacking overwhelming military superiority, the sultan believed that he was steering the safest course. But at this critical juncture action, not caution, was needed. Committing to a frontal assault on the crusaders' positions at the start of Acre's siege would have been a gamble, but one that Saladin stood a good chance of winning, albeit at considerable cost. With the decision to step back from the line in October, the chance to snuff out the Christian threat before it became fully embedded slipped away. It was not to return.[29]

Capitalising on the welcome breathing space they had been afforded, the crusaders set about securing their positions outside Acre. In mid-September they had begun throwing up rudimentary earthwork defences. Now, with the threat of an immediate offensive slackened, they 'heaped up turf ramparts and dug deep trenches from sea to sea to defend the tents', creating an elaborate system of semi-circular fortifications that enclosed Acre and offered far greater protection from Muslim assault, whether from the city's garrison or from Saladin. To hinder mounted attackers, the no-man's-land beyond the trenches was peppered with the medieval equivalent of minefields – deep, spike-laden, concealed pits, designed to cripple horse and rider. Reflecting on these measures, Saladin's sometime critic Ibn al-Athir sardonically observed: 'Now it became clear how well advised Saladin had been to retire.' At the same time, throughout October Muslim scouts reported the near-daily influx of Latin reinforcements, prompting Saladin to write to the caliph in Baghdad proclaiming that the Christians were being supplied by ships more numerous than the waves and bemoaning the fact that for every crusader killed 1,000 took his place.[30]

Hiatus

The coming of winter in December 1189 brought a further lull in the siege. Faced with roughening seas and lacking access to the safety of Acre's inner harbour, the Latin fleet was forced to sail north to Tyre and beyond in search of shelter. Conrad of Montferrat also returned to Tyre. Worsening weather forced a lull in hostilities as rain turned the ground between the crusaders' trenches and Saladin's camp at al-Kharruba to mud, across which it was impractical to launch attacks. The sultan sent the bulk of his troops home, remaining in person, while the Franks hunkered down to wait out the season, hoping to survive the predations of disease and hunger, devoting their energy to the construction of siege engines.

According to his confidant, Baha al-Din, Saladin now recognised 'how much importance the Franks . . . attached to Acre and how it was the target at which all their determined plans were directed'. The decision to winter outside the city indicates that the sultan now regarded it as the war's critical battleground. He may have lacked the nerve for an all-out assault on the crusader camp earlier that autumn, but at least he did show a new, steadfast determination to persevere with the campaign. Having spent the two years that followed Hattin scooping up easy conquests, avoiding drawn-out confrontations, he evidently decided that a line must be drawn at Acre and the Latin advance into Palestine halted in its tracks.

Knowing full well the devastation that would be rained upon Acre come spring, the sultan set about '[pouring in] sufficient provisions, supplies, equipment and men to make him feel confident that it was secure'. It was probably at this point that Saladin installed Abu'l Haija the Fat as the city's military commander, alongside Qaragush. Even the crusaders were impressed by these measures, with one later commenting that 'never was there a castle nor city that had so many arms, such defence, such provision of food, at such expense'. Amid the flurry of activity, the sultan suffered a grave personal loss when his close friend and shrewd counsellor Isa died of illness on 19 December 1189.[31]

The long months of stalemate were not solely the domain of grim-eyed exchanges and frenetic preparation. The winter afforded the first opportunities for fraternisation and the blossoming of a familiarity that would remain an undercurrent of the campaign. One of the last Latin ships to arrive in 1189 had carried a different breed of reinforcement: '300 lovely Frankish women, full of youth and beauty, assembled from beyond the sea [to offer] themselves for sin'. Saladin's secretary, Imad al-Din, took a certain scandalised pleasure in describing how these prostitutes, having set up shop outside Acre, 'brought their silver anklets up to touch their golden earrings [and] made themselves targets for men's darts', but noted with evident disgust that some Muslims also 'slipped away' to partake of their charms.

Another Muslim eyewitness noted that the Christian and Muslim enemies eventually 'got to know one another, in that both sides would converse and leave off fighting. At times people would sing and others would dance, so familiar had they become.' In the later periods the sheer proximity of the two entrenched sides must have contributed to this familiarity, as the Muslims were said to be 'face to face with the enemy . . . with both sets of camp fires visible to each other. We could hear the sound of their bells and they could hear our call to prayer.' The city's garrison, at least, earned the crusaders' begrudging respect, with one commenting that 'never was there a people as good in defence as these devil's minions'. This image of burgeoning friendship and acquaintance should not be stretched too far. Recent scholarship has unearthed an intriguing Latin survey of the forces amassed by Saladin at Acre, quite probably written during the siege. Characterised by a mixture of patchy knowledge and animosity, this document offers up precise details of Muslim troop characteristics and armament, peppered by persistent defamation and fantasy. Arabs were said to 'circumcise' their ears, while Turks were apparently renowned for indulging in homosexuality and bestiality, all in accordance with the supposed precepts of Muhammad.

The informal 'rules' of engagement that gradually built up between these entrenched foes also were sometimes transgressed. An understanding appears to have existed that troops leaving the safety of their camp to relieve themselves would not be attacked. The crusaders were therefore appalled when, on one occasion, '[a knight] doing what everyone has to do . . . was bent over' when a mounted Turk raced from his front line hoping to skewer him with his lance. Wholly unaware of the danger, the knight was warned in the nick of time by the shouts of 'Run, sir, run' from the trenches. He 'got up with difficulty . . . his business finished', just managing to dodge the first charge, and then, facing his enemy unarmed, felled the horseman with a well-thrown rock.[32]

THE STORM OF WAR

With the advent of 'the soft season of spring', open warfare returned, and the first battle to be fought was for dominion of the sea. In late March 1190, shortly after Easter, news reached Acre that fifty Latin ships were approaching from Tyre. In the course of the winter, Conrad had agreed a partial reconciliation with Guy, becoming the 'king's faithful man' in return for rights to Tyre, Beirut and Sidon. The fleet he now led south sought to re-establish Christian control over the Mediterranean seaboard to reconnect the crusaders' lifeline to the outside world. This was a struggle that Saladin could ill afford to lose, as perhaps his best hope of overall victory at Acre lay in isolating the Frankish besiegers. He resolved to resist the oncoming ships at all costs, prompting one of the twelfth century's most spectacular naval engagements.

The battle for the sea

When the Latin fleet appeared, driven down the coast by a north wind, around fifty of Saladin's ships sailed out of Acre's harbour in pairs to meet it, flying green and gold banners. The Franks possessed two main types of vessel: 'long, slender and low' galleys, fixed with battering rams and powered by two banks of oars (one below and one on deck); and 'galliots', shorter, more manoeuvrable warships with a single bank of oars. As the fleet approached, shield walls were erected on decks and the Christian ships formed into a V-shaped wedge, with the galleys at its point. With a cacophony of trumpets sounding on both sides, the two forces ploughed into one another and battle was joined.

Sea-borne combat was still a relatively rudimentary affair in 1190. Larger ships might try to ram and sink enemy craft, but on the whole fighting took place at close quarters and consisted of the exchange of short-range missiles and attempts to draw in opposing vessels with grappling hooks and board them. The greatest horror, as far as sailors were concerned, was Greek fire, because it could not be extinguished by water, and in this engagement both sides possessed supplies of this weapon. The Muslim fleet came close to gaining the upper hand on a number of occasions. One Frankish galley was bombarded with Greek fire and boarded, prompting its oarsmen to leap into the sea in terror. A small number of knights who were weighed down by their heavy armour, and who did not know how to swim anyway, chose to hold their ground 'in sheer desperation' and managed to win back control of the half-burnt vessel. In the end, neither side achieved an overwhelming victory, but the Muslim fleet came off the worst, being forced back behind Acre's harbour chain. One of their galleys was driven ashore and ransacked, its crew dragged on to the beach and summarily butchered and beheaded by a merciless pack of knife-wielding Latin women. In a grim aside, a crusader later noted that 'the women's physical weakness prolonged the pain of death' because it took them longer to decapitate their foes.

This battle cost Saladin control of the sea for the rest of 1190. The crusaders were able to police the waters around Acre, penning the sultan's remaining ships within the harbour and disrupting any attempts to resupply the city's garrison. For the next six months Acre's inhabitants lived on the edge of starvation. By late spring their stores of supplies were exhausted and they were forced to eat 'all their beasts, hooves and innards, necks and heads' and expel any old or weak prisoners (the young were kept to load catapults). Saladin made repeated attempts to break the naval cordon, with varying degrees of success. In mid-June, part of a twenty-five-ship-strong fleet managed to fight its way through. Around late August, the sultan arranged for a round-bellied transport ship to be packed with 400 sacks of wheat, as well as cheese, corn, onions and sheep. To beat the blockade it sailed from Beirut under the cloak of disguise. Its crew 'dressed up as Franks, even shaving their beards', while pigs were placed on deck in plain view and crosses flown. The crusaders were fooled and the vessel successfully ran the gauntlet. But these were meagre victories for a city that needed near-constant supply. At the start of September, Qaragush managed to smuggle out a letter informing Saladin that in two weeks Acre would be entirely empty of food. The sultan was so alarmed that he kept the news secret for fear that it would break his army's morale. Three more grain-laden supply ships were due from Egypt, but bad winds delayed their progress. Baha al-Din described how, on 17 September, Saladin stood on the shore 'like a bereft mother . . . his heart troubled', watching as they finally sailed up the coast towards Acre, knowing full well that the city would fall if they failed to get through. After fierce fighting 'the ships came safely into harbour, to be met like rains after drought'.[33]

One saving grace throughout all these struggles was that the crusaders never succeeded in taking control of Acre's inner harbour. Had they done so, the garrison's position would have quickly become untenable. Late in the summer of 1190 the Franks made a concerted effort to seize the Tower of Flies, the fort built on a rocky outcrop in the bay of Acre that controlled the chain guarding the port's harbour. They fortified two or three ships, creating what amounted to elaborate floating siege towers, but their assault failed when these were burned down by Greek fire.

With the exception of this attack, the Franks never attempted a naval assault on Acre and, in reality, from their perspective the battle for the sea functioned as a platform and an addendum to their land-based siege. Access to naval support was utterly indispensable in that it continued to furnish the crusaders with reinforcements, provisions and military supplies, and the blockade of Acre certainly added an important element of attrition to their investment, but for most of 1190 their overall strategy was grounded in warfare on land.

The struggle on land

Here the fighting season began again in earnest in late April and early May 1190. With spring, Saladin recalled his troops from Syria and Mesopotamia. On 25 April he moved his camp back to the front line at Tell Kaisan with the support of his son al-Afdal. Over the next two months they were reinforced by detachments from the likes of Aleppo, Harran and Mosul. At the same time, of course, with the sea open the crusader camp was again flooded by fresh recruits, many of whom were early arrivals from the armies of the French and English kings. Chief among them was Henry II of Champagne, count of Troyes, nephew of both Richard I and Philip Augustus. Henry reached Acre in August in the company of his uncles, Count Theobald V of Blois and Stephen, count of Sancerre, along with some 10,000 fighting men, and immediately took over military command of the siege. A large contingent of English crusaders arrived in late September, headed by Archbishop Baldwin of Canterbury, the formidable Hubert Walter, bishop of Salisbury, and Hubert's uncle, Ranulf of Glanville, once one of King Henry II of England's closest advisers.[34]

In spite of the renewed influx of western crusaders, Saladin should have possessed the manpower to balance, perhaps even overwhelm, the Christian besiegers during the long fighting season of 1190. But one factor stayed his hand – the coming of the Germans. As early as autumn 1189 Saladin had received reports that Emperor Frederick Barbarossa was marching to the Holy Land at the head of a quarter of a million crusaders – tidings that, not surprisingly, 'greatly troubled the sultan and caused him anxiety'. The impending threat posed by the expected arrival of this horde meant that from April to September the sultan was never able to direct the full might of his military resources, nor focus his strategic thinking, upon the problem at Acre. Convinced that the emperor's vast host would sweep south through Syria and Lebanon like an unstoppable tide, Saladin set about preparing for a bitterly fought war on two fronts. Almost as soon as the sultan's troops arrived at Acre that spring he began sending them away to bolster the defences of the north. Inland cities were ordered to store their harvests in case of siege, while along the coast Saladin judged that the likes of Latakia and Beirut would have no chance of resisting Frederick, and thus ordered their walls to be razed to the ground to prevent them becoming Latin strongholds. These measures made complete strategic sense – indeed Saladin would have been mad to ignore Barbarossa's approach – but they also served to cripple Muslim efforts at Acre by forcing a massive redirection of resources. In this way, even before they set foot in the Levant, the Germans made a significant contribution to the Third Crusade.[35]

Weakened and distracted, Saladin had to adopt a largely reactive approach to the defence of Acre. He could hope to frustrate the Franks' attempt to seize the city, but any plans actually to make a concerted attempt to annihilate the besiegers were again sidelined. By the first days of May the sultan had re-established a front-line position, penning in the crusaders between his armies and Acre's walls. This allowed Saladin to mount almost instantaneous counter-attacks to any Latin assault on the city, forcing the crusaders to fight their own draining struggle on two fronts. Meanwhile, the sultan sought to maintain contact with Qaragush and his garrison, but with the city subject to a close land and sea blockade this was no simple matter. Carrier pigeons were one of the mainstays of the communication and intelligence system that spanned the far-flung Ayyubid Empire, but at Acre they seem to have played a limited role, perhaps being too easy a target for enemy archers. Here, Saladin relied instead upon a group of guileful and courageous messengers who would seek to swim into Acre's inner harbour under cover of darkness, carrying letters, money and even flasks of Greek fire sealed in otter-skin bags. This was perilous work. On one mission an experienced swimmer named Isa, who 'used to dive and emerge on the far side of the enemy's ships', disappeared, only to be washed up drowned in the harbour a few days later, his consignment of messages and gold still tied round his waist.[36]

For the greater part of 1190, Saladin faced an enemy driven by one core objective – the breaching of Acre's landward defences. Lacking a single universally acknowledged leader (with power passing between the likes of King Guy, James of Avesnes and Henry of Champagne), their attacks sometimes lacked resolve, but the threat they posed was severe nonetheless. The Franks adopted an assault-based siege strategy, looking to overcome the city's walls through a combination of bombardment, scaling and sapping. Having constructed a number of catapults through the winter, they now initiated a near-daily barrage of stone missiles. These machines seem to have been of fairly limited strength, incapable of propelling truly massive boulders, so the attacks were probably designed to harass and injure the Muslim garrison as much as to weaken Acre's walls. Of course, this was no one-sided affair. Within the city, Qaragush had his own array of heavy weapons with which he sought to destroy the crusaders' siege engines, often with great success. One was said to be particularly massive, capable of loosing stones that on impact would bury themselves a foot into the ground.

Acre's landward walls were encircled by a dry moat, designed to hamper any ground assault and prevent large-scale siege towers from being drawn up against its battlements. The crusaders made arduous attempts to fill sections of this ditch with rubble, often under the cover of aerial bombardment. The garrison did its best to hamper these efforts, showering the workers with arrows, but they were determined. One Frankish woman, mortally wounded as she carried forward stones, even requested that her body be thrown into the moat to act as infill. By early May 1190, to the Muslims' horror, a path to the foot of the walls had been opened.

Panic now started to spread. For weeks Qaragush and Saladin had watched a frenzy of construction within the crusaders' camp, as three massive siege engines gradually rose into the air. Built with wood specially brought from Europe to a height of some sixty-five feet, these wheeled three-storey behemoths were covered in vinegar-soaked hide, to dampen the effect of fire, and hung with rope netting to weaken the impact of catapult attack. One Muslim eyewitness wrote that, towering above the battlements of Acre, '[they] seemed like mountains'. Around 3 May, King Guy, James of Avesnes and Ludwig of Thuringia packed them with troops – crossbowmen and archers on the roof, spear and pikemen below – and began inching the machines towards the city. This dreadful spectacle appalled the Muslims. In Saladin's camp 'everyone totally despaired for the city and the spirits of the defend[ers] were broken', while within Acre 'Qaragush was out of his mind with fear', preparing to negotiate a surrender. A swimmer was hurriedly dispatched to warn the sultan that collapse was imminent and Saladin quickly launched a counter-attack. Simultaneously, the garrison began pelting the towers with flasks of Greek fire once they came into range, but none of this halted their inexorable advance.

The day was saved by a young unnamed metalworker from Damascus. Fascinated by the properties of Greek fire, he had developed a variation on its formula which promised to burn with even greater intensity. Qaragush was sceptical, but eventually agreed to try this new invention, and the metalworker 'concocted the ingredients he had gathered with some naphtha in copper vats, until the whole mixture was like a burning coal'. Earlier in the day, fruitless attempts to use standard Greek fire had prompted the Franks to dance about and make jokes atop their towers, but when a clay pot of this new formulation struck, their jeers were silenced. 'Hardly had it hit the target before it burst into flames and the whole became like a mountain of fire', observed one Muslim onlooker. The two remaining towers soon suffered a similar fate. Trapped crusaders on the upper levels died in the conflagration, while below those who could escaped to watch their great engines 'burn to cinders'. For now, at least, Acre was safe.[37]

In the months that followed, the Muslims' superior mastery of combustible weapon technology proved a decisive element. In August, when the Franks sought to intensify their bombardment, operating in shifts through day and night, building ever more powerful catapults, Qaragush and Abu'l Haija launched a lightning sortie, sending 'Greek fire specialists' to burn the enemy's machines, killing seventy Christian knights in the process. In September a massive stone-thrower, built under the orders of Henry of Champagne at the cost of 1,500 gold dinars, was similarly dispatched in a matter of minutes. Not surprisingly, the crusaders developed an intense hatred of Greek fire. One unfortunate Turkish emir thus paid a heavy price when wounded in a skirmish beside a Frankish siege tower. He had been carrying a container of Greek fire, hoping to destroy the engine, but now a Latin knight 'stretched him out on the ground, emptying the contents of the phial on his private parts, so that his genitals were burned'.[38]

Other, more insidious, battles raged that summer. The careful nurturing of morale within one's own army and the struggle to break the will of the enemy had long been common features of medieval siege warfare. And, although events at Acre do not seem to have been marked by repeated acts of deliberately callous brutality or barbarism on either side, Qaragush's garrison occasionally employed such tactics. Latin dead had already been hung from Acre's battlements in November 1189 in an attempt to enrage the crusaders. Now, in 1190, Muslim troops occasionally dragged crosses and images of the Christian faith to the parapet to subject them to public defilement. This might involve beatings with sticks, spitting and even urination, although one soldier who attempted the latter was reportedly shot in the groin by a Frankish crossbowman.

The recurrent issues of any protracted investment – starvation and disease – also cast their shadows over Acre in 1190. Hunger and discontent seem to have prompted poorer sections of the crusader host to launch an ill-disciplined and ultimately fruitless attack on Saladin's camp in search of food on 25 July, at the cost of at least 5,000 lives. With their corpses rotting in the summer heat and great swarms of flies descending, making life unbearable in both camps, disease inevitably spread across the plains of Acre.

Saladin once again sought to cleanse the battlefield by throwing the remains of the Christian dead into the river, sending a gruesome mixture of 'blood, bodies and grease' downstream towards the crusaders. The tactic worked. One Latin described how 'no small number of [crusaders] died soon after [they arrived] from the foul air, polluted with the stink of corpses, worn out by anxious nights spent on guard, and shattered by other hardships and needs'. The lethal combination of malnutrition and atrocious sanitary conditions poisoned the camp for the rest of the season, and the mortality rate rocketed. Losses among the poor were severe, but even nobles were not immune: Theobald of Blois 'did not survive more than three months', while his compatriot Stephen of Sancerre 'also came and died without protection'. Ranulf of Glanville lasted just three weeks. Acre was fast becoming the graveyard of Europe's aristocracy.[39]

The fate of the German crusade

Elsewhere in the Near East another death was to change the course of the crusade. In late March 1190 Emperor Frederick Barbarossa secured terms with the Byzantines and led the German crusade across the Hellespont to Asia Minor. The Germans forged a route south-east through Greek territory, crossing into Turkish Anatolia in late April. Internal power struggles within the Seljuq sultanate of Konya meant that Frederick's earlier attempts to negotiate safe passage through to Syria had a limited impact on the ground, and the crusaders soon encountered concerted Muslim resistance. Despite supply shortages, Barbarossa managed to maintain discipline among his men – Muslim sources claimed that he threatened to cut the throat of any crusader deemed to have contravened orders – and the German marching column continued to make headway. On 14 May a major Turkish assault was beaten back and Frederick moved on to attack Konya itself, occupying the lower town of the Seljuq capital and forcing the Turks into temporary submission.

With the crossing of Asia Minor almost completed, Barbarossa pushed south towards the coast and the Christian territory of Cilician Armenia. The German crusade had suffered substantial losses in terms of men and horses, but all in all Frederick had achieved a striking success, prevailing where the crusades of 1101 and 1147 had failed. Then, just as the worst trials seemed to be over, disaster struck. Approaching Sifilke on 10 June 1190, the emperor impatiently decided to ford the River Saleph ahead of his troops. His horse lost its footing mid-stream, throwing Frederick into the river – on a scorching-hot day the water proved shockingly cold, and unable to swim, the German emperor drowned. His body was dragged ashore, but nothing could be done. Western Europe's most powerful monarch, the mightiest ruler ever to take the cross, lay dead.

This sudden unheralded cataclysm stunned Latins and Muslims alike. One Frankish chronicler remarked that 'Christendom suffered much harm by [Frederick's] death', while in Iraq another contemporary joyfully proclaimed that 'God saved us from his evil'. The German crusaders were gripped by a crisis of leadership and morale. Barbarossa's younger son Frederick of Swabia tried to salvage the expedition. Assuming command, he had the late emperor's body wrapped and embalmed, and then he led the way into northern Syria. But en route 'disease and death fell upon them [leaving them] looking as though they had been exhumed from their graves'. Thousands died, while others deserted. At Antioch, some of Barbarossa's remains were buried in the Basilica of St Peter, beside the site of the Holy Lance's discovery; his bones were then boiled and collected in a bag in the hope that they might be laid to rest in Jerusalem (as it was, they were eventually interred in the Church of St Mary in Tyre). Frederick of Swabia limped down the Syrian coast with what remained of the German army, facing attacks from Ayyubid troops stationed in the north.[40]

It is not clear precisely when news of Barbarossa's death reached Saladin – according to Baha al-Din, he was informed of the event by a letter from Basil of Ani, head of the Armenian Christian Church, but no date was provided. The tidings certainly caused celebration among the Muslims. A crusader wrote that 'inside Acre . . . there was dancing and playing of drums', and recalled that members of the Ayyubid garrison gleefully climbed the battlements to shout 'many times, in a loud voice . . .: "Your emperor has drowned."' Nonetheless, the sultan was still dispatching troops to defend Syria as late as 14 July 1190 and the full strength of his armies did not reassemble at Acre until early autumn. Thus, even though Barbarossa's demise crippled the German crusade, Saladin still lost vital military resources that summer. Frederick of Swabia eventually reached Acre in early October 1190 in the company of perhaps 5,000 troops. Saladin seems to have expected that, in spite of all their losses, the Germans' arrival would reinvigorate the crusader siege, but in real terms it did little to advance the Frankish cause.[41]

STALEMATE

In one sense the fighting season of 1190 had been a success for Saladin. Acre had shrugged off every Latin assault, its garrison countering the artifice of the Franks' experimental military technology. The sultan had managed, albeit with some difficulty, to maintain channels of communication and resupply with the city, while deploying his own troops to harass and distract the besieging crusaders. After twelve months' investment, Acre still held.

Nevertheless, in the wider scheme of things, Saladin had failed. Forced to redeploy his martial resources to meet the perceived threat of the German crusade, he lacked the manpower with which to seize the initiative at Acre. With armies at full strength, that summer he might have risked a concerted frontal assault on the Frankish positions and driven the crusaders from Palestine. As it was, by the time his troops had regrouped at Acre in early October, Saladin seems to have decided that, for now at least, the opportunity for decisive intervention had passed. This, combined with the onset of a 'bilious fever', prompted him to move his army back to a distant winter encampment at Saffaram (about ten miles south-east of Acre) in mid-October, effectively bringing the fighting season to a close. With his confidence evidently shaken, Saladin ordered the demolition of Caesarea, Arsuf and Jaffa – the key ports south of Acre – and even mandated the dismantling of Tiberias' walls. In the months that followed, Saladin faced a constant struggle to maintain his forces in the field. Some, like the lords of Jazirat and Sinjar, repeatedly petitioned to return to their lands; others, like Keukburi, were dispatched to oversee the governance of the sultan's neglected Mesopotamian interests and were lost to the *jihad*.[42]

In pulling back from the front line, just as he had a year earlier, Saladin was relying upon the ravages of nature to weaken his enemy, waiting to see if the crusaders could survive a second cruel winter huddled outside Acre. Before long the change of season began to bite. As in 1189, autumn's end heralded the closing of long-distance sea routes and the effective isolation of the Frankish host. By November, the crusaders' supplies were already running short, forcing them to attempt a foraging expedition south towards Haifa which was beaten back after just two days.

Ordeals

In late November Saladin at last disbanded his army for winter, once again remaining in person with only a small force to watch over Acre as the 'sea became rough [and the rains] heavy and incessant'. From the Muslim perspective, the months that followed proved far harsher and more trying than the winter of 1189. The city's garrison was faltering, while Saladin and his men were exhausted and ill-tempered. With supply lines stretched, there were widespread shortages of food and weapons, and too few doctors available to deal with the frequent outbreaks of illness. 'Islam asks aid from you', the sultan wrote in an imploring letter to the caliph, 'as a drowning man cries for help.' And yet, these problems were but a pale reflection of the torments faced by the crusaders. One Muslim eyewitness acknowledged this, writing that because 'the plain [of Acre] became very unhealthy' and 'the sea was closed to them', there 'was great mortality amongst the enemy' with 100 to 200 men perishing daily.

The Latins' suffering may have been obvious to onlookers, but the view from inside the Christian camp was even more anguished. Cut off from the outside world, the crusaders' stores of food simply ran out. By late December people had turned to skinning 'fine horses', eating their flesh and guts with gusto. As the famine intensified, one crusader wrote that there were 'those who had lost their sense of shame through their hunger [who] fed in sight of everyone on abominable food which they happened to find, no matter how filthy, things which should not be spoken of. Their dire mouths devoured what humans are not permitted to eat as if it were delicious.' This may be an indication that there were outbreaks of cannibalism.

Weakened by hunger, the Franks fell prey to illnesses such as scurvy and trench mouth:

A disease ran through the army . . . the result of rains that poured down such as have never been before, so that the whole army was half-drowned. Everyone coughed and sounded hoarse; their legs and faces swelled up. On one day there were 1,000 [men on] biers; they had such swelling in the faces that the teeth fell from their mouths.

The resultant mortality was on a scale not seen since the First Crusaders' siege of Antioch. Thousands died, among them such potentates as Archbishop Baldwin of Canterbury, Theobald of Blois and even Frederick of Swabia. These dark days of winter witnessed a collapse in Christian morale. One crusader commented 'there is no rage like that born of starvation', observing that, in the midst of this horror, anger and despair caused a loss of faith and desertion. 'Many of our people went to the Turks and turned renegade', he wrote; 'they denied [Christ], the Cross and baptism – everything.' Receiving these apostates, Saladin must have hoped that the siege of Acre would soon falter.

But still the crusaders clung on. Some resorted to grazing on grass and herbs 'like beasts', others turned to eating unfamiliar 'carob-beans' indigenous to the area, which they found 'sweet to eat'. Hubert Walter, bishop of Salisbury, played a major role in restoring some semblance of order to the chaos-stricken camp, organising charitable collections from the rich so that food could be distributed to the poor. When scores of hungry crusaders sinned by eating what little meat they could find during Lent, Hubert enforced a penance upon them – three blows on their backs with a stick, administered by the bishop himself, 'but not heavy blows', as he 'chastised like a father'. Finally, around late February or early March, the first small Christian supply ship bearing grain reached the camp to be greeted with great celebration, and with spring the crisis of supply ended. Having passed through a tempest of death and misery, the Franks were still thronged outside Acre.[43]

For Islam, the crusaders' tenacity spelled disaster. As he had a year earlier, Saladin sought to use the winter season to strengthen Acre, but this time his efforts met with less success. Al-Adil was sent to organise a supply depot at Haifa from which resources could be ferried from Egypt up the coast to the garrison. On 31 December 1190 seven fully laden transport ships reached Acre's harbour only to be dashed against the rocks and sunk by the treacherous seas. Food, weapons and money that could have sustained the city for months were lost. Then on 5 January 1191 an intense rainstorm caused a section of Acre's outer wall to collapse, suddenly exposing the city to attack. Racked by starvation and illness, the crusaders were in no position to capitalise on this opportunity and Saladin's men hurriedly filled the breach, but the omens for Islam were bleak. With a growing sense of apprehension, the sultan sought to reorganise Acre's defences. Abu'l Haija the Fat was relieved of his military command of the port on 13 February, to be substituted by al-Mashtub, although Qaragush was left in his post as governor. The exhausted troops of the garrison were also replaced, but Saladin's secretary Imad al-Din later criticised this measure, noting that a force of 20,000 men and sixty emirs was exchanged for just twenty emirs and far fewer troops because Saladin struggled to find volunteers willing to man the city.

The sultan's frustration is apparent in a letter sent to the caliph that same month, in which he warned that the pope might be coming to lead the crusaders and bemoaned the fact that, when Muslim troops arrived at Acre from the far corners of the Near East, their commanders' first question was when they could leave. At the same time, the manifold pressures of maintaining his enormous realm while locked in the struggle at Acre were beginning to tell. In March, Saladin begrudgingly assented to Taqi al-Din's repeated demands to be made ruler of the north-eastern cities of Harran and Edessa. While the sultan could ill afford to lose his nephew from the *jihad*, he needed to safeguard his control over the Upper Euphrates or risk the unravelling of his empire.[44]

By April 1191 Saladin's prospects, and those of Acre, seemed almost hopeless. For a year and a half the sultan had been immobilised by the crusaders' siege of the city, unable to consolidate fully his victories of 1187, cowed into a strategy of reactive defence. He had sought to turn back the vengeful tide that had swept from western Europe onto the shores of Palestine, and he had failed. Frederick Barbarossa's sudden death in June 1190 had been extraordinarily providential, but at Acre itself Saladin had been less fortunate, facing a seemingly indomitable Frankish enemy. Acre held, but so too did the Latin siege. Battered, but not broken, the crusaders had achieved a staggering feat of arms – the maintenance of a siege deep in enemy territory while beset by an opposing field army.

In one important regard, Saladin's handling of the titanic struggle outside Acre was laudable. For the first time in the war for the Holy Land, he had refused to back away from a prolonged and entrenched military confrontation, showing dogged determination through one and a half years and two harsh winters. Yet, in spite of all the obstacles he faced, the sultan's inability to crush the Christians between 1189 and 1191 must be harshly criticised. For he knew that all the Frankish might that had gathered before Acre, all the force of arms launched against its walls, were but tremors before the earthquake that would strike with the coming of the kings of England and France. And still Saladin lacked the will and vision to act. Now, with the gateway to the Holy Land ajar, Islam would have to face the full strength of Latin Christendom's crusading wrath.

15

THE COMING OF KINGS

Sailing down the coast of Palestine on the morning of Saturday 8 June 1191, King Richard I of England gained his first glimpse of the terrible spectacle that was the siege of Acre. The towers and ramparts of the city itself came into view, then the swarmed ranks of tens of thousands of crusaders, drawn 'from every Christian nation under heaven', 'the flower of the world' encircling its prey. Finally, 'he saw the slopes and the mountains, the valleys and the plains, covered with Turks and tents and men who had it in their hearts to harm Christianity', with Saladin in their midst. Three and a half long years after taking the cross, Richard had at last reached the Holy Land. The Franks greeted his appearance with rapturous celebration. One member of his army wrote of the festivities that followed that evening:

> Great was the joy, clear was the night. I do not believe that any mother's son ever saw or told of such elation as the army expressed over the king's presence. Bells and trumpets all sounded. Fine songs and ballads were sung. All were full of hope. So many lights and candles [were lit] that it seemed to the Turks in the opposing army that the whole valley was ablaze.

Within Saladin's camp, one of the sultan's advisers recorded that 'the accursed king of England came [with] great pomp, [at the head of] twenty-five galleys full of men, weapons and stores . . . he was wise and experienced and his coming had a dread and frightening impact on the hearts of the Muslims'. The Lionheart had arrived.[45]

JOURNEYING TO THE HOLY LAND

Richard had scored a notable victory even before he reached the Near East. The crusader armies of France and England sailed from Sicily in spring 1191. Philip II Augustus left Messina on 20 March and arrived in the Levant one month later. Richard I, meanwhile, headed for Crete on 10 April with a fleet that had grown to include more than 200 vessels. But after three days a gale blew around twenty-five of these ships off course to Cyprus – an island ruled since 1184 by the Byzantine Isaac Comnenus as an independent Greek territory. Among them was the craft carrying the Lionheart's sister Joanne and his fiancée Berengaria. Three ships were wrecked off the island and those who made landfall were badly treated by the local population. Some attempt was also made to take the two Latin princesses captive as they waited at anchor near Limassol, on the south coast.

After arriving on Rhodes around 22 April King Richard learned of these events and decided to launch an immediate naval assault on Cyprus, despite its status as a Christian polity and his position as a crusader. The Lionheart made a daring beach landing at Limassol on 5 May and readily beat back Isaac's troops, forcing the Greek to retreat to Famagusta on the eastern coast. During the lull in hostilities that followed, Richard and Berengaria were married in the chapel of St George in Limassol on 12 May.

Isaac then made half-hearted overtures towards peace, but Richard eventually sailed on to Famagusta, defeated the Greeks in battle for a second time and proceeded to subdue the entire island with remarkable efficiency. Isaac surrendered on 1 June and was promptly clapped in specially commissioned silver shackles (the Lionheart having promised not to place him in irons).

Richard thus began his crusading campaign with a major victory, albeit one scored against a fellow Christian territory. Cyprus' conquest provided the Angevin army with a massive influx of wealth and resources. The king levied a fifty per cent tax on the Cypriot populace and then, a few weeks after his departure, sold the island to the Templars for 100,000 gold bezants (although he only ever received the initial down payment of 40,000). The island also served as a critical staging post throughout the crusade. In the longer term, the Latin occupation of Cyprus would prove to have a profound bearing upon the future history of the crusades and the crusader states.

In the midst of the Cyprus campaign, Richard received an embassy from Guy of Lusignan. The Lionheart, as count of Poitou, was the feudal overlord of the Lusignan dynasty and Guy now sought to capitalise upon this bond, begging Richard to lend him support in the power struggle with Conrad of Montferrat. News also began to arrive from Palestine, intimating that Philip Augustus was making real progress at Acre. According to one crusader, 'when the [Angevin] king heard this, he gave a great and heartfelt sigh, [and said,] "God forbid that Acre should be won in my absence."' Stirred to action, the Lionheart left Cyprus on 5 June 1191 and, upon making landfall in Syria, had Isaac Comnenus interned in the Hospitaller castle of Marqab. Richard headed south, but was refused entry at Tyre by Conrad of Montferrat's garrison and so sailed on to reach Acre on 8 June.[46]

THE IMPACT OF THE KINGS

Richard the Lionheart's arrival, alongside that of Philip Augustus, transformed the Latins' prospects. The advent of these two monarchs revitalised the crusade, bringing new vigour and determination to the investment of Acre, supplying an empowering injection of resources – financial, human and material – that promised to bring this fiercely contested siege to a victorious end.

The arrival of Philip Augustus

In one sense, the rumours that Richard heard on Cyprus were right: King Philip had made significant progress at Acre since his arrival on 20 April 1191. While noting that he reached the city with a modest fleet of just six ships, Baha al-Din conceded that the French monarch was 'a great man and respected leader, one of their great kings to whom all present in the army would be obedient'. He came with much of the remaining might of the French nobility; men like the veteran crusader Count Philip of Flanders (who survived only to 1 June) and the proud and powerful Count Hugh of Burgundy. Although contemporary writers partisan to the Lionheart tended to downplay the French king's achievements at Acre, in reality Philip immediately made his presence felt, working to intensify the military pressure on Acre's garrison while consolidating the Frankish position.

Having 'ordered his crossbowmen and archers to shoot continuously so that no one could show a finger above the walls of the city', the king oversaw the erection of seven massive stone-throwing machines and the strengthening of the palisade surrounding the crusaders' trenches. On 30 May, with his catapults ready for action, Philip initiated a determined bombardment campaign of such intensity that 'stones rained on [Acre] night and day', forcing Saladin to move his troops back to the front line. Reaching Tell al-Ayyadiya by 5 June, the sultan launched daily attacks on the Latin trenches, hoping to interrupt their aerial offensive, but nothing seems to have stilled the French siege engines. At the same time, the crusaders were preparing for a frontal ground assault, making renewed attempts to fill sections of Acre's dry moat so that they could gain access to the walls. With the Franks throwing dead horses and even human remains into the ditch, the Muslim garrison was left with the desperate task of trying to empty the channel faster than the Latins could fill it. One Muslim witness described how the defenders were split into three groups: one 'going down to the moat and cutting up corpses and horses to make them easy to carry', another transporting this grisly burden to the sea and a third defending against Christian attack. It was said that 'no stout-hearted man could endure' such appalling work, 'yet they were enduring it', for now at least. One pro-French near-contemporary later observed that, with the momentum growing towards a Frankish assault, King Philip 'could easily have taken the city had he wished', but elected to wait for Richard's arrival so that they could share in the victory. This may have been an exaggeration, and it is doubtful that Philip truly would have shown such forbearance, but it is all too easy, amidst the glare of the Lionheart's legend, to forget that it was the Capetian and not the Angevin monarch who first breathed new, reinvigorating life into the Third Crusade.[47]

The Lionheart at Acre

Even so, Richard's grand, drama-laden landfall at Acre on 8 June did serve to tip the balance of military power in the Latins' favour. Comparing the two Christian monarchs, a Muslim eyewitness observed: '[The English king] had much experience of fighting and was intrepid in battle, and yet he was in their eyes below the king of France in royal status, although being richer and more renowned for martial skill and courage.' The Lionheart arrived in the Near East with many of England's and Normandy's most powerful nobles – the likes of Robert IV, earl of Leicester, and Roger of Tosny – men who held major estates on both sides of the Channel. He was also accompanied by an inner circle of *familiares*, or household knights – fiercely loyal warriors like Andrew of Chauvigny.[48]

Richard came to the Holy Land with more men, far deeper financial reserves and a much larger navy than King Philip. Indeed, at the head of the twenty-five-ship-strong advance guard of his fleet, the English monarch managed to score his first military success against Saladin even before setting foot on the Levantine mainland. Sailing south from Tyre, en route to Acre, Richard came across a huge Muslim supply ship in the region of Sidon. This vessel had set out from Ayyubid-held Beirut, packed with seven emirs, 700 elite troops, food, weapons and many phials of Greek fire, as well as 200 'very deadly snakes' which '[the Muslims] intended to let loose among the [Christian] army'. With a drop in the wind Richard managed to catch up to this craft and, seeing through its Muslim crew's attempt to pass themselves off as Frenchmen, launched an attack. Facing fierce resistance, unable to board and capture the ship intact, Richard settled for ramming and sinking it to ensure that its precious cargo never reached the enemy. To capitalise fully upon the demoralising effect of this defeat, a single prisoner was later mutilated and sent into Acre bearing news of the disaster.

Upon reaching the siege, Richard set up his camp to the north of the city, Philip having taken up a position to the east. The Lionheart immediately set about assessing 'how the city could be seized in the shortest time, what means, what cunning, what siege engines must be used'. But just as he was readying himself for war, barely a week after having set foot in the Holy Land, the king was unmanned by illness. In stark counterpoint to his naval triumph and the majesty of his arrival, Richard suddenly found himself confined to his tent for days by a scurvy-like affliction called *arnaldia* by contemporaries; soon his teeth and fingernails began to loosen and patches of his hair fell out. The humiliation must have been hard to bear, not least because sickness could so easily be interpreted as a sign of divine ill favour. In Saladin's camp the king's misery was seen as a blessing, because it 'discouraged [the Franks] from making their attacks'. Yet even in a state of infirmity, Richard proved himself capable of advancing the crusaders' cause.[49]

Showing a subtlety that might seem to belie his reputation for raw bellicosity, the English monarch immediately set about opening diplomatic channels of communication with Saladin. Experience in the West had taught the Lionheart that in the medieval world victory came to those who could marry the disciplines of politics and warfare. He showed absolutely no compunction in employing negotiation as a weapon in the struggle with the supposed 'infidel', although for now at least these contacts were kept secret from the crusader host. Richard began, even before the onset of his illness, by seeking a personal meeting with Saladin. An envoy was dispatched to request a parley, but the sultan responded with a courteous but firm rejection: 'Kings do not meet unless an agreement has been reached', he apparently replied; 'it is not good for them to fight after meeting and eating together.'

Richard soon came back with a proposal for an exchange of gifts and, on 1 July, released a North African 'whom they had captured a long time ago' as a sign of goodwill. A little later, Saladin received a visit from three Angevin envoys requesting 'fruit and ice' for their king. Richard seems to have delighted in asking for such delicacies, possibly as part of a mischievous diplomatic game, perhaps to gauge how far he could push the boundaries of hospitality, but also because he simply seems to have developed a taste for the finer things of the Orient, most notably peaches and pears. Saladin, himself an acute practitioner of the diplomatic arts, had the three Franks taken on a tour of his army's marketplace so that they might be dazzled by its spectacular array of shops, baths and supplies. Baha al-Din, who as part of Saladin's inner circle was privy to these early exchanges, soberly observed that such embassies were really spying missions, designed to gauge the level of Muslim morale, and that they were accepted so as to gain the same intelligence from the enemy. Richard was not alone in seeking to negotiate with Islam at Acre. Philip Augustus held his own private talks with the commanders of the city's garrison, although they similarly achieved little of substance. But the very fact that the two kings were competing in the field of diplomacy suggested that the ingrained rivalry that had so delayed their arrival in the Holy Land was still simmering.[50]

Rivalry or unity?

The initial signs upon Richard's arrival at Acre had suggested that unity of purpose might overcome discord. Philip went in person to greet the Lionheart as he disembarked, with the two monarchs 'showing each other every respect and deference'. The French king even held in check his anger at Richard's marriage to Berengaria, the final seal on his own sister's rejection. But cracks in the veneer of amity soon started to appear. Richard went out of his way to prove that his wealth exceeded that of his French counterpart, offering four gold bezants per month to 'any knight, of any land, who wished to take his pay' after Philip had tendered three. This may have smacked of pure, arrogant one-upmanship, but it had the very practical effect of further swelling the ranks of the Lionheart's army, and thus ensuring that he held the balance of military power among the crusaders.[51]

The thorny issue of the kingdom of Jerusalem's political future also served to perpetuate Angevin–Capetian rivalry. Ever since his disastrous defeat and capture at Hattin in 1187, Guy of Lusignan's right to the throne of Jerusalem had been open to challenge. Conrad, marquis of Montferrat, stalwart defender of Tyre, saviour of the Latin East, appeared to many to be the natural choice for the throne. When Conrad refused Guy access to Tyre, after the king's release from captivity, the dispute erupted into an open feud. The crisis then deepened in the early autumn of 1190 when Queen Sibylla (Baldwin IV's sister) and her two infant daughters succumbed to illness while staying in the crusader camp outside Acre. Their deaths were a dire blow to Guy's political security, removing as they did his only blood link to the throne of Jerusalem. With the legality of Guy's right to the crown now open to question, much of the surviving nobility of the Latin kingdom decided to back Conrad.

In November 1190 a rather unsavoury political solution was engineered. The bloodline of the Jerusalemite throne now devolved upon Sibylla's beautiful younger sister, Isabella, so a coalition of Guy's enemies arranged for her to be married to Conrad. There were a few details to be ironed out before this union could be finalised. Rumour had it that at least one of Conrad's two previous wives was still alive somewhere in the West. Worse still, Isabella already had a husband – Humphrey of Toron. Indeed, the couple were camped with the crusader army outside Acre. Abducted from her tent, browbeaten by her mother Maria Comnena into accepting a dubious annulment, Isabella finally acquiesced and was wed to Conrad. Decades later a papal commission would condemn their marriage as both bigamous and incestuous (because Isabella's sister had once been married to Conrad's brother) but for now the need for strong military leadership overruled the niceties of law. Conrad stopped short of having himself and Isabella crowned in Guy's stead, retiring instead to Tyre, leaving the 'king's' authority in tatters.

By the summer of 1191 the whole affair was in desperate need of resolution. Not surprisingly, Richard and Philip ended up backing different camps. As count of Poitou, the Lionheart was the overlord of the Lusignan family, so it was expected that Richard would lend his support to Guy, a fact confirmed when the latter came to Cyprus in May, supplicating himself before the king even before he arrived at Acre. Philip, meanwhile, promoted the interests of his relative Conrad, who had now returned to the siege. Outside Acre, on 7 May 1191, the French king acted as co-signatory to a charter – buying the support of the Venetians in return for trading privileges – in which Conrad boldly styled himself as 'king elect'. With the Genoese already allied to the French and the Pisans bought out by Richard, a complex web of overlapping factions and interrelated disputes looked set to rip the Third Crusade apart. And yet, the flames of open conflict never really took hold. With Richard's support, Geoffrey of Lusignan accused Conrad of treason in late June, but the marquis chose flight to Tyre over possible arrest and the quarrel was, for the moment, put to one side.[52]

In fact, despite the manifest tension and ill will between Richard and Philip, they managed to muster enough begrudging cooperation to ensure that progress was made on the military front. Throughout June and early July 1191 Angevin and Capetian troops coordinated and rotated their attacks – one force holding the trenches against Saladin while the other assaulted the city. Towards the end of June Philip became impatient with the delay caused by Richard's continued illness and decided to mount his own frontal assault on Acre, an attack that enjoyed little success. But even on this occasion, Richard's allies helped to defend the crusader camp, with Geoffrey of Lusignan alone killing ten Muslims with his battleaxe.

The crusaders' siege strategy

With some 25,000 crusaders deployed around Acre by early summer 1191, Richard and Philip implemented a relatively coherent and coordinated assault-based siege strategy. Teams of sappers were deployed to dig mines beneath the city's walls in the hope of collapsing its battlements, and intermittent attempts were also made to storm Acre's walls through frontal assault. Through June, however, the battle plan of both monarchs centred upon the use of incessant aerial bombardment to shatter both Acre's physical defences and its garrison's psychological resistance. Together the Frankish kings circled the city with a mighty array of stone-throwing catapults. So dreadful a destructive force had never before been witnessed on the field of crusading conflict and the Acre campaign marked something of a shift in the practice of siege warfare.

Of course, bombardment had been a feature of siegecraft in these holy wars from the very start, with both attackers and defenders using various types of stone-throwing engines. Till now, though, the relative weakness of these machines had limited the size and weight of projectiles that could be launched and their effective range. Besiegers might thus use catapult fire to injure and demoralise an enemy garrison, but usually there was little hope that bombardment alone could demolish the walls or towers of a well-fortified target.

Richard I, and perhaps also Philip Augustus, seem to have brought more advanced forms of catapult technology to bear during the siege of Acre, employing machines capable of projecting larger missiles further and with greater accuracy. The increased tempo of aerial attack established by Philip was further intensified after Richard's arrival, with more and more sections of Acre coming under near-continuous bombardment. By now the crusaders had christened the most powerful French catapult 'Mal Voisine', or 'Bad Neighbour', while nicknaming the Muslim stone-thrower that targeted it for counter-bombardment 'Mal Cousine', or 'Bad Relation'. Time and again Acre's garrison managed to damage 'Bad Neighbour', but Philip simply had it rebuilt, focusing its fire on the Cursed Tower in the city's north-eastern corner. The Franks paid for another engine, which they called 'God's own catapult', out of a communal fund – 'a priest, a man of great probity, always stood next to it', noted one contemporary, 'preaching and collecting money for its continual repair and for hiring people to gather stones for its ammunition'.

Among the stone-throwers operated by Richard's men were two newly built machines 'made with remarkable workmanship and materials' that could propel the massive catapult stones that the king had brought from Messina. It was rumoured among the Franks that just one of these missiles killed twelve of Acre's men and was later sent for inspection to Saladin, but this sounds like morale-boosting camp gossip and was not confirmed by Muslim witnesses. Another of the Lionheart's machines possessed such power that it could throw a missile into the heart of the city to reach Butchers' Row, a street which seems to have run clear down to the harbour.[53]

By late June the force of this intense crusader offensive was starting to tell. In Saladin's camp one observer noted that the Franks' 'constant battering of the city walls' meant that the battlements had begun to 'shake' and could be seen by the crusaders to be 'tottering'. 'The defenders in the city', he wrote, 'had become very weak and the noose around them very tight.' Troop shortages inside Acre meant that soldiers could not be rotated on and off duty on a regular basis, and most were going without sleep for days and nights. Messages began to arrive in the sultan's camp warning that the garrison, exhausted by the constant fighting, was faltering.

Saladin did what he could to relieve the pressure, launching regular counter-attacks on the Latin trenches. Throughout late spring and early summer the ranks of his army swelled as troops from around the empire returned to Acre. Indeed, at the end of June sizeable armies arrived from Mesopotamia and Egypt. But by then the crusaders were entrenched too firmly in their positions. From time to time Muslim raiding parties succeeded in breaking into the enemy camp – on one occasion they made a point of stealing the Franks' cooking pots – but they were always beaten back. At night, Saladin tried using more furtive tactics. Stealthy thieves were tasked with slipping past the Latin pickets, where, once among the tents, they would select a victim. Baha al-Din described how 'they seized men with ease by coming to them as they were sleeping, putting a knife to their throat, then waking them and saying through gestures, "If you speak, we shall cut your throat"', leading them away to captivity and interrogation. But, ultimately, these rather desperate attempts to halt the Christian offensive and erode crusader morale failed. By the start of July it was clear that Acre was on the verge of collapse. Surveying the city's defences from horseback, Saladin was said by one Muslim eyewitness to have been horrified: 'Tears flowed from his eyes . . . as he looked towards Acre and saw the torment she was in.' Badly shaken, 'that day he consumed no food at all [but] merely drank some cups of a drink that his doctor advised him to take. [He was] overcome by tiredness, dejection and grief.'[54]

THE FATE OF ACRE

Around 2 July 1191 the crusaders adjusted their strategy. Having battered Acre to the brink of submission, they now sought to exploit the damage done to the city's defences. The Cursed Tower had been weakened and a ten-metre length of nearby wall was beginning to crumble; to the north, a second major tower was close to collapse. With Latin sappers intensifying their efforts to undermine these targets, above ground the aerial barrage slackened and attention turned instead to the prosecution of a frontal assault, as the Franks set out 'with great seriousness of purpose' to break into Acre.

After the first day of these attacks Saladin received an urgent message from Qaragush and al-Mashtub stating that 'tomorrow, if you do not do something for us, we will seek terms and surrender the city'. An eyewitness in the Muslim camp reported that 'the sultan was devastated'. Appalled by this impending disaster, he ordered al-Adil to lead another frantic attack on the Christian camp on 3 July, but 'the Frankish infantry stood behind their defences like a solid wall with their weapons, their crossbows, bolts and arrows'. At the same time, near the Cursed Tower, French sappers completed a tunnel. Once set alight, this wood-packed mine caved in, bringing down much of the parapet above it. Scores of Franks raced towards the ruined barrier with scaling ladders, while the Muslim garrison mounted the rubble, girding themselves for hand-to-hand combat.

The first Latin up a ladder was Aubery Clements, marshal of France, one of Philip's leading knights. It was said later among the Christians' forces that, before climbing the breach, Aubery had called out defiantly: 'Either I shall die today, or God willing, I will enter Acre.' Upon reaching the top, Aubery's ladder collapsed beneath the weight of crusaders clamouring to follow him and the Frankish assault faltered. Suddenly isolated, Aubery was reported to have fought on alone with 'exceptional valour', leaving his stricken compatriots to watch from below as 'the Turks surrounded and crushed him, stabbing him to death'. That at least was the crusaders' version of events. Muslim witnesses testified that Aubery made a pathetic attempt to plead for his life, offering to arrange the withdrawal of the entire crusade, before being butchered by a zealous Kurd. The Latin attack may have foundered, but it had been a close-run affair, and the parlous state of Acre's defences sent a ripple of fear and panic through the city. That night three emirs fled the city in small boats under cover of night; one of them made the mistake of seeking refuge in Saladin's camp and was promptly thrown in irons. But in reality their actions merely reflected a truth that was now obvious to all: Acre was about to fall.[55]

The definitive breach came at the section of the northern defences

A late medieval depiction of Saladin, founder of the Ayyubid dynasty and champion of Islam.

The rocky outcrop in Galilee known as the Horns of Hattin, where Saladin confronted the Latins on 4 July 1187.

The nineteenth-century French artist Gustave Doré imagines the moment when the Muslims enveloped their quarry at Hattin.

The city of Acre – the remains of the Tower of Flies can be seen towards the bottom of this aerial photograph.

The effigy of Richard the Lionheart, king of England (1189–99). During the Third Crusade Richard confronted Saladin's forces, but proved unable to reconquer Jerusalem.

Crusader Castles

Above: The magnificent Hospitaller castle of Krak des Chevaliers.

Right: The defences of the Syrian 'crusader' fortress of Saone were bolstered by a deep trench, hewn through solid rock, with a single pillar left standing to support a bridge.

Below: The desert castle of Kerak helped to defend Jerusalem and to control passage through Transjordan.

Pope Innocent III – an ardent and enthusiastic advocate of the crusading cause.

Left: Emperor Frederick II of Germany, the most powerful secular ruler in Europe, cultivated an interest in learning and courtly pursuits like falconry.

Below: The Fifth Crusaders attacking Damietta used Oliver of Paderborn's floating siege tower to capture the Tower of the Chain.

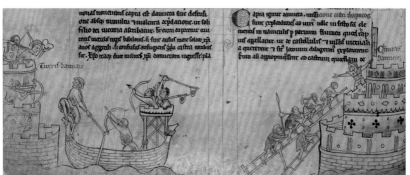

King Louis IX of France, clad in royal blue and golden fleur-de-lys, leading his troops at the Battle of Mansourah.

Mamluk warriors – Islam's military elite in the thirteenth century – in training.

The lion emblem from the Tower of Baybars in Cairo – an image used to mark the sultan's public works across the Near East. Baybars defeated the Mongols and unleashed a series of scouring attacks on the crusader states.

Acre, the thirteenth-century capital of Frankish Palestine, fell to the Mamluks in 1291. The titanic battle for the city was recalled in this nineteenth-century painting from the Salles des Croisades, Versailles.

The Longer Shadow

The monumental statue of Saladin erected by Syria's President Hafez Asad in 1992 outside the citadel of Damascus.

THE LAST CRUSADE.

Cœur-de-Lion (looking down on the Holy City). "MY DREAM COMES TRUE!"

The satirical periodical *Punch* sought to evoke echoes of the crusading past after General Allenby entered Jerusalem in 1917.

George W. Bush's decision to describe the 'War on Terror' as a 'crusade' after 9/11 played into the hands of Islamic extremists like Osama bin Laden.

targeted by Richard I. The ailing king, still too weak to walk, had taken to being carried to the front line on a regal stretcher, covered 'in a great silken quilt'. Shooting from behind the protection of a siege screen, he picked off hapless Muslim troopers with his crossbow, among them one warrior who had ill-advisedly elected to don Aubery Clements' armour. On 5 July his sappers torched another mine, toppling the northern tower and causing the partial disintegration of the adjoining walls. Just as at the Cursed Tower, the crusaders were now presented with a rubble-strewn fissure, through which it would be difficult to mount an overwhelming assault. Richard's response demonstrated both his ingenuity and his appreciation of the base realities of war. Knowing, as one contemporary dryly observed, that 'everyone is attracted by the smell of money', the king offered two gold coins to anyone who could carry off a stone from the damaged wall. This was near-suicidal work: arrows and crossbow bolts had to be dodged, the Muslims' furious hand-to-hand defence of the breach confronted. Yet many volunteered, particularly once the Lionheart raised the reward to three, and then four, gold coins. Despite the garrison's best efforts, over the next five days Richard's ploy bore fruit: by 11 July a substantial gap in the walls had been opened, albeit at great human and financial cost. Elsewhere, the crusaders' catapults were again put into action, ratcheting up the pressure to such an extent that, in despair, some Muslims chose to jump from the walls to their deaths.[56]

Negotiation

With defeat now seemingly imminent and all but inevitable, the commanders of Acre's garrison began exploring the option of surrender, even as intense fighting continued. The exact details and chronology of the city's capitulation are confused. It is possible that al-Mashtub and Qaragush opened channels of negotiation as early as 4 July and it thus would be wrong to give Richard more credit than Philip for finally bringing the siege to a successful conclusion. It was the combined might of the Angevin and Capetian armies that ultimately pummelled Acre into submission. What is clear is that the garrison had reached the limits of its physical and psychological endurance. One crusader eyewitness summarised the Muslims' predicament:

They were afraid of the miracle that they now beheld, how the whole world was coming [to] annihilate them; they saw their walls broken down, pierced and destroyed; they saw their people injured, killed and cut into pieces. [There] remained within the city 6,000 . . . but they were not sufficient.

A Muslim in Saladin's camp meanwhile observed, with stark clarity, that Acre's garrison 'looked death in the face' that July. Fearing that they would be butchered to a man once the city was stormed, the Muslims chose submission and life. Around 6 July Richard and Philip gave permission for Muslim envoys to leave the city under a banner of safe conduct, so that they might discuss terms of surrender with Saladin, but no deal was agreed. The sultan was still nursing hopes that total defeat might be averted. A plan was hatched to break the garrison out of the city during the night, but the scheme was betrayed to the Christians by a renegade *mamluk* who defected from the Ayyubid army. Forewarned of the attack, the crusaders put extra guards on duty and, although Saladin's troops spent the entire night under arms, no break in the Frankish lines could be found. At the same time, further Syrian reinforcements were arriving in the Muslim camp, exciting thoughts of a last-ditch counter-attack.

But in the crusader trenches Richard and Philip knew they had the upper hand. In the days that followed they adopted an iron-hard bargaining position, blankly refusing any offer that fell short of their ambitious demands. The precise nature of Saladin's involvement in these negotiations is unclear. Muslim eyewitnesses took pains to distance him from the entire process, striving to maintain his aura of invincibility. It was even said that, upon receiving a draft of the final terms, the sultan 'expressed his great disapproval', but that his planned condemnation of any surrender was wrecked by Acre's precipitous capitulation. Yet Christian contemporaries testified that Saladin 'agreed to the surrender of the town when it could no longer be defended', empowering its commanders to 'make the best peace terms that they could'. It is certainly unlikely that the crusader kings would have pursued peace talks without firm assurances that the sultan would honour a finalised settlement.[57]

Surrender

In any event, on 12 July 1191 a deal was struck that concluded the siege of Acre. The city and all its contents were to be surrendered to the Franks, the lives of the Muslims within spared. The captive garrison would then be held hostage as guarantors against the fulfilment of further punitive terms: the payment of 200,000 gold dinars; the return of the relic of the True Cross captured at Hattin; and the release of some 1,500 Frankish prisoners 'of common, unremarkable background', as well as 100 to 200 named captives of rank. Concessions of such magnitude signalled a categorical victory for Latin Christendom.

After close to two years of embittered struggle, the battle for Acre ended not in a feral, blood-stained sack, but in sudden peace. With the truce agreed, a public crier was sent out among the crusader armies to announce an immediate end to hostilities, ordering that 'no one should venture to do or say anything to insult or provoke any of the Turks; nor should they fire any more missiles at the walls or at any Turks they might happen to see on the ramparts'. A strange calm descended on the scene, as 'the Christians watched with very curious eyes as those Turkish people wandered around on the top of the walls that day'. The city gates were at last thrown open and the garrison marched out to make their submission. Witnessing this spectacle, many crusaders were taken aback: the faceless enemy of recent months was revealed, not as a savage rabble, but as 'men of admirable prowess [and] exceptional valour ... unaltered by adversity, their expressions resolute'. Some Franks showed less equanimity, bemoaning the desecration of Acre's 'broken and defaced' churches by this 'accursed race', but by and large the surrender passed without violent incident.[58]

Like their Muslim enemies, the soldiers of the Third Crusade had shown enormous resilience at Acre, tenaciously maintaining their siege through blistering heat and biting cold, facing hunger, disease and incessant battle. Thousands, perhaps even tens of thousands, perished in this endeavour – no accurate estimate of the overall number of dead is possible. Among the aristocracy, who are more readily traced, the losses were unprecedented: a patriarch, six archbishops and twelve bishops; some forty counts and 500 great nobles. The kings of England and France had not begun this struggle, but a good measure of the credit for bringing about its triumphant resolution was theirs. Before their arrival, the combatants had fought each other to a standstill. The resources and renewed vigour that Richard and Philip injected tipped the balance in the crusade's favour. Ultimately, this was a victory that the two monarchs could, and did, claim as their own. With the city's garrison disarmed, they moved in to claim their prize.

Back in the West, Richard and Philip had agreed to divide equally their conquests in the Holy Land. Their banners thus were jointly raised above Acre, with Richard occupying the royal palace and taking custody of al-Mashtub and half of the prisoners, while Philip acquired the Templars' old quarters, along with Qaragush and the remaining captives. However, their acquisitiveness left little in the way of spoils for others. In a move to assert royal rights, Richard stripped from the walls a banner belonging to Duke Leopold V of Austria, a crusader who had arrived at Acre that April. This has often been cited by historians as evidence of the Lionheart's hot-tempered, brutish nature, but this is to do him a disservice. Richard certainly lived to regret the ill feelings this episode engendered, but at the time his mind was on the robust defence of his inalienable rights and his treatment of Leopold received Philip's tacit approval. There were pockets of disgruntlement among the crusaders about the pitiful share of the spoils received; but for much of the Frankish host, the taste of life, free for now from the threat of death, was sweet. They swept into Acre 'with dancing and joy', where, one Latin contemporary rather primly observed, they were 'now free to enjoy themselves and be refreshed with much-desired rest'. In fact, before long most had lost themselves in the traditional soldierly recreations of drinking, gambling and whoring.[59]

The effect of Acre's fall

Acre's capture was by no means the end of the crusade, but it was a momentous step towards the reconquest of the Holy Land. In part this was because the port now could act as a beachhead for the armies of the Christian West, but this notion of Acre as the vital 'gateway to Palestine' should not be overplayed. Tyre, to the north, remained in Latin hands throughout and, had Acre not fallen, could have acted as a secondary foothold on the Levantine mainland. The real significance of Acre's fall lay elsewhere.

Saladin's Egyptian fleet, the jewel of his military arsenal, was moored within Acre's sheltered inner harbour. So essential as a lifeline to the city, the bulk of the sultan's navy – some seventy ships in all – had gradually been trapped within the encircled port as the siege progressed. The crusaders now took possession of this armada, vastly augmenting their own naval strength and, in a single blow, ending Saladin's hopes of challenging Christian control of the Mediterranean. For the remainder of the Third Crusade the Franks would enjoy unquestioned supremacy at sea.

Acre's capture also had less tangible effects. As a boost to Latin morale it was both timely and potentially energising. Perhaps now the crusaders could believe that the corner had been turned: that the horrors of 1187, of Hattin and Jerusalem's fall, were behind them; that they might once again triumph in God's war. The task of channelling this burgeoning confidence and conviction towards the conquest of the Holy City fell to Richard I and Philip Augustus.

In contrast, Saladin was confronted by an altogether more desolate reality. For twenty-one months he had dedicated himself to Acre's preservation, marshalling the resources of his vast empire in pursuit of this one task. Always before in the *jihad* he had shown a reluctance to commit to the grinding attrition of siege warfare. But here, at Acre, he had made his stand. And, faced by the seemingly innumerable armies of the Third Crusade, the sultan had failed. At critical moments – most notably in autumn 1189 and summer 1190 – his generalship had proved indecisive. Physically, he was weakened by repeated illness. Throughout the Acre campaign he struggled to muster sufficient manpower and resources, distracted by the demands of empire and the need to defend Syria against the Germans, battling all the while to galvanise a Muslim world wearied by long years of holy war.

In terms of loss of fighting manpower, even in terms of Acre's strategic significance as a port, this reversal was far from decisive. But the damage done to Saladin's martial reputation, to his image as the triumphant champion of Islam, was immeasurable. It was his aura of pious invincibility, so painstakingly cultivated, that had united Islam; the myth of Salah al-Din *al-Nasir* (the Defender), the idolised *mujahid*, that held his armies in the field. The cracks in that façade now ran deep. Surrounded by the 'cries, moans, weeping and wailing' of his shocked troops, Saladin ordered a general retreat to Saffaram, there to rebuild his reputation and contemplate revenge.[60]

THE ONE KING

Within days of Acre's conquest, Richard the Lionheart's role in the Third Crusade was transformed. He had left the West as a newly crowned king, one who exceeded Philip Augustus in age, wealth and military might, yet he still found himself operating partly in the Capetian monarch's shadow. But in mid-July 1191, rumours began to spread that Philip was preparing to leave the Holy Land. On 22 July, after Richard had sought to issue a joint proclamation confirming that the two rulers would remain in the East for three years or until

Jerusalem had been recovered, the French king came clean. With Acre conquered, he considered his crusading vow fulfilled and would now return to France with all haste. 'God's mercy! What a turnaround!' wrote one crusader.

Unpicking the motives behind Philip's shock decision is no simple matter, with contemporary testimony awash with contradiction and partisan polarisation. Different sources variously claimed that Philip was desperately ill; that Richard engineered a malicious rumour that the Capetian monarch's son and heir had died back in Europe; or that the cowardly French king callously abandoned the crusade, leaving his armies penniless. In truth, one overriding consideration seems to have shaped Philip's thinking: he was a king first and a crusader second. Holy war might be God's work, and Philip was willing to play his part in the struggle, but his heart was always dedicated to the preservation, governance and enlargement of his realm. With this latter thought in mind, an obvious opportunity had presented itself. Count Philip of Flanders had died at Acre that June, leaving King Philip as heir to a portion of his county, the prosperous region of Artois. To press home this valuable claim, the French sovereign needed to be in western Europe. Quite reasonably, Philip prioritised the interests of his kingdom above those of the crusade.

Whatever the reality of Philip's motivation, one thing was obvious. His departure was humiliating. Even some of Richard I's harshest critics in Europe denounced the French king's flight. To make matters worse, the vast majority of the French aristocracy chose to remain in the Holy Land, with only Philip of Nevers joining the sovereign's exodus. Philip Augustus' withdrawal may have garnered widespread condemnation among his contemporaries, prompting one modern commentator to declare that 'his crusading record remained a permanent slur upon his reputation', but this should not blind us to the fact that Philip did make a real contribution to the Third Crusade. Many were the kings of Latin Christendom who forswore their crusading oaths in this medieval age, never to set foot in Outremer –

among them, Richard's own father, the much-celebrated Henry II of England. Perhaps Philip did not weep, as one of his remaining supporters would have us believe, when his ship finally set sail into the west. But he had, nonetheless, advanced the cause of the holy war.[61]

For Richard I, the announcement of Philip's imminent departure was, in most respects, a blessing. True, he would be left to shoulder the financial burden of the entire expedition, but his pockets were deep enough for that. With the French king gone, the Lionheart would at last have uncontested control of the crusade. And, as virtually the entire contingent of French crusaders would remain in the Levant, deputised under the command of Hugh of Burgundy, the Latin host would not be weakened. Presented with this opportunity to forge his legend in the grand theatre of holy war, Richard wasted no time in seizing the initiative.

He began by seeking the most favourable solution to the dispute over the kingdom of Jerusalem's future. With Philip about to leave, a politically isolated Conrad of Montferrat was forced to make a begrudging submission to the English king on 26 July, agreeing to abide by the decision of a council of reconciliation that would inevitably favour Richard's interests. Two days later the Angevin and Capetian monarchs proclaimed their settlement. Guy of Lusignan was to remain king for the duration of his life. The revenues of his realm would be shared with Conrad, and then, upon Guy's death, the crown would pass to the marquis. Conrad, meanwhile, would be rewarded immediately with Tyre, Beirut and Sidon, to be held in hereditary right. Should both Guy and Conrad die, the kingdom would devolve upon Richard.

With this deal done, Richard turned to the one outstanding difficulty presented by Philip's return to Europe. The two monarchs had taken such pains to set out on crusade together precisely because neither could trust the other not to invade their lands in their absence. Once the French king reached the Latin West, the Angevin world would be ominously exposed. Richard did his best to minimise the danger, convincing Philip to swear a detailed oath of peace on 29 July.

In time-honoured manner, the Capetian king held a copy of the Gospels in one hand and touched saintly relics with the other, all to reinforce the sacred and binding nature of his promises. No attack on Angevin forces or lands would be made while Richard was still on crusade. Once the Lionheart returned to Europe, forty days' warning would be given before the resumption of hostilities. As further confirmation, Hugh of Burgundy and Henry of Champagne were to act as guarantors of this agreement.

On 31 July 1191 Philip sailed north to Tyre with Conrad, taking with him half of Acre's captive garrison, and a few days later the French king left the Holy Land and the Third Crusade. Oath or not, Richard remained deeply suspicious of Philip's intentions, immediately dispatching a group of his most trusted followers to shadow the king on his return journey and deliver warning of his homecoming to England and beyond. A letter composed by Richard on 6 August to one of his leading English officials offers a glimpse of his state of mind at this point, his desire to capitalise upon Philip's withdrawal playing alongside new fears:

Within fifteen days [of Acre's fall] the king of France left us to return to his own land. We, however, place the love of God and His honour above our own and above the acquisition of many regions. We shall restore the [Latin kingdom] to its original condition as quickly as possible, and only then shall we return to our lands. But you may know for certain that we shall set sail next Lent.

Up to this point, Richard had been able to focus upon the prosecution of the Third Crusade. With Philip by his side he had enjoyed a degree of confidence about the security of his western realm. From now on, his concerns would mount – each day spent in the East was time gifted to his rival. Never again could the Lionheart afford to be so single-minded in the pursuit of the Holy Land's recovery.[62]

IN COLD BLOOD

Richard's first concern, now that he possessed sole command of the crusade, was to see the terms of Acre's surrender fulfilled so that the reconquest of the Latin East might continue. With time now a burning issue, the maintenance of momentum became crucial. Barely two months of the normal fighting season remained, so a near-immediate march south would be necessary to achieve overall victory before the onset of winter. Richard needed a few weeks to rebuild Acre's fortifications to ensure that the city would be defensible in his absence, but at the same time he began pressuring Saladin for a precise timetable for the implementation of the peace settlement's terms.

Both sides now entered into a delicate, but potentially deadly, diplomatic dance. The sultan knew that, for Richard, speed was of the essence. But so long as the king still had thousands of prisoners and an immensely profitable treaty to cash in, he would effectively be immobilised. If negotiations could be strung out, the crusaders might even find themselves mired at Acre throughout that autumn and winter. The Lionheart, too, was clearly aware that his opponent would seek to employ just such delaying tactics. Both he and Saladin recognised that a game was being played; what they could not yet gauge was their adversary's temperament. Would the rules be adhered to, indeed, were their respective rules the same? And what risks and sacrifices would the other be prepared to countenance?

For both parties, the dangers inherent in a miscalculation were grave. Richard stood to lose a considerable fortune in ransom, and to forgo the repatriation of more than 1,000 Latin captives and Outremer's most revered relic. But more significantly, if he permitted postponement and procrastination to creep into proceedings, he risked the collapse of the entire crusade. For without forward progress, the expedition would surely founder under the weight of disunity, indolence and inertia. The equation confronting Saladin was perhaps simpler: the lives of some 3,000 captive Muslims balanced against the need to stifle the crusade.

The pact agreed on 12 July originally stipulated a timescale of thirty days for the fulfilment of terms. While Saladin showed a willingness to accommodate Frankish demands – allowing one group of Latin envoys to visit Damascus to inspect Christian prisoners and another to view the relic of the True Cross – he seemed equally determined to buy himself more time. Richard, inundated by delegations of silky-tongued, gift-laden Muslim negotiators, appeared to relent on 2 August. Even though his forces were nearly ready to move out of Acre, the Lionheart agreed to a compromise: the terms of the surrender would now be met in two to three instalments, the first of which would see the return of 1,600 Latin prisoners and the True Cross and the payment of half the money promised, 100,000 dinars. Saladin may well have read this as an indication that the English king could be manipulated, but if so he was badly mistaken. In fact, Richard had his own reasons for acceding to a short delay in proceedings – with Conrad of Montferrat stubbornly refusing to return Philip Augustus' share of the Muslim captives, now ensconced at Tyre, the Lionheart was, for the moment, in no position to meet his end of the bargain.

By mid-August, however, this difficulty had been redressed, the marquis forced into line by Hugh of Burgundy and the captives returned. With everything in place Richard was now eager to proceed. From this point forward, the contemporary evidence for this episode becomes increasingly muddled, with both Latin and Muslim eyewitnesses peppering their accounts with mutual recrimination, clouding the exact details of events. It does appear, however, that Saladin misjudged his opponent. Modern commentators have often suggested that the sultan was having difficulty amassing the money and prisoners required, but this is not supported by contemporary Muslim testimony. It seems more likely that, with the deadline for the first instalment – 12 August – now passed, he began deliberately to equivocate. To Richard's evident disgust, Saladin's negotiators now sought to insert new conditions into the deal, demanding that the entire garrison should be released upon settlement of the first instalment, with hostages exchanged as guarantors that the later payment of the remaining 100,000 dinars would be made. When the king responded with blunt refusal, an impasse was reached.

Settled in his camp at Saffaram, the sultan must have imagined that there was still room for negotiation, that Richard would tolerate further delay in the hope of an eventual resolution. He was wrong. On the afternoon of 20 August, Richard marched out of Acre in force, setting up a temporary camp beyond the old crusader trenches, on the plains of Acre. Watching from their vantage point on Tell al-Ayyadiya, Saladin's advance guard was puzzled by this sudden flurry of activity. They withdrew to Tell Kaisan, dispatching an urgent message to the sultan. Richard then showed his hand. The bulk of Acre's Muslim garrison – some 2,700 men – were marched out of the city, bound in ropes. Herded on to the open ground beyond the Frankish tents, they huddled, rank with fear and confusion. Were they to be released after all?

> Then as one man, [the Franks] charged them, and with stabbings and blows with the sword they slew them in cold blood, while the Muslim advance guard watched, not knowing what to do.

Too late to intervene, Saladin's troops mounted a counter-attack but were soon beaten off. With the sun setting, Richard turned back to Acre, leaving the ground stained red with blood and littered with butchered corpses. His message to the sultan possessed a stark clarity. This was how the Lionheart would play the game. This was the ruthless single-mindedness that he would bring to the war for the Holy Land.

No event in Richard's career has elicited more controversy or criticism than this calculated carnage. Describing a search of the plain made by Muslim troops on the following morning, Saladin's adviser Baha al-Din reflected on the event:

[They] found the martyrs where they had fallen and were able to recognise some of them. Great sorrow and distress overwhelmed them for the enemy had spared only men of standing and position or someone strong and able-bodied to labour on their building works. Various reasons were given for the massacre. It was said that they had killed them in revenge for their men who had been killed or that the king of England had decided to march to Ascalon to take control of it and did not think it wise to leave that number in his rear. God knows best.

Baha al-Din noted that the Lionheart 'dealt treacherously towards the Muslim prisoners', having received their surrender 'on condition that they would be guaranteed their lives come what may', at worst facing slavery should Saladin fail to pay their ransom. The sultan met the executions with a measure of shock and rage. Certainly, in the weeks that followed, he began ordering the summary execution of any crusader unfortunate enough to be captured. But equally, by 5 September, he had sanctioned the re-establishment of diplomatic contact with the English king and some members of his entourage went on to develop close, almost cordial, relations with Richard. On balance, they and Saladin seemed to have taken the whole grim episode for what it probably was: an act of military expediency, designed to convey a brutal, blunt statement of intent. More generally, the slaughter seems to have sent a tremor of fear and horror through Near Eastern Islam. Saladin recognised that, in the future, his garrisons might choose to abandon their posts rather than face a siege and possible capture. But even for Muslim contemporaries, the events of 20 August did not prompt the universal or unmitigated vilification of the English king. He remained both 'the accursed man' and '*Melec* Ric', or 'King Ric', the spectacularly accomplished warrior and general. In time, the massacre took its place alongside other crusader atrocities, like the sack of Jerusalem in 1099, as a crime that did not, in reality, spark an unquenchable firestorm of hatred, but could be readily recalled in the interests of promoting *jihad*.[63]

Of course, Richard's treatment of his prisoners also impacted upon his image within western Christendom, in some ways with a far more lasting and powerful effect. Calculated or otherwise, his actions could be presented as having contravened the terms agreed when Acre surrendered. Should Richard be seen to have broken his promise, he might be open to censure, the transgressor of popular notions regarding chivalry and honour. Fear of such criticism can be detected in the measured and carefully managed manner in which the king and his supporters sought to present the executions.

The dominant issue was justification. In Richard's own letter to the abbot of Clairvaux, dated 1 October 1191, he stressed Saladin's prevarication, explaining that because of this, 'the time limit expired, and, as the pact which he had agreed with us was entirely made void, we quite properly had the Saracens that we had in our custody – about 2,600 of them – put to death'. Some Latin chroniclers likewise sought to shift blame on to the sultan – affirming that Saladin began killing his own Christian captives two days before Richard's mass execution – and also explained that the Lionheart acted only after holding a council, and with the agreement of Hugh of Burgundy (who was now leading the French). Despite a few traces of censure in the West – the German chronicler 'Ansbert', for example, denounced the barbarity of Richard's act – the English king seems to have escaped widespread condemnation.

Meanwhile, assessments by modern historians have fluctuated over time. Writing in the 1930s, when the general view of the Lionheart as a rash and intemperate monarch still held sway, René Grousset characterised the massacre as barbarous and stupid, concluding that Richard was moved to act by raw anger. More recently, John Gillingham's forceful and hugely influential scholarship has done much to rejuvenate the king's reputation. In Gillingham's reconstruction of events at Acre, the Lionheart comes across as a calculating and clear-headed commander; one who recognised that the resources to feed and guard thousands of Muslim prisoners could not be spared, and thus made a reasoned decision, driven by military expediency.[64]

In truth, King Richard's motives and mindset in August 1191 cannot be recovered with certainty. A logical explanation for his actions exists, but this in itself does not eliminate the possibility that he was moved by ire and impatience.

16

LIONHEART

King Richard I of England was now free to lead the Third Crusade on to victory: Acre's walls had been rebuilt and its Muslim garrison ruthlessly dispatched; Richard had secured the support of many leading crusaders, including his nephew Henry II, count of Champagne; even Hugh of Burgundy and Conrad of Montferrat had shown at least nominal acceptance of the Lionheart's right to command, although Conrad remained ensconced in Tyre.[65] Now the expedition's next goal had to be determined. Little or nothing could be achieved by staying at Acre, but to leave the city by land would expose the crusade to the full ferocity of Saladin's troops. In the Middle Ages an army was at its most vulnerable while on the move in enemy territory. Richard's only alternative to a land advance was the sea, but he seems quickly to have rejected the idea of a strategy based purely on naval power. Large as his fleet now was, the transportation of the entire military machinery of the crusade would be a formidable challenge; even more significantly, should he fail to capture a suitable port to the south, the whole offensive would collapse. The Lionheart eventually settled on a combined approach – a fighting march that would hug the Mediterranean coastline south, closely shadowed and supported by the Latin navy.

This ruled out an inland advance on Jerusalem, but in any case the obvious route to the Holy City ran south along the coast road to Jaffa and then east into the Judean hills – a path similar to that taken by the First Crusaders almost a century earlier.

However, Richard's strategic intentions in summer 1190 are unclear. The Third Crusade had been launched to recover Jerusalem, but it is far from certain that this was the king's first objective that August. He may well have been planning to use the port of Jaffa as a springboard for a direct advance on the Holy City. But a more oblique approach also presented itself; one that targeted the coastal city of Ascalon to the south, disrupting Saladin's lines of communication with Egypt. Given the sultan's reliance upon Egypt's wealth and resources, this latter policy promised to cripple the Muslim military machine, opening the door to the eventual reconquest of Jerusalem, or, perhaps, to the seizure of the Nile Delta itself.

Of course, the lack of clarity surrounding Richard's plans was, in part, a direct result of the king's own deliberate evasiveness. It made perfect sense for him to conceal his strategy from Saladin, because this forced the sultan to dilute his resources by preparing for the defence of two cities rather than just one. Muslim sources certainly indicate that, to an extent, this ruse worked. By late August Saladin had heard rumours that the crusaders would march on Ascalon, but knew that once they reached Jaffa they could just as easily strike inland. Soberly informed by one of his generals that both Ascalon and Jerusalem would require garrisons of 20,000 men, the sultan eventually concluded that one of the two would have to be sacrificed.

In fact, it is quite possible that Richard had not yet settled upon a definitive goal. The bulk of his army might have had their eyes firmly fixed upon the Holy City, but he perhaps looked to retain a flexibility of approach, hoping to reach the intermediary objective of Jaffa and then decide. This might have seemed a sensible strategy at the time, but in truth the king was merely storing up problems for the future.

THE FINEST HOUR

Richard's immediate intention was to march the armies of the Third Crusade – totalling between 10,000 and 15,000 men – down the coast of Palestine, at least as far as the port of Jaffa. But it was not territorial conquest, nor even the pursuit of battle, that dominated the Lionheart's tactical outlook upon leaving the relative safety of Acre. Instead, survival was his guiding principle – the preservation of human manpower and military resources, to ensure that the crusading war machine reached Jaffa intact. This in itself presented enormous challenges. Richard knew that, while on the move, his army would be horribly vulnerable, subject to vicious, near-constant skirmishing attacks from enemy soldiers now baying with vengeful wrath for Frankish blood. He could also expect that Saladin would seek to lure the crusaders into open battle on ground of his choosing.

With all this in mind, it might at first glance be imagined that speed was the answer; that Richard's best chance lay in prosecuting the eighty-one-mile march to Jaffa as quickly as possible in the hope of evading the enemy. After all, the ground could be covered in four to five days and the king was short of time. In fact, Richard resolved to advance from Acre at an incredibly measured, almost ponderous pace. Latin military logic of the day dictated that control was the key to a successful fighting march: troops needed rigidly to maintain a tightly packed formation, relying upon strength of numbers and the protection afforded by their armour to weather the storm of enemy charges and incessant missile attacks. Richard set out to take this theory to extreme limits.

Historians have lavished praise upon the Lionheart's generalship in this phase of the expedition, describing the advance from Acre as 'a classic demonstration of Frankish military tactics at their best' and commending the crusaders' 'admirable discipline and self-control'. In many ways, this was Richard's finest hour as a military commander. One of his greatest moments of genius was the formulation of a strategy coordinating the land march with the southward progress of his navy. With the eastern Mediterranean now firmly in Latin control, the king sought to maximise the utility of his fleet. An army engaged in a fighting march could ill afford the burden of a large baggage train, but equally could not risk running out of food and weapons. Thus, while the land force was to carry ten days' supply of basic rations, made up of 'biscuits and flour, wine and meat', the vast bulk of the crusade's martial resources were loaded on to transport ships known as 'snacks'. These were to rendezvous with the march at four points along the coast – Haifa, Destroit, Caesarea and Jaffa – while more lightly stocked smaller boats would sail close to the shore, keeping pace with the army to offer near-constant support. One crusader wrote: 'So it was said that they would journey in two armies, one travelling by land, one by sea, for no one could conquer Syria any other way as long as the Turks controlled it.' Richard's coastline-hugging route south also promised to offer his troops protection from enemy encirclement. Wherever possible, the crusaders would advance with soldiers on the right flank practically wading in the sea, thereby eliminating any possibility of attack on that front. By these measures Richard hoped to minimise the negative impact of marching through enemy territory. This sophisticated scheme was evidently the product of advanced planning and probably relied in part upon the Military Orders' local knowledge. Success would depend upon the maintenance of martial discipline and in this regard Richard's force of personality and unshakeable valour would be critical.

In spite of all of this, neither the Lionheart's achievements nor the mechanistic precision of this march should be exaggerated. Even in this phase of the crusade Richard faced difficulties, a fact generally ignored by modern commentators. Indeed, his first problem – the actual commencement of the march – was nothing less than an embarrassment. One might expect that, as the expedition's only remaining monarch, Richard's authority would have been unquestioned; after all, he had even taken the trouble of paying potentially intractable French crusaders, like Hugh of Burgundy, to ensure their loyalty. Nevertheless, the English king had an inordinate amount of trouble actually convincing his fellow Franks to leave Acre.

The problem was that the port had become a comfortable, even enticing, refuge from the horrors of the holy war. Packed 'so full of people that it could hardly hold them all', the city had transformed into a fleshpot, offering up all manner of illicit pleasures. One crusader conceded that it 'was delightful, with good wines and girls, some very beautiful', with whom many Latin crusaders were 'taking their foolish pleasure'. Under these conditions Richard had to work hard to educe obedience. On the day after his massacre of the Muslim captives, he established a staging post on the plains south-east of the port, just beyond the old crusader trenches. His most loyal followers accompanied him, but others were reluctant. One supporter admitted that the Lionheart had to resort to a mixture of flattery, prayer, bribery and force to amass a viable force, and even then many were still left in Acre. Indeed, throughout the first stage of the fighting march stragglers continued to join the main army. To begin with at least, the restrained pace of Richard's advance – now so admired by military historians – seems primarily to have been adopted to allow these recruits to catch up.[66]

The march begins

The main army struck out south on Thursday 22 August 1191. To stamp out any residual 'wantonness' among his troops, Richard ordered that all women were to be left behind at Acre, although an exception was made for elderly female pilgrims who, it was said, 'washed the clothes and heads [of the soldiers] and were as good as monkeys at getting rid of fleas'. For the first two days, Richard rode in the rearguard of his forces, ensuring the maintenance of order, but despite expectations only negligible resistance was met. Saladin, unsure of the Lionheart's intentions and perhaps fearing a frontal attack on his camp at Saffaram, deployed only a token probing force at this stage. Having covered barely ten miles in two days, the

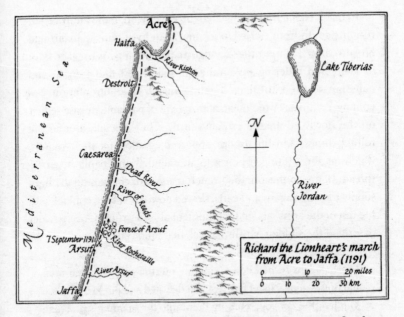

Richard the Lionheart's march
from Acre to Jaffa (1191)

0   10   20 miles
0   10   20   30 km

crusaders crossed the Belus River and made camp, resting for the whole of 24 August, 'wait[ing] for those of God's people whom it was difficult to draw out of Acre'.[67]

At dawn the next day Richard set out to cover the remaining distance to Haifa. The army was split into three divisions – the king taking the vanguard, a central body of English and Norman crusaders, and Hugh of Burgundy and the French bringing up the rear. For now, coordination between these groups was limited, but they were at least united by the sight of Richard's royal standard aloft in the centre of the host. As the crusade inched south, so too did the king's dragon banner at the army's heart, affixed to a huge iron-clad flagpole, drawn on a wheeled wooden platform and protected by an elite guard. Visible to all, including the enemy (who likened it to 'a huge beacon'), so long as it flew this totem signalled the Franks' continued survival, helping men to hold their fear in check in the face of Muslim onslaught. That Sunday, such resolve would be sorely needed.

To reach Haifa, Richard had led the crusade on to the sandy beach running south from Acre. Unbeknownst to the Latins, Saladin had broken camp that morning (25 August), dispatching his baggage train to safety and ordering his brother al-Adil to test the strength and cohesion of the Christians' fighting march. A confrontation was coming. As the day wore on an atmosphere of palpable unease settled on the slowly advancing crusader army. On their left, among the rolling dunes, Muslim troops appeared, shadowing their march, watching and waiting. Then a fog descended and panic began to spread. In the confusion, the French rearguard, containing the light supply train of wagons and carts, slowed down, breaking contact with the rest of the army, and at that moment al-Adil struck. One crusader described the sudden Muslim attack that followed:

> The Saracens rushed down, singling out the carters, killed men and horses, took a lot of baggage and defeated and put to rout those who led [the convoy], chasing them into the foaming sea. There they fought so much that they cut off the hand of a man-at-arms, called Evrart [one of Bishop Hubert Walter's men]; he paid no attention to this and made no fuss . . . but taking his sword in his left hand, stood firm.

With the rearguard 'brought to a standstill', and disaster impending, news of the attack raced up the line to Richard. Recognising that direct and immediate intervention would be necessary if a deadly encirclement of the French was to be avoided, the Lionheart rode back at speed. A Christian eyewitness described how 'galloping against the Turks [the king] went into their midst, quicker than a flash of lightning', beating off the Muslim skirmishers through sheer force of arms, reconnecting the rearguard with the main body of the army. With the enemy melting back into the dunes, the Latin army was left shaken but intact. Having survived this first challenge, the crusaders reached Haifa either that night or early the next morning, camping there throughout 26 and 27 August.[68]

It was clear that the crusaders would have to regroup. Modern scholarship has emphasised the skill with which Richard organised and upheld the Frankish marching formation upon leaving Acre. But this ignores the fact that, to a significant degree, the Lionheart and his men actually had to learn by their mistakes. One crusader wrote that, after the experiences of 25 August, the Franks 'made great efforts and conducted themselves more wisely'. While continuing to wait for the army to muster fully – for troops were still arriving from Acre, now mostly by ship – the king set about reordering his forces. Equipment was pared down; the poor especially had begun the march overburdened 'with food and arms', so that 'a number of them had to be left behind to die of heat and thirst'. At the same time, a far more structured marching order was established and this seems to have been followed for the remainder of the journey south.

The crusaders continued wherever possible to cling to the coastline, maintaining even closer contact with the fleet. Elite, battle-hardened Templars and Hospitallers were given the crucial job of holding the van and rearguard, while the king and a central mass of mounted knights were screened on the exposed left flank by dense ranks of well-armoured infantry. A Muslim eyewitness who beheld the army a few days later described this latter unit as an impenetrable 'wall'. Protected by 'full-length, well-made chain mail', all but invulnerable to light missile fire, 'arrows were falling on them with no effect', such that he saw 'Franks with ten arrows fixed in their backs, pressing on in this fashion quite unconcerned'. These infantrymen might use bow and crossbow fire to deter skirmishers, but in the main they focused upon sustaining their inexorable advance unabated. Recognising that this shielding role would take an enormous physical and psychological toll, Richard split the infantry into two divisions, rotating them in and out of service, leaving the rested group to recuperate as they marched on the protected right, seaward, flank alongside the army's lightened baggage train.[69]

Adopting this formation, the Christians left Haifa on 28 August, clear in the knowledge that they would, from this point on, face intense and unceasing harassment from Saladin's troops. Richard now took great care to conserve his army's energy, following each stage of the march with one or even two rest days. Muslim forces certainly trailed their every step, even picketing the Latins' camps at night, all the while looking for any opportunity to crack their marching order. What remained unclear, however, was whether the sultan would attempt to challenge them in a full-scale pitched battle. Historians have consistently misjudged Saladin's intentions in this regard, suggesting that he had from the start settled upon suitable ground to the south, near Arsuf. The richly detailed eyewitness testimony of Baha al-Din, who was with the sultan throughout this period, presents a very different picture. Saladin, it seems, was rather bewildered by Richard's tactics. Taken aback by the king's unexpected decision to take repeated rest days, the sultan misjudged the speed of the Frankish advance and therefore the length of time his own troops would have to stay in the field, prompting food shortages. For the moment, Saladin seemed to have been outplayed by the Lionheart, forced to adopt a reactive strategy shot through with desperation. Troops were indeed dispatched to stalk the Christians, but the sultan also began a rather frantic search for a suitable battlefield, personally reconnoitring the coastal route south, even assessing the vulnerability of the crusaders' likely campsites. Throughout this period he was actively looking to stop the Latins in their tracks.

For eight days the crusaders made slow, gruelling progress. Advancing from the ruined fortification at Destroit to Caesarea on Friday 30 August, they began to falter under the beating summer sun. A Latin marching in the army described how:

> The heat was so intolerable that some died of it; these were buried at once. Those who could not go on, the worn-out and exhausted, of whom there were often many, the sick and infirm, the king, acting wisely, had carried in the galleys and the small boats to the next stage.

The next day, en route to the grimly named Dead River, the Franks scored a notable success in the midst of a prolonged skirmish. Among the enemy on that day was Ayas the Tall, one of Saladin's most celebrated and ferocious *mamluks*, laying waste to all before him with a massive lance. When a lucky blow brought down his horse, Ayas, weighed down by his armour, was overrun and butchered. Baha al-Din admitted that 'the Muslims grieved for him greatly', but, perhaps more importantly, the victory helped to buoy Christian morale. So too did the crusaders' ritual each night of chanting en masse 'Holy Sepulchre, help us' before they settled down to snatch a few restless hours of sleep. But the undoubted key to their continued composure in the face of such unrelenting pressure was the presence of the Lionheart, unbending, ever ready to step into the fray, to bolster the line. Richard seems to have taken great care to monitor the mood of his men, seeking to ensure that he did not overstretch their endurance. By the start of September, with food shortages beginning to bite, arguments started breaking out. Infantrymen would swarm round the carcasses of 'the fattest of the dead horses' to have fallen during each day's march, brawling over their flesh, to the disgust of the steeds' knightly owners. The king interceded, proclaiming that he would replace any lost mount so long as the meat of the deceased animal was offered up to 'worthy men-at-arms'. Grateful Franks 'ate [the] horsemeat as if it were game. Flavoured with hunger rather than sauce, they thought it was delicious.'[70]

Of course, the benefits of Richard's visible presence came at considerable risk. Marching on from the Dead River on 3 September, a 'wild' stretch of coastline forced the crusaders to turn inland for a time. Saladin had chosen this moment to seek battle, personally leading three divisions of troops against the crusaders' massed ranks. Time and again the Muslims bombarded the Christians with arrows and then charged their lines. Baha al-Din watched the repeated attacks unfold:

I saw [Saladin] actually riding among the skirmishers as the enemy's arrows flew past him. He was attended by two pages with two spare mounts and that was all, riding from division to division and urging them forward, ordering them to press hard upon the enemy and bring them to battle.

The sultan emerged unscathed, but Richard was less fortunate. There, as always, in the thick of the fighting, the king was suddenly struck in the side by a crossbow bolt. Fortunately, he managed to stay in the saddle as combat raged on around him. This time he had been lucky: his armour had absorbed most of the impact and 'he was not seriously hurt'. But the episode highlighted the immense, but necessary, risks he took as a medieval warrior-king *par excellence*. Had he fallen that day, the whole crusade might soon have collapsed. Equally, however, without his tangible, seemingly indestructible, presence in the front line, Frankish resistance would probably have buckled. As it was, both he and Saladin survived this first confrontation. By the end of the day a rather shell-shocked Christian army had reached the River of Reeds. As they made camp on its banks they seem to have been unaware that, just a mile or so upstream, the Muslims too were pitching their tents. Baha al-Din reflected with some irony that 'we were drinking from the higher reaches while the enemy were drinking from the lower'.[71]

THE BATTLE OF ARSUF

Richard was now just twenty-five miles from Jaffa. Perilous and exhausting as the march had so far been, it had also proved a stunning success. But the king must have suspected that Saladin now would commit his every resource to halting the Frankish advance, for the loss of Jaffa would be a grave blow to Islam. The route ahead ran through the Forest of Arsuf to an obvious campsite beside the River Rochetaille, but beyond that a wide, sandy plain opened out before the small settlement of Arsuf itself was reached. Rumours were abroad in the Latin army that some sort of ambush or attack was imminent.

Richard let his troops rest beside the River of Reeds on 4 September, but that evening he made a masterful move. The unpredictable pace of the crusader march had already sown seeds of confusion and doubt in Saladin's mind, stifling his attempts to seize the initiative. Now the Lionheart played an unexpected and devious card, dispatching envoys to the Muslim advance guard to request peace talks with al-Adil.

The sultan had spent the day hurriedly scouting the forest and plain to the south, searching for a battlefield, before racing back north. Indeed, he moved with such haste that come nightfall many of his men were 'left scattered amongst the woods'. Saladin was beginning to lose control of his army. When news of Richard's request reached him that night he acceded, instructing his brother 'to spin out the talks'. With time, the sultan might be able to marshal his forces and mount an offensive.

Once again, however, the king of England had comprehensively outmanoeuvred his opponent. Richard was in no mood for actual negotiation; instead he had called for a parley to mislead Saladin as to his own intentions and, perhaps, to garner some intelligence regarding Muslim plans and preparedness. The Lionheart duly met al-Adil at dawn on 5 September in a private audience, but their conversation was neither prolonged nor cordial. The king bluntly demanded the return of the Holy Land and Saladin's retreat into Muslim territory. Unsurprisingly, al-Adil was outraged, but no sooner had the talks broken off than Richard ordered his army to advance into the Forest of Arsuf. Caught entirely flat-footed, the sultan was unable to respond, his troops left in disarray. Most crusaders still entered the forest in a state of anxiety, 'for it was said that [the Muslims] would set light to it, causing such a great fire that the [Christian] army would be roasted'. But thanks to their leader's skilful dissimulation, they passed through unhindered and unscathed to reach the Rochetaille. Richard rested his men on 6 September – taking this one last chance to draw breath before running the gauntlet to Arsuf and beyond. Saladin, meanwhile, held closed talks with al-Adil, furiously seeking a stratagem that might avert disaster.[72]

As he awoke on Saturday 7 September, the Lionheart must have known that the enemy would use the space afforded by the open plain ahead to mount another blistering assault. Perhaps he even sensed that the confrontation would be on a larger scale than that faced on 3 September. For the crusaders, that Saturday began as every day of the march had since leaving Haifa, with the rigorous structuring of troop formation. By this point the army contained some 15,000 men, of whom 1,000 to 2,000 were mounted knights. One crusader recorded that 'Richard, the worthy king of England, who knew so much about war and the army, set out in his own way who should go in front and who behind'. The Templars, as usual, were to take the lead, while their Hospitaller brethren held the rear with a strong force of archers and crossbowmen. With a mixed group of Poitevins, Normans and English holding the centre and Henry of Champagne commanding the left, inland flank, Richard and Hugh of Burgundy were to lead a mobile reserve that could range throughout the army, reinforcing points of weakness as necessary. As always, a tightly ordered formation was paramount; indeed, it was said that the Franks left the banks of the Rochetaille 'in such order, side by side and so close that any apple [thrown in their midst] could not have failed to strike man or beast'.

But according to the crusader Ambroise there was something different about that day's preparations. In his account, the king was readying his troops not just for a fighting march, but for battle. Ambroise, who followed Richard east on crusade and later composed an epic Old French verse history of the expedition, depicted 7 September 1191 as a day of deliberate confrontation; a day of glory on an almost Homeric scale. His hero, the Lionheart, was shown making a conscious, proactive decision to challenge Saladin head-on. Perceiving with almost supernatural foresight 'that they could not go forward without a battle', the king planned to deploy the Christians' most powerful weapon – the heavy cavalry charge – the moment the sultan overcommitted his forces. Timing was to be crucial, but with only the rudimentary medieval forms of battlefield communication available, Richard had to rely on an aural signal to initiate the attack. Ambroise described how 'six trumpets [were] placed in three different places in the army, which would sound when they were to turn against the Turks'.

Ambroise's account of Arsuf has been hugely influential: widely copied by contemporaries; often uncritically regurgitated by modern historians. The epic image of that Saturday morning on the coast of Palestine engendered by his depiction has long held sway: the resplendent crusader army beginning its march, primed, practically straining for the fight; like a nocked arrow, held quivering at full draw, ready for release. But detailed, colourful and alluring as Ambroise's vision is, other eyewitness reports challenge his narrative. Chief among these is a letter – one that has been extraordinarily undervalued by historians – composed by King Richard I himself. This missive, effectively a dispatch from the front lines to Garnier of Rochefort, Cistercian abbot of Clairvaux, was written not, like Ambroise's verse history, some six years later, but just three weeks after the Battle of Arsuf, on 1 October 1191. Its brief, almost passing description of events on 7 September, suggests that the Lionheart's primary concern that day was to reach the relative safety of the orchards at Arsuf with his army intact and not to seek a definitive confrontation with Saladin.

In the age of the crusades pitched battles were extremely rare. The risks involved, the element of chance, meant that shrewd generals avoided open conflict at all costs unless in possession of overwhelming numerical superiority. Richard's overall priority in this phase of the crusade was to reach Jaffa, and from there to threaten Ascalon and Jerusalem. To look for a decisive fight with Saladin when the sultan commanded equal, or perhaps even greater, military strength, and could chose his own ground, would have been tantamount to gambling the fate of the entire holy war on a dice roll. Perhaps the king did ready his men for battle at Arsuf, should it be thrust upon him – his letter does not say – but, even so, there is a significant, albeit subtle, difference between the preparation for conflict and its active pursuit.

For Saladin, in contrast, a decisive confrontation was all but essential. Facing the seemingly unstemmable Latin advance, he knew that without action he would be forced, in just a few days, to watch in abject impotence as the Lionheart reached Jaffa. Coming hard on the heels of Acre's surrender, the strategic and political consequences would be horrendous, Islam's hold over Palestine grievously destabilised, his own reputation as a *mujahid* gravely besmirched. The Franks must be stopped here, on the dusty plain of Arsuf. As Baha al-Din bluntly stated: '[The sultan had] every intention of bringing the enemy to pitched battle that day.'[73]

When the crusaders marched from the Rochetaille, soon after dawn, they were greeted by a menacing vision: there, where wooded hills ran down to the left edge of the plain, Saladin had arrayed the full strength of his army. Line upon line of troops stretched out before them, 'piled up, like a thick hedge'. Facing around 30,000 Muslim warriors, many of them mounted, the Franks were now outnumbered at least two to one. Around 9 a.m. the first wave of 2,000 enemy skirmishers raced down towards them and fighting began. As the morning progressed, Saladin committed practically his entire force, holding back only an elite unit of some 1,000 of the Royal Guard to spearhead a targeted assault, should a break appear in the Latin formation. For hour after hour, with the blistering sun now beating down on them, the Christians marched on, pummelled by the incessant onslaught.

One crusader described the overwhelming cacophony of the battlefield – a jumble of troops 'howling, shouting [and] baying', enemy trumpeters and drummers pulsing the terrible rhythm of combat – so that 'one could not have heard God thundering, such a racket was made'. The Muslims' primary weapon was an aerial bombardment of appalling intensity: 'never did rain or snow or hail falling in the heart of winter fall so densely as did the bolts which flew there and killed our horses', recalled one eyewitness, remarking that armfuls of arrows could have been gathered there like corn cut in the fields. Also among the enemy were troops few crusaders had encountered: terrifying black

Africans. A Latin eyewitness declared that 'they were called "blacks" –
this is the truth – [coming] from the wild land, hideous and blacker
than soot . . . a people who were very quick and agile'.

The horror of the relentless assault that morning was almost
unendurable.

[The Franks] thought their lines would be broken [and] did not
expect to survive one hour or to come out of it alive; know in truth
that [some] cowards could not help throwing down their bows and
arrows and taking refuge in the army . . . No man was so confident
that he did not wish in his heart that he had finished his
pilgrimage.[74]

King Richard's priority through all this was to maintain troop
discipline and keep his army moving forward in formation towards
Arsuf. Any pause or break in the line would be lethal, but the
temptation among his men to launch a counter-attack was nearly
irresistible. A messenger raced up the line from the Hospitaller
rearguard, begging for permission to retaliate, but the Lionheart
refused. For now, at least, order held. It was a testament to the king's
force of will and charisma as a general that, for so long, his authority
held in the face of such extraordinary pressure. The Christians were
now 'surrounded, like a flock of sheep in the jaws of wolves, so that
they could see nothing but the sky and their wicked enemies on every
side'. And yet, their advance continued.

With the Templar vanguard nearing the orchards of Arsuf, the
master of the Hospitallers himself, Garnier of Nablus, rode forward
to make a second petition to the king, bewailing the shame of
inaction, but once again the king demurred. Crucially, Richard's own
letter of 1 October indicates that the front ranks of the march now
reached the outskirts of Arsuf and began 'setting up camp', a fact
confirmed by Baha al-Din, who wrote that 'the first detachments of
[the Christian] infantry reached the plantations of Arsuf'. This gives
the lie to the notion that Richard was, throughout 7 September,

harbouring some grander strategy; holding his forces in check only so that they could be unleashed in open battle. Just as it had been throughout the journey from Acre, his priority at Arsuf was security and survival. But with that objective so near to realisation, the Lionheart's hand was forced.[75]

Looking back, Richard suddenly discovered that a crusader charge had begun. Without warning, two knights towards the rear – the marshal of the Hospitallers and Baldwin of Carew – had broken ranks. Driven by a mixture of anger, humiliation and bloodlust, 'they burst out of the line [and], with horses at full gallop, charged the Turks', screaming the name of St George. A ripple of realisation spread through the army and, within moments, thousands of crusaders had turned to follow their lead. The Hospitaller rearguard raced into battle. Then, as Richard watched in horror, Henry of Champagne, James of Avesnes and Robert, earl of Leicester, also committed the left flank and centre of the army to the charge.

This was the moment of decision. Richard may not have wanted battle, but with no hope of recalling his troops it was now upon him regardless. A failure to react would have been catastrophic, but the Lionheart showed no hesitation: 'He spurred his horse to the gallop [riding] faster than a bolt from a crossbow', leading his remaining forces with him. Not surprisingly, Ambroise's supposed trumpet signal was never sounded.[76]

A scene of carnage now lay before the king. The first crusader charge had resulted in a chaotic bloodbath, as the shocked front ranks of Saladin's army were routed and overrun. The injured were screaming, 'while others, wallowing in their own blood, breathed their last. A very great number were but headless corpses trodden under foot by friend or foe regardless.' But as Richard raced into the fray, the sultan rallied his troops and mounted a counter-attack. The king's own contribution to the battle is unclear. Richard downplayed his own prowess, offering this terse account of the encounter in his letter to the abbot of Clairvaux:

Our vanguard was proceeding and was already setting up camp at Arsuf, when Saladin and his Saracens made a violent attack on our rearguard, but by the grace of God's favourable mercy they were forced into flight just by four squadrons that were facing them.

Other Latin contemporaries, Ambroise among them, painted a more stirring scene of royal heroism, in which the Lionheart practically won the day single-handed:

King Richard pursued the Turks with singular ferocity, fell upon them and scattered them [and] wherever he went his brandished sword cleared a wide path on all sides ... He cut down that unspeakable race as if he were reaping the harvest with a sickle, so that the corpses of the Turks he had killed covered the ground everywhere for the space of half a mile.[77]

Perhaps his martial gallantry did not reach so epic a scale, but Richard's personal contribution may still have been the decisive factor that tipped the balance of the encounter. Time and again in the Middle Ages, warrior-kings, seen by their men in the thick of fighting, turned the tide of battle, assuring victory. Whatever the explanation, the Franks at Arsuf managed to repulse one, perhaps even two, Muslim counter-attacks. In the end, with most of his troops routed, Saladin was forced into a shameful retreat. Hotly pursued, he and the beleaguered remnants of his army melted into the surrounding forests, gifting the victory, such as it was, to the Christians.

The battle-weary Franks regrouped to limp into Arsuf, finally establishing a secure camp. Most collapsed in exhaustion, but as always there were some scavengers, 'greedy for gain', who were itching to pick over the dead and dying. As evening fell, they counted thirty-two Muslim emirs among the fallen, as well as some 700 enemy troops, most of whom had been slain in the first Latin charge. Meanwhile, at first count, Latin casualties appeared to be minimal.

That night, however, an unsettling rumour spread through the army. James of Avesnes, the respected crusader knight from Hainaut, was missing. At dawn the next day, a search party of Templars and Hospitallers scoured the battlefield, and eventually, there among the dead of Christendom and Islam, they located his mutilated corpse. It was said that, in the thick of the fray, his horse had fallen; thrown from his saddle, James had fought like a lion, but as the tide of the battle turned, his old comrade in arms, Count Robert of Dreux, had ignored his calls for aid. Abandoned, James made his last desperate stand, felling fifteen of the enemy, before being cut down. He was found, circled by Muslim dead, his 'face so smeared with congealed blood that they could hardly recognise it until it had been washed with water'. With great reverence, his body was carried back to Arsuf and buried in a ceremony attended by King Richard and Guy of Lusignan. 'Everyone wailed and wept and lamented over' his death; the Third Crusade had lost one of its longest-standing and most renowned warriors.[78]

The significance of Arsuf

The Battle of Arsuf has long been regarded as a historic crusader triumph. In seeking to construct an image of Richard I as the monumental hero of the holy war, Ambroise presented this engagement as a critical setpiece confrontation between the Lionheart and Saladin – an encounter that Richard actively sought, and one in which he achieved a resounding victory. This account of Arsuf has been widely accepted and Richard's success on 7 September 1191 has become one of the cornerstones of his martial reputation. Jean Flori, a recent biographer of the Lionheart, asserted that the battle revealed the king's 'skill in the "science of war"', adding that it 'was fought on Richard's terms', with the Angevin monarch having 'already drawn up his army in battle order'.[79]

In truth, the reconstruction of medieval battles is a phenomenally imprecise business and Richard's intentions cannot be defined with absolute certainty. On balance, though, the evidence makes it at least as likely that Richard did not want to fight a major battle at Arsuf. He may well have expected a Muslim attack on 7 September, but he seems to have remained focused upon his primary objective – reaching the proposed campsite at Arsuf and then continuing on to Jaffa. In the event, when the crusader rearguard broke ranks to launch an attack, the Lionheart's swift, resolute and valiant response did avert disaster, ultimately securing an opportunistic, but morale-boosting, victory. Crucially, his generalship was reactive, not proactive.

At the time, King Richard did not claim to have planned the battle – that notion seems only to have taken hold in the aftermath of the Third Crusade – but his letter of 1 October did state that the Muslims were badly stung at Arsuf. It declared:

> The slaughter among Saladin's more noble Saracens was so great, that he lost more on that day near Arsuf [than] on any day in the previous forty years . . . [Ever since] that day, Saladin has not dared do battle with the Christians. Instead he lies in wait at a distance, out of sight like a lion in his den, [waiting to kill] the friends of the cross like sheep.

Arabic sources acknowledged that the Ayyubids suffered a damaging defeat at Arsuf. Baha al-Din, who witnessed the battle, recorded that many 'met a martyr's death' and admitted that, although al-Adil and al-Afdal fought well, the latter was 'shaken by this day'. In real terms, though, Muslim manpower losses were by no means decisive – Saladin had been beaten from the field, but the holy war would go on. Within days the sultan was writing to his 'far-flung territories' requesting reinforcements. The telling damage, just as at Acre, was psychological. As Saladin struggled to reimpose control over his armies, his 'heart' was said to be 'full of feelings that God alone could know [and] the troops too were either wounded in the body or wounded in the heart'. The sultan's correspondence from this period strove to present a positive account of events, declaring that Muslim attacks had slowed the Frankish advance to such an extent that they took seventeen days over a two-day journey and celebrating the slaying of 'Sir Jak' (James of Avesnes). Even so, the truth of the matter could hardly be concealed. Once again, Saladin had tried and failed to stop the Third Crusade in its tracks.[80]

On 9 September 1191 the Franks resumed their march, reaching the River Arsuf without much difficulty. The next day, Richard arrived outside the ruins of Jaffa – the walls of the port town having been demolished on Saladin's orders in autumn 1190. Such was the devastation that the whole Latin army had to be quartered in the surrounding olive groves and gardens, but the crusaders rejoiced to find a great abundance of food, including grapes, figs, pomegranates and almonds. Before long, Christian ships began to arrive, ferrying supplies from Acre, and a defensible position was established on the Palestinian coast. Richard the Lionheart had led the Third Crusade to the brink of victory and Jerusalem now lay just over forty miles inland.

17

JERUSALEM

In late summer 1191 King Richard I of England prosecuted a remarkably controlled, ruthlessly efficient march south from Acre to Jaffa, subjecting Saladin to a humiliating, if not crushing, defeat along the way. Since his arrival in the Holy Land, the Lionheart had galvanised the Third Crusade; no longer mired and inert in the northern reaches of Palestine, the expedition now seemed poised on the threshold of victory. Success depended on momentum – only immediate and resolute action would preserve the brittle Frankish coalition and maintain pressure on a faltering enemy. But just when focused commitment to a clear military goal was needed, Richard hesitated.

DECISIONS AND DECEPTIONS

Around 12 September 1191, just a few days after reaching Jaffa, worrying reports from the south began filtering into the crusader camp. Saladin, it was said, had moved on Ascalon and even now was razing the Muslim-held port to the ground. With these rumours stirring up a mixture of incredulity, horror and suspicion, the king dispatched Geoffrey of Lusignan (who had now been appointed titular count of the region) and the trusted knight William of L'Estang to investigate. Sailing south, they soon caught sight of the city, and, as they drew closer, a scene of appalling devastation revealed itself. Ascalon was awash with flame and smoke, its terrified populace streaming away in forced evacuation while the sultan's men swarmed over the port's mighty defences, ripping wall and tower asunder.

This grave spectacle was the product of Saladin's newly resolute approach to the war. Still smarting from his humiliating defeat at Arsuf, the sultan had assembled his counsellors at Ramla on 10 September to re-evaluate Ayyubid strategy. Having tried and failed to confront the crusaders head-on during their march south from Acre, Saladin decided to adopt a more defensive approach. If Richard could not be crushed in open battle, then drastic steps would be taken to halt his advance – a scorched-earth policy to hamper Frankish movement, involving the destruction of key fortresses. The critical target was Ascalon, southern Palestine's main port and the stepping stone to Egypt. If the Franks captured the city intact then the Lionheart would have the perfect bridgehead from which to threaten Jerusalem and the Nile region. Saladin realised that he lacked the resources to fight a war on two fronts and, prioritising the protection of the Holy City, ordered that Ascalon's walls be razed to the ground. This cannot have been an easy decision – the sultan was said to have remarked, 'by God I would prefer to lose all my sons rather than demolish a single stone' – but it was necessary. Time was pressing, for if Richard marched on he might yet seize the port. Saladin therefore sent al-Adil to watch over the crusaders at Jaffa, and then raced south with al-Afdal to oversee the dreadful labour, driving his soldiers to work at a furious pace, day and night, fearful of the Lionheart's arrival.[81]

When Geoffrey and William brought news of what they had seen to Jaffa, King Richard still had a chance to act. Throughout the late summer he had been deliberately evasive about his objectives, but now a definite decision had to be made. To the Lionheart, the choice seemed clear: the seizure of Ascalon was the logical next step for the crusade. As a general he recognised that, to date, the expedition's achievements had been dependent upon naval superiority. While the crusade continued to hug the coastline, Latin domination of the Mediterranean could stave off isolation and annihilation by offering a lifeline of supply and reinforcement. So far, the Christians had not truly fought the Third Crusade in enemy territory; once they marched inland, the real battle would begin. Ascalon's seizure and refortification promised to destabilise further Saladin's hold over Palestine, creating a secure coastal enclave, while keeping Richard's options open for an eventual assault on Jerusalem or Egypt.

Richard arrived in Jaffa apparently expecting that, as king and commander, his will would be obeyed; that the march south could continue, almost without pause. But he had made a serious miscalculation. As a species of war, the crusade was governed not merely by the dictates of military science, nor by notions of politics, diplomacy or economy. This was a mode of conflict underpinned by religious ideology – one that relied upon the overwhelming and imperative devotional allure of a target like Jerusalem to create unity of purpose within a disparate army. And for the vast majority of those within Richard's amalgamated crusading host, marching south from Jaffa was tantamount to walking past the doorway to the Holy City.

At a council held outside Jaffa in mid-September 1191, the Lionheart was confronted by this reality. Despite his best efforts to press for an attack on Ascalon, a large number of Latin nobles resisted – among them Hugh of Burgundy and the French – arguing instead for the refortification of Jaffa and a more direct strike inland towards Jerusalem. In the end, as one crusader put it, 'the loud voice of the people prevailed' and a decision was made to stay put. Richard seems not to have recognised it at the time, but he had failed a critical test. The events at Jaffa exposed an ominous deficiency in his skills as a leader. The Lionheart had been well schooled in the affairs of war since childhood; since 1189 his skills and authority as a king had blossomed. But, as yet, he had not grasped the reality of crusading.

With the decision to halt at Jaffa, the crusade lost impetus. Work began to rebuild the port and its defences, even as Saladin completed Ascalon's destruction. Crusaders, shattered by the horrors of the march from Acre, now basked in the sudden break in hostilities. Among the constant flow of supply ships, vessels packed with prostitutes soon began to appear. With their arrival, bemoaned one Christian eyewitness, the army was again polluted by 'sin and filth, ugly deeds and lust'. As days turned to weeks, even the will to press on to the Holy City faltered and the expedition started to fragment. Some Franks actually sailed to Acre to enjoy more luxurious comforts, and eventually Richard had to travel north in person to goad these absentees back into action.[82]

On the road to Jerusalem

In the end, the Third Crusade remained stalled around Jaffa and its environs for the best part of seven weeks. This delay gave Saladin time to extend his scorched-earth strategy, demolishing the network of fortifications running from the coast inland to Jerusalem. Richard spent much of October 1191 reassembling his army and, only in the last days of that month, with the normal fighting season drawing to a close, did the expedition begin to advance on Jerusalem. It now faced a challenge unlike any encountered by previous crusades. Back in 1099, the First Crusaders had marched on the Holy City largely unopposed, and in their subsequent siege, arduous though it was, the Franks had encountered a relatively small, isolated enemy force. Now, almost a century later, the Latins could expect to meet far sterner resistance.

Saladin's power may have weakened in the years since 1187, but he still possessed formidable military resources with which to harass and oppose every step of a Christian approach on the Holy City. And should the crusaders reach Jerusalem, its actual conquest presented manifold difficulties. Protected by a full garrison and stout physical fortifications, the city's defences would be all but insurmountable, while any besieging army would undoubtedly face fierce counter-attacks from additional Muslim forces in the field. More troubling still was the issue of supply and reinforcement: once the Third Crusade left the coast behind, it would have to rely upon a fragile line of communication back to Jaffa; if broken, Richard and his men would face isolation and probably defeat.

The Lionheart's primary aim in the autumn of 1191 was the forging of a reliable chain of logistical support running inland. The main road to Jerusalem crossed the coastal plain east of Jaffa, through Ramla to Latrun, before arcing north-east to Beit Nuba in the Judean foothills and then winding east up to the Holy City (although there were alternatives, such as the more northerly route via Lydda). In the course of the twelfth century, the Franks had built a string of fortresses to defend the approaches to Jerusalem. Many of these had been controlled by the Military Orders, but all had fallen to Islam after Hattin.

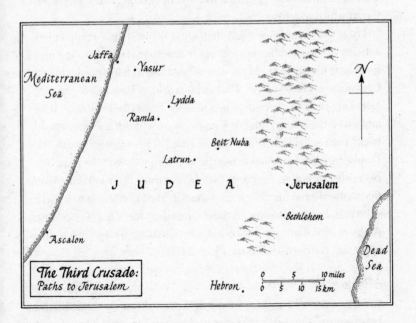

The Third Crusade:
Paths to Jerusalem

Saladin's recent shift in strategy had left the road ahead of the crusaders in a state of desolation. Every major fortified site – including Lydda, Ramla and Latrun – had been dismantled. On 29 October Richard marched on to the plains east of Jaffa and began the painstakingly slow work of rebuilding a string of sites running inland, starting with two forts near Yasur. In military terms, the war now devolved into a series of skirmishes. Marshalling his forces at Ramla, Saladin sought to hound the Franks, impeding their construction efforts while avoiding full-scale confrontation. Once the advance on Jerusalem began, the Lionheart frequently threw himself into the thick of these running battles. In early November 1192, a routine foraging expedition went awry when a group of Templars were attacked and outnumbered. When the news reached him, the king rode to their aid without hesitation, accompanied by Andrew of Chauvigny and Robert, earl of Leicester. The Lionheart arrived 'roaring' with bloodlust, striking like a 'thunderbolt', and soon forced the Muslims to retreat.

Latin eyewitnesses suggest that some of the king's companions actually questioned the wisdom of his actions that day. Chiding him for risking his life so readily, they protested that 'if harm comes to you Christianity will be killed'. Richard was said to have been enraged: 'The king's colour changed. Then he said "I sent [these soldiers] here and asked them to go [and] if they die there without me then would [that] I never again bear the title of king."' This episode reveals the Lionheart's determination to operate as a warrior-king in the front line of conflict, but it also suggests that, by this stage, he was taking risks that worried even his closest supporters. It is certainly true that there were real dangers involved in these skirmishes. Just a few weeks later, Andrew of Chauvigny broke his arm while skewering a Muslim opponent during a scuffle near Lydda.[83]

Talking to the enemy

Bold as Richard's involvement might have been in these inland incursions, his martial offensive was just one facet of a combined strategy. Throughout the autumn and early winter of 1191 the king sought to use diplomacy alongside military threat, perhaps hoping that, when jointly wielded, these two weapons might bring Saladin to the point of submission, forestalling the need for a direct assault on Jerusalem.

In fact, the Lionheart had reopened channels of communication with the enemy just days after the Battle of Arsuf. Around 12 September he sent Humphrey of Toron, the disenfranchised former husband of Isabella, to request a renewal of discussions with al-Adil. Saladin acceded, giving his brother 'permission to hold talks and the power to negotiate on his own initiative'. One of the sultan's confidants explained that '[Saladin] thought the meetings were in our interest because he saw in the hearts of men that they were tired and disillusioned with the fighting, the hardship and the burden of debts that was on their backs'. In all probability, Saladin was also playing for time and seeking to garner information about the enemy.[84]

In the months to come, reliable intelligence proved to be a precious commodity, and spies seem to have infiltrated both camps. In late September 1191 Saladin narrowly averted a potentially disastrous leak when a group of eastern Christians travelling through the Judean hills were seized and searched. They were found to be carrying extremely sensitive documents – letters from the Ayyubid governor of Jerusalem to the sultan, detailing worrying shortages of grain, equipment and men within the Holy City – which they had intended to present to King Richard. Meanwhile, to furnish a regular supply of Frankish captives for interrogation, Saladin engaged 300 rather disreputable Bedouin thieves to carry out night-time prisoner snatches. For Latin and Muslim alike, however, knowledge of the enemy's movements and intentions was always fallible. Saladin, for example, was apparently informed that Philip Augustus had died in October 1191. Perhaps more significantly, the Lionheart persistently overestimated Saladin's military strength for much of the remainder of the crusade.

Throughout autumn and early winter 1191, Richard eagerly

maintained a regular dialogue with al-Adil, and, to begin with at least, this contact seems to have been hidden from the Frankish armies. In part, the king must have been driven to negotiation by the rumour that Conrad of Montferrat had opened his own, independent, channel of diplomacy with Saladin. As always, the Lionheart's willingness to discuss avenues to peace with the enemy did not indicate some pacifistic preference for the avoidance of conflict. Negotiation was a weapon of war: one that might beget a settlement when combined with a military offensive; one that would certainly bring vital intelligence; and, crucially in this phase of the crusade, one that offered an opportunity to sow dissension among the ranks of Islam.

Even before leaving Jaffa, Richard entered into an intensive period of communication with al-Adil between 18 and 23 October. Initially, the king set out to gauge the enemy's attitude towards Jerusalem. He wanted to explore the possibility that Saladin might relinquish possession of a city that Richard bluntly stated 'is the centre of our worship which we shall never renounce, even if there were only one of us left'. But al-Adil conveyed an unequivocal response from the sultan, emphasising Islam's own reverence for the Holy City and urging the Lionheart 'not to imagine that we shall give it up, for we are unable to breathe a word of that amongst the Muslims'.

Richard then made an audacious change of tack – one that surprised his adversaries at the time and still confounds modern historians to this day. The king had already made a point of cultivating an amicable relationship with al-Adil, apparently describing him as 'my brother and my friend' in conversation. He now took the far grander step of proposing an extraordinary marriage alliance between Latin Christendom and Islam, in which al-Adil would be wed to Richard's own sister, Joanne. This union would form the basis of a peace agreement in which 'the sultan should give to al-Adil all the coastal lands that he held and make him king of [Palestine]', with Jerusalem to serve 'as the seat of [the royal couple's] realm'. This new polity would remain part of Saladin's empire, but

Christians would be given free access to the Holy City. Al-Adil and Joanne would command the region's castles, while the Christian Military Orders would take control of its villages. The pact would be sealed by an exchange of prisoners and the return of the True Cross. With a flourish of seeming magnanimity, the Lionheart proclaimed that the acceptance of this deal would bring the crusade to an immediate end and prompt his return to the West.

Because this offer was not recorded in any surviving contemporary Christian source (being mentioned only in Arabic texts) it is difficult accurately to assess how such an apparently outrageous arrangement might have been greeted by Richard's Frankish compatriots. The Lionheart seems to have kept the entire affair a closely guarded secret, even initially from his sister, but whether he took the whole idea seriously, or whether it was merely intended as a ruse, remains uncertain. What is clear is that al-Adil viewed it as a genuine proposal. In diplomatic terms, Richard's proposition possessed a masterful subtlety. Alive to the potential tensions between Saladin and al-Adil – the latter's position as trusted brother being balanced by the threat he posed to the sultan's son and heir – the English king made an offer that al-Adil could not ignore, but one that could also make him appear to be harbouring personal ambitions. Acutely aware of this implication, al-Adil refused to convey the news of Richard's scheme to Saladin in person, instead deputising Baha al-Din, instructing him to speak with strict caution.

Saladin actually agreed to the terms, although he may have believed that Richard would never go through with the plan and was merely trying to 'mock and deceive him'. Certainly, within a few days the Lionheart sent news that his sister would be unable to marry a Muslim and now suggested that al-Adil should convert to Christianity, leaving 'the door open for negotiations'.[85]

A few weeks later, with the Third Crusade now grinding out its advance on Judea, Richard once again requested a parley. He and al-Adil met in an opulently appointed tent, pitched just beyond the Muslim front line at Ramla, on 8 November 1191. The atmosphere was almost convivial. The pair exchanged 'foods, luxuries and presents', tasting delicacies from their respective cultures; Richard asked to hear some Arabic music and a female musician was duly ushered in to entertain him with singing and the playing of a harp. Having talked through the day, 'they parted', in the words of one Muslim witness, 'in amity and good spirits as firm friends', even though the Lionheart's repeated requests for a direct meeting with Saladin were declined.

Now, for the first time, the king's negotiations with the enemy became public knowledge in the crusader camp, prompting considerable criticism. One Christian eyewitness noted that Richard and al-Adil 'seemed to develop a sort of mutual friendship', exchanging gifts including seven camels and an excellent tent. The general feeling among the Franks appears to have been that this diplomacy was ill advised. The Lionheart was said to have been fooled by the façade of generosity and goodwill into delaying the advance on Jerusalem – an error 'for which he was much blamed and much criticised' – and outmanoeuvred by Saladin's brother, who 'trapped the overly credulous king with his shrewdness'. This notion of Richard as a befuddled pawn, manipulated by the devious political operator al-Adil, does not match up with the depiction of the Lionheart as a diplomat by Muslim sources. Indeed, the Mosuli chronicler Ibn al-Athir openly praised Richard, noting that 'the king [met with al-Adil] as a skilful stratagem'.

In fact, the English king seems to have been a wily negotiator. A different man might have felt stymied by Saladin's continued refusal of direct dialogue, but Richard sought to turn this factor to his advantage. On 9 November he sent the sultan an artful message, capitalising on the concessions made weeks earlier: 'You have said that you granted these coastal lands to your brother. I want you to be an arbitrator between him and me and to divide these lands between [us].' The Christians would need 'some hold on Jerusalem', but he wanted there to 'be no blame on [al-Adil] from the Muslims and none on me from the Franks'. Richard's rather devious underlying intention was to shift the whole basis of the negotiations, encouraging Saladin to think of himself as a magnanimous arbitrator and not an arch-opponent. At least some of the sultan's advisers 'were greatly impressed by this [approach]'.[86]

In the field of diplomatic machination, however, Saladin was, at the very least, Richard's equal. Throughout the autumn, the sultan had been in contact with Conrad of Montferrat, a fact he made no effort to hide from the Lionheart – indeed, Conrad's envoy even occasionally 'went riding with al-Adil, observing the Franks as the Muslims engaged them in battle', a spectacle which, it was believed, prompted the English king to redouble his own efforts at negotiation. Looking to exploit the rift between Richard and the marquis, Saladin pushed for a 'show of open hostility to the Franks from overseas', promising that if Conrad attacked crusader-held Acre he would be rewarded with an independent principality including Beirut and Sidon. The sultan juggled the negotiations with Richard and Conrad with panache, even lodging their respective envoys in different parts of his camp on the same day, all the while aiming, in the words of one of his advisers, 'to cause dissension amongst them'.

By 11 November, however, with the crusaders now threatening Ramla, Saladin was willing to deal in earnest. He assembled his counsellors to debate the relative merits of forging a truce with Conrad or Richard. The marquis' strength was certainly growing – he now had the backing of much of the nobility of the former Latin kingdom – but, ultimately, he was deemed less reliable than the Lionheart. Instead, the council backed an agreement with the English king based on an equitable division of Palestine that would see al-Adil and Joanne married and Christian 'priests in the shrines and churches of Jerusalem'. In the end, perhaps believing that he had Saladin backed into a corner, Richard responded to this significant offer with prevarication. For the union to be permissible, he argued, the pope would have to give his blessing and this would take three months. Even as the message was being delivered the Lionheart was readying his troops to advance on Ramla and beyond.[87]

TO TAKE THE HOLY CITY

By early November 1191 the work to refortify the region around Yasur had been completed. Richard took the next step towards Jerusalem on 15 November, moving the crusader army forward to a position between Lydda and Ramla. Saladin retreated before him, leaving the two settlements – their defences shattered – to the Franks and, in the weeks that followed, he moved back first to Latrun and then, around 12 December, took refuge in Jerusalem itself. Although Muslim forces continued to harry the Latins throughout this period, in some sense at least the path to the gates of the Holy City was now open.

But even as his men hurriedly sought to rebuild Ramla, the Lionheart had to confront a new enemy: winter. On the open plain, its onset brought a ferocious change in the weather. Lashed by driving rain, freezing in plummeting temperatures, the crusaders spent six miserable weeks stockpiling food and weapons at Ramla, securing the supply line back to Jaffa, before inching their way forward first to Latrun, and then on to reach the small dismantled fortress near Beit Nuba, at the foot of the Judean hills, soon after Christmas. They were now just twelve miles from Jerusalem.

Conditions within the army that December were appalling. One eyewitness wrote:

> It was cold and overcast . . . Rain and hail battered us, bringing down our tents. We lost so many horses at Christmas and both before and after, so many biscuits were wasted, soggy with water, so much salt pork went bad in the storms; hauberks rusted so that they could hardly be cleaned; clothes rotted; people suffered from malnourishment so that they were in great distress.

And yet, by all accounts, morale among the ordinary soldiers was high. After long months, and in some cases years, of struggle, they were now practically within sight of their goal. 'They had an indescribable yearning to see the city of Jerusalem and complete their pilgrimage', noted one Latin contemporary, while a crusader in the army recalled, 'no one was angry or sad . . . everywhere was joy and happiness and [everyone] said together "God, now we are going on the right way, guided by Your grace."' Enduring commitment to the cause of the holy war seems to have inspired them, even amidst the anguish of a winter campaign. Like their crusading forefathers back in 1099, they were now ready, desperate even, to besiege the Holy City, regardless of the risk and privation involved.[88]

The question was whether King Richard shared their fervour. As the new year of 1192 began, he had a crucial decision to make. The crusade had taken almost two months to advance just thirty miles towards Jerusalem. The line of communication with the coast still held but was subject to near-daily Muslim raids. Mounting a siege of the city in these conditions, in the bitter heart of winter, would be a mammoth undertaking and a huge gamble. And yet, the bulk of the Latin army clearly expected that an assault would be made.

Around 10 January, the Lionheart convened a council to debate the best course of action. Its shocking conclusion was that the Third Crusade should retreat from Beit Nuba, turning its back on Jerusalem. Officially it was said that a powerful lobby of Templars, Hospitallers and Latin barons native to the Levant persuaded Richard. The dangers of undertaking a siege while Saladin still possessed a field army were too severe, they argued, and anyway, the Franks lacked the manpower adequately to garrison the Holy City even if it did, by some miracle, fall. '[These] wiser men were not of the opinion that they should acquiesce in the common people's rash desires [to besiege Jerusalem]', recalled one contemporary, and instead they advised that the expedition 'should return and fortify Ascalon', cutting Saladin's supply line between Palestine and Egypt. In truth, the king probably packed the council with those sympathetic to his own views and knew only too well what its recommendations would be. For now, at least, Richard was not willing to stake the fate of the entire holy war on the outcome of so hazardous a campaign. On 13 January he broadcast the order to retire from Beit Nuba.

This was an earth-shattering pronouncement, but in recent scholarship Richard's decision has been viewed in a positive light. Championed by the likes of John Gillingham as an astute general whose decision making was governed by martial reality and not pious fantasy, the Lionheart has been widely praised for his cautious strategy. Hans Mayer, for example, concluded that 'in view of Saladin's tactics, [Richard's decision] was the right one'.[89]

In fact, the truth of the matter will never be known. One crusader eyewitness later concluded that the Franks missed an enormous opportunity to capture Jerusalem because they did not appreciate 'the distress, the suffering and the weakness' of the Muslim forces garrisoning the city, and to an extent he was right. Struggling to maintain his exhausted troops in the field, Saladin had been forced to disband the majority of his army after 12 December, leaving the Holy City dangerously undermanned. Ten days passed before Abu'l Haija the Fat arrived with Egyptian reinforcements. Throughout this period a decisive and determined move to assault Jerusalem might have broken Saladin's will, fracturing his already fragile hold over the Muslim alliance and plunging Near Eastern Islam into disarray. On balance, however, Richard was probably right to forgo such a massive gamble.

Even so, the Lionheart should not escape reproach for his conduct in this phase of the crusade. To date, historians have ignored a fundamental feature of his decision making. If, in January 1192, it was so obvious to Richard's military advisers and probably to the king himself that the Holy City was unconquerable and untenable, why had that same reality not been apparent months earlier, before the crusade ever left Jaffa? The king – the supposed master of military science – should surely have recognised in October 1191 that Jerusalem was a near-impossible military target and one that could never be retained. Writing in the early thirteenth century, Ibn al-Athir tried to reconstruct the Lionheart's thinking at Beit Nuba. He conjured up a scene in which Richard asked to see a map of the Holy City; once aware of its topography, the king supposedly concluded that Jerusalem could not be taken while Saladin still commanded a field army. But this is little more than an imaginative reconstruction. Richard's character and experience suggest that he would carefully have assembled the fullest possible picture of strategic intelligence before mounting the advance from Jaffa.

The Lionheart probably set foot on the road to Jerusalem in late October 1191 with little or no intention of actually prosecuting an attack on the city. This means that his advance was effectively a feint – the military component of a combined offensive in which a show of martial aggression augmented intensive diplomatic contact. Richard sought that autumn and winter to test Saladin's resolve and resources, but was ever ready to step back from the brink if a clear opportunity for victory failed to materialise. In all this, the king acted according to the best precepts of medieval generalship, but he failed to account for the distinct nature of crusading warfare.

The impact of the retreat upon Christian morale and the overall prospects of the crusade were catastrophic. Even Ambroise, the Lionheart's vocal supporter, acknowledged that:

> [When] it was realised that the army was to turn back (let it not be called retreat), then was the army, which had been so eager in its advance, so discouraged, that not since God created time was there ever seen an army so dejected and so depressed ... Nothing remained of the joy they had had before when they were to go to the [Holy] Sepulchre ... Everyone cursed the day he was born.

Now a stunned and bedraggled rabble, the army limped back to Ramla. From there, depression and disillusionment ripped the expedition apart. Hugh of Burgundy and many of the French decamped. Some returned to Jaffa, others went off to Acre, where food and earthly comforts were plentiful. Richard was left to lead a severely weakened force south-west to Ascalon.[90]

REGROUPING

The Lionheart reached the ruined port on 20 January 1192 amid horrendous storms that further dampened morale. As the crusaders struggled to come to terms with their retreat from Jerusalem, Richard did his best to recover from the first real setback of his campaign. He put his remaining troops to work rebuilding Ascalon, determined to salvage something from that dismal winter by making practical and visible progress on the coast. Henry of Champagne had remained loyal to his uncle and lent his aid to the project, but the refortifying of so devastated a city was a mammoth undertaking – one that would ultimately take five months of hard labour and cost Richard a fortune.

In late February, a crisis erupted in northern Palestine – one that revealed enduring divisions among the Franks. Even though the war for the Holy Land was far from over, the Latins began openly fighting over Acre. Genoese sailors tried to take control of the city, probably with the connivance of Conrad of Montferrat and Hugh of Burgundy, and it was only the fierce resistance put up by Richard's Pisan allies that prevented the port from being united with Tyre. Enraged by what he saw as a brazen act of betrayal, Richard travelled north to parley with Conrad, and the pair met halfway between Acre and Tyre. 'Long discussions' were apparently held, but no lasting agreement could be forged and the marquis returned to Tyre.[91]

Richard's military fortunes had turned in the hills of Judea, and now on the northern coast his gift for sure-footed diplomacy seemed also to desert him. Frustrated by his failure to bully Conrad into submission, the Lionheart immediately instituted an assembly and had the marquis officially deprived of the share of the kingdom of Jerusalem's revenue allotted to him in summer 1191. In truth, though, this was little more than an empty gesture. Conrad had two telling advantages: an unassailable centre of power at Tyre, and a growing body of support among Outremer's remaining Frankish barons, including the likes of Balian of Ibelin. The marquis may have been a devious, self-serving opportunist who was willing to negotiate with Saladin against the interests of the crusade, but his marriage to Isabella of Jerusalem gave him a claim to the throne. He also had proven himself a stronger leader than Guy of Lusignan (his rival for the Jerusalemite crown) and, unlike Richard, showed every sign of being committed to a permanent career in the Levant. That February the Lionheart chose to ignore the obvious, but eventually he would have to acknowledge the uncomfortable reality. Conrad could be neither broken nor turned and, therefore, he would have to be accommodated in any lasting political and military settlement in the Near East.

Around this time, channels of negotiation between Richard and Saladin were reopened. The sultan, once again, was represented by his brother al-Adil, while Humphrey of Toron spoke on the Lionheart's behalf. Meetings were held near Acre in late March and, at one point, it appeared that terms – including a partition of Jerusalem – might actually be agreed. In early April, however, Richard broke off the dialogue and sailed south to spend Easter in Ascalon. The reason for this sudden change of policy is uncertain, but it is likely that the king had heard rumours that Saladin's exhausted armies were showing signs of insubordination and that the sultan was also facing Muslim insurrection in Mesopotamia. Seizing upon this possible vulnerability, Richard seems to have convinced himself that he now had no need to agree to anything other than the most advantageous terms. Once back in Ascalon, he began preparing to launch a new offensive.

CRISIS AND TRANSFORMATION

On 15 April 1192 Robert, prior of Hereford, arrived in Ascalon having sailed east from Europe. He bore news that overturned all of Richard's plans. The king's aide and representative William of Longchamp had been exiled from England by Prince John, and

Richard's ambitious brother was now making moves to increase his own power in the kingdom. After ten months of crusading in the Holy Land, this was a stark reminder of Richard's duties and obligations as monarch of the Angevin realm. The Lionheart immediately recognised that, with a crisis looming in the West, he could ill afford to tarry in the Levant; but neither did he wish to abandon the crusade and return home a failure. Richard seems to have judged that he had time to dedicate one more fighting season to the cause of the cross. But to bring the Palestinian war to a swift and successful conclusion, he would need to unify the disparate Latin forces ranged across the Holy Land.

Reconciled to compromise, the Lionheart convened a council of crusader barons on 16 April. He announced that, in light of events in England, he might soon have to depart and instructed the assembly to resolve the issue of the Jerusalemite crown. A unanimous decision was reached, almost certainly with Richard's tacit approval, to offer the kingdom to Conrad of Montferrat. Guy of Lusignan, meanwhile, was to be compensated handsomely for his loss of status – Richard arranged for the Templars to sell Guy the island of Cyprus for 40,000 bezants, a move that allowed the Lusignan dynasty to establish a powerful and enduring lordship in the eastern Mediterranean. Henry of Champagne was deputised to sail north to Tyre and inform the marquis of his sudden promotion, and, more importantly, to persuade him to unite his forces, and those of Hugh of Burgundy, with the crusader army gathered at Ascalon so that the holy war might be waged.

Within a few short days Conrad received the news and by all accounts he was ecstatic. After months of waiting in the wings, proceeding ever with caution and cunning, his dreams of threading a path to regal power had been realised. For all his earlier intransigence and hesitation, the marquis immediately initiated preparations for a military campaign. Unbeknownst to Richard or the Franks, he also sent an urgent message to Saladin, explaining that an unexpected agreement had been reached among the Latins, and threatening that unless Saladin finalised 'a settlement [with Conrad] in the next few days', a full-scale confrontation would follow. According to a Muslim eyewitness in the sultan's court, Saladin took this approach extremely seriously. Threatened by impending civil unrest in Mesopotamia, 'the sultan believed . . . that the best plan was to make peace with the marquis' and on 24 April he dispatched an envoy to Tyre to finalise terms. In the last days of April 1192, then, King Richard and Saladin believed that they had found ways to conclude the war for the Holy Land: the one through renewed battle; the other through peace. The plans of both centred upon Conrad of Montferrat.[92]

On the evening of 28 April Conrad travelled to the French crusader Philip bishop of Beauvais' residence in Tyre to have supper. The pair seem to have struck up a friendship in the course of the crusade and Conrad was in a relaxed, celebratory mood. Riding home through the city later that night, attended by two guards, the marquis passed the Exchange building and entered a narrow street.

[There] two men were sitting on either side of the road. As [Conrad] came between them they rose up to meet him. One of them came and showed him a letter, and the marquis held out his hand to take it. The man drew a knife and plunged it into his body. The other man who was on the other side jumped onto the horse's rear and stabbed him in the side, and he fell dead.

Conrad's two assailants were subsequently revealed to have been members of the order of Assassins sent by Sinan, the Old Man of the Mountain. One of the pair was decapitated immediately; the other captured, interrogated and then dragged through the streets until he died. But though their link to the Assassins was established, the original instigator of the attack remained less certain. Hugh of Burgundy and the French in Tyre spread the rumour that King Richard had contracted the killing, while in some parts of the Muslim world it was rumoured that Saladin was involved. Given recent developments, however, neither ruler actually stood to gain much from Conrad's death. The truth of the matter is impossible to determine – Sinan may even have acted independently to eliminate the marquis, having deemed him to be a dangerous long-term threat to the balance of power in the Levant.[93]

The political situation among the Latins was in disarray. Hugh of Burgundy tried to seize control of Tyre, but he seems to have been thwarted by Conrad's widow Isabella, the heiress to the kingdom of Jerusalem. With yet another outbreak of infighting threatening, a new settlement was pushed through quickly. Count Henry of Champagne was chosen as a compromise candidate – because as nephew to both King Richard and Philip Augustus he represented Angevin and Capetian interests – and within a week he was married to Isabella and elected as titular monarch of Frankish Palestine.

The exact extent of the Lionheart's involvement in the engineering of this rapid solution is unclear. By and large, however, the new order suited his interests and those of the Third Crusade. Henry of Champagne's appointment finally united all the Latin armies in Palestine – from the native Franks of Outremer, to Hugh of Burgundy's French troops and Richard's Angevin forces. Given Henry's and Richard's recent history of alliance, there was also a good chance that the pair would be able to cooperate effectively.

Through May 1192 the Lionheart set about bolstering his foothold in southern Palestine, conquering the Muslim-held fortress of Darum, while the work of refortifying Ascalon neared completion and Count Henry and Duke Hugh mustered armies to the north. With Christian morale reinvigorated, the stage seemed set for the launch of a decisive campaign – although, given Richard's recent expansion down the coast towards Egypt, the target of any venture still might be subject to debate.

On 29 May, however, another Angevin messenger arrived from Europe with a dispatch confirming the Lionheart's worst fears. Ever since his rival Philip Augustus of France had left the crusade in midsummer 1191, Richard had been deeply concerned that the

Capetians might threaten Angevin territory in his absence. He now learned that King Philip had made contact with Prince John, and that together the pair were busy plotting. The envoy warned that unless something was done '[to restrain] this abominable treachery, there was a danger that very soon England would be taken from King Richard's authority'. The Lionheart was said to have been 'disturbed to hear this news, and afterwards . . . sat for a long time in silence, turning things over in his mind and weighing up what should be done'. In April he had resolved to remain in the Holy Land, but this latest grave report from the West reopened the issue. According to his supporter Ambroise, Richard was 'melancholy, downcast and saddened . . . his thinking confused'.[94] Christendom's great warrior had reached the critical moment of decision – would he fight on as a crusader, or heed the call of his Angevin realm and return home as a king?

18

RESOLUTION

With the approach of summer in 1192, Saladin began to reassemble his armies, girding Islam for a renewed Christian offensive. Over the preceding year the sultan had faced a series of ruinous setbacks. He had watched in impotent humiliation as Acre fell on 12 July 1191, and then suffered the shock of King Richard's cold-blooded execution of the city's Muslim garrison on 20 August. All efforts to halt the Lionheart's march south to Jaffa had failed and, on 7 September at Arsuf, Saladin's armies had been driven from the field of battle. Forced to reconsider his strategy, the sultan moved on to the defensive, demolishing the fortresses of southern Palestine, shadowing the crusaders' grinding inland advance, yet ultimately retreating within the confines of Jerusalem itself around 12 December, there to await attack.

Since the glory of his victories at Hattin and the Holy City in 1187, Saladin had remained resolute in his commitment to *jihad* – if anything, his dedication had deepened. But even so, he had gradually lost the initiative to the Franks. Debilitated by recurrent illness, hamstrung by the faltering morale and physical exhaustion of his troops, and distracted by the wider demands of his Ayyubid Empire, the sultan had been slowly driven to the edge of defeat.

Then, on 12 January 1192, the crusaders retreated from Beit Nuba, offering Islam a new lease of hope and gifting Saladin the chance to regroup and recover.

AYYUBID STRATEGY IN EARLY 1192

Having survived the Christian advance on Jerusalem, Saladin took stock of his position in the first months of 1192. The Ayyubid realm was in a worrying state of disrepair. After years of neglecting the management of his treasury, the sultan's financial resources were profoundly overstretched, and without a ready supply of money he was struggling to pay for the manpower and materials necessary for war. Egypt's continued prosperity offered a lifeline, but Richard's reoccupation of Ascalon posed a considerable threat to communications between Syria and the Nile region.

These economic woes were linked to a second concern: the dwindling availability and waning loyalty of his armies. Through the near-constant campaigning of the preceding four years, Saladin had made enormous demands of the troops drawn from his own domains in Egypt, Syria and the Jazira. Likewise, he had asked much of his allies in Mesopotamia and Diyar Bakr. It was a testament to Saladin's remarkable charisma as a leader, to the effectiveness of the political and religious propaganda he disseminated, and to the devotional appeal of *jihad* that even potential rivals such as the Zangid Izz al-Din of Mosul and Imad al-Din Zangi of Sinjar had continued to honour their commitments to the holy war by answering the Ayyubid sultan's calls to arms. But these demands could not be met indefinitely. If the conflict in Palestine continued unabated, it would be only a matter of time before the bonds of loyalty and common purpose uniting the Muslim world began to fracture. This was why Saladin took the risk of disbanding his army in December 1192.

To the sultan's dismay, these manifold problems were

compounded by the first flickerings of disloyalty within his own family. Back in March 1191, Saladin had allowed his trusted and able nephew Taqi al-Din to take possession of a parcel of territory in the Jazira, east of the Euphrates, which included the cities of Edessa and Harran. In November of that same year, in the midst of the Latins' advance on the Holy City, the sultan was deeply saddened by news of Taqi al-Din's death from illness. By early 1192, however, Taqi al-Din's adult son al-Mansur Muhammad began to show what one of Saladin's aides described as 'signs of rebellion'. Fearing that he might be deprived of an inheritance, al-Mansur sought to cajole his great-uncle, the sultan, into either confirming his rights to the Jaziran lands or granting other territory in Syria. The approach was evidently underlined with the implied threat that, if thwarted, al-Mansur would incite anti-Ayyubid insurrection in the north-east.

Saladin was appalled by this lack of fidelity in a member of his own bloodline, and his mood did not improve when al-Mansur attempted to use al-Adil as a mediator – indeed, the conniving tactic apparently left the sultan 'overcome with rage'. This whole affair proved to be a problematic distraction, one that rumbled on into early summer 1192. Saladin initially responded by sending his eldest son al-Afdal to subdue the Jazira in April, empowering him to request further aid from his brother al-Zahir in Aleppo if necessary. By late May, however, the sultan had relented. Al-Adil seems to have applied some pressure as an arbitrator, and the Emir Abu'l Haija also pointedly advocated leniency during an assembly held to discuss the case, observing that it was not possible to fight fellow Muslims and 'infidels' at the same time. Saladin duly granted al-Mansur lands in northern Syria and endowed al-Adil with rights to Harran and Edessa. However, this rather abrupt reconciliation caused something of a rift with al-Afdal. Angered by his father's vacillation and the decision to reward al-Adil, al-Afdal showed a marked reluctance to return to Palestine, tarrying first at Aleppo and then at Damascus, depriving Saladin of valuable manpower.[95]

In early 1192 Saladin faced financial insecurity, troop shortages and sedition. Not surprisingly, he further refined his approach to the holy war. During the preceding autumn he had adopted a more defensive strategy, avoiding decisive confrontations with the Franks but still maintaining relatively close contact with his enemy. From spring 1192 onwards, the sultan withdrew almost all of his soldiers from the field. Barring occasional skirmishing forays and opportunistic raids, the Ayyubid armies held fast in defensible positions across the length of Palestine, waiting to repel any Christian attack. In a related development, Saladin instituted a widespread work programme to strengthen his major fortresses and Jerusalem's battlements.

These preparations were reflective of a fundamental change of policy. In 1192 Saladin evidently concluded that he could no longer realistically expect to achieve outright victory against the Third Crusade. This realisation prompted him to re-engage with the diplomatic process – establishing dialogue with Richard I and Conrad of Montferrat. It also forced the sultan to re-evaluate his bargaining position. A deal based on a partition of the Holy Land, in which the Latins would retain control of a coastal strip of territory, was now deemed acceptable. As yet, however, Saladin retained two firm demands: Islam must retain dominion of Jerusalem; and Ascalon, the gateway to Egypt, must be abandoned.

Saladin's overarching strategy of defence and diplomacy was now underpinned by a singular objective – to survive the Third Crusade. He knew that the Latin Christians who had come east in their thousands to wage a war of reconquest would one day return home. King Richard, in particular, could not afford to remain in the Levant indefinitely. Saladin's goal was to withstand the storm: limiting his losses wherever possible; avoiding decisive confrontation at all costs; but bringing the Palestinian war to a swift conclusion, before the Ayyubid war machine collapsed. Then, once the crusaders had sailed from the eastern shores, the sultan could turn his mind to thoughts of recovery and reconquest.

THE CRUSADERS' SECOND ADVANCE ON JERUSALEM

Saladin had done his best to prepare for an attack on either Jerusalem or Egypt. In late May and early June 1192 troops from across the Near East began to regroup in the Holy City. The sultan also deployed a number of scouting forces, including one under Abu'l Haija, to monitor the movements of the Franks, who now were based in the region of Ascalon.

Indecision

On 6 June Saladin received an urgent warning that the crusaders were marching in strength north-east from Ascalon – a move that obviously heralded an advance on Jerusalem. It appeared that Richard and the Latins had resolved to make a second attempt to besiege and capture the Holy City. In fact, Richard had spent the first days of June in a tortured state of indecision. Badly shaken by the prospect of an alliance back in Europe between his acquisitive brother John and Philip Augustus, the Lionheart was torn between returning to the West and remaining in the Levant to fulfil his crusading vow. The English king's dilemma was compounded further by the thorny question of strategy. The Third Crusade's primary objective was the recovery of Jerusalem, but Richard still considered the city to be an unrealistic target. In some respects, the Franks were better placed to prosecute an inland campaign than they had been six months earlier. Now united, they could rely on stable summer weather and use the network of rebuilt fortifications established in late 1191. But in all other respects the proposition had not changed – the challenge remained almost insurmountable, the risks immense. Even if, by some miracle, the attack succeeded, Jerusalem would be virtually impossible to hold. Richard, therefore, favoured an attack on Egypt: a strike that would threaten the very foundations of the Ayyubid Empire, and likely force Saladin to agree a truce on terms of the Lionheart's choosing. In military terms, Richard's plan made sense, but it largely ignored the driving devotional dimension of crusader warfare. If the king was to press home his strategy – winning over the hearts and minds of the Christian host, persuading the Franks that the path to ultimate victory led through the Nile – he could afford none of the equivocation witnessed in autumn and winter 1191. He would have to offer clear-cut, compelling leadership, commanding with unfaltering vision and force of will.

Instead, after 29 May, Richard vacillated, withdrawing into private contemplation to ruminate on his options and stratagems. And as he did so, events began to overtake him. Popular opinion within the crusader army was crystallising. In the Lionheart's absence a group of Latin barons, presumably spearheaded by Hugh of Burgundy, held a council on 31 May and decided to march on Jerusalem with or without the Angevin monarch. News of this judgement was leaked, probably quite deliberately, and immediately spread through the army, eliciting a 'wildly joyful' reaction that left the troops dancing until after midnight.

Even Richard's most ardent promoter, Ambroise, admitted that the king became paralysed at this point, reflecting that he 'was not at all happy, but lay down, very upset about the news that he had heard', adding that 'he continually pondered [the tidings from England] in his tent and gave himself up to this pondering'. As the Lionheart wavered and the days passed, a potent surge of enthusiasm swept over the camp, with one thought at its core – the call of Jerusalem. According to Ambroise, Richard experienced a form of spiritual epiphany on 4 June, having wrestled with his conscience. As a result, the king abruptly proclaimed that 'he would remain in the [Holy Land] until Easter [1193] without turning back and that everyone should be prepared [to lay siege] to Jerusalem'. Perhaps the Lionheart did have a stirring change of heart, but it is far more likely that, in the face of mounting public pressure, he bowed to popular sentiment. He certainly seems to have harboured as yet unexpressed ambitions for an Egyptian campaign and continued to have deep misgivings about the viability of any assault on the Holy City. Nonetheless, he agreed to advance into Judea. This capitulation signalled that, for now at least, Richard had lost control of the Third Crusade. Thus, even as Saladin interpreted the Frankish mobilisation as a sign of new-found intent on 6 June, grievous fissures were starting to appear in the Christian command structure.[96]

The threat posed

Once begun, the crusaders' march on Jerusalem proceeded with remarkable rapidity. By 9 June the Franks had arrived at Latrun and, on the following day, they pushed on to Beit Nuba. In autumn 1191 it had taken the Christians months to reach this same position. Now, after only five days, they once again were within striking distance of the Holy City, just twelve miles from its hallowed walls. Saladin ordered Muslim raiding parties to harass the near-constant stream of Latin supply convoys coming inland from Jaffa, but other than intermittent skirmishing assaults, he made no serious attempt to threaten the crusaders' main forward camp at Beit Nuba. Instead, the sultan began positioning his troops within Jerusalem ahead of the impending attack.

After the first flurry of movement, however, the Frankish offensive seemed to stall. In fact, this delay was caused initially by the Latins' decision to wait for Henry of Champagne to bring further reinforcements from Acre. But as the days passed, the deep-seated divisions within the crusade that had remained submerged at Ascalon began to surface, and the Franks were soon locked in a furious argument over strategy and leadership.

On 20 June, Saladin's scouts reported that a large contingent of crusaders had moved off from Beit Nuba. This raised the sultan's suspicions, because at that very moment he was awaiting the imminent arrival of a massive supply caravan from Egypt. Concerned that the Franks might seek to intercept this column and appropriate the vital resources it contained, Saladin immediately dispatched troops to warn the Muslim convoy. The two Ayyubid parties rendezvoused successfully and were making watchful progress inland towards Hebron, when just before dawn on 24 June Richard I launched a searing attack. As Saladin feared, the Lionheart had been alerted to the caravan's movements by one of his spies and, galvanised by the prospect of rich plunder, immediately rushed south. The Angevin king spent three days tracking the caravan through his network of local informants and then unleashed a well-timed surprise assault. After a vicious fight the Latins prevailed. The bulk of the Muslim escort escaped, but they left behind a veritable hoard of booty: precious goods, including spices, gold, silver and silks; weapons and armour; tents; food supplies, including biscuits, wheat, flour, pepper, sugar and cinnamon; and 'a great many cordials and medicines'. Perhaps even more significantly, the Christians also took possession of literally thousands of camels, dromedaries, horses, mules and asses.

News of this disaster caused real alarm in Jerusalem. Not only had Saladin lost a plethora of much-needed supplies – all of which would now profit the enemy – he also recognised that the Latins could use the influx of pack animals to ferry further resources inland from Jaffa. When the crusaders' expeditionary force returned to Beit Nuba on 29 June, the sultan began 'to prepare the means to withstand a siege'. Baha al-Din, who was then present in the Holy City, recorded that his master 'started poisoning the water sources outside Jerusalem, destroying the pits and the cisterns, so that around Jerusalem there remained no drinking water at all', adding that the sultan also 'sent to muster his troops from all quarters and lands'.[97]

The choice

By the first days of July 1192 there seems to have been no question in Saladin's mind that the Franks were about to initiate their final drive towards Jerusalem. The moment of decisive confrontation – the crisis that he had hoped to avoid – was upon him. On Thursday 2 July the sultan assembled his most trusted emirs to discuss a plan of action. The meeting proved to be a grim-faced, earnest affair, as Saladin sat surrounded by the commanders and counsellors who had served him through long years of war and conquest. Abu'l Haija the Fat was there, although his legendary corpulence had now reached such a stage that he had trouble walking and needed 'a stool to sit on while in the presence of the sultan'.

Baha al-Din was also in attendance, and according to his account, Saladin set out to instil a sense of steadfast determination among his lieutenants by repeatedly reminding them of their duties and responsibilities: 'Know today that you are the army of Islam and its bulwark . . . There are no Muslims who can face the enemy but you [and] the Muslims in all lands depend on you.' In response, the emirs affirmed their willingness to fight to the death for Saladin, their lord and patron, and the sultan's heart was said to have been 'greatly cheered'.

Later that same day, however, after the meeting had broken up, Saladin received a private missive from Abu'l Haija warning that beneath the veneer of loyalty and unity insurrection was brewing. Many within the army were opposed to 'prepar[ing] for a siege', fearful that the catastrophe at Acre might be repeated. There was also a real danger that the long-standing resentment between the Kurds and Turks in Saladin's army might spill into open conflict. Abu'l Haija's advice was that the sultan should lead the bulk of his armies out of the Holy City while he still had the chance, leaving behind only a token garrison.

That evening the sultan summoned Baha al-Din and revealed the contents of Abu'l Haija's message. Baha al-Din recalled that 'Saladin felt a concern for Jerusalem that could move mountains and he was distressed by this communication. I remained in attendance upon him that night, a night wholly spent on the concerns of the holy war.' As dawn drew near, Saladin finally decided, with a heavy heart, to leave Jerusalem – 'he had been tempted to remain himself, but then his better sense rejected that because of the risk to Islam it involved'. The choice had been made; in the morning, on Friday 3 July, preparations for the exodus began. Saladin took the chance to visit the *Haram as-Sharif*, and there led a last Friday prayer in the sacred Aqsa mosque, where some four years earlier he had overseen the installation of Nur al-Din's glorious triumphal pulpit. Baha al-Din wrote: 'I saw [the sultan] prostrate himself and say some words, while his tears were falling on to his prayer rug.'

But then, as evening drew in, astonishing unforeseen news arrived – news that overturned Saladin's plans and reshaped the entire war for the Holy Land. Jurdik, the Syrian emir in command of the Ayyubid advance guard, reported that the Franks were in an evident state of confusion. His message described how that day 'the enemy all mounted up, stood in the field on horseback and then returned to their tents' and added that 'we have sent spies to discover what they are up to'. The very next morning, on 4 July 1192, five years to the day since the Battle of Hattin, the armies of the Third Crusade struck camp, turned their backs on Jerusalem and began to retreat towards Ramla. Amid great 'delight and rejoicing' it became clear that the Holy City had been saved.[98]

Frankish failure

The crusaders' departure left the Muslims in a state of gleeful disbelief. What had caused this sudden reversal? Jurdik's agents were able to piece together only a garbled version of events, reporting a dispute between Richard and the French. In fact, the seeds of the Frankish retreat had already been sown at Ascalon, when Richard lost his grip over the crusade and acceded to popular demands for a second inland advance. Once the expedition reached Beit Nuba on 10 June it rapidly became obvious that the Lionheart had no real intention of besieging Jerusalem, even though the French were determined that an attack should be attempted. On 17 June the crusade leaders met to debate the matter. Even two eyewitness Christian sources that were most biased in Richard I's favour freely admitted that the king was fiercely opposed to any further advance.

The Lionheart apparently offered three convincing arguments as to why a siege was unrealistic: the vulnerability of the Latin supply line back to the coast; the sheer scale of the Holy City's defences; and

Saladin's access to detailed intelligence regarding the Christians' strength and movements. The king also bluntly indicated that he was absolutely unwilling to lead the crusade in such a 'rash enterprise' because it would lead to 'terrible disgrace' for which he would be 'forever blamed, shamed and less loved'. This notable admission suggests that Richard was not simply considering the crusade's best interests, but was moved primarily by concerns about his own reputation. The king had obviously formulated this view while still in Ascalon, because he now lobbied for a switch of strategy, recommending that the Latins immediately commit to an Egyptian campaign – conveniently, he already had a fleet waiting at Acre to portage supplies to the Nile, and he pledged to pay for 700 knights and 2,000 men-at-arms of his own, and to offer financial support to any other participants. This was the scheme that Richard might have promoted at Ascalon had he not been dogged by hesitation and doubt.

However, the Lionheart had now allowed the crusader host to march, for a second time, to within a few hours of Jerusalem. In this position, any attempt to promote military realism over pious dedication would be fraught with difficulty. Even so, he tried to force through his plan, instituting what amounted to a rigged jury, which, unsurprisingly, concluded 'that the greatest good of the land would be to conquer [Egypt]'. When Hugh of Burgundy and the French rejected this pronouncement, declaring that 'they would not move on anywhere except to besiege Jerusalem', an impasse was reached.[99]

Having allowed the Third Crusade to reach this dreadful deadlock, the Lionheart's response was shockingly ineffectual. In an act of feeble petulance, he simply resigned as commander-in-chief, stating that he would stay with the expedition but no longer lead. Perhaps this was brinkmanship, designed to stun and silence dissenting voices, but if so it failed. In many respects, by abjuring his responsibilities at this critical juncture, Richard was merely acknowledging a crushing reality – the great Angevin king now possessed neither the power, nor the vision, to control the crusade.

On 20 June, intelligence of the Ayyubid caravan from Egypt

sparked action and a brief respite from discord, but once the expeditionary force returned to Beit Nuba on 29 June the wrangling resumed. Latin eyewitnesses described how the 'people [were] wailing and complaining', 'grieving' because of the continued failure to march on the Holy City. By early July the continued turmoil had effectively immobilised the crusade. The French seem to have made a last-ditch attempt to initiate an advance on 3 July, but without Richard's support this collapsed. With no way forward, the Christian host finally accepted the inevitable and began a dispirited retreat. According to Ambroise, when news spread through the army that 'they would not worship at the Holy Sepulchre which was four leagues away, their hearts were filled with sorrow and they turned back so disheartened and miserable that you never saw a chosen people so depressed and dismayed'.[100]

This reversal marked the nadir of Richard's crusading career. That summer he was guilty of a calamitous failure of leadership. His error was not the decision to step back from besieging Jerusalem – just as in January 1192, he rightly adhered to the dictates of military science and deemed the risks involved in an attack on the Holy City to be unacceptable. The fault lay in not manifesting this knowledge while still at Ascalon, in neglecting to assume firm control of the expedition, and in then allowing the Latin armies once again to be brought to within one day of the Holy City. The Third Crusade's prospects for success had already been severely impaired by Richard's mismanagement of the first abortive march on Jerusalem in late 1191. Now, in July 1192, this second reversal had a disastrous effect on Frankish morale and inflicted a lethal blow to Christendom's fortunes in the war for the Holy Land.

ENDGAME

By summer 1192 Saladin and Richard had fought one another to a standstill. The sultan had survived the crusaders' second inland advance and remained in possession of Jerusalem, but his Muslim armies were utterly exhausted and the Ayyubid Empire practically at the point of collapse. The Third Crusade, meanwhile, had suffered no deadly defeat, but its martial energy had been squandered through irresolute leadership. Frankish unity – so recently buoyed by Henry of Champagne's election as titular king of Latin Palestine – was now shattered irrevocably and the Latin coalition forces dispersed (with Hugh of Burgundy and the French congregating in Caesarea). Deprived of the requisite manpower and resources, the Lionheart's plan to open a new front in Egypt was eventually abandoned. At the same time, anxiety over events in Europe continued to figure heavily in Richard's thinking. With the forces of neither Christendom nor Islam able to win the Palestinian war, all that really remained was to settle upon a path to peace.

Much of that summer was given over to protracted negotiation as each side jockeyed for the most favourable terms, ever watchful for opportunities to gain diplomatic leverage. One such opening came in late July 1192, when Saladin sought to capitalise on Richard's temporary absence in Acre by leading a strike force on Jaffa. The sultan came within hours of conquering the port, but the Lionheart arrived by ship (having been alerted to the attack) to relieve the Frankish garrison. Wading ashore, the king spearheaded a fearless counter-attack, beating back the Muslim assault. Richard established a camp outside Jaffa and, in the days that followed, brazenly saw off all attempts to overrun his position, despite being heavily outnumbered. Attended by a small party of loyal supporters – including Henry of Champagne, Robert of Leicester, Andrew of Chauvigny and William of L'Estang – the king was said to have 'brandished his sword with rapid strokes, slicing through the charging enemy, cutting them down in two as he met them, first on this side, then on that'. Whatever his recent failings as a crusade commander, the Lionheart remained a warrior of unquestioned skill and fearsome repute. According to Muslim testimony, around 4 August Richard even rode out alone, lance in hand, before the Ayyubid lines, in an act of sheer defiance, 'but no one came out against him'. Soon after,

Saladin ordered the retreat, utterly incensed by his troops' deepening reluctance to confront this force of nature despite his exhortations to attack.

In truth, the sultan's anger – and the uncharacteristic recalcitrance of his soldiers outside Jaffa – can be at least partially explained by the fact that Richard had resorted to more devious tactics in the war of diplomacy. To Saladin's annoyance, his Angevin rival was making relentless, and increasingly successful, attempts to establish friendships with leading Ayyubid emirs. Already in 1191 the Lionheart had shown an interest in exploiting the potential for rivalry and suspicion between the sultan and his brother al-Adil. Now, in the second half of 1192, as the pace and intensity of negotiation quickened, Richard extended this ploy – re-establishing lines of communication with al-Adil, but also forging contacts with a number of other Muslim potentates drawn from Saladin's inner circle. The men he targeted were not necessarily openly disloyal to the sultan, but, like everyone else, they could sense that the crusade was drawing to a close. As such, they recognised that their role in any future settlement might be markedly improved if they served as mediators and peace brokers.

Richard deliberately conducted much of this contact in public – seemingly intent upon demonstrating to Saladin that his emirs' appetite for hard-bitten conflict was waning. Even outside Jaffa on 1 August, Richard invited a group of high-ranking Ayyubid commanders to visit his camp during a lull in the fighting. He spent the evening entertaining and joking with them, speaking of things both 'serious and light-hearted'. Unfortunately for Richard, the advantage accrued through this scheming was largely squandered when he fell gravely ill in mid-August. Up to this point he had stubbornly insisted that Ascalon – painstakingly rebuilt through his own efforts just months earlier – must remain in Christian hands, always adding that he had every intention of staying in the Levant until Easter 1193. By late August, however, with the Lionheart debilitated by fever, the haggling ceased.[101]

Through lengthy and convoluted diplomatic dialogue the terms of a three-year truce were eventually settled on Wednesday 2 September 1192. Saladin was to retain control of Jerusalem, but agreed to allow Christian pilgrims unfettered access to the Holy Sepulchre. The Franks were to hold on to the narrow coastal strip between Jaffa and Tyre conquered during the crusade, but Ascalon's fortifications were once again to be demolished. Strangely, no discussion over the fate of the Jerusalemite True Cross seems to have taken place – in any case, the revered Christian relic remained in Ayyubid hands.

Even at this final moment of accord, Saladin and Richard did not meet. Al-Adil brought the written treaty – the Arabic text of which was penned by the sultan's scribe Imad al-Din – to Richard at Jaffa. The ailing king was too weak even to read the document and merely offered his hand as a sign of truce. Henry of Champagne and Balian of Ibelin then swore oaths to uphold the terms, and the Templar and Hospitaller masters also indicated their approval. The next day, at Ramla, a Latin delegation that included Humphrey of Toron and Balian was ushered into Saladin's presence. There, 'they took his noble hand and received his oath to observe the peace on the agreed terms'. Key members of Saladin's family – al-Adil, al-Afdal and al-Zahir – and a number of leading emirs then proffered their own oaths. At last, with the elaborate rituals concluded, peace was achieved.[102]

In the month that followed, three delegations of crusaders made the journey to Jerusalem – achieving through truce what had been denied them in war. Among those who fulfilled their pilgrim vows were Andrew of Chauvigny and Hubert Walter, bishop of Salisbury. But Richard I made no attempt to travel to the Holy City. It may be that his continued ill health prevented him; or perhaps he deemed the prospect of visiting the Holy Sepulchre while Jerusalem yet remained in Muslim hands too shameful to bear. On 9 October 1192, after sixteen months in the Levant, the Lionheart began his journey back to Europe. As his royal fleet set sail, the king was said to have offered a prayer to God that he might one day return.

THE OUTCOME OF THE THIRD CRUSADE

In the end, neither Saladin nor Richard the Lionheart could claim victory in the war for the Holy Land. The Angevin king had failed to recapture Jerusalem or to recover the True Cross. But through his efforts and those of his fellow crusaders, Latin Christendom retained a foothold in Palestine, and the Frankish subjugation of Cyprus offered a further beacon of hope for Outremer's survival.

After leading Islam to victory in 1187, Saladin had faced a series of humiliating setbacks during the Third Crusade – at Acre, Arsuf and Jaffa. Despite unswerving devotion to the cause of *jihad*, he had also been wholly unable to prevent the Frankish reconquest of the coast. In siege and battle Richard had prevailed, while in the art of diplomacy the Lionheart had proved, at the very least, to be the sultan's equal. Yet, though beaten, Saladin remained undefeated. Jerusalem had been defended for Islam; the Ayyubid Empire endured. And now, the crusade's end and King Richard's departure offered the prospect of future triumphs – the chance to complete the work begun at Hattin.

The long road ends

Once news of King Richard's departure from the Holy Land had been confirmed, Saladin finally felt able to disband his armies. Thought was given to undertaking the pilgrimage to Mecca, but the needs of the empire soon took precedence. After touring his Palestinian territories, Saladin returned to Syria to spend a rainy winter resting in Damascus. Bidding farewell to al-Zahir, he was said to have counselled his son not to become too familiar with violence, warning that 'blood never sleeps'.

By early 1193, Saladin's health was in decline and he began to show worrying signs of exhaustion. Baha al-Din remarked that 'it was as though his body was full and there was a lassitude about him'. On 20 February the sultan fell ill, becoming feverish and nauseous. Through the days that followed his condition deteriorated. Together Baha al-Din and al-Fadil visited their master's chambers in the citadel each morning and each night, and al-Afdal was also in close attendance. By early March Saladin's fever had intensified, such that sweat soaked through his mattress to the floor and he began to slip in and out of consciousness. Baha al-Din described how on 3 March 1193:

> The sultan's illness grew ever worse and his strength dwindled further . . . [an *imam*] was called upon to spend the night in the citadel, so that if the death throes began, he would be with the sultan, [able] to rehearse his confession of faith and keep God before his mind. This was done and we left the citadel, each longing to give his own life to ransom the sultan's.

Just after dawn, as the *imam* recited the Koran beside him, Saladin died. He was fifty-five. His body was laid to rest in a mausoleum within the compound of the Grand Umayyad Mosque of Damascus. It remains there to this day.[103]

In his early career, Saladin had been driven by personal ambition and a hunger for renown to usurp power from the Zangids and forge a new and expansive Ayyubid Empire. He had also shown a ready willingness to defame his enemies, Muslim and Christian, through the use of propaganda. The sultan's dedication to *jihad* – a marked feature of his career only after his illness in 1186 – was ever coloured by a determination to lead Islam in the holy war, rather than serve as a lieutenant.

Nonetheless, Saladin does seem to have been inspired by authentic religious fervour and a genuine belief in the sanctity of Jerusalem. It has recently been suggested that after 1187, once the overriding goal of the Holy City's recapture was achieved, 'Saladin's emotional commitment to *jihad* faltered.' In fact, if anything, the sultan's devotion to this cause strengthened during the Third Crusade, even in the face of failure and defeat. It is also true that the sense of Muslim unity he engendered, while not absolute, was unparalleled in the twelfth century. Certainly, in the world of the crusades, adversaries and allies alike recognised that the sultan was a remarkable leader of men. Even his sometime critic, the great Iraqi historian and Zangid sympathiser Ibn al-Athir, wrote that:

> Saladin (may God have mercy on him) was generous, forbearing, of good character, humble, ready to put up with something that displeased him [and] much given to overlooking the faults of his followers . . . In short, he was a rare individual in his age, with many good qualities and good deeds, mighty in *jihad* against the infidels, for which his conquests are the proof.[104]

Above all else, one fundamental question underpins any attempt to judge Saladin's life and career: did he champion the cause of *jihad*, conquer and defend Jerusalem in pursuit of his own glory and gain, or in the wider interests of Islam? In the end, perhaps even the sultan himself remained unsure of the answer.

Richard the Lionheart's later career

Even as the Ayyubid sultan passed away, his nemesis Richard the Lionheart was facing a new struggle. Narrowly avoiding disaster when his ship was wrecked by a storm near Venice, the king continued his homeward journey overland. Travelling in disguise to evade his European enemies, he was captured nonetheless in Vienna by his old rival from the siege of Acre, Duke Leopold of Austria – apparently Richard's attempt to pass himself off as a lowly cook failed because he forgot to take off a fabulously bejewelled ring.

Confined in a lofty castle overlooking the Danube, the Lionheart was held prisoner for more than a year, causing political scandal throughout the West, and was released in February 1194 only after protracted negotiation and the payment of a massive ransom. By the late thirteenth century, however, a more romantic tale was circulating, in which the king's faithful minstrel, Blondel, doggedly searched across Europe for his supposedly 'missing' master, pausing at the foot of countless castles to sing a song that he and Richard had written together. The king did compose at least two doleful laments while in captivity (both of which survive to this day), but the story of Blondel is pure fiction – one more layer of myth in the legend of the Lionheart.

Despite all his fears, and prolonged absence, Richard returned to find that the Angevin realm remained his to rule – the king's loyal supporters had thwarted John's attempts at rebellion. Philip Augustus, however, had been able to take some advantage – seizing a number of castles along the border with Normandy – and Richard dedicated much of the next five years to campaigning against the Capetians. Embroiled in the affairs of Europe, he never returned to the Holy Land. At the end of the twelfth century the Lionheart's penchant for front-line combat finally caught up with him. While besieging the small castle of Chalus in southern France, he was struck in the shoulder by a crossbow bolt and badly injured. The wound turned gangrenous, and Richard died on 6 April 1199, at the age of forty-one. His body was buried at Fontevraud, beside his father Henry II, while his heart was interred at Rouen.[105]

Contemporaries remembered the Lionheart as a peerless warrior and superlative crusader: the king who brought the mighty Saladin to his knees. To a large extent, Richard can be credited with saving Outremer. Valorous and wily, adept in battle, he proved himself equal to the challenge of confronting the Ayyubid sultan. But for all his achievements in the holy war, the Angevin king always struggled to reconcile his various duties and obligations – torn between the need to defend his western realm and the desire to forge a legend in Palestine. Crucially, he also failed to understand the distinct nature and challenge of crusader warfare, and thus was unable to lead the Third Crusade to victory.

IV

THE STRUGGLE
FOR SURVIVAL

19

REJUVENATION

In the wake of the Third Crusade, anxious questions about the value and efficacy of Christian holy war began to surface in the West. The 'horrors' of 1187 – the Frankish defeat at Hattin and the Muslim reconquest of Jerusalem – had prompted Europe to launch history's largest and best-organised expedition to the East. Latin Christendom's greatest kings had led tens of thousands of crusaders to battle. And yet, the Holy City remained in the hands of Islam, as did that most treasured of Christ's relics, the True Cross. Given the physical, emotional and financial sacrifices made between 1188 and 1192, and the shocking failure, nonetheless, to achieve overall victory, it was inevitable that western Christendom would be moved to think again about crusading – looking inwards, to reconsider and reshape the idea and practice of fighting in the name of God.

TRANSFORMATION IN THE LATIN WEST

Fundamental shifts within Latin Europe also helped to kindle this 'reformation' in Christian holy war. Crusading had originally been born and fashioned in the world of the eleventh and early twelfth centuries. But by 1200, many essential features of western society were in flux: accelerating urbanisation was altering population patterns, stimulating social mobility and the empowerment of a merchant class, and centralised monarchical authority was strengthening in regions like France. More significant still were the associated changes in Europe's intellectual and spiritual landscape. From the start, crusade enthusiasm had been underpinned by the fact that almost all Latins felt an overwhelming need to seek redemption for their sins. But in the course of the twelfth century, attitudes towards penitential and devotional practice evolved, and new ideas about what a 'good Christian life' might actually entail began to percolate through the West.

One gradual change saw an increased emphasis on interior forms of spirituality, over external manifestations of piety. For the first time in the Middle Ages, what one truly thought, felt and believed was becoming as, or even more, important than what one said and did in public. In a parallel and related development, Man's relationship with God and Christ came to be seen in more personal and direct, 'internalised' terms. These notions possessed the potential to overturn the established frameworks of medieval religion. A salvific ritual like physical pilgrimage – one of the bedrocks of crusading – made far less sense, for example, if what truly mattered was heartfelt contrition. And if, as many theologians had begun to suggest, God's grace was omnipresent in everyone and everything, then why was it necessary to travel across half the Earth to seek His forgiveness at a site like Jerusalem? It would be many years before the full transformative force of this ideological revolution was felt in western Christendom, but early signs of influence were evident during the thirteenth century.

Latin Christianity also faced more immediate and urgent challenges around 1200. The first was heresy. Europe had once been a stronghold of religious orthodoxy and conformity, but over the last hundred years the West had experienced an outbreak of 'heretical' beliefs and movements of almost epidemic proportions. This ranged from the relatively innocuous rabble-rousing ravings of unordained demagogues to the inculcation of elaborately conceived, full-blown alternative faiths – like that of the dualistic Cathars, who believed in two Gods, one good, the other evil, and denied that Christ had ever lived in corporeal human form (and thus rejected the primary Latin tenets of Crucifixion, Redemption and Resurrection). Alongside those condemned as heretics by the Roman Church were others who strayed desperately close to the line, but nevertheless managed to garner papal approval. These included the Mendicant Friars – Franciscans and Dominicans – who advocated simple poverty and dedicated themselves to bringing God's word to the people with new vigour and clarity. The Church soon sought to harness the Friars' oratorical dynamism, not least to invigorate crusade preaching. But the Mendicants' evangelical enthusiasm also had the power to affect the objectives of a holy war; to weave a strand of conversion into the familiar background of conquest and defence.[1]

The world of the thirteenth century was to be one of new ideas and fresh challenges, in which crusading might have to fulfil different roles and assume novel forms. The critical question – soon apparent to contemporaries – was what all of this would mean for the war in the Holy Land.

POPE INNOCENT III

One man who wrestled with just this issue was Pope Innocent III – perhaps the mightiest and most influential Roman pontiff in all medieval history; certainly the most active and enthusiastic papal patron of the crusades in the central Middle Ages. Innocent was elected pope on 8 January 1198 and immediately brought a refreshing lease of exuberant vitality to the office. Over the preceding seventeen years, no fewer than five elderly popes had died in succession soon after elevation to the pontifical throne. Innocent, by contrast, was just thirty-seven, brimful with vigour, afire with ambition. In background, he was perfectly suited to his new role. Being born of Roman aristocracy, he possessed excellent political and ecclesiastical connections in central Italy. He had also been educated in Europe's finest centres of learning, studying Church law in Bologna and theology in Paris.

Moreover, the timing of Innocent's rise to power was fantastically propitious. Since the days of Pope Gregory VII and the eleventh-century Reform movement, papal authority had been stifled persistently by the combative predations of the German Hohenstaufen Empire. Rome's predicament only deepened in 1194 when Emperor Henry VI (Frederick Barbarossa's son and heir) also became king of Sicily through marriage, thereby encircling the Papal State from north and south. But in September 1197, Henry VI died unexpectedly of malaria, leaving behind only a three-year-old son, Frederick, as heir. The Hohenstaufen world was suddenly plunged into a crippling dynastic crisis that would rattle on for decades. This gave the papacy under Innocent III an extraordinary opportunity to act on the European stage relatively unhindered.[2]

Innocent's vision of papal authority

Pope Innocent was remarkably confident of the essential – and, in his opinion, divinely sanctioned – authority vested in the papal office. Innocent saw himself as Christ's earthly vicar (or representative). Earlier pontiffs may have dreamt of achieving meaningful, rather than simply theoretical, dominion over the entire Latin Church; Innocent's aspirations extended well beyond the ecclesiastical or spiritual sphere. Indeed, in his view, the pope should be the overlord of all western Christendom, perhaps even of all Christians on Earth; an arbiter of God's will whose power superseded that of temporal rulers; capable of making (and breaking) kings and emperors.

Innocent also possessed a clear vision of what he wished to achieve with this absolute power – the recovery of Jerusalem. He seems to have felt an earnest and authentic attachment to the Holy City; much of his pontificate would be dedicated, one way or another, to securing its reconquest. But like many of his generation in the West, the new pope had been dispirited by the Third Crusade's limited achievements. In his mind, the expedition's failure to retake Jerusalem could be traced to two overriding causes, and he had solutions for each.

God evidently was allowing the Franks to be defeated in the Levant as punishment for the manifest sins of all Latin Christendom. Therefore, the work of reform and purification in the West must be redoubled. Europe had to be brought – by force if necessary – to a new state of perfection: unified spiritually and politically under the righteous authority of Rome; purged of the dreadful, corrupting taint of heresy. And the faithful must be shepherded towards lives of virtue; given every possible opportunity to atone for their transgressions, so that they might find a path to salvation. By these means, the Latin world could be cleansed so that the Lord might lift Christianity to victory in the war for the Holy Land.

Pope Innocent also believed that the practice of crusading itself should urgently be amended, and seems to have concluded that functional measures would lead to spiritual rejuvenation. He set out, therefore, to refine the management and operation of holy war, so as to empower participants to act with greater purity of intent. Looking back over the last century, the pope perceived three fundamental problems: too many of the wrong people (especially non-combatants) were taking the cross; the expeditions were poorly funded; and they were also subject to ineffective command. Not surprisingly, Innocent was certain that he knew how to resolve these difficulties – the Latin Church would step forth, reaffirming its 'right' to direct the crusading movement, assuming control of recruitment, financing and leadership. The beauty of this whole scheme, as far as the pope was concerned, was that crusaders fighting in a 'perfected' holy war not only stood a better chance of driving Islam from Jerusalem; the very involvement of these Latins in a penitential expedition would serve simultaneously to expiate their sins, thus helping the whole of western Christendom along the road to rectitude.

With all this in mind, Innocent sought to launch a new crusade to the Holy Land once he became pope, issuing a call to arms on 15 August 1198. He visualised a glorious endeavour – the preaching, organisation and prosecution of which would be under his direct control – imagining that so orderly and sacred an expedition could not fail to win divine approval.

Summoning a crusade

During the first years of his pontificate, Innocent III set out to re-centre the mechanisms and machinery of crusading in Rome, hoping to institutionalise holy war as an endeavour governed by the papacy. In 1198 and 1199 he introduced a raft of innovative reforms, which came to form the backbone of his crusading policy throughout his time in office. Under Innocent, the spiritual reward (or indulgence) offered to crusaders was reconfigured and reinforced. Those taking the cross were given a firm promise of 'full forgiveness of their sins' and assured that their military service would absolve them of any punishment due, either on Earth or in the hereafter. Crusaders were required, however, to show 'penitence in voice and heart' for their transgressions – that is, external and internal remorse. Innocent's indulgence also carefully distanced the purificational force of holy war from the physical works of Man: it was no longer suggested that the suffering and hardship endured on campaign itself served to salve the soul; instead, the spiritual benefits gained through the indulgence were presented as a gift, mercifully granted by God as just reward for acts of merit. This was a subtle shift, but one that laid to rest some of the theological difficulties raised by crusading (such as God's relationship to Man). This formulation of the indulgence became the established 'gold standard' within the Latin Church, enduring virtually unchanged throughout the Middle Ages and beyond.

Innocent also tried to create a new financial system that placed the onus for crusade funding on the Church. This included a one-fortieth tax on almost all aspects of ecclesiastical income for one year and a ten per cent levy on papal revenue. The new pope set up donation chests in churches across Europe, into which lay parishioners were expected to place alms in support of the war effort. Crucially, the pope suggested that these monetary gifts, in and of themselves, would bring benefactors an indulgence similar to that enjoyed by actual crusaders. Over time, this notion would remould crusade ideology, and have far-reaching consequences for the whole history of the Roman Church.

Innocent openly acknowledged that the onerous burden of his duties in Rome made it impossible for him to lead a crusade in person, but in 1198 and 1199, he appointed a number of papal legates to represent his interests and oversee the holy war. He also placed precise limits on who was permitted to preach the crusade, enlisting the renowned French evangelist Fulk of Neuilly to trumpet the call. At the same time, the pope sought to impose stringent minimum terms of service on prospective crusaders, declaring that only after a set period of time spent fighting for the cross would an indulgence be earned (this began at two years, but was later downgraded to one year).

This all seemed wonderfully efficient. Yet, despite the verve and assurance of Innocent's vision, all his multifarious efforts elicited only a muted response: the anticipated hordes of enthusiastic warriors did not enlist (although many of the poor took the cross); the donation chests strewn across the West failed to fill. Innocent's first crusade encyclical had called for an expedition to start in March 1199, but that date soon came and went without any sign of action, and eventually a second call was made in December 1199. By this time, control of what would become the Fourth Crusade was already slipping through his fingers.

In fact, Innocent's conception of crusading was fundamentally flawed. Absolutist in tone, it made no provision for interactive collaboration between the Church and the secular leaders of lay society. The pope imagined that he would simply bend the kings and lords of Latin Christendom to his will, as mere tools of God's purpose. But this proved to be entirely unrealistic. From the First Crusade onwards, Europe's lay nobles had been utterly essential to the crusading movement. It was their febrile enthusiasm that could spark expanding waves of recruitment through the social networks of kinship and vassalage, and their military leadership that could direct the holy war. Innocent had certainly hoped to enrol knights, lords and even kings in his crusade, but only as obedient pawns, not equals or allies.

Historians used to suggest that Innocent deliberately limited the degree of royal involvement in the crusade, but this is not entirely true. To begin with, at least, he sought to broker a peace deal between Angevin England and Capetian France, and made some attempt at convincing King Richard I to take the cross. But when the Lionheart died in 1199, these nebulous plans somehow still to incorporate the Latin monarchy within the 'papal crusade' evaporated. After Richard's demise, his brother John was too busy battling to assume control of England and the Angevin realm to consider crusading. King Philip II Augustus of France equally made it clear that, until the Angevin succession was resolved, he would not leave Europe. And the ongoing power struggle in Germany precluded any direct Hohenstaufen participation. But even when it became obvious that there would be no crown involvement from these three realms, Innocent did not attempt to consult or recruit secular leaders from the upper aristocracy. He probably believed that the members of this class would flock to his cause of their own natural volition, eager to serve at his beck and call – but he was wrong, and this lapse of judgement would have tragic consequences for Christendom.[3]

THE FOURTH CRUSADE

Contrary to Pope Innocent III's hopes and expectations, the Fourth Crusade was shaped largely by the laity, being subject to secular leadership and the influence of worldly concerns. Real enthusiasm and widespread recruitment for the expedition among Europe's elite warriors only took hold after two prominent northern French lords – Count Thibaut III of Champagne and his cousin Louis, count of Blois – took the cross at a knightly tournament at Écry (just north of Rheims) in late November 1199. In February 1200 Count Baldwin of Flanders followed suit. All three men were drawn from the highest echelon of the Latin nobility, with connections to the royal houses of England and France. Each possessed an inestimable 'crusade pedigree' as multiple generations of their respective families had fought in the war for the Holy Land. Yet, although they appear to have been aware of Fulk of Neuilly's preaching of the crusade, there is no evidence to suggest that they were directly contacted or encouraged to enlist by any representative of the pope. Certainly, like most earlier crusaders, they regarded themselves as answering a call to arms issued and sanctioned by the papacy – but they do not seem to have perceived any special need to work alongside Rome in planning or executing their expedition. This resulted in a worrying disjuncture between their outlook and the idealised notions entertained by Innocent III.

Diversions to disaster

In April 1201, a group of crusader envoys – representing Thibaut, Louis and Baldwin – negotiated an ill-fated treaty with the Italian naval and commercial superpower of Venice. The agreement called for the construction of a vast fleet to transport 33,500 crusaders and 4,500 horses across the Mediterranean in return for the payment of 85,000 silver marks. This massive commission prompted the Venetians to call a temporary halt to their wider trading interests, putting all their energy into building the requisite number of ships in record time.

This scheme was unsound from its inception. The notion of using seaborne transport to reach the Holy Land had been popularised during the Third Crusade, with both the English and French contingents sailing to war. The problem was that sea travel was expensive and, in comparison to an overland march, required a massive initial outlay of hard cash. The fleets used by the Third Crusaders had to be underwritten by royal treasuries, and even then the requisite funds were not easily amassed. Lacking crown involvement or support, the Fourth Crusade inevitably struggled to foot the bill owed to Venice. The 1201 treaty was also predicated on the unrealistic assumption that every Latin who took the cross would agree to travel from the same port on a specified date, even though there was no precedent for this type of systematic departure and no commitment to embark from Venice was included in the crusading vow. The plan might just have worked had the secular leadership coordinated their efforts with the papacy to orchestrate a general muster – as it was, Innocent does not even seem to have been consulted about the deal with Venice. Realising that he was fast losing any semblance of control over the expedition, the pope grudgingly confirmed the treaty. From this point onwards, Innocent gradually found himself trapped between conflicting impulses: the desire to bring the crusade to heel by withdrawing his support; and the lingering hope that the campaign would still somehow find a way to enact God's will.

The Fourth Crusade's prospects were dealt a grievous blow in May 1201 when Thibaut of Champagne, though barely twenty years old, fell ill and died. Overall leadership passed to the north Italian nobleman Boniface of Montferrat – who, through his brothers William and Conrad, possessed his own notable 'crusade pedigree' – but Thibaut's demise nonetheless weakened recruitment in northern France. When the crusaders began to congregate at Venice from around June 1202 onwards, it quickly became obvious that there was a problem. By midsummer 1202, only around 13,000 troops had arrived. Far fewer Franks had taken the cross than predicted, and, of those who had enrolled, many chose to take ship to the East from other ports like Marseilles.

Even scraping together every available ounce of money, the crusade leaders were thus left with a massive financial shortfall. The Venetians had carried out their part of the bargain – the grand armada was ready – but they were still owed 34,000 marks. The expedition was saved from immediate collapse by the intervention of Venice's venerable leader, or doge, Enrico Dandalo. A wizened, half-blind octogenarian whose spirited character and unbounded energy belied his age, Dandalo possessed a shrewd appreciation of warfare and politics, and was driven by an absolute determination to further Venetian interests. He now offered to commute the crusaders' debt and to commit his own troops to join the Levantine war, so long as the crusade first helped Venice to defeat its enemies. In agreeing to this deal, the Fourth Crusade drifted from the path to the Holy Land.

Within months the expedition had sacked the Christian city of Zara on the Dalmatian coast, Venice's political and economic rival. Innocent was dismayed when he heard about this affront and reacted by excommunicating the entire crusade. At first, this act of censure – the ultimate spiritual sanction at the pope's disposal – seemed to stop the campaign in its tracks. But Innocent rather foolishly accepted the French crusaders' pledges of contrition and later rescinded their punishment (although the Venetians, who made no move to seek forgiveness, remained excommunicate). By this time, dissenting voices within the crusader host had begun to question the direction taken by the expedition; some Franks even left for the Holy Land under their own steam. The majority, however, continued to follow the advice and leadership offered by the likes of Boniface of Montferrat and Doge Dandalo.

When the plunder gathered from Zara's conquest proved insufficient, the crusade turned towards Constantinople and the Byzantine Empire. The 'just cause' cited for this extraordinary decision was that the crusaders planned to reinstate the 'legitimate' heir to Byzantium, Prince Alexius Angelus (son of the deposed Emperor Isaac II Angelus), who would then pay off the debt to Venice and finance an assault on the Muslim Near East. But there was a darker subtext at work. The Greeks had stifled Venetian ambitions to dominate Mediterranean commerce for decades. At the very least, Dandalo was hoping to install a 'tame' emperor on the throne, but perhaps he already had a more direct conquest in mind – certainly the doge was only too happy to usher the crusade towards Constantinople.

Once there, the expedition rapidly lost sight of its 'sacred' goal to recapture Jerusalem. After a short-lived military offensive, the existing imperial regime was toppled in July 1203 – at only limited cost in Greek blood – and Alexius was proclaimed emperor. But when he proved unable to redeem his lavish promises of financial reward to the Latins, relations soured. In January 1204 Alexius' grip on power faltered and he was overthrown (and then strangled) by a member of the rival Doukas family, nicknamed Murtzurphlus (or 'heavy-brow', on account of his prominent eyebrows). In spite of their own recent estrangement from the late emperor, the crusaders interpreted his deposition as a coup and characterised Murtzurphlus as a tyrannical usurper who must himself be removed from office. Girded by this cause for war, the Latins prepared for a full-scale assault on the great capital of Byzantium.

On 12 April 1204, thousands of western knights broke into the city and, in spite of their crusading vows, subjected its Christian population to a horrific three-day riot of violence, rape and plunder. In the course of this gruesome sack the glory of Constantinople was smashed, the city stripped of its greatest treasures – among them holy relics such as the Crown of Thorns and the head of John the Baptist. Doge Dandalo seized an imposing bronze statue of four horses and shipped it back to Venice, where it was gilded and erected above the entrance of St Mark's Basilica as a totem of Venetian triumph. It remains within the church to this day.

The Fourth Crusaders never did sail on to Palestine. Instead they stayed in Constantinople, founding a new Latin empire, which they dubbed Romania. Aping Byzantine practice, its first sovereign, Baldwin, count of Flanders, donned the elaborate jewel-encrusted robes of imperial rule on 16 May 1204 and was anointed emperor in the monumental Basilica of St Sophia – the spiritual epicentre of Greek Orthodox Christianity. Across the Bosphorus Strait in Asia

Minor, the surviving Greek aristocracy established their own empire in exile at Nicaea, awaiting revenge.

Causes and consequences

Contemporaries and modern commentators alike have been moved to ask what drove the Fourth Crusade to the ancient capital of the Byzantine Empire. It has been suggested that the diversion was the ultimate expression of a festering distrust and antipathy that had been an increasingly prominent characteristic of crusader–Byzantine relations during the twelfth century. After all, elements of the Second Crusade had considered attacking the Greek capital, and the Third Crusade had witnessed the forcible seizure of Cyprus, a Byzantine protectorate. Some have even intimated that the expedition was actually part of a complex anti-Greek conspiracy – that the seizure of Constantinople was the crusade's deliberate and intended goal from the outset. This is unlikely to have been true – not least because the entire endeavour was characterised by such an evident lack of effective organisation.

In fact, the crusade was set on its course by the poorly framed 1201 treaty with Venice and almost certainly reached the walls of Constantinople through a succession of unplanned, pragmatic decisions and a series of cumulative diversions. There may not have been a grand design at work, but that is not to say that the Latins' eventual bloody conquest of Constantinople did not suit Venetian interests or further the ambitions of some of the crusade's leaders.

The expedition also confirmed the abject failure of Innocent III's grand 'papal crusade' project. Events had shown that he was singularly unable to impose his will from Rome. In June 1203, when he first learned of the diversion to Constantinople, the pope had written to the crusade leaders explicitly forbidding any attack on the Christian metropolis, but this prohibition was ignored. Then, sometime before November 1204, Innocent received a letter from the new Latin Emperor Baldwin announcing the Byzantine capital's capture. Baldwin's missive evidently offered a heavily sanitised account of events, celebrating the conquest as a great triumph for Christendom and, despite his earlier misgivings, the Pope initially responded with jubilation. It seemed that, through God's inimitable will, the eastern and western Churches now had gloriously been united under Roman rule, and that with the foundation of the new Latin polity fresh succour might be brought to the Levantine crusader states. Only later did details of the crusaders' brutish avarice emerge, turning Innocent's joy to disgust, prompting him to rescind his initial approval and condemn the expedition's outcome as a disgraceful travesty.[4]

CONTROLLING THE FIRE

Innocent was appalled by the manner in which the Fourth Crusade spiralled out of control, but before long his innately pragmatic outlook and natural optimism prompted him to renew his interest in harnessing the power of holy war. In the course of the next decade, he repeatedly made attempts to utilise and control crusading. During this period, however, he redirected this weapon of papal policy towards new theatres of conflict and against different enemies. In part this was a response to emerging threats; thus, expeditions were launched against the pagan Livs of the Baltic and the Almohad Moors of Spain. And, despite his deep misgivings about the circumstances of its formation, Innocent also recognised that the newly formed empire of Latin Romania would need protection if it were to play any meaningful role in the wider struggle to recover the Holy Land. Other crusaders, therefore, were encouraged to reinforce Constantinople. The pope also concluded that crusades could play an important and direct role in his drive to purify western Europe itself. In 1209, he launched the so-called Albigensian Crusade against the Cathar heretics in south-eastern France, but the campaigns that followed proved to be shockingly brutal and largely ineffective, being subject to the self-serving acquisitiveness of northern French participants.

A popular outburst of ecstatic piety was witnessed in 1212, when, for reasons that remain uncertain (but may perhaps have been related to the preaching of the Albigensian Crusade), large groups of children and young adults in northern France and Germany spontaneously began to declare their dedication to the cause of the crusades. In the 'Children's Crusade' that followed, two boys, a young French shepherd from Vendôme named Stephen of Cloyes and one Nicholas of Cologne, apparently raised hordes of young followers, promising that God would oversee their journey to the Levant and then lend them the miraculous power to overthrow Islam, recapture Jerusalem and recover the True Cross. As innocents, they claimed, children would be able to fulfil God's divine purpose in a manner impossible for adults sullied by the taint of sin. Little reliable evidence survives regarding the fate of these 'crusaders', but for contemporaries then living in France, Germany and Italy – Innocent III included – their uprising served as a salutary reminder that the call of the cross could still move the hearts and minds of the masses.[5]

By 1213, Innocent realised that widening the focus of holy war had actually served to weaken the Latin East – distracting the West from the plight of the Holy Land – and thus set about a major rethink of policy. Withdrawing the crusading status of the conflicts in Spain, the Baltic and southern France, he rechannelled the full force of crusading enthusiasm towards the reconquest of Jerusalem, proclaiming a new, grand expedition: the Fifth Crusade. At the same time, he made renewed attempts to assert full papal control over the organisation and prosecution of sanctified violence.

He began by making even more strenuous attempts to regularise the preaching of the Fifth Crusade. Innocent appointed hand-picked bands of clergy to spread the call to arms, and regional administrators to oversee recruitment campaigns. He also encouraged the production of preaching manuals that contained model-sermons, and set out specific guidelines on the conduct of preachers. Although the crusade attracted relatively few recruits from France – the traditional heartland of enthusiasm – elsewhere the response was dramatic. Enraptured by masterful orators like the French cleric James of Vitry or the German preacher Oliver of Paderborn – whose sermons were frequently accompanied by 'miraculous' events such as the appearance of shining crosses in the sky – thousands of skilled knights from Hungary, Germany, Italy, the Low Countries and England took the cross.

Innocent's initiatives in the sphere of crusade finance had more problematic consequences. Until now, he had argued consistently that only trained warriors should be permitted to take the cross, believing that this would create a compact and efficient crusading army. In 1213 he performed what appeared to be a volte-face, declaring that as many people as possible should be encouraged to enlist, regardless of their suitability for the holy war. This opening of the floodgates may have been triggered, in part, by the recent Children's Crusade, which so patently demonstrated the breadth and depth of western crusade enthusiasm. Nonetheless, Innocent's scheme had a further twist. Years earlier, when he launched the Fourth Crusade, the pope had suggested that financial donations in aid of the holy war might be rewarded with an indulgence. Now, he refined and extended that notion. Innocent hoped many thousands would enrol in his new campaign, but he announced that anyone taking the cross who proved unable to fight in person could readily redeem their crusading vow by making a cash payment and still receive a religious reward. This extraordinary reform may have been well intentioned – designed to bring the crusade both financial and military resources, and to extend the redemptive power of holy war to a wider audience, but it established an extremely dangerous precedent. The idea that spiritual merit could be bought with money spawned the development of a comprehensive system of indulgences, perhaps the most widely criticised feature of later medieval Latin Catholicism and a key factor in the emergence of the Reformation. These looming long-term consequences were not apparent in 1213, but, even so, Innocent's innovation elicited scandalised criticism among some contemporaries and, in the course of the thirteenth century, led to grave abuses of the crusade movement.

Nonetheless, the pope would not be turned from his purpose. The call for a new crusade to the Holy Land was broadcast again in 1215 at a massive ecclesiastical council (the Fourth Lateran) convened by Innocent to discuss the state of Christendom. This spectacular assembly – then the largest of its kind – affirmed the elevation of papal power achieved during Innocent's pontificate. Ever obsessed with the drive to raise funds for the holy war, he renewed the deeply unpopular Church tax, this time at the even more scything rate of one-twentieth for three years, and appointed commissioners to ensure its careful collection.

Less than a year later, on 16 July 1216, Pope Innocent III died of a fever – one probably contracted while preaching the cross in the rain near Perugia (in central Italy) – even before the Fifth Crusade could begin.[6] Throughout his pontificate he had embraced holy war and, although the campaigns waged at his behest achieved only limited success, Innocent's willingness to support and amend the crusading movement did much to reinvigorate a cause that might otherwise have faltered. In many respects he shaped crusading into a form it would hold through the coming century and beyond. It is also true, however, that Innocent's monumental ambitions far outstripped the reality of papal authority and that his attempts to assert direct ecclesiastical control over crusading expeditions were ill conceived and unrealistic.

OUTREMER IN THE THIRTEENTH CENTURY

During the early thirteenth century, as the papacy sought to shape and to harness the might of crusading, the balance of power in the Near East underwent a series of convulsive changes. In the wake of the Third Crusade and the death of Saladin, Franks and Muslims alike were weakened and distracted by the eruption of convoluted succession crises in Palestine, Syria and Egypt. The Latin Christians struggling to survive in the Levant – nursing hopes of reconquest and expansion – had to embrace new approaches to Outremer's defence and to their interaction with Islam.

In the summer of 1216, the French churchman James of Vitry had urgent business to conduct in central Italy. Perhaps in his early fifties, James was an erudite cleric and ardent reformer, with a natural oratorical flair. He had already earned renown as a preacher of the Albigensian campaigns and the Fifth Crusade – his sermons may also have helped to stir into life the so-called Children's Crusade. James would go on to author an extremely valuable corpus of written material relating to the crusades, ranging from letters and historical accounts to collections of 'model' sermons. But in 1216 he had been elected as the new bishop of Acre and, before he could travel to the Levant, needed papal confirmation and consecration. James was expecting to meet with Pope Innocent III, but he arrived at Perugia on 17 July, the day after the pontiff's death. Entering the church in which Innocent's body had been laid in state before burial, James discovered that, overnight, looters had stripped the great pope's corpse of its lavish vestments; all that remained was a half-naked, decomposing cadaver, already stinking in the midsummer heat. 'How brief and vain is the deceptive glory of this world', James observed when describing the spectacle.

The next day Pope Honorius III was elected as Innocent's successor and James eventually received his confirmation. That autumn the bishop took ship from Genoa to the East – a perilous five-week journey, during which he endured severe late autumn storms that left the passengers on board able '[neither to] eat nor drink for the fear of death'. He arrived in Acre in early November 1216 and, in the months that followed, carried out an extensive preaching tour of Outremer, hoping to rejuvenate the spiritual fervour of its Christian populace in advance of the Fifth Crusade. The Near Eastern world he encountered was one of chronic political instability, in which old rivalries simmered on, even as new powers were emerging.[7]

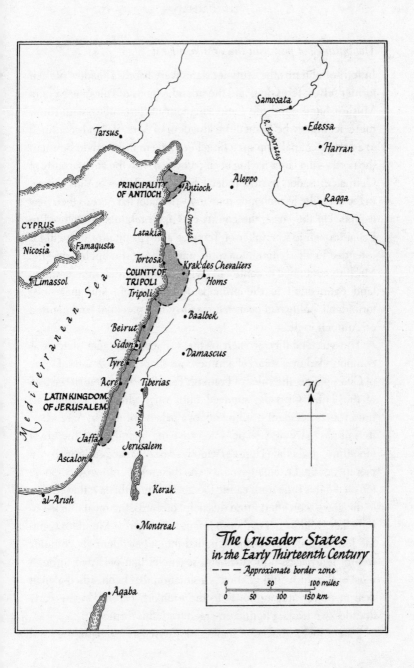

Samosata

R. Euphrates

Edessa

Harran

Tarsus

PRINCIPALITY
OF ANTIOCH   Antioch   Aleppo

Raqqa

CYPRUS   Latakia

Nicosia   Famagusta   Tortosa   Krak des Chevaliers

Limassol   COUNTY OF
TRIPOLI   Homs

Tripoli

Mediterranean Sea   Baalbek

Beirut

Sidon   Damascus

Tyre

Acre   Tiberias

LATIN KINGDOM
OF JERUSALEM

N

Jaffa   Jerusalem

Ascalon

Kerak

al-Arish

Montreal

R. Orontes

R. Jordan

The Crusader States
in the Early Thirteenth Century

--- Approximate border zone

| 0 | 50 | 100 miles |

| 0 | 50 | 100 | 150 km |

Aqaba

The balance of power in the Frankish East

In territorial terms the crusader states were barely a shadow of their former selves. Jerusalem and the inland regions of Palestine were in Muslim hands, and the Latin kingdom of 'Jerusalem' could now more accurately be termed the kingdom of Acre, its lands confined to a narrow coastal strip stretching from Jaffa in the south to Beirut in the north – the latter having been recovered with the aid of a party of German crusaders in 1197. Indeed, by the time James of Vitry arrived in the East, the Jerusalemite monarchy had adopted Acre as their new capital. Up the coast, the county of Tripoli retained a foothold in Lebanon, while a number of Templar and Hospitaller strongholds extended Frankish dominion some way to the north, but because the Muslims continued to control the region around Latakia there was no land connection to the principality of Antioch, and that once formidable polity had been reduced to a tiny parcel of land centred on Antioch itself.

The vulnerability of each of the surviving crusader states was compounded by a series of acrimonious succession disputes. Henry of Champagne, the ruler of Frankish Palestine appointed at the end of the Third Crusade, survived until 1197, when he died in an unfortunate accident – falling out of a palace window in Acre when its railings gave way. The sole surviving member of the royal bloodline, Isabella (Henry's widow), was married to Aimery, a member of the Lusignan dynasty, who then ruled until 1205, when he too died – this time from eating too much fish. Isabella followed him to the grave soon after. From this point onwards, the royal title fell to Isabella's child by her earlier marriage to Conrad of Montferrat, and the Jerusalemite succession spiralled into a bewilderingly complex web of marriages, minorities and regencies that persisted through most of the thirteenth century – a situation that bequeathed a great deal of power and authority to the Frankish barons. In the early decades two leading figures emerged from this turmoil.

Jean of Ibelin (Balian of Ibelin's son) served as regent for the royal heiress Maria between 1205 and 1210 and became the most important Latin baron in Palestine. Despite having lost their ancestral lands at Ibelin and Ramla to the Muslims, the Ibelin dynasty's fortunes prospered in this period. Jean was endowed with the valuable lordship of Beirut, and his family enjoyed a prominent connection to Frankish Cyprus.

Ibelin influence was challenged by the newcomer John of Brienne, a French knight from Champagne of middling aristocratic birth. John married Maria in 1210, and then, when she died in 1212, served as regent and effective ruler for their infant daughter Isabella II. Probably around forty years old, John was an experienced military campaigner with a crusade pedigree, but he lacked wealth and royal connections in the West. He spent much of his career seeking to assert his right to the Jerusalemite crown – styling himself as king despite the objections of the local nobility. John also made a further play for prominence in the north in 1214, marrying Princess Stephanie, heiress to the Armenian Christian kingdom of Cilicia.

Under the shrewd guidance of its latest Roupenid ruler King Leon I (ruling as Prince Leon II between 1187 and 1198, and then as king between 1198 and 1218), the eastern Christian realm of Cilicia became a dominant force in the politics of northern Syria and Asia Minor during the thirteenth century. Through a mixture of military confrontation and intermarriage Leon's Roupenid dynasty became intimately integrated into the history of Latin Antioch and Tripoli. Following Count Raymond III of Tripoli's death in 1187, the lines of succession in the county and principality became entwined, and a power struggle featuring Frankish and Armenian claimants (even more labyrinthine than that witnessed in Palestine) rumbled on until 1219, when Bohemond IV secured control of both Antioch and Tripoli.[8]

These protracted internecine conflicts enfeebled and distracted the Christians of Outremer in the early decades of the new century, severely curtailing any moves towards reconquest (and, in fact, similar problems would recur throughout the century). But the damage wrought by these petty squabbles was mitigated, at least in some measure, by the discord that likewise was afflicting Islam.

The fate of the Ayyubid Empire

After Saladin's death in 1193, the Ayyubid realm that he had constructed over two decades fragmented almost overnight. The sultan had intended the bulk of his territory to be divided between three of his sons in a form of confederacy, with the eldest, al-Afdal, holding Damascus and overall authority over Ayyubid lands. Al-Zahir was to command Aleppo and Uthman to rule Egypt from Cairo. In fact, the balance of power soon shifted in favour of Saladin's astute brother al-Adil. He had been left in control of the Jazira (north-western Mesopotamia), but his diplomatic guile and skill as a political and military strategist enabled him to outmanoeuvre his nephews. Al-Adil's rise was also facilitated by al-Afdal's incompetence in Damascus. There, al-Afdal quickly alienated many of this father's most trusted advisers and by 1196 was in no position to rule Syria. Acting, officially at least, as Uthman's representative, al-Adil seized power in Damascus that year – leaving al-Afdal to go into impotent exile in the Jazira. When Uthman died in 1198, al-Adil assumed full control of Egypt and, by 1202, al-Zahir had acknowledged his uncle's supremacy.

Through the first half of the thirteenth century, the lion's share of the Ayyubid world thus lay in the hands of al-Adil and his direct descendants, while al-Zahir and his line retained control of Aleppo. Al-Adil governed as sultan, installing three of his own sons as regional emirs: al-Kamil in Egypt, al-Mu'azzam in Damascus and al-Ashraf in the Jazira. Jerusalem played only a minor role in Ayyubid affairs and certainly did not function as any sort of capital. Despite its spiritual significance, Jerusalem's isolated position in the Judean hills meant that its political, economic and strategic value was limited. Although al-Adil and his successors made intermittent efforts to maintain and beautify the Holy Places, the city generally was neglected. Similarly, the notion of waging *jihad* against the Franks fell into abeyance, even though the Ayyubids still laid claim to titles imbued with the rhetoric of holy war.

In fact, al-Adil adopted a highly pragmatic approach to his dealings with Outremer, partly because of the more urgent threats posed by other rivals: the Zangid Muslims of Mesopotamia and Seljuq Turks of Anatolia; and the eastern Christians of Armenia and Georgia. Once in power, al-Adil agreed a series of truces with the Franks that ran almost unbroken through the early years of the thirteenth century (1198–1204, 1204–10, 1211–17) and were widely upheld. As sultan, al-Adil also forged ever closer commercial links with the trading powers of Venice and Pisa.

In spite of the relatively temperate nature of Muslim–Latin relations, the Ayyubids probably would have looked to achieve further territorial gains at Outremer's expense had it not been for a number of additional considerations underpinning the history of the crusader states and the wider Near East.[9]

The Military Orders

In the course of the thirteenth century, the religious movements that combined the professions of knighthood and monasticism – the Military Orders – assumed increasingly dominant and essential roles in Outremer's history. The problems that had beset the crusader states from their inception, those of isolation from the West and shortages of human and material resources, only deepened after the Third Crusade. The extension of the crusading ideal into the likes of Iberia and the Baltic, the holy wars against papal enemies and heretics, and the diversion of assets to defend the newly formed polity of Latin Romania all served to exacerbate the predicament of the Frankish Levant. So too did the endemic political factionalism within the surviving crusader states.

Against this background, the Templars and Hospitallers came into their own; and these two well-established orders were joined by a third major group – the Teutonic Knights. This movement was founded during the Third Crusade, when German crusaders set up a field hospital outside Acre around 1190. In 1199 Pope Innocent III confirmed their status as a new knightly order and they enjoyed a particularly close association with the Hohenstaufen dynasty and Germany. In the years that followed, the Teutonic Knights, like the Templars and Hospitallers before them, embraced an increasingly militarised role. By this point it had become customary for Templars to wear a white mantle emblazoned with a red cross, while the Hospitallers bore a white cross on a black background. Teutonic Knights, by contrast, adopted a white mantle with a black cross.

As a result of their increasing military, political and economic power, these three orders became the essential bedrocks of the Latin East, and their fundamental contribution to Outremer's continued survival was already apparent when James of Vitry arrived in Acre. The influence enjoyed by each of the orders was closely related to the papal support they continued to receive, because this preserved their independence from local ecclesiastical and political jurisdiction, as well as their exemption from tithes. The orders also possessed an incredible capacity to attract charitable donations from the nobles of Christian Europe, acquiring great swathes of land in the West. All three orders also accrued land on the island of Cyprus.

Their popularity and supranational status had long enabled the Military Orders to recruit new members (and thus supply Outremer with manpower) and to channel wealth from the West to the war for the Holy Land – with a levy, or 'responsion', of one-third on their income being sent east. By the late twelfth century, the orders had developed such an elaborate and secure international system of financial administration that they effectively became the bankers of Europe and of the crusading movement. In what was essentially the first use of a cheque, it became possible to deposit money in the West and receive a credit note that could then be cashed in the Holy Land.

The Military Orders' martial role also became ever more embedded. The Templars and Hospitallers could each field around 300 knights in the Levant, plus perhaps 2,000 sergeants (lower-status members). Simply in numerical terms this meant that they often contributed half or more of the total Frankish fighting force in times of war. Their highly trained, well-equipped troops were also willing and able to serve throughout the year and not just for limited periods as with an army raised through a normal feudal levy. Surviving copies of the 'Rules' (or written regulations) governing the lives of members indicate just how much emphasis was placed upon strict and absolute military discipline in the field. The Templar Rule, for example, provided detailed guidance on everything from marching to setting up camp and foraging, always with a strong emphasis on rigid obedience to a chain of command and unity of action – the critical prerequisites for success and survival among heavily armoured troops. Transgressions were punished harshly. Offenders might be temporarily deprived of their habit and thrown in irons, or even ejected from the order.

Alongside the undoubted strengths of the three main Military Orders, there were some difficulties and dangers to be faced in the course of the thirteenth century. With the weakening of royal and princely authority in the likes of Acre and Antioch, the capacity for the orders to pursue their own distinct goals and objectives increased, as did the potential for damaging rivalry between the three movements – the Templars and Hospitallers, for example, backed different parties during the dispute regarding the Antiochene succession. The orders' wider roles in other theatres of conflict, including the Teutonic Knights' extensive commitments on the Baltic frontier, also acted as a drain on the Levantine war effort.

Over time, groups like the Templars also experienced a gradual decline in the flow of donations from Latin patrons, partly related to shifts in attitudes towards religious life and the waning of interest in Outremer's fate. Because they stood in the front line of the holy war and were, over the decades, the recipients of such extraordinary largesse on the part of Latin Christendom's populace, the Military Orders also had to face significant, even swingeing, criticism when setbacks in the struggle against Islam were suffered. On the whole, these latter considerations only came into play after around 1250, and even then the Templars, Hospitallers and Teutonic Knights still retained access to massive reserves of manpower and wealth.[10]

Crusader castles

Through the twelfth and thirteenth centuries, the Military Orders became intimately associated with the great 'crusader' strongholds of the Near East because by 1200 they were the only Latin powers in the Levant who could afford the exorbitant costs associated with building and maintaining castles, and who also had the men needed to garrison these fortresses. With the massive haemorrhage of territory suffered after 1187, castles came to play an ever more vital role in defending the fragmented and exposed remnants of the crusader states. And dwindling numbers of Frankish settlers in the Levant further increased the reliance upon the physical defences offered by fortifications.

No medieval castle was entirely impregnable, nor could a fortress stop an invading army in its tracks. But strongholds did help the Military Orders to dominate portions of territory and defend frontiers; they also served as relatively secure outposts from which to launch raids and offensives, and functioned as administrative centres. In the thirteenth century, however, with far less land under their control than before, the Christians had to depend upon fewer fortresses that either were positioned near the sea (so as to facilitate support) or possessed highly evolved systems of defence. Under these conditions, only the Military Orders could develop and hold castles of sufficient size and strength.

Through the first half of the thirteenth century all three of the major orders devoted vast amounts of money and energy either to modifying and extending existing castles, or, in the case of the mighty Teutonic fortress of Montfort (inland from Acre), to designing and building new fortresses from scratch. From the 1160s, the Franks had begun to construct strongholds with more than one set of battlements – so-called 'concentric castles' – but this approach reached new heights after 1200. Huge advances were also made in stone-cutting techniques, the ability to erect the sturdier (but architecturally more complex) rounded forms of defensive tower and the employment of sloping walls to prevent sapping. In addition, improvements in the designs of vaulted ceilings enabled the Latins to construct massive storerooms and stables – essential for supplying large garrisons. During this golden age of castle building, the Military Orders constructed some of the most advanced fortifications of the medieval era.*

After arriving in the Levant, James of Vitry, the new bishop of Acre, toured many of these fortresses in early 1217 and described his visits in a letter written that spring. The most impressive fortress included in James' itinerary was Krak des Chevaliers, on the southern edge of the Ansariyah Mountains, overlooking the Bouqia valley. A Hospitaller possession since 1144, Krak had long been regarded as a formidable stronghold, not least because of its natural defences – being positioned on the end of a steeply sloping ridge. Saladin made no attempt to besiege the site after his victory at Hattin. In the early thirteenth century, the Hospitallers undertook a massive rebuilding programme (probably ongoing when James visited), and, when these alterations and improvements were completed, Krak had been shaped into a near-perfect fortress, capable of housing a garrison of 2,000 men.

Still standing to this day, the castle is arguably the most spectacular monument of the crusading age. Hewn from limestone, possessed of an elegant beauty of proportion, its unparalleled craftsmanship speaks of the same dedication to flawless precision and architectural excellence witnessed in the massive Gothic cathedrals that were constructed in western Europe at this same time. Its elaborate defensive system includes two lines of walls, with an inner moat and an outer circuit of rounded towers and box machicolations (protruding constructions that gave archers and

---

* The Templars' most important fortress, Pilgrims' Castle (or Athlit), was begun in 1218 with the help and initiative of Latin pilgrims, and was said to be capable of holding 4,000 men. The stronghold is now in a ruined state, but serves as an Israeli military base and, therefore, cannot be visited. The order also rebuilt the major inland castle of Safad, in northern Galilee, during the early thirteenth century.

defenders easier lines of fire). The castle is entered through a confined, upward-sloping tunnel, reinforced with numerous murder holes and gateways. And throughout, the quality of masonry is extraordinary – the limestone blocks were cut so precisely that virtually no mortar can be seen.[11]

Commerce and economy in Outremer

Much as the Military Orders and castles like Krak des Chevaliers helped to sustain Outremer's defensive integrity, the continued survival of the crusader states can actually be traced, above all, to another factor, beyond the sphere of war: trade. The Franks who settled in the East had maintained commercial contacts with the wider Levantine world through the twelfth century, but after the Third Crusade the scope, extent and significance of these links increased. Over time, the neighbouring Latin and Islamic powers of the Near East developed such close ties of commercial interdependence that the Muslims of Syria and Egypt preferred to allow the Christians to retain their meagre footholds along the coast, rather than risk any interruption of trade and income.

Frankish control of Syria's and Palestine's ports – the gateways to Mediterranean commerce – proved vital in this regard. Other wider forces also worked to Outremer's advantage. Until the thirteenth century, the Egyptian port of Alexandria had functioned as the economic hub of trade between East and West. After 1200, however, the pattern and flow of commercial traffic gradually shifted. The Latin conquest of Constantinople in 1204 affected the distribution of markets and, more critically still, the advent of the Mongols revitalised overland trade routes from Asia. The Latin East was the net beneficiary of these processes, while Egypt slowly lost its dominant position. Alexandria continued to enjoy a lively trade in high-value goods from the Indies, including spices like pepper, cinnamon and nutmeg, and drugs and 'medicines' such as ginger, aloe and senna leaves. Egypt likewise continued to be Europe's main supplier of alum (an essential ingredient for leather tanning). But in most other regards, Outremer became the Levant's leading centre of trade.

The simple fact that the Latins had been settled in the East for more than a century had given them time to establish and solidify the complex networks of transport and communication needed to exploit this opportunity. And the crusader states' economic vitality had been further buttressed in this same period by the investment in, and refinement of, the hugely profitable industrial production of goods like sugar cane, silk and cotton, and glassware that could be grown or manufactured in the remaining Latin territories and then shipped to the West and sold.

All of this meant that, in the course of the thirteenth century, Frankish cities like Antioch, Tripoli, Beirut and Tyre enjoyed remarkable prosperity. Without a doubt, though, Outremer's leading centre of commerce was Acre. After the Third Crusade, Acre became the new capital of Frankish Palestine and home to the realm's crown residence, the royal citadel. Within the confines of the 'old' twelfth-century city, each of the realm's leading powers had their own compound – from the Templars, Hospitallers and Teutonic Knights to the Italian merchants of Venice, Pisa and Genoa – and many of these became walled enclaves, enclosing multi-storey buildings. The city also contained numerous markets, some of which were covered to offer shelter from the intense heat of summer, and other buildings given over to industry. Acre's sugar plant had been dismantled by the Ayyubids in 1187, but glass and metal workshops remained, as did a street of tanneries, while a plant producing high-quality soap was situated in the Genoese quarter.

Before 1193 there had been large open expanses within the circuit of the city battlements, particularly in the landward areas to the north and east, away from the busier seaward promontory and docks. Now, Acre rapidly became heavily urbanised and densely populated, and this eventually led to the extension of the main walls northwards to incorporate the suburb known as Montmusard. And despite the fact that the many sections of the city had remarkably advanced sewage systems, this intensive growth meant that the crowded metropolis became subject to quite horrendous levels of pollution, and the associated dangers of illness and disease. Much of Acre's waste, including that from the royal slaughterhouse and fish market, was poured into the harbour, which became known as 'Lordemer' (the filthy sea). By the mid-thirteenth century, the situation had become so extreme that a church in the Venetian quarter had to have its main windows facing the port blocked off to prevent the wind blowing refuse on to the altar.

It was in this bustling capital that James of Vitry made his home after 1216, as the new Latin bishop. He found Acre to be a veritable den of iniquity – what he called 'a second Babylon', a 'horrible city . . . full of countless disgraceful acts and evil deeds', and people 'utterly devoted to the pleasures of flesh'. James was bewildered by the port's cosmopolitan character. Old French was still the main language of commerce, but along Acre's heaving streets a plethora of other western tongues – Provençal, English, Italian and German – mingled with Levantine languages, some spoken by visitors, others by eastern Christian and Jewish residents.

Acre was the most important meeting place between East and West in the thirteenth century. This was largely a function of the city's new role as the Mediterranean's leading entrepôt – the warehouse of the Levant, to which goods drawn from across Outremer, the Near East and beyond were brought before being shipped to the West. Acre also became a portal for the gradually increasing volume of return trade passing from Europe to the Orient.

An assortment of different goods passed through the city. Raw materials such as silk, cotton and linen fibres came in bales from local production centres in Palestine and the likes of Muslim-held Aleppo, while finished products, like silk clothing manufactured in Antioch, were also traded. Many commodities were both used in Acre itself and exported to more distant markets: sugar cane from Palestinian plantations; wine from Lower Galilee, Latakia and Antioch; dates from the Jordan valley. Soda ashes – produced by burning plantstuffs grown in areas of high saline concentration (like coastal regions) to give alkaline ashes – were used in dying textiles and soap making; they were also essential for glass production, and the glass manufactured locally made use of the excellent-quality sand found in the Belus River.

One marked development in the thirteenth century was the increase in commercial traffic heading from west to east. It became increasingly common for Latin merchants to travel into Muslim territory, trading woollen goods (especially those from Flanders) and saffron (the only western spice to find a market in the Orient) to the likes of Damascus, before returning to Acre with a new cargo of silks, precious and semi-precious stones.

In a normal year, Acre witnessed two periods of intense activity – just before Easter and at the end of summer – when the bulk of ships arrived from the West, bearing hordes of traders and travellers. At these times, the docks were awash with money-changers and touts offering to lead new arrivals to find accommodation or on guided tours of the city. The port already had a long history of functioning as the main point of arrival for Christian pilgrims to the Holy Land, but, with access to Jerusalem and other sacred sites curtailed after the Third Crusade, Acre emerged as a pilgrimage destination in its own right. The city possessed some seventy churches, shrines and hospitals to service the needs of these visitors, and a lively trade in locally produced devotional objects, including painted icons, sprang up. Acre also became the most important centre of book production in the Latin East, with a scriptorium employing some of the finest manuscript artists of the medieval period copying works of history and literature for a wealthy cosmopolitan clientele.[12]

Sustained by this range of commercial activity, Acre was one of the focal points of life in the Latin East. The city's history also stands as testament to the fact that international trade was the central pillar propping up Outremer through the thirteenth century.

20

NEW PATHS

Even as the forces of trade and commerce continued to shape life in Outremer, western Europe was preparing to mount another major offensive in the war for the Holy Land, timed to coincide with the end of the latest truce with the Ayyubids in 1217 – the campaign conceived and announced by Pope Innocent III before his death, known as the Fifth Crusade. By far and away the most powerful recruit for this expedition was Frederick II of Germany (the grandson of Frederick Barbarossa, the Third Crusader). Born in 1194 as heir to the Hohenstaufen dynasty, Frederick held claims to the mighty German Empire and the opulent kingdom of Sicily. But the precipitous death of his father Henry VI in 1197 left the infant prince somewhat in limbo, and Frederick grew up in Sicily, while other candidates contested the German succession.

Frederick was elevated to the Sicilian throne when he reached his majority in 1208. Judging the young monarch to be a trustworthy and pliable pawn, Innocent III decided to back Frederick's candidacy as crown ruler of Germany and he was proclaimed as the new king in 1211. His royal status was later reinforced by a crowning ceremony in Aachen (the traditional seat of power) in 1215. At this point Frederick II made two pledges: he took the crusading vow; and he promised not to exercise joint rule of Germany and Sicily, granting the latter to his own infant son Henry (VII). By this means, Pope Innocent believed that he had secured invaluable support for the holy war and safeguarded Rome from the dreaded threat of Hohenstaufen encirclement. The pope died still thinking that this deal would hold, but events would prove that he was sorely mistaken. It soon became clear that Frederick II had every intention of creating a unified Hohenstaufen realm – indeed, he aspired to rule a grand and expansive Christian empire, the strength and scale of which would surpass anything yet witnessed in the Middle Ages. His astounding career would cast a long shadow over the crusading movement.[13]

In 1216, with Innocent III dead and his successor Honorius III in power, Frederick began angling for his own advantage. His initial goal was to secure the imperial title – something that would require papal involvement in his coronation – without having to cede control of Sicily. To persuade Honorius of this arrangement's dubious merits, Frederick used his crusading vow as leverage, making it clear that he would only embark on the campaign once anointed as Hohenstaufen emperor. Delicate and prolonged negotiations followed, leaving the tantalising, and potentially disruptive, prospect of Frederick's involvement hanging over the Fifth Crusade.

THE FIFTH CRUSADE

While Frederick II and Pope Honorius haggled over terms, the first contingents of crusade troops from Austria and Hungary began to arrive in Palestine. In 1217 the Latins prosecuted three inconclusive forays into Ayyubid territory, but these early feints were mere precursors to the main expedition. With the arrival in summer 1217 of Frisian and German crusaders – among them the German preacher and scholar Oliver of Paderborn – the stage was set for a full attack. John of Brienne (now claiming the title of king of Jerusalem), the Military Orders, the Frankish barons of the Levant and James of Vitry, bishop of Acre, all joined the endeavour. By 1218 the Fifth Crusade was ready to set its sights on a new target.

The campaign's stated aim was still the recapture of Jerusalem from the Ayyubid Sultan al-Adil, but the Franks elected not to march against Muslim Palestine. Instead, in the words of James of Vitry: 'We planned to proceed to Egypt, which is a fertile land and the richest in the East, from which the Saracens draw the power and wealth to enable them to hold our land, and, after we have captured that land, we can easily recover the whole kingdom of Jerusalem.' This strategy echoed the plans formulated by Richard the Lionheart in the early 1190s, and, according to some of its leaders, the Fourth Crusade had also intended to strike against the Nile region before the expedition was rerouted to Constantinople. In fact, an Egyptian offensive probably had featured from the start in Pope Innocent III's conception of this new crusade.[14]

The Christians' primary objective was the city of Damietta, about one hundred miles north of Cairo – an outpost that Oliver of Paderborn described as 'the key to all Egypt'. The crusaders arrived by ship on the North African coast in May 1218, landing on the west side of a major branch of the Nile Delta, where it ran into the Mediterranean Sea. The heavily fortified city of Damietta lay a short distance inland, between the east bank of the Nile and a large inland body of saltwater known as Lake Mansallah. According to Oliver, the metropolis was protected by three lines of battlements, with a broad and deep moat situated beyond the first wall and a circuit of twenty-eight towers reinforcing the second.

Having elected John of Brienne as leader, the crusaders established a camp on the west bank of the river, opposite the city. Meanwhile, al-Adil's son al-Kamil, the emir of Egypt, marched north from Cairo and positioned his forces to watch over Damietta on the east side of the Nile. The first challenge confronting the Franks was to gain free access to the river. Their way was blocked by a sturdy chain, running between the city and a fortified island, known as the Tower of the Chain, in the mid-stream of the Nile. This chain prevented any ships

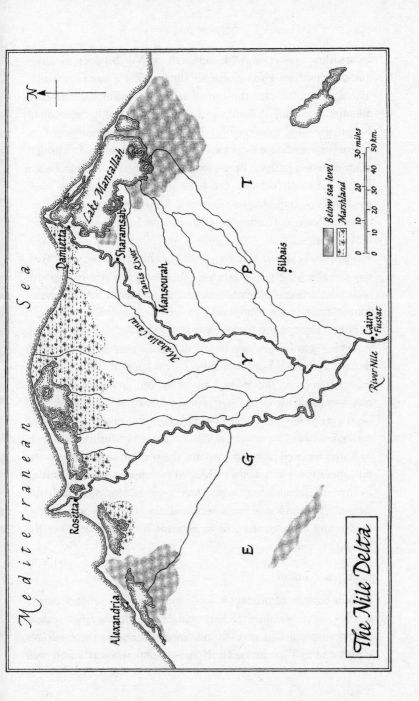

The Nile Delta

Mediterranean Sea

Alexandria
Rosetta
Damietta
Lake Mansallah
Sharamsah
Tanis River
Mansourah
Mahalla Canal
Cairo
Fustat
River Nile
Bilbais

EGYPT

Below sea level
Marshland

0   10   20   30 miles
0 10 20 30 40 50 km

from sailing upriver (and the section of the Nile between the tower and the west bank had become so silted up that it was impassable). Through the summer the crusaders made a number of fruitless attempts to capture this outpost, using fireships and bombardment. Eventually, the resourceful Oliver of Paderborn fashioned an ingenious waterborne siege tower out of two ships, with drawbridges controlled by a pulley system – what he described as 'a work of wood the likes of which had never before been wrought upon the sea' – and the Franks used this floating fortress to prosecute a successful attack on 24 August 1218. Cutting the chain, the crusaders assumed control of the river.

The Franks appeared to have the upper hand that summer. Their move to attack Egypt had taken al-Adil by surprise. It also coincided with a distracting, if ultimately ineffective, attempt by Saladin's exiled son al-Afdal to seize control of Aleppo with the aid of the Anatolian Seljuqs. Having spent the summer stabilising Syria, al-Adil was just marching into Egypt when he fell ill and died on 31 August. When the crusaders heard of his passing, they thought the shock of their recent success at the tower had killed him, and Oliver happily concluded that the late sultan would be 'buried in Hell'. Al-Adil had been a great champion of the Ayyubid cause, but although his demise weakened Islam, it did not prompt a collapse of Muslim resistance. Al-Kamil was well placed to step into the void left by his father – the only question was whether al-Kamil's brothers, al-Mu'azzam in Damascus and al-Ashraf in the Jazira, would lend him their full support. If not, al-Kamil might have to decide where his priorities lay: in resisting the crusaders; or in securing his supremacy over the Ayyubid realm.[15]

Cardinal Pelagius

From a position of strength in late summer 1218, the Fifth Crusade quickly lost momentum. In large part this was due to a new feature of the campaign. Thanks to the administrative and financial reforms introduced by Pope Innocent III, the expedition was relatively well funded and closely supported by an extensive fleet. This meant that crusaders were able to return to Europe without too much difficulty, even as new troop contingents arrived from the West to replace them. On the face of it, this practice seemed sensible because it allowed for the campaign to be rejuvenated by injections of fresh manpower. In reality, however, it had a detrimental effect upon the morale of those Franks who remained on the front line and hindered the development of the bonds of trust and familiarity between crusaders that had proved so essential to earlier expeditions.

The coming and going of Latin contingents also brought changes in leadership and associated shifts in strategic thinking. As the summer of 1218 drew to a close, a large number of Germans and Frisians sailed for home. At the same time, the Spanish churchman Pelagius, cardinal-bishop of Albano, arrived in the crusader camp along with forces from France, England and Italy. Pelagius – a forceful and stubborn character – came to the siege of Damietta as the papal legate, hoping to realise Innocent III's ambition for a Church-led crusade. Some modern historians have given the cardinal a withering press, one scholar declaring that he was 'hopelessly short-sighted [and] uncommonly pigheaded'. It also has been suggested that he immediately assumed overall command of the Fifth Crusade. Neither view is entirely accurate. In fact, Pelagius' authority and influence grew only gradually and, to begin with at least, he cooperated effectively with other prominent figures like John of Brienne. The cardinal's ecclesiastical leadership also helped to engender a renewed sense of religious devotion within the army, raising spirits and morale. This would prove to be an important factor amid the trials to come.

In the months that followed Pelagius' arrival, the Latins faced a challenge confronted by many crusader armies before them: a winter siege. Huddled on the west bank of the Nile, across from Damietta, they endured manifold torments. On the night of 29 November rough seas caused waves to break over the land and flood the Frankish camp, so that crusaders woke to find fish in their tents. Poor diet led to the outbreak of scurvy. Oliver of Paderborn described how 'corrupt flesh covered the gums and teeth' of those afflicted, 'taking away the power of chewing [and causing] a horrible blackness [to darken] the shins', while James of Vitry recalled seeing crusaders suffering from this wasting disease slip into a deathly coma, 'like those falling asleep'. All of the Christians were said to have been sick of the sight of sand, wishing only to behold fields of grass. Of course, the populace of Damietta were also suffering, as was al-Kamil in his encampment to the south. In early 1219 he was forced to return to Cairo to head off a coup, but the welcome arrival of his brother al-Mu'azzam averted the danger and al-Kamil was able to return to the siege before the Franks could take any meaningful advantage.[16]

Deadlock

The first eight months of 1219 passed in stalemate. The crusaders were sufficiently entrenched on their side of the Nile to be safe from attack, but they lacked manpower and resources either to overcome Damietta's defences or to drive al-Kamil from the field. The Latins' position worsened when a further wave of troops returned to the West in May. Throughout much of this period, hopes were high for the imminent arrival of Frederick II. All of the crusaders, including Pelagius, were waiting for the Hohenstaufen ruler to appear at the head of a vast, indomitable army – one that would trample all Ayyubid resistance under foot. The problem was that Frederick was still in Europe, wrangling with Rome over the coronation, and news eventually reached Egypt that he would not be joining the campaign until March 1220 at the earliest. James of Vitry recalled the mood in the army when he wrote: 'The majority of our men were in the grip of despair.'[17]

This period witnessed one of the strangest ever visitors to a crusading theatre of war. In summer 1219 the revered living saint Francis of Assisi – advocate of the mendicant principles of extreme poverty and ecstatic evangelism – arrived in the Christian camp. He had made his way to Egypt in the tattered rags of a holy man, believing that he could bring peace to the world (and success for the crusade) by converting the Muslims to Christianity. Crossing the lines of conflict under terms of parley, St Francis implored the bewildered Egyptian troops to lead him to al-Kamil. Taking him for a mad but harmless beggar, they agreed. In the bizarre audience that followed, al-Kamil politely refused Francis' offer to demonstrate the power of the Christian God by walking through fire, and the saint eventually went home empty-handed.

In spite of this remarkable sideshow, the siege ground on and the late summer brought further troubling developments. The relative success of the Egyptian harvest had always been closely linked to minor fluctuations in the annual Nile flood. That year the river failed to break its banks in many areas and this caused huge increases in the price of grain and food shortages. By September al-Kamil had recognised that Damietta's exhausted garrison was on the brink of collapse and, therefore, he offered the crusaders terms of truce. In exchange for an end to the siege he promised to return Jerusalem and most of Palestine to the Franks, and may also have pledged to hand back the True Cross. The castles of Kerak and Montreal in Transjordan were to remain in Ayyubid hands, but as compensation the Muslims would pay a handsome annual tribute.

This extraordinary proposition confirmed that the Ayyubids' real priorities lay in Egypt and Syria, rather than Palestine. The proposal also seemed set to bring the Holy Land back under Christian control, breathing new life into the kingdom of Jerusalem and all Outremer. Yet, at this critical juncture, the first clear sign of dissension among the expedition's leaders appeared. John of Brienne and the Teutonic Order expressed vocal support for the pact, as did many crusaders. But in the end, the views of Cardinal Pelagius – endorsed by the Templars, Hospitallers and Venetians – prevailed, and al-Kamil's offer was declined. Legitimate concerns were expressed about the defensive viability of a Frankish kingdom shorn of its Transjordanian fortresses – although, realistically, Kerak and Montreal were just as crucial to al-Kamil's hopes of maintaining secure lines of communication between Egypt and Damascus. The Venetians may also have been more interested in the commercial potential of Damietta than in Jerusalem's recovery. But the key consideration behind Pelagius' decision was the earnest belief that Frederick II's eventual arrival would facilitate even greater and more decisive gains.

With the close of negotiations, summer's end brought a further disruptive round of departures and arrivals for the crusader army. In early November 1219, al-Kamil made one last attempt to dislodge the Franks, launching a major offensive, but his troops were driven back. By this point, Damietta's populace was in a desperate state. On the night of 5 November, some Italian crusaders realised that one of the city's partially ruined towers had been left undefended. Rushing forward with a scaling ladder, they mounted the walls and soon called more troops forward. Within, the Latins were confronted by a ghastly spectacle. Oliver described how they 'found [the] streets strewn with the bodies of the dead, wasting away from pestilence and famine'; when houses were searched, enfeebled Muslims were discovered lying in beds beside corpses. The crusaders' eighteen-month investment had exacted a horrific toll upon the defenders – tens of thousands had perished. Nonetheless, the Franks celebrated their long-awaited success, plundering large amounts of gold, silver and silks. James of Vitry, meanwhile, supervised the immediate baptism of the surviving Muslim children.[18]

Once al-Kamil realised that Damietta had fallen, he hurriedly retreated some forty miles south along the course of the Nile, to retrench his position at Mansourah. In the event, he had more than enough time to prepare his defences, because, fresh from the flush of success, the Fifth Crusade was paralysed by indecision. The first contentious issue was the fate of Damietta itself. John of Brienne thought to claim it for himself – and later even minted coins affirming his right to the city – but Pelagius wished to hold Damietta (and the lion's share of the amassed spoils) in the interests of the papacy and Frederick II. A temporary compromise was eventually brokered that allowed John to hold the city until the German king appeared.

More problematic still was the issue of future strategy. The crusade had attacked Damietta as a means to an end, but intractable questions were now raised about the next step. Should the city be used as a bargaining chip to secure the return of the Holy Land on even more favourable terms than those already offered? Or might the Fifth Crusade consider a fully fledged assault on Egypt by marching up the Nile to crush al-Kamil and conquer Cairo?

To grasp victory

In an unprecedented feat of woeful indecision, the Fifth Crusade spent the next year and a half ensconced in Damietta considering these issues – ever haunted by the spectre of Frederick II's promised arrival. John of Brienne left Egypt, in part to pursue a claim to the crown of Cilician Armenia following the death of King Leon I, but also to supervise Palestine's defence against renewed attacks from al-Mu'azzam. As the months passed, however, John began to face widespread criticism for his absence from the crusade.

Back in Damietta, Pelagius assumed control of the remaining Frankish armies and did his best to maintain order. It was around this time that the cardinal had a mysterious book in Arabic – supposedly shown to the crusaders by Syrian Christians – translated and read aloud to the host. The text was purportedly a collection of prophecies written in the ninth century, relating revelations from St Peter the Apostle. The book appeared to 'predict' the events of the Third Crusade, as well as the fall of Damietta. It also declared that the Fifth Crusade would be brought to victory under the leadership of 'a great king from the West'. The whole episode might sound utterly fanciful, but Oliver of Paderborn and James of Vitry took the 'predictions' of this tome very seriously. Pelagius certainly used them to justify his continued refusal to negotiate with the Ayyubids and his determined patience in awaiting the advent of Frederick II.[19]

At last, on 22 November 1220, Pope Honorius III gave in to Frederick's demands and anointed him as emperor of Germany. In return, Frederick renewed his crusading vow. The coming of spring in 1221, therefore, seemed to herald a new dawn for the Fifth Crusade. That May, the first wave of Hohenstaufen crusaders arrived under the command of Ludwig of Bavaria and, bolstered by these reinforcements, Pelagius finally made the decision to push south and attack al-Kamil's now heavily fortified camp at Mansourah. Unfortunately for the Franks, the prosecution of this campaign was criminally inept. Even once the choice had been made, the Christians were slow to act, and the advance only began on 6 July 1221. The next day John of Brienne returned to Egypt and joined Pelagius' and Ludwig's force. A proportion of the crusader host was left to defend Damietta, but the Latins still mustered some 1,200 knights, around 4,000 archers and many other infantrymen. Their southward march down the east bank of the Nile was also shadowed by a sizeable Christian fleet.

The problem was that Pelagius had little knowledge of the terrain around Mansourah and seems to have been entirely ignorant of the Nile Delta's hydrology. By contrast, al-Kamil had chosen the location of his new encampment with great care and foresight. Positioned just south of a junction between the Nile and a secondary tributary – the Tanis River – running to Lake Mansallah, the Ayyubid base was practically unassailable. In addition, any attacking army would find themselves penned between two watercourses. The annual Nile flood of August was also fast approaching. This meant that if the crusaders tarried, their assault might be blunted not by Muslim swords, but by the unstemmable waters of the great river.

It was perhaps with a view to engineering just such a delay that al-Kamil now renewed his offer of truce on the same terms advanced in 1219. The postponement of hostilities also served al-Kamil's interests, because he was eagerly awaiting the arrival of reinforcements under both al-Ashraf and al-Mu'azzam. But despite some debate – and warnings from the Templars and Hospitallers about the growing concentration of Ayyubid forces in Egypt – Pelagius again declined to negotiate and the crusaders pressed on. It is impossible to judge whether al-Kamil would have honoured any deal settled at this late stage.

By 24 July the Franks had reached the settlement of Sharamsah, just a few days from Mansourah. There they repulsed a Muslim attack and Christian morale seems to have been buoyant. But, because of the imminent flooding of the Nile, John of Brienne counselled an immediate withdrawal to Damietta. His advice was overruled by Pelagius, who now seems to have been convinced that the Latins could grasp victory. In fact, they were marching into a well-prepared trap.

Continuing south, the Franks ignored a small tributary entering the Nile from the west. This was a grave error. The seemingly innocuous 'tributary' was actually the Mahalla Canal, a watercourse that rejoined the Nile miles to the south of Mansourah. Once the crusaders' army passed by with their fleet, al-Kamil sent a group of his own ships up the canal to enter the Nile and block any retreat, even sinking four vessels to ensure that the river was impassable. By 10 August the Christians had taken up a position in front of Mansourah, in the fork between the Nile and the Tanis. Around the same time, however, al-Ashraf and al-Mu'azzam arrived in Egypt and moved their troops to the north-east, thus blocking any land retreat. Soon after, the Nile flood began.

The Fifth Crusaders' position rapidly became untenable. With the swelling waters, their fleet proved impossible to control and overloaded ships began to sink. Some thought was given to making a fortified camp and waiting for reinforcement, but by the evening of 26 August the sheer desperation of the situation led to a sudden and chaotic retreat, with only the Templars in the rearguard holding discipline. At this point al-Kamil ordered the sluice gates used to moderate the Nile flood to be opened, inundating the fields and further isolating his enemy – the terrain became so muddy and waterlogged that the Franks were left wading up to their waists. After an agonising day spent trying to trudge their way north, Pelagius accepted the irretrievable reality of the Christian position and sued for terms of surrender on 28 August 1221.

Having twice been offered the Holy City of Jerusalem, the cardinal and his fellow crusaders now had to accept the humiliation of abject defeat. Al-Kamil treated the Franks with marked respect – keen to bring the whole sorry affair to a swift conclusion so that he could finally consolidate his hold over Egypt – but, nonetheless, he demanded the immediate return of Damietta and the release of all Muslim prisoners. The only concession was that the eight-year truce between Latin Christendom and the Ayyubids would not be extended to the newly anointed Emperor Frederick II. On 8 September, al-Kamil duly entered Damietta, reclaiming dominion of the Nile, and in the weeks that followed the Franks left Egypt empty-handed.

FREDERICK II'S CRUSADE

The crushing reversal of fortune suffered by the Fifth Crusaders sparked criticism across Latin Christendom in the early 1220s. Cardinal Pelagius stood accused of ineffectual and misguided leadership – to some his failures in Egypt proved the underlying folly of Innocent III's idealised vision of a Church-directed crusade. John of Brienne was also censured for neglecting his role as a field commander and for allowing the crusade to languish immobile at Damietta through 1220 and beyond. But perhaps the most forceful attacks were levelled against Frederick II, the great emperor who never did arrive in North Africa, despite all his promises. Even in 1221 he again had delayed his departure – distracted by an outbreak of political unrest in Sicily – and by late summer, with the disaster on the Nile and the crusade's end, the time for action had passed.[20]

Frederick had demonstrated that his overriding priority was the defence, consolidation and expansion of the Hohenstaufen Empire. These were not uncommon concerns for a medieval monarch. The same burdens of crown rule had impacted upon the crusading careers of Henry II and Richard I of England and Philip Augustus of France. Indeed, from one perspective, Frederick's dedication and determined ambition were commendable. But in the wake of the Fifth Crusade, the new emperor came under mounting pressure to make good his vows and enter the war for the Holy Land. This compulsion derived in part from public opprobrium, but it was driven most forcibly by the papacy. Honorius III was desperately concerned to renew the campaign for Jerusalem's recovery and assuage his own guilt over the Damietta expedition's dismal outcome. He also recognised that Frederick, now having encircled the Papal States, posed a clear threat to Roman sovereignty. The crusade might be a useful and effective means of controlling this potential enemy.

Stupor mundi

Frederick II was one of the most controversial figures in medieval history. In the thirteenth century he was lauded by supporters as *stupor mundi* (the wonder of the world), but condemned by his enemies as the 'beast of the apocalypse'; today historians continue to debate whether he was a tyrannical despot or a visionary genius, the first practitioner of Renaissance kingship. A paunchy, balding figure with bad eyesight, physically Frederick was rather unprepossessing. But by the 1220s, he was the Christian world's most powerful ruler: emperor of Germany and king of Sicily.

It has sometimes been suggested that Frederick had a distinctly unmedieval and enlightened approach to governance, religion and intellectual life, and that he brought this revolutionary perspective to the business of crusading, transforming the holy war and Outremer's fate with a wave of his mighty hand. In reality, Frederick was not quite so radical, either as a monarch or as a crusader. Through his upbringing in Sicily – with its own indigenous Arab population and long-established network of Muslim contacts – Frederick was familiar with Islam: he knew something of the Arabic language, retained the services of a loyal group of Muslim bodyguards and even possessed a harem. He also had an inquisitive mind, an avid interest in science and an absolute passion for falconry. But the notion of maintaining a cultured royal court was far from unique. The Iberian Christian kings of Castile were perhaps even more open to Muslim influence in this period. And Frederick was not always tolerant in his attitude to faith and Christian dogma, violently suppressing Sicilian Arab rebellion between 1222 and 1224 and opposing heretics within his realm.

Contemporaries and modern commentators alike have also alleged that the new Hohenstaufen emperor was distinctly disinterested in holy war. Yet, despite his failure to fight in the Fifth Crusade, Frederick would prove, in time, to be driven by an authentic commitment to the crusading cause. His approach to the struggle for dominion of the Holy Land was conditioned, however, by the firmly held belief that he was destined to extend his imperial authority across all Christendom. By leading a crusade, Frederick sought both to fulfil what he regarded as his natural obligation as a Christian emperor and to exercise his equally innate right to recover and rule the most sacred city of Jerusalem.[21]

Imperial crusader, Jerusalemite king

In the mid-1220s, Pope Honorius III repeatedly sought to bind Frederick to a new crusading pledge. Initially, the campaign was supposed to start in 1225, but by March 1224 the emperor was requesting a further delay because of the ongoing difficulty of maintaining order in Sicily. With the pope's patience now all but exhausted, a new agreement was formalised at San Germano (in north-western Italy) in June 1225. The treaty contained a number of strict provisions: Frederick was to recruit an army of 1,000 knights and fund their deployment in the Holy Land for two years; in addition, he had to provide 150 ships to transport crusaders to the East and furnish the master of the Teutonic Order, Herman of Salza (a close Hohenstaufen ally), with 100,000 ounces of gold. Most critically, the emperor promised, on pain of excommunication, to set out on crusade by 15 August 1227. Frederick accepted these terms partly because of his own willingness and determination to initiate an eastern campaign, but also to win support within the Hohenstaufen realm for a crusade tax – a levy that was unpopular because many feared, on past form, that its proceeds would end up in the imperial treasury. By agreeing to the Treaty of San Germano, Frederick was signalling categorically that, this time, he would redeem his vows. The move earned him the backing of his subjects, but it also left him tied to a dangerously precise schedule.

By this time the emperor had begun to lay diplomatic foundations for his expedition to the Near East. This brought him into contact with two Levantine rulers – John of Brienne and al-Kamil – both of whom evidently believed that they could manipulate Frederick for their own advantage. They had not counted on his guileful skills as a politician and a negotiator; his remarkable ability to mix pragmatism with resolute force. In the early 1220s John of Brienne still claimed the title of 'king of Jerusalem' through his role as regent to his daughter Isabella II, but faced an uphill battle to assert his legitimacy against Outremer's independent-minded Frankish barons, who by now had become particularly adept at using the laws and customs of the realm to limit royal authority. In 1223 John therefore agreed to a marriage alliance between Isabella and Emperor Frederick, imagining that Hohenstaufen backing would finally cement his own position as king. The union was duly formalised in November 1225 at a ceremony in Brindisi (southern Italy) attended by John and leading members of the Jerusalemite aristocracy. To John's surprise and disgust, as soon as the wedding finished, Frederick asserted his own rights to direct rule over Frankish Palestine and browbeat the assembled Latin nobles into submitting to his authority. This manoeuvre left John of Brienne disgruntled and disenfranchised, but it also rewrote the rules of crusade leadership – setting the stage for the coming expedition to be directed by an individual who uniquely combined the offices of crusader, Hohenstaufen emperor and Jerusalemite king.

Frederick also established a dialogue with al-Kamil, the Ayyubid sultan of Egypt, around 1226, although it is not clear which side initiated communication. Al-Kamil seems to have been aware of the emperor's planned expedition and, in order to diffuse any renewed threat to the Nile region, he proposed an unusual pact. Like his father al-Adil before him, the new sultan was far more interested in reaching diplomatic accommodations with the Franks – thereby safeguarding their shared commercial interests – than in waging a bloody and disruptive *jihad*. Al-Kamil's position as overlord of the Ayyubid confederation was also under threat in 1226. In the wake of the Fifth Crusade, relations with his brother al-Mu'azzam, emir of Damascus, had soured, and al-Mu'azzam had taken the rather drastic step of allying with the Khwarizmians – a band of ferocious Turkish mercenaries, driven out of Central Asia by the advent of the Mongols and now operating from northern Iraq. To balance this danger, al-Kamil invited Frederick to bring his armies to Palestine and, in exchange for a promise of aid against al-Mu'azzam, offered to return Jerusalem to the Latins. To iron out the details of this groundbreaking agreement, the sultan dispatched one of his most trusted lieutenants, Fakhr al-Din, as an envoy to the Hohenstaufen court. There, he and Frederick treated together on amicable terms, and the emperor even knighted Fakhr al-Din as a sign of their friendship.[22]

By 1227 Frederick II was primed to lead his crusade: endowed with unprecedented military and political authority, buttressed by a promising Ayyubid pact. His German and Sicilian crusading forces duly assembled at the port of Brindisi that August in preparation for departure to the Holy Land, but then disaster struck. Amid the summer heat a virulent illness (perhaps cholera) began to spread through the army. Faced with the threat of excommunication, the emperor knew he could not afford to delay and so the embarkation began on schedule. Frederick himself set sail on 8 September in the company of the leading German noble Ludwig IV of Thuringia, but within days they too became sick. Fearing for his health, the emperor turned back, making landfall at Otranto (south of Brindisi). There can be little doubt that the panic was real and the delay necessary – Ludwig died from the illness at sea. Frederick declared that he would restart his journey in May 1228 after convalescing in southern Italy, and sent the Teutonic Master Herman of Salza on to the Near East to watch over the crusader host. Conscious of how events might be interpreted in Rome, the emperor also dispatched a messenger to the pope.[23]

Honorius III had died in March that year, and his successor Pope Gregory IX was a hard-line reformer and a defender of papal prerogatives with little or no sympathy for the Hohenstaufen cause. Already suspicious of Frederick's motives, Gregory greeted the news with stern action rather than understanding. Seizing the opportunity to curb what he regarded as the excessive power of the empire, he immediately enacted the terms of the San Germano treaty and excommunicated Frederick on 29 September. This was a severe act of censure, particularly given the emperor's supposed status as a divinely ordained monarch; in theory, at least, it severed Frederick from the body of the Christian community, leaving him to be shunned by the faithful. The pope probably expected Frederick to seek reconciliation and absolution – to submit to Rome and make what would be a tacit admission of papal supremacy.

In fact, Frederick did nothing of the sort. Refusing to recognise his excommunication, he sent Riccardo Filangeri, one of his leading military officials, on to Palestine with 500 knights in April 1228. On 28 June the emperor followed, setting sail from Brindisi with a fleet of around seventy ships. He was taking a massive risk, leaving Sicily, in particular, exposed to the predations of an ambitious and unscrupulous pope – but Frederick now seems to have been determined finally to fulfil his crusading vow. He would arrive in the Holy Land as the most powerful leader ever to bear the sign of the cross, but also as an outcast, cut from the bosom of the Church.

Frederick II in the Near East

Over the preceding months, events had conspired further to diminish Frederick II's chances for success in the Levant. Two deaths reshaped his prospects. In late 1227 al-Mu'azzam died from a bout of dysentery, effectively nullifying the emperor's projected alliance with al-Kamil. Then, in May 1228, Frederick's young wife, Queen Isabella II of

Jerusalem, passed away after giving birth to a son. This infant, Conrad, became the heir both to the Hohenstaufen Empire and – through his mother's bloodline – to the kingdom of Jerusalem. In legal terms, this development weakened Frederick's authority in Palestine. No longer would he be acting as the husband of a living queen, but rather as regent to the new child heir.

These significant setbacks hardly caused the emperor to break stride. He arrived on Cyprus on 21 July 1228 and proceeded to reaffirm Hohenstaufen overlordship of the island – a right first established by his father at the end of the twelfth century. Frederick removed Jean of Ibelin (who had been acting as regent for the young King Henry I) from power, accusing him of financial corruption, and secured imperial rights to the royal revenues of Cyprus before sailing on to Tyre and then south to Acre in early September.

Once on the mainland, Frederick's excommunicate status caused only a limited degree of difficulty. The Latin Patriarch Gerold was distinctly uncooperative, and the Templars and Hospitallers were also slow to support the emperor's campaign, but this was probably the result of resentment over open Hohenstaufen favouritism towards the Teutonic Order. More troubling was the diminution in martial resources suffered that autumn. Having spent the summer helping the Teutonic Knights with the construction of their new castle of Montfort in the hills east of Acre, a fair proportion of the crusade army had sailed back to Europe. Without recourse to overwhelming military strength, Frederick turned instead to negotiation, reopening channels of communication with al-Kamil and direct dialogue with his representative Fakhr al-Din.

Given al-Mu'azzam's death and the resultant shift in the balance of power in the Ayyubid world, al-Kamil was reluctant to honour his promises to the emperor and thereby risk provoking criticism within Islam for having needlessly made concessions to the Franks. At the same time, however, the sultan's overriding priority was to secure full control over Damascus and not to become embroiled in a costly war with Frederick. To drive home the incipient threat of conflict, the emperor marched his remaining forces south from Acre to Jaffa in early 1229 – mirroring Richard the Lionheart's manoeuvre in 1191. The pressure began to tell, and as talks continued Frederick employed every artifice and argument to secure a favourable settlement and the return of the Holy City. At one point he extended the hand of cultured friendship by discussing questions of science and philosophy, but then shifted to threaten war; he argued that, to the Muslims, Jerusalem really was only a desolate ruin, but that its sanctity to the Christians was overwhelming. Worn down by these arguments, and with his eyes on Syria rather than Palestine, al-Kamil eventually conceded.

On 18 February 1229, Frederick agreed terms with the Ayyubid sultan. In return for a ten-year truce and Frederick's military protection against all enemies, even Christians, al-Kamil surrendered Jerusalem, Bethlehem and Nazareth, together with a corridor of land linking the Holy City with the coast. Muslims were to retain access to the *Haram as-Sharif*, with their own *qadi* to supervise this sacred area, but otherwise they were to abandon the city. For the first time in forty years the Holy Sepulchre would again be in Christian hands – an excommunicate emperor had achieved what no crusader since 1187 could, and all without spilling a single drop of blood.

At first glance, this impressive accomplishment might appear to be an extraordinary break with tradition – an act that overturned the established principles of crusading: the embracing of peace; the rejection of the sword. This certainly is how Frederick's recovery of Jerusalem has been presented by some modern historians – as proof that the emperor was gifted with a vision and sensibility beyond his times. Such a view relies upon simplification and distortion. While it is true that Frederick was the first crusade leader to secure such valuable gains through diplomacy, negotiation had played a prominent role in earlier campaigns. Indeed, the Hohenstaufen's methods and objectives bear close comparison to those employed by Richard the Lionheart during the Third Crusade. It is also worth noting that, like Richard, Frederick needed to gird his talk of truce with martial intimidation. He seems to have turned to diplomacy, not from some heartfelt desire to avoid bloodshed, but rather because it was the most expedient means available to achieve his goal.

Once the deal was struck in 1229, events proceeded apace. One Muslim chronicler described how 'after the truce the sultan sent out a proclamation that the Muslims were to leave Jerusalem and hand it over to the Franks. The Muslims left amid cries and groans and lamentations.' Frederick entered Jerusalem on 17 March 1229, visiting the Dome of the Rock and the Aqsa mosque in the company of a Muslim guide. In the Church of the Holy Sepulchre he proudly placed the imperial crown on his head with his own hands in a ceremonial affirmation of his unrivalled majesty. To publicise and glorify his achievement, that same day the emperor wrote a letter to King Henry III of England from Jerusalem. In this missive Frederick likened himself to the Old Testament King David and declared that '[God] exalted us on high among the princes of the world'. After this fleeting visit, the emperor returned to Acre.[24]

If Frederick thought his success would be greeted with jubilation, he was wrong. In his own letter, Patriarch Gerold condemned the emperor's conduct as 'deplorable', stating that his actions had been 'to the great detriment of the cause of Jesus Christ'. In part his anger was incited because Frederick's unilateral agreement with the Ayyubids had been formulated 'after long and mysterious conferences, and without having consulted any [native Franks]'. Along with the Templars and Hospitallers, Gerold also complained about the failure to secure control of a sufficient number of castles to defend the Holy City (many of which had previously belonged to the Military Orders) and pointed out that the emperor likewise had done nothing to supervise Jerusalem's refortification. Beneath the surface of all these attacks, however, was the quickening fear that Frederick would now be in a position to assert his full autocratic authority over the Latin kingdom.

The emperor may well have had a mind to impose his will, but troubling news from the West had begun to reach his ears. In his absence, Pope Gregory IX had launched a blistering invasion of southern Italy, aiming to capture Sicily and thus put an end to the Hohenstaufen encirclement of Rome. Even in light of Frederick's excommunication, this was a cynical and transparently self-serving ploy – one that later elicited widespread censure in Europe. To make matters worse, the pope sought to encourage recruitment for this campaign by offering participants spiritual rewards that seemed to echo those available to crusaders. Among those who spearheaded Gregory's cause were the two rivals from the Fifth Crusade, Cardinal Pelagius and John of Brienne, now reconciled.

With the threat to his western empire pressing, Frederick swiftly reached a compromise with the kingdom of Jerusalem's Latin nobility. Rather than appoint one of his own outsiders, he agreed to install two native barons to govern Palestine in his absence. This was little more than a temporary expedient, but it allowed the emperor hurriedly to depart for Italy. Even so, resentment at Frederick's high-handed tactics was stirring among a large number of Levantine Franks. Mindful of the heated atmosphere, the emperor tried to slip away from Acre on 1 May 1229 with a minimum of ceremony by taking ship at dawn. But according to one Latin chronicle, Frederick suffered a final indignity when a group of 'butchers and old people of the street' spotted him as he made his way down to the docks, and this angry mob 'ran along beside him and pelted him with tripe and bits of meat'. The Hohenstaufen emperor had recovered the Holy City for Christendom, but he was said to have left the Near East a 'hated, cursed and vilified' man.[25]

A NEW HORIZON

Frederick II returned to southern Italy in time to drive back the forces fighting in the name of Pope Gregory IX. Despite an atmosphere of anger and ill will, both sides recognised that, for now at least, reconciliation was in their best interests. In 1230 the emperor's excommunication was lifted, Gregory acknowledged the legality of the treaty brokered with al-Kamil in the East and a tense rapprochement was achieved. Meanwhile, in Palestine, the Franks gradually began to return to Jerusalem. For all their earlier complaints, Patriarch Gerold, the Templars and the Hospitallers all re-established a presence in the city, and slow work began on rebuilding its fortifications. With the Ayyubids still locked in an ongoing internecine struggle for supremacy, the terms of the 1229 truce held, and the Latins were left largely unthreatened.

Before long, though, the Christians were embroiled in squabbles of their own. In his rush to return westwards in 1229, Frederick had been forced to compromise his vision of direct Hohenstaufen hegemony of the Holy Land. But with the settlement in Italy, he dispatched Riccardo Filangeri to assert imperial rights over Cyprus and Palestine in 1231. Something of a hard-nosed autocrat, Filangeri proved to be deeply unpopular with much of the native Frankish nobility and clashed heavily with Jean of Ibelin, who now became the figurehead of anti-Hohenstaufen resistance. Through the remainder of the decade and beyond, the struggle to resist imperial authority simmered on – even leading Acre's local populace to declare their city an independent commune, separate from the kingdom of Jerusalem. Distracted by this hapless bickering, the Latins made little attempt either to consolidate their recent territorial gains or to exploit Ayyubid weakness.

To compound this situation, the barely contained animosity between Frederick II and Gregory IX resurfaced once more in 1239. The emperor was again excommunicated and, this time, the pope called for a fully fledged crusade against his Hohenstaufen opponent – now defamed as an enemy of Christendom and ally of Islam. Another crusade against the emperor was announced in 1244 and this led to open warfare that rumbled on until Frederick II's death in December 1250. Resolute in its desire to uphold and advance the strength of the Church, the papacy had finally embraced the idea of wielding the weapon of holy war against its political enemies. Similar calls to arms would follow for decades, even centuries, to come. These prompted some outcry, occasionally even vociferous condemnation, but nonetheless many willing recruits took the cross – content to fight on Latin soil against fellow Christians in return for an indulgence. Of all the criticisms levelled at the papacy by contemporaries for this dilution of the 'crusading ideal', the most telling was the frequent complaint that the true battlefield in the holy war lay in the East. It is certainly true that, over time, Rome's redirection of crusade armies – both within western Europe and to other theatres of conflict in Iberia, the Baltic and the faltering state of Latin Romania – served further to isolate and enfeeble Frankish Outremer.

The Barons' Crusade

These developments did not suddenly lead the papacy to abandon the Latin East. Rather, the Levant became one front among many, and it sometimes fell to secular leaders to prioritise the interests of the surviving crusader states. This was the case between 1239 and 1241 when two relatively small-scale expeditions (sometimes called the Barons' Crusade) were led by Thibaut IV of Champagne – a member of one of the West's great crusading dynasties – and by Henry III of England's brother, Richard of Cornwall. Their campaigns enjoyed a marked degree of success, partly because they adopted Frederick II's technique of forceful diplomacy, but primarily as a result of the fresh spiral of Ayyubid insecurity caused by al-Kamil's death in 1238. With various members of the late sultan's family vying for control of Egypt and Syria, Thibaut and Richard were able to play rival Ayyubids against one another, recovering Galilee and refortifying the southern coastal outpost of Ascalon.

In the wake of these successes, the kingdom of Jerusalem's Frankish nobility finally threw off the yoke of Hohenstaufen domination, declining to acknowledge the authority of Frederick's son and heir Conrad in around 1243. Tied up with events in Europe, the best response the emperor could muster was to install a new representative in Tripoli. From this point forward, the Jerusalemite crown shifted to the royal bloodline of Latin Cyprus, but in real terms power rested with the aristocracy.[26]

By 1244 the fortunes of Frankish Palestine seemed rejuvenated. Large swathes of territory had been reoccupied and Jerusalem, though still only sparsely populated, was in Christian hands. It looked as though the kingdom might return to the position of relative strength and security enjoyed before the ravages of 1187. But in truth, these signs of vitality were illusory and ephemeral. The Latins were actually in a desperately vulnerable state. Having alienated the Hohenstaufen Empire, their martial potency depended almost entirely upon the Military Orders and direct aid from the West in the form of crusades – a stream of support that might well diminish. Above all, the Franks' recent fortunes were a direct consequence of Ayyubid weakness. Should that Muslim dynasty recover or, perhaps worse still, be replaced by another force, the consequences for Outremer might be catastrophic.

The bane of Palestine

Through the tumult of the early 1240s, one Ayyubid rose to prominence: al-Salih Ayyub, al-Kamil's eldest son. By 1244 al-Salih had secured his position in Egypt, but, in so doing, lost Damascus to his uncle Ismail. With a view to reasserting his authority over Syria, al-Salih – like other Ayyubid rulers before him – looked to harness the feral brutality of the Khwarizmians, who were now under the command of their chief, Berke Khan. In response to al-Salih's summons, Berke led his mercenary horde of around 10,000 ravening troops into Palestine in early summer 1244. Seemingly acting of their own volition, the Khwarizmians proceeded to launch an unexpected attack on Jerusalem. At their approach thousands of Christians streamed out of the city, hoping to reach safety at the coast, leaving behind a small garrison of defenders. The refugees suffered terribly as they hurried west. Falling prey to Muslim raiders and bandits in the Judean hills and then being picked off by Khwarizmian outriders on the plains near Ramla, barely 300 reached Jaffa.

The situation back at the Holy City was worse still. The remaining Franks put up some resistance, but they were hopelessly outnumbered and outclassed. On 11 July 1244 Berke Khan's men broke into Jerusalem and went on the rampage. According to one Latin chronicler, the Khwarizmians 'found Christians who had refused to leave with the others in the Church of the Holy Sepulchre. These they disembowelled before the Sepulchre of Our Lord, and they beheaded the priests who were vested and singing mass at the altars.' Having ripped down the marble structure enclosing the Sepulchre itself, they proceeded to vandalise and loot the tombs of the great Frankish kings of Palestine – the likes of Godfrey of Bouillon and Baldwin I. It was said that 'they committed far more acts of shame, filth and destruction against Jesus Christ and the Holy Places and Christendom than all the unbelievers who had been in the land had ever done in peace or war'. With the work of destruction and desecration complete, Berke Khan led his forces to rendezvous near Gaza (in southern Palestine) with an army of around 5,000 warriors from Egypt.[27]

The shock of these atrocities goaded the Franks into action. Securing an alliance with Ismail of Damascus and another Muslim dissident, the emir of Homs, they marched south to confront the Egyptian–Khwarizmian coalition. Pooling the resources of the Frankish nobility and the Military Orders, the Christians managed to muster around two thousand knights and perhaps a further 10,000 infantrymen. This host – the largest field army amassed in the East since the Third Crusade – represented the Latin kingdom's full fighting manpower. Yet, even joined with its Muslim allies, it barely exceeded that of the enemy. There was considerable debate over the best strategy to employ. The emir of Homs, who had fought and bested the Khwarizmians before, counselled patient caution and the establishment of a well-defended camp, suggesting that Berke Khan's men would soon bore of any delay and disperse. However, the eager and overconfident Latins rejected this sage advice. On 18 October 1244 they launched an attack and battle was joined on the sandy plains near the village of La Forbie (north-east of Gaza).

For the Franks and their allies, the mêlée that followed was an unmitigated disaster. Lacking any clear numerical advantage, they had to rely upon closely coordinated action and a dose of luck – but they benefited from neither. To begin with, the Latins and the soldiers from Homs seem to have fought well, holding their ground. But in the face of an unrelenting Khwarizmian assault, the Damascene troops lost their nerve and fled. With their battle formation broken, the Franco-Syrian allies quickly became surrounded, and, though they bravely struggled on even as casualties mounted, the day ended in defeat. The losses sustained at La Forbie were appalling: of the 2,000 troops from Homs, 1,720 were killed or captured; only 36 Templar knights escaped out of 348; the Teutonic Order lost all but three knights from a force of 440. The master of the Templars was captured; his Hospitaller counterpart was slain. This was a calamity to match that endured at Hattin in 1187 – a crushing blow that shattered Outremer's remaining military strength. In the months that followed, half a century's worth of gradual territorial recuperation would be all but erased.

In a state of dread, the few Frankish survivors regrouped at Acre that autumn, 'weeping, shouting and crying as they went, so that it was grief to hear them'. Sending warnings to Cyprus and Antioch, they dispatched Bishop Galeran of Beirut 'to take solemn messages to the pope and to the kings of France and England [and to emphasise] that if swift decisions were not taken about the Holy Land, it would soon be completely lost'.[28] The grievous setbacks of 1244 that produced this heartfelt appeal mirrored those that five decades earlier had sparked the Third Crusade. But in that time the foundations of Christian holy war had begun to shift: customs and practices had changed; enthusiasms had waned or been refocused. Amid this new thirteenth-century reality, one obvious question must have gnawed at the minds of the Levantine Franks: would the Latin West once again mount a mighty crusade to save the Holy Land?

21

A SAINT AT WAR

Bishop Galeran of Beirut reached the West in 1245, bearing tidings of La Forbie and the Frankish army's destruction. In late June he attended a Church council convened by the new Pope Innocent IV at Lyons (south-eastern France), the papal court having fled Italy because of the conflict with Emperor Frederick II of Germany. Parlous as Outremer's predicament was, the pope and his prelates judged other issues to be more pressing: namely, their own survival. Frederick's excommunication was reconfirmed and, this time, he was officially deposed of his crown rights to Germany and Sicily – a move that prompted the outbreak of open warfare between the papacy and the Hohenstaufen Empire. Innocent IV was also concerned with directing resources to the Latin Empire of Romania, which was edging ever more certainly towards collapse. The pope agreed to proclaim a new crusade to the Near East, appointing the French cardinal-bishop Odo of Châteauroux as papal legate to the campaign, but it was evident that the Levantine cause was a relatively low priority.

Bishop Galeran's prospects of securing support from the great monarchs of Latin Europe also seemed dismal. Emperor Frederick obviously was in no position to leave the West. Henry III of England was preoccupied with the business of bringing his over-mighty nobles to heel, and even sought to ban Galeran from preaching the cross on English soil. Only one king would stand out in this sea of pre-occupation and indifference, responding to Outremer's call, a sovereign devoted to the war for the Holy Land – Louis IX of France, a man who would be canonised by the Roman Church as a saint.

KING LOUIS IX OF FRANCE

In 1244 King Louis was some thirty years old, tall, slight of frame, pale-skinned and fair-haired. By ancestry, his royal blood was infused with the crusading impulse, born as he was of an unbroken line – stretching back to Louis VII and Philip II – of Capetian kings who had waged the holy war. King Louis IX also inherited a French realm that had been transformed from its position of weakness in the early twelfth century. The long-lived Philip II had proved to be a gifted bureaucrat, and his forty-three-year reign saw huge improvements in governmental regulation and financial administration. Success, likewise, was achieved in the struggle with England, culminating in the conquest of Normandy and vast tracts of Angevin territory in western France.

After Philip's death in 1223, however, his son Louis VIII survived just three years. Thus, Louis IX was only twelve when he came to the throne. His forceful mother Blanche of Castile assumed the regency, ruling with assured competence; indeed, even as a full-grown man of thirty, King Louis had yet to emerge from Blanche's rather overbearing shadow.

Louis appears to have been a devout Christian. He gained a reputation for attending mass daily and for his keen interest in sermons. In 1238 he bought the Crown of Thorns, thought to have been worn by Jesus on the cross, looted from Byzantine Constantinople by the Fourth Crusade and then sold by the penniless ruler of Latin Romania. Over the next decade, Louis built a magnificent new chapel in the heart of Paris to house this relic of Christ's Passion – the Sainte-Chapelle – a towering masterpiece of the technologically advanced 'Gothic' style of architecture that had come to dominate western Europe. Louis was also a generous patron of religious houses across France. In his dealings with the papacy, the Capetian sovereign showed due deference and respect to the Latin Church, but not to the detriment of royal authority or his own spiritual beliefs. Thus, he allowed Frederick II's excommunication to be announced in France, but forbade the preaching of a crusade against the emperor on French soil.

Louis' early reign taught him something of war, but he had yet to reveal any spark of martial genius or strategic vision akin to that which had possessed Richard the Lionheart. The Capetian was capable, however, of inspiring loyalty and fidelity in his troops, not least through the assiduous care taken to ensure their wellbeing and morale. In fact, Louis' whole approach to the business of monarchy and generalship was heavily influenced by notions of honour, justice and obligation. These principles were at the heart of the codes of chivalric conduct that had solidified in the course of the later twelfth and early thirteenth centuries, and now informed almost every aspect of Christian knightly culture. Nascent ideals of chivalry had played a role in crusading from the start; certainly they formed a backdrop to the Third Crusade. But by the 1240s they were a dominant force, shaping the approach to, and prosecution of, holy war.

For Louis IX and those who followed him, crusading was a means to fulfil a debt of dutiful service owed to God and a struggle in which one's reputation might be preserved and advanced. Cherished renown was there to be earned through valorous feats of arms, although, of course, the danger of cowardice or failure – and thus the threat of deleterious shame – also hung in the air. Crusaders continued to be attracted by the spiritual reward of an indulgence, but while many still conceived of themselves as pilgrims, this idea of holy war as a devotional journey was increasingly balanced or even eclipsed by the image of crusading as a chivalric endeavour. This shift would have marked consequences on the battlefield, not least because of the inherent tension between seeking personal glory and following orders.

Louis may have harboured thoughts of enlisting in a crusade during the 1230s, and he lent financial support to the Barons' Crusade, but by late 1244 his determination to take the cross was hardening. By this stage, news of Jerusalem's capture by the Khwarizmians was probably circulating in the West, but Bishop Galeran had yet to report the shattering defeat at La Forbie. That winter the French king fell ill with a severe fever and in December he lay abed in Paris, 'so near dying that one of [his servants] wanted to draw the sheet over his face, maintaining that he was dead'. In the grip of this dire infirmity, Louis declared his unswerving determination to lead a crusade and was said to have 'asked for the cross to be given to him' there and then. The crusade became the enterprise through which he asserted his adulthood and independence – and the cause to which he would dedicate his life.[29]

THE PREPARATIONS FOR WAR

It would be almost four years before Louis IX embarked on his crusade. This delay was not the result of deliberate prevarication, but, rather, a consequence of the meticulous precision with which the king sought to prepare for the holy war. The expedition was to be dominated by the French. The conflict between the Hohenstaufen Empire and the papacy precluded German and Italian involvement, although Frederick II did make Sicily's ports and markets available to the Capetian monarch. A few prominent English nobles took the cross, in spite of Henry III's misgivings – most notably, the king's half-brother William Longsword.

In France, Louis' ardent enthusiasm and the efforts of the papal legate Odo of Châteauroux prompted widespread enrolment. All three of the king's brothers enlisted: Robert of Artois, Alphonse of

Poitiers and Charles of Anjou. A grand assembly held in Paris in October 1245 ended with many other leading counts, dukes and prelates committing to the expedition. The count of Champagne was busy in northern Spain, but many leading members of his household joined up, among them a twenty-three-year-old knight named John of Joinville, who had inherited the title of seneschal of Champagne (by this date, an office with oversight of lordly ceremony). As a participant in the coming crusade, Joinville came to know King Louis well and witnessed the holy war first-hand. Years later the seneschal wrote a vivid record of what he saw and experienced, albeit one that portrayed the French monarch in a heroic light. Joinville's Old French account – a mixture of personal memoir and royal biography (at times even hagiography) – offers one of the most visceral and illuminating insights into the human experience of crusading.[30]

Joinville's testimony, alongside a wealth of other contemporary evidence, makes it abundantly clear that Louis IX threw himself into the preparations for his forthcoming expedition with enormous energy. The elaborate measures taken reveal a commendable degree of foresight and an eye for detail. It is also apparent that the king's approach to planning grew from a belief that the crusade's success depended on both practical and spiritual considerations.

Louis adopted a remarkably clinical approach to the matter of logistical preparation, tapping into the increasing administrative sophistication of thirteenth-century France. He had no intention of leading a ramshackle foraging force into the East. Selecting Cyprus as his advance staging post, the king set about building up a supply of the food, weaponry and resources needed for war. After two years of stockpiling goods on the island the vast mounds of wheat and barley awaiting the army apparently resembled hills, while the stacks of wine barrels were, from a distance, easily mistaken for barns. Aigues-Mortes, a new fortified port on France's south-eastern coast, served as the expedition's European base of operations.

This feverish activity cost a fortune. The Capetian monarchy made an extraordinary financial commitment to the crusade and Louis amassed a sizeable war chest with which to fund the campaign. Royal accounts suggest that his expenditure during the first two years totalled two million *livres tournois* (gold 'pounds' of the weight accepted in Tours), much of which went on paying either wages or subsidies to French knights. Given that total royal income was no more than 250,000 *livres tournois* per annum in this period, the economic strain of mounting the campaign was massive. To help foot the bill, Louis was granted one-twentieth of all ecclesiastical revenues in France by the pope, and this was later increased to one-tenth for three years. Crown officials also extorted money from heretics and Jews, and, all in all, Louis was content to beg, borrow and steal in the name of the holy war. In addition, he encouraged other leading crusaders to raise their own funds and to contribute to the organisation of transport.[31]

Many earlier crusades had been derailed by the internal rivalries that beset Latin Christendom. This same hostile political environment had caused monarchs to delay or abandon their plans to campaign in the Levant because of anxiety caused by the potential consequences of a prolonged absence. But although Louis IX was conscious of his commitments to the realm of France, he evidently considered these to be outweighed by the absolute necessity to lead a crusade. Thus, before setting out for the East, the king conferred the regency of his Capetian domain upon his experienced mother Blanche. Likewise, he did his best to settle the political affairs of Europe: attempting to broker a settlement between the papacy and Frederick II; encouraging peace with England. But even when these steps enjoyed negligible success (as in the Hohenstaufen conflict with Rome) and the threats to France's safety and Louis' own position as king remained, he refused to postpone his departure or commute his pledge.

Alongside his efforts to bring harmony – and, as he saw it, Christian fellowship – to the West, in a more personal sense the Capetian king set about making peace with his people and with his soul. Louis clearly believed that his crusade would not prevail simply through the works of man, but that it had to be conducted in a spirit of contrite devotion and with a purified heart. He took the innovative step of instituting a series of enquiries, conducted in the main by Mendicant Friars, to settle any outstanding legal disputes within his realm, and to root out any corruption and injustice caused by himself, his officials or even his ancestors. As far back as the First Crusade, some of those taking the cross had sought to put their affairs in order and to resolve disputes before departure, but never on this scale.

Louis' crusade began in Paris on 12 June 1248 with an emotive, ritualised public ceremony designed to echo the piety of his crusading forebears. The king received the symbols of the crusading pilgrim – the scrip and staff – at Notre-Dame Cathedral and then walked barefoot to the royal Church of St Denis to take up the *Oriflame*, France's historic battle standard. From there he made his way south to the coast, departing with his army from Aigues-Mortes and Marseilles in late August.

Best estimates suggest that Louis led a total force of between 20,000 and 25,000 men. This included around 2,800 knights, 5,600 mounted sergeants and a further 10,000 infantry. In addition, some 5,000 crossbowmen fought in the crusade and significant advances in the accuracy and power of the bows they wielded enabled these troops to play an important role in the campaign. This was certainly not a vast host, but the king seems to have made a conscious decision to go to war with a select fighting force rather than a sprawling horde – he even left behind many thousands of other troops and non-combatants who, hoping to join the expedition, had gathered at Aigues-Mortes of their own accord.

Following the now established practice, the crusade made its journey to the Near East by sea. Louis travelled aboard a grand royal vessel, dubbed *Montjoie*, or 'Hill of Joy', the name given to the spot from which pilgrims to Jerusalem gained their first sight of the Holy City. But for most Franks the voyage to the eastern Mediterranean was a frightening and desperately uncomfortable affair. Normal transport craft offered perhaps 1,500 square feet of deck space (roughly equivalent to half the size of a modern tennis court) but had to carry around 500 passengers, and sometimes many more. Not surprisingly, one crusader likened sea travel to being locked in a prison. Lower decks were often used to ferry horses, although Louis also commissioned specially designed transports for this most precious cargo of animals, essential to the Latins' preferred style of mounted warfare.

John of Joinville described the experience of departing from Marseilles in late August 1248. Having boarded his ship, he watched as horses were led below decks through a door in the hull. This portal was then carefully sealed with caulking 'as is done with a barrel before plunging it into water, because once the ship is on the high seas, that door is completely submerged'. Urged on by the vessel's captain, all the crew and passengers sang a hymn popular with crusaders, 'Veni, Creator Spiritus' (Come, Creator Spirit), as the sails were unfurled and the journey began. But even with his morale lifted, Joinville admitted to feelings of intense trepidation over sea travel, observing that no one 'can tell when he goes to sleep at night, whether or not he may be lying at the bottom of the sea the next morning'. On this occasion, his fears proved unfounded, and the seneschal reached Cyprus about three weeks later, where King Louis had already arrived on 17 September.[32]

STORMING THE NILE

Upon reaching Cyprus, Louis IX made no precipitous move to initiate a military campaign; instead, he dedicated the following winter and spring to marshalling his forces and finalising strategy. The expedition was joined by troop contingents from Latin Palestine – including many leading Frankish nobles and substantial forces drawn from each of the three main Military Orders – and by the venerable patriarch of Jerusalem, Robert of Nantes (said to have been in his late seventies), who, together with the papal legate Odo of Châteauroux, oversaw the spiritual care of the army. Regardless of these arrivals, Louis' claim to supreme command of the crusade appears to have been undisputed.

A firm decision was made at this stage (if not earlier) to prosecute an Egyptian campaign, because of the continued vulnerability of Sultan al-Salih's Ayyubid regime. Louis' objective seems to have been the conquest of all Egypt. Rather than dabble in negotiation, either in advance of an assault or once initial territorial gains were made, he intended to crush the centre of Ayyubid power and then use the Nile region as a new base from which to recapture the rest of the Holy Land. This was an ambitious but not entirely unrealistic plan. After some debate weighing the relative merits of attacking Alexandria or Damietta, the latter eventually was chosen and Louis' crusade was set on course to follow in the footsteps of the Fifth Crusade.

The expedition emerged from months of nervous anticipation on Cyprus with an acknowledged leader and an agreed goal – two promising indicators. But the delay also had its costs. Intelligence of Louis' arrival allowed al-Salih to prepare his defences in Egypt. Illness (perhaps in the form of malaria) also cost the lives of some 260 Latin barons and knights – around one-tenth of the total force – even before the campaign properly began. For others, the prolonged period of inactivity sapped financial resources: like a number of his compatriots, Joinville almost ran out of money to pay his knights and was taken into service with King Louis.

By late spring, however, the preparations were complete. On 13 May 1249 a mighty fleet of around 120 large galleys and perhaps another 1,000 smaller vessels set sail from Cyprus. Joinville wrote that 'it seemed as if all the sea, as far as the eye could behold, was covered with the canvas of the ships' sails'. Storms and difficult winds dispersed some of the naval convoy, and it took twenty-three days to reach the Egyptian coast. Towards the end of the journey, the crusaders came across a group of four Muslim galleys. Three were promptly sunk by fire arrows and catapult stones shot from the Franks' deck-mounted engines, but one vessel escaped, albeit badly damaged, and seems to have issued a warning to the Muslims stationed on the North African coast.[33]

In early June, the Latins anchored offshore from Damietta. The Fifth Crusade had managed to land on the beaches north of the city and west of the Nile unheralded – Louis' men were not to enjoy the same luxury. Ranged along the seafront were thousands of Ayyubid troops under the command of Fakhr al-Din, the emir who had negotiated with Frederick II in the 1220s and had now risen to become one of al-Salih's leading generals. The mouth of the Nile also was guarded by a Muslim flotilla. Confronted by this entrenched opposition, Louis convened a war council on *Montjoie* and a decision was made to launch a massed landing the following morning. The king and his advisers must have known that they were about to take a huge gamble – attempting the most audacious amphibious assault in crusading history. Any lack of coordination among vessels arriving on the beach might leave isolated Frankish warriors to be annihilated. And if the brute force of the initial assault faltered and no foothold on the coast was gained, then the entire expedition might collapse with its first offensive.

The beach assault

As the sun rose on Saturday 5 June 1249, thousands of Latins huddled in their ships reciting prayers. All had been instructed to make confessions during the night. On *Montjoie*, Louis attended mass, as he did each morning. Then, across the fleet, the difficult work began of switching from large transport ships to shallower-draughted landing craft. John of Joinville and his men jumped into a longboat, which became so overloaded that it almost sank. Later he watched as one unfortunate knight mistimed his leap to a boat just as 'it drew away, so that he fell into the sea and drowned'.

Joinville described the scene on the delta coast with vivid clarity: 'The full array of the sultan's forces [were] drawn up along the shore. It was a sight to enchant the eye, for the sultan's [standards] were all of gold, and where the sun caught them they shone resplendent. The din this army made with its kettledrums and Saracen horns was terrifying to hear.' All around him, hundreds of craft were bearing down upon the beach, many of them brightly painted with coats of arms, streaming with pennons, their oarsmen straining to drive forward.

John of Joinville's longboat was among the first to reach land, pulling up directly in front of a pack of Muslim horsemen, who immediately charged forward. He described how, leaping into the shallow water, 'we stuck the sharp end of our shields into the sand and fixed our lances firmly in the ground with the points towards the enemy'. This bristling metal ring of protection saved Joinville and his men, for 'the moment [the charging enemy] saw the lances about to pierce their bellies, they wheeled around and fled'. Having survived their first encounter, John's party held their ground even as thousands more Latins reached the shoreline.[34]

Up and down the coast fierce fighting broke out, as the Muslims launched withering volleys of arrows and spears on to the landing craft. It soon became clear that not every Frankish boat was shallow enough to reach the sands. At this terrible moment there was a very real possibility that the attack might stall, but urgent orders went out to disembark and wade ashore. Some jumped too soon 'in their fervent eagerness' and drowned; others found themselves up to their waists or even armpits, but immediately began striding forward. Many knights struggled to disembark their horses so that they could fight astride a mount, while Christian crossbowmen sought to provide cover, unleashing a scouring rain of missiles that according to one crusader came 'so thick and so fast that it was a wonder to see'. Ferocious skirmishes broke out all along the shore, but the heavily armoured Frankish knights soon formed well-ordered units, and, once these beachheads were established on land, the Muslims' attacks became increasingly ineffective.

As the assault turned in the Latins' favour, Louis IX was watching from his own landing craft, beside Odo of Châteauroux. The plan was for the king to stay on board in safety, but when the Capetian sovereign saw his royal standard, the *Oriflame*, planted in the sands of Egypt, his patience broke. Against the papal legate's heated objections, Louis leapt overboard into chest-high water and forged his way forward, 'with his shield hung from his neck, his helmet on his head, and lance in hand, till he joined his people on the shore'. There, with his blood up, the king had to be held back from charging into combat.

Pockets of fighting continued until midday, but the Ayyubid defence was badly orchestrated and lacked determination. Fakhr al-Din eventually retreated inland towards Damietta. The Muslims were said to have lost 500 men, including three emirs and many horses, while the Franks suffered only limited losses. The entire landing had been a startling success. Many crusaders clearly felt that they had been lifted to victory by God's grace, one writing in a letter that the Latins fought 'like strong athletes of the Lord'.[35]

Even better fortune was to follow. King Louis must have expected and prepared for a hard-fought siege of Damietta, only too aware of the gruelling eighteen-month investment undertaken by the Fifth Crusade. As the day drew to a close, he began to ferry supplies ashore, preparing to fortify his position and, if necessary, to repel a counter-attack. But the very next day the Franks were astounded to discover that Damietta had been abandoned. Trails of smoke were seen rising above the city, and scouts returned to report that its garrison had fled, some by land, others down the Nile. In a single stroke, Louis had achieved the first goal of his campaign, establishing a foothold on the Nile and opening the doorway to Egypt. It was the most stunning opening foray of any crusade. In the sweltering heat of the North African summer, the image of the Ayyubids fleeing from the beaches and then forsaking Damietta seems to have burned into the minds of Louis and his compatriots. For them, it was an image to relish – one that seemed to speak of a Muslim world on the brink of collapse and to foreshadow ultimate Christian victory.

AYYUBID DECLINE

The crusaders assumed that their success in early June 1249 was born of their own martial superiority and the enfeebled state of Islam. But while these notions contained more than a grain of truth, they also concealed the underlying reality of the situation. Fakhr al-Din's decision to quit the field on 5 June does not appear primarily to have been a response to Latin ferocity. In fact, he conceded the beaches and then promptly marched the Egyptian field army south, straight past Damietta, because his real ambitions lay elsewhere. The city had been garrisoned by a regiment known as the Kinaniyya, renowned for their bravery; but horrified to find themselves deserted, they too absconded during the night. Pouring south, all of these forces regrouped at the main Ayyubid encampment, where Sultan al-Salih's grip on power was in terminal decline.

After the Muslim triumph at La Forbie in 1244, al-Salih had turned his back on the Khwarizmians. Judging this horde of untamed mercenaries to be too dangerous and uncontrollable to be trusted, he barred his former allies from entering Egypt. Left to ravage Palestine and Syria with little coherent purpose, the rampaging savagery that had driven the Khwarizmians eventually burned itself out, and in 1246 they were roundly defeated by a coalition of Syrian Muslims. In the years that followed, al-Salih moved to assume control of Damascus and to occupy further sections of Palestine.

Around this time, however, the sultan fell gravely ill with consumption. By 1249 his health was deteriorating rapidly and he was able to travel only when borne upon a litter. In one respect, therefore, King Louis IX's crusade was propitiously timed, because it coincided with a period of severe debility for the Ayyubid high command. Yet, even though al-Salih was dying, there were others eager to take his place, among them Fakhr al-Din. So it was that the emir readily abandoned his post at Damietta in early summer 1249, worried that if enmeshed in a prolonged engagement on the coast he might miss his opportunity to seize power when the sultan died. The outcome of events at the mouth of the Nile Delta enraged the ailing al-Salih. He seems to have suspected the real reason behind Fakhr al-Din's retreat, but lacked the confidence openly to punish such a prominent emir. The Kinaniyya were less fortunate, and the sultan had the entire regiment hanged.[36]

This brutalised atmosphere of mistrust, betrayal and rivalry was just one expression of a wider malaise affecting the Ayyubid realm across the Levant. After long decades of domination, the dynasty established by Saladin and his brother al-Adil was inching towards disintegration – bedevilled by ineffectual leadership and paralysed by internecine intrigue. But this did not mean that the Frankish conquest of Egypt or the Holy Land would proceed unopposed. In fact, even beyond Fakhr al-Din's dreams of glory, another extraordinarily potent force was rising to prominence in Egypt: the *mamluks*.

Mamluks – the swords of Islam

Mamluks, or slave soldiers, had been used by Muslim rulers in the Levant for centuries, playing significant roles in Zangid and Ayyubid armies through the twelfth and thirteenth centuries. These fiercely loyal, highly professional warriors were the product of an elaborate system of slavery and military training. Most were Turks from the Russian Kipchak steppes far to the north, beyond the Black Sea; captured as boys (usually between the ages of eight and twelve) by well-organised slave rings, they were sold to Islamic potentates in the Near and Middle East and then indoctrinated in the Muslim faith and trained in the arts of war.

Mamluks were prized not only for their unrivalled martial skill, but also for their fidelity. Because their welfare and survival were directly linked to just one master, they tended to be remarkably faithful – an unusual quality in the conniving quagmire of medieval Islamic power politics. Commenting on their commendable reliability, an eleventh-century Seljuq ruler observed that 'one obedient slave is better than 300 sons; for the latter desire their father's death, the former long life for his master'. Strange as it may sound, their loyalty was also a product of relatively rosy life prospects, as many prominent *mamluks* went on to enjoy command roles, liberty and prosperity.

Rulers from Nur al-Din to al-Kamil employed *mamluks* in positions ranging from 'royal' bodyguards to battlefield generals, but no sultan was more reliant upon their services than al-Salih. After about 1240 he became increasingly suspicious of the trustworthiness of his other retainers and soldiers, and built up a much larger *mamluk* army. The elite core of this force was a one-thousand-strong regiment known as the Bahriyya (a name derived from their garrison near Cairo on an island in the Nile, which in Arabic was known as the *bahr al-Nil*, or 'the sea of the Nile'). One Muslim contemporary recorded that the Bahriyya quickly 'became a mighty force, of extreme courage and boldness, from which the Muslims derived the greatest benefit'. To an extent, al-Salih's creation of this select band, alongside his wider use of other *mamluk* units, made perfect sense. The continued survival of his teetering political regime soon came to depend upon the Bahriyya's enduring support. But if and when al-Salih died, their loyalty to an Ayyubid successor might waver – indeed, the *mamluks* might begin even to question whether they should lead rather than follow.

For the time being, the balance held. Al-Salih lived on through the summer and autumn of 1249, establishing a well-protected base of operations for his army beside the fortified town of Mansourah – the same position taken up by his Ayyubid predecessors at the time of the Fifth Crusade. With the Muslim host thus entrenched, and its ranks bolstered by the presence of the Bahriyya, it was evident that King Louis' crusade would meet far stiffer resistance than that encountered at Damietta if it dared to venture south along the Nile.[37]

TO CONQUER EGYPT

The Frankish occupation of Damietta was followed by another period of cautious inactivity on Louis' part. The Capetian sovereign had no interest in using Damietta as a bargaining chip to achieve territorial concessions in Palestine – he aspired instead to conquer all Ayyubid Egypt and then, with Muslim resistance shattered, turn east towards Jerusalem. This strategy meant that, at some point, the crusade would have to march inland. The king seems to have been aware of some of the problems faced in Egypt by Cardinal Pelagius and John of Brienne twenty-eight years earlier, and a number of Christian eyewitnesses present at Damietta in 1249 refer explicitly to the reversals experienced by the Fifth Crusaders. Certainly, with the Nile flood pending, Louis made no immediate attempt to march south. Instead, the expedition waited out the summer.

Through these months, Louis and his advisers debated the next step in the campaign. The port of Alexandria was mooted as a possible target, but one of the king's brothers, Robert of Artois, apparently recommended a direct southward invasion, arguing that 'to kill the serpent, you must first of all crush its head'. With al-Salih's Ayyubid army now barracked at Mansourah, Louis' crusade, therefore, would face a similar strategic challenge to that confronted by Pelagius. But the experience of the Damietta landings pointed to Muslim weakness, and if success could be achieved on the Nile, the gains might be spectacular. A Muslim chronicler recognised the danger, noting that 'if the [Ayyubid] army at Mansourah were to be driven back just one stage to the rear, the whole of Egypt would be conquered in the shortest time'.[38]

Around 20 November 1249, with the floodwaters receding, Louis' army began its advance along the east bank of the Nile. In comparison to Pelagius, the king had a better – albeit not perfect – understanding of the delta's topography and a fuller appreciation of the challenge ahead. He set out to trace the route of the river south, marching in parallel with a fleet of 'many great and small boats loaded with foodstuffs, weapons, engines, armour and everything else needed in warfare'. Progress was slow, partly because a wind blowing from the south made it difficult to advance against the Nile's current, but a few early probing assaults by the Ayyubids were beaten back easily, and the Christians closed inexorably on Mansourah.

Towards the closing stages of the journey, Louis – like Pelagius before him – must have marched past the point where the Mahalla Canal joined the Nile, but this critical waterway was not mentioned in any of the Christian accounts of the advance and it appears that the Franks made no attempt to block or guard its course. At first glance this seems like sheer neglectful folly, given the decisive role the canal played in 1221. But in all probability neither Louis and his contemporaries, nor the Fifth Crusaders themselves, ever understood fully how al-Kamil managed to get a fleet on to the northern reaches of the Nile. And even if the French king did take the time to reconnoitre the canal in 1249, outside the main summer spate of the flood its low waters were probably deemed to be unnavigable.

In any case, the Franks completed their march on 21 December, taking up a position identical to that occupied by the Fifth Crusade, north of the fork between the Nile and the Tanis River. The Ayyubids had erected a tented camp on the opposite, southern banks of the Tanis, while billeting the bulk of their forces a little further to the south. The Bahriyya *mamluks*, meanwhile, had been quartered within Mansourah (which, since 1221, had grown from an encampment into a more permanent fortified settlement). In the course of Louis' march from Damietta, events within the Ayyubid court had moved on apace. After a long, crippling battle with illness, al-Salih died on 22 November. At this point, Fakhr al-Din forged an alliance with one of the late sultan's widows, Shajar al-Durr. According to Muslim sources, the pair made every effort to conceal al-Salih's demise: having his body carefully wrapped in a shroud and then spirited away in a coffin; forging his signature on documents that transferred overall command of the army to Fakhr al-Din; even continuing to set the dinner table each evening and claiming that the sultan was too ill to attend.

As far as Shajar al-Durr was concerned, this deception was designed to preserve the veneer of Ayyubid unity in the face of the crusader advance, and to allow the succession to the sultanate to be settled. To this end, Aqtay – commander of the elite Bahriyya *mamluks* – was sent to Mesopotamia to invite al-Salih's son and heir, al-Mu'azzam Turanshah, to assume control of Egypt. Fakhr al-Din agreed to this plan, both to avoid suspicion and because the scheme removed Aqtay (a potential rival) from the field. In private, though, Fakhr al-Din seems to have hoped that, given the distances involved and the enemy lands to be crossed, either the message would not get through or Turanshah would fail in any attempt to reach North Africa. In the words of one Muslim chronicler, Fakhr al-Din 'was aiming at sole and arbitrary rule'.

Despite all this convoluted intrigue, news of al-Salih's death eventually leaked out, causing alarm and unrest in Cairo. Before long, Louis IX also discovered that, as he later put it, 'the sultan of Egypt had just ended his wretched life' – tidings that only increased the king's hopes for victory.[39]

The main challenge now confronting the crusaders was somehow to breach the physical barrier of the fast-flowing Tanis River. Louis' stratagem, seemingly formulated in Damietta, was to build a causeway 'constructed of timber and earth' across the river. To achieve this goal, the king instructed his chief engineer Joscelin of Cornaut to oversee a two-stage plan. A pair of 'cat-houses' – movable towers with extending 'cats', or protective screens – were raised, under which labourers would be able to work on the causeway. At the same time, some eighteen stone-throwing engines brought from the coast were erected to provide covering fire. Once all these contraptions had been assembled and manoeuvred into position, the second, more perilous, phase of actual causeway construction began.

Unfortunately for the Franks, the Egyptian army had its own battery of sixteen ballistic engines on the south bank of the Tanis. As soon as the crusaders came into range, Fakhr al-Din initiated an incessant bombardment, 'using relays of men day and night' to sustain a constant barrage of 'stones, javelins, arrows [and] crossbow bolts [that] flew as thick as rain'. Like so many Muslim armies before them, the Ayyubids stationed at Mansourah also held a deadly technological advantage over their Christian foes: a ready supply of highly combustible Greek fire (or, as one Frank aptly named it, 'Hellfire'). Fakhr al-Din targeted the Latins' wooden 'cat-houses' with volleys of Greek fire to devastating effect. John of Joinville was ordered to man one of these vulnerable towers over a series of nights, and later frankly described the utter terror he and his men experienced, watching flasks of Greek fire hurtling through the darkened sky like 'dragon[s] flying through the air', with long 'tail[s] of fire stream[ing] behind' them. One day in early 1250 when John was not on duty, the Ayyubid barrage finally told, and the towers went down in flames. Thankful that this had not occurred on his watch, Joinville wrote, 'I and my knights praised God for such an accident.'[40]

Even with the 'cat-houses', the attempts to fashion a causeway had been failing because the river's fast-moving current eroded the structure. In the first week of February, Louis called off the futile efforts, and morale within the camp sank as it seemed an impasse had been reached. Around this same time, however, a Muslim traitor – variously described as a Bedouin or as a deserter from the Egyptian army – told the Latins about a ford some distance down the course of the Tanis that would give them access to the southern banks of the river. Offered this unexpected glimpse of hope, the French king immediately decided to use this ford to mount a direct attack on the Ayyubid camp.

Aware of the terrible risks involved in this operation, and of the lethal consequences of being caught and surrounded on the far side of the Tanis, Louis formulated his tactics with care. To avoid detection, the crossing would begin before daybreak. The depth of the ford and the need for swift engagement precluded the involvement of infantry, so only mounted knights and sergeants were selected. And with an eye to maintaining strict discipline, these men were drawn from the king's trusted French contingents and the Templar and Hospitaller Orders. The Franks of Outremer and the Teutonic Knights were to remain in place, defending the northern camp. Above all, it was imperative that the entire strike force reach the south bank and regroup before any attack was mounted. With this in mind, Louis 'commanded them all – great men and small – that no one should dare to break ranks'.[41]

The Battle of Mansourah

Before first light on Tuesday 8 February 1250, the king's plan was put into action. The Templars led the way, closely followed by a party of knights commanded by Louis' brother Count Robert of Artois, which included the Englishman William Longsword, earl of Salisbury. It soon became clear that the ford was deeper than expected, requiring horses to swim midstream, and the steep, muddy banks on either side caused some crusaders to fall from their mounts and drown. Nonetheless, hundreds of Franks began to emerge on the far shore.

Then, just as the sun was rising, Robert of Artois made a sudden and unexpected decision to launch an assault, charging at the head of his men towards the Ayyubids' riverside base. In the confusion, the Templars followed close behind, leaving Louis and the bulk of the strike force stranded in the ford. In this one instant, all hope of an ordered offensive evaporated. It is impossible to know what caused Robert to act so precipitously: perhaps he saw the chance for a surprise attack slipping away; or the promise of glory and renown may have spurred him on. As he rode off, those left behind – the king included – must have felt a mixture of shock, puzzlement and anger.

Even so, at first it looked as though Robert's audacity might win the day. Ploughing into the unsuspecting Muslim camp, where many were still asleep, the count's combined force of around 600 crusaders and Templars encountered only token resistance. Racing in among the enemy tents, they began the work of butchery. Fakhr al-Din, who was carrying out his morning ablutions, quickly threw on some clothes, mounted a horse and rode out, unarmed, into the tumult. Set upon by a party of Templars, he was cut down and slain by two mighty sword blows. Elsewhere the slaughter was indiscriminate. One

Frankish account described how the Latins were 'killing all and sparing none', observing that 'it was sad indeed to see so many dead bodies and so much blood spilt, except that they were enemies of the Christian faith'.[42]

This brutal riot overran the Ayyubid encampment and, had Robert now elected to hold the field, reorder his forces and await Louis' arrival, a stunning victory might well have been at hand. But this was not to be. With Muslim stragglers streaming towards Mansourah, the count of Artois made a woefully hot-headed decision to pursue them. As he moved to initiate a second charge, the Templar commander urged caution, but Robert chided him for his cowardice. According to one Christian account, the Templar replied: 'Neither I nor my brothers are afraid . . . but let me tell you that none of us expect to come back, neither you, nor ourselves.'

Together they and their men rode the short distance south to Mansourah and raced into the town. There the folly of their courageous but suicidal decision immediately became apparent. On the open plain, even in the Ayyubid camp, the Christians had been afforded the freedom to manoeuvre and fight in close-knit groups. But once in among the town's cramped streets and alleyways, that style of warfare proved impossible. Worse still, upon entering Mansourah, the Franks came face to face with the elite Bahriyya regiment quartered in the town. This was to be the Latins' first deadly encounter with these 'lions of battle'. A Muslim chronicler described how the *mamluks* fought with utter ruthlessness and resolve. Surrounding the crusaders 'on every side', attacking with spear, sword and bow, they 'turned their crosses upside down'. Of the 600 or so who rode into Mansourah barely a handful escaped, and both Robert of Artois and William Longsword were killed.[43]

Back on the banks of the Tanis, as yet unaware of the dreadful slaughter then just beginning in Mansourah, Louis was making a valiant attempt to retain control of his remaining troops, even as squadrons of mounted *mamluks* began racing forward to counter-attack. One crusader described how 'a tremendous noise of horns, bugles and drums broke out' as they drew near; 'men shouted, horses neighed; it was horrible to see or hear'. But in the thick of the throng, the king held his nerve and slowly fought his way forward to establish a position on the southern edge of the river, opposite the crusader camp. Here the Franks rallied to the *Oriflame* and made a desperate attempt to hold their ground, while the *mamluks* loosed 'dense clouds of bolts and arrows' and rushed in to engage in hand-to-hand combat. The damage sustained on that day was appalling. One of Joinville's knights took 'a lance-thrust between his shoulders, which made so large a wound that the blood poured from his body as if from a bung-hole in a barrel'. Another received a blow from a Muslim sword in the middle of his face that cut 'through his nose so that it was left dangling over his lips'. He carried on fighting, only to die later of his injuries. As for himself, John wrote: 'I was only wounded by the enemy's arrows in five places, though my horse was wounded in fifteen.'

The crusaders came close to routing – some tried to swim across the Tanis, and one eyewitness 'saw the river strewn with lances and shields, and full of men and horses drowning in the water'. For those fighting alongside the king it seemed as if there was an endless stream of enemies to face, and 'for every [Muslim] killed, another at once appeared, fresh and vigorous'. But through it all, Louis remained steadfast, refusing to be broken. Inspired by his resilience, the Christians endured wave upon wave of attack, until at last, at around three o'clock in the afternoon, the Muslim offensive slackened. As night fell, the battered Franks retained possession of the field.[44]

Latin sources described this, the Battle of Mansourah, as a great crusader victory, and in one sense it was a triumph. Holding out against horrendous odds, the Franks had established a bridgehead south of the Tanis. But the cost of this achievement was immense. The deaths of Robert of Artois and his contingent, alongside a large proportion of the Templar host, deprived the expedition of many of its fiercest warriors. In any battles still to come, their loss would be keenly felt. And though the crusaders had crossed the river, the town of Mansourah stood before them still, barring their advance.

BETWEEN VICTORY AND DEFEAT

In the immediate aftermath of the Battle of Mansourah, Louis IX was confronted by a pressing strategic dilemma. In theory the king had two options: to cut his losses and fall back across the Tanis; or to dig in on the south bank, in the hope of somehow overcoming the Ayyubid enemy. Choosing the former would have been tantamount to conceding defeat, for though this cautious tactic might have permitted the crusade to regroup, the chances of mounting a second cross-river offensive, with a now weakened army, were limited. Louis must also have recognised that the shame and frustration of forsaking a bridgehead won through the sacrifice of so many Christian lives would crush Frankish spirits, probably beyond repair. That night, or at dawn the following morning, the king could have ordered a withdrawal, but this act would have signalled the failure of his Egyptian strategy, effectively marking the crusade's end.

Given Louis' earnest belief that his endeavour enjoyed divine sanction and support, and the constant pressure placed upon him to uphold the tenets of chivalry and honour the achievements of his crusading ancestors, it is hardly surprising that he rejected any thought of retreat. Instead, he immediately began to consolidate his position south of the river, scavenging materials from the overrun Muslim camp – including wood from the fourteen remaining engines – to improvise a stockade, while also digging a shallow defensive trench. At the same time, a number of small boats were lashed together to create a makeshift bridge across the Tanis, linking the old northern camp and the crusaders' new outpost. By these measures, the Franks sought to prepare themselves for the storm of war that would surely come. And for now, Louis seems to have clung to the memory of the sudden victory at Damietta, convinced that Ayyubid resistance was about to collapse.

Three days later, the king's hopes suffered a first blow. On Friday 11 February, the *mamluks* initiated a massive onslaught, spearheaded by the Bahriyya, which lasted from dawn till dusk. Thousands of Muslims surrounded the crusader camp, intent upon dislodging the Franks through aerial bombardment and bloody close-quarter combat. Christians later declared that they attacked 'so persistently, horribly and dreadfully' that many Latins from Outremer 'said that they had never seen such a bold and violent assault'. The *mamluks'* unbridled ferocity terrified the crusaders, one of whom wrote that they 'hardly seemed human, but like wild beasts, frantic with rage', adding that 'they clearly thought nothing of dying'. Many Franks were carrying injuries from the Battle of Mansourah – Joinville, for example, was no longer able to don armour because of his wounds – but, nonetheless, they fought back manfully, aided by raking showers of crossbow bolts unleashed from the old camp across the river. Once again Louis kept his nerve and the Christians held their ground, but only through the sacrifice of hundreds more dead and injured, among them the master of the Templars, who had lost one eye on 8 February and now lost another and soon died from his wounds.

The Latins demonstrated immense fortitude in the two dreadful mêlées endured that week. They also claimed to have killed some 4,000 Muslims in this second encounter. There are no figures in Arabic chronicles with which to confirm this count, but, even if accurate, these losses seem to have done little to dent the Ayyubids' overwhelming numerical superiority. The crusader army had survived, albeit in a terribly weakened state. From this point onwards, it must have been obvious that they were in no position to mount an offensive of their own. At absolute best, they could hope to retain their precarious foothold on the south bank. And if Mansourah was not to be attacked, then how could the war be won?

In the days and weeks that followed, this question became ever more imperative. The Egyptians carried out regular probing attacks, but otherwise were content to confine the Christians within their stockade. By late February, with no possible hint of progress in the campaign, the atmosphere in the camp began to darken, and the crusaders' predicament was only exacerbated by the outbreak of illness. This was partly linked to the enormous number of dead piled upon the plain and floating in the water. Joinville described seeing scores of bodies dragged down the Tanis by the current, until they piled up against the Franks' bridge of boats, so that 'all the river was full of corpses, from one bank to another, and as far upstream as one could cast a small stone'. Food shortages were also starting to take hold, and this led to scurvy.[45]

In this situation, the supply chain down the Nile to Damietta became an essential lifeline. So far, the Christian fleet had been free to ferry goods to the camps at Mansourah, but this was about to change. On 25 February 1250, after long months of travel from Iraq, the Ayyubid heir to Egypt, al-Mu'azzam Turanshah, arrived at the Nile Delta. He immediately brought new impetus to the Muslim cause. With the Nile flood long abated, the Mahalla Canal contained too little water to be entered to the south, but Turanshah had some fifty ships portaged across land to the canal's northern reaches. From there, these vessels were able to sail down to the Nile, bypassing the Frankish fleet at Mansourah. Joinville admitted that this dramatic move 'came as a great shock to our people'. Turanshah's ploy was virtually identical to the trap sprung against the Fifth Crusade, and for Louis' expedition it spelled disaster.

Over the next few weeks Ayyubid ships intercepted two Christian supply convoys heading south from Damietta. Cut off by this blockade, the crusaders soon found themselves in a hopeless position. A Latin contemporary described the awful sense of desperation that now gripped the army: 'Everyone expected to die, no one supposed he could escape. It would have been hard to find one man in all that great host who was not mourning a dead friend, or a single tent or shelter without its sick or dead.' By this stage, Joinville's wounds had become infected. He later recalled lying in his tent in a feverish state;

outside, 'barber-surgeons' were cutting away the rotting gums of those afflicted with scurvy, so they might eat. Joinville could hear the cries of those enduring this gruesome surgery resounding through the camp, and likened them to those 'of a woman in labour'. Starvation also began to take a heavy toll among men and horses. Many Franks happily consumed carrion from dead horses, donkeys and mules, and later resorted to eating cats and dogs.[46]

The price of indecision

By early March 1250, conditions in the main Christian camp on the south bank of the Tanis were unbearable. One eyewitness admitted that 'men said openly that all was lost'. Louis was largely responsible for this ruinous state of affairs. In mid-February, he had failed to make a realistic strategic assessment of the risks and possible rewards involved in maintaining the crusaders' southern camp, holding on to the forlorn hope of Ayyubid disintegration. He also grossly underestimated the vulnerability of his Nile supply line and the number of troops needed to overcome the Egyptian army at Mansourah.

Some of these errors might have been mitigated had the king now acted with decisive resolution – recognising that his position was utterly untenable. The only logical choices remaining were immediate retreat or negotiation, but throughout the month of March Louis embraced neither. Instead, as his troops weakened and died all around him, the French monarch seems to have been paralysed by indecision – unable to face the fact that his grand Egyptian strategy had been thwarted. It was not until early April that Louis finally took action, but by this stage he was too late. Seeking to secure terms of truce with the Ayyubids, he seems to have offered to exchange Damietta for Jerusalem (raising yet another parallel with the Fifth Crusade). A deal of this sort might have been acceptable in February 1250, perhaps even in March, but by April the Muslim stranglehold was clear to all. Turanshah knew that he held a telling advantage and, sensing that victory was close at hand, rebutted Louis' proposal. All that remained now to the Christians was to attempt a retreat north, across the forty miles of open ground to Damietta.[47]

On 4 April orders were passed through the lines of the exhausted Latin host. The hundreds, perhaps even thousands, of sick and wounded were to be loaded on to boats and ferried down the Nile in the vain hope that some craft might evade the Muslim cordon. The remaining able-bodied crusaders were to march overland to the coast.

By this stage Louis himself was suffering with dysentery. Many leading Franks urged him to flee, either by ship or on horseback, so as to avoid capture. But in a valiant, if somewhat foolhardy, show of solidarity, the king refused to abandon his men. He had led them into Egypt; now he hoped to guide them back out to safety. An ill-conceived plan was hatched to escape under cover of darkness, leaving the tents standing in the southern camp so as not to warn the Muslims that an exodus was under way. Louis also ordered his engineer, Joscelin of Cornaut, to cut the ropes holding the bridge of boats in place once the Tanis had been crossed.

Unfortunately the whole scheme quickly fell apart. Most of the crusaders made it back to the north shore at dusk, but a group of Ayyubid scouts realised what was happening and raised the alarm. With enemy troops bearing down on his position, Joscelin seems to have lost his nerve and fled – certainly the bridge remained in place, and packs of Muslim soldiers crossed over to give chase. In the failing light, panic spread and a chaotic rout began. One Muslim eyewitness described how 'we followed on their tracks in pursuit; nor did the sword cease its work among their backsides throughout the night. Shame and catastrophe were their lot.'

Earlier that same evening, John of Joinville and two of his surviving knights had boarded a boat and were waiting to push off. He now watched as wounded men, left in the confusion to fend for themselves in the old northern camp, started to crawl to the banks of the Nile, desperately trying to get on to any ship. He wrote: 'As I was urging the sailors to let us get away, the Saracens entered the [northern] camp, and I saw by the light of the fires that they were slaughtering the poor fellows on the bank.' Joinville's vessel made it out into the river and, as the current took the craft downstream, he made good his escape.[48]

By daybreak on 5 April 1250, the full extent of the disaster was apparent. On land, disordered groups of Franks were being keenly pursued by *mamluk* troops who had no interest in showing clemency. Over the next few days, many hundreds of retreating Christians were slain. One band got to within a day of Damietta, but were then surrounded and capitulated. Throughout the host, the great symbols of Frankish pride and indomitability fell: the *Oriflame* 'was torn to pieces'; the Templar standard 'trampled under foot'.

Riding north, the aged Patriarch Robert and Odo of Châteauroux somehow managed to elude capture, but, after the first twenty-four hours, shattered by their exertions, they were unable to go on. Robert later described in a letter how, by chance, they stumbled across a small boat tied up on the shore and eventually reached Damietta. Few were so fortunate. Most of the ships carrying the sick and injured were ransacked or burned in the water. John of Joinville's boat made slow progress downstream, even as he beheld terrible scenes of carnage on the banks, but his craft was finally spotted. With four Muslim vessels bearing down on them, Joinville turned to his men, asking if they should land and try to fight their way to safety, or stay on the water and be captured. With disarming honesty, he described how one of his servants declared: 'We should all let ourselves be slain, for thus we shall go to paradise', but admitted that 'none of us heeded his advice'. In fact, when his boat was boarded, Joinville lied to prevent his execution on the spot, saying that he was the king's cousin. As a result he was taken into captivity.[49]

In the midst of all this mayhem, King Louis became separated from most of his troops. He was now so stricken with dysentery that he had to have a hole cut in his breeches. A small group of his most loyal retainers made a brave attempt to lead him to safety, and eventually they took refuge in a small village. There, cowering, half dead, in a squalid hut, the mighty sovereign of France was captured. His daring attempt to conquer Egypt was at an end.

THE PENITENT KING

Louis IX's errors of judgement at Mansourah – perhaps most notably his failure to learn fully from the mistakes of the Fifth Crusade – were now compounded by his own imprisonment. Never before had a king of the Latin West been taken captive during a crusade. This unparalleled disaster placed Louis and the bedraggled remnants of his army in an enormously vulnerable position. Seized by the enemy outright, with no chance to secure terms of surrender, the Franks found themselves at the mercy of Islam. Relishing the triumph, one Muslim witness wrote:

A tally was made of the number of captives, and there were more than 20,000; those who had drowned or been killed numbered 7,000. I saw the dead, and they covered the face of the earth in their profusion. . . . It was a day of the kind the Muslims had never seen; nor had they heard of its like.

Prisoners were herded into holding camps across the Delta and sorted by rank. According to Arabic testimony, Turanshah 'ordered the ordinary mass to be beheaded', and instructed one of his lieutenants from Iraq to oversee the executions – the grisly work apparently proceeded at the rate of 300 a night. Other Franks were offered the choice of conversion or death, while higher-ranking nobles, like John of Joinville, were held aside because of their economic value as hostages. Joinville suggested that King Louis was threatened with torture, being shown a gruesome wooden vice, 'notched with interlocking teeth', that was used to crush a victim's legs, but this is not hinted at elsewhere. Despite his illness and the ignominious circumstances of his capture, the monarch seems to have held his dignity.[50]

In fact, Louis' circumstances were markedly improved by Turanshah's own increasingly uncertain position at this time. Since his arrival at Mansourah, the Ayyubid heir had favoured his own soldiers and officials, thereby alienating many within the existing Egyptian army hierarchy – including the *mamluk* commander Aqtay and the Bahriyya. Keen to secure a deal that would consolidate his hold over the Nile region, Turanshah agreed to negotiate and, in mid-to late April, terms were settled. A ten-year truce was declared. The French king would be released in return for Damietta's immediate surrender. A massive ransom of 800,000 gold bezants (or 400,000 *livres tournois*) was set for the 12,000 other Christians in Ayyubid custody.

In early May, however, it suddenly seemed that even the fulfilment of these punitive conditions might not bring the Christians to liberty, because the Ayyubid coup – so long awaited by Louis at Mansourah – finally took place. On 2 May Turanshah was murdered by Aqtay and a vicious young *mamluk* in the Bahriyya regiment, named Baybars. The ensuing power struggle initially saw Shajar al-Durr appointed as figurehead of Ayyubid Egypt. In reality, though, a seismic shift was now under way – one that would lead to the gradual but inexorable rise of the *mamluks*.

In spite of these dynastic upheavals, the Muslim repossession of Damietta went ahead as planned and Louis was released on 6 May 1250. He then set about collecting the funds with which to make an initial payment of half the ransom – 200,000 *livres tournois* – 177,000 of which was raised from the king's war chest and the remainder taken from the Templars. This massive sum took two days to be weighed and counted. On 8 May Louis took ship to Palestine with his leading nobles, among them his two surviving brothers, Alphonse of Poitiers and Charles of Anjou, and John of Joinville. As yet, the vast majority of the crusaders remained in captivity.

In adversity's wake

All Louis IX's hopes of subjugating Egypt and winning the war for the Holy Land had ended in failure. But in many ways the true and remarkable depth of the French king's crusading idealism only became apparent after this humiliating defeat. In similar circumstances, shamed by such an unmitigated debacle, many a Christian monarch would have sloped off back to Europe, turning his back on the Near East. Louis did the opposite. Realising that his men would likely remain rotting in Muslim captivity unless he continued to pressure the Egyptian regime for their release, the king chose to remain in Palestine for the next four years.

In this time, Louis served as overlord of Outremer and, by 1252, had secured the liberation of his troops. Working tirelessly, he set about the unglamorous task of bolstering the kingdom of Jerusalem's coastal defences – overseeing the extensive refortification of Acre, Jaffa, Caesarea and Sidon. He also established a permanent garrison of one hundred Frankish knights in Acre, paid for by the French crown at an annual cost of around 4,000 *livres tournois*.

Given the ardent self-promotion typical of other crusade leaders – from Richard the Lionheart to Frederick II of Germany – Louis also showed an extraordinary willingness to accept responsibility for the dreadful setbacks experienced in Egypt. The king's supporters tried their best to transfer the blame to Robert of Artois, emphasising that it had been his advice that led to the march on Mansourah in autumn 1249 and criticising the count's reckless behaviour on 8 February 1250. But in a letter written in August 1250, Louis himself praised Robert's bravery, describing him as 'our very dear and illustrious brother of honoured memory', and expressing the hope and belief that he had been 'crowned as a martyr'. In the same document, the king explained the crusade's failure and his own incarceration as divine punishments, meted out 'as our sins required'.[51]

Eventually, in April 1254, Louis travelled home to France. His mother Blanche had died two years earlier, and the Capetian realm had become increasingly unstable. The king returned from the Holy Land a changed man, and his later life was marked by extreme piety and austerity – wearing a hair shirt, he ate only meagre rations of the blandest food and engaged in seemingly constant prayer. At one point Louis even considered renouncing his crown and entering a monastery. He also harboured a heartfelt, lingering desire to launch another crusade, thereby, perhaps, to win redemption.

The Egyptian expedition reshaped King Louis' life, but the events on the Nile also had a wider effect upon Latin Europe. The crusade of 1250 had been carefully planned, financed and supplied; its armies led by a paragon of Christian kingship. And still it had been subjected to an excoriating defeat. After one and a half centuries of almost unbroken failure in the war for the Holy Land, this latest reversal prompted an outpouring of doubt and despair in the West. Some even turned their backs on the Christian faith. In the second half of the thirteenth century – as Outremer's strength continued to fade and new, seemingly invincible, enemies emerged on to the Levantine stage – the chances of mounting another crusade to the East seemed bleak indeed.

V

VICTORY IN
THE EAST

22

LION OF EGYPT

For more than half a century after Saladin's death in 1193, members of his Ayyubid dynasty dominated Near Eastern Islam. Saladin had brought doom and defeat to the Christian Franks living in the Levant, reconquering Jerusalem and holding back Richard the Lionheart's Third Crusade. But wrapped up in their own petty rivalries, later Ayyubids proved willing to live in relative peace alongside the remaining crusader states. And with Muslims and Christians both keen to maintain mutually profitable trade links, negotiation, accommodation and truce became the order of the day. The Islamic rulers of Damascus, Cairo and Aleppo still claimed to be champions of *jihad*, but their struggle turned inwards, to be expressed in works of spiritual purification and religious patronage. Rather than embrace the external militaristic form of *jihad* by waging holy war, the Ayyubids sought, in the main, to limit conflict – ever conscious that aggression might provoke a dangerous and disruptive western European crusade.

This delicately balanced *modus vivendi* was to be dramatically overturned when two new oriental superpowers – the Mamluks and the Mongols – rose to prominence in the Levant. Each was imbued with fearsome military strength, unlike anything yet witnessed in the age of the crusades, and their monumental clash reshaped the fate of the Holy Land and the history of the crusades. Overshadowed by these two behemoths, Latin Outremer became the third, sometimes almost incidental, challenger in the struggle for mastery of the East.

NEW POWERS IN THE NEAR EAST

A new Islamic dynasty – the Mamluk sultanate, governed by members of the *mamluk* (slave soldier) military elite – seized power in Egypt in the wake of King Louis IX of France's failed crusade. A convoluted and brutal power struggle raged throughout the 1250s, as various *mamluk* leaders sought to overthrow the last vestiges of Ayyubid authority in the Nile region. The elite Bahriyya *mamluk* regiment was forced to flee Egypt in 1254, when their commander Aqtay was murdered by the ruthless warlord Qutuz, spearhead of a rival *mamluk* faction. Three years later, Shajar al-Durr – widow of the last great Ayyubid Sultan al-Salih – was executed, and Qutuz gradually assumed control of Egypt, while still governing in the name of a young puppet-sultan, al-Mansur Ali.

Meanwhile, the Bahriyya went into exile under the leadership of Baybars – one of the conspirators in the 1250 murder of the Ayyubid heir, Turanshah. Born around 1221, Baybars was a tall, dark-skinned Kipchak Turk, the hardy, bellicose people of the Russian steppes, known in the ancient world as the Cumans. He was said to possess a remarkably powerful voice, but Baybars' most striking feature was his blue eyes, one of which held a small but distinct white fleck the size of the eye of a needle. Taken into slavery at the age of fourteen, Baybars began *mamluk* training, and then passed through the hands of a number of owners before eventually being recruited into al-Salih's new Bahriyya corps in 1246. There his martial skill and leadership qualities were soon recognised, and he fought against King Louis' crusaders in the Battle of Mansourah in 1250.

In the mid- to late 1250s, Baybars and the Bahriyya served a succession of ineffectual Ayyubid emirs who were trying desperately to cling to power in Syria, Palestine and Transjordan. Among them was al-Nasir Yusuf, the nominal ruler of Aleppo and Damascus – an emir born of a noble bloodline, being Saladin's grandson, but singularly incapable of facing the violent challenges of this turbulent era of shifting allegiances and emerging world powers. During this period, Baybars honed his abilities as a military commander, scoring a number of impressive successes, but also enduring some chastening defeats. Throughout, he was closely supported by a fellow *mamluk* and Kipchak Turk, Qalawun, perhaps his closest friend and comrade in arms. With an ever watchful eye upon events in Egypt, Baybars twice attempted to invade the Nile region and depose Qutuz, but, being heavily outnumbered, he proved unable to achieve a significant victory.

By 1259, Baybars had shown himself to be an adept general with an obvious appetite for advancement, but as yet he had not been given the chance to realise his ambitions or evident potential. That opportunity would come, both for Baybars and indeed for the entire Mamluk regime, with the appearance of a new, devastating threat to the Muslim Near East.[1]

Around the year 1206 a warlord named Temüjin united the nomadic Mongol tribes of the vast east Asian steppe grasslands of Mongolia and assumed the title of Chinggis, or Genghis, Khan (literally 'stern ruler'). Genghis and his followers were driven by a boundless hunger for war and came to believe, within the tenets of their pagan faith, that the Mongols were destined by a heavenly decree to conquer the entire world. Through sheer strength of will Genghis transformed the feuding Mongol tribes into an unstoppable army, harnessing the innate resilience of his people and their peerless skills as horsemen and archers.

For the next fifty years, first under Genghis Khan and then, after his death in 1227, under his sons, the Mongols exploded across the face of the Earth. They were a force unparalleled in the medieval world, perhaps in all human history. Unrelenting and utterly uncompromising in their approach to warfare, they expected enemies to show immediate wholesale submission or face total annihilation. And by 1250 their dominions stretched from China to Europe, from the Indian Ocean to the northern wastes of Siberia. This exponential expansion inevitably brought the Mongols into contact with the Christian and Muslim worlds.

Having subjugated northern China, the Mongols began their westward advance in 1229, crushing the Islamic rulers of northern Iran – a move which prompted the Khwarizmians to flee into northern Iraq and eventually culminated in the Khwarizmian invasion of the Holy Land in 1244. Between 1236 and 1239 the Mongol horde defeated the eastern Christians of Georgia and Greater Armenia and, in 1243, invaded Asia Minor, overwhelming the Seljuq Turkish dynasty that had ruled there since the eleventh century. Through the 1230s Mongol armies also conquered the southern steppelands of Russia, establishing a polity that came to be known as the Golden Horde. Ironically, this caused many of the Kipchak Turks native to this region to become refugees. Flooding southwards, they fell into the clutches of slave traders and thus massively increased the availability of *mamluk* recruits for the Muslims of Egypt.

Driving further west, the Mongols eventually encountered the Latin Christians of Europe, where their advent was greeted with a mixture of fear, confusion and uncertainty. News that the Muslims of Iran had been defeated by an unknown force from the distant lands of the East reached the Fifth Crusaders in Egypt in 1221, causing many Franks to imagine that the Mongols might actually be valuable allies. At first this view gained credence, because the shadowy Mongols were equated with the ancient legend of Prester John – a powerful Christian king, prophesied to emerge from the East in Christendom's darkest hour. Over time, it also became clear that Nestorian Christians (a sect long settled in Central Asia) had managed to gain some influence among the Mongols, even converting the wives of some leading warlords.

But Latin Christendom slowly realised that the Mongols, or Tartars as they came to be known in Europe, were not merely a distant foreign power, but an immediate and potentially lethal threat. In 1241 the Mongol army pushed on from Russia and spent the next year ravaging and terrorising Poland, Hungary and eastern Germany, causing untold destruction. Even in the wake of this devastating incursion, the rulers of western Europe – locked in their own disputes – were slow to react, and many continued to nurse ideas of accommodation or alliance. From the late 1240s onwards, the Roman papacy sent two missionary embassies to the Mongols, led by groups of Friars. These Frankish envoys travelled thousands of miles to visit the lavish Mongol court at Qaraqorum (in Mongolia), hoping to convert the Great Khan to Christianity; they returned with blunt ultimatums instructing Rome to submit to Mongol authority. During his time on Cyprus, Louis IX also made contact with the Tartars. In 1249 he sent his own representatives to the Mongols in Iran, but when this embassy returned in 1251 to find Louis in Palestine, it likewise bore a stark demand that he begin paying an annual tribute, which, needless to say, he ignored.

In spite of this uncompromising approach to diplomacy, the Mongol Empire actually started to decay in the second half of the thirteenth century, corroded by dynastic struggle and the problems attendant on governing such an immense realm. Nonetheless, they remained an awe-inspiring force. In the 1250s, the new Great Khan Möngke (Genghis Khan's grandson) initiated a renewed wave of expansion into the Muslim world of the Middle East and beyond, placing his brother Hülegü in command of a massive host of tens of thousands of warriors, alongside the leading Mongol general Kitbuqa. Marching through southern Iran in 1256, this mighty army turned towards Baghdad, where an enfeebled member of the Abbasid dynasty still claimed the title of Sunni caliph. In February 1258 Hülegü crushed Baghdad, putting in excess of 30,000 Muslims to the sword and destroying much of the once great capital. He went on to subjugate most of Mesopotamia, establishing what came to be known as the Mongol Ilkhanate of Persia (stretching from Iraq to the borders of India). Hülegü then crossed the Euphrates to arrive on the borders of Syria and Palestine in 1259.

Not surprisingly, the coming of the Mongols terrified the peoples of northern Syria. The Christians continued to harbour the hope that Hülegü might prove to be an ally against Islam, encouraged by the fact that his wife was a Nestorian. King Hethum of Cilician Armenia had submitted to Mongol rule as far back as 1246, and had been allowed to retain partial autonomy in return for the payment of an annual tribute. Hethum now convinced his son-in-law Bohemond VI (ruler of both the principality of Antioch and the county of Tripoli) to ally with Hülegü's army. Al-Nasir, the Ayyubid ruler of Aleppo and Damascus, had also been paying the Mongols tribute since 1251 in the hope of forestalling a direct invasion, but in autumn 1259, with the horde now marching into Syria, the limitations of the policy of appeasement became apparent.[2]

The Battle of Ayn Jalut

While the advent of the Mongols brought panic and chaos to much of the Muslim Near East, their arrival infused the Mamluk world with a new sense of unity and purpose. In November 1259, Qutuz used the Mongol threat to justify his overthrow of the existing young sultan and had himself proclaimed as the new ruler of Egypt. At the same time, al-Nasir's grip on power was faltering. Stationed near Damascus, the Ayyubid emir seems to have been wholly immobilised by fear as the Mongols advanced on Aleppo – certainly he did nothing to react, even as streams of refugees poured into southern Syria from as far afield as Persia.

In early 1260 Hülegü laid siege to Aleppo, with the aid of Hethum and Bohemond VI, and by the end of February the city had been captured and subjected to a six-day-long orgy of violence. Bohemond personally set fire to the city's main mosque and although he was later excommunicated by the Latin Church for aiding the Mongols, the prince made significant territorial gains as a result of the 1260 pact, including the reassertion of Frankish control over the port

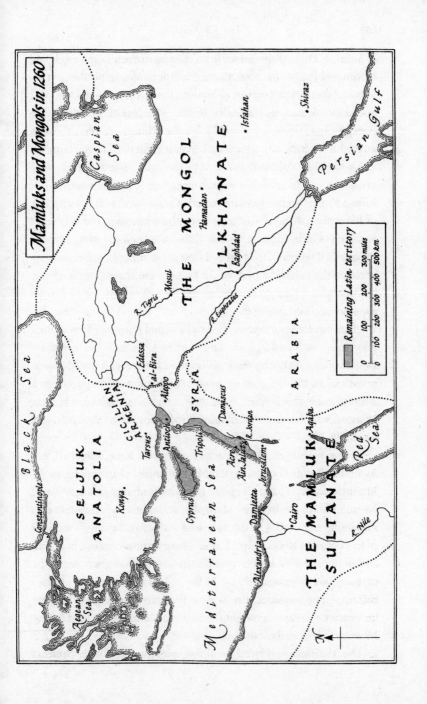

Mamluks and Mongols in 1260

Black Sea

SELJUK ANATOLIA

Constantinople

Konya

Aegean Sea

Caspian Sea

THE MONGOL ILKHANATE

Hamadan

Mosul

R. Tigris

Edessa

Tal-Bira

CICILIAN ARMENIA

Tarsus

Aleppo

Antioch

SYRIA

Damascus

Isfahan

Shiraz

Persian Gulf

Baghdad

R. Euphrates

ARABIA

Tripoli

Acre

Ain Jalut

R. Jordan

Jerusalem

Mediterranean Sea

Cyprus

Damietta

Alexandria

Cairo

THE MAMLUK SULTANATE

R. Nile

Aqaba

Red Sea

Remaining Latin territory

0   100   200   300 miles

0   100   200   300   400   500 km

N

of Latakia. Hülegü moved on from Aleppo to overcome the likes of
Harim and Homs, and soon attained full dominion of northern Syria.
News of these events caused al-Nasir to flee Damascus and the city's
populace elected to surrender to the Mongols rather than face
Aleppo's fate. Thus, in March 1260, the Mongol general Kitbuqa
arrived to occupy Islam's ancient Syrian capital. The cowering al-
Nasir was soon captured and sent to Hülegü – where, for the time
being, he was treated as a valuable hostage – but news arrived of
Möngke's death, and Hülegü decided to leave Syria with the vast bulk
of his army, returning east to oversee the succession of his brother
Kublai as Great Khan. This left Kitbuqa in command of Mongol
Syria, albeit with a much-reduced host at his disposal, but even so he
received the surrender of Ayyubid Transjordan that summer.

With the Mongols having swept into the Holy Land largely
unopposed, overturning the Ayyubid world, it was now questionable
whether any Levantine power had the will and resources to stem their
advance. The Franks of the kingdom of Jerusalem did not share
Bohemond of Antioch's ready willingness to side with the Mongols,
conscious of the fact that to do so might simply be to exchange a
Muslim enemy for another, even more dangerous, pagan foe. Hoping
to avoid any direct confrontation, the Latins adopted a policy of
neutrality.[3]

By the middle of 1260, therefore, only one force remained that
might be capable of opposing the Mongol horde – Mamluk Egypt. By
this time, Baybars had recognised that his Ayyubid paymasters would
be unable to resist the Mongols, and thus he negotiated a
rapprochement with Qutuz, travelling with the remaining members
of the Bahriyya to Cairo in March. There a tense concord held, but
a current of mutual animosity and suspicion swirled just beneath the
surface. Both men were aware of the other's ambition and Qutuz's
role in Aqtay's murder was fresh in Baybars' mind. One Muslim
chronicler acknowledged that the profound hatred each held for the
other was clear in their eyes.

The Mamluks now faced a defining question: whether to confront or placate the Mongols. On this issue, at least, Qutuz and Baybars were in resolute agreement. Early that summer, an embassy from Hülegü arrived in Cairo demanding Mamluk surrender. The envoys were summarily butchered, their bodies cut in half and their heads hung from one of Cairo's gates. With this extraordinarily defiant statement of intent the Mamluks went to war. Rather than wait in Egypt, in the hope of repelling an invasion on home ground, they chose to confront Kitbuqa head-on, while his army was still in a weakened state. If successful, this bold strategy promised to bring the Mamluks near-total dominion of the Near East. But the risks were colossal, for they involved direct battle with the Mongols – an invincible enemy, before which all other armies had fallen.

In midsummer 1260 the Mamluks marched out of Egypt, rallying some additional Muslim troops who had formerly served the Ayyubids. Baybars was appointed as commander of the Mamluk vanguard and, together with Qutuz, formulated a plan of attack. Some attempt was made to draw the Franks into an active alliance. They refused, holding to their policy of neutrality, but did permit the Muslim host to march north unhindered through Latin territory to Acre. News of this advance brought Kitbuqa, then based in Baalbek (Lebanon), south, with additional troops levied from Georgia, Cilician Armenia and Muslim Homs.

The great battle to decide the Near East's fate took place at Ayn Jalut, in Galilee – where Saladin had sought to confront the Franks in 1183. Leading the vanguard, Baybars found the Mongol army camped beside this small settlement, at the foot of Mount Gilboa. He and Qutuz then led their Mamluk army south-east down the Jezreel valley and launched their attack on 3 September 1260. The opposing armies appear to have been roughly equal in terms of numbers – with somewhere between 10,000 and 12,000 troops in each host – so, by the norms of medieval warfare, both sides were taking a perilous gamble. Qutuz and Baybars demonstrated skill and bravery in command, withstanding two massive charges, and, at a key moment, the Muslims from Homs positioned on the Mongol left wing fled the field. This turned the battle in the Mamluks' favour, as they managed to surround the Mongols and slay Kitbuqa. In one of the epochal moments of history, the seemingly unstoppable tide of Mongol expansion was halted by the new champions of Islam.

Only one arm of the great Mongol Empire had been defeated, and the spectre of retaliation remained – as yet unable to return to the Near East, an incensed Hülegü responded to news of the setback by executing al-Nasir. But the victory at Ayn Jalut proved critical in sealing the future ascendancy of the Mamluk sultanate. In the immediate wake of the battle, Qutuz assumed control of Damascus and Aleppo, installing two of his allies as governors. Baybars' ambitions and expectations were slighted by these arrangements, because Qutuz broke a promise to reward him with the rule of Aleppo (perhaps understandably judging that it would be folly to establish a rival in power so far from Egypt). Together, the sultan and his disgruntled general set out on the triumphant return journey to Egypt.[4]

Around 22 October 1260, Qutuz and his emirs were crossing the Egyptian desert en route to Cairo when the sultan called a pause to the march so that he might engage in one of his favourite pastimes – hare coursing. Baybars and a small group of *mamluks* agreed to accompany him on the hunt, but once away from the main camp, they murdered Qutuz. Numerous and varying accounts of the coup survive, but it appears that Baybars asked the sultan for a favour (probably the gift of a slave girl), and, when Qutuz acceded, reached out to kiss the sultan's hand. At that moment, Baybars gripped Qutuz's arms to prevent him from drawing a weapon, and another emir struck him in the neck with his sword. After that first attack, the other conspirators rushed in and the sultan died beneath a cascade of blows.

Baybars seems to have been the plot's ringleader, but his position was not yet assured. Riding back to the camp, a council of all the leading Mamluk emirs was convened in the royal pavilion. Given their shared tribal Turkish roots, there was a strong sense of equality among these elite *mamluks* and an expectation that any new leader should be chosen from their ranks through election. Not to be denied, Baybars declared that, as Qutuz's murderer, he had earned the right to power, while sweetening his demand with promises of reward and patronage for supporters. By these means – through blood and persuasion – Baybars emerged as the new Mamluk sultan, the man who would now be responsible for leading the Muslim Near East against the Mongols and the Latins.[5]

BAYBARS AND THE MAMLUK SULTANATE

In the autumn of 1260, Baybars was patently aware of the fragility of his hold on the sultanate. He moved swiftly to assume authority in Cairo, occupying the great citadel – the seat of power built by Saladin – and rewarding a wide circle of emirs with offices and wealth. In addition, the surviving Bahriyya *mamluks* were established as his personal bodyguards. Their old regimental barracks on the Nile were later rebuilt and placed under the command of the sultan's most trusted emirs, including Qalawun.

Baybars' most urgent concerns were the legitimisation of his own rule and the wider entrenchment of Mamluk power in Egypt. But the new sultan also possessed the political and strategic vision to recognise, and adapt to, the new Levantine world order. In decades past, Muslim leaders had sought to unite Islam and, in some cases, tried actively to combat the Franks in the Holy Land. Now, the imperative had changed and a different paradigm had been created. After 1260, the critical frontiers lay to the north and east of Syria, whence the primary enemy – the Mongol Empire – might once again seek to destroy Islam. To combat this threat, these borders must be protected and the Near East transformed into a united and impervious fortress state.

The Latin Christians were a secondary danger. Geographically their remaining settlements lay within the Syrian, Lebanese and Palestinian territory that Baybars now wished to unify and secure against the Mongols. He rightly judged that, in the wake of setbacks like the Battle of La Forbie, the Franks of Outremer were effectively emasculated. On their own, they posed little concern. But as allies to an external force – be it in the form of a Mongol horde or a western crusade – they might open a troublesome and distracting second front within the confines of the Near East. As such, the crusader states were embedded irritants that had to be neutralised.

Aware of these challenges, Baybars dedicated much of the early 1260s to radically reshaping the Muslim Near East, founding a potent, authoritarian regime. At the same time, he set out to ready the Mamluk state for the onset of war – be it against Mongol or Christian enemies. By these means, the new sultan spent his first years in power assiduously preparing for what he hoped would be ultimate victory in the struggle for control of the Holy Land.

The protector of Islam

At first, Baybars' hold on power was relatively precarious: he inherited a Mamluk state that was only partially formed; and he had been involved in the assassination of two former sultans, Turanshah and Qutuz. Against this somewhat tainted background, civil insurrection or counter-coup threatened, and the loyalty of his fellow *mamluk* emirs was by no means assured. But in late 1260, the new sultan also stood to benefit from some significant advantages. In the aftermath of the Mongol invasion and the Battle of Ayn Jalut, the remaining vestiges of Ayyubid power in Syria and Palestine were all but shattered, and the Holy Land was ripe for Mamluk domination. Thus, in contrast to the likes of Nur al-Din and Saladin, who laboured for decades to unite the Near East, Baybars was able to assert control of Damascus and Aleppo within the first years of his reign, installing regional governors who answered to Cairo.

In addition, Baybars was able to draw upon the triumph achieved at Ayn Jalut to legitimate his claim to power. Presenting himself as the saviour of Islam, he had a monument erected on the battlefield, and demolished Qutuz's grave to downplay any suggestion that the late sultan also might have played a 'heroic' role in the confrontation. In later years, Baybars' chancellor and official biographer, Abd al-Zahir, reconfigured the history of the battle in his account of the sultan's life, presenting it as a victory won almost single-handedly by Baybars. The sultan also sought to promote his own cult of personality, embodied in his lion emblem (depicting a lion walking to the left, with a raised forepaw). This distinctive heraldic device was placed on Baybars' coinage and used to mark public buildings and bridges constructed in his name. And while it is true that the Mamluk state was threatened by potent enemy forces in the 1260s, these evident dangers enabled Baybars to enact an unprecedented programme of militarisation and to enjoy unparalleled autocratic authority.[6]

Baybars took a number of masterful steps to consolidate his hold on the sultanate. To ground the new Mamluk regime within the framework of Islam's traditional legal and spiritual hierarchy, he re-established the Sunni Abbasid caliphate. In June 1261, Baybars claimed to have found one of the few surviving members of the Abbasid dynasty. The man's pedigree was carefully assessed by a hand-picked committee of Cairene jurists, theologians and emirs and then confirmed as the new Caliph al-Mustansir. Baybars then made a ritual oath of allegiance to the caliph, swearing to uphold and defend the faith; to rule justly, according to the law; to serve as a protector of Sunni orthodoxy; and to wage *jihad* against the enemies of Islam. In return, al-Mustansir invested Baybars as the sole, all-powerful sultan of the entire Muslim world, an act that not only confirmed his rights to Egypt, Palestine and Syria, but also provided tacit authorisation for a massive campaign of expansion. In a final public affirmation of his regime's legitimacy, Baybars was invested with sultanly apparel: a black rounded turban of the sort customarily worn by the Abbasids; a violet robe; shoes adorned with golden buckles; and a ceremonial sword. Dressed in this finery, he and the caliph rode, in state procession, through the heart of Cairo. From this point onwards, Baybars took great care to endorse caliphal authority, so long as it did not impinge upon his own power. Both the caliph and sultan were named in the Friday prayer; likewise, Mamluk coinage bore both their names.

To reinforce the aura of tradition and continuity developing around the sultanate, Baybars consciously sought to connect himself with two Muslim rulers. The first, al-Salih Ayyub (Baybars' own former master), was now presented as the last legitimate Ayyubid sultan, with Baybars as his direct and rightful heir – an agile manipulation of the past that conveniently ignored the bloody turmoil of the 1250s. The sultan also modelled himself upon Saladin, the conqueror of the Franks and idealised *mujahid*. Imitating his famed generosity as a patron of the faith, Baybars set about restoring Cairo's now dilapidated al-Azhar mosque. In addition, he established a new mosque in Cairo and a *madrasa* beside al-Salih's tomb. The sultan also visited Jerusalem and there restored the Dome of the Rock and the Aqsa mosque – both of which had become somewhat run down under later Ayyubid rule.

Similar echoes were present in a number of civil measures adopted in these early years. Styling himself as the archetypal 'just ruler', Baybars abolished the war taxes imposed by Qutuz, established palaces of justice in Cairo and Damascus and also ordered fair prices to be paid to merchants for goods sequestered by the state. By these diverse means, the sultan engendered widespread popular support among his subjects in the Near East and this helped to insulate his position against other *mamluk* challengers.[7]

Centralised power in the Mamluk state

While working to legitimise the Mamluk sultanate and his own claim to power, Baybars also took bold steps towards governmental and administrative centralisation. Mamluk Cairo was turned into the unquestioned capital of the Muslim Near East, and the office of sultan was imbued with a degree of despotic authority never before witnessed in the medieval era. In stark contrast to many of his predecessors, Baybars carefully monitored state finances and controlled the Mamluk treasury – measures that gave him the wealth to pay for critical reforms.

As sultan, Baybars expected his will to be obeyed without hesitation across the Mamluk world, and he made ready use of both direct force and propaganda to ensure submission and compliance on the part of regional governors. Emirs who failed to levy troops for war in short order, for example, were hung by their hands for three days. Anyone foolish enough to attempt insurrection could expect summary punishment, with torments ranging from blinding or dismemberment to crucifixion. Like other rulers before him – including Nur al-Din and Saladin – Baybars drew upon the fear of external threats to justify his autocratic behaviour, but new emphasis was placed upon the Mongols as the prime enemy of the state. Thus, when the sultan wished to remove the petty Ayyubid princeling al-Mughith from power in Transjordan in 1263, accusations of consorting with the Ilkhanate of Persia were levelled, and letters supposedly from Hülegü to al-Mughith were produced as evidence.

But even beyond guile and brutality, the true cornerstone of Baybars' authority in the Near East was communication. He was the first Muslim in the Middle Ages to master the business of ruling a pan-Levantine empire from Egypt because he made huge investments in message-carrying networks. Many centuries earlier, the Byzantines and early Abbasids had made use of a courier-based postal structure, but this had long since fallen out of use. Baybars created his own *barid*, or postal system, using relays of horse-borne messengers, hand-picked and well rewarded for their reliability. Changing mounts at carefully maintained post stations positioned along key routes through the Mamluk realm, these men could routinely bring a message from Damascus to Cairo in four days, or three in an emergency. Use of the *barid* was strictly limited to the sultan, and letters were always brought directly to Baybars, no matter what he was doing – on one occasion he even had a messenger report to him in the bath. To ensure the smooth and swift transfer of information, major roads and bridges were carefully repaired, and the *barid* was also supplemented by pigeon post and a system of signal fires. This remarkable (and admittedly costly) feat of organisation allowed

Baybars to maintain contact with the far reaches of the Mamluk state – in particular the northern and eastern borders with the Mongols – and meant that he could react to both military threats and civil disorder with unprecedented speed.[8]

Allied to Baybars' own particularly forceful and energetic brand of rulership, this raft of practical and administrative reforms served to consolidate the Mamluk state and cement 'royal' power by the mid-1260s. However, Baybars' regime was not without its faults. The success of this intensely centralised approach to government depended heavily upon the sultan's personal qualities and skills, and this raised obvious questions about how readily the mantle might be passed on to a successor. Seeking to overturn the notion that a Mamluk sultan should be elected, Baybars tried to lay the foundations for his own familial dynasty in August 1264 by appointing his four-year-old son Baraka as joint ruler. Given the emphasis placed on merit rather than heritage among the *mamluk* elite, it remained to be seen whether this plan would be realised.

Baybars also developed a potentially disruptive association with the *sufi* (holy man) mystic Khadir al-Mihrani in these early years. Supposedly a prophet, but regarded by many in the Mamluk court as a philandering fraud, Khadir befriended Baybars in 1263 during one of the sultan's visits to Palestine. Impressed by the *sufi*'s predictions of numerous future Mamluk conquests (many of which later came true), Baybars soon rewarded him with property in Cairo, Jerusalem and Damascus. Khadir was given unfettered access to the sultan's inner circle and was said to have been privy to matters of state, all to the chagrin of Baybars' leading *mamluk* lieutenants. This strange relationship suggests that even a cold-blooded despot like Baybars could be seduced by flattery – it also was a chink in his defences that, in time, would have to be sealed.

Mamluk diplomacy

Given the time and resources Baybars expended within the Muslim Levant while building his Mamluk state in the early 1260s – and the strident militarism evident in his later career – it would be easy to imagine that the sultan adopted an insular approach to the outside world, turning inwards to spurn diplomacy. In fact, he was an active and adept player on the international stage. Baybars used negotiation to pursue three interlocking goals: to forestall any possibility of an alliance between the Latin West and the Mongols; to sow dissension within the Mongol ranks by encouraging rivalry between the Golden Horde and the Persian Ilkhanate; and to maintain access to a ready supply of slave recruits from the Russian steppes.

Within his first year in office, Baybars established contact with the late Emperor Frederick II's bastard son, King Manfred of Sicily (1258–66). Seeking to perpetuate the tradition of close relations between Egypt and the Hohenstaufen, and to support Manfred's anti-papal policies, the sultan dispatched envoys to the Sicilian court with exotic gifts, including a group of Mongol prisoners, complete with their horses and weaponry – testament to their shattered reputation for invincibility. After Manfred's death, Baybars renewed contact with his rival and successor, King Louis IX of France's acquisitive brother, Charles of Anjou.

The sultan likewise opened channels of negotiation with the Golden Horde in 1261. The Mongol ruler of this region, Berke Khan (1257–66), had converted to Islam and was engaged in a heated power struggle with the Ilkhanate of Persia. Baybars flattered Berke's religious affiliation by including his name in the Friday prayers at Mecca, Medina and Jerusalem, and by establishing equitable relations he retained access to the steppe-land slave markets within the Golden Horde and secured the Mamluk sultanate's northern borders with Asia Minor. To ensure the safe and efficient passage of Kipchak slaves from the Black Sea to Egypt, the sultan also forged pacts with the Genoese – the main transporters of slave cargo in the Mediterranean basin. These Italian merchants had recently lost the so-called 'War of St Sabas' – a two-year struggle with Venice over economic and political pre-eminence in Acre and Palestine. When this fractious civil war ended with Genoese defeat in 1258, they relocated to Tyre and, through the 1260s and beyond, proved only too happy to trade with the Mamluks. To ensure that Genoese ships continued to enjoy unhindered access to the Bosphorus Strait, Baybars forged additional contacts with the newly reinstated Byzantine Emperor Michael VIII Palaeologus, who had returned to Constantinople in 1261 with the final collapse of Latin Romania.[9]

For a *mamluk* inculcated in the arts of war rather than the intrigues of court politics, Sultan Baybars managed this tangled web of diplomatic interests with a surprisingly deft and assured hand – all the while manoeuvring to isolate the Mongol Ilkhanate and Latin Outremer.

Perfecting the Mamluk military machine

Between 1260 and 1265 Baybars was phenomenally active in the fields of diplomacy and statecraft. But ever mindful of the need to undertake urgent and extensive preparations for war, he simultaneously set the Mamluk state on the path to militarisation. The sultan's underlying goal was to prosecute *jihad* against the Mongols and the Levantine Franks – scoring victories that would cement further his position and reputation, achieving conquests that would secure Muslim dominion over the Levant.

From the start, work proceeded apace to strengthen the Mamluk world's physical defences. In Egypt, Alexandria's fortifications were bolstered and the mouth of the Nile at Damietta was partially sealed to prevent another naval incursion up the delta akin to that mounted by Louis IX. Across Syria, battlements destroyed by the Mongols at the likes of Damascus, Baalbek and Shaizar were repaired. To the northeast, along the course of the Euphrates River – now the effective frontier with the Persian Ilkhanate – the castle of al-Bira became a strategic linchpin. The fortress was strengthened and heavily garrisoned, and its security closely monitored by Baybars via the *barid*. Al-Bira proved its worth in late 1264, when it successfully withstood the first serious offensive by Ilkhanid forces. This attack, brought on by a lull in the war between the Golden Horde and Mongol Persia, caused the sultan to rally his forces for war, but even as he prepared to march from Egypt reports arrived indicating that the Ilkhanids had already broken off their fruitless siege of al-Bira and retreated.

Above and beyond any reliance on castles, however, Sultan Baybars regarded the army as the bedrock of the Mamluk state. Adopting and extending the existing system of *mamluk* recruitment, he purchased thousands of young male slaves, drawn from Kipchak Turkish and, later, Caucasian stock. These boys were trained and indoctrinated as *mamluk* troops, and then at the age of eighteen freed to serve their masters within the Mamluk sultanate. This approach created a constantly self-rejuvenating military force – what one modern historian has called a 'one-generation nobility' – because children born of *mamluks* were not regarded as being part of the martial elite, although they were permitted to enrol in the army's second-tier *halqa* reserves.

Baybars ploughed massive financial reserves into building, training and refining the Mamluk army. In total, the number of *mamluks* was increased fourfold, to around 40,000 mounted troops. The core of this force was the 4,000-strong royal *mamluk* regiment – Baybars' new elite, schooled and honed in a special practice facility within the citadel of Cairo. Here recruits were taught the arts of swordsmanship – learning to deliver precise strikes by repeating the same cut up to 1,000 times a day – and horse archery with powerful composite recurve bows. The sultan emphasised rigid discipline and rigorous military drilling across every section of the Mamluk host. In the course of his reign, two massive hippodromes were constructed in Cairo – training arenas where the essential skills of horsemanship and combat could be perfected. Whenever in the capital, Baybars himself came daily to practise the warrior craft, setting a standard of professionalism and dedication. His *mamluks* were encouraged to experiment with new weapons and techniques, some archers even attempting to use arrows doused in Greek fire from horseback.[10]

Once of adult age, *mamluks* were paid, but also were expected to maintain their own horses, armour and weaponry. To ensure his forces were outfitted properly, Baybars instituted troop reviews, in which the entire army, in full martial regalia, would parade past the sultan in a single day (in part to ensure that equipment was not being shared). Failure to attend these displays was punishable by death. Fear was also used to maintain order while on campaign. The drinking of wine was banned on many expeditions, and any soldier caught contravening this injunction was summarily hanged.

To reinforce the human component of the Mamluk armed forces, Baybars invested in some forms of heavier armament. Close attention was paid to the development of siege weaponry, including sophisticated counter-weight catapults, or trebuchets. These engines became the mainstay of Mamluk siegecraft. Capable of being dismantled, borne to a target and then readily reconstructed, the largest could propel stones weighing in excess of 500 pounds. In addition to raw military power, Baybars also placed great value upon accurate and up-to-date intelligence. He therefore maintained an extensive network of spies and scouts across the Near East and received reports from agents embedded in Mongol and Frankish societies. The sultan also showed generous patronage to the nomadic Bedouin Arabs of the Levant, and thereby won their valuable support, both in military conflicts and in the gathering of information.

Through these diverse methods, Baybars constructed the most formidable Muslim army of the crusading era; a force more numerous, disciplined and ferocious than any yet encountered in the war for the Holy Land – the perfect military machine of its day.[11] Having carefully legitimised and consolidated his hold on power, the sultan turned in 1265, with a united Islamic Near East behind him, to wield this deadly weapon in the name of *jihad*.

THE WAR AGAINST THE FRANKS

Unlike his Ayyubid predecessors, Sultan Baybars showed little or no interest in reaching an accommodation with Outremer. Rather than appease the Franks to preserve commercial links and stave off a western European crusade, he sought simply and completely to eradicate the Latin presence in the Levant. Baybars calculated that, by this means, the flow of trade might be forced back through Mamluk Egypt and that, with no bridgehead in the Holy Land, any attempts by the West to mount an invasion would surely fail. The sultan was always conscious of the need to maintain a watchful eye on the Mongol threat, but this did not prevent him from initiating a series of merciless strikes against the crusader states.

While the work of preparation proceeded apace in the Mamluk world through the early 1260s, Baybars carried out a number of incidental exploratory raids into Frankish Palestine, the only notable product of which was the destruction of the church in Nazareth. To preclude any premature outbreak of full-scale hostilities, the sultan agreed to some limited truces with various factions within the Latin kingdom – a realm that was now in an appallingly disunited and feeble state. The most useful pact was that forged with John of Ibelin, count of Jaffa, one of the last great barons of Outremer. In 1261, Baybars accepted John's entreaties for peace, and in return used the port at Jaffa to transport grain supplies from Egypt to Mamluk territories in Palestine. By 1265, however, with the Mongol siege of al-Bira having faltered, Baybars' offensive against the Franks began in earnest.

A *path of destruction*

For the next three years, Sultan Baybars prosecuted a brutal campaign of conquest and devastation, waging war on a scale not witnessed since the days of Hattin in 1187. To provide a formal justification for his attack, the sultan accused the Franks of encouraging the recent Mongol invasion of Mamluk territory to the north. Then, in early 1265, he initiated his own assault. In the past, Baybars' first objective might have been to confront the Frankish field army, but now only a tattered remnant of this force remained. The sultan thus was free to begin the task of eliminating Latin settlements relatively unhindered.

In February the Mamluk host made camp in the woods near the fortified coastal town of Arsuf. Baybars had a massive tent erected next to the royal pavilion, within which five trebuchets were reassembled in secret. With the siege train prepared, the army marched on the Latin port of Caesarea on 27 February. Appearing suddenly and unheralded, the Muslims quickly secured control of the lower town, while the Christian populace retreated into the citadel – one of those recently refortified with the aid of King Louis IX. The sultan deployed his trebuchets, commencing heavy bombardment with stones and Greek fire, while a siege tower was raised, upon which he himself fought. By 5 March, the battered defenders had taken flight in a number of ships sent from Acre, abandoning Caesarea, and Baybars ordered the town and citadel to be razed to the ground.

Again, without announcing his target, the sultan moved south on 19 March and laid siege to Arsuf, which by this date was encircled by a major moat and possessed a sturdy keep. At first, Mamluk units under the direction of Qalawun tried to create a path to Arsuf's walls by filling sections of its moat with vast quantities of wood (felled from local forests), but the defenders managed to burn these piles of timber during the night. After this initial setback, Baybars subjected the town to an incessant aerial barrage, and the garrison eventually capitulated on 30 April 1265 and was taken captive. In the face of this terrifying offensive, the hopelessly outnumbered Franks based in Acre were all but impotent. Even when the nominal ruler of the kingdom of Jerusalem, Hugh of Lusignan, arrived from Cyprus on 23 April with a small party of reinforcements, no move was made to counter the Mamluk invasion. In early May Baybars instructed his troops to demolish Arsuf, and, in triumph, led his Christian prisoners back to Egypt, forcing them to enter Cairo with broken crosses hung around their necks. That summer, the sultan wrote to inform Manfred of Sicily of these successes. In a stark demonstration of the casual disregard for Outremer's future now prevalent in some western circles, Manfred responded by sending congratulatory gifts to Egypt. Others, including the papacy, began to consider action upon hearing of the Mamluk aggression.

In this first wave of attack, Baybars struck with speed and efficiency. His methods and achievements revealed the Mamluks' grasp of siegecraft and their overwhelming numerical and technological supremacy. The sultan had also indicated an ability to employ stealth so as to prevent his Latin quarry from preparing for an attack. In future campaigns Baybars took extreme steps to maintain this element of surprise. Always suspicious of enemy spies and scouts, he used messengers to deliver sealed orders to his generals, containing details of the next target that were only to be read once on the march. Most crucially of all, the sultan had shown that, in the case of Caesarea and Arsuf, his intention was destruction, not occupation. All along the Mediterranean coast his policy would be to wipe the Latin ports from the face of the Holy Land, closing, one by one, the doorways that linked Outremer with the West.

Breaking the Franks

Baybars renewed his attacks in spring 1266. One army of around 15,000 troops was sent north under Qalawun to ravage the county of Tripoli, where it swept up a number of minor fortresses, all of which were razed. Later that summer, a second Mamluk force was dispatched, this time to punish the Armenian Christians of Cilicia for their alliance with the Mongols. The Muslim host invaded in August 1266 and proceeded to lay waste to a succession of Armenian settlements. This unrelenting campaign left Hethum's Cilician kingdom in a severely weakened state.

Meanwhile, the sultan led the bulk of his forces on a series of scouring raids up the coast, enacting a devastating scorched-earth strategy around the likes of Acre, Tyre and Sidon. The Mamluk host then turned inland to attack the major Templar fortress of Safad in Galilee, the last Latin bulwark in the Palestinian interior. According to Baybars' chancellor, this castle was targeted because 'it was a lump in Syria's throat, and an obstacle to breathing in Islam's chest'. The siege began on 13 June 1266 with a mixture of bombardment and sapping, and though the Templars put up strong resistance, they were eventually forced to sue for terms on 23 July. Conditions of surrender were agreed that supposedly allowed the Franks safe conduct to the coast, but these were never realised. Whether through blunt deceit or, as most Muslim sources suggest, because the Templars were found still to be armed as they marched from Safad, Baybars ordered the garrison's execution. Some 1,500 Christians were duly led to a nearby hill – the site upon which the Templars traditionally themselves had executed Muslim captives – and the entire party was beheaded. One sole surviving Frank was spared and sent to Acre to relate the news of these events, and thus inspire fear.[12]

In the aftermath of this massacre, Baybars refortified Safad with great care and at considerable expense, and garrisoned the fortress with Muslim troops. In addition to the strengthening of battlements, two mosques were also built within its confines. This established the second arm of the sultan's strategy: the retention of major inland strongholds to act as centres of Mamluk administration and military domination. In the months that followed, he overran a series of other castles and settlements in Palestine, including Ramla. By the end of the summer, Galilee and the Palestinian interior were under Mamluk control.

Having suffered two years of unmitigated defeat, the Latins of Outremer were left in total disarray, unsure of how to react to this seemingly unstoppable enemy. In October 1266 Hugh of Lusignan bravely tried to lead a raiding party of about 1,200 men into Galilee, but around half of this force was butchered by the Muslim force now stationed at Safad. From this point onwards the Franks began clamouring to secure terms of peace with the Mamluks, no matter how punitive. In some cases, Baybars was happy to neutralise and isolate potential opponents while the work of conquest and destruction progressed elsewhere. In 1267, for example, the master of the Hospitallers agreed a humiliating ten-year treaty covering the castles of Krak des Chevaliers and Marqab, agreeing to forsake the tribute monies traditionally extracted from local Muslims and acknowledging Baybars' right to annul the treaty whenever he wished. However, when the Franks of Acre desperately tried to negotiate a truce in March that same year, Baybars flatly refused and, in May, made another destructive incursion into the city's environs, terrorising the population and burning the harvest. According to one Latin chronicler, the Mamluks 'killed more than 500 of the common people' taken prisoner in the fields, and then 'sliced all the hair off their heads, to below their ears'. These scalps were then supposedly hung from a 'cord around the great tower at Safad'. This story is not confirmed in any Muslim source, but it indicates clearly the level of horror either experienced or imagined by the Christians during Baybars' dreadful assaults.[13]

The fate of Antioch

Baybars' assiduous preparations in the early 1260s had borne considerable fruit. The outposts of the Latin kingdom of Jerusalem were being picked off virtually at will and the power of Cilician Armenia had been all but broken. Even so, the Mamluks had yet to conquer one of Outremer's great cities – to crush a crusader state and drive home the message that the days of Latin dominion in the Levant were ending. In 1268, with the Ilkhanid Mongols still showing no sign of launching a new invasion, the sultan decided that the time for such a statement was ripe. As his target, he chose the territory of Bohemond VI, lord of Tripoli and Antioch – the Frankish prince who had collaborated with the Mongols in 1260.

With his sights firmly set on the north, Baybars marched out of Egypt that spring. He briefly paused at Jaffa. The truce agreed with John of Ibelin had elapsed (and John himself had died in 1266) and the sultan brusquely refused to renew terms of peace. The port promptly fell to his attack in half a day, and was demolished. After this short interruption, Baybars led his armies into the county of Tripoli, marching up the coast in early May, leaving a trail of desolation behind them. Contemporary Muslim testimony described how 'the churches [were] razed from the face of the earth . . . the dead were piled up on the shore like islands of corpses'.

Bohemond VI was ensconced in Tripoli, readying himself to resist a siege, but the Mamluks bypassed the city. Baybars' target was Antioch. Advancing north via Apamea, he arrived outside the ancient city on 15 May 1268. Antioch's power as a crusader state had long since waned, but its great walls still stood, holding a population numbered in the tens of thousands. The sultan appears at first to have encouraged the Antiochenes to negotiate terms of capitulation, but they brazenly refused, choosing to rely upon the same walls that had held back the First Crusaders for eight months and had later repelled numerous Muslim warlords, from Il-ghazi to Saladin. This was to prove a foolish and fatal error. The Mamluk host surrounded the city on 18 May and, within a day, Baybars' troops broke in near the citadel on Mount Silpius. A bloody and savage massacre followed, echoing that enacted by the Franks at the moment of their own conquest, almost exactly 170 years earlier. In retribution for their stubborn refusal to submit, the sultan locked the city gates so that none could escape.

Glorying in the triumphant horror of this moment, Baybars wrote to Bohemond VI to describe Antioch's sack. In mocking terms he congratulated the Frankish ruler for not having been in the city, 'for otherwise you would be dead or a prisoner', and described how, if present, 'you would have seen your knights prostrate beneath the horses' hooves . . . flames running through your palaces, your dead burned in this world, before going down to the fires of the next'. The city's fall brought the Mamluks a huge amount of plunder – it was said to have taken two days simply to divide the loot – but, once they had picked it clean, Baybars' men left Antioch in a state of utter ruination; one from which it would not recover for centuries. The few remaining Templar outposts to the north were immediately abandoned, while the Antiochene patriarch was permitted to linger in his castle at Cursat (just to the south) for a few more years, but only as a Mamluk subject. The principality of Antioch – once Outremer's great northern bastion – had been overwhelmed, reduced to a tiny, isolated enclave at the port of Latakia. Only the imperilled husks of two crusader states now remained: the county of Tripoli and the kingdom of Jerusalem.[14]

In three years of hardened campaigning, Sultan Baybars had demonstrated the unrivalled strength of the Mamluk military machine, laid bare his own hunger for conquest and for the prosecution of *jihad*, and exposed the wretched weakness of the Franks. In 1269 he allowed his victorious armies to pause for breath, and, that same summer, permitted himself the luxury of performing the *Hajj*, although even then he travelled in secret so as not to leave the sultanate unduly vulnerable to any threat, external or internal. With this affirmation of his Islamic faith completed, Baybars returned to Syria and began touring his dominions through the autumn. At this moment, he seems to have been absolutely confident of his ability finally to eliminate the last vestiges of Latin settlement and to resist any renewed threat of Mongol invasion.

But by then, tidings of Outremer's devastation and the emergence of the terrible Mamluk scourge of the Levant had reached the West. Old champions and new were taking up the cross, eyes set to the East, for one last chance to reclaim the Holy Land.

23

THE HOLY LAND RECLAIMED

By the end of the 1260s, little remained of the once mighty crusader settlements of Outremer. The Franks were confined now to a coastal strip running north from the Templars' Pilgrims' Castle (south of Haifa), through the likes of Acre, Tyre, Tripoli and Marqab, to the outpost at Latakia. Only a handful of inland castles still stood, including the headquarters of the Teutonic Order at Montfort and the redoubtable Hospitaller fortress, Krak des Chevaliers. Internal rivalry among the Latins was rife, with various claimants contesting the Jerusalemite throne, the Italian merchants of Venice and Genoa fighting over trading rights and even the Military Orders embroiled in petty politics. Centralised authority had devolved to such an extent that each Frankish city functioned as an independent polity. The shock of Antioch's conquest in 1268 did nothing to arrest this spiralling descent into disunity and decay.

Sultan Baybars, meanwhile, had achieved major victories against the Christians, manifestly affirming his commitment to *jihad*. His pitiless approach to holy war had reduced the crusader states to a position of almost prone vulnerability. But the sultan had to be mindful of the continued threat posed by the Mongols. The problems that, for years, had left them paralysed in Mesopotamia, Asia Minor and Russia – including protracted dynastic upheavals and the open hostility between the Golden Horde and the Ilkhanate of Persia – now were starting to diminish. A forceful new Ilkhan, Abaqa, had come to power in 1265 and immediately initiated attempts to secure an anti-Mamluk alliance with western Europe. Another destructive Ilkhanid assault on Islam threatened. Yet, in spring 1270, even as Baybars looked to deal with this northern menace, news reached him in Damascus that the French were preparing again to mount a crusade from the West. Remembering only too well the havoc caused in Egypt by the last Latin invasion in 1249, the sultan immediately returned to Cairo to brace Muslim defences.

KING LOUIS' SECOND CRUSADE

Back in Rome, Pope Clement IV was deeply alarmed by the vicious Mamluk campaigning that began in 1265. Recognising that the war for the Holy Land was being lost, in August 1266 Clement started to formulate plans for a relatively small but swiftly deployed crusade. He recruited a band of troops, mostly from the Low Countries – instructing them to depart no later than April 1267 – and opened coalition talks with Abaqa and the Byzantine Emperor Michael VIII. In late summer 1266, however, King Louis IX of France caught wind of this expedition. A veteran of the holy war, now in his early fifties and ever more stringent in his religious devotions, Louis sensed a chance to lay the troubled memories of Mansourah to rest. That September he privately informed the pope of his wish to join the crusade. In some respects, Louis' enrolment – publicly confirmed by a crusading vow on 25 March 1267 – was a boon, for it promised to result in a far larger and more potent campaign. With this in mind, Clement postponed the smaller endeavour that he had originally envisaged. Somewhat ironically, this delay (the result of Louis' enthusiasm) left Baybars free to crush Antioch in 1268.

Just as he had done in the 1240s, Louis made careful financial and logistical preparations for his second crusade. Recruitment was not as buoyant for this campaign – the king's old comrade-in-arms John of Joinville was one who did not enlist. But given the setbacks endured by previous expeditions, and the concerns expressed in some quarters about the papacy's apparent abuse of the crusading ideal, the number of participants was surprisingly substantial. The most notable figure to take the cross was the future King Edward I of England, then known as the Lord Edward. Fresh from winning the civil war that had threatened the reign of his embattled father King Henry III, Edward committed to the crusade in June 1268 and, putting aside any animosity with France, later agreed to coordinate his expedition with that of King Louis.

In November 1268, however, Clement IV died, and because of divisions with the Church over Rome's dealings with the ambitious and, by some accounts, untrustworthy Charles of Anjou (Louis IX's surviving brother and now the king of Sicily), no papal successor was appointed until 1271. During this interregnum, the sense of urgency that Clement had sought to instil in the crusaders quickly dissipated. With momentum lost, the departure was delayed until summer 1270. In the interim, renewed attempts were made to contact the Mongol Ilkhan Abaqa, and in March 1270 Charles of Anjou also took the cross.

After Louis finally embarked from Aigues-Mortes in July 1270, his second crusade proved to be a pathetic anticlimax. For reasons that have never been satisfactorily explained, but may well have been related to the machinations of his scheming brother Charles, Louis detoured from his declared route to Palestine. Instead, he sailed to Tunis (in modern Tunisia), which was then ruled by an independent Muslim warlord, Abu Abdallah. The French king arrived in North Africa seemingly expecting Abu Abdallah to convert to Christianity and collaborate in an attack on Mamluk Egypt. When he failed to do so, plans for a direct assault on Tunis were laid – but the attack never came. In the midsummer heat, disease took hold in the crusader camp and, in early August, Louis himself fell ill. Over the course of three weeks his strength ebbed. On 25 August 1270, the pious crusader monarch Louis IX died, his final act a fruitless campaign far from the Holy Land. Legend has it that his last whispered words were 'Jerusalem, Jerusalem'. The king's dreams of recovering that sacred city had come to nothing, but his earnest devotion was unmistakeable. In 1297 Louis was canonised as a saint.[15]

In the wake of Louis' demise, efforts were made in mid-November to sail on to the Levant, but when a large portion of the fleet sank in a heavy storm, most Franks returned to Europe. Only Charles of Anjou gained from the whole affair, securing a treaty with Abu Abdallah that brought Sicily rich tribute payments. Edward of England, alone of the leading crusaders, refused to be turned from his purpose and insisted on continuing his journey to the Near East with a small fleet of thirteen ships.

TIGHTENING THE NOOSE

Some six months earlier, in May 1270, Baybars had returned to Cairo to prepare Egypt for King Louis' expected invasion. He took this threat seriously, putting the Nile region on high alert, and later demolished the battlements at Ascalon and filled its harbour with rocks and timber to render it unusable. But that autumn, news of the French king's death reached Cairo, bringing relief and leaving the sultan free to ready the Mamluk army for another campaign.

The impregnable fortress

In early 1271, Baybars marched north to target the remaining Latin outposts in the southern reaches of the Ansariyah range – once the border zone between Antioch and Tripoli. This area was dominated by a supposedly impregnable Hospitaller castle: Krak des Chevaliers. Since the crusades began, no Muslim commander had ever made a serious attempt to invest this fortress, perched on a steep-sloped ridge, dominating the surrounding region. Significantly strengthened by an extensive building programme earlier in the thirteenth century, Krak's defences now stood as a perfect expression of cutting-edge Frankish castle technology. Yet even in the face of this seemingly insurmountable challenge, Baybars was not to be deterred. Arriving in force with an array of ballistic weaponry, he laid siege to the stronghold on 21 February.

Krak could only be approached along the ridge from the south, and this was where the Hospitallers had positioned their sturdiest battlements: double walls, lined with hefty rounded towers; an inner moat, leading on to an angled glacis (sloping stone wall) to prevent sapping. Nonetheless, the Mamluks concentrated their bombardment in this sector and, after more than a month, the barrage eventually told, causing a section of the southern outer walls to collapse. This was not the end of the affair, because the Hospitallers were able to retreat to the inner ward – a compact citadel that was virtually indestructible. Realising that overcoming this keep would probably cost many Muslim troops their lives and would certainly result in structural damage to the castle itself, Baybars switched tactics. In early April he had a forged letter presented to the Latin garrison commander. This missive, purportedly from the Hospitaller master, instructed the knights to seek terms and surrender. It is not certain whether they really were duped by the sultan's ruse, or merely seized upon this opportunity to capitulate with a modicum of honour. In any case, the Hospitallers submitted on 8 April 1271 and were granted safe passage to Tripoli. After this famous triumph, Baybars was said to have declared proudly that 'these troops of mine are incapable of besieging any fort and leaving it [unconquered]'. Carefully repaired, Krak des Chevaliers became a Mamluk command centre in northern Syria.

Fresh from his unprecedented success, the sultan amassed troops for a decisive assault on Tripoli. In May, Muslims swarmed over a number of outlying forts and, in a confident mood, Baybars again wrote to Bohemond VI, this time warning the count of Tripoli that chains had been readied for his incarceration. The sultan ordered the main advance on 16 May, but at that same moment he received a report of Lord Edward's arrival with a crusader host at Acre. Unsure of the precise level of threat posed to Palestine, Baybars called off the Tripolitan invasion and readily acceded to Bohemond's pleas for truce, agreeing a ten-year peace.[16]

The Lord Edward of England

Travelling via Damascus, the sultan moved into northern Palestine, ready to counter an attack from Acre by Edward's crusaders. It soon became clear, however, that the English prince had arrived with only a limited contingent of troops. Finding himself free to act, Baybars promptly laid siege to the castle of Montfort – the headquarters of the Teutonic Order, in the hills east of Acre. Once again, victory soon followed. After three weeks of heavy bombardment and sapping, the fortress surrendered on 12 June and, in this case, was then demolished.

In July 1271, Edward mounted a short-lived incursion into Muslim territory east of Acre, but soon turned back when his soldiers fell ill, unaccustomed to the heat and the local food. This type of fleeting foray caused the sultan little concern. His main worry was the possibility of an alliance between the English crusaders and the Ilkhanid Mongols. In fact, Christian sources make it clear that, upon his arrival in the Levant, Edward immediately dispatched envoys to Abaqa, but it seems that no reply was forthcoming. Even so, that autumn – whether by coincidence or design – the Mongols and Latins managed to launch offensives that were roughly simultaneous. In October, Ilkhanid troops marched into northern Syria and ravaged the region around Harim. Meanwhile, in late November Edward mounted a second punitive raid into the area south-east of Caesarea. Neither attack was made in force, however, nor was any real determination shown, and, rather than lead in person, Abaqa sent one of his field commanders. Baybars was forced to redeploy a few *mamluk* divisions, but easily quelled these two minor incursions.

With such limited resources at his disposal, there was little more that Edward could do. When fighting in the West he had proved himself to be a skilled general and a cold-blooded campaigner –

qualities that would come to the fore during his reign as king of England – but Edward was given no real opportunity to exercise these talents in Palestine. Even so, the English crusade did benefit Outremer: halting the attack on Tripoli and prompting Baybars to re-evaluate his strategic priorities. The recent Ilkhanid offensive may have been repelled, but it seemed to presage a new era of Mongol aggression and highlighted the potential perils of an alliance between Abaqa and the Franks. With all this in mind, the sultan decided to buy security in Palestine, agreeing a ten-year truce with the kingdom of Jerusalem on 21 April 1272. The deal brought the Latins minor territorial concessions and a pledge of pilgrim access to Nazareth. Baybars was willing to use negotiation to neutralise the kingdom of Jerusalem, but he had already decided to employ more violent means to deal with the lingering and unpredictable threat posed by the Lord Edward.

At some point during the preceding months, the sultan had hired an Assassin to murder the English crusader. Through a slow and painstaking deception, this Muslim gained entry into Acre – claiming to seek baptism – and then inveigled himself into Edward's service. One evening in May he caught the crusader off guard in his chambers, and attacked him suddenly with a dagger. Reacting instinctively, Edward deflected the blow and the blade inflicted only a minor injury, perhaps to his hip. The assailant was cudgelled to death and, fearing that poison might have been involved, the English prince was immediately given an antidote. This may have been an unnecessary measure; in any case, after a few weeks' convalescence, Edward was returned to health. Having survived his brush with death, he left the Near East in late September 1272.[17]

Shifting focus

With treaties in place binding the Franks to peace in Palestine and Tripoli, Baybars turned his attention to the Mongols. In late 1272 Abaqa launched another, more concerted, offensive that was driven back only after a series of hard-fought engagements in which Qalawun distinguished himself. The sultan now resolved to deal directly with the Ilkhanid problem. Rather than await further invasions, he decided to take the fight to his enemy – returning to Egypt, he began to lay plans for the most ambitious campaign of his career.

In 1273 Baybars endured two distractions. For years, his disreputable *sufi* confidant Khadir al-Mirani had been a cause of irritation and suspicion for the sultan's leading emirs. Khadir acquired a well-earned reputation for rampant sexual deviancy and rapacious adultery; he was also given to desecrating the sacred sites of other religions – causing significant damage to the likes of the Holy Sepulchre. In May 1273, the emirs finally pinned him down on irrefutable charges of embezzlement and forced the sultan to recognise his soothsayer's crimes at a tribunal convened in Cairo. A death penalty was prescribed, but this soon was commuted to imprisonment when Khadir prophesied that his own death would be immediately followed by that of Baybars. In July that same year, the sultan also moved against the Assassins. The Isma'ili Order had maintained a weakening presence on the western flanks of the Ansariyah range through the thirteenth century. Despite having called upon their services in 1272, Baybars now judged their continued independence to be unacceptable. Mamluk forces were thus detailed to seize possession of the Assassins' remaining fortresses, including Masyaf, and from this point onwards the remnants of the Order were controlled by the sultanate.

Beyond these minor diversions, Baybars trained the full force of his energy and resources in the mid-1270s towards the preparations for an attack on Ilkhanid territory. Rejecting a frontal strike on Iraq – probably on the grounds that Mamluk and Mongol forces were too evenly balanced for such a blunt strategy – the sultan carefully laid the foundations for an invasion of Asia Minor (now an Ilkhanid protectorate). In early 1277 he led his armies from northern Syria into Anatolia and there scored a startling success – defeating the Mongol host stationed in Asia Minor at Elbistan in April. Leaving behind some 7,000 enemy dead, Baybars immediately had himself proclaimed sultan of Anatolia, but his victory was short-lived. With another large Ilkhanid army on its way, the Mamluks were worryingly isolated and faced the prospect of being cut off from Syria. In a tacit acknowledgement that he had overstretched his forces, the sultan ordered a swift retreat. He had proved that the Mongol menace might be countered, but he had also to accept that they could not be decisively defeated on their own territory.

Baybars' determination to cripple Ilkhanid Persia had drawn him away from the war against the Franks. That struggle might still have been completed, but upon his return to Damascus in mid-June 1277 the sultan contracted a severe case of dysentery. One of his last acts was to dispatch a messenger, ordering the release of the soothsayer Khadir. On 28 July, Baybars, the Lion of Egypt, died. His message duly arrived in Cairo, but the pardon came too late. Khadir had already been strangled by Baraka, Baybars' son and heir. Whether by chance, or through Baraka's superstitious desire to hasten his father's demise, Khadir's prediction had come true.[18]

Baybars – scourge of the Franks

Sultan Baybars never achieved full victory in the struggle for mastery of the Holy Land. But in the course of his astonishing career he had defended the Mamluk sultanate and Islam against the Mongols and inflicted the most grievous damage upon the crusader states, causing wounds that surely would prove fatal. Historians have long recognised Baybars' achievements in the *jihad*, highlighting the stark shift in policy heralded by his reign: the overturning of Ayyubid appeasement and détente; the uncompromising pursuit of war, albeit on two fronts. Less effort has been made to place the sultan in the context of the wider crusading era and to judge his methods and accomplishments alongside those of twelfth-century Muslim leaders.

In a sense, Baybars mixed and perfected the modes of rule adopted by these forerunners. Like the *atabeg* Zangi, he used fear to pacify his subordinates and maintain military discipline. But Baybars also sought to secure the support and loyalty of his subjects by harnessing the inspirational power of religious devotion and by employing manipulative propaganda – techniques utilised by Nur al-Din and Saladin. In common with all three of these predecessors, Baybars – as a Kipchak *mamluk* – was an outsider; as they had done, he looked to legitimise his rule and dynasty, and to cultivate a reputation as Islam's paramount *mujahid*.

Even so, in many respects Baybars' qualities and successes surpassed those of Zangi, Nur al-Din and even Saladin. The Mamluk sultan was a more attentive and disciplined administrator, alive in a way Saladin had never been to the financial realities of statecraft and war. At best, the Zangids and Ayyubids had imposed a fragile semblance of unity upon Near Eastern Islam – Baybars achieved near-hegemonic power over the Levant and created an unsurpassed and obedient Muslim army. Circumstance and opportunity undoubtedly played their parts, but perhaps, above all, it was Baybars' personal traits that set him apart. During the seventeen years of his sultanate, his unbridled energy saw him travel some 25,000 miles, prosecuting thirty-eight campaigns. Martial genius brought him more than twenty victories against the Latins. Most crucially, the sultan was an unrelentingly ruthless adversary, whose ambition was not tempered by the humanity or compassion witnessed under Saladin. Undoubtedly a brutal, even callous, despot, Baybars nonetheless brought Islam closer than ever to triumph in the war for the Holy Land.

TESTS AND TRIUMPHS

Baybars intended the Mamluk sultanate to pass to his son and supposed co-ruler, Baraka, but he proved to be an inept successor, alienating the existing inner circle of *mamluk* emirs. An unruly power struggle followed, which saw Baraka overthrown and Qalawun emerge from the infighting to claim the title of sultan in November 1279. However, even then Qalawun was not able to assert full control over the Muslim Near East until 1281.[19]

Qalawun and the Mamluk sultanate

During his first years in office, Qalawun faced a quickening tide of Mongol aggression. The Ilkhan Abaqa took advantage of the disarray afflicting the Mamluks to send a sizeable raiding force into northern Syria in 1280, prompting the general evacuation of Aleppo. By 1281 it was clear that the full-scale invasion, always feared by Baybars, was soon to begin. This ominous spectre actually enabled Qalawun to enforce a greater degree of unity upon the Mamluk realm, but it also forced him to renew peace treaties with the Franks. The sultan even agreed terms with the Hospitallers in Marqab, in spite of the fact that they had used the opportunity of the Mongols' 1280 offensive to pillage Muslim territory.

With Mamluk agents embedded in the Persian Ilkhanate reporting that Abaqa was readying his host, Qalawun held his own troops at Damascus from spring 1281 onwards. A massive Ilkhanid army crossed the Euphrates that autumn – perhaps numbering in the region of 50,000 Mongols, plus a further 30,000 allied Georgian, Armenian and Seljuq Turkish soldiers. Even after putting almost every available Mamluk regiment into the field, Qalawun was probably outnumbered; nonetheless, a decision was taken to march north to Homs and confront the enemy. Battle was joined upon the plains north of the city on 29 October 1281. Drawing upon the fearsome discipline and skill-at-arms instilled in the Mamluk war machine by Baybars, Qalawun achieved a second historic victory over the Mongols – echoing the glories of Ayn Jalut – and the broken Ilkhanid horde limped back across the Euphrates. With Mamluk supremacy confirmed, the immediate danger of Mongol attack abated. Qalawun spent the next years consolidating his hold over the sultanate, but by the mid-1280s he was free to redirect his attention to Outremer's annihilation.[20]

Turning on Outremer

In spite of recent Mamluk difficulties, the Levantine Franks remained in a vulnerable and disunited state. The Latin kingdom of Jerusalem was riven by leadership disputes that culminated in the likes of Beirut and Tyre declaring their independence. In the county of Tripoli, Bohemond VII (who succeeded upon his father's death in 1275) was in open conflict with the Templars – nervous of the order's excessive power at Tortosa – and faced a rebellion by the southern port of Jubail. Meanwhile, the Italian mercantile states were locked in yet another embittered trade war, this time involving Venice, Pisa and Genoa. By the 1280s, the Genoese were emerging from this fracas as the dominant force and began to establish a stranglehold over eastern Mediterranean commerce.

The crusader states could also entertain little hope of receiving aid from the West. In the early 1270s, while Baybars was focusing his attention upon the Mongols, a new pope, Gregory X, was finally elected as Clement IV's replacement. At the time of Lord Edward's crusade and before his elevation to the papal throne, Gregory had visited Acre and was thus only too aware of Outremer's problems. Once installed in Rome, he set out to energise the Latin West and to address the widespread criticisms levelled at crusading. These included the condemnation of crusades against Christians, cynicism over the redemption of the crusading vow in return for money and disquiet over the excessive burden of crusade taxation. In addition, some dissenting voices suggested that the Levantine Franks actually needed support from a permanent professional fighting force, paid for by the West, and not ill-defined, intermittent crusade expeditions. Pope Gregory instituted a number of enquiries into the state of the crusading movement, but he was also determined to aid the war effort in the Near East. Having convened the Second Council of Lyons in May 1274, Gregory announced plans for a new crusade to begin in 1278. Through force of will he secured the support of France, Germany and Aragon (in northern Spain), and proposed to fund the endeavour by taxing the Church a tenth for six years. But for all its vision, the pope's grand scheme came to nothing. When Gregory died in 1276, the projected crusade collapsed and concerns about Outremer's fate once again slipped into the background, amidst the tangled intrigues of western European political life.[21]

Qalawun, therefore, was able to strike against the remaining Frankish outposts with relative impunity from the mid-1280s. Keen to exploit any opportunity to overturn the treaties earlier agreed with the Christians, the sultan condemned the Hospitallers for attacking Muslim lands and launched his own campaign against Marqab in May 1285. Mamluk sappers managed to collapse one of the stronghold's towers, and the defenders duly surrendered their order's second great Syrian castle. Just as at Krak des Chevaliers, Marqab was repaired and a Mamluk garrison installed. In April 1287 Qalawun maintained the pressure in the north by seizing Latakia, claiming that the 'Antiochene' port was not covered by his pact with Tripoli.

That autumn Tripoli was weakened by its own succession crisis, following the death of Bohemond VII. A civil war broke out, in which the Genoese sought to assume control of the city and thereby establish a new commercial centre in Lebanon. This culminated in a rival group of Italians actually appealing to Qalawun for intervention. Happy to be presented with such a ready excuse both to invade Tripoli and to prevent Genoa from challenging Alexandria's resurgent economic might, the sultan mustered his forces. The Franks continued with their petty squabbles, oblivious to the imminent danger. Only the master of the Templars, William of Beaujeu – who evidently had his own informers inside the Mamluk world – recognised that Qalawun was about to mount a major siege, but William's warnings largely went ignored.

The Mamluk host assembled at Krak des Chevaliers and then swooped down on Tripoli, initiating a siege on 25 March 1289. After a month of bombardment, the city was stormed on 27 April and a bloody sack began. Hundreds, perhaps even thousands, of men were massacred, while the women and children were taken captive. Some Latins escaped on ships down the coast. Others, on smaller craft, took refuge on the tiny island of St Thomas, just offshore, but were hotly pursued by Qalawun's soldiers and soon butchered. Fighting within the Mamluk army, a noble from Hama named Abu'l Fida later wrote: 'After looting [the city] I went by boat to this island, and found it heaped with putrefying corpses; it was impossible to land there because of the stench.'

Upon Tripoli's conquest, Qalawun ordered the city to be razed to the ground and a new settlement built nearby, a move perhaps designed to intimate his willingness to eradicate all memory of the Franks. In the weeks that followed, the last few outposts of the county of Tripoli fell in quick succession; the Latin governor of Jubail was allowed to remain, but only in return for paying a hefty tribute. Like Baybars before him, Qalawun had destroyed a crusader state. His gaze now turned south, to the last vestiges of Frankish settlement in Palestine – to the city of Acre – and preparations began for an all-out attack on the capital of Latin Outremer.[22]

1291 – THE SIEGE OF ACRE

The shock of Tripoli's collapse finally caused at least some Latin Christians to recognise that disaster was looming. In Europe, Pope Nicholas IV made strident efforts to rejuvenate Gregory X's plans for a major crusade. Nicholas also sought to offer immediate aid, sending 4,000 *livres tournois* to the Latin patriarch of Jerusalem and providing thirteen galleys to assist in Acre's defence. In February 1290 the pope called for a new crusade that would, rather optimistically, aim to achieve the 'total liberation of the Holy Land'. Banning all commercial contact with the Mamluks, Nicholas announced a departure date for the expedition of June 1293. In response, King James II of Aragon promised to send troops to the Levant, while Edward I, now king of England, sent a military contingent to Acre in 1290, under the command of Otho of Grandson, a veteran of Edward's crusade in the early 1270s. Around Easter 1290 a contingent of some 3,500 Italian crusaders also set sail for Palestine. Alongside these signs of activity, however, other moves were afoot. Despite his assurances to the pope, James of Aragon negotiated a treaty with the Mamluks, pledging not to aid the crusade in return for promises that Aragonese pilgrims would be permitted to visit Jerusalem. Qalawun also reconciled with the Genoese.[23]

By this stage, the Mamluks were busily readying themselves for the campaign, but Qalawun still sought a pretext on which to rescind the standing treaty with Acre. This came in August 1290, when a number of the recently arrived Italian crusaders attacked a group of Muslim merchants in Acre. After the Franks refused to hand over the culprits for summary justice, the sultan declared war. That autumn the Mamluk host was about to march from Egypt when Qalawun fell ill and died on 10 November 1290. For once, his heir al-Ashraf Khalil was able to take power without great difficulty. After a brief interruption, Khalil set himself the task of completing the work begun by his father.

The last battle

Both Qalawun and Khalil recognised that the city of Acre – heavily fortified, with two lines of walls and numerous towers, and densely garrisoned – would be no easy target. The Muslim operation, therefore, was planned with great care and forethought. Mamluk strategy was founded on two principles: overwhelming numerical superiority, with tens of thousands of *mamluk* cavalry assisted by squadrons of infantry and specialist teams of sappers; and the deployment of the extraordinary arsenal of siege machinery built up since the days of Sultan Baybars. In the last days of winter 1291, Khalil ordered around one hundred ballistic engines to be brought to Acre from across the Mamluk Levant. Some of these weapons truly were monstrous in scale and power. Abu'l Fida was in the siege train of a hundred ox-drawn wagons transporting the pieces of one massive trebuchet nicknamed 'Victorious' from Krak des Chevaliers. He complained that, marching through rain and snow, the heavily laden column took a month to cover a distance that was usually an eight-day ride.

On 5 April 1291 Sultan Khalil's troops encircled Acre from the north shore above Montmusard to the coast south-east of the harbour, and the siege began. At this point, the city contained many members of the Military Orders – including the masters of the Temple and Hospital – and, in time, the severity of the threat now posed to Acre brought other reinforcements by sea, among them King Henry II (titular monarch of Jerusalem) with 200 knights and 500 infantry from Cyprus. Even so, the Christians were hopelessly outnumbered.

Khalil set about the task of crushing Acre with methodical determination. With his forces ranged in a rough semi-circle around the city, an aerial barrage began. The largest trebuchets, like 'Victorious' and another known as 'Furious', had been reassembled and were now pummelling Acre's battlements with massive boulders. Meanwhile, scores of smaller ballistic devices and squads of archers were deployed behind siege screens to shower the Franks with missiles. Mammoth in scale, unremitting in its intensity, this bombardment was unlike anything yet witnessed in the field of crusader warfare. Teams of Mamluk troopers worked in four carefully coordinated shifts, through day and night. And, each day, Khalil ordered his forces to make a short forward advance – gradually tightening the noose around Acre, until they reached its outer fosse. Eyewitness Latin testimony suggests that, as these efforts proceeded apace, possible terms of surrender were discussed. The sultan apparently offered to allow the Christians to depart with their movable property, so long as the city was left undamaged. But the Frankish envoys are said to have refused, concerned at the dishonour that would be suffered by King Henry through such an absolute concession of defeat.

As the Mamluks pounded Acre, the Christians made some vain attempts to launch counter-attacks. Stationed on the northern shore, Abu'l Fida described how 'a [Latin] ship came up with a catapult mounted on it that battered us and our tents from the sea'. William, master of the Templars, and Otho of Grandson also tried to prosecute a bold night-time sortie, hoping to wreak havoc within the enemy camp and torch one of the massive Mamluk trebuchets. The raid went awry when some of the Christians tripped over the guy ropes of the Muslim tents, raising a commotion. Thus alerted, scores of Mamluks rushed into the fray, routing the Franks and slaying eighteen knights. One unfortunate Latin 'fell into the latrine trench of one of the emir's detachments and was killed'. The next morning, the Muslims proudly presented the heads of their vanquished foes to the sultan.[24]

By 8 May, Khalil's inexorable advance had brought the Mamluk lines close enough to the city for sappers to be deployed on the outer walls. They quickly turned Acre's advanced sewerage system to their advantage, using outflows to start their tunnels. Just as in the Third Crusaders' siege of Acre in 1191, the work of undermining was focused particularly upon the city's north-eastern corner, but with Acre now protected by double walls there were two lines of defence to breach. The first collapsed at the Tower of the King on Tuesday 15 May and, by the following morning, Khalil's troops had taken control of this section of the outer battlements. With panic rising in the city, women and children began to evacuate by ship.

The sultan now prepared the Mamluks for a full-strength frontal assault through the breached Tower of the King, towards the inner walls and the Accursed Tower. At dawn on Friday 18 May 1291, the signal for the attack began – the thunderous booming of war drums that created 'a terrible, terrifying noise' – and thousands of Muslims began racing forward. Some threw flasks of Greek fire, while archers loosed arrows 'in a thick cloud [that] seemed to fall like rain from the heavens'. Driven forward by the overwhelming force of this onslaught, the Mamluks broke through two gates near the Accursed Tower and began rushing into the city proper. With Acre's defences punctured, the Franks tried to make a last desperate stand to contain the incursion, but one eyewitness admitted that attacking the Muslim horde was like trying to hurl oneself 'against a stone wall'. In the thick of the fighting, the Templar Master William of Beaujeu was mortally wounded when a spear pierced his side. Elsewhere, John of Villiers, master of the Hospital, took a lance thrust between his shoulders. Grievously injured, he was dragged back from the walls.

Before long, the Christian defenders were overrun and the sack of Acre began. One Latin, then in the city, wrote that the 'day was terrible to behold. The [ordinary people of the city] came fleeing through the streets, their children in their arms, weeping and despairing, and fleeing to sailors to save them from death', but hunted down, hundreds were slaughtered and abandoned infants were said to have been trampled under foot. Abu'l Fida confirmed that 'the Muslims killed vast numbers of people and gathered immense [amounts of] plunder' once Acre fell. As the Mamluks surged through the city, masses of desperate Latins tried to escape in any remaining boats, and there was utter chaos at the docks. Some got away, including King Henry and Otho of Grandson. Half dead, John of Villiers was carried to a boat and sailed to safety. But the Latin patriarch fell into the water and drowned when his overburdened craft became unstable. Elsewhere, some Latins chose to remain and face their fate. Khalil's troops found a band of Dominican Friars singing 'Veni, Creator Spiritus' – the same crusader hymn intoned by Joinville in 1248 – in their convent, and butchered them to a man.[25]

Many Christians sought to take refuge in the fortified compounds of the three main Military Orders, and some managed to hold out for days. The robust Templar citadel was eventually undermined by sappers and collapsed on 28 May, killing the Templars within. Those sheltering in the Hospitallers' quarter surrendered on promise of safe conduct from Khalil, but Muslim chronicles testify to the fact that the sultan deliberately broke this promise, leading his Christian prisoners out of the city and on to the surrounding plains. Almost exactly one hundred years earlier, Richard the Lionheart had violated his own pledge of clemency to Acre's Ayyubid garrison, executing some 2,700 captives. Now, in 1291, Khalil herded the Latins into groups and 'had them slaughtered as the Franks had done to the Muslims. Thus Almighty God was revenged on their descendants.'

Acre's fall was a final and fatal disaster for the Latin Christians of Outremer. Recalling the city's sack, one Frankish eyewitness who fled by boat declared that 'no one could adequately recount the tears and grief of that day'. The Hospitaller Master John of Villiers survived to pen a letter to Europe describing his experiences, although he admitted that his wound made it difficult to write:

> I and some of our brothers escaped, as it pleased God, most of whom were wounded and battered without hope of cure, and we were taken to the island of Cyprus. On the day that this letter was written we were still there, in great sadness of heart, prisoners of overwhelming sorrow.

For the Muslims, by contrast, the glorious victory at Acre affirmed the efficacy of their faith, sealing their triumph in the war for the Holy Land. One witness described in amazement how, 'after the capture of Acre, God put despair into the hearts of the other Franks left in Palestine'. Christian resistance crumbled. Within a month, the last outposts at Tyre, Beirut and Sidon had been evacuated or abandoned by the Franks. That August, the Templars withdrew from their strongholds at Tortosa and Pilgrims' Castle. With this, the days of Outremer – the crusader settlements on the mainland Levant – were brought to an end. Reflecting upon the wonder of this event, Abu'l Fida wrote:

> These conquests [meant that] the whole of Palestine was now in Muslim hands, a result that no one would have dared to hope for or to desire. Thus the [Holy Land was] purified of the Franks, who had once been on the point of conquering Egypt and subduing Damascus and other cities. Praise be to God![26]

CONCLUSION
THE LEGACY OF THE CRUSADES

With Acre's fall and the loss of Outremer's last remaining strongholds, Latin Christendom's political and military presence on the mainland Levant came to a definitive end. The final conquest of the crusader states helped further to validate Mamluk authority, and the sultanate's power in the Near East held for more than two centuries. In the West, however, the kingdom of Jerusalem's collapse caused widespread shock and anxiety. Not surprisingly, explanations were sought and recriminations levelled. The Levantine Franks were derided for their sinfulness and propensity to factionalism, the Military Orders criticised for pursuing international interests rather than focusing upon the Holy Land's defence.

Commercial contact between Europe and the Muslim Near East continued long after 1291 and Cyprus remained under Frankish rule until the late sixteenth century. But the mainland Levant remained a target of holy war. From the 1290s onwards, many detailed treatises were composed in Europe, advancing various plans and methods to secure Jerusalem's reconquest. New expeditions to the Near East were discussed, some were even launched – one culminating in the brief capture of the Egyptian port of Alexandria in 1365. Through the fourteenth century and beyond, many more crusades were preached and wars fought against the likes of heretics, Ottoman Turks and the papacy's political enemies. The Templars were dissolved as an order in 1312, after accusations of abuses and neglect spearheaded by an acquisitive French monarchy, but other Military Orders survived through the Middle Ages. The Hospitallers established new headquarters, first on Cyprus and then on Rhodes and later Malta, while the Teutonic Order carved out their own independent state in the Baltic. Yet, despite all of this, no crusade ever reclaimed the Holy City, and Islam's hold over the Levant did not weaken until the early twentieth century.[1]

CAUSES AND OUTCOMES

To begin with, the crusades were, at the very least, as much acts of Christian aggression as wars of defence. It is certainly true that Islam had initiated its own unprovoked surge of invasion and expansion in the seventh century, but the mercurial vigour of this onslaught had long since slackened. The First Crusade was not launched in response to an overwhelming and impending threat, nor was it the immediate result of any catastrophic loss. Jerusalem, the campaign's averred goal, had been conquered by Muslims some four centuries earlier – hardly a recent injury. The accusations of widespread or systematic abuse of Christian subjects or pilgrims by the Islamic overlords of the Levant also appear to have had little basis in fact. After the First Crusade's seemingly miraculous success and the foundation of the crusader states, the war for the Holy Land was perpetuated by cycles of violence, vengeance and reconquest, in which Christians and Muslims alike perpetrated acts of savage brutality.

A conflict unlike any other?

Through two centuries, diverse forces combined to fuel and propel this struggle. These ranged from the ambition of popes to achieve Rome's 'divinely ordained' ecclesiastical primacy, to the economic aspirations of Italian merchants; from notions of social obligation and bonds of kinship, to an emerging sense of chivalric duty. Leaders – Muslim and Christian, secular and spiritual – came to realise that the ideals of holy war could be harnessed to justify programmes of unification and militarisation, even to facilitate the imposition of autocratic governance. In this respect, the crusader wars conformed to a paradigm common to many periods of human history – the attempt to control and direct violence, ostensibly for the common good, but often to serve the interests of ruling elites.

In the case of Latin Christian crusades and Islamic *jihad*, however, this 'public' warfare was imbued with a compelling religious dimension. This did not necessarily lead to a conflict marked by uniquely barbaric acts of violence or especially entrenched enmity. But it did mean that many of those involved in the contest for control of the Holy Land earnestly believed that their actions were enmeshed with spiritual concerns. Popes like Urban II and Innocent III preached crusades to affirm their own authority, but they also did so in the hope of helping Christians find a path to salvation. Venetian crusaders may have had an eye for earthly profit, yet, just like other participants in these holy wars, they seem to have been moved by a heartfelt desire to attain a spiritual reward. Even a power-hungry warlord like Saladin – content to exploit the struggle for his own ends – evidently experienced a quickening sense of pious dedication to Jerusalem's reconquest and defence. Of course, not all crusaders, Frankish settlers or Muslim warriors felt these religious impulses in equal measure, but the pulse of faith, pervasive and enduring, resounded through the two-century-long battle for the Levant.

This devotional element infused these wars with a distinct character, inspiring remarkable feats of resilience, fortitude and, on occasion, intolerance. It also helps to explain how and why tens of thousands of Christians and Muslims continued to participate in this protracted struggle across so many decades. The enthusiasm of Near Eastern Islam is more easily understood. *Jihad* was a devotional obligation rather than a voluntary form of penance, and generations of Muslims could take inspiration from a mounting succession of Zangid, Ayyubid and Mamluk victories. The lasting appeal of crusading in western Europe is more striking taken against a backdrop of an endless sequence of depressing defeats and the redirection of holy wars into new theatres of conflict. The very fact of continued recruitment, through the twelfth and thirteenth centuries and beyond, illustrates the compelling allure of taking the cross – of participating in an endeavour that fused the ideals of military service and penance – and ultimately purifying the soul of sin. From 1095 onwards, Latin Christians wholeheartedly accepted the idea that crusading was a permissible and efficacious form of devotion. There is virtually no sign of concern over the union of violence and religion among medieval contemporaries. And even when criticism of the crusading movement gathered pace, the questions raised related to issues such as wavering commitment and finance, not the basic principle that God would support and reward wars fought in his name.[2]

Accounting for victory and defeat

If the continued attraction of crusading was noteworthy, so too was the associated survival of Frankish Outremer for close to 200 years. Even so, there is no escaping the fact that, in the end, the Latins lost the war for the Holy Land. The path from the First Crusade's victory in 1099 to Acre's fall in 1291 was by no means simply a spiral of defeat and decay. But equally, from the Second Crusade's failure at Damascus in 1148 to King Louis IX of France's ignominious capture in Egypt in 1250, there hardly was a tide of success. Whenever historians have sought to explain this trend, the focus generally has turned to Islam – to the supposed resurgence of *jihadi* enthusiasm and the shift to Muslim unification across the Near and Middle East. Yet in reality, until the advent of the Mamluks, enthusiasm for holy war was sporadic and pan-Levantine accord ephemeral at best. Of course, events within Islam did impact upon the outcome of the crusades, but there were other, perhaps even more powerful, issues at work.

The very nature of crusading itself was a fundamental cause of Christendom's ultimate defeat in the struggle for mastery of the eastern Mediterranean. The idea of holy war did not remain static between 1095 and 1291. It was subject to evolution and development – although these changes were not always apparent to contemporaries – and underwent some adjustment in response to wider developments in religious thinking, including the incorporation of mission and conversion as means to overcome non-Christian opponents. Throughout, however, crusading expeditions remained badly suited to the business of defending or reconquering the Holy Land. To survive, the crusader states desperately needed external martial assistance, but in the form of permanent (or at least long-standing) and obedient military forces. More often than not, crusades actually brought short-lived injections of massed armies – often adulterated by non-combatants – led by independent-minded potentates fixated upon their own objectives.

The fact that Outremer's needs were not met by the crusading movement should come as no surprise, because this form of holy war was not expressly designed to fulfil such a purpose. Instead, at an elemental level, crusades were constructed as a voluntary and personal form of penance. Participants might expect to pursue an established goal – the capture of a particular target or the defence of a region. They also might envisage themselves as fulfilling a duty of service owed to God, as bringing succour to fellow Christians, even as imitating the labours and suffering of Christ himself. Yet always, at the heart of the crusading impulse, lay the promise of individual salvation: a guarantee that the penalties owing for confessed sins would be cancelled out by the completion of an armed pilgrimage. This was the overwhelming allure of a crusade – its capacity to eradicate the taint of transgression, to offer an escape from damnation. And this was why hundreds of thousands of Latins took the cross in the course of the Middle Ages.

The febrile aura of religiosity that enveloped most crusading expeditions could instil a unity of purpose and an unparalleled determination in its participants, empowering them to undertake unimaginable feats of arms. It was this sense of divine sanction and spiritual devotion that helped Louis IX's troops to survive the Battle of Mansourah, that enabled the Third Crusaders to endure the gruelling siege of Acre and led the Franks to risk total annihilation by marching on Jerusalem in 1099. Burning with enthusiasm, crusaders could prevail against seemingly insurmountable odds, but this fiery passion often also proved to be impossible to control. Crusade armies were made up of thousands of individuals, each ultimately intent upon forging their own path to redemption. As such, they could not be led or governed in the same way as other, more conventional military forces. Raymond of Toulouse discovered this to his cost at Marrat and again at Arqa during the First Crusade; so too did Richard the Lionheart when he twice retreated from Jerusalem. Arguably, no Christian king or commander ever truly learned how to harness the force of the crusading tempest.

In the course of the thirteenth century, popes like Innocent III strove to control crusading through increased regulation and the effective institutionalisation of holy war. But they faced the converse problem: how to tame fervour without smothering the fire that lent these sanctified campaigns their strength? They also failed to find a workable formula, and new ideas about reconfiguring the whole basis of crusading activity – with professional forces stationed semi-permanently in the Near East – came too late and incited little response.

Some historians have suggested that Christendom was defeated in the war for the Holy Land because of a gradual slump in crusade enthusiasm after 1200 – a malaise supposedly brought on by papal manipulation and dilution of the 'ideal'. This view is somewhat simplistic. True, the thirteenth century did not witness the same massive expeditions that had punctuated the period between 1095 and 1193, but a plethora of smaller-scale campaigns still enjoyed substantial recruitment, even when directed against new enemies and into different theatres of conflict. If anything, the decline came in Latin

Europe's direct concern for the fate of the Holy Land, but this apparent deterioration likewise should not be exaggerated. The huge campaigns of the twelfth century were themselves only spawned in the wake of seismic shocks – the fall of Edessa and the Battle of Hattin – and otherwise western Christendom often remained immune to Outremer's urgent appeals for assistance. Domestic problems and concerns, from succession disputes and dynastic rivalries to failed harvests and outbreaks of heresy, might only too easily trump the needs of the embattled crusader states. Evocative and potent as the fate of Jerusalem and the Holy Land might be, the course of crusading history proves that most Latins living in Europe did not exist in a permanent state of anxiety over events in the East and thus were rarely willing to upend their lives at home to save a distant, if sacred, outpost.

In reality this was a function of another, decidedly practical consideration that impacted upon the outcome of the battle for the Near East. In physical and conceptual terms, the Levant was simply a long way from western Europe. Christians living in France, Germany or England faced journeys covering thousands of miles to reach the Holy Land. The huge distances involved caused significant difficulties when it came to mounting military expeditions or even maintaining regular contact with the Latin settlements in the East. The comparison is by no means perfect, but the other major territorial contest being played out between Latins and Muslims – the so-called Spanish *Reconquista* – ended in Christian victory at least in part because of the basic fact of Iberia's relative geographical proximity to the rest of Europe. Outremer's problems of separation were partially alleviated by the rise of the Military Orders as supranational institutions and the growth in trans-Mediterranean trade, but the gap was never fully bridged. At the same time, the Levantine Franks failed to cooperate fully or effectively with the eastern Christian allies, from the Byzantine Empire to Cilician Armenia, who could have helped to mitigate their isolation, and allowed themselves to become embroiled in countless highly disruptive internal power struggles.

For all these reasons, Outremer found itself in a precarious state of vulnerability throughout much of the twelfth and thirteenth centuries. Nonetheless, it took a concomitant degree of strength and advantage for Islam to be capable of exploiting Frankish weakness. The crusader wars were not fought, in the first instance, in the political or cultural heartlands of Eastern Islam, but rather in the frontier zone between Egypt and Mesopotamia, and neither can the Holy Land be characterised in any way as a uniformly Muslim society. Yet even so, in the long run Islam did benefit from the physical propinquity of the Levantine battlefield and the inescapable fact that it was waging a war on what was tantamount to home ground. The Muslim world was also lifted to victory in this prolonged struggle by the insightful and charismatic leadership offered by Nur al-Din and Saladin, and by Baybars' unflinching ruthlessness.[3]

CONSEQUENCES IN THE MEDIEVAL WORLD

The crusades have been presented as an international conflagration that reshaped the world: dragging Europe out of the Dark Ages towards the beckoning light of the Renaissance; consigning Islam, militarised and radicalised in the pursuit of victory, to centuries of insular stagnation. Some have characterised these holy wars as apocalyptic conflicts that left indelible scars of ethnic and religious hatred, initiating an unending cycle of hostility. Such grand assertions rely upon simplification and exaggeration. Huge changes were undoubtedly wrought across the medieval world between 1000 and 1300. This was a period marked by population growth, migration and urbanisation; advances were made in learning, technology and cultural expression; and international commerce was extended. Yet the precise role of the crusades remains debatable. Any attempt to pinpoint the effect of this movement is fraught with difficulty, because it demands the tracing and isolation of one single thread within the weave of history – and the hypothetical reconstruction of the world, were that strand to be removed. Some impacts are relatively clear, but many observations must, perforce, be confined to broad generalisations. It is certain that the war for the Holy Land was not the sole influence at work in the Middle Ages. But equally, this Levantine struggle did have a significant impact upon medieval history, especially in the Mediterranean basin.

The eastern Mediterranean

The threats posed by the Franks, both real and imagined, presented the Muslim world with an enemy to rally against and a cause for which to fight. This enabled Nur al-Din and then Saladin to resurrect the ideal of *jihad*. It also allowed them to impose a degree of unity upon Near and Middle Eastern Islam that, while yet imperfect, still far outstripped anything witnessed since the early era of Muslim expansion. The process reached its ultimate expression, with the added and overriding danger presented by the Mongols, when the Mamluks forged a unitary state under Baybars and Qalawun.

However, for all the contact between Muslims and Latins witnessed in this era – through war and peace – Islam's attitude towards western Christendom was not radically altered. Old prejudices remained, among them popular misconceptions about the worship of Christ and God as an indication of polytheism, as well as entrenched antipathy towards the use of figurative religious images, forbidden in Islam, and wild assertions of Frankish sexual impropriety. Familiarity does not seem to have bred much in the way of understanding or tolerance. But equally, contrary to the suggestion of some scholars, the advent of the crusades did not prompt widespread deterioration in Muslim relations with indigenous eastern Christians. There were some intermittent signs of a hardening in attitudes, particularly in cases where native Christians living under Islamic rule were suspected of aiding or spying for the Franks, but, broadly speaking, little changed until the rise of the more fanatical Mamluks.

For both Islam and the West, perhaps the most striking transformation wrought by the crusades related to trade. Levantine

Muslims already maintained some commercial contacts with Europe before the First Crusade through Italian seaborne merchants, but the volume and importance of this economic interaction were revolutionised in the course of the twelfth and thirteenth centuries, largely as a result of the Latin settlement of the eastern Mediterranean. The crusades and the presence of the crusader states reconfigured Mediterranean trade routes – perhaps most powerfully after Constantinople's conquest in 1204 – and played a critical role in solidifying the power of the Italian mercantile cities of Venice, Pisa and Genoa. Europe's adoption of Arabic numerals can also be dated to around 1200 and likely resulted from trade with Islam, though this cannot definitively be connected to contact with the 'crusader' world.

The Franks residing in Outremer did not live in a hermetically sealed environment. Pragmatic reality and political, military and commercial expediency meant that these Latins were brought into frequent contact with the native peoples of the Levant, including Muslims and eastern Christians, and later the Mongols. In this way, the crusades created one of the frontier environments in which Europeans were able to interact with and, in theory, absorb 'eastern' culture. The 'crusader' society that developed in Outremer certainly was marked by a degree of assimilation, though whether this was the result of conscious choice or an organic process remains uncertain. There can be no doubt that the social milieu found in the Latin East was utterly unique. This was not the result of an unprecedented degree of connection with Islam – indeed, this type of contact was as, if not more, common in medieval Iberia and Sicily; nor was it a consequence of the ongoing holy war in the Near East. Instead, the distinctive character of 'crusader' Outremer was born of the extraordinary array of different Levantine influences encountered – from Greek and Armenian to Syriac, Jewish and, of course, Muslim – and the mixture of so many western European influences, drawn from the likes of France and Germany, Italy and the Low Countries.[4]

Western Europe

Historians have long recognised that interaction between western Christendom and the Muslim and wider Mediterranean worlds during the Middle Ages played an important, perhaps even critical, role in advancing European civilisation. These contacts resulted in the absorption of artistic influences and the transference of scientific, medical and philosophical learning – all of which helped to stimulate far-reaching changes in the West, and ultimately contributed to the Renaissance. Gauging the relative importance of different spheres of contact within this process is all but impossible. Thus, while the art and architecture of the 'crusader' Levant exhibited unquestionable signs of intercultural fusion, 'crusader' styles of manuscript illumination or castle design cannot reliably be tracked back to the West and categorically isolated as the sole inspiration for any given European exemplar. By its nature, the textual transmission of knowledge is easier to trace. In this area of exchange Outremer played a notable role – as witnessed in the translations made at Antioch – but its importance was secondary to the plethora of copied and translated texts that poured out of Iberia in the Middle Ages. At best, we can conclude that the crusades opened a door to the Orient, but by no means was it the only portal of contact.

Other forms of change brought about by the crusades in Latin Europe can more easily be determined. On a practical level, large-scale expeditions had a huge political, social and economic impact upon regions such as France and Germany, culminating as they did in the interruptive disappearance of whole kinship groups and sections of the nobility. The absence of the ruling classes, and especially crown monarchs, could cause widespread instability and even regime change. The advent of the Military Orders and the spread of their power to virtually every corner of the West had an obvious and profound effect upon medieval Europe – as new and formidable players on the Latin stage, these orders possessed the might to rival established secular and ecclesiastical authorities. The popularity of crusading served to increase the authority of the papacy and to reconfigure the practice of medieval kingship. It also influenced the emerging notions of knighthood and chivalry. By creating a new form of penitential activity, these holy wars likewise altered devotional practice – a process that accelerated markedly in the thirteenth century with the vast extension of crusade preaching, the commutation of vows and the system of indulgences.

Throughout this period, it is true that more Latin Christians stayed in the West than were actively engaged in crusading activity or fighting in the war for the Holy Land. But by the same token, between 1095 and 1291, few living in Europe remained wholly untouched by the crusades – whether through participation, taxation or the broader formulation of a communal Latin Christian identity within society.[5]

THE LONGER SHADOW

In February 1998 a radical terrorist network, describing itself as the 'World Islamic Front', declared its intention to wage 'Holy War against Jews and Crusaders'. This organisation, led by Osama bin Laden, has come to be known as al-Qaeda (literally, the 'base' or 'foundation'). Five days after al-Qaeda's 11 September attacks on New York and Washington in 2001, US President George W. Bush walked on to the south lawn of the White House and, before a crowded huddle of international journalists, affirmed America's willingness to defend its soil, warning that 'this crusade, this war on terrorism, is going to take a while'. Later, in October that same year, bin Laden responded to the approaching allied invasion of Afghanistan. He characterised this operation as a 'Christian crusade', stating that 'this is a recurring war. The original crusade brought Richard from Britain, Louis from France and Barbarossa from Germany. Today the crusading countries rushed as soon as Bush raised the cross. They accepted the rule of the cross.'[6]

How can it be possible that this language of medieval holy war has found a place in modern conflicts? This rhetoric seems to suggest that the crusades have somehow continued unabated since the Middle Ages, leaving Islam and the West pitted against one another – locked in an undying and embittered war of religion. In fact, there is no unbroken line of hatred and discord connecting the medieval contest for control of the Holy Land to today's struggles in the Near and Middle East. The crusades, in reality, are a potent, alarming and, in the early twenty-first century, distinctly dangerous example of the potential for history to be appropriated, misrepresented and manipulated. They also prove that a constructed past can still create its own reality, for the crusades have come to have a profound bearing upon our modern world, but almost entirely through the agency of illusion.

Among the root causes of this phenomenon is the disjuncture between popular and collective interest in, and perception of, the medieval crusading era, across what might broadly be termed the Muslim world and the West. At a basic level this difference can be shown in terminology. From around the mid-nineteenth century onwards, the crusades came to be known in Arabic as *al-hurub al-Salabiyya* (the 'Cross' wars), a term that underlines the elements of Christian faith and military conflict. In English, however, the word 'crusade' has largely been disassociated from its medieval and devotional origins – taken now to denote striving in the interests of a cause that is often presented as just. The term 'crusade' is strewn with casual abandon through media and popular culture in the West. Indeed, it is quite possible to speak of a crusade against religious fanaticism, even of a crusade against violence. Western interpretation of the Arabic word *jihad* is equally jarring. Many Muslims consider that the idea of *jihad* relates, first and foremost, to an inner spiritual struggle. But in the West the word is commonly thought to embody a single meaning: the waging of a physical holy war. As with so many of our modern attitudes to the crusader era, this problem with terminology emerged only in the last two centuries. To an extent, however, the divergence of Western and Islamic memories and perceptions occurred in the more immediate aftermath of Outremer's eradication.

Later medieval and early-modern perceptions

Between the fourteenth and sixteenth centuries, with Europe still engaged in struggles against other Muslim enemies (most notably the Ottoman Turkish Empire), the medieval crusades attained a semi-mythic status. Certain, supposedly central, 'heroes' were lionised. Godfrey of Bouillon was included, alongside the likes of Alexander the Great and Augustus Caesar, among the 'Nine Worthies' – the most revered figures in human history. Richard the Lionheart was celebrated as a legendary warrior-king, while Saladin was actually widely praised for his chivalric demeanour and noble character. In Dante's conception of the afterlife, depicted in his famous *Divine Comedy* (1321), Saladin appeared in the first level of Hell, the plane reserved for virtuous pagans.

However, with the coming of the Reformation after 1517 and later the birth of Enlightenment thinking, European theologians and scholars undertook a broad reassessment of Christian history. By the eighteenth century, the crusades had been consigned to a dark and distinctly undesirable medieval past. The British scholar Edward Gibbon, for example, asserted that these holy wars were an expression of 'savage fanaticism', born of religious faith. The French intellectual Voltaire, meanwhile, condemned the crusade movement as a whole, but reserved some admiration for particular individuals – with King Louis IX praised for his piety and Saladin described as 'a good man, a hero and a philosopher'.[7]

By contrast, throughout the late medieval and early-modern periods of Mamluk and Ottoman rule, Near and Middle Eastern Islam exhibited very little interest in the crusades. Most Muslims seem to have regarded the war for the Holy Land as a largely irrelevant conflict, fought in a bygone age. True, the barbarous Franks had invaded the Levant and carried out acts of violence, but they had been roundly punished and defeated. Islam, quite naturally, had prevailed and the era of Frankish intrusion was brought to an unequivocal and triumphant end. When 'heroic' figures were drawn as exemplars from this period, they tended to differ from those selected in the West. Far less attention was paid to Saladin. Instead Nur al-Din's piety was applauded, while Baybars became prominent in folklore from the fifteenth century onwards. Throughout these centuries there appears to have been no sense that crusader aggression had sparked a perpetual holy war, or that Frankish atrocities still somehow demanded retribution.[8]

To understand how the crusades emerged from the dusty corners of history, seemingly to become relevant to the modern world, the academic study and social, political and cultural recollection of these wars since 1800 must be traced in Islam and the West.

The crusades in western history and memory

By the early nineteenth century a broad consensus, informed by Enlightenment thinking, had emerged in the West. Medieval crusaders were scorned for their brutish and misguided barbarity, though occasionally lauded for their bravery. However, attitudes were soon to be tempered by a potent strand of romanticism for a more idealised vision of the Middle Ages. This trend was evoked in the wildly popular and hugely influential fiction penned by the British author Sir Walter Scott. His novel *The Talisman* (1825), set at the time of the Third Crusade, portrayed Saladin as the 'noble savage', gallant and wise, while presenting King Richard I as a rather tempestuous thug. Scott's book, along with works including *Ivanhoe* (1819), and those by other authors, helped to engender a vision of the crusades as grand, daring adventures.[9]

Around the same time, some European scholars began to engage in historical parallelism – the desire to see the modern world reflected in the past – depicting the crusades and the creation of the crusader states in triumphalist terms as commendable exercises in proto-colonialism. This trend started the process of separating crusading (and the very word 'crusade') from its religious and devotional context, allowing the war for the Holy Land to be celebrated as an essentially secular endeavour. Writing in the early nineteenth century, the French historian François Michaud published a widely disseminated, three-volume account of these holy wars (along with four further volumes of sources), peppered with misleading statements and misrepresentations of history. Michaud applauded the 'glory' earned by the crusaders, noting that their objective was 'the conquest and civilisation of Asia'. He also identified France as the movement's spiritual and conceptual epicentre, stating that 'France would one day become the model and centre of European civilisation. The holy wars contributed much to this happy development and one can perceive this from the First Crusade onwards.' Michaud's publications were both a product of, and further stimulus to, potent sentiments of French nationalism – a drive to formulate a national identity that saw the war for the Holy Land dragged into a fabricated reconstruction of 'French' history.[10]

Romanticised, nationalistic enthusiasm for the crusades was by no means the preserve of France. The newly created state of Belgium adopted Godfrey of Bouillon as its hero, while, across the Channel, Richard the Lionheart was embraced as an iconic English champion. Both men were immortalised in striking equestrian statues in the mid-nineteenth century. Godfrey's image stands in Brussels' Grand Place, while Richard sits astride his horse, sword raised, outside the Houses of Parliament in London. Throughout the nineteenth century the tendrils of interest spread far and wide. Benjamin Disraeli, the future British prime minister, was fascinated by the crusades – travelling to the Near East in 1831, even before he was elected to Parliament; and later publishing a novel, *Tancred: or The New Crusade*, about a young nobleman with a crusading heritage. The American writer Mark Twain also toured the Holy Land, visiting the battlefield at Hattin, and was much impressed by the sight of a sword, once reputedly owned by Godfrey of Bouillon, which stirred 'visions of romance [and the] memory of the holy wars'.

In 1898 Kaiser Wilhelm II of Germany went to extraordinary lengths to enact his crusading fantasies. Decked out in mock-medieval regalia during a visit to the Levant, he processed on horseback into Jerusalem and then journeyed to Damascus to pay his respects to Saladin, whom the kaiser regarded as 'one of the most chivalrous rulers in history'. On 8 November he laid a wreath on the Ayyubid sultan's rather dilapidated tomb and later paid for his mausoleum's restoration.[11]

Of course, not all western study of the crusades in this period was coloured by fanciful notions of romanticism and nationalistic imperialism. Through these same years a strong trend towards a more precise, detached and empirical approach was gathering pace. But even in the 1930s, the French crusade historian René Grousset made comparisons between France's involvement in the crusades and the return of French rule to Syria in the early twentieth century. And it was the more impassioned and intemperate accounts that exerted most influence over popular perceptions. The potency and potential perils of such facile modern parallelism became apparent in the context of the First World War. In the course of this conflagration, France was granted a mandate to govern 'Greater Syria' by the League of Nations – and French diplomats sought to reinforce claims to this territory by citing crusade history.

The British, meanwhile, were mandated to administer Palestine. Arriving in Jerusalem in December 1917, General Edmund Allenby was evidently conscious of the offence which might be caused within Islam by any tinge of crusading rhetoric or triumphalism (not least because there were Muslim troops serving in the British Army). In stark contrast to Kaiser Wilhelm, Allenby entered the Holy City on foot, and was said to have issued strict orders forbidding his troops from making references to the crusades. Unfortunately, his caution did not prevent sections of the British media from revelling in the event's supposed medieval echoes. Indeed, the satirical English periodical *Punch* published a cartoon headed 'The Last Crusade', depicting Richard the Lionheart looking down on

Jerusalem from a hill-top, with the caption: 'My dream comes true!' Later, an apocryphal, but nonetheless enduring, rumour spread that Allenby had himself proclaimed: 'Today the wars of the crusades are ended.'

In fact, even then, the word 'crusade' – already disassociated from religion – was starting to be detached in the English language from its medieval roots. In 1915 the British Prime Minister David Lloyd George described the First World War as 'a great crusade' in a rallying speech. By the time of the Second World War, General Dwight D. Eisenhower's D-Day orders, issued for 6 June 1944, contained the exhortation to Allied troops: 'You are about to embark on a great crusade.' Eisenhower's 1948 account of the war was entitled *Crusade in Europe*.[12]

Modern Islam and the crusades

After a sustained period of marked disinterest, the Muslim world began to exhibit the first flickers of renewed curiosity about the crusades in the mid-nineteenth century. Around 1865, the translation of French histories by Arabic-speaking Syrian Christians led to the first uses of the term *al-hurub al-Salabiyya* (the 'Cross' wars) for what before had been known as the wars of the *Ifranj* (the Franks). In 1872, an Ottoman Turk, Namik Kemal, published the first 'modern' Muslim biography of Saladin – a work seemingly written to refute Michaud's triumphalist history that had recently been translated into Turkish. Kaiser Wilhelm's 1898 visit to the Near East either coincided with, or perhaps fuelled, another burst of interest, for in the following year the Egyptian scholar Sayyid 'Ali al-Hariri produced the first Arabic history of the crusades, entitled *Splendid Accounts of the Crusading Wars*. In this book al-Hariri wrote that the Ottoman Sultan Abdulhamid II (1876–1908) recently had sought to characterise western occupation of Muslim territory as a new 'crusade', and al-Hariri stated that the sultan 'rightly remarked that Europe is now carrying out a crusade against us in the form of a political campaign'. Around the same time, the Muslim poet Ahmad Shaqwi wrote a verse questioning why Saladin had been forgotten by Islam until the reminder provided by Kaiser Wilhelm.[13]

In the years that followed, Muslims from India to Turkey and the Levant began to comment on the similarity between medieval crusader occupations and modern western encroachments – a comparison that, of course, had been espoused vocally and enthusiastically in the West for decades. A gathering fascination with Saladin as a heroic Muslim figurehead is also evidenced by the opening of a new university in Jerusalem named after the sultan in 1915. These two related phenomena were accelerated by events towards the tail end of the First World War: the establishment of the British and French mandates in the Levant; the extensive reporting of Allenby's supposed reference to the crusades; and the widespread popularisation of historical parallelism in Europe. By 1934 one prominent Arabic author was moved to suggest that 'the West is still waging crusading wars against Islam under the guise of political and economic imperialism'.

The critical change came, however, after the Second World War, with the UN-mandated foundation of the state of Israel in 1948 – the realisation of what has been called Zionism. That October, the commentator 'Abd al-Latif Hamza wrote that 'the struggle against Zionists has reawakened in our hearts the memory of the crusades'. From 1948 onwards, the Muslim world engaged in an increasingly active re-examination of the medieval war for the Holy Land. Arab-Islamic culture already had a long tradition – stretching back to the central Middle Ages and beyond – of seeking to learn from the past. It is not surprising, therefore, that across the Near and Middle East, scholars, theologians and radical activists now started to refine and affirm their own historical parallels; to harness crusade history for their own purposes.[14]

The principles of 'crusade parallelism'

This process of historical appropriation continues to this day. The crusader period was, and is, exceptionally well suited to the needs of

Islamic propagandists. Having come to an end almost 800 years earlier, the precise events of this era are sufficiently cloudy to be readily reshaped and manipulated: useful 'facts' can be selected; any uncomfortable details that do not correlate with a particular ideology are easily discarded. The crusades can also be used to construct a valuable didactic narrative, because they encapsulate both 'western' attack and eventual Islamic victory. Jerusalem's role likewise is critical. In reality, the political and even the devotional importance accorded by Muslims to the Holy City varied and wavered in the course of the Middle Ages, even as it did in later centuries. But the medieval struggle for dominion of this site helps modern ideologues to cultivate an idea of Jerusalem – and most especially of the *Haram as-Sharif*, or Temple Mount – as a sacred and inviolable stronghold of the Muslim faith.

Over the past sixty years, a wide range of Islamic groups and individuals, from politicians to terrorists, have sought to draw comparisons between the modern world and the medieval crusades. On points of detail and emphasis there are important differences in the messages and ideas they propagate, but there is also a relatively consistent substructure underpinning all of their various arguments, dominated by two ideas. The first is that the West, as an invading colonial power, is now committing crimes against the Muslim world, just as it did 900 years ago; recreating the medieval crusades in the modern era. However, Israel's creation, with Western support, added a new strand to the story. In the twentieth-century incarnation of this struggle, it is not just imperialist crusaders but also Jews who are seeking to occupy the Holy Land. Together they are supposed to be joined in a 'Crusader-Zionist' alliance against Islam. Propagandists seek to lend an aura of credibility to this strange juxtaposition by pointing out that Israel occupies roughly the same territory as the Frankish kingdom of Jerusalem. In recent decades, however, the geographical focus of this ideology has rapidly been expanded. New western, and notably American-led, interventions in the Near and Middle East and Central Asia have been positioned alongside the

Arab–Israeli conflict and the plight of the Palestinians, adding to the crimes of the so-called 'Crusader-Zionist' alliance. These include the two Gulf Wars, the struggle against the Taliban and al-Qaeda in Afghanistan and the stationing in the sacred Muslim territory of Saudi Arabia of US troops, described by Osama bin Laden as 'Crusader hosts [who] have spread in it like locusts'.[15]

The second pillar of 'crusade parallelism' relates to the supposed capacity for Islam to learn valuable lessons from the medieval era. In 1963, the Muslim author Sa'id Ashur published a two-volume *History of the Crusades* in Arabic, in which he claimed that the situation facing modern Muslims was very similar to that of the Middle Ages, and therefore it was 'incumbent upon us to study the movement of the crusades minutely and scientifically'. Numerous Islamic ideologues have sought to find inspiration in the medieval war for the Holy Land. Some have argued for the unification of Islam, by force if necessary, and the unflinching and relentless pursuit of *jihad*, in supposed imitation of the Muslims of the Middle Ages. Many propagandists suggest that Islam must be willing to patiently face a long battle – after all, it took eighty-eight years to reclaim Jerusalem from the Franks and almost two centuries to destroy Outremer. Crucially, Muslim 'heroes' of the crusader era have also been raised as exemplars – most notably Saladin. Indeed, in the course of the twentieth century, the Ayyubid sultan has been widely mythologised as the central Islamic champion of the medieval war for the Holy Land. It is now Saladin, not Sultan Baybars, who has gained cult status across the Arabic-speaking world. His defeat of the western Christians in the Battle of Hattin is revered as one of the greatest victories in Muslim history, and his subsequent recapture of Jerusalem is the subject of intense pan-Islamic pride and celebration.[16]

Arab Nationalism and Islamism

Diverse ideals have been constructed upon these two foundation stones – the idea of a renewed crusader offensive and the need to draw instruction from the Middle Ages. In fact, the true power of this manipulative approach to the past has proved to be its remarkable flexibility, for Muslim adherents of two diametrically opposed ideologies – Arab Nationalism and Islamism – have sought with equal enthusiasm to appropriate crusading history.

The precepts of Arab Nationalism are essentially secular in character: positing the separation of spiritual and temporal authority in Islam; and advocating the governance of Arab Muslim states by political, rather than religious, leaders. As such, Arab Nationalist leaders have shown little interest in the crusades as wars of religion, focusing instead upon the notion of threatening foreign imperialism and the propaganda value of forging comparisons between their own lives and the achievements of Saladin. Gamal Abdel Nasser, Egypt's prime minister (and later president) from 1954 to 1970, was one of the first proponents of Arab Nationalist ideology. He claimed that Israel's creation was 'a substitute for the crusades', instituted when 'imperialism signed a pact with Zionism'. Nasser also made repeated attempts to liken himself to Saladin. It was no coincidence that Youseff Chahine's famous 'historical' epic *Saladin* (1963) – in its day the highest-budget Arabic film in history – was produced in Egypt, with a star actor who bore a striking resemblance to Nasser.

Commenting on the Arab–Israeli conflict in 1981, Syria's President Hafez Asad encouraged Muslims to 'go back to the Crusaders' invasion. Although they fought us for 200 years, we did not surrender or capitulate.' Asad also styled himself as 'the Saladin of the twentieth century' and in 1992 erected a larger-than-life statue of his hero in the heart of Damascus. The Iraqi Arab Nationalist leader Saddam Hussein was even more obsessed with Saladin. Conveniently forgetting Saladin's Kurdish heritage and instead emphasising their shared birthplace of Tikrit, Saddam went to extraordinary lengths to connect their two careers. Iraqi stamps and banknotes depicted Saladin standing alongside Saddam and the exteriors of his palaces were decorated with golden statues of the president dressed as Saladin. Saddam even ordered the production of a children's picture book, *The Hero Saladin*, in which he himself was named as 'the second Saladin'.[17]

Islamism is the polar opposite of Arab Nationalism in terms of ideology – espousing the notion that Islam must be governed as a theocracy. Nonetheless, Islamists have, if anything, been even more strident in their attempts to establish spurious links between the medieval crusades and the modern world. Given its spiritual perspective, Islamist propaganda presents the crusades as aggressive religious wars waged against the *Dar al-Islam* (Islamic territory), the only response to which can be violent physical *jihad*. One of the most influential Islamist ideologues, Sayyid Qutb (who was executed in Egypt for treason in 1966), described western imperialism as a 'mask for the crusading spirit', stating that 'the crusader spirit runs in the blood of all westerners'. He also declared that there was a conspiracy of 'international Crusaderism' behind the West's Levantine interventions, citing Allenby's supposed reference to the medieval crusades as proof.

Qutb's ideas have influenced many radical Islamist organisations, from Hamas to Hezbollah. But in the twenty-first century the most dangerous proponents of his particular brand of extremism have been Osama bin Laden and his ally Ayman al-Zawahiri – the leading voices of the terrorist network known as al-Qaeda. Their rhetoric was littered with references to the crusades in the lead-up to 2001. When, just after 9/11, George W. Bush ill-advisedly chose to characterise his proposed 'war on terrorism' as a 'crusade' (a term carefully avoided since), he simply played into al-Qaeda's hands. Indeed, in late 2002, bin Laden released a statement declaring that 'one of the most important positive results of the raids on New York and Washington was the revelation of the truth regarding the conflict between the Crusaders and the Muslims [and] the strength of the hatred which the Crusaders feel towards us'. Then, in March 2003, after the US-led invasion of Iraq, bin Laden added: 'The Zionist-Crusader campaign on [Islam] today is the most dangerous and rabid ever . . . [to learn] how to resist these enemy forces from outside, we must look at the previous Crusader wars against out countries.' This inflammatory and misleading propaganda, grounded in the manipulation of history, has shown little sign of abating.[18]

THE CRUSADES IN HISTORY

'Crusade parallelism' has played a distinct role in shaping the modern world – one that, in recent times, has been widely misunderstood. The manipulation of the history and memory of the war for the Holy Land began with nineteenth-century romanticism and western colonial triumphalism. It has been perpetuated by political propaganda and ideological invective in the Muslim world. The purpose of identifying and examining this process is not to condone or condemn the ideologies of imperialism, Arab Nationalism or Islamism – but rather to expose the crude simplicity and glaring inaccuracy of the 'historical' parallels evoked in their name. The political, cultural and spiritual resonances of the distant crusades have been manufactured by an imaginary view of the past; one that trades in caricature, distortion and fabrication, not the medieval realities of reciprocal violence, diplomacy and trade, enmity and alliance that lay at the heart of crusading.

Of course, humankind has always shown a proclivity for the deliberate misrepresentation of history. But the dangers attendant upon 'crusade parallelism' have proven to be particularly intense. Over the last two centuries, a fallacious narrative has taken hold. It suggests that the crusades were pivotal to the relationship between Islam and the West because they engendered a deep-rooted and irrevocable sense of mutual antipathy, leaving these two cultures locked in a destructive and perpetual war. This notion – of a direct and unbroken trail of conflict linking the medieval and modern eras – has helped to cultivate a pervasive, and almost fatalistic, acceptance that a titanic clash of civilisations is inevitable. Yet dark, brutal, even savage as they sometimes were, the crusades left no permanent marks upon western Christian or Muslim society. In truth, the war for the Holy Land had been all but forgotten by the end of the Middle Ages and was only resurrected centuries later.

Perhaps the crusades do have things to tell us about our world. Most, if not all, of their lessons are common to other eras of human history. These wars lay bare the power of faith and ideology to inspire fervent mass movements and to elicit violent discord; they affirm the capacity of commercial interests to transcend the barriers of conflict; and they illustrate how readily suspicion and hatred of the 'other' can be harnessed. But the notion that the struggle for dominion of the Holy Land – waged by Latin Christians and Levantine Muslims so many centuries ago – does, or somehow should, have a direct bearing upon the modern world is misguided. The reality of these medieval wars must be explored and understood if the forces of propaganda are to be assuaged, and incitements to hostility countered. But the crusades must also be placed where they belong: in the past.

ACKNOWLEDGEMENTS

I owe many debts of gratitude to those who helped me through six years spent researching and writing this book. My colleagues in the Department of History at Queen Mary University of London have been wonderfully supportive throughout, and I particularly would like to thank Virginia Davis, Julian Jackson, Peter Hennessy, Miri Rubin, Peter Denley, Yossi Rapoport, Dan Todman and Alice Austin. My students, not least those on my Special Subject 'The First Crusade' and the London MA in Crusader Studies, also have been a great source of inspiration.

Peter Edbury kindly read the first draft of this work (when it was considerably longer than it is now!), and I also benefited enormously from the friendship and the assistance offered by Sue Edgington and William Purkis. Andrew Gordon and John Saddler shaped my early vision of the book, while the patience and encouragement of Mike Jones at Simon & Schuster, Dan Halpern and Matt Weiland at Ecco enabled me to complete the project. Sue Phillpott's astute eye helped to refine the text, and I am especially grateful to Katherine Stanton for her judicious editorial guidance and the great care she has taken in preparing this book for publication. My agents Peter Robinson and George Lucas have always been stalwart sources of support and advice. The numerous discussions of the crusading world I enjoyed with Tony To, Don MacPherson and Kario Salem also helped to spark my idea of switching perspectives between Christendom and Islam in this work.

I would like to offer heartfelt thanks to all those who have stood by me through these years. To James Ellison, the finest of friends and colleagues; to John Hardy, a true friend through all seasons; to Steve Jones and Stuart Webber, who always knew not to ask how the book was going; and to Robert and Maria Oram, Simon Bradley, Anthony Scott, Daniel Richards, Julie Jones and Lizzie Webber for their unfailing support. I am most grateful to my family for their encouragement, and wish to thank Per Asbridge, Camilla Smith, Jane Campbell, Margaret Williams and Craig Campbell. My parents have shown enormous kindness, as always, and without their help it would have been all but impossible to write this book. At the centre of my life, throughout, have been Christine and Ella, my wife and daughter. It is their patience and love that has sustained me, above and beyond all else, and they who deserve my deepest thanks.

Thomas Asbridge
September 2009
West Sussex

CHRONOLOGY

27 November 1095	Pope Urban II's sermon on the First Crusade at Clermont
18 June 1097	Nicaea surrenders to the First Crusade
1 July 1097	Battle of Dorylaeum
3 June 1098	First Crusade sacks Antioch
28 June 1098	Battle of Antioch against Kerbogha of Mosul
15 July 1099	First Crusade captures Jerusalem
May 1104	Battle of Harran
28 June 1119	Roger of Antioch slain at the Field of Blood
June 1128	Zangi assumes control of Aleppo
December 1144	Zangi conquers Edessa
1 December 1145	Pope Eugenius III proclaims the Second Crusade
September 1146	Zangi assassinated; Nur al-Din assumes control of Aleppo
July 1148	Failure of the Second Crusade's siege of Damascus
29 June 1149	Battle of Inab
19 August 1153	Latins conquer Ascalon
April 1154	Nur al-Din occupies Damascus
11 August 1164	Nur al-Din defeats the Franks near Harim
March 1169	Saladin assumes the title of vizier of Egypt
September 1171	Abolition of the Fatimid caliphate in Egypt
15 May 1174	Death of Nur al-Din; that October Saladin assumes control of Damascus
25 November 1177	Battle of Mont Gisard
12 June 1183	Saladin occupies Aleppo
May 1185	Death of King Baldwin IV of Jerusalem

4 July 1187	Battle of Hattin
2 October 1187	Saladin retakes Jerusalem
29 October 1187	Pope Gregory VIII issues call for the Third Crusade
November 1187	Richard the Lionheart takes the cross
28 August 1189	Guy of Lusignan lays siege to Acre
10 June 1190	Death of Frederick Barbarossa in Asia Minor
8 June 1191	Richard the Lionheart arrives at Acre
12 July 1191	Third Crusaders occupy Acre
20 August 1191	Richard I executes Muslim prisoners outside Acre
7 September 1191	Battle of Arsuf
13 January 1192	Richard I orders first retreat from Beit Nuba
4 July 1192	Third Crusade makes its second retreat from Beit Nuba
2 September 1192	Treaty of Jaffa finalised
4 March 1193	Death of Saladin
15 August 1198	Pope Innocent III issues call for the Fourth Crusade
12 April 1204	Fourth Crusade sacks Constantinople
November 1215	Pope Innocent III presides over the Fourth Lateran Council
5 November 1219	Fifth Crusade captures Damietta
17 March 1229	Frederick II Hohenstaufen enters Jerusalem
11 July 1244	Khwarizmians sack Jerusalem
18 October 1244	Battle of La Forbie
5 June 1249	King Louis IX of France lands in Egypt
8 February 1250	Battle of Mansourah
April 1250	Louis IX taken captive by Turanshah
February 1258	Mongols sack Baghdad
3 September 1260	Battle of Ayn Jalut
June 1261	Baybars invested as Mamluk sultan
19 May 1268	Baybars sacks Antioch
8 April 1271	Hospitallers surrender Krak des Chevaliers to Baybars
27 April 1289	Qalawun captures Tripoli
18 May 1291	Mamluk conquest of Acre

NOTES

Abbreviations

RHC Occ.   *Recueil des historiens des croisades, Historiens occidentaux,*
            5 vols, ed. Académie des Inscriptions et Belles-Lettres
            (Paris, 1844–95).
RHC Or.   *Recueil des historiens des croisades, Historiens orientaux,* 5
            vols, ed. Académie des Inscriptions et Belles-Lettres (Paris,
            1872–1906).

INTRODUCTION

1. During the Middle Ages and beyond, crusades were fought in other
   theatres of conflict, but at the height of their popularity and
   significance – between 1095 and 1291 – the Christian campaigns
   primarily targeted the Near East. As a consequence, this book
   concentrates upon events in the Holy Land. A broad interpretation of
   the Holy Land's geographical extent has been adopted. By one
   definition this region might be deemed to equate roughly to the borders
   of the modern state of Israel, including those areas under Palestinian
   authority. But in the medieval era, western European Christians often
   had a more vaguely defined notion of the 'Holy Land', sometimes
   including other devotionally significant sites – such as the city of
   Antioch (now in south-eastern Turkey) – within its confines. In the age
   of the crusades, Muslim contemporaries also tended to refer both
   specifically to *al-Quds* (the 'Holy City') and more broadly to an area
   known as *Bilad al-Sham* (the Coast). The wars for the Holy Land
   examined in this book, therefore, relate to conflicts ranging across
   modern Israel, Jordan, Lebanon and Syria, and parts of Turkey and
   Egypt. In recent times, it has become common to refer, in an
   overarching sense, to this region as the Middle East, but this is actually

somewhat inaccurate. Strictly speaking, the coastal territories are the Near East, with the Middle East lying beyond the expanse of the Euphrates River. This work also makes use of the term 'the Levant' to describe the eastern Mediterranean lands – a word derived from the French *lever* (to rise), and related to the sun's daily appearance in the east. For overviews of recent advances in crusader studies scholarship see: G. Constable, 'The Historiography of the Crusades', *The Crusades from the Perspective of Byzantium and the Muslim World*, ed. A. E. Laiou and R. P. Mottahedeh (Washington, DC, 2001), pp. 1–22; M. Balard, *Croisades et Orient Latin, XIe–XIVe siècle* (Paris, 2001); R. Ellenblum, *Crusader Castles and Modern Histories* (Cambridge, 2007); C. Hillenbrand, *The Crusades: Islamic Perspectives* (Edinburgh, 1999); N. Housley, *Contesting the Crusades* (Oxford, 2006); N. Housley, *Fighting for the Cross* (New Haven and London, 2008); A. Jotischky, *Crusading and the Crusader States* (Harlow, 2004); H. E. Mayer, *The Crusades*, trans. J. Gillingham, 2nd edn (Oxford, 1988); T. F. Madden, *The New Concise History of the Crusades* (Lanham, 2006); N. Jaspert, *The Crusades* (New York and London, 2006); J. Richard, *The Crusades, c. 1071–c. 1291*, trans. J. Birrell (Cambridge, 1999); J. S. C. Riley-Smith (ed.), *The Oxford Illustrated History of the Crusades* (Oxford, 1995); J. S. C. Riley-Smith, *The Crusades: A History*, 2nd edn (London and New York, 2005); C. J. Tyerman, *God's War: A New History of the Crusades* (London, 2006).

2. B. S. Bachrach, 'The pilgrimages of Fulk Nerra, count of the Angevins, 987–1040', *Religion, Culture and Society in the Early Middle Ages*, ed. T. F. X. Noble and J. J. Contreni (Kalamazoo, 1987), pp. 205–17.

3. Raoul Glaber, *Opera*, ed. J. France, N. Bulst, P. Reynolds (Oxford, 1989), p. 192. On the Late Antique period, the conversion of Europe and early Christianity see: R. Fletcher, *The Conversion of Europe* (New York, 1998); P. Brown, *The Rise of Western Christendom* (Oxford, 1996); B. Hamilton, *The Christian World of the Middle Ages* (Stroud, 2003). On the Franks see: E. James, *The Franks* (Oxford, 1988). On the use of the term 'Franks' in the crusading context see: J. S. C. Riley-Smith, *The First Crusaders, 1095–1131* (Cambridge, 1997), pp. 64–5. On the Carolingian era and early medieval world see: R. McKitterick, *The Frankish Kingdoms under the Carolingians 751–987* (London, 1983); R. McKitterick, *The Early Middle Ages: Europe 400–1000* (2001); C. Wickham, *Framing the Early Middle Ages: Europe and the Mediterranean, 400–800* (Oxford, 2005).

4. Popes argued that because Christ's chief apostle St Peter had been Rome's first prelate, his successors should be recognised not only as the head of the Latin Church in the West, but also as the supreme spiritual

power across the whole Christian world. Not surprisingly, this view did not sit well with the likes of the Greek Orthodox patriarch in Constantinople, and a dispute over this principle and wider doctrine caused an open split, or 'schism', between these two arms of 'European' Christianity in 1054. On the medieval papacy, Pope Gregory VII and the papal Reform movement see: W. Ullmann, *A Short History of the Papacy in the Middle Ages* (London, 1974); C. Morris, *The Papal Monarchy: The Western Church from 1050 to 1250* (Oxford, 1989); H. E. J. Cowdrey, *Pope Gregory VII, 1073–1085* (Oxford, 1998); U.-R. Blumenthal, *The Investiture Controversy: Church and Monarchy from the Ninth to the Twelfth Century* (Philadelphia, 1988).

5. Raoul Glaber, *Opera*, p. 60; M. G. Bull, *Knightly Piety and the Lay Response to the First Crusade: The Limousin and Gascony, c. 970–c. 1130* (Oxford, 1993), p. 158. On medieval religion, monasticism and pilgrimage see: M.G. Bull. 'Origins', *The Oxford Illustrated History of the Crusades*, ed. J. S. C. Riley-Smith (Oxford, 1995), pp. 13–33; B. Hamilton, *Religion in the Medieval West* (London, 1986); C. H. Lawrence, *Medieval Monasticism: Forms of Religious Life in Western Europe in the Middle Ages*, 3rd edn (London, 2001); J. Sumption, *Pilgrimage: An Image of Mediaeval Religion* (London, 1975); B. Ward, *Miracles and the Medieval Mind*, 2nd edn (London, 1987); D. Webb, *Medieval European Pilgrimage, c. 700–c.1500* (London, 2002); C. Morris, *The Sepulchre of Christ and the Medieval West: From the Beginning to 1600* (Oxford, 2005).

6. The heavy costs of functioning as a knight or *miles* (pl. *milites*) – particularly those related to equipment and training – made it difficult for less affluent men to operate as *milites*, although, as yet, the group was not the exclusive domain of the nobility. Virtually all male members of the lay aristocracy were expected to carry out the duties of a knight, and most wealthy lords retained the service of a number of *milites* as vassals, under contract to protect and farm a parcel of land in return for military service. This convention made it possible for poorer individuals to achieve the status of a *miles*, acquiring the tools of the trade through employment. On medieval knighthood and European warfare see: J. France, *Western Warfare in the Age of the Crusades* (London, 1999).

7. I. S. Robinson, 'Gregory VII and the Soldiers of Christ', *History*, vol. 58 (1973), pp. 169–92; F. H. Russell, *The Just War in the Middle Ages* (Cambridge, 1975); T. Asbridge, *The First Crusade: A New History* (London, 2004), pp. 21–31.

8. Over time Sunni Islam also developed four distinct 'schools' of law or *madhabs*: the Hanafi, Shafi'i, Hanbali and Malaki. During the crusader period these various 'schools' gained popularity and support with

different groups and in different regions. The Syrian city of Damascus was a Hanbali centre, for example, while the Zangid Turkish dynasty tended to support the Hanafites and the Kurdish Ayyubids were Shafi'ites.

9. On the history of medieval Islam, the rise of the Seljuqs, and the Near East on the eve of the First Crusade see: H. Kennedy, *The Prophet and the Age of the Caliphates: The Islamic Near East from the Sixth to the Eleventh Century* (London, 1986); J. Berkey, *The Formation of Islam: Religion and Society in the Near East, 600–800* (Cambridge, 2003); C. Cahen, 'The Turkish invasion: The Selchükids', *A History of the Crusades*, ed. K. M. Setton, vol. 1, 2nd edn (Madison, 1969), pp. 135–76; Hillenbrand, *The Crusades: Islamic Perspectives*, pp. 33–50; C. Cahen, *Introduction à l'histoire du monde musulman médiéval, Initiation à l'Islam*, vol. 1 (Paris, 1982); C. Cahen, *Orient et Occident aux temps des croisades* (Paris, 1983); P. M. Holt, *The Age of the Crusades: The Near East from the Eleventh Century to 1517* (London, 1986), pp. 1–22; T. el-Azhari, *The Saljuqs of Syria during the Crusades 463–549 A.H./1070–1154 A.D.* (Berlin, 1997); S. Zakkar, *The Emirate of Aleppo 1004–1094* (Beirut, 1971); J.-M. Mouton, *Damas et sa principauté sous les Saljoukides et les Bourides 468–549/1076–1154* (Cairo, 1994); M. Yared-Riachi, *La politique extérieure de la principauté de Damas, 468–549 A.H./1076–1154 A.D.* (Damascus, 1997); A. F. Sayyid, *Les Fatimides en Égypte* (Cairo, 1992).

10. The basic building block of Muslim armies was the *'askar* – the personal military entourage of a lord or emir. These forces were dominated by highly trained professional 'slave-soldiers' (who came to be termed *mamluks*), initially drawn from the Turkic peoples of Central Asia and the steppe-lands of Russia, but later supplemented by Armenians, Georgians, Greeks and even eastern European Slavs. Within the Seljuq world, large armies were commonly levied through the use of the *'iqta* system – whereby an emir was granted rights to the revenues from a parcel of land in return for an obligation to field his *'askar* for wars and campaigns. This procedure later was adopted in Egypt. On medieval Islamic warfare see: H. Kennedy, *The Armies of the Caliph* (London, 2001); Hillenbrand, *The Crusades: Islamic Perspectives*, pp. 431–587.

11. On Islamic *jihad* in the Middle Ages see: E. Sivan, *L'Islam et la Croisade* (Paris, 1968); Hillenbrand, *The Crusades: Islamic Perspectives*, pp. 89–103; B. Z. Kedar, 'Croisade et *jihad* vus par l'ennemi: une étude des perceptions mutuelles des motivations', *Autour de la Première Croisade*, ed. M. Balard (Paris, 1996), pp. 345–58; H. Dajani-Shakeel and R. A. Mossier (eds), *The Jihad and its Times* (Ann Arbor, 1991); R. Firestone, *Jihad. The Origins of Holy War in Islam* (Oxford, 2000); D.

Cook, *Understanding Jihad* (Berkeley, 2005). According to Shi'ite theology the duty to wage an external *jihad* would not become active until the Last Days. Thus the Isma'ili Shi'ites of Egypt and Twelver Shi'ites like the Munqidh clan of Shaizar fought wars against the Franks, but did not regard themselves as being engaged in a holy war.

12. Al-Azimi, 'La chronique abrégée d'al-Azimi', ed. C. Cahen, *Journal Asiatique*, vol. 230 (1938), p. 369; J. Drory, 'Some observations during a visit to Palestine by Ibn al-'Arabi of Seville in 1092–1095', *Crusades*, vol. 3 (2004), pp. 101–24; Hillenbrand, *The Crusades: Islamic Perspectives*, pp. 48–50.

PART I: THE COMING OF THE CRUSADES

1. In spite of the historic significance of this speech, no precise record of Urban's words survives. Numerous versions of his address, including three by eyewitnesses, were written after the end of the First Crusade, but all were coloured by hindsight and none can be regarded as authoritative. Nonetheless, by comparing these accounts with references to the 'crusade' in letters composed by the pope in 1095–6, the core features of his message can be reconstructed. For the primary source accounts of Pope Urban II's sermon at Clermont see: Fulcher of Chartres, *Historia Hierosolymitana (1095–1127)*, ed. H. Hagenmeyer (Heidelberg, 1913), pp. 130–38; Robert the Monk, *Historia Iherosolimitana*, *RHC Occ.* III, pp. 727–30; Guibert of Nogent, *Dei gesta per Francos*, ed. R. B. C. Huygens, *Corpus Christianorum, Continuatio Mediaevalis*, 127A (Turnhout, 1996), pp. 111–17; Baldric of Bourgueil, bishop of Dol, *Historia Jerosolimitana*, *RHC Occ.* IV, pp. 12–16. For the letters written by Urban at the time of the First Crusade see: H. Hagenmeyer, *Die Kreuzzugsbriefe aus den Jahren 1088–1100* (Innsbruck, 1901), pp. 136–8; 'Papsturkunden in Florenz', ed. W. Wiederhold, *Nachrichten von der Gesellschaft der Wissenschaften zu Göttingen*, Phil.-hist. Kl. (Göttingen, 1901), pp. 313–14; *Papsturkunden in Spanien. I Katalonien*, ed. P. F. Kehr (Berlin, 1926), pp. 287–8. An English translation of these accounts and letters is given in: L. and J. S. C. Riley-Smith, *The Crusades: Idea and Reality*, 1095–1274 (London, 1981), pp. 37–53.

2. On Pope Urban II and the Clermont sermon see: A. Becker, *Papst Urban II. (1088–1099)*, *Schriften der Monumenta Germaniae Historica* 19, 2 vols (Stuttgart, 1964–88); H. E. J. Cowdrey, 'Pope Urban II's preaching of the First Crusade', *History*, vol. 55 (1970), pp. 177–88; P. Cole, *The Preaching of the Crusades to the Holy Land, 1095–1270* (Cambridge, Mass., 1991),

pp. 1–36; J. S. C. Riley-Smith, *The First Crusaders, 1095–1131* (Cambridge, 1997), pp. 60–75. More generally on the preaching and progress of the First Crusade see: J. S. C. Riley-Smith, *The First Crusade and the Idea of Crusading* (London, 1986); J. France, *Victory in the East: A Military History of the First Crusade* (Cambridge, 1994); J. Flori, *La Première Croisade: L'Occident chrétien contre l'Islam* (Brussels, 2001); T. Asbridge, *The First Crusade: A New History* (London, 2004). For an account that is dated and somewhat unreliable, but lively nonetheless, see: S. Runciman, 'The First Crusade and the foundation of the kingdom of Jerusalem', *A History of the Crusades*, vol. 1 (Cambridge, 1951). The main primary sources for reconstructing the history of the First Crusade are: *Gesta Francorum et aliorum Hierosolimitanorum*, ed. and trans. R. Hill (London, 1962); Fulcher of Chartres, *Historia Hierosolymitana (1095–1127)*, ed. H. Hagenmeyer (Heidelberg, 1913); Raymond of Aguilers, *Le 'Liber' de Raymond d'Aguilers*, ed. J. H. Hill and L. L. Hill (Paris, 1969); Peter Tudebode, *Historia de Hierosolymitano itinere*, ed. J. H. Hill and L. L. Hill (Paris, 1977); Caffaro di Caschifellone, 'De liberatione civitatum orientis', ed. L. T. Belgrano, *Annali Genovesi*, vol. 1 (Genoa, 1890), pp. 3–75; Ekkehard of Aura, 'Hierosolimita', *RHC Occ.* V, pp. 1–40; Ralph of Caen, *Gesta Tancredi in expeditione Hierosolymitana*, *RHC Occ.* III, pp. 587–716; *Historia Belli Sacri*, *RHC Occ.* III, pp. 169–229; Albert of Aachen, *Historia Iherosolimitana*, ed. and trans. S. B. Edgington (Oxford, 2007); H. Hagenmeyer, *Die Kreuzzugsbriefe aus den Jahren 1088–1100* (Innsbruck, 1901); Anna Comnena, *Alexiade*, ed. and trans. B. Leib, 3 vols (Paris, 1937–76), vol. 2, pp. 205–36, vol. 3, pp. 7–32; Ibn al-Qalanisi, *The Damascus Chronicle of the Crusades, extracted and translated from the Chronicle of Ibn al-Qalanisi*, trans. H. A. R. Gibb (London, 1932), pp. 41–9; Ibn al-Athir, *The Chronicle of Ibn al-Athir for the crusading period from al-Kamil fi'l-Ta'rikh*, trans. D. S. Richards, vol. 1 (Aldershot, 2006), pp. 13–22; Matthew of Edessa, *Armenia and the Crusades, Tenth to Twelfth Centuries: The Chronicle of Matthew of Edessa*, trans. A. E. Dostourian (Lanham, 1993), pp. 164–73. For a selection of translated sources see: E. Peters (ed.), *The First Crusade: The Chronicle of Fulcher of Chartres and other source materials*, 2nd edn (Philadelphia, 1998). For an introduction to these sources see: S. B. Edgington, 'The First Crusade: Reviewing the Evidence', *The First Crusade: Origins and Impact*, ed. J. P. Phillips (Manchester, 1997), pp. 55–77. See also: S. D. Goitein, 'Geniza Sources for the Crusader period: A survey', *Outremer*, ed. B. Z. Kedar, H. E. Mayer and R. C. Smail (Jerusalem, 1982), pp. 308–12.

3. Fulcher of Chartres, pp. 132–3; Robert the Monk, p. 729; Guibert of Nogent, p. 113; Baldric of Bourgueil, p. 13.

4. Fulcher of Chartres, p. 134; Guibert of Nogent, p. 116; Hagenmeyer, *Kreuzzugsbriefe*, p. 136; Robert the Monk, pp. 727–8; B. Hamilton, 'Knowing the enemy: Western understanding of Islam at the time of the crusades', *Journal of the Royal Asiatic Society*, 3rd series, vol. 7 (1997), pp. 373–87.

5. Hagenmeyer, *Kreuzzugsbriefe*, p. 136; Fulcher of Chartres, pp. 134–5; Baldric of Bourgueil, p. 15; J. A. Brundage, 'Adhémar of Le Puy: The bishop and his critics', *Speculum*, vol. 34 (1959), pp. 201–12; J. H. Hill and L. L. Hill, 'Contemporary accounts and the later reputation of Adhémar, bishop of Le Puy', *Mediaevalia et humanistica*, vol. 9 (1955), pp. 30–38; H. E. Mayer, 'Zur Beurteilung Adhemars von Le Puy', *Deutsches Archiv für Erforschung des Mittelalters*, vol. 16 (1960), pp. 547–52. Urban appears to have woven an assortment of additional themes into his 'crusading' message: that fighting in the name of the papacy as a 'soldier of Christ' fulfilled quasi-feudal obligations to God, lord of 'the kingdom of Heaven'; that joining the expedition would allow one to follow in the footsteps of Christ by imitating the suffering of his Passion; that the Last Days were approaching, and that only the conquest of Jerusalem could usher in the prophesied Apocalypse.

6. On Urban as the progenitor of crusading, attitudes towards martyrdom and the development of the crusading ideal see: C. Erdmann, *The Origin of the Idea of Crusade* (Princeton, 1977); J. T. Gilchrist, 'The Erdmann thesis and canon law, 1083–1141', *Crusade and Settlement*, ed. P. W. Edbury (Cardiff, 1985), pp. 37–45; E. O. Blake, 'The formation of the "crusade idea"', *Journal of Ecclesiastical History*, vol. 21 (1970), pp. 11–31; H. E. J. Cowdrey, 'The genesis of the crusades: The springs of western ideas of holy war', *The Holy War*, ed. T. P. Murphy (Columbus, 1976), pp. 9–32; J. Flori, *La formation de l'idée des croisades dans l'Occident Chrétien* (Paris, 2001); J. S. C. Riley-Smith, 'Death on the First Crusade', *The End of Strife*, ed. D. Loades (Edinburgh, 1984), pp. 14–31; H. E. J. Cowdrey, 'Martyrdom and the First Crusade', *Crusade and Settlement*, ed. P. W. Edbury (Cardiff, 1985), pp. 46–56; J. Flori, 'Mort et martyre des guerriers vers 1100. L'exemple de la Première Croisade', *Cahiers de civilisation médiévale*, vol. 34 (1991), pp. 121–39; C. Morris, 'Martyrs of the Field of Battle before and during the First Crusade', *Studies in Church History*, vol. 30 (1993), pp. 93–104; J. S. C. Riley-Smith, *What Were the Crusades?*, 3rd edn (Basingstoke, 2002); C. J. Tyerman, 'Were there any crusades in the twelfth century?', *English Historical Review*, vol. 110 (1995), pp. 553–77; C. J. Tyerman, *The Invention of the Crusades* (London, 1998).

7. Guibert of Nogent, p. 121; Anna Comnena, vol. 2, p. 207; E. O. Blake and C. Morris, 'A hermit goes to war: Peter and the origins of the First

Crusade', *Studies in Church History*, vol. 22 (1985), pp. 79–107; C. Morris, 'Peter the Hermit and the Chroniclers', *The First Crusade: Origins and Impact*, ed. J. P. Phillips (Manchester, 1997), pp. 21–34; J. Flori, *Pierre l'Ermite et la Première Croisade* (Paris, 1999); Riley-Smith, *The First Crusade and the Idea of Crusading*, pp. 49–57; J. S. C. Riley-Smith, 'The First Crusade and the persecution of the Jews', *Studies in Church History*, vol. 21 (1984), pp. 51–72; R. Chazan, *European Jewry and the First Crusade* (Berkeley, 1987); Asbridge, *The First Crusade*, pp. 78–89, 100–103.

8. This estimate tends towards the calculations made by J. France, *Victory in the East*, pp. 122–42. For other recent contributions to this vexed question see: B. Bachrach, 'The siege of Antioch: A study in military demography', *War in History*, vol. 6 (1999), pp. 127–46; Riley-Smith, *The First Crusaders*, p. 109; J. S. C. Riley-Smith, 'Casualties and the number of knights on the First Crusade', *Crusades*, vol. 1 (2002), pp. 13–28.

9. Guibert of Nogent, p. 87; J.H. and L.L. Hill, *Raymond IV, Count of Toulouse* (Syracuse, 1962).

10. William of Malmesbury, *Gesta Regum Anglorum*, vol. 1, ed. and trans. R. A. B. Mynors, R. M. Thomson and M. Winterbottom, vol. 1 (Oxford, 1998), p. 693; Anna Comnena, vol. 3, pp. 122–3; R. B. Yewdale, *Bohemond I, Prince of Antioch* (Princeton, 1917); R. L. Nicholson, *Tancred: A Study of His Career and Work in Their Relation to the First Crusade and the Establishment of the Latin States in Syria and Palestine* (Chicago, 1940).

11. J. C. Andressohn, *The Ancestry and Life of Godfrey of Bouillon* (Bloomington, 1947); P. Gindler, *Graf Balduin I. von Edessa* (Halle, 1901); C. W. David, *Robert Curthose, Duke of Normandy* (Cambridge, Mass., 1920); W. M. Aird, *Robert Curthose, Duke of Normandy* (Woodbridge, 2008); J. A. Brundage, 'An errant crusader: Stephen of Blois', *Traditio*, vol. 16 (1960), pp. 380–95; *Gesta Francorum*, p. 7; J. A. Brundage, *Medieval Canon Law and the Crusader* (Madison, 1969), pp. 17–18, 30–39, 115–21; J. A. Brundage, 'The army of the First Crusade and the crusade vow: Some reflections on a recent book', *Medieval Studies*, vol. 33 (1971), pp. 334–43; Riley-Smith, *The First Crusaders*, pp. 22–3, 81–2, 114; Mayer, *The Crusades*, pp. 21–3; Riley-Smith, *The First Crusade and the Idea of Crusading*, p. 47; France, *Victory in the East*, pp. 11–16; Asbridge, *The First Crusade*, pp. 66–76; Housley, *Contesting the Crusades*, pp. 24–47.

12. Anna Comnena, vol. 2, pp. 206–7, 233. On Byzantine history see: M. Angold, *The Byzantine Empire, 1025–1204: A Political History*, 2nd edn (London, 1997). On crusader–Byzantine relations during the First Crusade see: R.-J. Lilie, *Byzantium and the Crusader States 1096–1204*, trans. J. C. Morris and J. E. Ridings (Oxford, 1993), pp. 1–60; J. H. Pryor,

'The oaths of the leaders of the First Crusade to emperor Alexius I Comnenus: fealty, homage, *pistis, douleia*', *Parergon*, vol. 2 (1984), pp. 111–41; J. Shepard, 'Cross purposes: Alexius Comnenus and the First Crusade', *The First Crusade: Origins and Impact*, ed. J. P. Phillips (Manchester, 1997), pp. 107–29; J. Harris, *Byzantium and the Crusades* (London, 2006), pp. 53–71.

13. Albert of Aachen, p. 84; Anna Comnena, vol. 2, pp. 220–34; Asbridge, *The First Crusade*, pp. 103–13.

14. Raymond of Aguilers, pp. 42–3; *Gesta Francorum*, p. 15; Fulcher of Chartres, p. 187; Albert of Aachen, pp. 118–20.

15. *Gesta Francorum*, p. 15; Hagenmeyer, *Kreuzzugsbriefe*, pp. 138–40; Anna Comnena, vol. 2, pp. 230, 234.

16. Fulcher of Chartres, pp. 202–3; W. G. Zajac, 'Captured property on the First Crusade', *The First Crusade: Origins and Impact*, ed. J. P. Phillips (Manchester, 1997), pp. 153–86.

17. *Gesta Francorum*, pp. 18–21; Fulcher of Chartres, pp. 192–9; France, *Victory in the East*, pp. 170–85; Asbridge, *The First Crusade*, pp. 133–7.

18. Albert of Aachen, pp. 138–40. The quotation has been abridged. *Gesta Francorum*, p. 23.

19. T. S. Asbridge, *The Creation of the Principality of Antioch 1098–1130* (Woodbridge, 2000), pp. 16–19; France, *Victory in the East*, pp. 190–96; Albert of Aachen, p. 170.

20. I myself espoused this assumption in 2004. Asbridge, *The First Crusade*, pp. 153–7.

21. Hagenmeyer, *Kreuzzugsbriefe*, p. 150; Raymond of Aguilers, pp. 47–8.

22. *Gesta Francorum*, p. 42; Fulcher of Chartres, p. 221; Albert of Aachen, pp. 208–10, 236–8; Hagenmeyer, *Kreuzzugsbriefe*, p. 150; Matthew of Edessa, pp. 167–8.

23. Fulcher of Chartres, pp. 224–6; Asbridge, *The First Crusade*, pp. 169–96. On the debate regarding Taticius' departure see: Lilie, *Byzantium and the Crusader States*, pp. 33–7; J. France, 'The departure of Tatikios from the army of the First Crusade', *Bulletin of the Institute of Historical Research*, vol. 44 (1971), pp. 131–47; France, *Victory in the East*, p. 243. On the first siege of Antioch see also: R. Rogers, *Latin Siege Warfare in the Twelfth Century* (Oxford, 1992), pp. 25–38.

24. Hagenmeyer, *Kreuzzugsbriefe*, p. 151; Raymond of Aguilers, p. 58. On the First Crusaders' relations with Near Eastern Muslims see: M. A. Köhler, *Allianzen und Verträge zwischen frankischen und islamischen Herrschern in Vorderren Orient* (Berlin, 1991), pp. 1–72; T. Asbridge, 'Knowing the enemy: Latin relations with Islam at the time of the First Crusade', *Knighthoods of Christ*, ed. N. Housley (Aldershot, 2007), pp. 17–25; Albert of Aachen, p. 268.

25. Fulcher of Chartres, p. 233; Albert of Aachen, pp. 282–4; *Gesta Francorum*, p. 48.

26. *Gesta Francorum*, p. 48; Peter Tudebode, p. 97; Albert of Aachen, pp. 298–300. This quotation has been abridged.

27. Raymond of Aguilers, p. 75; *Gesta Francorum*, pp. 65–6.

28. T. Asbridge, 'The Holy Lance of Antioch: Power, devotion and memory on the First Crusade', *Reading Medieval Studies*, vol. 33 (2007), pp. 3–36.

29. Matthew of Edessa, p. 171; Ibn al-Athir, vol. 1, p. 16; Albert of Aachen, p. 320.

30. Ibn al-Qalanisi, p. 46. On the Battle of Antioch see: France, *Victory in the East*, pp. 280–96; Asbridge, *The First Crusade*, pp. 232–40.

31. Raymond of Aguilers, p. 75; C. Morris, 'Policy and vision: The case of the Holy Lance found at Antioch', *War and Government in the Middle Ages: Essays in honour of J. O. Prestwich*, ed. J. Gillingham and J. C. Holt (Woodbridge, 1984), pp. 33–45.

32. Fulcher of Chartres, pp. 266–7; Raymond of Aguilers, p. 101; T. Asbridge, 'The principality of Antioch and the Jabal as-Summaq', *The First Crusade: Origins and Impact*, ed. J. P. Phillips (Manchester, 1997), pp. 142–52. For alternative readings of these events see: Hill, *Raymond IV, Count of Toulouse*, pp. 85–109; J. France, 'The crisis of the First Crusade from the defeat of Kerbogha to the departure from Arqa', *Byzantion*, vol. 40 (1970), pp. 276–308.

33. Raymond of Aguilers, pp. 120–24, 128–9; Fulcher of Chartres, pp. 238–41.

34. Albert of Aachen, p. 402.

35. Fulcher of Chartres, pp. 281–92. On medieval Jerusalem see: A. J. Boas, *Jerusalem in the Time of the Crusades* (London, 2001); J. Prawer, 'The Jerusalem the crusaders captured: A contribution to the medieval topography of the city', *Crusade and Settlement*, ed. P. W. Edbury (Cardiff, 1985), pp. 1–16; France, *Victory in the East*, pp. 333–5, 337–43.

36. Raymond of Aguilers, pp. 139–41; Albert of Aachen, pp. 410–12. On the siege of Jerusalem see: France, *Victory in the East*, pp. 332–55; Rogers, *Latin Siege Warfare*, pp. 47–63; Asbridge, *The First Crusade*, pp. 298–316.

37. Raymond of Aguilers, pp. 141–2; Albert of Aachen, p. 422.

38. Raymond of Aguilers, pp. 146–8; Albert of Aachen, p. 416.

39. Raymond of Aguilers, pp. 148–9; Fulcher of Chartres, pp. 296–9.

40. Raymond of Aguilers, p. 150; *Gesta Francorum*, p. 91; Robert the Monk, p. 868.

41. Ibn al-Athir, pp. 21–2; Fulcher of Chartres, pp. 304–5; B. Z. Kedar, 'The Jerusalem massacre of 1099 in the western historiography of the crusades', *Crusades*, vol. 3 (2004), pp. 15–75.

42. Historians continue to debate the precise nature of Godfrey's title. He may well also have employed the appellation 'prince', but it is relatively certain that he did not style himself as 'king of Jerusalem'. On this debate see: J. S. C. Riley-Smith, 'The title of Godfrey of Bouillon', *Bulletin of the Institute of Historical Research*, vol. 52 (1979), pp. 83–6; J. France, 'The election and title of Godfrey de Bouillon', *Canadian Journal of History*, vol. 18 (1983), pp. 321–9; A. V. Murray, *The Crusader Kingdom of Jerusalem: A Dynastic History 1099–1125* (Oxford, 2000), pp. 63–77.

43. Peter Tudebode, pp. 146–7; France, *Victory in the East*, pp. 360–65; Asbridge, *The First Crusade*, pp. 323–7.

44. On the 1101 crusade see: Riley-Smith, *The First Crusade and the Idea of Crusading*, pp. 120–34; J. L. Cate, 'The crusade of 1101', *A History of the Crusades*, ed. K. M. Setton, vol. 1, 2nd edn (Madison, 1969), pp. 343–67; A. Mullinder, 'The Crusading Expeditions of 1101–2' (unpublished Ph.D. thesis, University of Wales, Swansea, 1996).

45. On the evolving debate surrounding the centrality of the *Gesta Francorum* as a source for the First Crusade and on the identity of its author see: A. C. Krey, 'A neglected passage in the *Gesta* and its bearing on the literature of the First Crusade', *The Crusades and Other Historical Essays presented to Dana C. Munro by his former students*, ed. L. J. Paetow (New York, 1928), pp. 57–78; K. B. Wolf, 'Crusade and narrative: Bohemond and the *Gesta Francorum*', *Journal of Medieval History*, vol. 17 (1991), pp. 207–16; C. Morris, 'The *Gesta Francorum* as narrative history', *Reading Medieval Studies*, vol. 19 (1993), pp. 55–71; J. France, 'The Anonymous *Gesta Francorum* and the *Historia Francorum qui ceperunt Iherusalem* of Raymond of Aguilers and the *Historia de Hierosolymitano Itinere* of Peter Tudebode', *The Crusades and Their Sources: Essays Presented to Bernard Hamilton*, ed. J. France and W. G. Zajac (Aldershot, 1998), pp. 39–69; J. France, 'The use of the anonymous *Gesta Francorum* in the early twelfth-century sources for the First Crusade', *From Clermont to Jerusalem: The Crusades and Crusader Societies, 1095–1500*, ed. A. V. Murray (Turnhout, 1998), pp. 29–42; J. Rubenstein, 'What is the *Gesta Francorum* and who was Peter Tudebode?', *Revue Mabillon*, vol. 16 (2005), pp. 179–204.

46. Kedar, 'The Jerusalem massacre of 1099', pp. 16–30; *La Chanson d'Antioche*, ed. S. Duparc-Quioc, 2 vols (Paris, 1982); *The Canso d'Antioca: An Occitan Epic Chronicle of the First Crusade*, trans. C. Sweetenham and L. Paterson (Aldershot, 2003). For a discussion of Robert the Monk's account see: C. Sweetenham, *Robert the Monk's History of the First Crusade* (Aldershot, 2005), pp. 1–71. On the role of memory see: Asbridge, 'The Holy Lance of Antioch', pp. 20–26; S. B.

Edgington, 'Holy Land, Holy Lance: religious ideas in the Chanson d'Antioche', *The Holy Land, Holy Lands and Christian History, Studies in Church History*, ed. R. N. Swanson, vol. 36 (Woodbridge, 2000), pp. 142–53; S. B. Edgington, 'Romance and reality in the sources for the sieges of Antioch, 1097–1098', *Porphyrogenita*, ed. C. Dendrinos, J. Harris, E. Harvalia-Crook and J. Herrin (Aldershot, 2003), pp. 33–46; Y. Katzir, 'The conquests of Jerusalem, 1099 and 1187: Historical memory and religious typology', *The Meeting of Two Worlds: Cultural Exchange between East and West in the Period of the Crusades*, ed. V. P. Goss (Kalamazoo, 1986) pp. 103–13; J. M. Powell, 'Myth, legend, propaganda, history: The First Crusade, 1140–c.1300', *Autour de la Première Croisade*, ed. M. Balard (Paris, 1996), pp. 127–41.

47. Ibn al-Qalanisi, pp. 44, 48; Ibn al-Athir, pp. 21–2; al-Azimi, pp. 372–3; C. Hillenbrand, 'The First Crusade: The Muslim perspective', *The First Crusade: Origins and Impact*, ed. J. P. Phillips (Manchester, 1997), pp. 130–41; Hillenbrand, *The Crusades: Islamic Perspectives*, pp. 50–68.

48. Hillenbrand, *The Crusades: Islamic Perspectives*, pp. 68–74; J. Drory, 'Early Muslim reflections on the Crusaders', *Jerusalem Studies in Arabic and Islam*, vol. 25 (2001), pp. 92–101; D. Ephrat and M. D. Kahba, 'Muslim reaction to the Frankish presence in Bilad al-Sham: intensifying religious fidelity within the masses', *Al-Masaq*, vol. 15 (2003), pp. 47–58; W. J. Hamblin, 'To wage *jihad* or not: Fatimid Egypt during the early crusades', *The Jihad and its Times*, ed. H. Dajani-Shakeel and R. A. Mossier (Ann Arbor, 1991), pp. 31–40. Al-Sulami was particularly unusual, because he identified accurately that the Franks were waging a holy war targeting Jerusalem. He also considered the crusade to be part of a wider Christian offensive against Islam that included conflicts in Iberia and Sicily. E. Sivan, 'La genèse de la contre-croisade: un traité Damasquin du début du XIIe siècle', *Journal Asiatique*, vol. 254 (1966), pp. 197–224; N. Christie, 'Jerusalem in the *Kitab al-Jihad* of Ali ibn Tahir al-Sulami', *Medieval Encounters*, vol. 13.2 (2007), pp. 209–21; N. Christie and D. Gerish, 'Parallel preaching: Urban II and al-Sulami', *Al-Masaq*, vol. 15 (2003), pp. 139–48.

49. The term 'crusader states' is somewhat misleading, as it gives the impression that these settlements were exclusively populated by crusaders and that their history might be interpreted as an example of ongoing crusading activity. The vast majority of the surviving First Crusaders returned to the West in 1099, leaving Outremer to face perpetual manpower shortages and to rely upon the influx of new settlers, most of whom had not formally taken the cross. The issue of the continued influence of crusading ideology over the history of the Latin

East is a more vexed question. J. S. C. Riley-Smith, 'Peace never established: the Case of the Kingdom of Jerusalem', *Transactions of the Royal Historical Society*, 5th series, vol. 28 (1978), pp. 87–102.

50. For an overview of the history of the crusader states in the first half of the twelfth century see: Mayer, *The Crusades*, pp. 58–92; Richard, *The Crusades*, pp. 77–169; Jotischky, *Crusading and the Crusader States*, pp. 62–102. For a detailed and lively (if not always entirely reliable) account of this period see: S. Runciman, 'The kingdom of Jerusalem and the Frankish East 1100–1187', *A History of the Crusades*, vol. 2 (Cambridge, 1952). For more detailed regional studies see: J. Prawer, *Histoire du Royaume Latin de Jérusalem*, 2nd edn, 2 vols (Paris, 1975); J. Richard, *The Latin Kingdom of Jerusalem*, trans. J. Shirley, 2 vols (Oxford, 1979); A. Murray, *The Crusader Kingdom of Jerusalem: A Dynastic History 1099–1125* (Oxford, 2000); C. Cahen, *La Syrie du Nord à l'époque des Croisades et la principauté Franque d'Antioche* (Paris, 1940); T. Asbridge, *The Creation of the Principality of Antioch* (Woodbridge, 2000); J. Richard, *La comté de Tripoli sous la dynastie toulousaine (1102–1187)* (Paris, 1945); M. Amouroux-Mourad, *Le comté d'Édesse, 1098–1150* (Paris, 1988); C. MacEvitt, *The Crusades and the Christian World of the East* (Philadelphia, 2008). The main chronicle and narrative primary sources for Outremer's early history are: Fulcher of Chartres, *Historia Hierosolymitana (1095–1127)*, ed. H. Hagenmeyer (Heidelberg, 1913); Albert of Aachen, *Historia Iherosolimitana*, ed. and trans. S. B. Edgington (Oxford, 2007); Walter the Chancellor, *Bella Antiochena*, ed. H. Hagenmeyer (Innsbruck, 1896); Orderic Vitalis, *The Ecclesiastical History of Orderic Vitalis*, ed. and trans. M. Chibnall, vols 5 and 6 (Oxford, 1975); William of Tyre, *Chronicon*, ed. R. B. C. Huygens, *Corpus Christianorum, Continuatio Mediaevalis*, 63–63A, 2 vols (Turnhout, 1986); Ibn al-Qalanisi, *The Damascus Chronicle of the Crusades, extracted and translated from the Chronicle of Ibn al-Qalanisi*, trans. H. A. R. Gibb (London, 1932); Ibn al-Athir, *The Chronicle of Ibn al-Athir. Part 1*, trans. D. S. Richards (Aldershot, 2006); Kemal ad-Din, *La Chronique d'Alep, RHC Or.* III, pp. 577–732; Anna Comnena, *Alexiade*, ed. and trans. B. Leib, vol. 3 (Paris, 1976); John Kinnamos, *The Deeds of John and Manuel Comnenus*, trans. C. M. Brand (New York, 1976); Matthew of Edessa, *Armenia and the Crusades, Tenth to Twelfth Centuries: The Chronicle of Matthew of Edessa*, trans. A. E. Dostourian (Lanham, 1993); Michael the Syrian, *Chronique de Michel le Syrien, patriarche jacobite d'Antioche (1166–1199)*, ed. and trans. J. B. Chabot, 4 vols (Paris, 1899–1910); Anonymous Syriac Chronicle, 'The First and Second Crusades from an Anonymous Syriac Chronicle', ed. and trans. A. S. Tritton and H. A. R. Gibb, *Journal of the Royal Asiatic Society*, vol.

92 (1933), pp. 69–102, 273–306.

51. Albert of Aachen, p. 514. Murray, *The Crusader Kingdom of Jerusalem*, pp. 81–93; B. Hamilton, *The Latin Church in the Crusader States. The Secular Church* (1980), pp. 52–5.

52. William of Tyre, p. 454; Fulcher of Chartres, p. 353.

53. On the foundation of the Latin Church in Palestine and relations between the patriarch and king of Jerusalem see: Hamilton, *The Latin Church in the Crusader States*, pp. 52–85; K.-P. Kirstein, *Die lateinischen Patriarchen von Jerusalem* (Berlin, 2002). On the Jerusalemite True Cross see: A. V. Murray, '"Mighty against the enemies of Christ": The relic of the True Cross in the armies of the kingdom of Jerusalem', *The Crusades and Their Sources: Essays Presented to Bernard Hamilton*, ed. J. France and W. G. Zajac (Aldershot, 1998), pp. 217–37.

54. Fulcher of Chartres, pp. 387–8, 460–61; J. Wilkinson (trans.), *Jerusalem Pilgrimage 1099–1185* (London, 1988), pp. 100–101; Albert of Aachen, p. 664. A northern-French cleric, Fulcher of Chartres began the First Crusade in the company of Count Stephen of Blois-Chartres, but later gravitated to Baldwin of Boulogne's contingent, becoming his chaplain. Fulcher accompanied Baldwin to Edessa and then, with him, relocated to Jerusalem in 1100, remaining resident in the Holy City for the next three decades. In the earliest years of the twelfth century, Fulcher composed a history of the First Crusade (based, in part, upon the *Gesta Francorum*). He later extended his account to cover events in Outremer between 1100 and 1127, at which point his chronicle came to an abrupt end. As the work of a well-informed witness, Fulcher's *Historia* is an invaluable source. V. Epp, *Fulcher von Chartres: Studien zur Geschichtsschreibung des ersten Kreuzzuges* (Düsseldorf, 1990).

55. Fulcher of Chartres, pp. 397, 403. On Outremer's relations with the Italian mercantile communities see: M.L. Favreau-Lilie, *Die Italiener im Heiligen Land vom ersten Kreuzzug bis zum Tode Heinrichs von Champagne (1098–1197)* (Amsterdam, 1989).

56. In 1103, Muslim Acre was saved from an earlier Frankish siege by the timely arrival of a Fatimid fleet. It is possible that the Genoese may have carried out some ill-disciplined pillaging after Acre's fall in 1104.

57. This incident was recorded in Latin and Muslim sources: Albert of Aachen, pp. 808–10; Ibn al-Qalanisi, pp. 108–10.

58. On the relationship between the Jerusalemite crown and the Frankish aristocracy see: Murray, *The Crusader Kingdom of Jerusalem*, pp. 97–114; S. Tibble, *Monarchy and Lordships in the Latin Kingdom of Jerusalem 1099–1291* (Oxford, 1989).

59. Fulcher of Chartres, pp. 407–24; Albert of Aachen, pp. 580–82. On the

first Battle of Ramla and the two campaigns that followed in 1102 and
1105 see: R. C. Smail, *Crusading Warfare 1097–1193* (Cambridge,
1956), pp. 175–7; M. Brett, 'The battles of Ramla (1099–1105)', *Egypt
and Syria in the Fatimid, Ayyubid and Mamluk Eras*, ed. U.
Vermeulen and D. De Smet (Leuven, 1995), pp. 17–39. On Fatimid
warfare see: B. J. Beshir, 'Fatimid military organization', *Der Islam*,
vol. 55 (1978), pp. 37–56; W. J. Hamblin, 'The Fatimid navy during the
early crusades: 1099–1124', *American Neptune*, vol. 46 (1986), pp.
77–83.

60. William of Malmesbury, p. 467; Fulcher of Chartres, p. 446; Albert of
Aachen, p. 644.

61. A Muslim pilgrim from Iberia, Ibn Jubayr, journeyed through the Terre
de Sueth seventy years later and bore witness to the fact that the
cooperative Latin–Muslim agrarian exploitation of this fertile region
continued, seemingly unaffected by the war brewing between Saladin
and the kingdom of Jerusalem. Ibn Jubayr described how 'the
cultivation of the valley is divided between the Franks and the
Muslims ... They apportion crops equally, and their animals are
mingled together, yet no wrong takes place between them.' Ibn Jubayr,
The Travels of Ibn Jubayr, trans. R. J. C. Broadhurst (London, 1952), p.
315.

62. Matthew of Edessa, p. 192. On the early history of Frankish Antioch see:
Asbridge, *The Creation of the Principality of Antioch*, pp. 47–58.

63. Ibn al-Qalanisi, p. 61; Ralph of Caen, p. 712; Smail, *Crusading Warfare*,
pp. 177–8, no. 6.

64. Ralph of Caen, pp. 713–14. A Norman priest who joined Bohemond's
1107–08 crusade and then settled in the principality of Antioch, Ralph
of Caen wrote a history of the First Crusade and the crusader states to
c. 1106. His account focused upon the careers of Bohemond and
Tancred. For an introduction to Ralph's account see: B. S. Bachrach
and D. S. Bachrach (trans.), *The Gesta Tancredi of Ralph of Caen*
(Aldershot, 2005), pp. 1–17.

65. Albert of Aachen, p. 702; Ralph of Caen, pp. 714–15; Asbridge, *The
Creation of the Principality of Antioch*, pp. 57–65.

66. Anna Comnena, vol. 3, p. 51. To date, the standard work of Bohemond's
venture is: J. G. Rowe, 'Paschal II, Bohemund of Antioch and the
Byzantine empire', *Bulletin of the John Rylands Library*, vol. 49 (1966),
pp. 165–202. Rowe's arguments are ripe for revision. See also: Yewdale,
Bohemond I, pp. 106–31.

67. It is possible that Tancred fought alongside Ridwan of Aleppo in a
second conflict against Chavli of Mosul and Baldwin of Edessa in 1109.
Ibn al-Athir, vol. 1, p. 141; Asbridge, *The Creation of the Principality of*

Antioch, pp. 112–14.

68. Albert of Aachen, pp. 782, 786, 794–6; Asbridge, *The Creation of the Principality of Antioch*, pp. 114–21. On the early history of the Latin Church in northern Syria and the ecclesiastical dispute between Antioch and Jerusalem see: Hamilton, *The Latin Church in the Crusader States*, pp. 18–51; J. G. Rowe, 'The Papacy and the Ecclesiastical Province of Tyre 1110–1187', *Bulletin of John Rylands Library*, vol. 43 (1962), pp. 160–89; Asbridge, *The Creation of the Principality of Antioch*, pp. 195–213.

69. Contemporaries were aware of the obstacle presented by the Belus Hills, with one Latin eyewitness, Walter the Chancellor (p. 79), commenting on the protection afforded to Antioch by the 'mountains [and] crags', but modern historians have largely ignored the significance of the Belus Hills. Being of such limited altitude, they rarely appear on maps of the region. I stumbled (almost literally) upon the range when travelling through this beautiful, yet rugged, area on foot, an experience which led me to re-evaluate the impact of this topographic feature upon Antiochene history. P. Deschamps, 'Le défense du comté de Tripoli et de la principauté d'Antioche', *Les Châteaux des Croisés en Terre Sainte*, vol. 3 (Paris, 1973), pp. 59–60; Asbridge, *The Creation of the Principality of Antioch*, p. 50; T. Asbridge, 'The significance and causes of the battle of the Field of Blood', *Journal of Medieval History*, vol. 23.4 (1997), pp. 301–16.

70. Matthew of Edessa, p. 212; T. Asbridge, 'The "crusader" community at Antioch: The impact of interaction with Byzantium and Islam', *Transactions of the Royal Historical Society*, 6th series, vol. 9 (1999), pp. 305–25; Asbridge, *The Creation of the Principality of Antioch*, pp. 65–7, 134–9.

71. Fulcher of Chartres, p. 426; Runciman, A *History of the Crusades*, vol. 2, p. 126; Smail, *Crusading Warfare*, p. 125; Richard, *The Crusades*, p. 135; Ibn al-Qalanisi, p. 137.

72. On the Assassins see: M. G. S. Hodgson, *The Secret Order of the Assassins* (The Hague, 1955); B. Lewis, *The Assassins* (London, 1967); B. Lewis, 'The Isma'ilites and the Assassins', A *History of the Crusades*, ed. K. M. Setton, vol. 1, 2nd edn (Madison, 1969), pp. 99–132; F. Daftary, *The Isma'ilis: Their History and Doctrines* (Cambridge, 1990).

73. Smail, *Crusading Warfare*, pp. 143–8, 178–9; Asbridge, *The Creation of the Principality of Antioch*, pp. 70–73.

74. Albert of Aachen, pp. 866–8. In the midst of his bout of illness in early 1117 King Baldwin's ability to dominate Palestine's Frankish aristocracy was curbed. Having failed to produce an heir, Baldwin was all but compelled by the Latin nobility to repudiate his third wife Adelaide (the

widowed mother of the young count of Sicily, Roger II) on grounds of
bigamy, in order to avoid the prospect of a Sicilian ruler acceding to the
Jerusalemite throne. Murray, *The Crusader Kingdom of Jerusalem*, pp.
115–17.

75. Kemal al-Din, p. 617; C. Hillenbrand, 'The career of Najm al-Din Il-
Ghazi', *Der Islam*, vol. 58 (1981), pp. 250–92. King Baldwin II came to
power in Jerusalem in 1118 only after a disputed succession in which
Baldwin I's brother Eustace of Boulogne was an alternative candidate.
H. E. Mayer, 'The Succession of Baldwin II of Jerusalem: English
Impact on the East', *Dumbarton Oaks Papers*, vol. 39 (1985), pp. 139–47;
A. Murray, 'Dynastic Continuity or Dynastic Change? The Accession
of Baldwin II and the Nobility of the Kingdom of Jerusalem', *Medieval
Prosopography*, vol. 13 (1992), pp. 1–27; A. Murray, 'Baldwin II and his
Nobles: Baronial Faction and Dissent in the Kingdom of Jerusalem,
1118–1134', *Nottingham Medieval Studies*, vol. 38 (1994), pp. 60–85.

76. Walter the Chancellor, pp. 88, 108; Ibn al-Qalanisi, pp. 160–61; Smail,
Crusading Warfare, pp. 179–81.

77. Walter the Chancellor, p. 78; Asbridge, 'The significance and causes of
the battle of the Field of Blood', pp. 301–16. There may have been some
truth to the accusations of sexual impropriety – even his supporter
Walter the Chancellor hinted at this misdemeanour – but otherwise,
Roger seems to have ruled, unchallenged, as a legitimate prince in his
own right. The notion that he had unlawfully deprived Bohemond II of
his inheritance was probably disseminated posthumously, both to
account for the offender's death and to validate the young prince-
designate's position. Unfortunately for Roger, the slur stuck and ever
since he has generally been painted as an ill-fated, grasping regent. On
attitudes towards Roger's status and moral probity see: Asbridge, *The
Creation of the Principality of Antioch*, pp. 139–43; T. Asbridge and S.
E. Edgington (trans.), *Walter the Chancellor's The Antiochene Wars*
(Aldershot, 1999), pp. 12–26.

78. Murray, *The Crusader Kingdom of Jerusalem*, pp. 135–46; H. E. Mayer,
'Jérusalem et Antioche au temps de Baudoin II', *Comptes-rendus de
l'Académie des Inscriptions et Belles-Lettres, Nov.–Déc. 1980* (Paris, 1980);
T. Asbridge, 'Alice of Antioch: a case study of female power in the
twelfth century', *The Experience of Crusading 2: Defining the Crusader
Kingdom*, ed. P. W. Edbury and J. P. Phillips (Cambridge, 2003), pp.
29–47.

79. '*Liber ad milites Templi de laude novae militiae*', *Sancti Bernardi Opera*,
vol. 3, ed. J. Leclercq and H. M. Rochais (Rome, 1963), pp. 205–39. For
a collection of primary sources relating to the Templars translated into
English see: M. Barber and K. Bate (trans.), *The Templars: Selected*

Sources Translated and Annotated (Manchester, 2002). On the history of Templars and Hospitallers see: M. Barber, *The New Knighthood. A History of the Order of the Templars* (Cambridge, 1994); H. Nicholson, *The Knights Templar* (London, 2001); J. S. C. Riley-Smith, *The Knights of St John in Jerusalem and Cyprus, 1050–1310* (London, 1967); H. Nicholson, *The Knights Hospitaller* (Woodbridge, 2001); A. Forey, *The Military Orders. From the Twelfth to the Early Fourteenth Centuries* (London, 1992). On castles in the crusader states during the twelfth century see: Smail, *Crusading Warfare*, pp. 204–50; H. Kennedy, *Crusader Castles* (Cambridge, 1994); R. Ellenblum, 'Three generations of Frankish castle-building in the Latin kingdom of Jerusalem', *Autour de la Première Croisade*, ed. M. Balard (Paris, 1996), pp. 517–51.

80. Lilie, *Byzantium and the Crusader States*, pp. 109–41; Harris, *Byzantium and the Crusades*, pp. 74–92.

81. William of Tyre, p. 656; H. E. Mayer, 'The Concordat of Nablus', *Journal of Ecclesiastical History*, vol. 33 (1982), pp. 531–43. On Outremer's relations with western Europe in the period see: J. P. Phillips, *Defenders of the Holy Land. Relations between the Latin West and East, 1119–87* (Oxford, 1996). On the progress and consequences of the dispute between King Fulk and Queen Melisende see: H. E. Mayer, 'Studies in the History of Queen Melisende of Jerusalem', *Dumbarton Oaks Papers*, vol. 26 (1972), pp. 93–183; H. E. Mayer, 'Angevins versus Normans: The New Men of King Fulk of Jerusalem', *Proceedings of the American Philosophical Society*, vol. 133 (1989), pp. 1–25; H. E. Mayer, 'The Wheel of Fortune: Seignorial Vicissitudes under Kings Fulk and Baldwin III of Jerusalem', *Speculum*, vol. 65 (1990), pp. 860–77; B. Hamilton, 'Women in the Crusader States. The Queens of Jerusalem (1100–1190)', *Medieval Women*, ed. D. Baker (*Studies in Church History, Subsidia*, 1) (1978), pp. 143–74; J. S. C. Riley-Smith, 'King Fulk of Jerusalem and "the Sultan of Babylon"', *Montjoie: Studies in Crusade History in Honour of Hans Eberhard Mayer*, ed. B. Z. Kedar, J. S. C. Riley-Smith and R. Hiestand (Aldershot, 1997), pp. 55–66.

82. Melisende Psalter, Egerton 1139, MS London, British Library; J. Folda, *The Art of the Crusaders in the Holy Land, 1098–1187* (Cambridge, 1995), pp. 137–63; L.-A. Hunt, 'Melisende Psalter', *The Crusades: An Encyclopaedia*, ed. A. Murray, vol. 3 (Santa Barbara, 2006), pp. 815–17. On crusader art in general see: J. Folda, *Crusader Art in the Twelfth Century* (Oxford, 1982); J. Folda, *The Nazareth Capitals and the Crusader Shrine of the Annunciation* (University Park, PA, 1986); J. Folda, *The Art of the Crusaders in the Holy Land, 1098–1187* (Cambridge, 1995); J. Folda, 'Art in the Latin East, 1098–1291', *The Oxford Illustrated History of the Crusades*, ed. J. S. C. Riley-Smith

(Oxford, 1995), pp. 141–59; J. Folda, 'Crusader Art. A multicultural phenomenon: Historiographical reflections', *Autour de la Première Croisade*, ed. M. Balard (Paris, 1996), pp. 609–15; J. Folda, *Crusader Art in the Holy Land, 1187–1291* (Cambridge, 2005); J. Folda, *Crusader Art: The Art of the Crusaders in the Holy Land, 1099–1291* (Aldershot, 2008); H. W. Hazard (ed.), *Art and Architecture of the Crusader States (History of the Crusades*, vol. 4) (Madison, Wis., 1977); L.-A. Hunt, 'Art and Colonialism: The Mosaics of the Church of the Nativity at Bethlehem and the Problem of Crusader Art', *Dumbarton Oaks Papers*, vol. 45 (1991), pp. 65–89; N. Kenaan-Kedar, 'Local Christian Art in Twelfth-century Jerusalem', *Israel Exploration Journal*, vol. 23 (1973), pp. 167–75, 221–9; B. Kühnel, *Crusader Art of the Twelfth Century* (Berlin, 1994); G. Kühnel, *Wall Painting in the Latin Kingdom of Jerusalem* (Berlin, 1988).

83 In the nineteenth and early twentieth centuries, the crusader states were commonly interpreted, in a positive light, as a form of proto-colonialism. Particularly among French scholars such as Emmanuel Rey, the forces of integration, adaptation and acculturation were emphasised, and Outremer was painted as a glorious Franco-Syrian nation. In contrast, by the mid-twentieth century the opposite viewpoint was being championed by the likes of the Israeli academic Joshua Prawer: the crusader states were presented as oppressive, intolerant colonial regimes in which Latin conquerors exploited the Levant for their own material benefit and that of their western European homelands, while staunchly maintaining their own Frankish identity through the imposition of an apartheid-like separation from the indigenous population. E. G. Rey, *Les Colonies Franques de Syrie au XIIe et XIIIe siècles* (Paris, 1883); J. Prawer, 'Colonisation activities in the Latin Kingdom of Jerusalem', *Revue Belge de Philologie et d'Histoire*, vol. 29 (1951), pp. 1063–1118; J. Prawer, *The Latin Kingdom of Jerusalem: European Colonialism in the Middle Ages* (London, 1972); J. Prawer, 'The Roots of Medieval Colonialism', *The Meeting of Two Worlds: Cultural Exchange between East and West during the Period of the Crusades*, ed. V. P. Goss (Kalamazoo, 1986), pp. 23–38. For the record of an illuminating symposium on this issue held in 1987 see: 'The Crusading kingdom of Jerusalem – The first European colonial society?', *The Horns of Hattin*, ed. B. Z. Kedar (Jerusalem, 1992), pp. 341–66. For more up-to-date overviews see: Jotischky, *Crusading and the Crusader States*, pp. 123–54; Ellenblum, *Crusader Castles and Modern Histories*, pp. 3–31.

84. Fulcher of Chartres, p. 748. In exceptional circumstances, Muslim nobles might even be granted land within a crusader state. One such figure, Abd al-Rahim, gained the friendship of Alan, lord of al-Atharib, after 1111, and was granted possession of a nearby village and served as

an administrator on the principality of Antioch's eastern frontier. R. Ellenblum, *Frankish Rural Settlement in the Latin Kingdom of Jerusalem* (Cambridge, 1998); H. E. Mayer, 'Latins, Muslims and Greeks in the Latin Kingdom of Jerusalem', *History*, vol. 63 (1978), pp. 175–92; B. Z. Kedar, 'The Subjected Muslims of the Frankish Levant', *Muslims under Latin Rule*, ed. J. M. Powell (Princeton, 1990), pp. 135–74; Asbridge, 'The "crusader" community at Antioch', pp. 313–16; J. S. C. Riley-Smith, 'The Survival in Latin Palestine of Muslim Administration', *The Eastern Mediterranean Lands in the Period of the Crusades*, ed. P. Holt (Warminster, 1977), pp. 9–22.

85. Usama ibn Munqidh, *The Book of Contemplation*, trans. P. M. Cobb (London, 2008), pp. 144, 147, 153. On Usama's life and work see: R. Irwin, 'Usamah ibn-Munqidh, an Arab-Syrian gentleman at the time of the crusades', *The Crusades and Their Sources: Essays Presented to Bernard Hamilton*, ed. J. France and W. G. Zajac (1998), pp. 71–87; P. M. Cobb, *Usama ibn Munqidh: Warrior-Poet of the Age of the Crusades* (Oxford, 2005); P. M. Cobb, 'Usama ibn Munqidh's *Book of the Staff*: Autobiographical and historical excerpts', *Al-Masaq*, vol. 17 (2005), pp. 109–23; P. M. Cobb, 'Usama ibn Munqidh's Kernels of Refinement (*Lubab al-Adab*): Autobiographical and historical excerpts', *Al-Masaq*, vol. 18 (2006); N. Christie, 'Just a bunch of dirty stories? Women in the memoirs of Usamah ibn Munqidh', *Eastward Bound: Travel and Travellers, 1050–1550*, ed. R. Allen (Manchester, 2004), pp. 71–87. Alongside this adoption of customs there appears to have been some adaptation of dress to suit the Levantine climate – including greater use of silk by the aristocracy and high clergy – but this was not universal. Frankish envoys from Outremer visiting the great Muslim leader Saladin in February 1193 were said to have scared the sultan's infant son to tears because of 'their shaven chins and their cropped heads and the unusual clothes they were wearing'. Baha al-Din Ibn Shaddad, *The Rare and Excellent History of Saladin*, trans. D. S. Richards (Aldershot, 2001), p. 239.

86. Ibn Jubayr, pp. 316–17, 321–2. It has to be noted, however, that Ibn Jubayr travelled through only a small corner of Outremer, and that this section of his journey took only a few weeks; so his testimony may not be wholly representative. It is also clear that he wrote his account in part to advocate fairer treatment for Muslim peasants living under Moorish rule in Spain, so he may even have sanitised his description of Latin lordship.

87. In 1978 Hans Mayer concluded that 'Muslims [in the kingdom of Jerusalem certainly] had no freedom of worship' (Mayer, 'Latins, Muslims and Greeks in the Latin Kingdom of Jerusalem', p. 186), but his analysis has since been rebutted convincingly (Kedar, 'The

Subjected Muslims of the Frankish Levant', pp. 138–9). Not all Muslims residing in Outremer were peasants or farmers: in Nablus, for example, Usama ibn Munqidh stayed at a Muslim-run inn. Nonetheless, some Muslim Hanbali peasant villagers living near Nablus (and within the lordship of Baldwin of Ibelin) decided to leave Frankish territory as refugees and resettle in Damascus in the 1150s. The Muslim chronicler Diya al-Din recorded that Baldwin increased the poll tax imposed on the villagers fourfold (from one to four dinars), and that 'he also used to mutilate their legs'. It is worth noting, however, that Hanbalis held particularly hard-line views regarding the Franks and even Diya al-Din acknowledged that the group's leader 'was the first to emigrate out of fear for his life and because he was unable to practise his religion'. J. Drory, 'Hanbalis of the Nablus region in the eleventh and twelfth centuries', *Asian and African Studies*, vol. 22 (1988), pp. 93–112; D. Talmon-Heller, 'Arabic sources on Muslim villagers under Frankish rule', *From Clermont to Jerusalem. The Crusades and Crusader Society, 1095–1500*, ed. A. Murray (Turnhout, 1998), pp. 103–17; D. Talmon-Heller, 'The Shaykh and the Community: Popular Hanbalite Islam in 12th–13th Century Jabal Nablus and Jabal Qasyun', *Studia Islamica*, vol. 79 (1994), pp. 103–20; D. Talmon-Heller, '"The Cited Tales of the Wondrous Doings of the Shaykhs of the Holy Land" by Diya' al-Din Abu 'Abd Allah Muhammad b. 'Abd al-Wahid al-Maqdisi (569/1173–643/1245): Text, Translation and Commentary', *Crusades*, vol. 1 (2002), pp. 111–54.

88. Fulcher of Chartres, pp. 636–7; Ibn al-Qalanisi, pp. 162–3, 246. Zangi also agreed an 'armistice' with Frankish Antioch that apparently allowed hundreds of 'Muslim merchants and men of Aleppo and traders' to operate in the Latin principality. This trading pact held until 1138, when it was broken by Prince Raymond (perhaps because of the arrival of the Byzantine imperial army in northern Syria). On trade and commerce in the crusader states see: E. Ashtor, *A Social and Economic History of the Near East in the Middle Ages* (London, 1976); J. H. Pryor, *Commerce, Shipping and Naval Warfare in the Medieval Mediterranean* (London, 1987); D. Jacoby, 'The Venetian privileges in the Latin kingdom of Jerusalem: Twelfth- and thirteenth-century interpretations and implementation', *Montjoie: Studies in Crusade History in Honour of Hans Eberhard Mayer*, ed. B. Z. Kedar, J. S. C. Riley-Smith and R. Hiestand (Aldershot, 1997), pp. 155–75. For a selection of articles by the same author see: D. Jacoby, *Studies on the Crusader States and on Venetian Expansion* (London, 1989); D. Jacoby, *Commercial Exchange across the Mediterranean* (Aldershot, 2005).

89. C. Burnett, 'Antioch as a link between Arabic and Latin culture in the twelfth and thirteenth centuries', *Occident et Proche-Orient: contacts*

scientifiques au temps des croisades, ed. I. Draelants, A. Tihon and B. van den Abeele (Louvain-la-Neuve, 2000), pp. 1–78. William of Tyre, the Latin historian of Outremer, was certainly intrigued by Islam. Around the 1170s he researched and wrote a detailed history of the Muslim world, but he probably could not read Persian or Arabic himself and had to rely on translators. Unfortunately, no manuscripts of this text have survived to the modern day – but this in itself may suggest that the work gained only a limited audience in the West. P. W. Edbury and J. G. Rowe, *William of Tyre: Historian of the Latin East* (Cambridge, 1988), pp. 23–4.

90. C. Burnett, 'Stephen, the disciple of philosophy, and the exchange of medical learning in Antioch', *Crusades*, vol. 5 (2006), pp. 113–29. Al-Majusi's *Royal Book* detailed a remarkable range of medical treatments, some practical even by modern standards, some staggeringly bizarre. The section 'On the adornment of the body' included advice on how to remove unwanted hair and deal with cracks in lips and hands, curbing the growth of breasts and testicles, and dealing with body odour. Elsewhere, the section 'About the regimen of travellers on land and sea' was a mine of information useful to pilgrims: heat-stroke could be alleviated by pouring cooled rosewater over the head; bodily parts affected by frostbite should be rubbed with oils and grey squirrel fur; and a cure for seasickness was a syrup made from sour grapes, pomegranate, mint, apple and tamarind. The suggestion that an infestation of lice could be resolved by rubbing the body down with a mercury poultice was not quite so judicious.

91. It is worth considering what this evidence actually reveals about Outremer in the twelfth century. Did the patrons who commissioned works expressly demand pieces that reflected the variegated culture of the East; did they employ Latin craftsmen who absorbed oriental styles and techniques, either through deliberate study or organic transmission? If so, then it might reasonably be suggested that a flourishing, immersive artistic culture was developing in the Frankish Levant. It is possible, however, that more practical considerations were also at play; that Latin patrons simply employed the best craftsmen available. Usama ibn Munqidh, pp. 145–6; S. Edgington, 'Administrative regulations for the Hospital of St John in Jerusalem dating from the 1180s', *Crusades*, vol. 4 (2005), pp. 21–37. On the Church of the Holy Sepulchre, crusader architecture and material culture in Outremer see: Folda, *The Art of the Crusaders*, pp. 175–245; A. Boas, *Crusader Archaeology: The Material Culture of the Latin East* (London, 1999); N. Kenaan-Kedar, 'The Figurative Western Lintel of the Church of the Holy Sepulchre in Jerusalem', *The Meeting of Two Worlds, Cultural Exchange between*

East and West during the Period of the Crusades, ed. V. P. Goss (Kalamazoo, 1986), pp. 123–32; N. Kenaan-Kedar, 'A Neglected Series of Crusader Sculpture: the ninety-six corbels of the Church of the Holy Sepulchre', *Israel Exploration Journal*, vol. 42 (1992), pp. 103–14; D. Pringle, 'Architecture in the Latin East', *The Oxford Illustrated History of the Crusades*, ed. J. S. C. Riley-Smith (Oxford, 1995), pp. 160–84; D. Pringle, *The Churches of the Latin Kingdom of Jerusalem*, 3 vols (Cambridge, 1993–2007).

92. B. Hamilton, 'Rebuilding Zion: the Holy Places of Jerusalem in the Twelfth Century', *Studies in Church History*, vol. 14 (1977), pp. 105–16; B. Hamilton, 'The Cistercians in the Crusader States', *Monastic Reform, Catharism and the Crusade* (1979), pp. 405–22; B. Hamilton, 'Ideals of Holiness: Crusaders, Contemplatives, and Mendicants', *International History Review*, vol. 17 (1995), pp. 693–712; A. Jotischky, *The Perfection of Solitude: Hermits and Monks in the Crusader States* (University Park, PA, 1995); A. Jotischky, 'Gerard of Nazareth, Mary Magdalene and Latin Relations with the Greek Orthodox Church in the Crusader East in the Twelfth Century', *Levant*, vol. 29 (1997), pp. 217–26; B. Z. Kedar, 'Gerard of Nazareth, a neglected twelfth-century writer of the Latin East', *Dumbarton Oaks Papers*, vol. 37 (1983), pp. 55–77; B. Z. Kedar, 'Multidirectional conversion in the Frankish Levant', *Varieties of Religious Conversion in the Middles Ages*, ed. J. Muldoon (1997), pp. 190–97; B. Z. Kedar, 'Latin and Oriental Christians in the Frankish Levant', *Sharing the Sacred: Contacts and Conflicts in the Religious History of the Holy Land*, ed. A. Kofsky and G. Stroumsa (1998), pp. 209–22; B. Z. Kedar, 'Convergences of Oriental Christian, Muslim and Frankish worshippers: the case of Saydnaya and the knights Templar', *The Crusades and the Military Orders*, ed. Z. Hunyadi and J. Laszlovszky (Budapest, 2001), pp. 89–100.

93 Even Ibn Jubayr – the source of so many revealing insights into trans-cultural encounters – peppered his testimony with the language of hate and prejudice: describing Baldwin IV of Jerusalem as 'the accursed king' and a 'pig', and characterising Acre as a stinking hotbed of 'unbelief and impiety' that he hoped God would destroy (pp. 316, 318). Hillenbrand, *The Crusades: Islamic Perspectives*, pp. 257–429.

94. C. Hillenbrand, 'Abominable acts: the career of Zengi', *The Second Crusade: Scope and Consequences*, ed. J. P. Phillips and M. Hoch (Manchester, 2001), pp. 111–32; Holt, *The Age of the Crusades*, pp. 38–42; H. Gibb, 'Zengi and the fall of Edessa', *A History of the Crusades*, vol. 1, ed. K. M. Setton and M. W. Baldwin (Philadelphia, 1958), pp. 449–62.

95. In 1140 Zangi gained mention of his name in the *khutba* (Friday prayer) as overlord of Damascus, but this was really an empty honorific.

William of Tyre, p. 684.

96. Matthew of Edessa (Continuation), p. 243; William of Tyre, p. 739; Bernard of Clairvaux, 'Epistolae', Sancti Bernardi Opera, vol. 8, ed. J. Leclercq and H. M. Rochais (Rome, 1977), pp. 314–15.

97. On the history and significance of assigning numbers to crusading expeditions see: Constable, 'The Historiography of the Crusades', pp. 16–17.

98. Calixtus II, Bullaire, ed. U. Roberts (Paris, 1891), vol. 2, pp. 266–7; D. Girgensohn, 'Das Pisaner Konzil von 1153 in der Überlieferung des Pisaner Konzils von 1409', Festschrift für Hermann Heimpel, vol. 2 (Göttingen, 1971), pp. 1099–100; Bernard of Clairvaux, 'Epistolae', p. 435.

99. For the text of Quantum praedecessores see: R. Grosse, 'Überlegungen zum kreuzzugeaufreuf Eugens III. von 1145/6. Mit einer Neueedition von JL 8876', Francia, vol. 18 (1991), pp. 85–92. On the history of the Second Crusade see: V. Berry, 'The Second Crusade', A History of the Crusades, vol. 1, ed. K. M. Setton and M. W. Baldwin (Philadelphia, 1958), pp. 463–511; G. Constable, 'The Second Crusade as Seen by Contemporaries', Traditio, vol. 9 (1953), pp. 213–79; M. Gervers (ed.), The Second Crusade and the Cistercians (New York, 1992); A. Grabois, 'Crusade of Louis VII: a Reconsideration', Crusade and Settlement, ed. P. W. Edbury (Cardiff, 1985), pp. 94–104; J. P. Phillips and M. Hoch (eds), The Second Crusade: Scope and Consequences (Manchester, 2001); J. P. Phillips, The Second Crusade: Extending the Frontiers of Christendom (London, 2007). The main primary sources for the Near Eastern element of the Second Crusade are: Odo of Deuil, De profectione Ludovici VII in Orientem, ed. and trans. V. G. Berry (New York, 1948); Otto of Freising, Gesta Frederici seu rectius Chronica, ed. G. Waitz, B. Simon and F.-J. Schmale, trans. A. Schmidt (Darmstadt, 1965); William of Tyre, pp. 718–70; John of Salisbury, Historia Pontificalis, ed. and trans. M. Chibnall (London, 1956), pp. 52–9; John Kinnamos, The Deeds of John and Manuel Comnenus, trans. C. M. Brand (New York, 1976), pp. 58–72; Niketas Choniates, O' City of Byzantium: Annals of Niketas Choniates (Detroit, 1984), pp. 35–42; Ibn al-Qalanisi, pp. 270–89; Ibn al-Athir, The Chronicle of Ibn al-Athir for the Crusading Period from al-Kamil fi'l-Ta'rikh, trans. D. S. Richards, vol. 2 (Aldershot, 2007), pp. 7–22; Sibt ibn al-Jauzi, 'The Mirror of the Times', Arab Historians of the Crusades, trans. F. Gabrieli, pp. 62–3; Michael the Syrian, Chronique de Michel le Syrien, patriarche jacobite d'Antioche (1166–1199), ed. and trans. J. B. Chabot, vol. 3 (Paris, 1905); Anonymous Syriac Chronicle, 'The First and Second Crusades from an Anonymous Syriac Chronicle', ed. and trans. A. S. Tritton and H. A. R.

Gibb, *Journal of the Royal Asiatic Society*, vol. 92 (1933), pp. 273–306.

100. On St Bernard and the Cistercians see: G. R. Evans, *Bernard of Clairvaux* (New York, 2000); C. H. Berman, *The Cistercian Evolution* (Philadelphia, 2000).

101. Odo of Deuil, pp. 8–9; Bernard of Clairvaux, '*Epistolae*', pp. 314–15, 435; Phillips, *The Second Crusade: Extending the Frontiers of Christendom*, pp. 61–79.

102. '*Vita Prima Sancti Bernardi*', *Patrologia Latina*, J. P. Migne, vol. 185 (Paris, 1855), col. 381; Tyerman, *God's War*, p. 280; J. Phillips, 'Papacy, empire and the Second Crusade', *The Second Crusade: Scope and Consequences*, ed. J. P. Phillips and M. Hoch (Manchester, 2001), pp. 15–31; G. A. Loud, 'Some reflections on the failure of the Second Crusade', *Crusades*, vol. 4 (2005), pp. 1–14. Despite Graham Loud's convincing refutation of the arguments posited by Jonathan Phillips in 2001, Phillips made a rather ill-advised attempt in 2007 to defend his suggestion that Pope Eugenius was involved in Conrad's recruitment. By contrast, Phillips' observations on the impact of memory and kinship upon recruitment are persuasive (Phillips, *The Second Crusade: Extending the Frontiers of Christendom*, pp. 25, 87–98, 99–103, 129–30).

103. 'Chevalier, Mult es Guariz', *The Crusades: A Reader*, ed. S. J. Allen and E. Amt (Peterborough, Ontario, 2003), pp. 213–14. For an introduction to crusader songs see: M. Routledge, 'Songs', *The Oxford Illustrated History of the Crusades*, ed. J. S. C. Riley-Smith (Oxford, 1995), pp. 91–111.

104. Helmold of Bosau, *Chronica Slavorum*, ed. and trans. H. Stoob (Darmstadt, 1963), pp. 216–17; Eugenius III, '*Epistolae et privilegia*', *Patrologia Latina*, J. P. Migne, vol. 180 (Paris, 1902), col. 1203–4; Constable, 'The Second Crusade as Seen by Contemporaries', pp. 213–79; A. Forey, 'The Second Crusade: Scope and Objectives', *Durham University Journal*, vol. 86 (1994), pp. 165–75; A. Forey, 'The siege of Lisbon and the Second Crusade', *Portuguese Studies*, vol. 20 (2004), pp. 1–13; Phillips, *The Second Crusade: Extending the Frontiers of Christendom*, pp. 136–67, 228–68.

105. Lilie, *Byzantium and the Crusader States*, pp. 142–69; Phillips, *Defenders of the Holy Land*, pp. 73–99; P. Magdalino, *The Empire of Manuel Komnenos, 1143–1180* (Cambridge, 1994).

106. Odo of Deuil, pp. 16–17.

107. Suger, '*Epistolae*', *Recueil des historiens des Gaules et de la France*, ed. M. Bouquet et al., vol. 15 (Paris, 1878), p. 496; William of Tyre, pp. 751–2.

PART II: THE RESPONSE OF ISLAM

1. Ibn al-Qalanisi, p. 266; Hillenbrand, *The Crusades: Islamic Perspectives*, pp. 112–16; Hillenbrand, 'Abominable acts: the career of Zengi', pp. 111–32; C. Hillenbrand, '*Jihad* propaganda in Syria from the time of the First Crusade until the death of Zengi: the evidence of monumental inscriptions', *The Frankish Wars and Their Influence on Palestine*, ed. K. Athamina and R. Heacock (Birzeit, 1994), pp. 60–69; H. Dajani-Shakeel, '*Jihad* in twelfth-century Arabic poetry', *Muslim World*, vol. 66 (1976), pp. 96–113; H. Dajani-Shakeel, '*Al-Quds*: Jerusalem in the consciousness of the counter-crusade', *The Meeting of Two Worlds*, ed. V. P. Goss (Kalamazoo, 1986), pp. 201–21.

2. Ibn al-Athir, vol. 1, p. 382; Hillenbrand, 'Abominable acts: the career of Zengi', p. 120.

3. Ibn al-Qalanisi, pp. 271–2; Ibn al-Athir, vol. 2, p. 222; William of Tyre, p. 956. On Nur al-Din's career see: H. Gibb, 'The career of Nur ad-Din', *A History of the Crusades*, vol. 1, ed. K. M. Setton and M. W. Baldwin (Philadelphia, 1958), pp. 513–27; N. Elisséeff, *Nur al-Din: un grand prince musulman de Syrie au temps des Croisades*, 3 vols (Damascus, 1967); Holt, *The Age of the Crusades*, pp. 42–52; Hillenbrand, *The Crusades: Islamic Perspectives*, pp. 117–41.

4. Ibn al-Qalanisi, p. 272; Ibn Jubayr, p. 260. In the centuries before the crusading era, Aleppo was ruled first by the Seleucids during the Hellenistic period (that followed Alexander the Great's conquests), and then prospered for six centuries under the Romans before falling to the Arabs in 637 CE, assuming something of a secondary role to Damascus. The city's fortunes were rejuvenated under the Iraqi Hamdanid dynasty (944–1003) and, when conquered by the Seljuq Turks in 1070, it stood as a bastion on the frontier with Byzantium.

5. Ibn al-Qalanisi, pp. 274–5; Michael the Syrian, vol. 3, p. 270; Matthew of Edessa, Continuation, pp. 244–5; Ibn al-Athir, vol. 2, p. 8.

6. Ibn al-Athir, vol. 1, p. 350; Ibn al-Qalanisi, pp. 280–81.

7. Ibn al-Qalanisi, pp. 281–2. The esteemed German historian Hans Mayer went so far as to describe the attack on Damascus as 'incredibly stupid' and even 'ridiculous' (Mayer, *The Crusades*, p. 103). On this debate see: M. Hoch, *Jerusalem, Damaskus und der Zweite Kreuzzug: Konstitutionelle Krise und äussere Sicherheit des Kreuzfahrerkönigreiches Jerusalem, AD 1126–54* (Frankfurt, 1993); M. Hoch, 'The choice of Damascus as the objective of the Second Crusade: A re-evaluation', *Autour de la Première Croisade*, ed. M. Balard (Paris, 1996), pp. 359–69; Phillips, *The Second Crusade: Extending the Frontiers of Christendom*, pp. 207–18.

8. Sibt ibn al-Jauzi, p. 62; Ibn al-Athir, vol. 2, p. 22; Ibn al-Qalanisi, p. 286; 'Die Urkunden Konrads III. und seines Sohnes Heinrich', ed. F. Hausmann, *Monumenta Germaniae Historica, Diplomata*, vol. 9 (Vienna, 1969), n. 197, p. 357; William of Tyre, pp. 760–70; A. Forey, 'The Failure of the Siege of Damascus in 1148', *Journal of Medieval History*, vol. 10 (1984), pp. 13–24; M. Hoch, 'The price of failure: The Second Crusade as a turning point in the history of the Latin East', *The Second Crusade: Scope and Consequences* (Manchester, 2001), pp. 180–200; Phillips, *The Second Crusade: Extending the Frontiers of Christendom*, pp. 218–27.

9. Ibn al-Athir, vol. 2, pp. 39–40; Lilie, *Byzantium and the Crusader States*, pp. 163–4.

10. Ibn al-Athir, vol. 2, pp. 1–4, 222–3. One source offering a modicum of balance was authored by Ibn al-Qalanisi (d. 1160), who wrote his *Damascus Chronicle* while living in that city during the mid-twelfth century, but even he ended up writing under Zangid rule. Ibn al-Qalanisi twice held the office of *ra'is* – leader of townspeople and head of the urban militia (Ibn al-Qalanisi, pp. 7–14). On the Arabic sources for this period see: F. Gabrieli, 'The Arabic historiography of the crusades', *Historians of the Middle East*, ed. B. Lewis and P. M. Holt (London, 1962), pp. 98–107; D. S. Richards, 'Ibn al-Athir and the later parts of the *Kamil*', *Medieval Historical Writing in the Christian and Islamic Worlds*, ed. D. O. Morgan (London, 1982), pp. 76–108; A. M. Eddé, 'Claude Cahen et les sources arabes des Croisades', *Arabica*, vol. 43 (1996), pp. 89–97.

11. For Sir Hamilton Gibb, the renowned British scholar of Arabic history, the change came in 1149. Gibb declared that this was 'the turning-point in [Nur al-Din's] own conception of his mission and in the history of Muslim Syria. In the eyes of all Islam he had become a champion of the faith, and he now consciously set himself to fulfil the duties of that role' (Gibb, 'The career of Nur ad-Din', p. 515). Just over a decade later, in 1967, Nikita Elisséeff published an influential three-volume biography of the 'great Muslim prince of Syria', refining this view. Elisséeff argued that it was only after 1154 that Nur al-Din truly was driven by authentic devotion to *jihad* and an overwhelming desire to reconquer Jerusalem (Elisséeff, *Nur al-Din*, II, p. 426). In 1991, Michael Köhler adopted a less sympathetic tone, suggesting that Nur al-Din was never truly dedicated to the struggle to reclaim the Holy City, but merely used *jihad* propaganda after 1157 to further his political aims (Köhler, *Allianzen und Verträge*, pp. 239, 277). On this issue see: Hillenbrand, *The Crusades: Islamic Perspectives*, pp. 132–41.

12. On the Battle of Inab see: Ibn al-Qalanisi, pp. 288–94; Ibn al-Athir, vol.

2, pp. 31–2; William of Tyre, pp. 770–74; John Kinnamos, p. 97; Matthew of Edessa, Continuation, p. 257; Michael the Syrian, vol. 3, pp. 288–9; Abu Shama, 'Le Livre des Deux Jardins', *RHC Or.* IV–V, pp. 61–4.

13. Ibn al-Athir, vol. 2, pp. 31–2, 36; Ibn al-Qalanisi, p. 295; Gibb, 'The career of Nur ad-Din', pp. 515–16; Holt, *The Age of the Crusades*, p. 44; Mayer, *The Crusades*, pp. 107–8; Richard, *The Crusades*, p. 171; Jotischky, *Crusading and the Crusader States*, p. 111.

14. The Zangid supporter Ibn al-Athir later argued that in the early 1150s 'Nur al-Din had no route to hinder [the Franks] because Damascus was an obstacle between [them]'. It was feared, so the chronicler asserted, that the Franks would soon occupy that ancient metropolis, because they were sucking it dry of wealth through hefty annual tribute payments that 'their agents used to enter the city and collect . . . from the population' (Ibn al-Athir, vol. 2, p. 71). Nur al-Din was only too aware of the power of these arguments and actively engaged in a propaganda war against Damascus, sponsoring the composition of poetry decrying the city's policy of allying with the Franks. On the kingdom of Jerusalem in the period see: Mayer, 'Studies in Queen Melisende', pp. 95–183; M. W. Baldwin, 'The Latin states under Baldwin III and Amalric I 1143–74', *A History of the Crusades*, vol. 1, ed. K. M. Setton and M. W. Baldwin (Philadelphia, 1958), pp. 528–62.

15. Ibn al-Qalanisi, pp. 296–327. Elisséeff echoed the view that Nur al-Din prioritised the Holy War after occupying Damascus, claiming that after 1154 the emir proceeded solely 'in the name of *jihad* against the crusaders and to help the revitalisation of Sunni Islam' (Elisséeff, *Nur al-Din*, II, p. 426). Hillenbrand, *The Crusades: Islamic Perspectives*, p. 134.

16. Ibn Jubayr, pp. 271–2, 279; R. Burns, *Damascus* (London, 2004), p. 169. Damascus developed around an oasis formed by a delta of the Barada River that flows out of the mountains of Lebanon. Muslims conquered the city in the seventh century CE, during the first rush of Arab-Islamic expansion, and it remained the capital of the Umayyad Empire and seat of the caliphate until 750.

17. Ibn al-Qalanisi, p. 340; B. Hamilton, 'The Elephant of Christ: Reynald of Châtillon', *Studies in Church History*, vol. 15 (1978), pp. 97–108.

18. William of Tyre, pp. 860–61; Phillips, *Defenders of the Holy Land*, pp. 100–39; Lilie, *Byzantium and the Crusader States*, pp. 163–87.

19. Ibn al-Athir, vol. 2, pp. 141–2; William of Tyre, pp. 873–4.

20. Ibn al-Athir, vol. 2, pp. 146–50; William of Tyre, pp. 874–7; Cahen, *La Syrie du Nord*, pp. 408–9.

21. Elsewhere in his realm, Nur al-Din promoted a similar building programme: in 1159 he sponsored the building of the *Madrasa al-*

Shu'aybiyya in Aleppo, one of forty-two Islamic teaching colleges built in the city during his rule, half of which enjoyed his personal patronage. Nur al-Din's pulpit survived intact for eight hundred years. But in 1969 it was destroyed by a fire lit by a fanatical Australian. Hillenbrand, *The Crusades: Islamic Perspectives*, pp. 118–67; D. S. Richards, 'A text of Imad al-Din on twelfth-century Frankish-Muslim relations', *Arabica*, vol. 25 (1978), pp. 202–4; D. S. Richards, 'Imad al-Din al-Isfahani: Administrator, litterateur and historian', *Crusaders and Muslims in Twelfth-Century Syria*, ed. M. Shatzmiller (Leiden, 1993), pp. 133–46; E. Sivan, 'The beginnings of the *Fada'il al-Quds* literature', *Israel Oriental Studies*, vol. 1 (1971), pp. 263–72; E. Sivan, 'Le caractère sacré de Jérusalem dans l'Islam aux XIIe–XIIIe siècles', *Studia Islamica*, vol. 27 (1967), pp. 149–82; N. Elisséeff, 'Les monuments de Nur al-Din', *Bulletin des Études Orientales*, vol. 12 (1949–51), pp. 5–43; N. Elisséeff, 'La titulaire de Nur al-Din d'après ses inscriptions', *Bulletin des Études Orientales*, vol. 14 (1952–4), pp. 155–96; I. Hasson, 'Muslim literature in praise of Jerusalem: *Fada'il Bayt al-Maqdis*', *The Jerusalem Cathedra* (Jerusalem, 1981), pp. 168–84; Y. Tabbaa, 'Monuments with a message: propagation of *jihad* under Nur al-Din', *The Meeting of Two Worlds*, ed. V. P. Goss (Kalamazoo, 1986), pp. 223–40.

22. Ibn al-Qalanisi, p. 303.
23. William of Tyre, p. 903; Ibn al-Athir, vol. 2, p. 62; C. F. Petry (ed.), *Cambridge History of Egypt: Islamic Egypt, 640–1517* (Cambridge, 1998); Y. Lev, *State and Society in Fatimid Egypt* (Leiden, 1991); Y. Lev, 'Regime, army and society in medieval Egypt, 9th–12th centuries', *War and Society in the Eastern Mediterranean, 7th–15th Centuries*, ed. Y. Lev (Leiden, 1997), pp. 115–52.
24. Ibn al-Athir, vol. 2, p. 138; William of Tyre, pp. 864–8. For the Latin perspective on the Egyptian campaigns of the 1160s see: Mayer, *The Crusades*, pp. 117–22; Phillips, *Defenders of the Holy Land*, pp. 140–67.
25. William of Tyre, p. 871; Ibn al-Athir, vol. 2, p. 144; M. C. Lyons and D. E. P. Jackson, *Saladin.The Politics of the Holy War* (Cambridge, 1979), pp. 6–9.
26. Ibn al-Athir, vol. 2, pp. 144, 163; William of Tyre, p. 922; Lyons and Jackson, *Saladin*, pp. 9–25; Smail, *Crusading Warfare*, pp. 183–5.
27. Ibn al-Athir, vol. 2, pp. 175, 177; Lyons and Jackson, *Saladin*, pp. 25–9.
28. Holt, *The Age of the Crusades*, pp. 48–52; Mayer, *The Crusades*, p. 122; Jotischky, *Crusading and the Crusader States*, pp. 115–16; Madden, *The New Concise History of the Crusades*, p. 68. On Saladin's rule in Egypt see: Y. Lev, *Saladin in Egypt* (Leiden, 1999); Lyons and Jackson, *Saladin*, pp. 31–69.
29. This colourful story makes a fine tale and, while it could be factual, it is recorded only in Ayyubid sources and thus remains uncorroborated.

It is possible that some of its details may have been fabricated to justify a clampdown on the Fatimid court. Lyons and Jackson, *Saladin*, pp. 33–4.

30. Ibn al-Athir, vol. 2, p. 180. On Outremer's relations with Byzantium and the West in this period see: J. L. La Monte, 'To What Extent was the Byzantine Emperor the Suzerain of the Latin Crusading States?', *Byzantion*, vol. 7 (1932), pp. 253–64; R. C. Smail, 'Relations between Latin Syria and the West, 1149–1187', *Transactions of the Royal Historical Society*, 5th series, vol. 19 (1969), pp. 1–20; Lilie, *Byzantium and the Crusader States*, pp. 198–209; Phillips, *Defenders of the Holy Land*, pp. 168–224.

31. One Arabic chronicler suggested that al-Adid was poisoned, but even if Saladin was indeed involved in engineering the caliph's rather timely death, a subtler form of assassination had been preferred to the traditional Egyptian bloodbath. Lyons and Jackson, *Saladin*, pp. 44–8.

32. Lyons and Jackson, *Saladin*, pp. 46–9, 61–5; Ibn al-Athir, vol. 2, pp. 197–200, 213–14.

33. Baha al-Din Ibn Shaddad, *The Rare and Excellent History of Saladin*, trans. D. S. Richards (Aldershot, 2001), p. 49.

34. Ibn al-Athir, vol. 2, pp. 221–2; William of Tyre, p. 956.

35. Baha al-Din, p. 28; Imad al-Din al-Isfahani, *Conquête de la Syrie et de la Palestine par Saladin*, trans. H. Massé (Paris, 1972); Ibn al-Athir, vol. 2, pp. 223–409; Abu Shama, 'Le Livre des Deux Jardins', IV, p. 159–V, p. 109; Gabrieli, *Arab Historians of the Crusades*, pp. 87–252; Lyons and Jackson, *Saladin*, pp. 435–6. On the sources for Saladin's life see: H. A. R. Gibb, 'The Arabic sources for the life of Saladin', *Speculum*, vol. 25.1 (1950), pp. 58–74; D. S. Richards, 'A consideration of two sources for the life of Saladin', *Journal of Semitic Studies*, vol. 25 (1980), pp. 46–65. On Saladin's career from 1174 onwards see: S. Lane-Poole, *Saladin and the Fall of the Kingdom of Jerusalem* (London, 1898); H. Gibb, 'Saladin', *A History of the Crusades*, vol. 1, ed. K. M. Setton and M. W. Baldwin (Philadelphia, 1958), pp. 563–89; H. A. R. Gibb, 'The armies of Saladin', *Studies in the Civilization of Islam*, ed. S. J. Shaw and W. R. Polk (London, 1962), pp. 74–90; H. A. R. Gibb, 'The Achievement of Saladin', *Studies in the Civilization of Islam*, ed. Shaw and Polk, pp. 91–107; H. A. R. Gibb, *The Life of Saladin* (Oxford, 2006); A. Ehrenkreutz, *Saladin* (Albany, 1972); Lyons and Jackson, *Saladin*, pp. 71–374; H. Möhring, 'Saladins Politik des Heiligen Krieges', *Der Islam*, vol. 61 (1984), pp. 322–6; H. Möhring, *Saladin: The Sultan and His Times 1138–1193*, trans. D. S. Bachrach (Baltimore, 2008); Hillenbrand, *The Crusades: Islamic Perspectives*, pp. 171–95. On the adoption of the title 'sultan' see: P. M. Holt, 'The sultan as idealised ruler: Ayyubid and Mamluk prototypes', *Suleyman the Magnificent and His Age*, ed. M.

Kunt and C. Woodhead (Harrow, 1995), pp. 122–37.

36. Lyons and Jackson, *Saladin*, pp. 73–4.

37. Lyons and Jackson, *Saladin*, pp. 79–84; Baha al-Din, p. 51; William of Tyre, p. 968.

38. Lyons and Jackson, *Saladin*, pp. 85–6.

39. The first truce was apparently concluded in secret with the count of Tripoli in spring 1175 (just before the first battle against the Aleppan–Mosuli coalition), to forestall the opening of a second front against the Christians. In July that same year, the sultan entered into a more public dialogue with a high-level diplomat from the kingdom of Jerusalem. Admittedly, Muslim and Latin sources seem to agree that Saladin got the better deal in these negotiations, promising to release some Frankish captives from Homs in return for firm assurances that there would be no moves to counter his campaigns against Aleppo. Lyons and Jackson, *Saladin*, pp. 86–110.

40. William of Tyre, pp. 953–4.

41. Lewis, *The Assassins*, pp. 116–17.

42. Lyons and Jackson, *Saladin*, p. 130; S. B. Edgington, 'The doves of war: the part played by carrier pigeons in the crusades', *Autour de la Première Croisade*, ed. M. Balard (Paris, 1996), pp. 167–76; D. Jacoby, 'The supply of war materials in Egypt in the crusader period', *Jerusalem Studies in Arabic and Islam*, vol. 25 (2001), pp. 102–32.

43. William of Tyre, pp. 961–2.

44. B. Hamilton, 'Baldwin the leper as war leader', *From Clermont to Jerusalem*, ed. A. V. Murray (Turnhout, 1998), pp. 119–30; B. Hamilton, *The Leper King and His Heirs: Baldwin IV and the Crusader Kingdom of Jerusalem* (2000).

45. William of Tyre, p. 961. Piers Mitchell published a useful study of Baldwin IV's leprosy as an appendix to Bernard Hamilton's biography of the leper king (Hamilton, *The Leper King*, pp. 245–58).

46. *Anonymi auctoris Chronicon ad AC 1234 pertinens*, ed. I. B. Chabot, trans. A. Abouna, 2 vols (Louvain, 1952–74), p. 141.

47. William of Tyre, p. 991; Ibn al-Athir, vol. 2, p. 253; Baha al-Din, p. 54; Lyons and Jackson, *Saladin*, pp. 121–6; Hamilton, *The Leper King*, pp. 132–6.

48. Lyons and Jackson, *Saladin*, pp. 130–33.

49. The excavation of the castle at Jacob's Ford, pioneered by Professor Ronnie Ellenblum of the Hebrew University of Jerusalem, represents a massive breakthrough in the field of crusader studies. This dig offers an astonishingly detailed glimpse of the crusading world – the equivalent of a freeze-frame image of the twelfth century – because Jacob's Ford is the first castle to be discovered as it was in 1179, with its slaughtered

garrison still within its walls. Many of the physical and material finds from the site can be dated with incredible precision to the morning of Thursday 29 August 1179, because they lay beneath buildings known to have burned and collapsed when the fortress fell. Somewhat ironically, the fact that the stronghold was incomplete actually adds to its archaeological value, because its remains provide an invaluable insight into the construction techniques of medieval castle builders. William of Tyre, p. 998; M. Barber, 'Frontier warfare in the Latin kingdom of Jerusalem: the campaign of Jacob's Ford, 1178–9', *The Crusades and Their Sources: Essay Presented to Bernard Hamilton*, ed. J. France and W. G. Zajac (Aldershot, 1998), pp. 9–22; R. Ellenblum, 'Frontier activities: the transformation of a Muslim sacred site into the Frankish castle of Vadum Jacob', *Crusades*, vol. 2 (2003), pp. 83–97; Hamilton, *The Leper King*, pp. 142–7; Lyons and Jackson, *Saladin*, pp. 133–43.

50 Lilie, *Byzantium and the Crusader States*, pp. 211–30. Not surprisingly, given the obvious advantages accrued by Saladin at al-Salih's death, some rumours circulated suggesting that Ayyubid agents had poisoned the Zangid heir. However, Saladin's initially slow and relatively inept reaction to al-Salih's demise (which allowed Imad al-Din Zangi to seize power in Aleppo) probably indicates that the sultan was not involved. Lyons and Jackson, *Saladin*, pp. 143–60.

51. Lyons and Jackson, *Saladin*, pp. 165–70; Hamilton, *The Leper King*, pp. 172–5.

52. Lyons and Jackson, *Saladin*, pp. 170–75; Hamilton, *The Leper King*, pp. 175–7.

53. William of Tyre, p. 1037.

54. This territorial expansion prompted Saladin to redistribute power and responsibility within his realm. His brother al-Adil, who since 1174 had governed Egypt, was summoned to Syria to take possession of Aleppo – perhaps with some suggestion that he might be able to pursue semi-independent expansion in the Jazira. The sultan's nephew Taqi al-Din was promoted, taking over responsibility for the Nile region. Saladin's other trusted nephew Farrukh-Shah had died of ill-health in late 1182; for the time being he was replaced in Damascus by Ibn al-Muqqadam. Lyons and Jackson, *Saladin*, p. 202.

55. It was once popular to suggest that the kingdom of Jerusalem's Latin nobility were, at this time, divided into two distinct and opposing factions, vying for power and influence as Baldwin IV's health and authority waned. On the one hand, it was suggested, were the 'Native Barons', including Count Raymond III of Tripoli and the Ibelins, who were familiar with the political and military realities of life in the Levant and thus willing to adopt a cautious approach in their dealings with

Saladin and Islam; and on the other, the aggressive upstart 'Court Party', including Guy of Lusignan and Sibylla, Agnes and Joscelin of Courtenay and Reynald of Châtillon, who were supposedly headstrong newcomers. The problem with this picture, enthusiastically presented by the likes of Steven Runciman in the 1950s, was that it bore little relation to reality. The make-up and policies of these 'factions' were never so clear-cut, nor were the members of the 'Court Party' ill-informed new arrivals – Reynald of Châtillon and the Courtenays, for example, were well-established figures in Outremer. This traditional image of endemic political factionalism in the 1180s is also suspect because it tends, uncritically, to incorporate the views and prejudices of William of Tyre, who was himself closely embroiled in events and an ardent supporter of Raymond of Tripoli. P. W. Edbury, 'Propaganda and Faction in the Kingdom of Jerusalem: The Background to Hattin', in *Crusaders and Muslims in Twelfth-Century Syria*, ed. M. Shatzmiller (1993), pp. 173–89; Hamilton, *The Leper King*, pp. 139–41, 144–5, 149–58.

56. Ernoul, *La Chronique d'Ernoul*, ed. L. de Mas Latrie (Paris, 1871), pp. 69–70; Abu Shama, p. 231; Lyons and Jackson, *Saladin*, pp. 185–8; Hamilton, 'The Elephant of Christ', pp. 103–4; Hamilton, *The Leper King*, pp. 179–85.

57. These included Raymond of Tripoli who, after the attempted coup of 1180, had spent two years in the county of Tripoli (effectively in a state of exile from Palestine) before being reconciled with Baldwin IV in spring 1182. William of Tyre, pp. 1048–9; R. C. Smail, 'The predicaments of Guy of Lusignan, 1183–87', *Outremer*, ed. B. Z. Kedar, H. E. Mayer and R. C. Smail (Jerusalem, 1982), pp. 159–76.

58. William of Tyre, p. 1058.

59. Ibn Jubayr also provided a detailed description of the commercial taxes imposed by both Muslims and Latins upon 'foreign' traders. Under normal circumstances Muslim merchants passing through either Transjordan or Galilee paid the Franks a toll. This raises the possibility that Saladin targeted these two regions, in part, to open them to commerce free from Christian levies. Ibn Jubayr, pp. 300–301.

60. Lyons and Jackson, *Saladin*, pp. 234–9. According to Ibn al-Athir (vol. 2, p. 309), Nasir al-Din 'drank wine, indulging excessively, and by the morning he was dead. Some have related – and the responsibility for this is theirs – that Saladin arranged for a man, called al-Nasih, who was from Damascus, to go to him, carouse with him and give him a poisoned drink. Come the morning, al-Nasih was nowhere to be seen.'

61. Lyons and Jackson, *Saladin*, pp. 239–41; Ehrenkreutz, *Saladin*, p. 237; Ellenblum, *Crusader Castles and Modern Histories*, pp. 275ff.

62. William of Tyre, p. 968. Around the same time, Ibn Jubayr (p. 311)

applauded Saladin's 'memorable deeds in the affairs of the world and of religion, and his zeal in waging holy war against the enemies of God', noting that 'his efforts for justice, and his stands in defence of Islamic lands are too numerous to count'. This evidence is significant because it was not coloured by later events.

63. Lyons and Jackson, *Saladin*, pp. 243–6.

64. P. Balog, *The Coinage of the Ayyubids* (London, 1980), p. 77; N. Jaspert, *The Crusades*, p. 73.

65. Ibn al-Athir, vol. 2, p. 320; Hillenbrand, *The Crusades: Islamic Perspectives*, pp. 175–85.

66. Imad al-Din, p. 22; C. P. Melville and M. C. Lyons, 'Saladin's Hattin Letter', *The Horns of Hattin*, ed. B. Z. Kedar (Jerusalem, 1992), pp. 208–12.

67. Imad al-Din, p. 23. On Saladin's defeat of the Franks see: *Libellus de expugnatione Terrae Sanctae per Saladinum, Radulphi de Coggeshall Chronicon Anglicanum*, ed. J. Stevenson, Rolls Series 66 (London, 1875), pp. 209–62. A translation of this text is available in: J. A. Brundage, *The Crusades: A Documentary Survey* (Milwaukee, 1962), pp. 153–63. On the Battle of Hattin see: Smail, *Crusading Warfare*, pp. 189–97; P. Herde, 'Die Kämpfe bei den Hörnen von Hittin und der Untergang des Kreuzritterheeres', *Römische Quartalschrift für christliche Altertumskunde und Kirchengeschichte*, vol. 61 (1966), pp. 1–50; Lyons and Jackson, *Saladin*, pp. 255–66; B. Z. Kedar, 'The Battle of Hattin revisited', *The Horns of Hattin*, ed. B. Z. Kedar (Jerusalem, 1992), pp. 190–207.

68. Imad al-Din, p. 25. My own experience of walking through Israel from the Lebanese border to Jerusalem in July 1999 made me realise just how vital water would be during a midsummer campaign. My water consumption peaked at an extraordinary seventeen litres per day! Luckily I had plenty of opportunities to fill my water bottles – in 1187 the Latins were not so fortunate.

69. Eracles, 'L'Estoire de Eracles empereur et la conqueste de la Terre d'Outremer', *RHC Occ.* II (Paris, 1859), pp. 62–5; Ibn al-Athir, vol. 2, p. 321; Imad al-Din, p. 26.

70. Imad al-Din, p. 26; Ibn al-Athir, vol. 2, p. 322.

71. Ibn al-Athir, vol. 2, p. 323; Imad al-Din, p. 26.

72. Ibn al-Athir, vol. 2, pp. 323–4. This famous episode was recorded in numerous Muslim and Christian accounts, with minor variations on Reynald's attitude (with some western sources claiming that he remained defiant to the last) and on whether Saladin killed Reynald with his own hand. For example, see: Melville and Lyons, 'Saladin's Hattin Letter', p. 212; Imad al-Din, pp. 27–8; Baha al-Din, pp. 74–5; *La Continuation de Guillaume de Tyr (1184–1197)*, ed. M. R. Morgan (Paris,

1982), pp. 55–6.

73. Imad al-Din, pp. 28–9; Ibn al-Athir, vol. 2, p. 324.

74. Imad al-Din, p. 31. A similarly horrific spectacle of clumsy butchery had been played out for the amusement of spectators in 1178. On that occasion Imad al-Din himself was asked by Saladin to participate in a mass execution of Christian captives, but turned aside when he discovered that his allotted victim was but a boy. Lyons and Jackson, *Saladin*, pp. 131–2. Melville and Lyons, 'Saladin's Hattin Letter', pp. 210, 212; Z. Gal, 'Saladin's Dome of Victory at the Horns of Hattin', *The Horns of Hattin*, ed. B. Z. Kedar (Jerusalem, 1992), pp. 213–15.

75. '*Historia de expeditione Friderici Imperatoris*', *Quellen zur Geschichte der Kreuzzuges Kaiser Friedrichs I*, ed. A. Chroust, *Monumenta Germaniae Historica: Scriptores rerum Germanicarum in usum scholarum* (Berlin, 1928), pp. 2–4; *La Continuation de Guillaume de Tyr*, pp. 56–8. Acre's immense wealth and valuable landed estates were distributed among three of Saladin's most prominent lieutenants – al-Afdal, Taqi al-Din and Isa – although even Imad al-Din later admitted that the sultan might have been better advised to retain at least some of this booty for his own treasury. On Saladin's strategy after Hattin see: W. J. Hamblin, 'Saladin and Muslim military theory', *The Horns of Hattin*, ed. B. Z. Kedar (Jerusalem, 1992), pp. 228–38.

76. Ibn al-Athir, vol. 2, p. 328; Runciman, *A History of the Crusades*, vol. 2, p. 471.

77. These hugely influential ideas can be traced through modern scholarship. In the 1950s Hamilton Gibb wrote that Jerusalem surrendered 'on terms that confirmed – if confirmation were needed – [Saladin's] reputation for limitless courtesy and generosity' ('Saladin', p. 586). Around the same time, Steven Runciman – whose three-volume account of the crusades often is marred by historical imprecision, but remains widely read – argued that the sultan specifically mentioned the events of 1099 in his dealings with Balian. Runciman added that 'Saladin, so long as his power was recognised, was ready to be generous, and he wished Jerusalem to suffer as little as possible', and the historian went on to contrast the 'humane' Muslims with the Franks who had 'waded through the blood of their victims' (*A History of the Crusades*, vol. 2, pp. 465–6). In 1988 these sentiments were echoed by Hans Mayer, affirming that Jerusalem's inhabitants 'had reason to be grateful that they were at the mercy of a merciful enemy' (*The Crusades*, pp. 135–6). And Carole Hillenbrand, in her benchmark study of the crusades from an Islamic perspective (1999), highlighted Saladin's magnanimity, arguing that for Muslim chroniclers 'the propaganda value of the bloodless conquest of Jerusalem by Saladin count[ed] for much more than the

temptation, soon overcome, to exact vengeance' (*The Crusades: Islamic Perspectives*, p. 316).

78. Imad al-Din, *Arab Historians of the Crusades*, pp. 156–8. Massé's text claimed at this point (p. 46, n. 2) that Imad al-Din's account was replicated by Abu Shama (even though this is not the case) and, therefore, Massé did not present this part of the text. For this reason the Gabrieli translation has been cited here. Baha al-Din, pp. 77–8; Lyons and Jackson, *Saladin*, pp. 273–6; Richard, *The Crusades*, p. 210. References to the precedent set by the First Crusade appear only in later sources: Ibn al-Athir, vol. 2, p. 332; *La Continuation de Guillaume de Tyr*, pp. 66–7.

79. Saladin may have sought to engineer the negotiated surrender of Jerusalem in early September while engaged in the siege of Ascalon, but the Franks refused. *La Continuation de Guillaume de Tyr*, pp. 61–3; Lyons and Jackson, *Saladin*, pp. 271–2.

80. Imad al-Din, *Arab Historians of the Crusades*, p. 158; Ibn al-Athir, vol. 2, pp. 333–4. The Hospital of Jerusalem also was permitted to stay open for one year, so as not to cause undue harm to its patients, after which point it was transformed into a college of Islamic law. In response to lobbying from Isa, Saladin agreed to allow 'eastern' Christians to remain in the Holy City if they accepted subject status and paid a ransom plus the customary poll tax owed by non-Muslims living under Islamic rule.

81. Lyons and Jackson, *Saladin*, pp. 275–6.

82. Hillenbrand, *The Crusades: Islamic Perspectives*, pp. 188–92, 286–91, 298–301, 317–19.

83. Ibn al-Athir, vol. 2, p. 335; Hillenbrand, *The Crusades: Islamic Perspectives*, p. 316.

PART III: THE TRIAL OF CHAMPIONS

1. The Third Crusade is the first expedition for which modern historians have access to full and detailed eyewitness sources from both Latin Christians and Muslims. Among the western observers was Ambroise, a Norman cleric who went on crusade with Richard the Lionheart and then, between 1194 and 1199, wrote an Old French epic verse poem recounting the expedition – *The History of the Holy War* – running to more than 12,000 lines. Ambroise's account seems to have been used by another crusader, Richard de Templo, in constructing his Latin narrative history of the crusade, the *Itinerarium Peregrinorum et Gesta Regis Ricardi* (the *Itinerary of the Pilgrims and Deeds of King Richard*). The narrative accounts, biographies and letters written by three highly

placed officials within Saladin's court – Imad al-Din, Baha al-Din and the *Qadi* al-Fadil – offer invaluable insights into the Muslim perspective on the crusade. They can also be usefully compared to the testimony of the Mosuli historian Ibn al-Athir, who was not a partisan of Saladin's Ayyubid dynasty. In spite of this abundance of primary source material, there is a surprising dearth of authoritative modern scholarship focusing specifically on the Third Crusade. Therefore, I have devoted the third part of this current work to the Third Crusade. The main primary sources for this expedition include: Baha al-Din, pp. 78–245; Imad al-Din, pp. 63–434; Ibn al-Athir, vol. 2, pp. 335–409; Abu Shama, 'Le Livre des Deux Jardins', *RHC Or.* IV, pp. 341–522, V, pp. 3–101; Ambroise, *The History of the Holy War: Ambroise's Estoire de la Guerre Sainte*, ed. and trans. M. Ailes and M. Barber, 2 vols (Woodbridge, 2003) (all the following references to Ambroise relate to the Old French verse edition in volume I). *Itinerarium Peregrinorum et Gesta Regis Ricardi, Chronicles and Memorials of the Reign of Richard I*, vol. 1, ed. W. Stubbs, Rolls Series 38 (London, 1864). For a translation and useful introduction to the complexities surrounding this text see: *Chronicle of the Third Crusade: A Translation of the Itinerarium Peregrinorum et Gesta Regis Ricardi*, trans. H. Nicholson (Aldershot, 1997). *La Continuation de Guillaume de Tyr*, pp. 76–158. For a translation of this text and a number of other related sources see: P. W. Edbury (trans.), *The Conquest of Jerusalem and the Third Crusade: Sources in Translation* (Aldershot, 1996). For further reading on these sources see: C. Hanley, 'Reading the past through the present: Ambroise, the minstrel of Reims and Jordan Fantosme', *Mediaevalia*, vol. 20 (2001), pp. 263–81; M. J. Ailes, 'Heroes of war: Ambroise's heroes of the Third Crusade', *Writing War: Medieval Literary Responses*, ed. F. Le Saux and C. Saunders (Woodbridge, 2004); P. W. Edbury, 'The Lyon *Eracles* and the Old French Continuations of William of Tyre', *Montjoie: Studies in Crusade History in Honour of Hans Eberhard Mayer*, ed. B. Z. Kedar, J. S. C. Riley-Smith and R. Hiestand (Aldershot, 1997), pp. 139–53. Secondary works that do shed light on the Third Crusade include: S. Painter, 'The Third Crusade: Richard the Lionhearted and Philip Augustus', *A History of the Crusades*, vol. 2, ed. K. M. Setton (Madison, 1969), pp. 45–85; Lyons and Jackson, *Saladin*, pp. 279–363; H. Möhring, *Saladin und der dritte Kreuzzug* (Wiesbaden, 1980); J. Gillingham, *Richard I* (New Haven and London, 1999); Tyerman, *God's War*, pp. 375–474.

2. 'Annales Herbipolenses', *Monumenta Germaniae Historica, Scriptores*, ed. G. H. Pertz et al., vol. 16 (Hanover, 1859), p. 3.

3. E. Haverkamp, *Medieval Germany, 1056–1273* (Oxford, 1988); E.

Hallam, *Capetian France, 987–1328*, 2nd edn (Harlow, 2001); W. L. Warren, *Henry II* (London, 1973); J. Gillingham, *The Angevin Empire*, 2nd edn (London, 2001).

4. *'Historia de expeditione Friderici Imperatoris'*, pp. 6–10. The text of *Audita Tremendi* is also translated in: Riley-Smith, *The Crusades: Idea and Reality*, pp. 63–7.

5. Gerald of Wales, *Journey through Wales*, trans. L. Thorpe (London, 1978), p. 204. On the preaching of the Third Crusade see: C. J. Tyerman, *England and the Crusades* (Chicago, 1988), pp. 59–75; Tyerman, *God's War*, pp. 376–99. According to Muslim testimony, Latin preachers in Europe also made use of tableau paintings depicting Muslim atrocities – including the desecration of the Holy Sepulchre – to incense audiences and spur recruitment. Baha al-Din, p. 125; Ibn al-Athir, vol. 2, p. 363. This notion is not corroborated in western sources.

6. Routledge, 'Songs', p. 99. Other poets expanded on these ideas. In particular, those not taking the cross were accused of cowardice and a reluctance to fight. In some circles it became common to humiliate non-crusaders by giving them 'wool and distaff', the tools for spinning, to suggest that they were fit only for women's work – a distant precursor to the white feather.

7. *Itinerarium Peregrinorum*, p. 33; Routledge, 'Songs', p. 108.

8. *Itinerarium Peregrinorum*, pp. 143–4.

9. Gillingham, *Richard I*, pp. 1–23. In 1786 the English historian David Hume derided Richard for neglecting England, but the tide of criticism really began with William Stubbs, who in 1867 described the Lionheart as 'a bad son, a bad husband, a selfish ruler and a vicious man' and 'a man of blood . . . too familiar with slaughter'. In France, René Grousset's work of 1936 endorsed this view, characterising Richard as a 'brutal and impolitic knight', while A. L. Poole's 1955 history of medieval England observed that 'he used England as a bank on which to draw and overdraw in order to finance his ambitious exploits elsewhere'. By 1974 the American academic James Brundage declared that Richard had been a 'peerlessly efficient killing machine . . . [but] in the council chamber he was a total loss', confidently concluding that he was 'certainly one of the worst rulers that England has ever had'. During the Victorian era, at least, this damning appraisal was at odds with the popular romanticisation of Richard's reign, promoted in works of fiction by the likes of Walter Scott. In the mid-nineteenth century a monumental bronze statue of the Lionheart astride his horse was erected outside the Houses of Parliament in London – a tribute to the 'great English hero' paid for by public subscription. Other recent academic studies of Richard I include: J. L. Nelson (ed.), *Richard Coeur*

de Lion in History and Myth (London, 1992); J. Gillingham, 'Richard I and the Science of War', *War and Government: Essays in Honour of J. O. Prestwich*, ed. J. Gillingham and J. C. Holt (Woodbridge, 1984), pp. 78–9; R. A. Turner and R. Heiser, *The Reign of Richard the Lionheart: Ruler of the Angevin Empire* (London, 2000); J. Flori, *Richard the Lionheart: Knight and King* (London, 2007). In addition to the evidence presented in Ambroise and the *Itinerarium Peregrinorum*, the main primary sources for Richard I's career and crusade include: Roger of Howden, *Gesta Regis Henrici II et Ricardi I*, 2 vols, ed. W. Stubbs, Rolls Series 49 (London, 1867); Roger of Howden, *Chronica*, vols 3 and 4, ed. W. Stubbs, Rolls Series 51 (London, 1870). On Howden see: J. Gillingham, 'Roger of Howden on Crusade', *Medieval Historical Writing in the Christian and Islamic Worlds*, ed. D. O. Morgan (London, 1982). Richard of Devizes, *The Chronicle of Richard of Devizes of the Time of Richard the First*, ed. and trans. J. T. Appleby (London, 1963); William of Newburgh, *Historia Rerum Anglicarum, Chronicles of the Reigns of Stephen, Henry II and Richard I*, vol. 1, ed. R. Howlett, Rolls Series 82 (London, 1884); Ralph of Coggeshall, *Chronicon Anglicanum*, ed. J. Stevenson, Rolls Series 66 (London, 1875); Ralph of Diceto, *Ymagines Historiarum, The Historical Works of Master Ralph of Diceto*, vol. 2, ed. W. Stubbs, Rolls Series 68 (London, 1876).

10. *Itinerarium Peregrinorum*, p. 143.

11. Roger of Howden, *Gesta*, vol. 2, pp. 29–30. On Philip Augustus see: J. Richard, 'Philippe Auguste, la croisade et le royaume', *La France de Philippe Auguste: Le temps des mutations*, ed. R.-H. Bautier (Paris, 1982), pp. 411–24; J. W. Baldwin, *The Government of Philip Augustus: Foundations of French Royal Power in the Middle Ages* (Berkeley and London, 1986); J. Bradbury, *Philip Augustus, King of France 1180–1223* (London, 1998); J. Flori, *Philippe Auguste, roi de France* (Paris, 2002).

12. On Frederick Barbarossa and his crusade see: P. Munz, *Frederick Barbarossa: A Study in Medieval Politics* (London, 1969); F. Opll, *Friedrich Barbarossa* (Darmstadt, 1990); E. Eickhoff, *Friedrich Barbarossa im Orient: Kreuzzug und Tod Friedrichs I* (Tübingen, 1977); R. Chazan, 'Emperor Frederick I, the Third Crusade and the Jews', *Viator*, vol. 8 (1977), pp. 83–93; Lilie, *Byzantium and the Crusader States*, pp. 230–42; H. E. Mayer, 'Der Brief Kaiser Friedrichs I an Saladin von Jahre 1188', *Deutsches Archiv für Erforschung des Mittelalters*, vol. 14 (1958), pp. 488–94; C. M. Brand, 'The Byzantines and Saladin, 1185–92: Opponents of the Third Crusade', *Speculum*, vol. 37 (1962), pp. 167–81. It was once thought that Frederick contacted Saladin himself at this point, but the two Latin letters purporting to be copies of their correspondence are now regarded as forgeries. However,

it is likely that Barbarrosa had established some form of diplomatic contact with Saladin in the 1170s.

13. Gerald of Wales, '*Liber de Principis Instructione*', *Giraldi Cambriensis Opera*, vol. 8, ed. G. F. Warner, Roll Series 21 (London, 1867), p. 296.

14. The tithe had an additional impact on recruitment because all those joining the crusade were exempt; as a result, Roger of Howden observed that 'all the rich men of [the Angevin realm], both clergy and laity, rushed in crowds to take the cross'. Roger of Howden, *Gesta*, vol. 2, pp. 32, 90.

15. Roger of Howden, *Gesta*, vol. 2, pp. 110–11. On the question of naval transport see: J. H. Pryor, *Geography, Technology and War: Studies in the Maritime History of the Mediterranean 649–1571* (Cambridge, 1987); J. H. Pryor, 'Transportation of horses by sea during the era of the crusades: eighth century to 1285 A.D., Part I: To c. 1225', *The Mariner's Mirror*, vol. 68 (1982), pp. 9–27, 103–25.

16. Roger of Howden, *Gesta*, vol. 2, pp. 151–5; Gillingham, *Richard I*, pp. 123–39.

17. Lyons and Jackson, *Saladin*, pp. 277, 280–81.

18. Ibn Jubayr, p. 319; D. Jacoby, 'Conrad, Marquis of Montferrat, and the kingdom of Jerusalem (1187–92)', *Dai feudi monferrini e dal Piemonte ai nuovi mondi oltre gli Oceani* (Alessandria, 1993), pp. 187–238.

19. Roger of Howden, *Gesta*, vol. 2, pp. 40–41; Ibn al-Athir, vol. 2, p. 337.

20. Imad al-Din, p. 108. For a discussion of Baha al-Din's career see Donald Richards' introduction to his own translation of Baha al-Din's *History of Saladin* (Baha al-Din, pp. 1–9). See also: Richards, 'A consideration of two sources for the life of Saladin', pp. 46–65.

21. Lyons and Jackson, *Saladin*, pp. 296, 307.

22. Ambroise, pp. 44–5, indicating that Guy was accompanied by 400 knights and 7,000 infantry. *Itinerarium Peregrinorum*, p. 61, noting around 700 knights and a total force of 9,000.

23. Ibn Jubayr, p. 318; *Itinerarium Peregrinorum*, pp. 75–6. On the siege of Acre and siege weaponry see: Rogers, *Latin Siege Warfare*, pp. 212–36, 251–73. On the geography of Acre see: D. Jacoby, 'Crusader Acre in the thirteenth century: Urban layout and topography', *Studia Medievali*, 3rd series, vol. 10 (1979), pp. 1–45; D. Jacoby, 'Montmusard, suburb of crusader Acre: The first stage of its development', *Montjoie: Studies in Crusade History in Honour of Hans Eberhard Mayer*, ed. B. Z. Kedar, J. S. C. Riley-Smith and R. Hiestand (Aldershot, 2000), pp. 205–17.

24. *La Continuation de Guillaume de Tyr*, p. 89; Ambroise, p. 45. Mount Toron was also known as Tell al-Musallabin or Tell al-Fukhkhar.

25. Abu Shama, pp. 412–15; *Itinerarium Peregrinorum*, p. 67.

26. Ambroise, p. 46; *Itinerarium Peregrinorum*, p. 67.

27. Imad al-Din, p. 172; Lyons and Jackson, *Saladin*, pp. 301–2.

28. Baha al-Din, p. 102–3; *Itinerarium Peregrinorum*, pp. 70, 72.

29. Baha al-Din, p. 104; Tyerman, *God's War*, pp. 353–4.

30. *Itinerarium Peregrinorum*, p. 73; Ibn al-Athir, vol. 2, p. 369.

31. Baha al-Din, pp. 107–8; Ambroise, p. 52.

32. Imad al-Din, *Arab Historians of the Crusades*, trans. F. Gabrieli, pp. 204–6; Baha al-Din, pp. 27, 100–101; Ambroise, pp. 55, 58; B. Z. Kedar, 'A Western survey of Saladin's forces at the siege of Acre', *Montjoie: Studies in Crusade History in Honour of Hans Eberhard Mayer*, ed. B. Z. Kedar, J. S. C. Riley-Smith and R. Hiestand (Aldershot, 2000), pp. 113–22.

33. Ambroise, pp. 52, 55; *Itinerarium Peregrinorum*, pp. 80, 82; Baha al-Din, pp. 124, 127.

34. Saladin was joined by his son al-Zahir of Aleppo and Keukburi of Harran on 4 May; by Imad al-Din Zanki, lord of Sinjar, on 29 May; by Sanjar Shah, lord of Jazirat, on 13 June; by Mosuli troops under 'Ala al-Din, son of Izz al-Din Masud, on 15 June; and by Zayn al-Din of Irbil in late June or early July. Baha al-Din, pp. 109–12.

35. Baha al-Din, p. 106. Lyons and Jackson, *Saladin*, pp. 312–13, 316. Saladin dispatched troops to Manbij, Kafartab, Baalbek, Shaizar, Aleppo and Hama. Among those who left the environs of Acre was al-Zahir.

36. Baha al-Din, p. 124.

37. Baha al-Din, pp. 110–11; Ibn al-Athir, vol. 2, p. 373; Ambroise, p. 55.

38. Baha al-Din, p. 123; Ambroise, p. 59.

39. *La Continuation de Guillaume de Tyr*, p. 105; *Itinerarium Peregrinorum*, p. 74; Ambroise, p. 56.

40. *La Continuation de Guillaume de Tyr*, p. 98; Ibn al-Athir, vol. 2, p. 375.

41. Ambroise, pp. 52, 61–3. Frederick of Swabia's presence, as a ruler largely bereft of manpower, raised uncomfortable questions about leadership and King Guy's status. Baha al-Din (pp. 128–31) believed that, soon after his arrival, Frederick spearheaded a new offensive against Acre, employing experimental military technology. This involved the medieval equivalent of a tank – a huge wheeled structure, clad with metal sheets, housing a massive iron-tipped battering ram. But Latin eyewitnesses gave all the credit for this initiative to the French and, in any case, once the 'tank' reached the foot of the walls it was quickly crushed and burned beneath a barrage of boulders and Greek fire.

42. Baha al-Din, pp. 130, 132; Lyons and Jackson, *Saladin*, pp. 318–20. Around the same time, work to shore up the defences of Alexandria and Damietta was proceeding apace in Egypt, and instructions were broadcast through Syria to store grain from the recent harvest in case of invasion.

43. Baha al-Din, pp. 140, 143; Lyons and Jackson, *Saladin*, pp. 323–4; *Itinerarium Peregrinorum*, pp. 127, 129–30; Ambroise, pp. 68–71, 73.

44. Baha al-Din, pp. 141–2; Lyons and Jackson, *Saladin*, pp. 323–5.

45. Ambroise, p. 38; Baha al-Din, p. 150.

46. *Itinerarium Peregrinorum*, pp. 204–5; P. W. Edbury, *The Kingdom of Cyprus and the Crusades, 1191–1374* (Cambridge, 1991), pp. 1–12.

47. Baha al-Din, pp. 145, 149–50; *La Continuation de Guillaume de Tyr*, pp. 109, 111.

48. Baha al-Din, p. 146; R. Heiser, 'The Royal *Familiares* of King Richard I', *Medieval Prosopography*, vol. 10 (1989), pp. 25–50.

49. *Itinerarium Peregrinorum*, pp. 206, 211; Baha al-Din, p. 155.

50. Baha al-Din, pp. 153, 156, 159.

51. *Itinerarium Peregrinorum*, p. 211; Ambroise, p. 74.

52. *Codice Diplomatico della repubblica di Genova*, ed. C. Imperiale di Sant' Angelo, 3 vols (Genoa, 1936–42), ii, n. 198, pp. 378–80; J. S. C. Riley-Smith, *The Feudal Nobility and the Kingdom of Jerusalem 1174–1277* (London, 1973), pp. 112–17.

53. *Itinerarium Peregrinorum*, pp. 218–19. The precise details of these siege weapons – their origins and exact designs – are unclear, because the contemporary sources are frustratingly imprecise. It is possible that some use was made of counterweight technology in these stone-throwers (traction-powered devices being the established norm). It is also possible that the technology and materials for these engines were brought from Europe, or that captured engineers contributed to their development. The dating of Philip's independent assault is problematic and it may have occurred at any point between 17 June and 1 July. Hugh of Burgundy, the Templars and Hospitallers all appear to have manned their own catapults. Richard does seem to have built a siege tower at Acre, protected by 'leather, cords and wood', but this structure does not appear to have played a major role in the assault.

54. Baha al-Din, pp. 155–7.

55. Baha al-Din, pp. 156–7; *Itinerarium Peregrinorum*, pp. 223–4.

56. Ambroise, p. 80; *Itinerarium Peregrinorum*, p. 225.

57. Ambroise, pp. 82, 84; Baha al-Din, p. 161; *La Continuation de Guillaume de Tyr*, p. 125.

58. Baha al-Din, p. 161; Imad al-Din, p. 318; *Itinerarium Peregrinorum*, p. 233; Ambroise, p. 84.

59. *Itinerarium Peregrinorum*, pp. 233–4.

60. Baha al-Din, p. 162; Lyons and Jackson, *Saladin*, p. 331; Gillingham, *Richard I*, p. 162; Pryor, *Geography, Technology and War*, pp. 125–30.

61. Ambroise, p. 85; Rigord, '*Gesta Philippi Augusti*', *Oeuvres de Rigord et de Guillaume le Breton*, ed. H. F. Delaborde, vol. 1 (Paris, 1882), pp.

116–17; Howden, *Gesta*, vol. 2, pp. 181–3; Gillingham, *Richard I*, p. 166.

62. '*Epistolae Cantuarienses*', *Chronicles and Memorials of the Reign of Richard I*, ed. W. Stubbs, vol. 2, Rolls Series 88 (London, 1865), p. 347.

63. Baha al-Din, pp. 164–5; Imad al-Din, p. 330; Ibn al-Athir, vol. 2, p. 390; Lyons and Jackson, *Saladin*, pp. 331–3.

64. Howden, *Chronica*, vol. 3, pp. 127, 130–31; Howden, *Gesta*, vol. 2, pp. 187, 189; Ambroise, pp. 87–9; *Itinerarium Peregrinorum*, pp. 240–43; *La Continuation de Guillaume de Tyr*, pp. 127–9; '*Historia de expeditione Friderici Imperatoris*', p. 99; R. Grousset, *Histoire des Croisades*, 3 vols (Paris, 1936), vol. 3, pp. 61–2; Gillingham, *Richard I*, pp. 166–71.

65. Richard also had the significant advantage of enjoying close relations with the leaders of the two main Military Orders. Robert of Sablé, who was appointed to the vacant post of master of the Templars in 1191, was one of the Lionheart's leading vassals from the Sarthe valley and had served as one of five fleet commanders during the journey to the Levant. Garnier of Nablus, who was elected as Hospitaller master in late 1189 or early 1190, was the former prior of England and grand commander of France. He travelled to the Near East with Richard's contingent.

66. Smail, *Crusading Warfare*, p. 163; Gillingham, *Richard I*, p. 174; J. F. Verbruggen, *The Art of Warfare in Western Europe during the Middle Ages* (Woodbridge, 1997), pp. 232–9; Ambroise, pp. 91–2.

67. Ambroise, p. 92.

68. Baha al-Din, p. 170; Ambroise, p. 93.

69. Ambroise, p. 94; Baha al-Din, p. 170.

70. Ambroise, p. 96; *Itinerarium Peregrinorum*, pp. 253, 258–9; Baha al-Din, p. 171.

71. Ambroise, p. 97; Baha al-Din, pp. 171–2.

72. Baha al-Din, pp. 172–3; Ambroise, p. 98; Lyons and Jackson, *Saladin*, p. 336.

73. Ambroise, pp. 99–107; *Itinerarium Peregrinorum*, pp. 260–80; Howden, *Chronica*, vol. 3, pp. 130–33; Baha al-Din, pp. 174–6; Imad al-Din, p. 344.

74. Ambroise, pp. 100–101, 103.

75. *Itinerarium Peregrinorum*, p. 264; Howden, *Chronica*, vol. 3, p. 131; Baha al-Din, p. 175.

76. *Itinerarium Peregrinorum*, pp. 268–9; Ambroise, p. 104.

77. *Itinerarium Peregrinorum*, p. 270; Howden, *Chronica*, vol. 3, pp. 129–31. Richard authored another letter on that same day (this time addressed generally to the people of his realm) which had even less to say about the battle, commenting simply that 'as we were nearing Arsuf Saladin came swooping down upon us'.

78. *Itinerarium Peregrinorum*, pp. 274–7; Ambroise, pp. 107–9. Richard I

described James of Avesnes as the 'best of men whose merits had made him dear to the whole army' and as the 'pillar' of the crusade (Howden, *Chronica*, vol. 3, pp. 129–31). Ambroise recalled the circumstances of James' death, noting that 'there were some who did not come to his rescue, which gave rise to much talk; this was one of the barons of France, they said, the count of Dreux, he and his men. I have heard so many speak ill of this that the history cannot deny it.' Unfortunately, no further explanation was offered of Robert of Dreux's failure to help James.

79. Flori, *Richard the Lionheart*, pp. 137–8. Many historians have expressed similar views, suggesting that Richard actively sought battle at Arsuf. These include: Gillingham (*Richard I*, pp. 173–8) who acknowledged that his account of Arsuf was based on Ambroise's testimony and described the battle as the 'height of Richard's fame', characterising the king's handling of the encounter as 'masterful'; Verbruggen (*The Art of Warfare*, p. 232) who described Arsuf as 'the last great triumph of the Christians in the Near East'; and S. Runciman ('The kingdom of Acre and the later crusades', *A History of the Crusades*, vol. 3 (Cambridge, 1954), p. 57) who applauded the Lionheart's 'superb generalship'. Tyerman (*God's War*, pp. 458–9) downplayed the importance of the battle, but nonetheless maintained that Richard wanted to engage Saladin in combat and launch a heavy cavalry charge. Others, like J. P. Phillips (*The Crusades 1095–1197* (London, 2002), pp. 146, 151), praised Richard's 'brilliant generalship at Arsuf', while ignoring the question of whether or not the king deliberately sought battle. Smail (*Crusading Warfare*, p. 163) did describe Arsuf as a natural event that was merely part of the process of a fighting march, but still believed that Richard had planned the crusader charge (pp. 128–9).

80. Baha al-Din, pp. 175–7; Lyons and Jackson, *Saladin*, pp. 338–9.

81. Baha al-Din, p. 178; Lyons and Jackson, *Saladin*, pp. 338–42.

82. *Itinerarium Peregrinorum*, p. 284; Ambroise, p. 114. There can be little doubt that Richard was contemplating an Egyptian campaign from that autumn onwards, as letters to the Genoese dating from October 1191 refer to plans to 'hasten with all our forces into Egypt' the following summer 'for the advantage' of the Holy Land. *Codice Diplomatico della repubblica di Genova*, vol. 3, pp. 19–21. Richard showed a deft diplomatic touch in managing to curry the support of the Genoese, while still maintaining the backing of his established allies, the Pisans. Favreau-Lilie, *Die Italiener im Heiligen Land*, pp. 288–93.

83. *Itinerarium Peregrinorum*, p. 293; Ambroise, pp. 118–19; Gillingham, 'Richard I and the Science of War', pp. 89–90; D. Pringle, 'Templar castles between Jaffa and Jerusalem', *The Military Orders*, vol. 2, ed. H.

Nicholson (Aldershot, 1998), pp. 89–109.

84. Baha al-Din, p. 179.

85. Baha al-Din, pp. 185–8; Imad al-Din, pp. 349–51. Gillingham, *Richard I*, pp. 183–5; Lyons and Jackson, *Saladin*, pp. 342–3. The Old French Continuation of William of Tyre (*La Continuation de Guillaume de Tyr*, p. 151) mentioned the proposed union between al-Adil and Joanne, but this text (also known as the Lyon *Eracles*) originated in the mid-thirteenth century. The reason for Joanne's refusal is unclear. Baha al-Din recorded that she flew into a rage when Richard finally presented his plan to her. Imad al-Din, however, believed that she had been willing to enter into such a union, but had been compelled to refuse by the Latin clergy.

86. Baha al-Din, pp. 193–5; Imad al-Din, pp. 353–4; Ibn al-Athir, vol. 2, p. 392; *Itinerarium Peregrinorum*, p. 296; Ambroise, p. 120. Imad al-Din saw Richard's approaches as duplicitous. Baha al-Din, meanwhile, argued that Saladin's real 'aim was to undermine the peace talks'. He recorded a personal conversation in which the sultan emphasised that peace would not end the danger to Islam. Predicting the collapse of Muslim unity after his death and a resurgence in Frankish power, Saladin apparently stated: 'Our best course is to keep on with the *jihad* until we expel them from the coast or die ourselves.' Baha al-Din concluded that 'this was his own view and it was only against his will that he was persuaded to make peace'. However, this was probably propaganda designed to maintain Saladin's image as an undefeated *mujahid*.

87. Baha al-Din, pp. 194–6.

88. Ambroise, pp. 123–4; *Itinerarium Peregrinorum*, p. 304.

89. *Itinerarium Peregrinorum*, p. 305; Ambroise, p. 126; Mayer, *The Crusades*, p. 148; Gillingham, *Richard I*, p. 191; Phillips, *The Crusades*, p. 151.

90. Ambroise, p. 126; Ibn al-Athir, vol. 2, p. 394.

91. *Itinerarium Peregrinorum*, p. 323; D. Pringle, 'King Richard I and the walls of Ascalon', *Palestine Exploration Quarterly*, vol. 116 (1984), pp. 133–47.

92. Baha al-Din, p. 200.

93. *La Continuation de Guillaume de Tyr*, p. 141. Richard certainly struggled to clear himself of blame and suspicion, his guilt being widely reported in the courts of Europe. Eventually his supporters devised a solution that exonerated the Lionheart – producing a letter in 1195, purportedly from the Old Man Sinan himself (but almost certainly a forgery), affirming that the Assassins had acted because of a historic grudge against the marquis. Gillingham, *Richard I*, pp. 199–201.

94. *Itinerarium Peregrinorum*, p. 359; Ambroise, p. 153.

95. Baha al-Din, pp. 199–202; Lyons and Jackson, *Saladin*, pp. 346–8.

96. Ambroise, p. 153.

97. *Itinerarium Peregrinorum*, p. 390; Baha al-Din, pp. 208–9.

98. Baha al-Din, pp. 209–12.

99. Ambroise, pp. 163–5; *Itinerarium Peregrinorum*, pp. 379–82.

100. *Itinerarium Peregrinorum*, p. 393; Ambroise, p. 172. Many Latin Christian contemporaries were dismayed by this second retreat. Eyewitnesses, like Ambroise, clearly acknowledged that it was King Richard who foiled the attempt to besiege Jerusalem. Back in the West, however, other chroniclers presented a different version of events, exculpating the Lionheart of blame. Roger of Howden (*Chronica*, vol. 3, p. 183) actually recorded that Richard had been determined to capture the Holy City, but was stymied by the French, who were reluctant to participate because the king of France had ordered them to return to Europe. Ralph of Coggeshall (pp. 38–40), meanwhile, affirmed that Richard had been about to lead the army on to Jerusalem when Hugh of Burgundy, the Templars and the French refused to fight, fearing that Philip Augustus would be angry with them if they helped the Angevin king capture the Holy City. Ralph added that it was discovered later that Hugh had shamefully entered into a secret alliance with Saladin. Ironically, the notion that the French had foiled the Lionheart's attempts to conquer Jerusalem stuck and, by the mid-thirteenth century, had become embedded in popular memory. Gillingham, *Richard I*, pp. 208–10; Lyons and Jackson, *Saladin*, pp. 353–4. M. Markowski ('Richard the Lionheart: Bad king, bad crusader', *Journal of Medieval History*, vol. 23 (1997), pp. 351–65) criticised Richard's conduct during the Third Crusade, branding him 'a failure as a crusade leader', but on rather different grounds – namely that 'any good crusade leader should have done what the army expected' by launching an assault on Jerusalem whether it was militarily viable or not.

101. *Itinerarium Peregrinorum*, p. 422; Baha al-Din, pp. 223, 225–6. The most influential of the Lionheart's new allies were: al-Mashtub – the Kurdish emir who had served Saladin since 1169, commanded Acre's garrison in 1191 and recently (and perhaps deliberately) had been released by Richard; and another of Saladin's field commanders, Badr al-Din Dildirim al-Yaruqi. Both served as mediators and negotiators through the summer of 1192.

102. Baha al-Din, p. 231; Imad al-Din, pp. 388–91. On the consequences of this accord see: J. H. Niermann, 'Levantine peace following the Third Crusade: a new dimension in Frankish-Muslim relations', *Muslim*

World, vol. 65 (1975), pp. 107–18.

103. Baha al-Din, pp. 235, 239, 243.

104. Hillenbrand, *The Crusades: Islamic Perspectives*, p. 195; Ibn al-Athir, vol. 2, pp. 408–9. See also: Lyons and Jackson, *Saladin*, pp. 361–74; Möhring, *Saladin: The Sultan and his Times*, pp. 88–104.

105. On Richard I's later career see: Gillingham, *Richard I*, pp. 222–348. On the legends surrounding Richard's life see: B. B. Broughton, *The Legends of King Richard I (The Hague*, 1966).

PART IV: THE STRUGGLE FOR SURVIVAL

1. Morris, *Papal Monarchy*, pp. 358–86, 452–62, 478–89; B. Z. Kedar, *Crusade and Mission. European Approaches towards the Muslims* (Princeton, 1984); R. I. Moore, *The Formation of a Persecuting Society. Power and Deviance in Western Europe, 950–1250*, 2nd edn (Oxford, 2007); M. D. Lambert, *Medieval Heresy: Popular Movements from the Gregorian Reform to the Reformation*, 3rd edn (Oxford, 2002); C. H. Lawrence, *The Friars: The Impact of the Early Mendicant Movement on Western Society* (London, 1994).

2. H. Roscher, *Innocenz III und die Kreuzzüge* (Göttingen, 1969); H. Tillman, *Pope Innocent III* (Amsterdam, 1980); J. Sayers, *Innocent III: Leader of Europe* (London, 1994); B. Bolton, *Innocent III: Studies on Papal Authority and Pastoral Care* (Aldershot, 1995); J. C. Moore, *Pope Innocent III: To Root Up and to Plant* (Leiden, 2003); J. M. Powell (ed.), *Pope Innocent III: Vicar of Christ or Lord of the World?* (Washington, DC, 1994); Morris, *Papal Monarchy*, pp. 417–51. Henry VI died before he could participate in a planned crusade to the Holy Land. Nonetheless, a number of German crusaders did fight in the Near East in 1197–8. C. Naumann, *Die Kreuzzug Kaiser Heinrichs VI* (Frankfurt, 1994).

3. Innocent III, *Die Register Innocenz' III*, ed. O. Hageneder and A. Haidaicher, vol. 1 (Graz, 1964), p. 503.

4. M. Angold, 'The road to 1204: the Byzantine background to the Fourth Crusade', *Journal of Medieval History*, vol. 25 (1999), pp. 257–68; M. Angold, *The Fourth Crusade: Event and Context* (Harlow, 2003); C. M. Brand, 'The Fourth Crusade: Some recent interpretations', *Mediaevalia et Humanistica*, vol. 12 (1984), pp. 33–45. Harris, *Byzantium and the Crusades*, pp. 145–62; J. Pryor, 'The Venetian fleet for the Fourth Crusade and the diversion of the crusade to Constantinople', *The Experience of Crusading: Western Approaches*, ed. M. Bull and N. Housley (Cambridge, 2003), pp. 103–23; D. Queller and T. F. Madden, *The Fourth Crusade: The Conquest of Constantinople, 1201–1204*, 2nd

edn (Philadelphia, 1997).

5. J. R. Strayer, *The Albigensian Crusades* (Ann Arbor, 1992); M. D. Costen, *The Cathars and the Albigensian Crusade* (Manchester, 1997); M. Barber, *The Cathars: Dualist Heretics in Languedoc in the High Middle Ages* (London, 2000); G. Dickson, *The Children's Crusade: Medieval History, Modern Mythistory* (Basingstoke, 2008).

6. J. M. Powell, *Anatomy of a Crusade 1213–1221* (Philadelphia, 1986), pp. 1–50.

7. James of Vitry, *Lettres*, ed. R. B. C. Huygens (Leiden, 1960), pp. 73–4, 82; James of Vitry, 'Historia Orientalis', *Libri duo quorum prior Orientalis . . . inscribitur*, ed. F. Moschus (Farnborough, 1971), pp. 1–258; James of Vitry, *Historia Occidentalis*, ed. J. Hinnebusch (Freiburg, 1972); C. Maier, *Crusade Propaganda and Ideology: Model Sermons for the Preaching of the Cross* (Cambridge, 2000).

8. On the crusader states in the first half of the thirteenth century see: Mayer, *The Crusades*, pp. 239–59; J. S. C. Riley-Smith, *The Feudal Nobility and the Kingdom of Jerusalem, 1174–1277* (London, 1973); P. W. Edbury, *John of Ibelin and the Kingdom of Jerusalem* (Woodbridge, 1997); Cahen, *La Syrie du Nord*, pp. 579–652.

9. On the Ayyubid world after Saladin see: Holt, *The Age of the Crusades*, pp. 60–66; Hillenbrand, *The Crusades: Islamic Perspectives*, pp. 195–225; R. S. Humphreys, *From Saladin to the Mongols: The Ayyubids of Damascus 1193–1260* (Albany, 1977); R. S. Humphreys, 'Ayyubids, Mamluks and the Latin East in the thirteenth century', *Mamluk Studies Review*, vol. 2 (1998), pp. 1–18; E. Sivan, 'Notes sur la situation des Chrétiens à l'époque Ayyubide', *Revue de l'Histoire des Religions*, vol. 172 (1967), pp. 117–30; A.-M. Eddé, *La principauté ayyoubide d'Alep (579/1183–658/1260)* (Stuttgart, 1999).

10. In broad terms, the common pattern through all three orders was to have a division between full knights, who were expected to have between three and four horses; sergeants, the less well-equipped subordinates to knights; and priest-brothers, the ordained clerics not involved in fighting, who were responsible for overseeing the spiritual wellbeing of the brother knights. It was also usually possible to enter orders on a temporary basis for set period, such as one year. A. Forey, 'The Military Orders, 1120–1312', *The Oxford Illustrated History of the Crusades*, ed. J. S. C. Riley-Smith (Oxford, 1995), pp. 184–216; J. Upton-Ward (trans.), *The Rule of the Templars* (Woodbridge, 1992).

11. P. Deschamps, 'Le Crac des Chevaliers', *Les Châteaux des Croisés en Terre Sainte*, vol. 1 (Paris, 1934); Kennedy, *Crusader Castles*, pp. 98–179; C. Marshall, *Warfare in the Latin East, 1192–1291* (Cambridge, 1992).

12. James of Vitry, *Lettres*, pp. 87–8; D. Jacoby, 'Aspects of everyday life in

Frankish Acre', *Crusades*, vol. 4 (2005), pp. 73–105; D. Abulafia, 'The role of trade in Muslim–Christian contact during the Middle Ages', *Arab Influence in Medieval Europe*, ed. D. A. Agius and R. Hitchcock (Reading, 1994), pp. 1–24; D. Abulafia, 'Trade and crusade, 1050–1250', *Cross-cultural Convergences in the Crusader Period*, ed. M. Goodich, S. Menache and S. Schein (New York, 1995), pp. 1–20.

13. D. Abulafia, *Frederick II: A Medieval Emperor* (London, 1988); W. Stürner, *Friedrich II*, 2 vols (Darmstadt, 1994–2000).

14. James of Vitry, *Lettres*, p. 102. On the Fifth Crusade see: Powell, *Anatomy of a Crusade*, pp. 51–204; J. Donavan, *Pelagius and the Fifth Crusade* (Philadelphia, 1950); T. C. Van Cleve, 'The Fifth Crusade', *A History of the Crusades*, vol. 2, ed. K. M. Setton (Madison, 1969), pp. 377–428.

15. Oliver of Paderborn, 'The Capture of Damietta', *Christian Society and the Crusades 1198–1229*, ed. E. Peters, trans. J. J. Gavigan (Philadelphia, 1971), pp. 65, 70, 88.

16. Mayer, *The Crusades*, p. 223; Oliver of Paderborn, p. 72; James of Vitry, *Lettres*, p. 116.

17. James of Vitry, *Lettres*, p. 118.

18. Oliver of Paderborn, p. 88.

19. J. M. Powell, 'San Francesco d'Assisi e la Quinta Crociata: Una Missione di Pace', *Schede Medievali*, vol. 4 (1983), pp. 69–77; Powell, *Anatomy of a Crusade*, pp. 178–9.

20. Powell, *Anatomy of a Crusade*, pp. 195–204.

21. Abulafia, *Frederick II*, pp. 251–89; F. Gabrieli, 'Frederick II and Muslim culture', *East and West* (1958), pp. 53–61; J. M. Powell, 'Frederick II and the Muslims: The Makings of a Historiographical Tradition', *Iberia and the Mediterranean World of the Middle Ages*, ed. L. J. Simon (Leiden, 1995), pp. 261–9.

22. Abulafia, *Frederick II*, pp. 148–201; T. C. Van Cleve, 'The Crusade of Frederick II', *A History of the Crusades*, vol. 2, ed. K. M. Setton (Madison, 1969), pp. 429–62; R. Hiestand, 'Friedrich II. und der Kreuzzug', *Friedrich II: Tagung des Deutschen Historischen Instituts in Rom im Gedenkjahr 1994*, ed. A. Esch and N. Kamp (Tübingen, 1996), pp. 128–49; L. Ross, 'Frederick II: Tyrant or benefactor of the Latin East?', *Al-Masaq*, vol. 15 (2003), pp. 149–59.

23. H. Kluger, *Hochmeister Hermann von Salza und Kaiser Friedrich II* (Marburg, 1987).

24. Ibn Wasil, *Arab Historians of the Crusades*, trans. F. Gabrieli (London, 1969), p. 270. Sibt ibn al-Jauzi (pp. 273–5) described an outpouring of grief thus: 'news of the loss of Jerusalem spread to Damascus, and disaster struck the lands of Islam. It was so great a tragedy that public

ceremonies of mourning were instituted.' Roger of Wendover, *Flores Historiarum*, ed. H. G. Hewlett, 3 vols, Rolls Series 84 (London, 1887), vol. 2, p. 368.

25. Matthew Paris, *Chronica Majora*, ed. H. R. Luard, 7 vols, Rolls Series 57 (London, 1872–83), vol. 3, pp. 179–80. On the authenticity of this letter see: J. M. Powell, 'Patriarch Gerold and Frederick II: The Matthew Paris letter', *Journal of Medieval History*, vol. 25 (1999), pp. 19–26. Philip of Novara, *Mémoires*, ed. C. Kohler (Paris, 1913), p. 25; B. Weiler, 'Frederick II, Gregory IX and the liberation of the Holy Land, 1230–9', *Studies in Church History*, vol. 36 (2000), pp. 192–206.

26. Kings of the Hohenstaufen line were still acknowledged as titular absentees until 1268. M. Lower, *The Barons' Crusade: A Call to Arms and its Consequences* (Philadelphia, 2005); P. Jackson, 'The crusades of 1239–41 and their aftermath', *Bulletin of the School of Oriental and African Studies*, vol. 50 (1987), pp. 32–60.

27. Rothelin Continuation, 'Continuation de Guillaume de Tyr de 1229 à 1261, dite du manuscrit de Rothelin', *RHC Occ.* II, pp. 563–4. This text is available in translation: J. Shirley (trans.), *Crusader Syria in the Thirteenth Century* (Aldershot, 1999), pp. 13–120.

28. Rothelin Continuation, p. 565.

29. Matthew Paris, *Chronica Majora*, vol. 4, p. 397. On Louis IX's career and crusade see: J. Richard, *Saint Louis: Crusader King of France*, trans. J. Birrell (Cambridge, 1992); W. C. Jordan, *Louis IX and the Challenge of the Crusade: A Study in Rulership* (Princeton, 1979); J. Strayer, 'The Crusades of Louis IX', *A History of the Crusades*, vol. 2, ed. K. M. Setton (Madison, 1969), pp. 487–518; C. Cahen, 'St Louis et l'Islam', *Journal Asiatique*, vol. 258 (1970), pp. 3–12. On Louis' piety see: E. R. Labande, 'Saint Louis pèlerin', *Revue d'Histoire de l'Église de France*, vol. 57 (1971), pp. 5–18.

30. John of Joinville, *Vie de Saint Louis*, ed. J. Monfrin (Paris, 1995). This text is available in translation: C. Smith (trans.), *Chronicles of the Crusades: Joinville and Villehardouin* (London, 2008). See also: C. Smith, *Crusading in the Age of Joinville* (Aldershot, 2006). A wonderfully rich collection of additional western and Arabic primary sources is available in translation in: P. Jackson (trans.), *The Seventh Crusade, 1244–1254: Sources and Documents* (Aldershot, 2007). See also: A.-M. Eddé, 'Saint Louis et la Septième Croisade vus par les auteurs arabes' *Croisades et idée de croisade à la fin du Moyen Âge, Cahiers de Recherches Médiévales (XIIIᵉ–XVᵉ s)*, vol. 1 (1996), pp. 65–92.

31. Jordan, *Louis IX and the Challenge of the Crusade*, pp. 65–104.

32. John of Joinville, p. 62; J. H. Pryor, 'The transportation of horses by sea during the era of the Crusades', *Commerce, Shipping and Naval Warfare*

in the Medieval Mediterranean, ed. J. H. Pryor (London, 1987), pp. 9–27, 103–25.

33. John of Joinville, p. 72

34. John of Joinville, pp. 72–6.

35. Matthew Paris, *Chronica Majora*, vol. 6, *Additamenta*, p. 158; Rothelin Continuation, p. 590; John of Joinville, p. 78; P. Riant (ed.), 'Six lettres aux croisades', *Archives de l'Orient Latin*, vol. 1 (1881), p. 389.

36. Humphreys, *From Saladin to the Mongols*, pp. 239–307.

37. Nizam al-Mulk, *The Book of Government or Rules for Kings*, trans. H. Darke (London, 1960), p. 121; Ibn Wasil, *The Seventh Crusade*, trans. P. Jackson, p. 134; D. Ayalon, 'Le régiment Bahriyya dans l'armée mamelouke', *Revue des Études Islamiques*, vol. 19 (1951), pp. 133–41; R. S. Humphreys, 'The emergence of the Mamluk army', *Studia Islamica*, vol. 45 (1977), pp. 67–99.

38. John of Joinville, p. 90; Ibn Wasil, *The Seventh Crusade*, trans. P. Jackson (Aldershot, 2007), p. 141.

39. Rothelin Continuation, p. 596; Ibn Wasil, *The Seventh Crusade*, pp. 133–40; *Historiae Francorum Scriptores ad Ipsius Gentis Origine*, ed. A. du Chesne, vol. 5 (Paris, 1649), p. 428.

40. Rothelin Continuation, p. 600; Matthew Paris, *Chronica Majora*, vol. 6, *Additamenta*, p. 195; John of Joinville, pp. 100–102.

41. Rothelin Continuation, p. 602.

42. Rothelin Continuation, pp. 603–4.

43. Rothelin Continuation, pp. 604–5; Ibn Wasil, *The Seventh Crusade*, p. 144.

44. Rothelin Continuation, p. 606; John of Joinville, pp. 110, 116.

45. Rothelin Continuation, p. 608; John of Joinville, pp. 142–4.

46. John of Joinville, pp. 144, 150; Rothelin Continuation, p. 609.

47. Rothelin Continuation, p. 610. It is perhaps possible that, in these dark days, King Louis IX moved beyond rational decision making, turning instead to God, to pray for a miracle. Such a circumstance was far from inconceivable in the context of a crusade. But given Louis' views on the need to balance divine aid with practical human responsibility, it is unlikely that he would simply rely on supernatural intervention.

48. Sibt ibn al-Jauzi, *The Seventh Crusade*, trans. P. Jackson (Aldershot, 2007), p. 159; John of Joinville, p. 150.

49. Matthew Paris, *Chronica Majora*, vol. 6, *Additamenta*, p. 195; John of Joinville, pp. 156–8.

50. Sibt ibn al-Jauzi, *The Seventh Crusade*, p. 160; John of Joinville, p. 166.

51. *Historiae Francorum Scriptores ad Ipsius Gentis Origine*, p. 429.

PART V: VICTORY IN THE EAST

1. D. Ayalon, *Le phénomène mamelouk dans l'orient Islamique* (Paris, 1996); R. Amitai-Preiss, *Mongols and Mamluks: The Mamluk–Ilkanid War, 1260–1281* (Cambridge, 1995). The classic study of Baybar's career is: P. Thorau, *The Lion of Egypt: Sultan Baybars I and the Near East in the Thirteenth Century*, trans. P. M. Holt (London, 1992). See also: A. A. Khowaiter, *Baybars the First* (London, 1978). For a translation of excerpts from Ibn 'Abd al-Zahir's biography of Baybars see: S. F. Sadaque, *The Slave King: Baybars I of Egypt* (Dacca, 1956). D. P. Little, *An Introduction to Mamluk Historiography* (Montreal, 1970); P. M. Holt, 'Three biographies of al-Zahir Baybars', *Medieval Historical Writing in the Christian Worlds*, ed. D. Morgan (London, 1982), pp. 19–29; P. M. Holt, 'Some observations on Shafi' b. ibn 'Ali's biography of Baybars', *Journal of Semitic Studies*, vol. 29 (1984), pp. 123–30; Y. Koch, 'Izz al-Din ibn Shaddad and his biography of Baybars', *Annali dell'Istituto Universitario Orientale*, vol. 43 (1983), pp. 249–87.
2. D. Morgan, *The Mongols*, 2nd edn (Oxford, 2007); J.-P. Roux, *Genghis Khan and the Mongol Empire* (London, 2003); P. Jackson, *The Mongols and the West, 1221–1410* (Harlow, 2005); J. Richard, *La papauté et les missions d'Orient au Moyen Âge* (Rome, 1977); J. D. Ryan, 'Christian wives of Mongol khans: Tartar queens and missionary expectations in Asia', *Journal of the Royal Asiatic Society*, 3rd series, vol. 8.3 (1998), pp. 411–21; P. Jackson, 'Medieval Christendom's encounter with the alien', *Historical Research*, vol. 74 (2001), pp. 347–69.
3. D. Morgan, 'The Mongols in Syria, 1260–1300', *Crusade and Settlement*, ed. P. W. Edbury (Cardiff, 1985), pp. 231–5.
4. P. Jackson, 'The crisis in the Holy Land in 1260', *English Historical Review*, vol. 95 (1980), pp. 481–513; Amitai-Preiss, *Mongols and Mamluks*, pp. 26–48; J. M. Smith, 'Ayn Jalut: Mamluk success or Mongol failure', *Harvard Journal of Asiatic Studies*, vol. 44 (1984), pp. 307–47; P. Thorau, 'The battle of Ayn Jalut: A re-examination', *Crusade and Settlement*, ed. P. W. Edbury (Cardiff, 1985), pp. 236–41.
5. Thorau, *The Lion of Egypt*, pp. 75–88.
6. Thorau, *The Lion of Egypt*, pp. 91–119.
7. Hillenbrand, *The Crusades: Islamic Perspectives*, pp. 225–46; D. P. Little, 'Jerusalem under the Ayyubids and Mamluks 1197–1516 AD', *Jerusalem in History*, ed. K. J. Asali (London, 1989), pp. 177–200.
8. Thorau, *The Lion of Egypt*, pp. 103–5.
9. P. M. Holt, 'The treaties of the early Mamluk sultans with the Frankish states', *Bulletin of the School of Oriental and African Studies*, vol. 43

(1980), pp. 67–76; P. M. Holt, 'Mamluk–Frankish diplomatic relations in the reign of Baybars', *Nottingham Medieval Studies*, vol. 32 (1988), pp. 180–95; P. M. Holt, *Early Mamluk Diplomacy* (Leiden, 1995).

10. D. Ayalon, 'Aspects of the Mamluk phenomenon: Ayyubids, Kurds and Turks', *Der Islam*, vol. 54 (1977), pp. 1–32; D. Ayalon, 'Notes on Furusiyya exercises and games in the Mamluk sultanate', *Scripta Hierosolymitana*, vol. 9 (1961), pp. 31–62; H. Rabie, 'The training of the Mamluk Faris', *War, Technology and Society in the Middle East*, ed. V. J. Parry and M. E. Yapp (London, 1975), pp. 153–63.

11. The sultan also tried, but failed, to develop an elephant cavalry. Efforts were made to construct a Mamluk fleet – Islam having enjoyed little or no presence on the Mediterranean since the Third Crusade – but Baybars' ships seem to have been relatively poorly designed, and most sank during a later attempt to assault Cyprus.

12. Thorau, *The Lion of Egypt*, p. 168.

13. 'Les Gestes des Chiprois', *Recueil des historiens des croisades, Documents arméniens*, vol. 2, ed. Académie des Inscriptions et Belles-Lettres (Paris, 1906), p. 766. This text is translated in: P. Crawford (trans.), *The 'Templar of Tyre': Part III of the 'Deeds of the Cypriots'* (Aldershot, 2003).

14. Ibn 'Abd al-Zahir, *Arab Historians of the Crusades*, trans. F. Gabrieli (London, 1969), pp. 310–12.

15. William of Saint-Parthus, *Vie de St Louis*, ed. H.-F. Delaborde (Paris, 1899), pp. 153–5.

16. Ibn al-Furat, *Arab Historians of the Crusades*, trans. F. Gabrieli (London, 1969), p. 319.

17. S. Lloyd, 'The Lord Edward's Crusade, 1270–72', *War and Government: Essays in Honour of J. O. Prestwich*, ed. J. Gillingham and J. C. Holt (Woodbridge, 1984), pp. 120–33; Tyerman, *England and the Crusades*, pp. 124–32.

18. Thorau, *The Lion of Egypt*, pp. 225–9, 235–43.

19. L. Northrup, *From Slave to Sultan: The Career of al-Mansur Qalawun and the Consolidation of Mamluk Rule in Egypt and Syria (678–689 A.H./1279–1290 A.D.)* (Stuttgart, 1998); P. M. Holt, 'The presentation of Qalawun by Shafi' b. ibn 'Ali', *The Islamic World from Classical to Modern Times*, ed. C. E. Bosworth, C. Issawi, R. Savory and A. L. Udovitch (Princeton, 1989), pp. 141–50.

20. Amitai-Preiss, *Mongols and Mamluks*, pp. 179–201.

21. Richard, *The Crusades*, pp. 434–41; P. M. Holt, 'Qalawun's treaty with the Latin kingdom (682/1283): negotiation and abrogation', *Egypt and Syria in the Fatimid, Ayyubid and Mamluk Eras*, ed. U. Vermeulen and D. de Smet (Leiden, 1995), pp. 325–34.

22. Abu'l Fida, *Arab Historians of the Crusades*, trans. F. Gabrieli (London,

1969), p. 342; R. Irwin, 'The Mamluk conquest of the county of Tripoli', *Crusade and Settlement*, ed. P. W. Edbury (Cardiff, 1985), pp. 246–50.

23. Richard, *The Crusades*, pp. 463–4.

24. Abu'l Fida, *Arab Historians of the Crusades*, pp. 344–5; 'Les Gestes des Chiprois', p. 811; D. P. Little, 'The fall of 'Akka in 690/1291: the Muslim version', *Studies in Islamic History and Civilisation in Honour of Professor David Ayalon*, ed. M. Sharon (Jerusalem, 1986), pp. 159–82.

25. Abu l-Mahasin, *Arab Historians of the Crusades*, trans. F. Gabrieli (London, 1969), p. 347; 'Les Gestes des Chiprois', pp. 812, 814; Abu'l Fida, *Arab Historians of the Crusades*, p. 346.

26. Abu l-Mahasin, *Arab Historians of the Crusades*, p. 349; 'Les Gestes des Chiprois', p. 816; J. Delaville le Roulx (ed.), *Cartulaire général de l'ordre des Hospitaliers 1100–1310*, vol. 3 (Paris, 1899), p. 593; Abu'l Fida, *Arab Historians of the Crusades*, p. 346.

CONCLUSION: THE LEGACY OF THE CRUSADES

1. M. Barber, *The Trial of the Templars* (Cambridge, 1978); N. Housley, 'The Crusading Movement, 1274–1700', *The Oxford Illustrated History of the Crusades*, ed. J. S. C. Riley-Smith (Oxford, 1995), pp. 260–93; N. Housley, *The Later Crusades* (Oxford, 1992).

2. E. Siberry, *Criticism of Crusading, 1095–1274* (Oxford, 1985). Historians have yet to demonstrate whether or not the warfare carried out during the crusading era was unusually violent or extreme in comparison to other medieval conflicts. This is one fundamental area of enquiry in which further research is urgently needed.

3. For a readable attempt to place crusading within the wider context of Christian and Muslim relations see: R. Fletcher, *The Cross and the Crescent* (London, 2003).

4. Hillenbrand, *The Crusades: Islamic Perspectives*, pp. 257–429; Housley, *Contesting the Crusades*, pp. 144–66; C. J. Tyerman, *Fighting for Christendom: Holy War and the Crusades* (Oxford, 2004), pp. 79–92, 155–70.

5. C. J. Tyerman, 'What the crusades meant to Europe', *The Medieval World*, ed. P. Linehan and J. L. Nelson (London, 2001), pp. 131–45; Tyerman, *Fighting for Christendom*, pp. 145–54.

6. J. S. C. Riley-Smith, 'Islam and the crusades in history and imagination, 8 November 1898–11 September 2001', *Crusades*, vol. 2 (2003), p. 166.

7. Constable, 'The Historiography of the Crusades', pp. 6–8; Tyerman, *The Invention of the Crusades*, pp. 99–118.

8. Hillenbrand, *The Crusades: Islamic Perspectives*, pp. 589–600; R. Irwin, 'Islam and the Crusades, 1096–1699', *The Oxford Illustrated History of the Crusades*, ed. J. S. C. Riley-Smith (Oxford, 1995), pp. 217–59.

9. E. Siberry, 'Images of the crusades in the nineteenth and twentieth centuries', *The Oxford Illustrated History of the Crusades*, ed. J. S. C. Riley-Smith (Oxford, 1995), pp. 365–85; E. Siberry, *The New Crusaders: Images of the Crusades in the Nineteenth and Early Twentieth Centuries* (Aldershot, 2000); E. Siberry, 'Nineteenth-century perspectives on the First Crusade', *The Experience of Crusading, 1. Western Approaches*, ed. M. G. Bull and N. Housley (Cambridge, 2003), pp. 281–93; R. Irwin, 'Saladin and the Third Crusade: A case study in historiography and the historical novel', *Companion to Historiography*, ed. M. Bentley (London, 1997), pp. 139–52; M. Jubb, *The Legend of Saladin in Western Literature and Historiography* (Lewiston, 2000).

10. Riley-Smith, 'Islam and the crusades in history and imagination', pp. 155–6. This desire to reconnect with the medieval past found further expression at Versailles, outside Paris. King Louis Philippe of France dedicated five rooms – the *Salles des Croisades* – of this palace to monumental paintings depicting scenes from the crusades. French nobles with a family history of crusading were permitted to display their coats of arms in these chambers, and 316 emblems were originally hung when the *Salles* opened in 1840. However, voluble protests over exclusion meant that they were closed, almost immediately, for another three years, so that additional aristocratic dynasties could be represented. This prompted a furious trade in forged documents purporting to prove crusading pedigree, supplied (for a handsome price) by a sharp-witted opportunist named Eugène-Henri Courtois. These forgeries remained undetected until 1956.

11. Siberry, 'Images of the crusades in the nineteenth and twentieth centuries', pp. 366–8, 379–81; Riley-Smith, 'Islam and the crusades in history and imagination', pp. 151–2; J. Richard, 'National feeling and the legacy of the crusades', *Palgrave Advances in the Crusades*, ed. H. Nicholson (Basingstoke, 2005), pp. 204–22.

12. Siberry, 'Images of the crusades in the nineteenth and twentieth centuries', pp. 382–5.

13. E. Sivan, 'Modern Arab Historiography of the Crusades', *Asian and African Studies*, vol. 8 (1972), p. 112; Hillenbrand, *The Crusades: Islamic Perspectives*, pp. 590–92; Riley-Smith, 'Islam and the crusades in history and imagination', p. 155.

14. Sivan, 'Modern Arab Historiography of the Crusades', pp. 112–13.

15. B. Lewis, 'License to Kill: Usama bin Ladin's Declaration of *Jihad*', *Foreign Affairs* (November/December 1998), p. 14.

16. Sivan, 'Modern Arab Historiography of the Crusades', p. 114;
    Hillenbrand, *The Crusades: Islamic Perspectives*, pp. 592–600.
17. E. Karsh, *Islamic Imperialism* (London, 2006), pp. 134–5; U. Bhatia,
    *Forgetting Osama bin Munqidh, Remembering Osama bin Laden: The
    Crusades in Modern Muslim Memory* (Singapore, 2008), pp. 39–40, 53.
18. Hillenbrand, *The Crusades: Islamic Perspectives*, pp. 600–602; Bhatia,
    Forgetting Osama bin Munqidh, Remembering Osama bin Laden, pp.
    23, 52–3.

INDEX

(page numbers in *italic* type refer to maps)

THOMAS ASBRIDGE is Reader in Medieval History at Queen Mary University in London, and an internationally renowned expert on the history of the Crusades. He has written and presented a major BBC TV series on the Crusades. His acclaimed *The First Crusade* and *The Greatest Knight* are also available from Simon & Schuster.